The Composition of the Pentateuch

THE ANCHOR YALE BIBLE REFERENCE LIBRARY is a project of international and interfaith scope in which Protestant, Catholic, and Jewish scholars from many countries contribute individual volumes. The project is not sponsored by any ecclesiastical organization and is not intended to reflect any particular theological doctrine.

The series is committed to producing volumes in the tradition established half a century ago by the founders of the Anchor Bible, William Foxwell Albright and David Noel Freedman. It aims to present the best contemporary scholarship in a way that is accessible not only to scholars but also to the educated non-specialist. It is committed to work of sound philological and historical scholarship, supplemented by insight from modern methods, such as sociological and literary criticism.

JOHN J. COLLINS
General Editor

THE ANCHOR YALE BIBLE REFERENCE LIBRARY

THE COMPOSITION OF THE PENTATEUCH

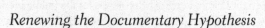

Renewing the Documentary Hypothesis

Joel S. Baden

Yale
UNIVERSITY PRESS
New Haven & London

Published with assistance from the foundation established in memory of
Philip Hamilton McMillan of the Class of 1894, Yale College.

Set in Postscript Electra type by Newgen North America.
Printed in the United States of America.

Library of Congress Cataloging-in-Publication Data

Baden, Joel S., 1977–
The composition of the Pentateuch : renewing the documentary
hypothesis / Joel S. Baden.
p. cm. — (The Anchor Yale Bible reference library)
Includes bibliographical references and index.
ISBN 978-0-300-15263-0 (alk. paper)
1. Bible. O.T. Pentateuch—Criticism, Redaction. 2. Documentary hypothesis
(Pentateuchal criticism) 3. Bible. O.T. Pentateuch—Criticism,
interpretation, etc. I. Title.
BS1225.52.B3325 2012
222'.1066—dc23
2011034207

A catalogue record for this book is available from the British Library.

For Baruch

CONTENTS

ACKNOWLEDGMENTS

This project was commissioned by Prof. John Collins, the general editor of the Anchor Yale Bible and a wonderful colleague, and so thanks are due first and foremost to him for his support in this and other endeavors. The book was written mostly during my sabbatical from the Yale Divinity School, for which I am grateful to Dean Harold Attridge. My other Hebrew Bible colleagues at YDS, Profs. Robert Wilson and Carolyn Sharp, have been continual sources of encouragement.

I am grateful to Prof. Candida Moss, who has been endlessly generous with her advice and constant support in this and other projects, and most of all with her friendship. She has been a close companion throughout the writing of this book, and it would not have been possible without her.

This book benefited immeasurably from regular discussions of issues both large and small, theoretical and technical, with my colleagues from the University of Chicago, Profs. Simeon Chavel and Jeffrey Stackert. They were kind enough to read portions of it and engage in lengthy conversations, far beyond the bounds of collegiality or even friendship. They will undoubtedly recognize their insights on many pages, and I owe them both much.

I am also grateful to the efforts of the anonymous readers of the manuscript, whose insightful remarks were tremendously helpful. I am grateful too to Jennifer Banks, my editor at Yale University Press, who helped shepherd this project from beginning to end, and who was a source of support and good cheer throughout.

My family suffered through long hours of my absence while I was writing this book, and I deeply appreciate their patience and understanding. This book will forever be linked in my mind with the arrival of Iris, who brightened every day (and many nights) with her presence; like her sister before her, she arrived just in time for the good part at the end.

This book is dedicated to my teacher, mentor, and friend Baruch Schwartz. He knows why, and so do all who have benefited from his guidance, his teaching, and his work. I can only hope that this volume repays him for a mere fraction of what he has given to me.

Introduction

THE SALE OF JOSEPH, GENESIS 37:18–36

¹⁸They saw him from afar, and before he came close to them they conspired to kill him. ¹⁹They said to one another, "Here comes that dreamer! ²⁰Come now, let us kill him and throw him into one of the pits; and we can say, 'A savage beast devoured him.' We shall see what comes of his dreams!" ²¹But when Reuben heard it, he tried to save him from them. He said, "Let us not take his life." ²²And Reuben went on, "Shed no blood! Cast him into that pit out in the wilderness, but do not touch him yourselves"—intending to save him from them and restore him to his father. ²³When Joseph came up to his brothers, they stripped Joseph of his tunic, the ornamented tunic that he was wearing. ²⁴They took him and cast him into the pit. The pit was empty; there was no water in it. ²⁵Then they sat down to a meal. Looking up, they saw a caravan of Ishmaelites coming from Gilead,

¹⁸וַיִּרְא֤וּ אֹתוֹ֙ מֵֽרָחֹ֔ק וּבְטֶ֙רֶם֙ יִקְרַ֣ב אֲלֵיהֶ֔ם וַיִּֽתְנַכְּל֥וּ אֹת֖וֹ לַהֲמִיתֽוֹ׃ ¹⁹וַיֹּאמְר֖וּ אִ֣ישׁ אֶל־אָחִ֑יו הִנֵּ֗ה בַּ֛עַל הַחֲלֹמ֥וֹת הַלָּזֶ֖ה בָּֽא׃ ²⁰וְעַתָּ֣ה ׀ לְכ֣וּ וְנַֽהַרְגֵ֗הוּ וְנַשְׁלִכֵ֙הוּ֙ בְּאַחַ֣ד הַבֹּר֔וֹת וְאָמַ֕רְנוּ חַיָּ֥ה רָעָ֖ה אֲכָלָ֑תְהוּ וְנִרְאֶ֕ה מַה־יִּהְי֖וּ חֲלֹמֹתָֽיו׃ ²¹וַיִּשְׁמַ֣ע רְאוּבֵ֔ן וַיַּצִּלֵ֖הוּ מִיָּדָ֑ם וַיֹּ֕אמֶר לֹ֥א נַכֶּ֖נּוּ נָֽפֶשׁ׃ ²²וַיֹּ֨אמֶר אֲלֵהֶ֣ם ׀ רְאוּבֵ֗ן אַל־תִּשְׁפְּכוּ־דָם֙ הַשְׁלִ֣יכוּ אֹת֗וֹ אֶל־הַבּ֤וֹר הַזֶּה֙ אֲשֶׁ֣ר בַּמִּדְבָּ֔ר וְיָ֖ד אַל־תִּשְׁלְחוּ־ב֑וֹ לְמַ֗עַן הַצִּ֤יל אֹתוֹ֙ מִיָּדָ֔ם לַהֲשִׁיב֖וֹ אֶל־אָבִֽיו׃ ²³וַֽיְהִ֕י כַּֽאֲשֶׁר־בָּ֥א יוֹסֵ֖ף אֶל־אֶחָ֑יו וַיַּפְשִׁ֤יטוּ אֶת־יוֹסֵף֙ אֶת־כֻּתָּנְתּ֔וֹ אֶת־כְּתֹ֥נֶת הַפַּסִּ֖ים אֲשֶׁ֥ר עָלָֽיו׃ ²⁴וַיִּ֙קָּחֻ֔הוּ וַיַּשְׁלִ֥כוּ אֹת֖וֹ הַבֹּ֑רָה וְהַבּ֣וֹר רֵ֔ק אֵ֥ין בּ֖וֹ מָֽיִם׃ ²⁵וַיֵּשְׁבוּ֮ לֶֽאֱכָל־לֶחֶם֒ וַיִּשְׂא֤וּ עֵֽינֵיהֶם֙ וַיִּרְא֔וּ וְהִנֵּה֙ אֹרְחַ֣ת יִשְׁמְעֵאלִ֔ים בָּאָ֖ה מִגִּלְעָ֑ד וּגְמַלֵּיהֶ֣ם נֹֽשְׂאִ֗ים נְכֹאת֙ וּצְרִ֣י וָלֹ֔ט הוֹלְכִ֖ים לְהוֹרִ֥יד מִצְרָֽיְמָה׃ ²⁶וַיֹּ֥אמֶר יְהוּדָ֖ה אֶל־אֶחָ֑יו מַה־בֶּ֗צַע כִּ֤י נַהֲרֹג֙ אֶת־אָחִ֔ינוּ וְכִסִּ֖ינוּ אֶת־דָּמֽוֹ׃ ²⁷לְכ֞וּ וְנִמְכְּרֶ֣נּוּ לַיִּשְׁמְעֵאלִ֗ים וְיָדֵ֙נוּ֙ אַל־תְּהִי־ב֔וֹ כִּֽי־אָחִ֥ינוּ בְשָׂרֵ֖נוּ ה֑וּא וַֽיִּשְׁמְע֖וּ אֶחָֽיו׃ ²⁸וַיַּֽעַבְרוּ֩ אֲנָשִׁ֨ים מִדְיָנִ֜ים סֹֽחֲרִ֗ים וַֽיִּמְשְׁכוּ֙ וַיַּֽעֲל֤וּ אֶת־יוֹסֵף֙ מִן־הַבּ֔וֹר וַיִּמְכְּר֧וּ אֶת־יוֹסֵ֛ף לַיִּשְׁמְעֵאלִ֖ים בְּעֶשְׂרִ֣ים כָּ֑סֶף וַיָּבִ֥יאוּ אֶת־יוֹסֵ֖ף מִצְרָֽיְמָה׃ ²⁹וַיָּ֤שָׁב רְאוּבֵן֙ אֶל־הַבּ֔וֹר וְהִנֵּ֥ה אֵין־יוֹסֵ֖ף בַּבּ֑וֹר וַיִּקְרַ֖ע אֶת־בְּגָדָֽיו׃ ³⁰וַיָּ֥שָׁב אֶל־אֶחָ֖יו וַיֹּאמַ֑ר הַיֶּ֣לֶד אֵינֶ֔נּוּ וַאֲנִ֖י אָ֥נָה אֲנִי־בָֽא׃ ³¹וַיִּקְח֖וּ אֶת־כְּתֹ֣נֶת יוֹסֵ֑ף וַֽיִּשְׁחֲטוּ֙ שְׂעִ֣יר

1

their camels bearing gum, balm, and ladanum to be taken to Egypt. ²⁶Then Judah said to his brothers, "What do we gain by killing our brother and covering up his blood? ²⁷Come, let us sell him to the Ishmaelites, but let us not do away with him ourselves. After all, he is our brother, our own flesh." His brothers agreed. ²⁸When Midianite traders passed by, they pulled Joseph up out of the pit. They sold Joseph for twenty pieces of silver to the Ishmaelites, who brought Joseph to Egypt. ²⁹When Reuben returned to the pit and saw that Joseph was not in the pit, he rent his clothes. ³⁰Returning to his brothers, he said, "The boy is gone! Now, what am I to do?" ³¹Then they took Joseph's tunic, slaughtered a kid, and dipped the tunic in the blood. ³²They had the ornamented tunic taken to their father, and they said, "We found this. Please examine it; is it your son's tunic or not?" ³³He recognized it, and said, "My son's tunic! A savage beast devoured him! Joseph was torn by a beast!" ³⁴Jacob rent his clothes, put sackcloth on his loins, and observed mourning for his son many days. ³⁵All his sons and daughters sought to comfort him; but he refused to be comforted, saying, "No, I will go down mourning to my son in Sheol." Thus his father bewailed him. ³⁶The Midianites, meanwhile, sold him in Egypt to Potiphar, a courtier of Pharaoh and his chief steward.

32וַיְשַׁלְּחוּ אֶת־עֳדִים וַיָּבִיאוּ אֶת־הַכְּתֹנֶת בַּדָּם: כְּתֹנֶת הַפַּסִּים וַיָּבִיאוּ אֶל־אֲבִיהֶם וַיֹּאמְרוּ זֹאת מָצָאנוּ הַכֶּר־נָא הַכְּתֹנֶת בִּנְךָ הִוא אִם־לֹא: 33וַיַּכִּירָהּ וַיֹּאמֶר כְּתֹנֶת בְּנִי חַיָּה רָעָה אֲכָלָתְהוּ טָרֹף טֹרַף יוֹסֵף: 34וַיִּקְרַע יַעֲקֹב שִׂמְלֹתָיו וַיָּשֶׂם שַׂק בְּמָתְנָיו וַיִּתְאַבֵּל עַל־בְּנוֹ יָמִים רַבִּים: 35וַיָּקֻמוּ כָל־בָּנָיו וְכָל־בְּנֹתָיו לְנַחֲמוֹ וַיְמָאֵן לְהִתְנַחֵם וַיֹּאמֶר כִּי־אֵרֵד אֶל־בְּנִי אָבֵל שְׁאֹלָה וַיֵּבְךְּ אֹתוֹ אָבִיו: 36וְהַמְּדָנִים מָכְרוּ אֹתוֹ אֶל־מִצְרָיִם לְפוֹטִיפַר סְרִיס פַּרְעֹה שַׂר הַטַּבָּחִים:

The story of Joseph's brothers selling him into slavery in Egypt is well known.[1] The images of Joseph being thrown into the pit, of a brother pleading with the others to spare Joseph's life, of the taking of Joseph to Egypt by a band of traders, and of the falsification of the evidence of Joseph's death are vivid in our traditional collective consciousness. To some extent, however, familiarity with the outlines of this story can obscure the significant—in places insurmountable—narrative inconsistencies and outright contradictions. To step back and read this text with fresh eyes is to realize just how problematic the narrative is as it stands.

There are some aspects of this text that appear strange—repetitions, awkward transitions, apparent gaps—but these could plausibly be attributed to authorial style.[2] The brothers seem to decide to kill Joseph twice, once described in narrative ("they conspired to kill him," v. 18) and once in dialogue ("let us kill him," v. 20). Reuben's plan to save Joseph ("cast him into that pit," v. 22—that is, instead of killing him with our hands) is identical to the brothers' original plan to kill him ("let us throw him into one of the pits," v. 20—that is, to dispose of his body after we have killed him). Judah's argument for not killing Joseph ("let us not do away with him ourselves," literally, "let our hands not be against him," v. 27) is almost a duplication of Reuben's ("do not touch him yourselves," literally, "do not stretch a hand against him," v. 22)—and when Judah proposes his plan, the brothers had already accepted, and even carried out, that of Reuben.[3] These issues can perhaps be interpreted away on a case-by-case basis, but taken together they present a challenge to any reader.

There are, however, problems in the text that cannot be easily resolved, problems that preclude any straightforward reading of the plot. These derive from the narrative presence and action of both Ishmaelites and Midianites in the sale of Joseph. When we read the text as it stands, according to its plain meaning, these two foreign groups are the source of great confusion. The Ishmaelite traders arrive on the scene first (v. 25), leading Judah to persuade his brothers that rather than kill Joseph, they ought to sell him; they will be just as effectively rid of him, and even profit in the process (vv. 26–27). Before the transaction can take place, however, the Midianite traders pass by, and though it was the brothers who had planned to sell Joseph to the caravan of Ishmaelites, it is the Midianites, according to the plain reading of the text, who pull Joseph from the pit, and it is the Midianites who sell him to the Ishmaelites.[4] The Midianites, therefore, appear to frustrate Judah's plans, as it is they who reap the benefits of selling Joseph to the Ishmaelites. If the brothers are present for this, they are strikingly silent.

Far more difficult is the notice at the end of v. 28 that the Ishmaelites, upon purchasing Joseph, brought him to Egypt. This is expected in light of what preceded in v. 25, where the Ishmaelites are said to be heading toward Egypt. But it is expressly contradicted by what follows at the end of the chapter in v. 36: "The Midianites, meanwhile, sold him in Egypt to Potiphar."⁵ If this were not problem enough, Genesis 39:1 states that Potiphar bought Joseph "from the Ishmaelites who had brought him there."

Interpreters have had to come to terms with these apparent contradictions and inconsistencies from the earliest stages of biblical interpretation to the present. For precritical interpreters, the unity of the text was never in question, and they were therefore forced to find ways to eliminate or otherwise explain away the narrative problems.⁶ In the second-century-BCE book of Jubilees, the Midianites and the abduction of Joseph are removed from the story entirely; Joseph's brothers sell him to the Ishmaelites, who bring him to Egypt and sell him to Potiphar (Jub 34:11). This elimination of the narrative problem by means of the wholesale elimination of the Midianites is attested elsewhere in postbiblical texts of the early period.⁷ In Josephus's retelling, as in Jubilees, the brothers sell Joseph to the Ishmaelites, and they in turn sell him to Potiphar in Egypt.⁸ In the *Testament of Joseph,* Joseph is sold by his brothers to the Ishmaelites (10:6), but we find also a rather lengthy and convoluted story (11:1–16:5), not found in Genesis, in which the trader to whom the Ishmaelites give Joseph for safekeeping is accused by Potiphar of having stolen him from Canaan.⁹ This added narrative may be the means by which this text tries to reconcile the biblical accounts of Joseph being both abducted and sold. It does so, however, without mentioning the Midianites. In Philo, the Ishmaelites are not mentioned by name either, being called simply merchants traveling from Arabia to Egypt, though they perform precisely the same role as the Ishmaelites—they pass by, they buy Joseph from the brothers, and they in turn sell him into Egypt.¹⁰ Pseudo-Philo is perhaps most extreme in that the Midianites and the Ishmaelites are absent; indeed, there are no merchants whatsoever. The brothers themselves are the ones who bring Joseph to Egypt.¹¹

Common to all of these early interpretations is their form: in each, the biblical story is retold in one way or another, thereby giving the author the chance to reshape the narrative slightly and eliminate the problem of the Ishmaelites and Midianites. In later generations, in the rabbinic sources, the simple removal of unwanted elements from the biblical text was no longer feasible, and new ways of interpreting away the contradictions were developed. From a midrashic exposition of the passage found in Genesis Rabbah, it is clear that the rabbis recognized that the notice in Genesis 37:36 of the Midianites selling Joseph to Egypt, rather than the Ishmaelites in v. 28, was a problem. Rather than eliminating one of the merchants from the story as had earlier interpreters, they multiplied them, creating a chain of sales from the brothers to Egypt that took into account all of the various named entities: "How many deeds of sale were written on his account? R. Judan and R. Huna disagree. R. Judan maintained, Four. His brothers sold him to the Ishmaelites, the Ishmaelites to the merchants, the merchants to the Midianites, and the Midianites into Egypt. R. Huna said, Five: the Midianites to the Egyptians, and the Egyptians to Potiphar."[12] In both rabbinic proposals, we have not only the Midianites and the Ishmaelites, but, as a way of bridging the gap between them, the "merchants." These unknown characters are ostensibly derived by the rabbis from the descriptive term used for the Ishmaelites in v. 28; "Ishmaelite merchants passed by" became "Ishmaelites and merchants passed by." This is, of course, classically midrashic, in that it sees a problem in the text, assumes that there is a gap in the narrative to be filled that would resolve the problem, and finds (or creates), within the text itself, a possible, if not plausible, solution.

Medieval Jewish exegetes similarly struggled with this text. Rashi followed the classical midrash: "Midianites passed by—This was another caravan: Scripture indicates that he was sold many times. And the sons of Jacob drew up Joseph from the pit, and they sold him to the Ishmaelites, and the Ishmaelites to the Midianites, and the Midianites to Egypt."[13] Rashi made explicit the interpretation that it was not the Midianites who drew Joseph from the pit and sold him to the Ishmaelites, as the syntax of the biblical text would indicate, but rather the brothers who pulled him out. The subsequent sale of Joseph from the Ishmaelites to the Midianites described by Rashi is not found in the text but is necessitated by the statement in v. 36 that it was the Midianites who sold Joseph to Egypt.[14] Thus Rashi, with the classic midrash, invented at least one step in the chain of sales to account for the biblical contradiction. Note, however, that he did not then explain what is meant by Potiphar buying Joseph "from the hand of the Ishmaelites" in 39:1.[15]

Rashi's grandson, Rashbam, attempted in his commentary to hold as closely as possible to the plain meaning of the text.[16] He rejected the classical view and reverted to a reading that followed the syntax: "Before those Ishmaelites arrived, different people—Midianites—passed by there, saw Joseph in the pit, and pulled him out. These Midianites sold Joseph to the Ishmaelites. It is to be understood that the brothers did not know [of the sale]."[17] This reading is an explicit rejection of Rashi's statement that it was the brothers who pulled Joseph out of the pit[18] and draws the necessary conclusion that the brothers must not have known about it.[19] Yet Rashbam created a problem for himself regarding 37:36, where the "Medanites" are said to have sold Joseph into Egypt; since Rashbam had already made clear that the Midianites sold Joseph to the

Ishmaelites, he had to find a way to understand this apparent inconsistency. Rather than take the classical approach and invent yet another sale of Joseph from the Ishmaelites to the Medanites, Rashbam brought evidence from elsewhere in Genesis to argue that in fact the Ishmaelites and the Medanites were one and the same people: "Medan, Midian, and Ishmael were all brothers, and according to the plain meaning of Scriptures, Medan and Ishmael are one and the same. The text can then claim that the Medanites were the ones who sold him and still claim that it was the Ishmaelites who brought him down to Egypt, since they are the same people according to the plain meaning of Scripture."[20] Rashbam's interpretation here rests on the genealogical note in Genesis 25:2 that Medan and Midian were, like Ishmael, sons of Abraham, although by his second wife, Keturah. Yet his use of this information is decidedly selective, since he argued only that the Ishmaelites and Medanites should be equated, rather than all three groups; furthermore, this equation is never drawn or required anywhere else in the biblical corpus, which is to say, it is useful only for this particular passage. Despite Rashbam's greater fidelity to the plain meaning of the biblical narrative—or perhaps precisely because of it—his interpretation requires almost as much inventiveness as the classical view.

Abraham ibn Ezra took a similar approach to that of Rashbam, but rather than differentiating between the Midianites and the Medanites (and saying that it was the Medanites who were the same as the Ishmaelites), he equated the Ishmaelites and the Midianites directly (and implicitly acknowledged that the Medanites and Midianites were the same group). He understood "When Midianite merchants passed by" in 37:28 as "When the Ishmaelite merchants passed by them." He explained, "Scripture refers to the Ishmaelites as Midianites because the Midianites are called Ishmaelites. The book of Judges similarly says concerning the kings of Midian, because they were Ishmaelites (Judg 8:24)."[21] Rather than derive the equation of tribes from the genealogical information in Genesis as had Rashbam, ibn Ezra drew on a passage in Judges in which the kings of Midian, defeated by Gideon, are said to wear earrings because they were Ishmaelites (who tend to wear earrings, as the biblical author assumes everyone knows). The use there of "Ishmaelites" to describe the Midianites seems most logically to be a description of the Midianites in terms that the author's contemporary audience would understand—that is, these Midianite people are like the well-known Ishmaelites—rather than, as ibn Ezra read it, an actual historical or ethnological identification—that is, the Midianites are Ishmaelites.[22] Yet one might wonder that the Bible draws this equivalence between the two groups only in Judges, rather than at every point where the Ishmaelites or Midianites are referred to; it is especially curious that such an equation is not explicitly drawn in Genesis 37, where without it, as we have seen, confusion reigns. Furthermore, of course, the fact that this "single" group seems to arrive twice is difficult to understand.[23] Ibn Ezra's solution is well grounded in the biblical text but is no less midrashic for that.

Further, the fact that both ibn Ezra and Rashbam used other biblical passages as the basis for their interpretations only highlights the issue: neither was able to understand the text of Genesis 37 on its own terms. Despite their adherence in principle to *peshat*—the plain meaning of the text in its immediate narrative context—here they were forced into the standard midrashic technique of finding a single verse elsewhere in the Bible, unrelated to the passage at hand, in order to create a reading that eliminates the textual problem. In so doing, they (and their predecessors) actually further underscored the textual difficulty. Nevertheless, the two opposing interpretations of Rashbam and ibn Ezra became the standard possibilities for understanding this passage: either the Midianites sold Joseph to the Ishmaelites—in which case we are left with the problem of 37:36—or the brothers sold Joseph to the Ishmaelites—in which case we have to understand the Ishmaelites and Midianites to be the same people, despite their different names and moments of appearance in the narrative. Each solution has its problems.

Naḥmanides proposed a novel interpretation, acknowledging that the Ishmaelites and Midianites were different groups but having them work together to effect the sale and transfer of Joseph to Egypt. He understood the Midianites (merchants, as per 37:28) to have hired camels from the Ishmaelites (the caravan, 37:25); the brothers sold Joseph to the Midianites, who became his rightful owners, while the Ishmaelites, with their camels, did the actual transporting of Joseph.[24] Naḥmanides also directly countered ibn Ezra's equation of the Midianites and Ishmaelites, asking of Judges 8:24 (and as applied also to our text), "Why should 'kings of Midian' be called in the name of Ishmael their brother?"[25] The harmonistic character of this solution, clever though it may be, is evident.[26]

The same difficulty was noted, and very similar solutions to it were also offered, by some of the major Christian commentators. Augustine took the position, familiar from Rashbam, that the Ishmaelites and Midianites are the same, since they are both descendants of Abraham.[27] Martin Luther also equated the two groups, though on different grounds.[28] He claimed that the "band (*'ōrḥat*) of Ishmaelites" means a mixed company of merchants, traveling together: "Such also was the company of Ishmaelites and Midianites, who were joined together in business transactions, commercial relations, and agreements, as is common also among very different and remote nations."[29] Despite this, Luther recognized the difficulty in the text and was at least willing to allow for the possibility of a succession of sales, as in Genesis Rabbah: "I do not reject the opinion about the triple selling, for it will also be stated about the Midianites that they sold him to Potiphar."[30] In the end, Luther found the question largely uninteresting: "Whether these or those sold Joseph is of little import. This much is sure, that he was sold."[31]

John Calvin also seems to have been familiar with the rabbinic notion that Joseph changed hands multiple times, even at the very site of his first sale, and acknowledged that the solution of Rashbam and Augustine that equates the Ishmaelites and Midianites is difficult: "Some think that Joseph was twice sold in the same place. For it is certain, since Median was the son of Abraham and Keturah, that his sons were distinct from the sons of Ishmael: and Moses has not thoughtlessly put down these different names."[32] He did not accept this reading; his solution, however, is as midrashic as any that preceded him: "But I thus interpret the passage: that Joseph was exposed for sale to any one who chose, and seeing the purchase of him was declined by the Midianites, he was sold to the Ishmaelites."[33]

Text-critical investigation reveals that at least some scribes involved in the transmission of the Septuagint were also disturbed by the apparent inconsistency in this story and sought to correct it by changing "Ishmaelites" to "Midianites" or vice versa. Thus for "Midianites" in 37:28, two marginal glosses in manuscripts from the tenth and eleventh centuries read "Ishmaelites"; one manuscript omits "Ishmaelites" from the verse; and one from the twelfth century creates a wonderful hybrid form, "Ishmadianites." The same sources, plus at least one other from the tenth century, replace "Midianites" with "Ishmaelites" in 37:36 as well.[34]

The European Enlightenment in the eighteenth century saw the rise of critical biblical scholarship, and the nineteenth century witnessed in particular the development of source criticism, in which midrashic approaches were generally rejected in favor of a theory of composite authorship; this movement and its continuation to the present are the subject of this book and will be explored in detail in the following pages. Even in the critical era, however, scholars writing from a variety of perspectives have continued to argue for the coherence and unity of the biblical text, frequently employing many of the same arguments as their precritical predecessors.

In some cases, these scholars wrote from an explicitly anti-source-critical perspective, whether confessionally Christian or Jewish. On the Christian side we find arguments such as that of Alfred Cave: "Ishmaelite is a synonym for Arab, and Midianites are a tribe of Arabs."[35] This is obviously similar to some of the precritical approaches, but Cave went even further, denying that the text is problematic at all: "One would have thought that a single reading of the verse concerned [37:28] would have silenced the objection. . . . If the original writer of the passage saw no difficulty in calling Midianites Ishmaelites, of what weight is modern punctiliousness?"[36] Where even Augustine, Calvin, and Luther saw a difficulty, Cave insisted that he saw none. Similarly, A. H. Finn argued that "this verse [37:28] connects the two names so closely that the writer must have considered them interchangeable," again using the very existence of the verse as evidence for its innate coherence.[37]

The Jewish commentator Benno Jacob explicitly followed Rashbam in adhering strictly to the grammar of 37:28 and stating that it was the Midianites who pulled Joseph from the pit and sold him to the Ishmaelites.[38] To avoid the same difficulties Rashbam encountered in 37:36, Jacob claimed that "the Midianites sold him in Egypt" meant "by the hand of the Ishmaelites," to whom they had sold him earlier.[39] He based this conclusion on the phrase *'el-miṣrāyim*, which he claimed indicates that the Midianites did not really go to Egypt, for otherwise it would have read *miṣrāymāh* (as it does regarding the Ishmaelites in v. 25). By this interpretation Jacob removed the difficulty of the discrepancy between 37:28, 37:36, and 39:1, but at the cost of having to render 37:36 in a decidedly nonliteral manner.[40]

In recent decades one of the major trends in biblical scholarship has been the rise of modern literary criticism. Without necessarily rejecting the source-critical approach, some scholars have undertaken to read and analyze the text in its final form, as a means of understanding the Bible as it stands before us first and foremost. Frequently, these scholars engage in broad readings of the Joseph narrative, in which the precise details of the story, such as who exactly sold Joseph, are relatively less important. Barbara Green follows the line of Rashbam and Jacob in taking the Midianites as the subject in the sale of Joseph to the Ishmaelites in 37:28.[41] This reading fits best into her broader interest in the issue of who knows what happened in the story, among Jacob, the brothers, the reader, and the narrator. She does not, however, deal in the body of her text with the problem of 37:36 for this reading but relegates it to an endnote in which she reveals her ambivalence about the importance of such details: "Dismissing the notion that the two groups are historically the same, since whatever the fact may be, the narrator makes two steps, I suggest either that the Midianites are referenced by 37:36 as the initiators of the sale with Ishmaelites invisible middlemen, or—better—that what we witness from our vantage point in Canaan needs repositioning to make sense to us, standing in Egypt as we are at 39:1."[42] By presenting two possibilities—neither of which accords with the plain meaning of the text—Green makes clear that the actual facts of what happened according to the narrator are of little importance in the greater scheme of the narrative.[43]

J. P. Fokkelman, one of the foremost modern literary critics of the Bible, has a brief structural analysis of Genesis 37:18–33 in which he discovers an intricate chiasm in the text, one that, he claims, reveals the coherence of the narrative:[44]

A		18–20	conspiracy by the brothers: kill Joseph!
			"A savage beast devoured him!"
B		21–22	speeches by Reuben: no, throw him into the pit
C		23–24	brothers cast Joseph into the pit
D		25	a caravan passes by
X		26–27	proposal by Judah: sell Joseph
D'		28	Joseph sold to caravan
C'		29	Reuben finds the pit empty, rends his clothes
B'		30	and mourns; speech to his brothers
A'		31–33	they deceive Jacob with the coat,
			Jacob concludes: Joseph must be dead.
			"A savage beast devoured him!"

There are many attractive features of this structure, including the centrality of Judah's role in the selling of Joseph, but Fokkelman does not address, nor even recognize, the substantive contradiction of the Midianites and Ishmaelites. Rather, he privileges the discernment of formal structure over the narrative coherence of the passage. In short, he does not take into account, either positively or negatively, the main textual difficulty.

Edward L. Greenstein has written an essay in which he attempts to read the final form of Genesis 37 as a meaningful whole, even while acknowledging that it is contradictory.[45] Like many others, he finds in 37:28 two possible readings: one in which the Midianites sell Joseph, which he terms the "syntactic" reading, and one in which the brothers sell him, which he calls the "allusive" reading.[46] These two readings stand in conflict and do not allow the reader to choose one over the other. This imposed ambiguity, then, produces in the reader "the realization that, in the view of our narrative, [who sold Joseph] is not crucial to our understanding of the story. . . . It is important, rather, to perceive that the descent of Joseph to Egypt and his subsequent rise to power there reveal divine providence in history."[47] Greenstein's work highlights the narrative incoherence of the final form even as it seeks to find a way to understand it. Yet it is clear that the ability to impose a sort of after-the-fact sense on a problematic text does not lead to the conclusion that the text was intentionally composed in a problematic manner, and Greenstein, at least, admits as much.

For some scholars, however, the very textual inconsistencies that render the narrative difficult are used as an indication of the author's particular literary style and therefore as evidence of the compositional unity of the passage. Readings in this vein can take many forms. Thus Robert E. Longacre, in undertaking a "textlinguistic and sociolinguistic" analysis of the Joseph story, follows ibn Ezra in taking Judges 8:24 as his proof that the Ishmaelites and Midianites are to be identified—even going so far as to use the contradiction between 37:36 and 39:1 as evidence for this equation.[48] He correctly asks, however, "why, if the caravan is identified in 37:25, is it renamed and re-identified in 37:28?"[49] His answer is grounded in his literary analysis: "Here, I believe, we must tie this matter into the fact that 37:23–28 is the Peak of its episode. Suspense and elaboration are characteristic of Peak. . . . Graphically, the text first applies the term 'Ishmaelites' to the caravan seen from afar, and then on closer view calls them 'Midianite merchants.' Suspense of this sort is appropriate to the high point of a story."[50] Yet it must be asked what sort of suspense is created by changing the names of the merchants.

Antony Campbell and Mark O'Brien also see the interchange of "Midianite" and "Ishmaelite" as an element of authorial style, albeit in a different fashion. They read the text as intentionally presenting numerous "options" for reading: "One option: Joseph stripped, dropped down the well, and left to die; no Reuben rescue, no Ishmaelites, no Midianites. Another option: Joseph sold to passing Ishmaelites. Another option: Joseph 'lifted' by the Midianites . . . thwarting any sale by the brothers, and leaving open the possibility of the Midianites selling to Potiphar (cf. 37:36) or to the Ishmaelites (cf. 39:1). A further option: no sale of Joseph, but the rescue planned by Reuben (cf. v. 22b) and thwarted by the Midianites."[51] Unlike Longacre, Campbell and O'Brien recognize the inconsistencies in the narrative, but they make this part of the narrative technique of the author: "Can the various repetitions and doublets be accounted for as enhancements, enriching the story with options and the like? Exposure to the text affirms this."[52] We must wonder, however, how a reader, ancient or modern, is to understand a narrative that contains multiple options for a single event. We should also ask why such options are present only in certain sections of the Bible and are entirely absent in others. Campbell and O'Brien do not provide a solution to the problems the text presents; they simply affirm that the text is problematic.

W. Lee Humphreys, in an investigation of "the poetics of the Joseph novella," deals with the problem of the Ishmaelites and Midianites by offering the two standard possibilities we have already encountered: either the two groups are to be identified, in which case "they sold Joseph" in 37:28 refers to the brothers, or they are to be kept separate, in which case "the Midianites seem to appear just in time to steal even this brief success from the brothers."[53] More than Campbell and O'Brien, Humphreys finds meaning in the presence of multiple possibilities: "As the text now stands, syntactical ambiguity signals a breakdown in the ability of the brothers fully to shape events."[54] No real solution to the problem is offered here—just a way of making sense of it.

E. J. Revell also sees the alternation of names as part of the author's rhetorical technique, "with the intention of presenting to the reader different aspects of the same referent."[55] He argues that "Midianites" is used "where the character is agent, as with the traders," and "Ishmaelites" is used "where other characters perceive them, or sell to or buy from them . . . and so can be seen to represent their viewpoint."[56] He concludes that "the contrasting terms can be seen as used to highlight the distance between the world of the narrative and that of the narrator."[57] His observation as to how these names are used is well taken, but he depends on the assumption that "Ishmaelites" and "Midianites" have relatively narrower and broader usages and connotations for the ancient Israelite audience. It is also unclear what purpose such a rhetorical distancing of narrative from narrator would serve.

Whether writing from the precritical perspective in which the unified composition of the text was taken for granted, from the anticritical perspective, or from what we might term the postcritical perspective of the modern literary approach, the difficulty of reading the end of Genesis 37 as it stands is apparent. Examination of some of the various attempts throughout history to read the sale of Joseph as a unified narrative reveals a number of marked consistencies. The solutions to the textual problem do not—indeed, apparently cannot—rest on the plain meaning of the passage alone. New narrative elements must be introduced, or selective appeals made to unrelated biblical passages, or novel theories of reading imposed on the text. Insofar as the plain meaning of the text in all of these cases is subordinated to an externally derived hermeneutic, these methods may all be lumped under the term "midrash."

The critical method, specifically the Documentary Hypothesis, that is the subject of this book is grounded in the fundamental denial of such midrashic attempts to understand the text. Given the contradictions and inconsistencies found in Genesis 37 and throughout the Pentateuch, the unity of the text cannot be taken for granted, nor is it enough to recognize the textual difficulties and attempt to read around them, as it were. The Documentary Hypothesis is the attempt to understand how the text came to be the way it is, to wit: problematic, and in parts incoherent.

Chapter 1

THE DOCUMENTARY HYPOTHESIS

The critical study of the composition of the Pentateuch begins, in practical terms, and began, in terms of the history of scholarship, with the attempt to read the pentateuchal narrative from beginning to end as a unified whole. The nearly immediate consequence of such an attempt is and was the recognition that the canonical text, when read as a human literary product rather than as a divinely inspired work, presents insurmountable literary problems; indeed, any attempt to read the Pentateuch as a unified whole, or even many of its individual pieces, is difficult, if not impossible. The traditional ascription of the Pentateuch to Moses, which had been questioned in part from very early times, was already largely rejected by the leading scholars of the seventeenth century.

The rabbis of the Talmud stated that "Moses wrote his book and the Balaam pericope and Job. Joshua wrote his book and eight verses of the Torah" (*b. Bab. Bat.* 14b). The eight verses in question are those that the rabbis deemed it impossible for Moses to have written: Deuteronomy 34:5–12, beginning with "Moses died there" and continuing through his burial and the assessment of his stature as a prophet. It is not going too far to say that this rabbinic dictum opened the door for the further elaborations of this question during the medieval period and beyond. Of particular note is the great medieval commentator Abraham ibn Ezra (on Deut 1:2), who identified in addition to the entire last chapter of Deuteronomy (which he referred to as the "secret of the twelve," after its twelve verses) a few other verses that he thought it improbable, if not impossible, for Moses to have written. The sentence "The Canaanites were then in the land" in Genesis 12:6, for example, seems to have been written in a period when the Canaanites were no longer in the land; according to the biblical narrative, this was not the case until after the death of Moses, when Joshua and the Israelites conquered Canaan. Similarly, in Deuteronomy 1:1, when Moses is said to deliver his speech "on the other side of the Jordan," the sentence seems to have been written on this side of the Jordan—that is, on the Israelite side—a place that, again, Israel did not occupy until after Moses's death. The other verses ibn Ezra identified were Genesis 22:14 (in which the mountain where Abraham sacrificed Isaac is called Moriah or the mountain of Yahweh, which points to a time after Solomon built the temple there), Deuteronomy 3:11 (in which the giant bed of King Og is said to be kept as something of a wonder in the city of Rabbah in the territory of the Ammonites, even though Moses and the Israelites have just conquered Og), and Deuteronomy 31:22 (where Moses is said to write down the song contained in Deut 32 "on that day," as if it took place some time in the past, even though Moses dies on the same day he writes the song, so that it should, if written by Moses, read "on this day").[1] The end of the precritical belief in Mosaic authorship of the entire Pentateuch was sounded already by Thomas Hobbes in 1651: "And first, for the Pentateuch, it is not argument enough that they were written by Moses, because they are called the five Books of Moses; no more than these titles, The Book of Joshua, the Book of Judges, the Book of Ruth, and the Book of the Kings, are arguments sufficient to prove, that they were written by the Judges, by Ruth, and by the Kings."[2] Fewer than forty years later, the scholar Richard Simon was able to write regarding the texts challenging Mosaic authorship, "I know that one can suggest responses to most of these passages and to some others which it would be pointless to produce: but with the little thought that one might give to these responses, one would find them more subtle than true; and I don't believe that it would be necessary, or even wise, to resort to these kinds of ways around the problem, since the most knowledgeable Fathers have freely admitted that the Pentateuch, at least in the form it is now, cannot be attributed in its entirety to Moses."[3]

The Pentateuch itself makes no claim for Mosaic authorship; the tradition that Moses wrote the five books was both an unintentional by-product of inner-biblical developments and an intentionally articulated article of faith for both Jewish and Christian religious groups.[4] Although the precise manner by which Mosaic authorship came to be the authoritative view is perhaps lost to us, some evidence is available from within the biblical corpus. It is related to the referential range of the word "Torah." The word means "a teaching" or "a law," that is, a single legal or ritual prescription. It is used this way, for example, in Leviticus 6:2: "This is the law of the burnt offering," a statement that stands as the heading for the subsequent sacrificial prescriptions.[5] The book of Deuteronomy, however, applies the word more broadly, to encompass the collection of laws found in Deuteronomy 12–26. Thus in Deuteronomy 4:8, Moses says, "What great nation has perfect laws and rules like all of this Torah which I am setting before you today?" Here the term explicitly connotes the plurality of laws contained in the subsequent chapters, and in those alone: "which I am setting before you today" can only mean the laws delivered by Moses to the people on the plains of Moab, that is, the laws of Deuteronomy 12–26. Throughout Deuteronomy, the term is similarly used self-referentially: "this Torah" is a purely deuteronomic expression.[6] The only place that the phrase occurs outside of Deuteronomy is in Numbers 5:30, where it refers back to the preceding single law. In Deuteronomy, when Moses is said to have set "this Torah" down in writing (Deut 31:9; see also 31:24), the phrase refers, as it does everywhere in the book, to the laws of Deuteronomy alone.

The books following Deuteronomy, Joshua through Kings (the Deuteronomistic History), stretch the term even further. They use a new expression, "the [book of the] Torah of Moses." This phrase no longer refers just to the laws of Deuteronomy 12–26, but rather to the book of Deuteronomy as a whole, including Moses's speeches before and after the giving of the law. Joshua 8:31, for example, describes the building of the altar on Mount Ebal, "as Moses, the servant of Yahweh, had commanded the Israelites, as is written in the book of the Torah of Moses"; this refers to Deuteronomy 27:2–8.[7]

In the final books of the Hebrew Bible, Ezra, Nehemiah, and Chronicles, we again find the phrases "the book of Moses" and "the (book of the) Torah of Moses." We also, however, find the word "Torah" used on its own, as if the referent is a well-known entity to the listener or reader. Throughout these books, the Torah referred to seems to be not only Deuteronomy, as in Joshua–Kings, but the entire canonical Pentateuch. The famous example from 2 Chronicles 35:12–13 serves to demonstrate this. While in Deuteronomy 16:7 the Passover sacrifice is to be "boiled," in Exodus 12:8–9 it is to be "roasted in fire," and definitively not boiled; 2 Chronicles 35:12–13 says that the Israelites "boiled [not "roasted," as in the New Jewish Publication Society translation] the Passover sacrifice in fire"—thereby combining the two pentateuchal laws—"as is written in the book of Moses." Similar citation of elements from both Deuteronomy and elsewhere in the Pentateuch in Ezra, Nehemiah, and Chronicles serves to indicate that the term "Torah" had come to mean the canonical Pentateuch.[8]

We have in the Hebrew Bible, then, an interesting semantic phenomenon: while the use of the word "Torah" and the phrase "Torah of Moses" was continuous through the biblical period, the precise referent of "Torah" changed, gradually taking on a wider meaning, from a single law or collection of laws (Deut 12–26) to a book in which those laws were found (Deuteronomy) and finally to the entire corpus in which that book—and others with other laws—

were found (the Pentateuch), which is what the word means to this day. When this late meaning is read back into the earlier uses of the phrase, it was but a small step to understand the phrase "Torah of Moses" in Joshua–Kings, and especially the statement near the end of Deuteronomy that "Moses wrote this Torah" (Deut 31:9), as signifying that Moses was the author of the entire Pentateuch. Through this semantic expansion and the inner-biblical and postbiblical interpretive process, the idea of Mosaic authorship became a textually warranted claim.

NARRATIVE PROBLEMS

During the Reformation, when the challenging of authoritative claims, religious and otherwise, was the order of the day, scholars began to insist on a close reading of the pentateuchal narrative on its own terms, as a history of Israel from the creation of the world until the death of Moses. Under these circumstances, it was not long before the literary problems of the text became undeniable.[9] The hallmark of a unified composition, one created by a single author, is internal consistency: consistency of language and style, consistency of theme and thought, and, above all, consistency of story. Every narrative makes certain claims about the way events transpired—who, what, when, where, how, and why. When these elements are uniform throughout a text, there is no pressing need to inquire as to its unity. In the Pentateuch, however, historical claims made in one passage are undermined or contradicted outright in another. The problems identified by the Reformation scholars are the same as those we struggle with today and can be classified in three major overlapping groups: contradictions, doublets, and discontinuities.

Contradictions in the pentateuchal narrative come in a variety of forms, from the smallest of details to the most important of historical claims. On the minor end are ostensibly simple disagreements about the names of people and places. Is Moses's father-in-law named Reuel (Exod 2:18) or Jethro (Exod 3:1)? Is the mountain in the wilderness where Yahweh appeared to the people called Sinai (Exod 19:11) or Horeb (Exod 3:1; Deut 1:6)? Of somewhat more significance are disagreements about where, when, and even why an event took place. In Numbers 20:23–29, Aaron dies on Mount Hor; according to Deuteronomy 10:6, however, he dies in Moserah. In Numbers 3–4, after Moses has descended from the mountain and is receiving the laws, the Levites are assigned their cultic responsibilities; but according to Deuteronomy 10:8, the Levites were set apart at a site in the wilderness called Jotbath.[10] In Numbers 20:2–13, Moses is forbidden from crossing the Jordan because of his actions at the waters of Meribah, when he brought forth water from the rock; but then according to his own words in Deuteronomy 1:37–38, Moses was prohibited from entering the promised land not because of anything he did, but because of the sins of the people in the episode of the spies. Major contradictions, with important historiographical and theological ramifications, are also present in the text. The premier example of these is the creation story in Genesis 1 and 2: in what order was the world created? was it originally watery or dry? were male and female created together, or was woman made from man's rib? is man the culmination of creation, or the beginning? Other examples are equally problematic. For the cult: was the Tent of Meeting in the center of the Israelite camp (Num 2–3) and did Yahweh dwell there constantly (Exod 40:34–38), or was it situated well outside the camp (Exod 33:7), and does Yahweh descend to it only to speak with Moses (Exod 33:8–11)? For prophecy: could there be other prophets like Moses after his death (Deut 18:15), or not (Deut 34:10–12)? These contradictions, from minor to major, are difficult, and frequently impossible, to reconcile.

The second category of narrative inconsistency is doublets: stories that are told twice. In order to qualify as a literarily problematic repetition, two passages must not only tell a similar story, but do so in a way that renders them mutually exclusive: they must be events that could not possibly happen more than once. Thus one of the most often cited doublets in the Pentateuch, the patriarch passing off his wife as his sister in a foreign land (Gen 12:10–20; 20; 26:6–11) — which is actually a triplet — does not count. As hard as it is to believe that Abraham would pull the same trick twice, and that Isaac would do the same a generation later, there is nothing in these stories that prohibits such a reading. The two stories about Abraham and Sarah are set in different regions (Egypt and Gerar), with different characters (Pharaoh and Abimelech), while the story about Isaac and Rebekah, although set in Gerar with Abimelech, obviously features different protagonists at a different time. On the grounds of narrative alone, all three stories could well belong to a single author.

There are truly problematic doublets, however. The city of Luz is renamed Bethel by Jacob in Genesis 28:19, as he is on his way from his father's house to stay with his uncle Laban. The city of Luz is again renamed Bethel by Jacob in Genesis 35:15, on his way from his uncle Laban's house to rejoin his father in Canaan. (Not to mention that Abraham had already built an altar at Bethel, already not called Luz, in Gen 12:8.) Similarly, the site of Beersheba is given its name on the basis of the oath sworn (*nišbā‘*) between Abraham and Abimelech in Genesis 21:31. It is named again by Isaac in Genesis 26:33, on the basis of the oath sworn between him and Abimelech. Jacob's own name is changed to Israel when he wrestles with the divine being in Genesis 32:29. Jacob's name is changed to Israel again by God at Bethel in Genesis 35:10. These doublets are mutually exclusive: in each case, the naming or renaming is recounted as if it is happening for the first and only time.

More striking are the narratives relating the thirst of the Israelites in the wilderness. In Exodus 17:1–7, just after they have crossed the sea and before they arrive at the mountain in the wilderness, the people complain that they have no water to drink; Yahweh responds by telling Moses to strike a rock, from which water will come forth. Moses strikes the rock, the water comes forth, and the place is named Massah and Meribah. In Numbers 20:2–13, well after the Israelites have left the mountain, in the midst of their wilderness wandering, the people complain that they have no water to drink; Yahweh responds by telling Moses to speak to a rock, from which water will come forth. Moses strikes the rock, the water comes forth, and the place is named "the waters of Meribah." In these stories not only is the same name given to two different places, and for the same reason, but the stories themselves are remarkably similar.

In fact, all of these doublets, and others not discussed here, overlap with the previous group, that is, narrative contradictions. For the double telling of a single event entails two competing historical claims about, at the very least, when that event happened. As we have seen, not only when, but also the characteristics of where, who, how, and why may vary from passage to passage, even when the central "what" remains the same.

Contradictions and doublets can be found both across pentateuchal texts, as described above, and within individual pericopes; that is, the same problems exist on both the macro level and the micro level. The standard example of this is the beginning of the flood story, in Genesis 6:17–7:5. In 6:17–22, God tells Noah that he is going to bring a flood and instructs him to bring into the ark two of each kind of animal; we are then told that "Noah did so; just as God had commanded him, so he did" (v. 22). In 7:1–5, Yahweh tells Noah that he is going to bring a flood and instructs him to bring into the ark two of each unclean animal and seven pairs of every clean animal; we are then told that "Noah did just as Yahweh commanded him" (v. 5). The story thus presents the same events happening twice—God's announcement of the flood, instructions about the animals, and the fulfillment of those instructions by Noah—which marks it as a doublet. The story also tells us that on the one hand, Noah is to bring two of every animal (and he does so), and on the other, that he is to bring two of every unclean and seven of every clean animal (and he does so)—a glaring contradiction.

Similarly, in Numbers 14, after the episode of the spies, Yahweh tells Moses that the first generation of the Exodus will die before reaching the promised land, all except for Caleb (Num 14:21–24). Immediately thereafter, he speaks again and says almost the same thing: the first generation of the Exodus will die before reaching the promised land, all except for Caleb and Joshua (vv. 29–35). Virtually the same message is delivered twice in a row—it is a doublet—but there is a significant distinction in the content, a disparity in precisely who is to survive—and it therefore also entails a contradiction.

The third category of narrative problems may be called discontinuities. In these cases, the natural course of events of a story is interrupted by what appears to be an unrelated narrative. In Exodus 24:1–2, Yahweh commands Moses to go up the mountain with Aaron, Nadab, Abihu, and seventy of the Israelite elders. They do so—but not until 24:9. In between, in vv. 3–8, Moses performs a covenant ceremony with the people on the basis of the laws in Exodus 20:19–23:33 that Yahweh gave to Moses on the mountain—the same mountain that Moses is told to go up in 24:1 before he has even come back down (in v. 3). In vv. 9–11, Moses and the others go up the mountain, as instructed in vv. 1–2; in v. 12, however, Moses is again instructed to ascend the mountain, even though he is already there.

These types of discontinuities can also have significant and troublesome chronological components. The story of Isaac's blessing of Jacob instead of Esau in Genesis 27 takes place as Isaac is dying (v. 1), as Esau explicitly recognizes (v. 41). Yet Isaac does not die until Genesis 35:28–29—at least twenty-one years later (the time that Jacob served Laban).[11] Although perhaps not always technically contradictions, these discontinuities prevent the natural reading of the narrative as a continuous whole.

Alone, the evidence of the narrative problems that plague the pentateuchal text speaks only to the discontinuity of the whole and results in the isolation of one passage from the next, or the compositional distinctiveness of one pericope in relation to another. One might, on this basis, think that the Pentateuch is no more than a compilation of individual elements, originally independent from one another: Genesis 1 would be one text, and Genesis 2 another; Numbers 20 a third, and Deuteronomy 10 a fourth. Such a theory was, in fact, proposed early in scholarship. Suggested in part by scholars of the seventeenth century, the Fragmentary Hypothesis, as it came to be known, reached its fullest expression in the late eighteenth and early nineteenth centuries.[12]

Yet this theory was short-lived. It was quickly recognized that alongside the narrative difficulties in the text—indeed, hand in hand with them—are marked continuities, historical claims of one passage that are assumed and incorporated and developed in another.[13] Thus the story of Aaron's death in Numbers 20:23–29, although contradicted by Deuteronomy 10:6, is explicitly referred back to in Deuteronomy 32:50–51. At the same time, Numbers 20:23–29 presumes information from earlier passages: Aaron is said to be stripped of his vestments, which are then placed on his son Eleazar (vv. 25–26, 28); these are the official priestly garments first described in Exodus 28, made in Exodus 39, and placed on Aaron in the ceremony of Leviticus 8:6–9. The watery chaos of Genesis 1, although contradicted by the description of the earth in Genesis 2, is a central image for part of the flood story, in which the destruction of the world is represented as a return to the primordial chaos (Gen 7:11; 8:1–2a). At the same time, the rain that brings life to the dusty earth in Genesis 2 becomes, ironically, the agent of its destruction in other passages of the flood story (7:4, 12). Jacob's naming of Bethel in Genesis 35, although a doublet of the previous naming in Genesis 28, is recalled in detail by Jacob on his deathbed in Genesis 48:3–4 (see further case study V); this latter passage, in turn, in which Jacob calls the deity El Shaddai, is connected with God's statement to Moses in Exodus 6:3: "I appeared to Abraham, Isaac, and Jacob as El Shaddai." This brief list points out only some of the most obvious links, and only for a handful of texts; of course every one of these passages depends on many others and is itself the basis for yet others.

When the Pentateuch is read with a careful eye toward the narrative inconsistencies and continuities alike, the individual fragments coalesce into four strands or sources, each of which is internally consistent, and markedly distinct, in its historical claims. Furthermore, each of these sources is recognizable as an independently composed text—a document that once stood on its own, only later to be incorporated with the others. The original independence of the documents is to be seen in the coherence, continuity, and completeness of each (see further chapters 2, 3, and 4). This claim—four originally independent documents that have been subsequently combined and interwoven—is the central assertion of the Documentary Hypothesis.

THE FOUR DOCUMENTS

The first of these documents, in order of appearance, begins in Genesis 1 with the creation of the world and continues through the primeval history (including the flood), the patriarchs, the Exodus, the revelation at Sinai, the wilderness wandering, and the death of Moses. The second source begins in Genesis 2 with the creation of man and covers the same overarching narrative as the first. The third begins in Genesis 15 with God making a covenant with Abraham, before continuing on the same path as the others. The fourth document comprises the majority of the book of Deuteronomy and is, with the exception of an introduction and a few narrative transitions, the final speech of Moses to the Israelites before his death on the plains of Moab.

One of the most significant discrepancies among the first three sources—and importantly for our current purposes, the one that gives rise to the scholarly nomenclature—is when and how God's proper name, Yahweh, came to be known. According to the first strand, in Exodus 6:2–6, God appeared to the patriarchs as El Shaddai, "God Almighty," but did not tell them his true name. And this was indeed the case: in Genesis 17:1 God introduces himself to Abraham as El Shaddai; in 28:3 Isaac blesses Jacob in the name of El Shaddai; in 35:11 God introduces himself to Jacob as El Shaddai; and Jacob, in recalling this theophany on his deathbed in 48:3, again uses this title. It is not until Exodus 6:2–6 that God tells Moses that his true name is Yahweh. Before this point in the narrative of the first document, logically enough, none of the characters uses the divine name; they say either El Shaddai or employ the generic title Elohim, "God." According to the third document, too, God revealed his true name only to Moses (in this case, however, in Exod 3:14–15), and only because Moses asked. El Shaddai is not mentioned, but rather the earlier phrase "the God of your fathers" (see Gen 31:5, 42; 46:1). Now, however, God reveals himself with the obscure cipher "Ehyeh-Asher-Ehyeh" (Exod 3:14), which is quickly explained as something of a pun on the name Yahweh (3:15). As in the first source, in the third the characters (almost) never use the divine name but exclusively the title Elohim. In contrast to these two sources, in the second, Yahweh's name has been known and used since the earliest times: in Genesis 4:26, Enosh, in the third generation of humanity, begins to invoke Yahweh by name. And, not unexpectedly, in this document the characters in Genesis all regularly use the name Yahweh when referring to the deity.

On the basis of these distinct concepts of how and when the divine name was revealed, scholars gave the second source, which uses Yahweh throughout, the title "Yahwist," or "J" (from the German spelling, "Jahwist"). The third source, which introduces the divine name only in Exodus 3, was given the title "Elohist," or "E," since its characters use this name until the time of Moses. And the first source, though once also known as "Elohist," is now called "P," for "Priestly," in light of its close attention to all things cultic. The fourth source, which is contained entirely in Deuteronomy, is called "D," for "Deuteronomist."

Although I follow the standard nomenclature in this book, it needs to be noted that the names "Yahwist" and "Elohist" are not particularly helpful; indeed, because they imply that the use of the name "Yahweh" or the title "Elohim" is the primary means by which the sources are identifiable, they are largely misleading. These names originate from an early period of pentateuchal scholarship in which the alternation of the divine designations was seen as the single overriding key to the disentanglement of the sources in Genesis, to the neglect of all other narrative inconsistencies.[14] The use of either Yahweh or Elohim was understood to be a stylistic choice, with two important and detrimental results: first, Genesis was divided into only two strands—the Yahwist and the Elohist—and second, these two sources ceased to be found after (unsurprisingly) Exodus 2, that is, the last chapter before the name Yahweh is formally introduced in E.[15] This two-source analysis did in fact solve many of the narrative problems, insofar as much of J was largely isolated from the rest of Genesis; many problems remained, however, since P and E, with their competing historical claims, were still viewed as a single strand. For example, according to E, Benjamin is born to Rachel in Bethel, where Rachel dies in childbirth (Gen 35:16b–18), while according to P, Benjamin is born, like his siblings, in Paddan-Aram (35:22b–26); both of these contradictory claims were attributed by Jean Astruc to the Elohist—even though Isaac's sending of Jacob to Paddan-Aram in Genesis 28:1–5, and his return from there in 33:18, Astruc attributed to the Yahwist.[16] This two-source theory (again, only for Genesis), today known as the Older Documentary Hypothesis, was therefore an important step but was both literarily unsatisfying and methodologically misleading. The breakthrough occurred when scholars came to realize that the varying divine appellations in Genesis were related to the narratives in Exodus 3 and 6, and that the latter explained the former.[17] Once the use of the divine name in Genesis was understood not as a stylistic choice, but simply as one of many distinct historical claims inherent in the respective sources, the single older "Elohist" strand could be correctly seen as, in fact, two strands, each of which has a similar (though not identical) view on the revelation of the divine name to Moses, but each of which also has very different ideas on almost everything else.[18] Furthermore, connecting the divine designations in Genesis to Exodus 3 and 6 meant that the source analysis of Genesis could be—in fact, had to be—extended finally into the rest of the Pentateuch, where the analysis depends not on the use of Yahweh or Elohim, since in all the sources the characters now know the divine name, but rather on the multitude of other distinct historical claims in each document. Previously, scholars tended to rely on separate theories to explain the composition of Genesis and the rest of the Pentateuch: a documentary solution for Genesis and a fragmentary or supplementary solution for Exodus–Deuteronomy.[19] Now the whole could be understood in a uniform light. Although the understanding of the import of the divine designations in Genesis had fundamentally changed, the nomenclature for the documents remained; thus the formerly single Elohist was divided into the "older Elohist" and the "younger Elohist."[20] When these names were finally recognized as being unwieldy, the older Elohist became known as P, and the younger Elohist remained E.[21]

Although the four documents cover much the same territory—even D, which takes place in a single day, begins with Moses recalling the history of Israel from the theophany on the mountain to the end of the wilderness wandering—they each do so in a unique way. The basic history of Israel is the same, but the details differ on virtually every point. We have already seen that the two documents that describe the creation, P and J, do so in almost entirely contrary ways. The same two sources also describe the flood differently, and in each case, as we have noted, in line with their variant views on creation. Only J, however, describes the garden of Eden, Cain and Abel, and the Tower of Babel.

All three documents that tell the story of the patriarchs—P, J, and E—agree on their names and order—Abraham, Isaac, and Jacob—as well as their respective wives and children (for the most part), but they diverge widely in the details of the plot. In all three, Abraham receives a promise of land and progeny. In J, this happens before he leaves his homeland; in P, it happens after he has already entered Canaan. In P and E, this promise is accompanied by a covenant—yet the covenants are completely different, that of P being the covenant of circumcision and that of E involving a detailed sacrificial rite (and no circumcision). P and J describe the birth of Hagar's son Ishmael; E never names him. The destruction of Sodom and Gomorrah is known to both P and J, but only J tells the story of Abraham's negotiation with God. J and E contain stories of Abraham (and Isaac) passing off their wives as their sisters in a foreign court (although at different times and places); P does not. Only E describes the sacrifice of Isaac. Only P tells of Abraham's purchase of a burial plot for Sarah and the rest of the family, and only P has all the patriarchs and matriarchs (except Rachel) being buried there. Although all the sources know that Isaac married Rebekah, only J contains a narrative of how this happened. Although all the sources know that Isaac was the father of Jacob and Esau, only J tells the story of their birth and the trickery of Jacob in procuring Isaac's blessing. According to J, Jacob goes to Haran to escape from Esau and chances upon his mother's family there, where he marries Leah and Rachel and has twelve sons; according to P, Jacob goes to his mother's family in Paddan-Aram for the express purpose of finding a wife. All three documents know that a cult site was founded by a patriarch at Bethel, but in P it is Jacob, after his return from Paddan-Aram; in E it is Jacob, though before his time with Laban; and in J it is Abraham, in his initial sojourn through Canaan. Only J and E describe the struggles of Jacob against Laban, or Rachel and Leah's travails in child-bearing. Only J and E describe the affair of

Dinah and Shechem; P does not know that Dinah ever existed. Both P and E tell of Rachel's death, and only in E is it connected with the birth of Benjamin; in P, Benjamin has already been born, and in J, Rachel is still alive (see case study V). Although all three know that Joseph went down to Egypt, that there was a famine, and that Jacob and his family came to Egypt to join Joseph there, only J and E describe this process in detail; only J tells the story of Joseph and his Egyptian master's wife, only E tells the story of Joseph's and Pharaoh's dreams. According to P, Jacob's family dwells in Rameses; J tells us that his family dwells in Goshen.

In the Exodus narrative, we find the same situation. Only E tells the story of Moses's birth; only J tells of Moses killing the Egyptian. According to J, Moses's father-in-law is named Reuel; according to E, he is named Jethro. In P, Moses never leaves Egypt. These three documents describe God instructing Moses to lead the Israelites out of Egypt. Only J tells of the burning bush. In P and E, this theophany is accompanied by the revelation to Moses of God's true name, Yahweh; in J, as noted, this name was known to humanity from primeval times. Only P and J tell the story of the plagues in detail, and though they agree on some of the plagues, they disagree on others: P tells of blood, frogs, lice, boils, hail, locusts, and darkness; J has blood, frogs, insects (not lice), pestilence, hail, and locusts. Only in J do the Israelites have to escape hastily and at night. P and J describe the Israelites' escape from the Egyptians at a body of water but do so in entirely different terms (see case study IV). P, J, and D describe the giving of manna to feed the people in the wilderness; E never mentions manna. Only P and J tell the story of getting water from a rock; in J, this takes place before the theophany in the wilderness, whereas in P it takes place long after. Only E tells of the battle against the Amalekites, and only E and D describe the appointing of judges to assist Moses.

As for the theophany at the mountain in the wilderness, the most significant discrepancy is the identification of the mountain itself: in P and J, it is Sinai; in E and D, Horeb. The Decalogue and the tablets on which it is written are known only to E and D; P and J never mention either. In P, the theophany is unaccompanied by a covenant. All four sources know that Moses went up the mountain, sometimes more than once. But what he did there, and how long he stayed, is different in each case. The instructions for and construction of the Tabernacle are told only in P. The Tent of Meeting, as already mentioned, is presented differently in P and E; D and J never refer to it. The ark does not exist in E. Joshua does not exist in J. Miriam exists only in E. The episode of the golden calf is told only in E and D.

In the wilderness wandering, all four documents describe the Israelites as difficult. Only one story is found in multiple sources, however: the episode of the spies, which is told in P, J, and D, but not in E. Even here, the accounts differ as to what area of Canaan the spies explored, who went, what kind of report they brought back, who the offending party was, and how they were punished. Otherwise, the stories narrated in the various sources do not overlap (with the exception of D, which tells some stories parallel to those of J and E; see chapter 4). Thus the Israelites' desire for meat is told only in J—in P, they had received meat along with the manna before the theophany. The prophesying elders are known only to E (see case study II). The leprosy of Miriam is told only in E. The revolt of Dathan and Abiram is only in E. The revolt of Korah is only in P. The death of Aaron is only in P. The plague of serpents is only in E. The war against Midian is described only in P; in E, the same territory is known as the land of the Amorites and was conquered earlier. Both P and E describe the assignment of Transjordanian land to the tribes of Gad and Reuben; in P, however, this is not to be accomplished until after the Israelites have conquered Canaan, and then it is to be done by Joshua and Eleazar, while in E, it is done on the spot by Moses.

I present this rather lengthy list to illustrate the two competing factors at work in reading the pentateuchal documents: although their stories follow the same basic outline, they do so in divergent ways. And despite its length, this list is only partial and covers merely a selection of the broadest and most obvious differences among the strands. Each narrative contains a multitude of historical claims that stand in stark contradiction to those of the other sources, but these can be demonstrated only through the detailed study of a given passage.

It should be clear from this list that many individual episodes are told in only one of the documents; only a few are told in more than two. As a result, the majority of pericopes in the Pentateuch are, in fact, unified texts, in which a search for multiple strands is unjustified. The division of sources, in these cases, comes between pericopes, in the transition from one story to another. For example, the sacrifice of Isaac (Gen 22), the purchase of Sarah's burial plot (Gen 23), and the wooing of Rebekah (Gen 24) occur in three essentially discrete narratives, one after the other; each belongs to a different source (E, P, and J, respectively). At the same time, however, there are stories that are told in more than one document. In some of these, the two (or three) strands that contain the narrative situate it at different times in Israel's history—for example, Moses getting water from a rock or the establishment of a cult site at Bethel. But in some, the same story is told at the same time, and it is in these cases that we are faced with truly composite narratives. The clearest example of this is the flood narrative in P and J. Both situate the flood, naturally, in the primeval period, and they are interwoven into a single narrative of a single flood. Yet the process for identifying the original strands in these closely interwoven passages is precisely the same as that for identifying them elsewhere: the historical claims of each narrative are distinctive enough from those of the other, and continuous enough with themselves, that it is simply a matter of reading carefully and following the threads.

To this point I have discussed only the narrative portions of the Pentateuch and left the laws to one side. Yet the laws exhibit many of the same features that we have seen in the narratives: specifically, doublets and contradictions. The feature that is not present in the laws is the compositional alternation or interweaving that we find in the narratives. The pentateuchal laws exist in three discrete blocks: the laws of the so-called Covenant Code, in Exodus 20–23; the priestly code in Leviticus and Numbers; and the deuteronomic code in Deuteronomy 12–26. The repetitions in these laws are glaring: for example, all three have festival calendars; all three have slave laws; all three have asylum laws; two tell the Israelites not to boil a kid in its mother's milk; two have an altar law; two have the kosher laws; two have tithing laws. The contradictions are equally telling. In Exodus 20:21–23, the law states that the Israelites can make an altar of stone wherever they like; in Deuteronomy 12:13–14, the law states that they are to sacrifice only at the centralized cultic site (that is, the Temple in Jerusalem). And while Deuteronomy 12:15–16 allows for animals to be killed and eaten anywhere in the country, Leviticus 17:2–7 requires that all animals that are killed for food be brought to the Temple and presented as an offering. According to Numbers 18:21–32, the Israelites are to tithe annually, and those tithes are to go directly to the Levites; according to Deuteronomy 14:22–29, only every third year are tithes to go to the Levites, while in the other two years the Israelites are permitted to spend their tithes on a feast to be consumed at the Temple. In both Exodus 21:2 and Deuteronomy 15:12 a Hebrew slave is to be released in the seventh year; in Leviticus 25:40, however, he is to serve until the jubilee year.

It is clear that the three law codes are, like the narratives, independent and mutually exclusive. It is a mistake, however, to consider the laws as distinct from the narratives. Whether one believes that the laws and the narratives were composed separately or not, it remains the case that the laws are embedded in narrative contexts. Each law code claims to be the single law code given by God to Moses at the mountain in the wilderness. This is a historical claim, no different in type from others that we find in the pentateuchal sources. And when read in this light, it becomes clear that the law codes belong integrally to the narrative sources. The Covenant Code is a part of E; the priestly laws are part of P; and the deuteronomic laws stand at the center of D. Thus it is E's claim that God gave Moses the laws of the Covenant Code the first time Moses went up the mountain and that Moses delivered them to the people immediately thereafter and ratified them with a covenant (Exod 24:3–8). It is P's claim that God gave Moses the laws of Leviticus and Numbers at the foot of the mountain (whereas what Moses received on the mountain itself was the blueprint for the Tabernacle, the prerequisite for all the subsequent laws). It is D's claim that God gave Moses the laws on the mountain but that Moses did not deliver them to the Israelites until his final address on the plains of Moab. Further, the content of the laws is itself a historical claim: each source states not just that God gave laws at a certain time in a certain place, but that these are the specific laws he gave — these and not others. Although the laws are distinct in form, they are not distinct literarily; they are part of the narrative, both in content and in context.

DISTINGUISHING THE DOCUMENTS

When the pentateuchal narrative is separated into its constituent strands on the basis of narrative flow alone — when the reader follows the historical claims of each passage and of the whole — other features of the individual documents emerge with varying degrees of clarity. The first category of these we might call thematic: those elements that give the overarching narrative of a given source its shape and focus. In P, these thematic elements may be most prominent. We notice first the strong structural aspects of the source: the repeated "these are the generations" markers in Genesis; the heavy use of genealogies throughout; the regular reporting of characters' ages and other important dates; and the use of formulaic introductory and concluding phrases. Also readily apparent, and responsible for the name of the source, is P's focus on the affairs of the cult, and particularly of the priesthood: for instance, the establishment of the Tabernacle, the presence of Yahweh in it, the elevation of Aaron and the ordination of the Aaronid priesthood, the relegation of the Levites to cultic servants, the levitical revolt of Korah. P's narrative as a whole tends to be, somewhat confusingly, both elliptical and expansive: although some periods are passed over with only the barest of outlines, such as Jacob's travels outside of Canaan or Joseph's descent into Egypt, some events are described in excruciating detail, such as the purchase of a burial plot in Mamre (Gen 23) and the instructions for and construction of the Tabernacle (Exod 25–31, 35–40).

J is different — less highly structured and less interested in priestly affairs. There is a marked propensity in J toward etiology, both of the obvious kind ("therefore the place was called X") and the broader kind (as in Yahweh's addresses to the serpent, Eve, and Adam in Gen 3). Family affairs figure strongly in J's patriarchal narratives: Cain and Abel, Jacob and Esau, Judah and Tamar. Far more than the other documents, J takes up preexisting songs and poems into its narrative, incorporating them at the appropriate time to lend color or depth to the narrative: the song of Lemech (Gen 4:23–24), the blessing of Jacob (Gen 49), the song of the sea (Exod 15), the song of the well (Num 21:17–18), the blessing of Moses (Deut 33). J tends to represent the deity working behind the scenes to affect the course of history, rather than directly interfering; the seminal statement of this for J is Genesis 45:5–8 (and further in 50:20).

E is marked first by a concentration on prophecy: the strongly prophetic description of Moses, and even of Abraham (Gen 20:7, 17), and a focus on questions of prophetic authority. Probably connected with this theme is the regular appearance of God to humans in visions and dreams rather than directly (for example, Gen 15:1; 20:3; 31:24); Moses is the explicitly noted exception (Num 12:6–8). In line with this, divine messengers play a particularly prominent role in the E stories, both in the patriarchal narratives and as a constant presence in the wilderness (see Exod 23:20).

Structurally, D is notable for being set almost exclusively as Moses's farewell speech. It is further marked by alternations of narrative and rhetorically charged exhortations (for example, Deut 9:23 [narrative], 24 [rhetoric], 25–29 [narrative]). Hand in hand with its unique form is D's repeated insistence on the theme of Israel's disobedience, in the past and even in the future (Deut 31:29). At the same time, Moses's stalwart leadership and blamelessness is equally important in D.

These thematic and structural features of the four documents emerge only once the literary analysis, done on the basis of the narrative flow, has been completed. The recognition of overarching themes in a given source is a secondary stage of the analysis, not a primary one: the analysis cannot begin with the identification of themes and then proceed to the discovery of the documents. This is because themes are, for the most part, not unique to a given source, but rather are more prominent in one source than the others, or differently configured. We cannot assume, therefore—as some scholars have, with unfortunate results—that every positive mention of Aaron necessarily belongs to P (see Exod 4:14–16, J); that every etiology belongs to J (see Gen 35:15, P); that every depiction of Moses as a prophet belongs to E (see Exod 8:8–9, J); that all references to ages and dates belong to P (see Gen 37:2, J); that every interpolated song or poem belongs to J (see Num 21:27–30, E); or that every appearance of a divine messenger belongs to E (see Gen 19:1, J). If such assumptions are followed, the resulting narratives are unreadable. Such is only to be expected: the identifying feature of a narrative is not its theme, but its plot, and it is from the plot and the ways in which the coherent story is told that the theme emerges, secondarily. As with any literary work, the message and structure of each document are apparent only once the document has been read in its entirety. And in order to understand the themes of any of the sources, the sources must first be separated on the more objective grounds of narrative continuity.

A second category of features that emerges once the documents have been separated on narrative grounds is that of style and terminology. We have already seen that the mistaken early view that the divine designations in Genesis were a stylistic feature led to an erroneous understanding of the composition of the text. We would be similarly in error were we to understand the name of the mountain in the wilderness (Sinai or Horeb) as merely a terminological choice, rather than as the names of two distinct locations.[22] There are, however, authentic stylistic and terminological features of each document. Only P uses the word *g-w-h,* "to perish." While all the sources use the preposition *bᵊṭerem,* "before," only J uses the word *ṭerem* alone in this way. Only E uses the common noun *hannāhār,* "the river," to designate the Euphrates. Only P uses the phrase *mᵊ'ōd mᵊ'ōd,* "very very." The list can go on.

What is true of themes is even more the case with style and terminology: these observations can be made only after the sources have been isolated. There is a fundamental underlying principle in play here: all of the documents are written in good ancient Hebrew, and their authors all had access, one must assume, to the entirety of the Hebrew language. To say that a document doesn't use a particular term, then, is not to say that it could not use it; in other words, these observations are descriptive, not prescriptive. Unfortunately, as with the category of themes, all too often in the history of scholarship style and terminology have been used in order to identify sources, rather than to describe them; thus we encounter scholars who produce vast lists of words and phrases that "belong" to the various documents and rely on those lists (or the lists of other scholars) to then distinguish the sources.[23] When this has occurred, the resulting textual analyses invariably produce problematic narratives. This is especially true even when scholars have recognized that a certain word or phrase is only typical of a given document, rather than unique to it; in other words, if a word has appeared nine times out of ten in one source, then it is assumed that the eleventh example is from that same source. Yet the very existence of the word in another source makes such a conclusion methodologically untenable: if a document uses a word even once, it can use it more than once. Furthermore, even if a word never appears elsewhere in a given source, that is not a reason to deny that a passage containing the word can belong to said source if the passage fits narratively into the source. However, there are words and phrases that are typical of a document, even if they are not unique to it. This is true of almost all literature: some words and phrases are particularly important or meaningful within the context of a given work, and though they may be used by others, that does not mean that they are any less central to the first.

Far more useful than identifying words and phrases that occur only in a single document are those examples in which a single entity is referred to by one source using one word and by another source using another word. For instance, whereas both P and J use the word *šipḥāʰ* to designate a female servant, E uses *ʾāmāʰ*. Even more valuable are those examples in which a single word is used with distinctive meanings in various sources. For instance, J and E use the word *minḥāʰ*, "gift," to refer to any sort of presentation, but in P this word only and always has the specific meaning of "grain-offering." Equally compelling is the evidence of linguistic differences among the sources; for example, J and P, even in identical narrative contexts, use different forms of the verb "to beget."[24] Even in these cases, however, we are still dependent on the correct division of the text according to narrative flow for our appreciation of the stylistic and terminological distinctions among the documents.

As should by now be clear, it is the primary and fundamental claim of this book—in contrast to almost all previous source-critical scholarship—that the literary analysis of the Pentateuch must begin with and be carried out on the basis of the narrative consistencies and contradictions. We cannot start with the diversity of theme or language and divide the text on these bases. The literary analysis of the Pentateuch is grounded in the basic inability to read the text as a whole, and that inability is not manifested in the variety of themes or style. Our reading of the Pentateuch is not undermined by the collocation of disparate themes or by the use of different words for "female servant." Instead, what makes the reading of the Pentateuch problematic is its lack of narrative flow, and only by addressing this problem first and foremost can we be responding authentically to the text before us.

This argument can be carried forward into the area of the dating of the documents as well. The popularization of the Documentary Hypothesis in the late nineteenth century, and its acceptance in the wider field of biblical studies, was a result of the association of the sources with various historical settings, so that the literary analysis of the text had direct implications for the history of Israel and Israelite religion.[25] Although some features of the sources may suggest broad historical settings—J's advancement of the tribe of Judah lends itself to a pro-Davidic/Solomonic reading; P's focus on the cult might belong to a period in which the Temple stood and functioned; E's polemic against the northern calf shrines of Dan and Bethel implies its composition at a time when those shrines still existed; D's requirement of cult centralization fits well with the Hezekian and Josianic reforms—for the most part these settings overlap chronologically or are simply too broad to be fit into any clear chronological framework with respect to the other sources. Indeed, attempts to order the documents chronologically (that is, to date them relatively) and situate them temporally (to date them absolutely) with any specificity are based more on a given scholar's a priori historical beliefs than on the texts themselves. We must be careful not to confuse the literary question with the historical one. Like thematic and stylistic considerations, the dating of the documents can be accomplished only after the sources have been isolated on other grounds. And at that point, the various datings of the documents have no effect on the literary analysis: if it could be demonstrated somehow that J is from the tenth century BCE and that P is from the third century BCE, while E is from the second millennium BCE and D was written during the Hoover administration, the literary evaluation of the text and the isolation of the sources on the grounds of narrative flow would be precisely the same. In this book, then, I will not discuss the dating of the documents. The separation of the literary analysis, on the grounds of narrative flow alone, from all other secondary considerations of the individual sources, be it theme, style, or potential historical setting, must be maintained if the analysis is to retain any degree of objectivity.

As long as it is remembered that considerations of narrative flow must always be primary in the analysis of the Pentateuch, the elements of theme, style, and historical setting, though secondary, do add considerably to the Documentary Hypothesis as a whole. As Sean McEvenue puts it, "Such observations do not prove source divisions, but they do confirm probabilities, just as travelling does not prove geographic facts but does confirm one's trust in maps."[26] What makes the theory compelling is not that it resolves only the narrative problems, but that the secondary elements of theme and style fit beautifully into the source division revealed by the narrative analysis. We see in the individual documents a confluence of all the literary aspects: the separation of the narratives, the identification of coherent themes, and consistent style align, so that there is a convergence of evidence.[27] Thus those who would oppose the Documentary Hypothesis on one basis—who would say that the use of stylistic features to isolate sources is invalid and produces flawed results—are both correct, in that such a procedure is methodologically faulty, and incorrect, in that the Documentary Hypothesis does not rest on the grounds of style alone. Rather, its elegance derives from the observation that the stylistic evidence falls in line with the narrative and thematic distinctions—as long as it is remembered that no single word or phrase or theme must always belong to a single document but may instead be predominant, central, or differently used in one source while still being used in others.

Since almost the beginning of the Documentary Hypothesis, scholars have attempted to discern within each source further layers. J was thus divided into J^1, J^2, and J^3; P into P^1, P^2, and P^3, etc.[28] In some cases this type of analysis is undoubtedly correct: few scholars today would deny that, for example, P is in fact at least two layers, P and H (which stands for Holiness Code: the laws in Lev 17–26, and perhaps some further material in Exodus and Numbers).[29] In some cases, claims for multiple layers are considerably more speculative in nature and less textually justified. Yet insofar as these layers are seen as the literary prehistory of a single source, the Documentary Hypothesis itself is largely unconcerned with them. The Documentary Hypothesis is intended to account for the penultimate stage of the text, the existence of the sources immediately before their combination into the canonical whole. If it could be demonstrated that there were fifteen recensions of D, it would not matter, as long as the last of them was the D that was incorporated into the Pentateuch we now have. The attempt to discern the original layers of each source is by no means unimportant—indeed, it is of great value—but it is, like so much else, a secondary stage of analysis that can only follow the separation of the four sources.

The Documentary Hypothesis must be recognized for what it is: a hypothesis. It is a proposed literary solution to the literary problems of the Pentateuch, no more, no less. It does not purport to date the texts or to be the key to the history of Israelite religion. It does not intend to address the issue of the oral transmission of Israelite traditions or the combination thereof. It is only an attempt to understand how the book we call the Pentateuch came to look the way that it does. All other considerations are secondary. To that end, it must be judged against alternative solutions proposed to solve the same problems. It is not a method, comparable to structural analysis; it is in fact misleading even to call it "source criticism," since it is not a specific critical approach like form criticism or tradition criticism. It is a hypothesis—it just happens to be the most economical, clearest, and most complete solution currently available for the literary complexities of the canonical text.

In this book, I explore the Documentary Hypothesis in two ways. First, I present five case studies of individual pentateuchal passages. These are meant to serve both as a demonstration of the Documentary Hypothesis at work—as a proof for the statements made above, the "showing" to accompany the preceding "telling"—and as something of a guide for the reader, a how-to for the analysis of other pentateuchal texts. Thus each one begins with the assumption that a text is unified until shown to be otherwise and continues with the analysis through the disentanglement of the sources. Each also contains discussion of how the sources discovered in this passage fit into their respective documents as a whole, as well as engagement with alternative views. Interwoven with these case studies are five chapters dealing with specific issues regarding the individual sources of the Documentary Hypothesis. This interplay of textual analysis and thematic discussion should help readers to attain a clearer understanding of the Documentary Hypothesis both in practice and in theory. Ideally, the case studies and the discursive chapters will be convincing illustration that the Documentary Hypothesis remains the best explanation for the composition of the Pentateuch.

Case Study I

The Sale of Joseph, Genesis 37:18–36

The text of Genesis 37:18–36 and its textual difficulties were presented in the introduction and do not require repeating here. It should be recalled, however, that the problems of the passage do not stem from any verbal or terminological confusion; for instance, the divine name makes no appearance in this chapter, and the interchange of "Jacob" and "Israel" creates no difficulties. Rather, the textual issues of this chapter derive entirely from the confused, contradictory narrative—that is, the plot and the historical claims of the story—and any resolution of these issues must in turn derive first and foremost from the resolution of the narrative continuity of the passage.[1] In the introduction, I noted that there are a number of textual difficulties, some of which may be attributed to authorial choice, but the central problem of the Ishmaelites and Midianites is irresolvable in any straightforward reading of the biblical text.[2] It is also worth remembering that the problematic parts of the passage broke down nicely into pairs: two decisions by the brothers to kill Joseph, two plans to throw Joseph into a pit, two arguments for saving him, two passing tribes. When these observations are taken into account, the solution becomes little more than the connection of individual elements in the various pairs, recognizing both the discontinuities and continuities in the text.[3]

Because the Ishmaelite/Midianite problem is the driving force behind the need for literary analysis of the chapter, it is sensible to start the analysis with the separation of these variations. Thus the arrival of the Ishmaelites in v. 25 will belong to one story (hereafter story A), and the passing by of the Midianites in v. 28aα[1] will belong to another (story B). To story B we may also add the rest of v. 28aα, "they pulled Joseph up out of the pit." I noted in the introduction that the syntax of the verbs in this verse suggests that the Midianites are the subject throughout; at the same time, however, the idea of the Midianites selling Joseph to the Ishmaelites is untenable narratologically. The natural break in this verse is between "out of the pit" and "they sold." The evidence for this is

34

in the repetition of the explicit direct object, "they pulled Joseph up out of the pit. They sold Joseph"; as it stands, this repetition is awkward and unnecessary.[4] The central distinction between the two stories can therefore be identified: in story A, "they"—that is, the brothers—sell Joseph to the Ishmaelites, just as Joseph says, in 45:5: "because you [the brothers] sold me hither." In story B, the Midianites steal Joseph from the pit without the brothers' knowledge, again just as Joseph says, in 40:15: "I was kidnapped from the land of the Hebrews."

The arrival of the Ishmaelites in story A is inseparable from Judah's reaction to their arrival in vv. 26–27. These verses are a single speech with a rhetorically structured argument.[5] The actual sale of Joseph to the Ishmaelites—that is, the fulfillment of Judah's plan—is found in v. 28aβb, which we have already separated from v. 28aα. In this analysis, the act of selling Joseph follows directly on the brothers' agreement to Judah's plan to sell him at the end of v. 27, as it naturally should: "'Let us sell him to the Ishmaelites, but let us not do away with him ourselves. After all, he is our brother, our own flesh.' His brothers agreed. . . . They sold Joseph for twenty pieces of silver to the Ishmaelites, who brought Joseph to Egypt."[6]

Judah's plan is clearly a response to a previous initiative. There are, however, two mentions of the brothers' decision to kill Joseph, one in v. 18, and one in vv. 19–20.[7] To which does Judah's plan refer? The two-part description of what the brothers intended to do according to Judah—kill Joseph and "cover his blood"—matches perfectly with the two-part plan described in v. 20: "Let us kill him and throw him into one of the pits."[8] We have here both elements: the killing (with the same verb, *h-r-g*), and the hiding of the fact. Verses 19–20, like vv. 26–27, are indivisible, even exhibiting some of the same structural features.[9]

We have, to this point, assigned vv. 19–20, 25–27, and 28aβb to story A. If we return to story B, so far identified only as v. 28aα, we can certainly connect with it v. 36, the sale of Joseph into Egypt by the Midianites.[10] Verse 28aα also contains, however, mention of the pit from which the Midianites took Joseph. This must connect back to v. 24, in which the brothers throw Joseph into an empty pit (though all but Reuben think that it has water in it). Verse 24, in turn, is the fulfillment of Reuben's plan (to save Joseph, not to kill him) in vv. 21–22.[11] The use of the definite article, "the pit," *habbōrāʰ*, seems to presuppose that a specific pit has already been identified, that is, by Reuben in v. 22 ("that pit," *habbôr hazzeʰ*)—in story A the brothers only planned to throw Joseph's body into "one of the pits" (v. 20).[12] The notice that there was no water in the pit is crucial to Reuben's plan to return and remove Joseph. And in story B, as in story A, the act follows immediately upon the plan: "Reuben went on, 'Shed no blood! Cast him into that pit . . .' and they took him and cast him into the pit." This cannot be the same pit mentioned in vv. 19–20 in story A. There, the pit is to be used to hide Joseph's corpse after he has already been killed. Moreover, the plan in vv. 19–20 goes unfulfilled, as Judah's speech in vv. 26–27 explicitly supplants it with the sale of Joseph to the Ishmaelites. The pit in vv. 21–22, 24, and 28aα is used not to hide Joseph's body, but as the means by which Joseph is to be saved, as Reuben plans, or the means by which he is actually to be killed, as the other brothers think.[13]

Reuben's plan in vv. 21–22, like Judah's in vv. 26–27, is a response to a previous initiative to kill Joseph, as both the opening words, "Reuben heard," and the repeated pleas "do not strike him," "shed no blood," and "do not touch him yourselves" indicate. Judah's plan, as we saw, matched perfectly with vv. 19–20; Reuben's plan, therefore, is to be connected with the more general decision to kill Joseph in v. 18.[14] The existence of Reuben's plan, and more importantly the brothers' implementation of it, makes it impossible for Judah's plan in vv. 26–27 to be read as part of the same story. How could Judah suggest to the brothers that Joseph should not be killed when the brothers think that it is already a fait accompli—or, even if they have seen through Reuben's plan (for which there is no indication in the text), they have already decided not to kill Joseph?[15]

The plan of Reuben to hide Joseph in the pit and the removal of Joseph by the Midianites are part of story B, and therefore also must be Reuben's response when he finds that Joseph is no longer in the pit, in vv. 29–30. We can thus assign to story B vv. 18, 21–22, 24, 28aα, 29–30, and 36.

We are left with only a few unassigned verses: v. 23, in which Joseph is stripped of his tunic, and the continuous section of vv. 31–35,[16] in which the brothers fake Joseph's death and bring his bloodied tunic back to their father. The actions of vv. 31–35 are precisely those already planned in story A, in v. 20: "we can say, 'A savage beast has devoured him.'" The only difference is that now, with Joseph having been sold rather than killed, the brothers have to find a source of the blood to put on Joseph's tunic, hence the slaughter of the kid.[17] In vv. 31–35 we see the tying together of a number of the elements in story A: the tunic, the lie about Joseph's death by a wild beast, and Jacob's preference for Joseph over the other sons, which ties in with Joseph's dreams in the beginning of the chapter and thus also with the brothers' decision to kill Joseph in vv. 19–20.[18] The presence of the tunic in this part of the story indicates that v. 23, the removal of the tunic, belongs also to story A. This is further supported by the verbal connection between vv. 23 and 19–20: the first words of v. 23, "When Joseph came up to his brothers," hearken back to the end of v. 19, "Here comes that dreamer."[19]

Finally, we may take another look at the first words of v. 25: "they sat down to a meal." These words have little connection to what immediately follows in story A, the passing of the Ishmaelites, or to what immediately precedes it, the stripping of Joseph in v. 23; we surely cannot expect that the brothers will have stripped him of his tunic and then sat down to a meal with him.[20] On the other hand, they do fit with v. 24 in story B, in which Joseph is already in the pit. More crucially, the meal in v. 25aα connects nicely with v. 28aα, the passing of the Midianites. The brothers' meal provides the narrative rationale for where the brothers were when this happened, and why they, or at least Reuben, did not prevent it.[21]

The preceding analysis is based entirely on narrative continuity: which parts of the story contradict each other, and which naturally continue and build on each other. By simply following the story in its plain meaning, the two strands emerge naturally from the text. When viewed individually, the results are striking:[22]

STORY A

¹⁹וַיֹּאמְרוּ אִישׁ אֶל־אָחִיו הִנֵּה בַּעַל הַחֲלֹמוֹת הַלָּזֶה בָּא׃ ²⁰וְעַתָּה לְכוּ וְנַהַרְגֵהוּ וְנַשְׁלִכֵהוּ בְּאַחַד הַבֹּרוֹת וְאָמַרְנוּ חַיָּה רָעָה אֲכָלָתְהוּ וְנִרְאֶה מַה־יִּהְיוּ חֲלֹמֹתָיו׃ ²³וַיְהִי כַּאֲשֶׁר־בָּא יוֹסֵף אֶל־אֶחָיו וַיַּפְשִׁיטוּ אֶת־יוֹסֵף אֶת־כֻּתָּנְתּוֹ אֶת־כְּתֹנֶת הַפַּסִּים אֲשֶׁר עָלָיו׃ ²⁵וַיִּשְׂאוּ עֵינֵיהֶם וַיִּרְאוּ וְהִנֵּה אֹרְחַת יִשְׁמְעֵאלִים בָּאָה מִגִּלְעָד וּגְמַלֵּיהֶם נֹשְׂאִים נְכֹאת וּצְרִי וָלֹט הוֹלְכִים לְהוֹרִיד מִצְרָיְמָה׃ ²⁶וַיֹּאמֶר יְהוּדָה אֶל־אֶחָיו מַה־בֶּצַע כִּי נַהֲרֹג אֶת־אָחִינוּ וְכִסִּינוּ אֶת־דָּמוֹ׃ ²⁷לְכוּ וְנִמְכְּרֶנּוּ לַיִּשְׁמְעֵאלִים וְיָדֵנוּ אַל־תְּהִי־בוֹ כִּי־אָחִינוּ בְשָׂרֵנוּ הוּא וַיִּשְׁמְעוּ אֶחָיו׃ ²⁸וַיִּמְכְּרוּ אֶת־יוֹסֵף לַיִּשְׁמְעֵאלִים בְּעֶשְׂרִים כָּסֶף וַיָּבִיאוּ אֶת־יוֹסֵף מִצְרָיְמָה׃ ³¹וַיִּקְחוּ אֶת־כְּתֹנֶת יוֹסֵף וַיִּשְׁחֲטוּ שְׂעִיר עִזִּים וַיִּטְבְּלוּ אֶת־הַכֻּתֹּנֶת בַּדָּם׃ ³²וַיְשַׁלְּחוּ אֶת־כְּתֹנֶת הַפַּסִּים וַיָּבִיאוּ אֶל־אֲבִיהֶם וַיֹּאמְרוּ זֹאת מָצָאנוּ הַכֶּר־נָא הַכְּתֹנֶת בִּנְךָ הִוא אִם־לֹא׃ ³³וַיַּכִּירָהּ וַיֹּאמֶר כְּתֹנֶת בְּנִי חַיָּה רָעָה אֲכָלָתְהוּ טָרֹף טֹרַף יוֹסֵף׃ ³⁴וַיִּקְרַע יַעֲקֹב שִׂמְלֹתָיו וַיָּשֶׂם שַׂק בְּמָתְנָיו וַיִּתְאַבֵּל עַל־בְּנוֹ יָמִים רַבִּים׃ ³⁵וַיָּקֻמוּ כָל־בָּנָיו וְכָל־בְּנֹתָיו לְנַחֲמוֹ וַיְמָאֵן לְהִתְנַחֵם וַיֹּאמֶר כִּי־אֵרֵד אֶל־בְּנִי אָבֵל שְׁאֹלָה וַיֵּבְךְּ אֹתוֹ אָבִיו׃

STORY B

¹⁸וַיִּרְאוּ אֹתוֹ מֵרָחֹק וּבְטֶרֶם יִקְרַב אֲלֵיהֶם וַיִּתְנַכְּלוּ אֹתוֹ לַהֲמִיתוֹ׃ ²¹וַיִּשְׁמַע רְאוּבֵן וַיַּצִּלֵהוּ מִיָּדָם וַיֹּאמֶר לֹא נַכֶּנּוּ נָפֶשׁ׃ ²²וַיֹּאמֶר אֲלֵהֶם רְאוּבֵן אַל־תִּשְׁפְּכוּ־דָם הַשְׁלִיכוּ אֹתוֹ אֶל־הַבּוֹר הַזֶּה אֲשֶׁר בַּמִּדְבָּר וְיָד אַל־תִּשְׁלְחוּ־בוֹ לְמַעַן הַצִּיל אֹתוֹ מִיָּדָם לַהֲשִׁיבוֹ אֶל־אָבִיו׃ ²⁴וַיִּקָּחֻהוּ וַיַּשְׁלִכוּ אֹתוֹ הַבֹּרָה וְהַבּוֹר רֵק אֵין בּוֹ מָיִם׃ ²⁵וַיֵּשְׁבוּ לֶאֱכָל־לֶחֶם ²⁸וַיַּעַבְרוּ אֲנָשִׁים מִדְיָנִים סֹחֲרִים וַיִּמְשְׁכוּ וַיַּעֲלוּ אֶת־יוֹסֵף מִן־הַבּוֹר ²⁹וַיָּשָׁב רְאוּבֵן אֶל־הַבּוֹר וְהִנֵּה אֵין־יוֹסֵף בַּבּוֹר וַיִּקְרַע אֶת־בְּגָדָיו׃ ³⁰וַיָּשָׁב אֶל־אֶחָיו וַיֹּאמַר הַיֶּלֶד אֵינֶנּוּ וַאֲנִי אָנָה אֲנִי־בָא׃ ³⁶וְהַמְּדָנִים מָכְרוּ אֹתוֹ אֶל־מִצְרָיִם לְפוֹטִיפַר סְרִיס פַּרְעֹה שַׂר הַטַּבָּחִים׃

¹⁹They said to one another, "Here comes that dreamer! ²⁰Come now, let us kill him and throw him into one of the pits; and we can say, 'A savage beast devoured him.' We shall see what comes of his dreams!" ²³When Joseph came up to his brothers, they stripped Joseph of his tunic, the ornamented tunic that he was wearing. ²⁵Looking up, they saw a caravan of Ishmaelites coming from Gilead, their camels bearing gum, balm, and ladanum to be taken to Egypt. ²⁶Then Judah said to his brothers, "What do we gain by killing our brother and covering up his blood? ²⁷Come, let us sell him to the Ishmaelites, but let us not do away with him ourselves. After all, he is our brother, our own flesh." His brothers agreed. They sold Joseph for twenty pieces of silver to the Ishmaelites, who brought Joseph to Egypt. ³¹Then they took Joseph's tunic, slaughtered a kid, and dipped the tunic in the blood. ³²They had the ornamented tunic taken to their father, and they said, "We found this. Please examine it; is it your son's tunic or not?" ³³He recognized it, and said, "My son's tunic! A savage beast devoured him! Joseph was torn by a beast!" ³⁴Jacob rent his clothes, put sackcloth on his loins, and observed mourning for his son many days. ³⁵All his sons and daughters sought to comfort him; but he refused to be comforted, saying, "No, I will go down mourning to my son in Sheol." Thus his father bewailed him.

¹⁸They saw him from afar, and before he came close to them they conspired to kill him. ²¹But when Reuben heard it, he tried to save him from them. He said, "Let us not take his life." ²²And Reuben went on, "Shed no blood! Cast him into that pit out in the wilderness, but do not touch him yourselves"—intending to save him from them and restore him to his father. ²⁴They took him and cast him into the pit. The pit was empty; there was no water in it. ²⁵Then they sat down to a meal. ²⁸When Midianite traders passed by, they pulled Joseph up out of the pit. ²⁹When Reuben returned to the pit and saw that Joseph was not in the pit, he rent his clothes. ³⁰Returning to his brothers, he said, "The boy is gone! Now, what am I to do?" ³⁶The Midianites, meanwhile, sold him in Egypt to Potiphar, a courtier of Pharaoh and his chief steward.

We may now turn to the question of determining to which source documents these stories belong. There are a few hints: in story B the focus is on Reuben, and in story A the main actor is Judah; the deception of Jacob in story A links thematically to Jacob's deception of Isaac in Genesis 27 (J), involving as it does both mistaken clothing and the use of an animal's carcass;[23] the use of the imperative *hakker-nā'* in v. 32 is repeated and serves as a keyword for the J story in Genesis 38:25;[24] and finally, the concept in story A of "covering the blood" of Joseph is distinctly reminiscent of the same motif in the J narrative of Genesis 4:1–16, when Cain attempts to cover the blood of his slain brother, Abel.[25] These clues point to the assignment of story A to J and story B to E. It is most important to observe that the two stories in Genesis 37 connect narratively and thematically with the J and E stories from earlier in Genesis and continuing on throughout the Joseph narrative.[26]

When viewed independently, the differences between the two stories emerge clearly. In E, the brothers not only want to kill Joseph, but actually try to do so, with only Reuben knowing that the boy is safe because the pit is empty.[27] Having accomplished this, they sit down to eat, but while they are preoccupied the Midianites come by and steal Joseph from the pit. Reuben returns to the pit alone, as according to his plan, but the boy is not there; the story concludes with the information (not available to the characters) that the Midianites have taken Joseph to Egypt and sold him there. In J, the brothers plan to kill Joseph and go as far as removing his precious tunic—which, like Joseph's dreams, appears only in the J story—but before they can go any further they see the Ishmaelites, and Judah devises the plan to sell, rather than kill, Joseph. Having sold him successfully, the brothers return to their plan of lying about Joseph's whereabouts to their father.

Perhaps more remarkable than the ease with which the canonical text breaks down into two independently coherent stories is the fact that in this separation, not a single word of the biblical text has been altered: nothing removed, nothing added, nothing even moved out of its original place in its source document. The compilation of the two into a single story, moreover, is readily understood to be based purely on the logic and chronology of the narrative. No part of the ordering and interweaving of these two texts depends on or even suggests any ideological or theological intentionality on the part of the compiler (for more on this term, which is used throughout, and on the process of compilation in general, see chapter 6).[28] The decision of the brothers to kill Joseph in v. 18 (E) had to precede the same in vv. 19–20 (J), since it is in v. 18 that we find the notice that Joseph is at a distance from the brothers. Reuben's plan, vv. 21–22 (E), had to follow immediately on the decision to kill Joseph, since they begin with

"Reuben heard": that is, he heard the brothers plan to kill Joseph.[29] The disrob-
ing of Joseph (v. 23; J) had to precede the throwing of him into the pit (v. 24; E),
for the obvious reason that the brothers could not remove Joseph's tunic after he
was already in the pit. Because the arrival of the Ishmaelites and Judah's plan to
sell Joseph to them form a naturally continuous story (vv. 25aβ–27; J), the notice
that the brothers sat down to a meal (v. 25aα; E) had to come first; there is no
other place for it in the remainder of the narrative. The removal of Joseph from
the pit (v. 28aα; E) had to precede his sale (v. 28aβb; J).[30] The sale, in turn, had
to precede Reuben's return to the pit to find Joseph missing (vv. 29–30; E). The
entire continuous conclusion to J, vv. 31–35, followed this, as was only natural;
note in particular that the subject of v. 31, "they," links back nicely to "his brothers" in v. 30. Had v. 36, the conclusion to E, come before v. 31, it would appear
that the Midianites were the ones who slaughtered the kid and dipped Joseph's
tunic in the blood.

In short, throughout the process of combining the two stories into a single
narrative, the compiler had very little choice in what piece went where, at least
if he had any interest in preserving a semblance of narrative logic and chronology in the final product.

In critical scholarship, the major alternative to the documentary solution
to the problems of the text has always been the supplementary model, that is,
the notion that the text attained its current form through the accretion to an
original text of secondary insertions, alternative variants, or redactional layers.
Although the ease and simplicity of the documentary approach as presented
above is probably the best rebuttal to such analyses, we must nonetheless con-
tend with the supplementary approach directly.

The scholars who take the vast majority of the text as being original, with
only the barest of secondary additions, are those who generally view the text
as a unity but are unable to overcome the glaring difficulty of the Ishmael-
ite/Midianite problem. The foremost proponent of this approach is Umberto
Cassuto, who was committed to opposing the Documentary Hypothesis.[31] He
pointedly rejected the attempts of Benno Jacob and others to read the text as
it stands, recognizing in such readings many of the problems discussed in the
introduction. His solution was to ascribe the two mentions of the Midianites (in
vv. 28aα and 36) to marginal glosses that had migrated through scribal error into
the body of the text.[32] These glosses would represent an ancient variant tradition to that found in the majority of the passage, one in which the Midianites,
rather than the Ishmaelites, sold Joseph into Egypt. By calling the insertions
"marginal glosses," Cassuto was able to couch his solution in the language of
text criticism, rather than source criticism, but this is only a superficial altera-

tion. Cassuto's "glosses" have no versional evidence to support them; they are transparently a means of removing unwanted material from the text. Further, his solution resolves only the Ishmaelite/Midianite problem. While this is admittedly the most glaring of the difficulties in Genesis 37, there are others that Cassuto leaves to stand.

Later scholars, less opposed to the idea of layers of composition but equally opposed to the Documentary Hypothesis, have seen these Midianite references as additions to an otherwise unified text, but for other reasons. Thus George Coats saw the insertion of the Midianites in v. 28aα as a means of alleviating the guilt of the brothers in the selling of Joseph into slavery by attributing it to the passing Midianites.[33] It is not clear that this puts the brothers in a much better position: they are still guilty of wanting to kill Joseph, planning to sell him, losing him, and covering up the fact. Herbert Donner's solution was similar:[34] he claimed that a later editor realized that when Joseph's brothers sell him to the Ishmaelites in v. 28aβb, there is no notice of their removing Joseph from the pit; this editor therefore added that the Ishmaelites—whom he called "Midianites" on the basis of their equation in Judges 8:24—were the ones who had done this. Thus v. 28aα was added. The final verse of the chapter was written on the basis of 39:1 and was inserted to provide an inclusio for the insertion of Genesis 38, also considered secondary;[35] the use of "Midianites" rather than "Ishmaelites" in 37:36 was done on the same basis as v. 28aα. In both cases, it seems clear that the presence of the Midianites was deemed problematic enough to warrant their removal from the original text; what is less obvious, in fact, nearly inexplicable, is why they should then have been added in at a later stage.[36]

Where the preceding scholars saw the Midianites as the insertion, some scholars have gone the opposite route and viewed the Ishmaelites as secondary. This requires that three verses be considered additions to the text. Claus Westermann argued that vv. 25–27 and 28aβb are a secondarily inserted variant tradition (not unlike Cassuto).[37] Westermann, however, suggested that the two variants, the Midianites and Ishmaelites, are maintained together in the text "for the benefit of the listener or reader . . . who likewise know[s] the variants in the patriarchal narratives."[38] Again, the other duplications and contradictions in the text are left to stand. In addition, the "insertion" of vv. 25–27 and 28aβb has narratological, thematic, and verbal resonances only with select parts of the rest of the passage—that is, those that we have identified as J.[39] What is more, as noted above, Judah's speech seems totally unfamiliar with the plan of Reuben; why would a later editor add a speech that does not move the narrative forward, but rather takes it a step backward? Finally, we must ask what the contours of this "variant tradition" were: was it otherwise identical to the plot of the "original" layer of the passage? was there more to it that was not preserved? if not, why not? This sort of fragmentary approach raises many more questions about the *Sitz im Leben* of the fragments than it answers about the final form.

A similar but more convoluted suggestion was brought by Samuel Loewenstamm.[40] He claimed that the original version of the story was from E and included the majority of what is now the canonical text. This base text had then been reworked by a J-redactor, who added vv. 25–27 and 28aβb. According to Loewenstamm, however, this J-redactor also deleted from the original E text vv. 28aα, 29–30, and 36, that is, those most contradictory to the newly added material. How did these deleted verses find their way back into the canonical text? They were returned by the final redactor, who, one assumes, got them from the authentic E text, which must have still existed in some form, even though the verses made the text more difficult to read.

The aforementioned scholars, whether seeing the Midianites or Ishmaelites as secondary, all considered only a few verses, two or three, to be secondary additions. There are, as we have seen, two difficulties with this approach. First, what is ascribed to the "original" layer of the passage is not a perfectly readable, coherent, logical narrative but contains numerous duplications and confusions. Second, there is no obvious justification for the insertion, since there is little obvious reason for anyone to have complicated the passage, in either direction. The variety of explanations for why these verses may have been inserted only adds to the feeling that this is an ad hoc explanation, intended mainly to explain away the most egregious narrative problem while making light of, or indeed ignoring, all of the others.

On the other end of the spectrum are those scholars who hold to something very close to the classical source division, at times even referring to the two layers as J and E, but who nevertheless maintain that one of the stories is a supplement to the other, original, narrative. For some, the J story is the original layer, while E is a revision of it. Robert Coote claims that everywhere it appears, including in this passage, E is a layer of revision of J, albeit a thorough one.[41] One wonders, however, why the author of the Elohistic revision of J, who intended, as Coote claims, to change the original J narrative of "Judah and Joseph" into "the history of Joseph" alone,[42] would bother inserting the plan of Reuben and the presence of the Midianites; how do these contribute to E's purported propagandistic purpose? And can it merely be chance that both E and J are readable as continuous texts? Why would the author of E bother to write his insertions in such a way when he might much more simply have added a word or phrase here and there?[43]

The same basic treatment is found in the work of Hans-Christoph Schmitt, but he attributes to the "Reuben layer" a theological, rather than political, agenda.[44] This layer emphasizes, according to Schmitt, the hand of God in what happens to Joseph: even though Reuben plans to save his brother, God sends the Midianites to ensure that Joseph goes to Egypt, and Reuben's grief in vv. 29–30 is an important statement of humanity's powerlessness in the face of God's desires. While this theological interpretation of the "Reuben layer" is attractive, even convincing, it does not require that the "layer" be seen as a supplement to an earlier, presumably less theological, *Grundschrift*.[45] All of the theological meaning Schmitt finds in this layer functions within the layer itself, without any necessary interaction with the "Judah layer." Schmitt's argument for a supplementary reading in this passage is based, it would seem, on the notion that a more theologically minded author must be later than, and written in response to, one who is less so. There is, however, no textual reason to believe this.[46]

Some scholars take E, or the "Reuben variant," as the original layer, with J as the supplement; this approach is similar to that of Westermann, but with a broader view of what is included in the secondary layer.[47] The object of this revision is unclear, though it is usually attributed to the political priority of Judah in ancient Israel and the attempt of a later Judean author to revise in Judah's favor an originally northern text. Regardless of the motivation, the textual questions remain: why would he insert a plan from Judah that is narratologically implausible? why invent the arrival of the Ishmaelites, when Judah simply could have suggested that the brothers sell Joseph to the Midianites who were already in the text? why are the thematic and verbal links only within this added material, rather than interacting with the rest of the chapter?

Of the scholars who see a larger block of supplementary material, essentially one full source according to the classical documentary approach, it must be asked why one should understand the material as supplementary at all. When the "layer" has its own identifiable plot, differentiated from that of the base text, and even its own theological or other conceptual identity, verbal or stylistic profile, and internal coherence, are these not the hallmarks of an independent writing? It is the coherence and continuity of the "supplement" that raises doubts: if an editor or re-writer wanted to alter, for whatever reason, the original text of the story of the sale of Joseph, why would he bother connecting the pieces of his own insertions, since they would never be read as anything other than part of the larger whole? It is entirely unexpected to find that "supplements" to an original text form in themselves a coherent, continuous narrative.

In the final analysis, it is the nature of the J and E stories identified above—that is, continuous, coherent, and complete—that stands as the sharpest rebuttal to any theory of gradual growth, secondary insertions, or redactional layering. The basis for many nondocumentary analyses has been the claim that the chapter cannot be divided into two independently coherent narratives, but we have seen above, as others have before, that in fact it can. Each story represents a fully conceived, internally consistent narrative, a distinct historical claim, relating how Joseph was sold and transported to Egypt. Neither has any gaps that are filled by the other; reading them in isolation is, in fact, far simpler than trying to understand them in light of each other.[48] It cannot be claimed even that one is a revision of the other; they are simply two different ways of narrating the same underlying tradition of Joseph's descent to Egypt. The conclusion of E. A. Speiser regarding v. 28 serves to describe the entirety of the chapter: "This single verse alone provides a good basis for a constructive documentary analysis of the Pentateuch; it goes a long way, moreover, to demonstrate that E was not just a supplement to J, but an independent and often conflicting source."[49]

Chapter 2

CONTINUITY

The J Source

The J source has long been considered one of the most secure elements of the Documentary Hypothesis—a coherent, continuous, virtually complete account of Israel's history from creation through the death of Moses. It is therefore unsurprising that attacks against the Documentary Hypothesis in the past thirty years or so have centered on the denial of the existence of J. This denial was announced most influentially and stridently by Rolf Rendtorff in his seminal work *The Problem of the Process of Transmission in the Pentateuch* and has been taken up in much of the scholarship that followed him, culminating in the publication of a paired set of essay collections, *Abschied vom Jahwisten* and *A Farewell to the Yahwist?*[1] Understanding how some scholars came to the position that the J document is illusory requires going back in the history of scholarship to the development of the methods known as form and tradition criticism. Once we have established the development and contours of this fundamentally antidocumentary view, we can return to the question of whether and how J can still be maintained as a central element in the Documentary Hypothesis.

FORM AND TRADITION CRITICISM

The broad acceptance of the classical four-source Documentary Hypothesis in the late nineteenth and early twentieth centuries led to a rise in new methods of understanding the growth of the Pentateuch. These new approaches focused not on the literary formation of the text but rather on the preliterary development of the genres and traditions that the literary sources took up. Over time, however, these preliterary investigations resulted in new theories regarding the composition of the text, theories that ostensibly pose a significant challenge to the Documentary Hypothesis.

Form criticism, inaugurated by Hermann Gunkel in the early twentieth century, is the study of the development and social origins of the various genres that are found in the biblical text.[2] Briefly drawn, the method involves the identification of a genre, or form—such as myth, genealogy, law, etiological tale—and the subsequent attempt to discern the *Sitz im Leben* of that genre, the cultural setting in which it originally would have been used. This approach was fundamentally preliterary: the earliest forms of the genres were understood to be oral and to belong in the public sphere.

The clearest examples of form-critical analysis may come from the study of the psalms. On the basis of a set of formal markers—keywords, rhetorical structure, and sometimes meter, among others—a given psalm may be identified as part of a particular genre, such as a psalm of thanksgiving, a psalm of praise, a lament, or a royal psalm.[3] Though these categories are not always perfectly applicable to every psalm, they provide a general rubric into which most psalms may fit. For example, Psalm 30 may be formally analyzed as a psalm of thanksgiving.[4] Its dominant feature is a rather vague story of deliverance from some trouble (vv. 2–4, 7–13a), and it uses the keyword "praise," or "thank" (*y-d-h*; vv. 5, 10, 13b). There is further some suggestion of a public recitation, as vv. 5–6 are addressed to some other party. These elements are found over a range of psalms (including Pss 18, 32, 92, 116, 118, and 138, and parts of others), helping us place Psalm 30 in the larger genre of psalms of thanksgiving. The *Sitz im Leben* of this genre is then the topic of inquiry. Given the frequent references to some sort of public reading, as well as the exhortation to the audience to praise Yahweh, it is logical to assume that the psalm of thanksgiving was originally recited at a site of public worship, probably the Temple, at a time of community gathering. It must be remembered that the *Sitz im Leben* refers to the genre, not to the specific psalm.[5] This analysis does not suggest that Psalm 30 itself was read aloud, though it may have been. Rather, Psalm 30 was written in the genre of the thanksgiving psalm, and its formal features are traceable to an originally oral recitation in a specific cultic setting.

One reason that the psalms are relatively easy to analyze form-critically is that the individual textual blocks are, for the most part, clearly separated: each psalm is a form-critical unit. There are elements of the Pentateuch that are similarly clear: for example, the genealogy of Genesis 5, the collection of tribal sayings in Genesis 49, the hymn in Exodus 15, or the laws of Exodus 20:23–23:33. Each of these can be firmly assigned to a genre, and that genre can be assigned a probable *Sitz im Leben*. Much of the pentateuchal narrative, however, is not so readily broken down into genres. The examples given stand out precisely because they are not narrative, though they are embedded in narratives. The narrative proper presents more difficulties: can one really distinguish with certainty between a "tale" and a "legend"? Or, in a narrative in which the deity is the protagonist, can one readily distinguish the "myth" even from "history"? Some of these problems exist because biblical scholars borrowed both terminology and classifications from nonbiblical literature, notably from Scandinavian folklore, and it is not always apparent that the same labels fit the two distinct corpora.[6] Different scholars use different terms, such that there is little homogeneity in the literature.[7] Gunkel referred to virtually all the narrative of Genesis as "legend," though he distinguished between various types of legend.[8] Beyond the problem of terminology, there has been broad disagreement regarding the means by which the form of a text is established: on the basis of content, or linguistics, or structure.[9] One may agree, however, that there are some patent generic differences in the diverse narratives of the Pentateuch: etiological narratives are distinct from battle reports, birth stories from tales of rebellion. Thus we may justifiably assume that the etiology of Mahanaim in Genesis 32:2–3 belongs to the genre of local etiology, stories that describe how a particular place got its name, and that this genre has its *Sitz im Leben* in particularly localized oral traditions.[10] These types of stories would have been told by the residents of a given place, among themselves or perhaps to visitors, about how the place received its name. Again, however, the actual story of Genesis 32:2–3 only participates in the genre; the text itself has no *Sitz im Leben*. We cannot leap from our assessment of the genre to the assumption that the residents of Mahanaim actually told this story about Jacob, though neither can we necessarily rule it out; the form-critical method simply does not address this specifically textual question.

What form criticism does provide is an interpretive key for a given text. Knowing the genre of a text allows the reader to recognize a set of meanings not necessarily evident from the words themselves. A reader who is not conversant with the genres of ancient Israelite literature, oral or written, is at a distinct disadvantage.[11] Form criticism allows for an important diachronic analysis as well. Once the genre of a text is established, and the features of the passage that belong to the genre are identified, the scholar is able to understand more clearly the manner in which the text applies and particularizes that genre for its own purposes. This type of analysis, sometimes called rhetorical criticism, and perhaps best considered as a process distinct from that of form criticism, brings the broad characterization of genre into play with the specific literary aspects of the text itself.[12] It is primarily an act of appreciation, a method for studying the narrative art of the biblical author, and it highlights the features of a passage that the author has marked as important over and above the simple generic category he has used in writing the passage. Especially in cases of a single genre being used multiple times, as, for example, the stories of the endangered matriarch in Genesis 12:10–20; 20; 26:1–11, the ability to recognize the manner in which each story has departed from or expanded upon the basic genre allows for far greater precision in exegesis.[13]

Like form criticism, tradition criticism probes the preliterary history of the pentateuchal narratives. The product of the combined efforts of Gerhard von Rad and Martin Noth in the mid-twentieth century, tradition criticism inquires not about the form of the preliterary story but about its content. To again take the example of Genesis 32:2–3, a tradition-critical analysis of these verses would suggest that this etiology is fundamentally associated with the town of Mahanaim.[14] Tradition criticism attempts, in a way not found in form criticism, to attribute a plausible historical scenario to the earliest underlying traditions. Thus, for example, the story of Jacob's treaty with Laban in Genesis 31:43–54 is associated with the authentic memory of a treaty between some segment of Israel and some segment of Aram.[15] Tradition criticism is multilayered: it recognizes that the traditions about Jacob are distinct from those about the other patriarchs, that the traditions about Jacob and Esau are distinct from those about Jacob and Laban, and that the traditions about Jacob in Shechem are distinct from those about Jacob in Bethel, despite the fact that on the literary level all of these elements are interwoven and intrinsically connected. As each layer is pulled back, we get closer to the earliest manifestation of the individual traditions; from there we can see how they have come together into the larger traditions and cycles of stories in which they are now found, expanding outward to encompass the entire scope from creation through conquest. In terms of the history of traditions, then, the individual traditions about the patriarchs came together at some point to form a larger tradition complex, or theme, of the patriarchs—so too the primeval history, the Exodus, the wilderness wanderings, and the conquest. And these "major themes," as Noth called them, then came together to form the overarching pentateuchal narrative found in each of the pentateuchal sources.

At the same time, tradition criticism addresses the question of the relative age of various pentateuchal traditions. Thus Noth posited that the traditions of Isaac were older than those of Abraham.[16] Similarly, one may inquire about the relative age of individual manifestations of a single tradition: Noth considered the etiology of Beersheba in Genesis 26:32–33 to be tradition-critically earlier than the version in 21:27–31.[17] It must be stressed that these evaluations of the age of traditions are not evaluations of the age of the pentateuchal stories themselves. The text of Genesis 26:32–33 may well be younger than that of 21:27–31, even if the tradition contained in it is considered older. The aim is not to date passages of the Pentateuch, but rather to understand the development of the traditions that the pentateuchal authors took up and reshaped. "Compared with oral transmission," Noth wrote, "literary fixations are secondary, and the time and circumstances of their appearance provide no direct indication of the origin and significance of the traditions absorbed in them."[18] Like form criticism, tradition criticism, in its original manifestation, was not addressed to the literary question of the composition of the Pentateuch.

Gunkel, von Rad, and Noth, despite some differences in the details, all fundamentally accepted the Documentary Hypothesis.[19] Indeed, form and tradition criticism depend on the correct separation of the sources from each other. The canonical text cannot be used as the basis for either form-critical or tradition-critical analyses for the simple reason that the canonical text is a conflation of various forms and traditions. To start from the canonical text is to start with a false data set; it is only after the original sources, with their original stories, with their original forms and traditions, have been isolated that these preliterary investigations can move forward. A few examples of this should serve to make the point.

Genesis 48:1–12 relates Jacob's encounter with Joseph's sons Manasseh and Ephraim. Verses 5–6 describe in what appears to be technical language Jacob's adoption of the boys. If we read this section in the canonical text, therefore, we may consider vv. 1–12 as a whole to participate in the genre of adoption report.[20] Yet the source-critical analysis of this passage assigns vv. 3–7 alone to P. The adoption language, and therefore the form of adoption report, is confined exclusively to these verses; when they are removed, it is apparent that what remains belongs not to the genre of adoption report, as there is no adoption language therein, but rather to the genre of deathbed blessing, and the parallels with other texts that belong to this genre are readily apparent. The canonical text here is misleading; genre cannot be assigned to it because it is composed of two distinct genres that have been interwoven. Only after the source division has been carried out can we make informed and accurate form-critical assessments.

Similarly, the theophany Jacob experiences in 28:10–22 can in its canonical form be understood as *hieros logos* of the cult site of Bethel.[21] Yet when the sources of this passage are separated, it becomes clear that this is true only of E. The E story connects the theophany with the erection of a cultic pillar and the naming of the site Bethel and is indeed a *hieros logos*. The J story, on the other hand, is a theophany accompanied by a promise of divine assistance on Jacob's journey and so belongs more properly to a genre one might call promise narra-tive. Not only is there no establishment of a cultic site, the story is not even lo-cated at any particular place to which a *hieros logos* could be attached (for more on this, see case study V). Again, the source division reveals two distinct genres within a single canonical story; to apply form-critical analysis to the canonical text is to miss or misread the genres present in the text.

We may use the same examples to demonstrate the dependence of tradi-tion criticism on source analysis. In Genesis 48, as already noted, there are two sources: one from P, in which Jacob adopts Manasseh and Ephraim (vv. 3–7), and one from E, in which Jacob blesses Joseph's sons, including the important switching of their birth order such that Ephraim receives the more substantial blessing (vv. 17–19). Each of these stories contains important evidence of earlier traditions. In P, the adoption of Manasseh and Ephraim is a means by which the tribes by those names became central to the larger Israelite nation even though they were not among Jacob's twelve sons.[22] In E, the switching of the blessings stands as an explanation for the greater importance of the tribe and territory of Ephraim in Israel, even though Manasseh was traditionally the first-born.[23] Reading the text canonically, as if it were all from a single author, one might draw conclusions regarding the tradition history by which these two elements were brought together.[24] When we recognize that they derive from two separate sources, we can avoid this error and see that the traditions were separate until the sources in which they were transmitted were brought together.

In the case of Genesis 28:10–22, the canonical text is unclear about the pre-cise tradition underlying the *hieros logos* of Bethel. One cannot be certain whether the tradition held that Jacob founded a cultic site there because he saw the divine messengers ascending and descending the stairs or because Yahweh appeared to him and promised him divine protection. When the sources are separated and we understand that only the divine messengers belong to the *hieros logos*, a clearer picture of the tradition that may underlie the narrative emerges, and we can (more) reasonably conjecture what the local tradition of Bethel held regarding the foundation of the sanctuary there.

Although both form and tradition criticism were developed as means for un-derstanding the preliterary development of the Pentateuch, it was perhaps in-evitable that over time the methods would be applied to the literary stage. Form and tradition criticism became tools by which scholars evaluated the compo-sition of a single text, or the relationships among various texts. In both cases this move was methodologically problematic: the questions asked by a method aimed at the preliterary stage (form or tradition criticism) were now being answered in terms of a literary investigation (source criticism).

The Joseph story, comprising Genesis 37 and 39–47 by most accounts, has been the subject of intensive form-critical scrutiny. Since its identification as a "novella" by Gunkel, it has been further defined by von Rad as belonging to the tradition of wisdom writings.[25] That genre definitions can apparently be applied to the entirety of the story has led a number of commentators to argue for the compositional unity of these chapters.[26] If the text is divided among sources, it is claimed, its form is necessarily destroyed, and therefore the division is illegitimate.[27] Such analyses explicitly prioritize the form of the text over its content. As we have already seen, the Joseph story contains narrative contradictions that cannot be overlooked, such as how Joseph came to Egypt, who purchased him, and where in Egypt Jacob's family settled when they arrived. Scholars who argue for the unity of the text on form-critical grounds must go to great lengths to explain these contradictions as features of a unified composition.[28] Thus George Coats, for example, attributes the contradiction of the Midianites and Ishmaelites in Genesis 37 to "glosses"; other contradictions he leaves unnoted.[29] Such explanations, however, are by definition ad hoc, since they derive from the a priori conclusion that the text is a unity. Especially in the cases of scholars who use such contradictions as evidence of composite authorship elsewhere in the Pentateuch, the arguments for the unity of the Joseph story reveal themselves as special pleading. When the Joseph story is understood as in fact three independent and distinct Joseph stories (the J and E narratives observed in case study I plus the considerably briefer P account; see chapter 5), the "form" of the canonical whole identified by scholars is indeed destroyed; but in its place are three distinctive forms, each of which deserves its own analysis.

In this case, both form and source criticism begin with an attempt to read the text as it is received; source criticism takes the content, the historical claims of the narrative, as the definitive starting point for analysis, while form criticism prioritizes the structure and formal features of the text. Only the historical claims of the narrative are intrinsic to the text; the genre and structure identified by form critics is an abstract construction, even when a well-grounded one. To take the scholar's own delineation of the text's form as the starting point for compositional analysis is to ignore the actual words of the text in question. More to the point, it is not the purpose of form criticism to address the question of a text's composition; that is the realm of source criticism. Thus when form-critical studies make claims for demonstrating the unity of a text, they must be weighed against the source-critical assessment of whether the text was ever written by a single author at a single time. If not, as in the case of the Joseph story, then form-critical analysis addresses the form of a new text, one that is the result of compilation, and any genres that are extrapolated from it may be either coincidental or artificially constructed.

At the same time, ironically, the form-critical assessment of the unity of the Joseph story apparently requires the elimination of some passages from the narrative. Foremost among these is Genesis 38, which, given its undeniably digressive nature, is treated as a secondary insertion into the story.[30] It is also argued that the description of Joseph's acquisition of Egyptian property for the Pharaoh in Genesis 47:13–26, because it appears "isolated and extraneous to the overall story,"[31] is treated as a later expansion of the text.[32] The rationales for treating these passages as secondary are formal: because they do not seem to participate in the plot development of the "novella," they cannot belong to it. Yet the "novella" is a modern critical genre construction. The biblical author—in both of these cases the author of J—was not constrained to follow the "novella" form, and there is no reason that he could not have written a digression in Genesis 38 or an etiology of Egyptian land practice in Genesis 47. Neither is contradictory to the historical claims of the J story; there are no literary disjunctures or other problems to indicate that they should be eliminated. Here, again, form-critical criteria are being used to render judgment on the source criticism of the text. We may say, on form-critical grounds, that the elements of Genesis 38 and 47:13–26 are not part of the main genre being employed by the biblical author; this is, however, a judgment of the genre of the Joseph story—not of the actual Joseph story itself. The source criticism of the Joseph story indicates that the author of J did include these elements; thus from a form-critical perspective, the Joseph story, even specifically J's Joseph story, does not comprise a single genre, but a combination of different genres. Again, the use of form-critical criteria to determine the composition of the text results in a false data set; in this specific case, the argument is also clearly circular.

In terms of tradition criticism, we may take as a first example the treatment of Exodus 24:1–2, 9–11 by Ernest Nicholson. Over a series of articles, he argued for the antiquity of the basic tradition in these verses, that seventy Israelite elders ascended the mountain and beheld Yahweh.[33] Nicholson asserts that the early tradition did not feature the characters of Moses, Aaron, Nadab, and Abihu mentioned in vv. 1–2.[34] This may be so; the validity of Nicholson's basic position is not at issue here. What is methodologically problematic is his description of the growth of the tradition in terms of the actual text of Exodus. Thus he argues that vv. 1b–2 are late and that v. 1a, "though probably earlier than verses 1b–2, cannot be regarded as the original introduction to verses 9–11."[35] Nicholson has leapt here from the realm of tradition to that of text. His basic argument, that the tradition in its earliest form did not include the figures referred to in the text of vv. 1–2, may be profitably discussed. The text of vv. 1–2, however, is integrally bound up with the rest of the passage in question and on a literary level cannot be removed from it; in literary terms, vv. 1–2 are manifestly the original introduction to vv. 9–11. Nicholson, by referring to the actual text rather than to the traditions contained in it , suggests that the original tradition of Exodus 24:1–2, 9–11 was fixed in form and that it can be extracted from the pentateuchal text; what is left, therefore, is secondary—no longer to the oral tradition, but to the fixed literary form of the story. In fact, Exodus 24:1–2, 9–11 is not only by any measure a compositional unity in its own right, but belongs squarely as part of the larger J story of Moses and the Sinai event.[36] It may be that in writing his narrative the author of J was the first to introduce Moses, Aaron, Nadab, and Abihu to the earlier tradition of the theophany before the seventy elders. But every word of Exodus 24:1–2, 9–11 is J's, even those parts that are founded on an earlier tradition. As a text, as words on the page, this passage is a single layer; it may have a preliterary history, but it has no literary prehistory that can be revealed. As Jean-Louis Ska rightly states, "[Nicholson's] argument of course holds true only of the early tradition, and not for the present text."[37] Whence the J author derived the tradition of the theophany in Exodus 24, and which elements of the tradition he added, or which elements had accreted to the basic tradition before J adopted it, are the questions of tradition criticism. The actual words in the text of Exodus 24, and how they belong together compositionally, are the questions of source criticism.

THE EUROPEAN APPROACH

The convergence of tradition criticism and source criticism evident in Nicholson's analysis of Exodus 24, and the confusion of text and tradition, came to full fruition in the late twentieth century with Rendtorff's *The Problem of the Process of Transmission in the Pentateuch* and the critical approach this work promulgated.[38] As form and tradition criticism began to be used as methods for addressing the literary problems of the text, rather than the preliterary questions for which they were designed, it is not surprising that different conclusions as to the composition of the Pentateuch were reached, as the preceding examples demonstrate. Form-critical and tradition-critical analyses of the composition of the text resulted in an entirely new set of theories about the literary growth of the Pentateuch. Rendtorff's argument centers on the claim that form and tradition criticism are fundamentally at odds with source criticism. The adherence of Gunkel, von Rad, and Noth to the Documentary Hypothesis, which I have argued above is in fact a necessary prerequisite to their methods, was taken by Rendtorff as a failure of will, the influence of scholarly tradition preventing these scholars from recognizing the contradictions inherent in their own work.[39] The alternative Rendtorff proposed was to begin with the form-critical and tradition-critical analysis and only secondarily to assess the question of sources. The task of the scholar, according to Rendtorff, is to identify in each passage the "smallest literary unit" from which the final form of the text grew. The recognition of a pure generic form underlying a passage was no longer to be understood as an indication of the way in which the biblical author employed and reconfigured a genre, but as evidence of the original text itself, which has been secondarily expanded. Layers of accreted traditions in a passage were no longer to be understood as the result of a lengthy preliterary combination and expansion of potentially reconstructable oral traditions, but as the result of a lengthy literary process of textual supplementation. With only one or two exceptions, this approach has found acceptance throughout continental Europe, where the majority of pentateuchal research has been carried out in the past few generations; for lack of a better term, I call it "the European approach." This is not to dismiss the contributions of the handful of scholars outside continental Europe who adhere to these theories; it is simply an acknowledgment that the origin and continuing center of scholarship along these lines is in Europe.

Rendtorff's largely programmatic work formed the conceptual basis for a number of major contributions to pentateuchal criticism. First and foremost are the two books of Erhard Blum, Rendtorff's student, which provide a comprehensive analysis of the entire Pentateuch according to Rendtorff's model.[40] A similarly comprehensive treatment is undertaken by Christoph Levin; although Levin ostensibly takes a different approach when analyzing the text, and with quite different results, he still adheres to the basic concept of textual supplementation espoused by Rendtorff.[41] Reinhard Kratz also treats the entire Pentateuch, finding numerous supplementary layers throughout.[42] Ska, in a number of articles and in an introduction to the Pentateuch, accepts major portions of Rendtorff's model, as does Konrad Schmid in his many contributions.[43] There are major works on the individual books of the Pentateuch from scholars of the European approach: David Carr on Genesis, Jan Gertz on Exodus, Christophe Nihan on Leviticus, Reinhard Achenbach on Numbers, and Thomas Römer on Deuteronomy.[44] The European approach has been applied to the legal corpora by Eckart Otto in numerous books and articles. In short, Rendtorff's influence can be felt in the analysis of virtually every aspect of the Pentateuch from a range of important contemporary scholars—of which the preceding is by no means an exhaustive list. Though there is little agreement on the details of the analysis from scholar to scholar, all accept and assume the fundamental principles of Rendtorff's model: the absence of continuous sources and the existence of sequential literary supplementation as the explanation for the composition of the Pentateuch.

In essence, the European approach takes the tradition-critical results of Noth's analysis and applies them directly to the text, rather than to the preliterary stage. Each traditional unit becomes a textual unit; the growth of the tradition becomes the growth of the text. The challenge this procedure presents to the Documentary Hypothesis is posed by Rendtorff in terms of the convergence of results: "One is only justified in accepting continuous 'sources' in the Pentateuch when, at the end of the tradition-historical inquiry, the source theory offers the most enlightening answer to the questions which arise from the final shape of the text."[45] If another answer is reached, as is claimed, then the conclusion is drawn that the Documentary Hypothesis is invalid.

The methodological crux is therefore the issue of what should be the starting point for the analysis. Rendtorff lays out the issue clearly: "The different 'sources' of the Pentateuch was the answer to a particular question, namely: is the final form of the Pentateuch as it lies before us a unity or not? Source division as used hitherto makes sense only as an answer to this question."[46] This is generally an accurate description of the documentary approach. As described in chapter 1, the Documentary Hypothesis is an attempt to provide a rationale for the largely incoherent state of the canonical Pentateuch. Technically the question is not "is the Pentateuch as it lies before us a unity or not," as Rendtorff puts it, but rather "how can we best explain the literary features of the Pentateuch as it lies before us." The solution—not the question—is that the text is not a unity. On the other side is the form-critical approach: "As soon as access to the pentateuchal texts is set in the context of the form-critical method, the statement of the question is basically altered. The Pentateuch as a whole as it lies before us is no longer the point of departure, but rather the concrete individual text, the 'smallest literary unit.' The work begins as it were at the opposite end."[47] The methodological distinction here is clear: whereas source criticism begins with the canonical text, form criticism, as defined by Rendtorff at least, begins with the smallest literary unit.[48] Whereas source criticism takes seriously the continuity of one passage to another, the European approach searches strenuously to separate each textual unit by any means possible.[49]

The isolation of these "smallest literary units," and the concomitant assumption that they were originally independent of one another, only brought together in a series of successive redactional stages, hearkens back to the Fragmentary Hypothesis of the late eighteenth and early nineteenth centuries (see chapter 1). In the original incarnation of the Fragmentary Hypothesis, the focus was entirely on the textual aspects that differentiated one passage from the next, with no consideration given to the aspects that connected one passage to another some chapters later. The undoing of the original Fragmentary Hypothesis was essentially the accepted recognition that there are such connections, that, as Hermann Hupfeld demonstrated, the individual pieces could be aligned into three continuous, internally consistent, and self-referential narratives. In the new Fragmentary Hypothesis of the twentieth century, these connections are not ignored as in the past; they are, rather, systematically removed from the text. They are deemed redactional additions, inserted with the explicit intention of connecting two originally unconnected literary works. A few examples follow.

Blum claims that the final verses of the story of Jacob at Bethel in Genesis 28 — in which Jacob vows that Yahweh will be his god, that he will turn his stone pillow into a cult center, and that he will tithe if he is granted protection on his journey and returns safely to his father's house — are a secondary addition linking the original Jacob-at-Bethel cult etiology to the independent Jacob-Esau-Laban cycle.[50] These verses were written to link the two stories, he writes, because they contain both the theme of the stone pillow and the cult site at Bethel — that is, elements of the preceding Jacob-at-Bethel narrative — and the theme of Jacob's flight from Esau in Canaan to live with Laban, as well as that of his subsequent return to Canaan — that is, the basic elements of the Jacob-Esau-Laban cycle. In other words: the verses containing the strongest textual data for the intentional, intrinsic, coherent connection of the story in Genesis 28 with the rest of the life of Jacob are precisely the verses that are identified and removed as secondary additions.[51]

Blum considers the first of the stories of the endangered matriarch (Gen 12: 10–20) to be distinct from its context and therefore a tradition that has been secondarily inserted.[52] Yet Abraham's travel to Egypt in this passage is explicitly referred to in the first verses of the subsequent chapter (13:1, 3–4), which also refer back to Abraham's journey through Canaan and the altar he had built at Bethel in 12:8. In 13:1–4, Abraham makes the return journey from Egypt, back through the Negev up to Bethel, to the place where he had started. These verses are not only perfectly integrated into their context, they are essential to it, as they provide the link from the episode in Egypt to the settlement of Abraham and Lot in Canaan. It is precisely because they serve this linking purpose that Blum considers 13:1, 3–4 to be additions: since the units of 12:10–20 and 12:6–8; 13:2, 5–13, 18 are originally independent, the verses that link them must be secondary.[53]

The third of the endangered matriarch stories, in Genesis 26, is considered by Levin to be an independent textual unit, with no original relationship to the other stories of this type in Genesis 12:10–20 and Genesis 20.[54] Genesis 26:1 begins, however, with the statement that "there was a famine in the land—aside from the previous famine that occurred in the days of Abraham." This is an explicit reference to the episode of Genesis 12:10–20. So too is the beginning of Yahweh's speech to Isaac in v. 2: "Do not go down to Egypt." These direct references ostensibly mark the two stories as coming from the same hand (in contrast to the story of Gen 20, in which there are no references to Gen 12 or 26 and to which no reference is made in either). Because the references in 26:1–2 link two texts that Levin judges to be originally independent, he claims that these verses must be considered secondary.[55]

Achenbach isolates the original narrative of Numbers 20:14–21 by removing from it the verses in which Moses recollects the Exodus (vv. 14b–16), verses that contain both specific narrative claims (the divine messenger who leads the people through the wilderness; cf. Exod 23:20–24; 32:34[56]) and specific language ("all the hardships that have befallen us," Num 20:14; cf. Exod 18:8) that connect Numbers 20:14–21 with other passages; naturally, all of the texts to which Numbers 20:14b–16 refer are also attributed to a redactional layer.[57] The verses that establish the connection of Numbers 20:14–21 to a larger narrative are no longer to be considered evidence that such a larger narrative exists; they are, rather, taken as precisely the opposite: evidence that the text was originally independent.

Just as the smallest literary units are deemed independent, linked only by secondary additions, so too the larger literary units (comprising the now-connected smaller units), Noth's tradition complexes, were originally independent of each other according to the European approach. As in the smaller units, the verses that serve to connect the larger narrative complexes into the broader pentateuchal narrative are judged to be secondary. For example, it is commonly claimed that the larger traditions of the patriarchs and the Exodus were unconnected before they were joined together in P.[58] On purely tradition-critical grounds, this claim has merit: as many have recognized, the patriarchal narratives and the Exodus story seem, in their earliest forms, to have provided alternative and competing explanations for the origin of Israel.[59] The literary evidence brought in support of the contemporary claim that the actual texts of the patriarchal narratives and the Exodus story were originally independent is the lack of reference to the Exodus in Genesis or to the patriarchs in Exodus through Numbers.[60] Of course, there are numerous examples of just such references—but those verses too are deemed secondary.[61] For example, in Genesis 50:25, Joseph makes his brothers promise that "when God has taken notice of you, you shall carry up my bones from here." This promise is fulfilled in Exodus 13:19, just at the point of the Israelites' departure from Egypt: "And Moses took with him the bones of Joseph, who had exacted an oath from the children of Israel, saying, 'God will be sure to take notice of you: then you shall carry up my bones from here with you.'" Thus in Genesis we have reference to the Exodus; in the story of the Exodus we have reference to an episode in Genesis. This explicit link of the patriarchal and Exodus stories, in a clearly nonpriestly context, stands as a challenge to the theory. Both verses are therefore deemed late insertions.[62] In a similar manner, the nonpriestly primeval history has been claimed to be originally a separate literary unit from the patriarchal narratives.[63] This type of argument has extended so far as to claim that in the references in Deuteronomy to "the land that I swore on oath to give to your fathers,"[64] the "fathers" refer not to the patriarchs of Genesis, but to the first generation of the Exodus.[65] And when the "fathers" are specified in the text as "Abraham, Isaac, and Jacob," the names are deemed secondary.[66]

Axel Graupner asks the appropriate questions of this procedure: "The examination into the tradition-historical independence of the Pentateuch themes is by no means new, but was produced by G. von Rad and M. Noth. From this perspective, texts which present connections that cover different themes are certainly secondary. Does this judgment count, however, also from a literary-critical perspective? In the non-priestly Tetrateuch the blocks of themes are separable only if one eliminates or glosses over the unequivocal connections evident in the text. To what extent, however, is such a procedure methodologically permissible and sensible?"[67] There is a circularity to the European approach.[68] The identification of the smallest literary unit depends on the removal of the literary links to other texts; the removal of those links is done on the basis of the identification of the smallest literary unit. It is rather simple by this mechanism to prove that the Jacob-at-Bethel story and the Jacob-Esau-Laban cycle are not the work of a single author: we simply remove the signs of authorial activity— cross-reference, foreshadowing, thematic resonance, verbal similarity—and label them "secondary." And what we are left with are two unconnected texts: the smallest literary units.[69] The method itself is suspect—no less the theory that stands behind it. As Sean McEvenue pointedly states—he offers telling comparisons with the Odyssey, Dante, Goethe's *Faust*, the *Canterbury Tales*, and the *Decameron*—"The hypothesis implies an outrageous principle, namely that any segment of a longer story which does not explicitly refer to, or explicitly depend on, the overarching narrative, must be considered as written in isolation from, and independently of, the larger text."[70] A similar critique is brought by Damian Wynn-Williams: "A more serious difficulty with Rendtorff's approach is that by subordinating literary criticism to the concerns of traditio-historical criticism as he advocates, one runs the danger of arbitrarily relegating such textual phenomena as episodic interrelatedness and cross-referencing to the level of editorial re-working. While it is most probable that some structural elements in the final text were introduced by later editors or redactors, it cannot simply be presumed that the earliest stages of the tradition were unstructured or without interconnections."[71]

We may raise a corollary set of concerns regarding the fragmentary aspects of the European approach: where, why, and how these smallest literary units were preserved. In the leap from tradition to text, this question has been essentially overlooked. A brief oral tradition, for example an etiology, is readily imagined; a short written text comprising that tradition, on the other hand, is perhaps less so. We are talking no longer about the production and preservation of local tradition, but of an actual piece of text, tangible and perishable—not an orally transmitted tradition, but a written document. To take the Jacob-at-Bethel story as our example again: this story is ostensibly the narrative etiology of the Bethel cult site. Its creation and transmission should therefore naturally be located at Bethel and would presumably be the work of the local priesthood, who would be responsible for both its invention and its preservation down through the generations. These assumptions are logical enough, at least for the oral tradition of the founding of the Bethel cult. But they do not translate easily to the realm of the written text. We are forced to imagine that the Bethel priesthood decided to set down in writing a handful of lines telling the story of their cult's founding by the local patriarch. Such a text would not be necessary to preserve the tradition: on the one hand, this brief story would not require a written text for its transmission from generation to generation, and on the other hand, the precise wording of such a story would not be crucially important.[72] This is a story—a tradition—for which an oral transmission makes more sense.

Furthermore, the setting of these sorts of fragments into writing is most comprehensible as part of the process of placing them into a larger context, in which they are given new meaning by being part of an overarching narrative whole. Only when Jacob's stop at Bethel is a crucial part of a larger movement from Canaan to Mesopotamia and back, part of a larger theme of divinely promised and threatened possession of the land, part of a narrative of fraternal and cross-generational struggle and deception, is it necessary to have the story preserved in writing and in a precisely worded form.[73] We might even suggest that a fragment like the Jacob-at-Bethel story is not sensible even as an independent oral tradition: we need some context, after all, for who Jacob is, what he is doing at Bethel in the middle of the night, and what his relationship is to the deity. This context would be supplied by the body of Jacob traditions already extant in the local community—that is, the traditions represented in the other Jacob stories in Genesis, as well as, we can surmise, many others that did not find their way into the text.[74]

There is finally the question of the physical object of the literary fragment. Longer documents, scrolls, products of a central elite, are easily understood. But this purported text, the Jacob-at-Bethel story, is no more than six or seven verses long. In terms of length, this is roughly equivalent to a scrap of papyrus— or better, perhaps, a standard ostracon.[75] In terms of content, this is a reasonably close ancient equivalent of the plaques found outside buildings throughout the eastern United States reading "George Washington slept here." However, it is hardly conceivable that this text was written on the walls of the Bethel sanctuary—and even if it was, it is even less conceivable that it was collected from there by the editor of the Jacob cycle.[76] We must ask where this scrap of text resided before it was taken up into the larger Jacob text. It is unclear what medium is imagined in the European approach even for the larger Jacob cycle (the combination of the various Jacob traditions/texts), or proto-Genesis (the combination of the Jacob cycle with that of Abraham and Joseph), or the various redactions and revisions of the biblical text, but given Israelite practice, we may assume that a papyrus scroll is envisioned.[77] It is hard to imagine, however, a piece of papyrus containing the six or seven lines of the Jacob-at-Bethel story. There is no evidence for scrolls of that length at any time in Israelite history.[78]

Perhaps more to the point: we have virtually no evidence from ancient Israel of locally manufactured or preserved narrative texts, even granting the relatively static nature of these narratives. Letters, trade documents, military instructions, agricultural data, individual prayers—these are the local texts we have, and the common element in all of them is their essential ephemerality: ironically, these documents, such as they are, were not intended to be preserved for all time, or even for an extended period. We have no examples in the corpus of ancient Israelite inscriptions of a local etiology, or any traditional narrative.[79] Although it is an argument from silence, the state of the evidence to date supports the theory that these types of local traditions, inasmuch as we have to assume that they were preserved and transmitted, were preserved and transmitted orally. The written text of the Jacob-at-Bethel story, isolated from its narrative context, is not only unheard of in ancient Israel, it is virtually unimaginable.

The isolation of the smallest literary units in the Pentateuch according to the European approach is a revival of the Fragmentary Hypothesis, but the manner in which these units are thought to have been combined and added to hearkens back to another early theory, known as the Supplementary Hypothesis.[80] According to this theory, there was an original stratum of the Pentateuch (at the time presumed to be something close to what we now call P) that was expanded by a series of supplementary layers, each building on the previous. In the modern version of the European approach, the original stratum is the collection of independent fragments, or multiple collections (such as an Abraham cycle, a Jacob cycle, an Exodus story). As these pieces were put together, the redactors responsible also added new material: not just the cross-references necessary for bridging the previously independent episodes, but also entirely new episodes, or new versions of earlier traditions.

Methodologically, there is a significant lack of control in this approach. In both the original and the renewed Supplementary Hypothesis, the number and scope of the supplementary layers are restricted only by the scholar's imagination. Heinrich Ewald, one of the founders of the Supplementary Hypothesis in the nineteenth century, identified six layers in the Pentateuch;[81] it is not unusual to find even more in modern scholarship (see below). Which texts belong to which stratum, which individual phrases or verses are redactional (and to which redactor they are to be attributed), which corpus they cover—only Genesis? Genesis and Exodus? the Pentateuch? Hexateuch? Enneateuch?— all of these questions are decided differently by each scholar.[82] Because each supplementary layer is credited with both inserting new material and adjusting the old, virtually any text, no matter how coherent or integrated into its context, is liable to be considered the product of successive redactions.

We may take, for example, Levin's analysis of Genesis 27:1–45, the ostensibly unified story of Jacob tricking Isaac into giving him Esau's blessing.[83] Levin isolates an original independent narrative in this chapter, which has the basic contours of the final form (vv. 1–3aα, 3b–4, 5b, 14, 18a, 24–25, 27 [only the words "he blessed him and said"], 28, 30 [without the first clause], 31–33a, 41b): Isaac calls for Esau to bring him a final meal before he dies, but Jacob preempts his brother and receives the blessing; Esau comes in, discovers the trick, and vows to kill Jacob. To this basic narrative, Levin says, was added a redactional layer that introduces the dominant role of Rebekah into the story (vv. 5a, 6, 7 [without "before Yahweh"], 8–10, 15a [without the phrase "the clothes which were there in the house"], 15b, 17, 26–27a [through "his clothes"], 27b [from "see . . ."], 42–44, 45aββb): her overhearing of Isaac instructing Esau, her passing on the information to Jacob and telling him what to do, the entire motif of Jacob feeling and smelling like his brother, Rebekah's overhearing Esau plan to kill Jacob, and her instructions to Jacob to flee to Haran. The author of this layer is also responsible for the notice in Genesis 25:28 that Isaac favored Esau, while Rebekah favored Jacob. A third layer is discernible, according to Levin, in Isaac and Jacob's first interaction, in which Jacob identifies himself as the firstborn and asks for the blessing (vv. 18b–19). The author of this layer is also responsible for the story of the purchase of Esau's birthright in 25:29–34; according to this author's reinterpretation of the story, Jacob is not being deceptive when he claims to be the firstborn; in fact Esau, by asking for the blessing, is not holding to the previous agreement.

These three layers were thoroughly reworked and brought into line with the larger narrative complex Levin sees as stretching from Genesis 2 through Numbers 24 by a redactor whom he calls the Yahwist, although with a very different meaning from that indicated by the traditional term (vv. 7b [only the words "before Yahweh"], 20, 27b , 29aα, 30a [only the first clause], 33b–34, 38b–40a, 45aα). In this layer there is a greater emphasis on the blessing, both here and elsewhere in the Pentateuch; it is in part via the blessing that the originally disparate narrative elements were brought together. Genesis 27 is thereby linked with Genesis 24:31, 26:29, and Numbers 22:12, where the same sort of redactional emphasis is found. The references to Yahweh in the chapter belong to this layer as well; no longer does Jacob (or Rebekah) act alone, but rather Yahweh's hand is to be seen behind their actions. This aspect connects the story with Genesis 10:9 and 24:12, 27. The rivalry of the brothers is a theme supplied by the author of this redactional layer, both here and in Genesis 4:11–12, 5:29, 8:21–22, and 9:25. Other aspects of this redaction, both thematic and linguistic, connect it with Genesis 12:3; 32–33; and Numbers 24:9.

The newly expanded narrative of Genesis 27 was then further supplemented. A layer was added that introduced the identification of Esau as Edom (vv. 11–13, 16, 21–23); this same layer can be found also in 25:25, 27, 30, 34. Another redactor added the theme of Judah's ascendance over Edom, or at least the allusions to such (vv. 29aβ , 36b–38a, 41a); the same redactor's hand is at work in 9:25–27. Another redactor added the prophecy of Edom's independence from Judah in v. 40. Yet another added the etymology for Jacob's name in vv. 35–36a. The final redactor inserted v. 46, which ties the rest of Genesis 27 to the priestly material in 26:34–35 and 28:1–9. To this final redaction were added two postredactional additions: the identification of Esau's "gear" as his quiver and bow (v. 3aβ) and the description of Esau's clothes, which Rebekah gave to Jacob, as his good clothes that were in the house (v. 15a [from "the elder"]).

On a broader scale, we may take as a second example Kratz's analysis of the Exodus narrative.[84] He isolates as the earliest traditions/texts a victory of Yahweh over the Egyptians (Exod 12:37; 13:20; 14:10b, 19b, 20, 24, 25b, 30a) and the song of Miriam in Exodus 15:20–21. These traditions were originally independent of each other, linked only secondarily by the insertion of a variety of redactional elements. These include the figure of Moses (who was the center of his own traditional story, now unrecoverable), the sea, and the wilderness itinerary. The pillars of cloud and fire and the miracle at the sea from the song of Miriam were secondarily brought together into a single story, and the wilderness itinerary was gradually expanded; in combination with the Moses traditions, this redaction created for the first time "the remarkable idea that the origins of Israel lie with Moses and the Hebrews in Egypt."[85] This larger narrative complex "was revised and expanded several times"[86]—above all by the priestly material and only subsequently by the nonpriestly, in Kratz's view postpriestly, plagues cycle (which in its original form included only four plagues) and by further elaboration of the wilderness itinerary. While some of these layers belong only within the framework of the nonpriestly Exodus narrative (including the wilderness wandering), some interact with the later priestly material, and some take into account the secondary linking of the Exodus and patriarchal traditions. In all, the final form of the canonical book of Exodus seems to comprise at least ten distinct layers, according to Kratz.[87]

Though these examples may be drawn from the extreme end of the spectrum, they are different only in degree, not in kind. Both adhere to the essential form-critical and tradition-critical methods of the European approach, with the fragmentary/supplementary conclusions drawn from it. We may see in these examples the lack of control the European approach entails. Levin finds ten layers in Genesis 27; Kratz finds five;[88] Jacques Vermelyen identifies four;[89] Blum considers it a unity.[90] Nothing in the method prohibits scholars from identifying as many layers as desired: the isolation of the smallest literary unit is largely subjective, and even more so the identification of the successive layers added to it.

An interesting effect of the transition from tradition to text in the European approach is the fundamentally altered concept of tradition. For von Rad and Noth, the process by which the independent traditions aggregated into the larger traditional complexes, including the overarching tradition of the pentateuchal narrative from creation through the conquest, was a lengthy oral one.[91] The written texts by which those traditions were transmitted, the source documents of the Pentateuch, agreed substantially with each other on so many points because the traditions they took up into their writings were common Israelite traditions, the product of generations of cultural and geographical agglomeration. By the time the J, E, and P authors set their pens to papyrus, each was familiar from the oral tradition, as was the rest of Israel's general populace, with the notion that, for example, there were three patriarchs, Abraham, Isaac, and Jacob, and that they were related genealogically, in that order.[92] When traditions became equated with texts, however, the notion of the common Israelite tradition silently disappeared, along with the notion of oral transmission altogether.[93] Now the relationship of Abraham to Isaac, or Moses to Aaron, became a literary phenomenon, the product of two independent texts being combined by a redactor.[94] Even the Abraham cycle on its own could no longer be assumed to be known to anyone beyond the person who wrote it, because it no longer has an oral existence: the tradition is the text, and the text is the work of an author, not a culture. It is therefore possible according to this approach to say that the common ancient Israelite knew nothing of Adam, Noah, Abraham, Isaac, Jacob, Joseph, Moses, or Aaron. Not only is the growth of the Pentateuch an elite literary phenomenon, even the stories and characters contained in it become exclusive property of the elite literary community. Ironically, the extrapolation of tradition-critical analysis to the literary realm did away with one of the basic insights of tradition criticism.[95]

A second effect of the European approach concerns the purpose of the redactional linking and supplementing of earlier materials. Without recourse to the older tradition-critical claim that the oral traditions grew to their present shape by an organic gradual process of cultural accretion, scholars in the European approach need to provide a rationale for the combination of individual texts into larger wholes. Thus to each redactional layer is assigned a motivation—ideological, political, theological—and the texts assigned to that layer are those that conform to the theorized motivation. Each successive layer is thereby understood to reorient the preceding material according to its own worldview.

While the idea of such theologically oriented additions is not unique to this theory—indeed, this is how many scholars have understood the priestly material for decades (see chapter 5)—its application across the board is fundamentally new. The effect this new conception has on the understanding of the smallest literary units, in turn, is equally revolutionary. The claim that the theological elements in the nonpriestly text are those that bind the independent texts together is an implicit claim that the original independent texts were essentially free of theological import.

For example, the story of Abraham, or, better, the story of Abraham and Lot (Gen 12–13, 18–19), is understood according to the European approach to be, in its earliest form, the explanation for the division of land between Israel and its neighbors.[96] The elements of this story that carry the theological weight—Yahweh's command to settle in Canaan, promises of land and offspring, the dialogue between Abraham and Yahweh over the fate of Sodom and

Gomorrah—are precisely those elements that are considered secondary links between the original, nontheological material.[97] Yet this concept of the nature of the traditions is decidedly beyond what we find even in Noth's analysis. For Noth, although the traditions regarding Abraham were originally independent of the traditions regarding Jacob, each already contained, in its independent form, the concept of the divine promise.[98] It is hard indeed to imagine what meaning these narratives, or even their underlying traditions, would have had without the theological element. All that the Abraham-Lot cycle provides is a series of settlements and genealogies. The fundamental questions that drive the narrative—where does this Abraham come from? how does he know where to go? what right has he to the land?—these questions, basic to the understanding and appreciation of the narrative both as a story and as an etiology, are answered by the concepts of divine command and promise. The theological and ideological claims are intrinsic to the comprehension of the text, of its being set down in writing, and of its traditional origins in the first place.

In truth, there is a claim being made here about the nature of the development of Israelite thought and religion: the early texts—not the orally transmitted traditions, but the actual first writings—are considered relatively simple, containing mostly single, straightforward concepts, couched in terms of plain human movement and relationships. The more complex, highly developed ideas, whether theological, ideological, or political, are a later development.[99] It is difficult not to associate this perspective with that of Gunkel, in his classically disparaging statements about ancient Israelites: "the ancient listener['s] receptive power was very limited. . . . One or two lines . . . was all that the average listener of the day could grasp at one time."[100] "Theologically complex" equals "later," virtually by definition.

By taking theological interests and statements as a central piece of evidence for the original or secondary status of a text, scholars using the European approach subtly transform the analysis of the text from a literary evaluation to a theological one. Not only are subjective decisions made about what type of theological statement is appropriate at a given stage of the development of the tradition, but the understanding of the composition of the Pentateuch as a whole is fundamentally shifted. The disjunctures and contradictions in the narrative, and in the laws as well, are relegated to a by-product of the theological reinterpretations of the text. This results in a reading of the Pentateuch, at each stage of its development, primarily through a theological lens; no longer do we have to deal with stories, but rather with ideas and themes. In this way the basic unreadability of the final form of the text, and of the various stages of its development according to the European approach, is set aside as an unnecessary concern, if not in the division of the text into its various elements, then in the conception of their subsequent combination.

Though there is something appealing about this, insofar as it imbues every stage of the text's development with significant meaning, the theological reckoning of the development of the Pentateuch runs into trouble, especially in the later layers of redaction. If the European approach relies on the notion that each supplementary layer reshapes and reorients the previous stage according to its own ideas, then the presence of contradictory theological claims, retained from the earlier stages of the text, necessarily challenges the new arguments of the last layer. If, for one example, the lines in Genesis 37 about the Midianites stealing Joseph from the pit were added to remove the guilt of selling Joseph from the brothers (see case study I), they are dramatically undermined by Joseph's statement in 45:4 that the brothers did in fact sell him and the important theological message that is attached to that statement in 45:5–8. If the priestly material is taken as a redactional layer rather than as an independent source (see chapter 5), then the fundamental claim of P that there was no cult before Sinai is rendered virtually moot by the presence in the theoretically P-oriented text of numerous stories in which the patriarchs, and even Moses, build altars and offer sacrifices. As Graham Davies cogently observes, "The combination of the new Priestly passages with the older material could not but serve to blur the important distinctions that the Priestly author wanted to make."[101] This is true not only of P, but of any redactional layer that retains the text it wishes to reinterpret. Thus when Exodus 33:7–11 is taken as a deliberate correction of the priestly depiction of the Tabernacle,[102] one cannot help but be confused by the predominance in the "corrected" text of the innumerable references to the Tabernacle according precisely to the priestly view, as opposed to the relatively few that conform to that of Exodus 33:7–11. In short, the latest layer does not always succeed in reconfiguring the text in its own image; if that is understood as the purpose of the redaction, then we have to reckon with fairly inept redactors. This was a weakness of the Supplementary Hypothesis in the early nineteenth century, and it remains a weakness in the modern incarnation of the theory.

In addition to the altered concepts of tradition and theology in the European approach, we may consider as a final point the way in which the notion of the author has been radically changed. By stripping the text down to the barebones narrative, by eliminating the overarching themes, theological ideas, and literary connections as secondary, the European approach leaves us with authors who are responsible only for the most basic stories. The traits we associate with authorship, and with literature in general, are denied to the biblical authors.

Digression and resumption, foreshadowing and back-referencing and cross-referencing, development of theme and character, integration of multiple ideas, comment on and explanation of events, and especially variety of expression — all of the authorial techniques that make up literature, both ancient and modern, are eliminated as secondary.[103] It is not coincidental that Rendtorff declared that "the Pentateuch is no longer regarded primarily as a literary product."[104] Yet the only way such a claim is defensible — if indeed it is, given that the only Pentateuch we have is a written one — is by systematically removing all traces of literary technique from the text.

The challenge of the European approach, as posited by Rendtorff, was the claim that the smallest literary units do not necessarily combine to form the documents of the classical source-critical theory. Yet because they do not necessarily do so does not mean that they cannot. As the variety of reconstructions offered by scholars attests, the smallest literary units can be isolated in an almost unlimited number of ways, as can the process by which they were brought together. The European approach does not, therefore, stand as a contradiction of the Documentary Hypothesis. It is, rather, an alternative explanation for how the Pentateuch came to look the way that it does. As such, it must be judged accordingly. The methodological objections raised in this chapter are not intended to disprove the European approach, for, barring the discovery of the text of J somewhere in the desert, it would be impossible to do so. The issue at hand is not one of possibility, for there are many possible ways the Pentateuch may have taken shape, beyond the documentary and the European models. The issue is, rather, one of probability. It is in this light that both the method and the results of the European approach must be evaluated: is it probable that this is how the Pentateuch came to look as it does? Or better: are the theories espoused by adherents of the European approach more probable than the Documentary Hypothesis?

THE J SOURCE

With this question in mind we may return to the J document. Rendtorff was not far off the mark when he observed that "if one does not succeed in demonstrating this chief source convincingly, then the hypothesis as a whole can scarcely be maintained."[105] For scholars of the European approach, as we have seen, there is no such thing; the nonexistence of J has been perhaps the central element of the European approach. The denial of a J document, however, entails the elimination of a vast number of literary connections across a substantial set of pentateuchal texts. The argument in favor of the J document, therefore, consists primarily of the demonstration that its constituent pieces are remarkably well integrated and that the document does indeed cohere well as a literary whole—and that the literary connections evident in the source are so integral to it that they cannot be removed without doing grave literary damage both to the individual episodes that constitute the document and to the overall literary work. I undertake this demonstration not primarily on terminological or stylistic grounds (including the use of the name Yahweh), but rather on the basis of the continuity and consistency of the narrative and the themes expressed in it. In the following overview I also touch only briefly on the distinctions between the historical claims of J and those of the other sources (many of which will be noted in the chapters and case studies to follow).

The primeval history in J comprises the account of creation and Adam and Eve's expulsion from Eden in Genesis 2–3, the story of Cain and Abel and the genealogy of Cain in Genesis 4, the flood narrative in Genesis 6–9*,[106] the Table of Nations in Genesis 10*, and the story of the Tower of Babel in Genesis 11:1–9. Though each of these episodes may reflect an independent tradition, they are integrally connected by continuity of narrative, character, and theme. The story of Cain and Abel in Genesis 4 begins with the notice that "the man knew his wife Eve," a name she is given only in the J account of Genesis 3:20.[107] Eve's statement upon bearing Cain, "I have gained a male child with the help of Yahweh," directly reflects the curse of difficulty in childbirth that was laid on her in 3:16. Cain's offering of the fruits of the soil in 4:3 is rejected by Yahweh in 4:5 because it consisted of produce from the ground that Yahweh had cursed in 3:17–19.[108] Yahweh's address to Cain in 4:7 parallels the address to Eve in 3:16. The uniquely J curse on the ground in 3:17–19 is mentioned again in Yahweh's curse on Cain in 4:11–12: "you shall be more cursed than the ground"; now Cain cannot even work the ground to bring forth food, as Adam his father had. The violence inaugurated with Cain reaches a new apex with his descendant Lemech (4:23–24). At the end of Genesis 4 Seth is born, as a replacement for the deceased Abel (4:25), and it is Seth's descendant Enosh—pointedly not of Cain's line—who begins the formal worship of Yahweh (4:26).[109]

Noah's birth in Genesis 5:29 is accompanied by an etymology that explicitly picks up on the historical claim that Yahweh had cursed the ground in 3:17–19: "this one will provide us relief . . . out of the very soil which Yahweh cursed." Yet the wickedness of humankind evident in the line of Cain and Lemech drives Yahweh to bring the flood (6:5–7).[110] The J flood story—which is, when disentangled from that of P, perfectly complete and coherent[111]—is related to both the evils of Cain's lineage, in its inception, and the curse on the earth, in its conclusion (8:21–22). Noah's curse on Canaan and its correlative blessing on Shem and Jephet (9:25–27) are closely related to the subsequent Table of Nations in Genesis 10*, in which the national entities signified by these ancestors are laid out. Finally, the Tower of Babel story in Genesis 11:1–9 completes humankind's expansion from a single man in a single place—Adam in the garden of Eden—to a diverse humanity, across the entire face of the earth, and prepares the ground for Yahweh's selection of a single family from among the now disparate peoples, languages, and locations. Although it is possible that the traditions underlying the primeval history in J were originally independent, there can be little doubt that the actual written texts constitute an integrally connected narrative. This is true, as we will see, for the entire J document.

The transition from the history of humankind to the history of Abraham and his family is marked by the beginning of Yahweh's address to Abraham in Genesis 12:1: "Go forth from your native land [literally, "from your land, from your birthplace"], and from your father's house." Each of these locations is increasingly specific, highlighting the singular personage of Abraham. The promise of 12:1–3 picks up on two of the main themes from the primeval period in J, and specifically from the final episode of the Tower of Babel: the land—from which Abraham goes and to which he comes, with the final notice that "all the families of the earth shall bless themselves by you"—and the concept of a name, which in the Tower of Babel story is a negative element because it is actively sought by the builders of the tower, but which in Genesis 12:2 is a distinctly positive feature, as it is bestowed upon Abraham by Yahweh. The rationale for the selection of Abraham and his line is clear, if implicit, from the preceding narratives: the entire primeval history in J—from the disobedience of Adam and Eve in the garden to Yahweh's recognition of humankind's inherent evil after the flood to the hubris of the builders of the Tower of Babel—stands as evidence that Yahweh cannot count on humanity as a whole to provide the devoted loyalty and worship that he requires. Abraham and his line will be chosen from the whole of humanity to be a singularly loyal people, to serve in that role as an example for others, and in return Yahweh will bless them. The primeval period is recounted in J for this primary purpose: to explain the selection of Abraham in 12:1–3.[112] The primeval period and the patriarchal period are interdependent and mutually explanatory.

The continuity of Genesis 12–13 is clear (see the discussion above). Only when Lot has occupied the plains of the Jordan has Abraham truly come into sole possession of the promised land, and thus it is only at this point that Yahweh can, in 13:14–17, give him the full promise of land and progeny only hinted at in 12:1–3.

The question of progeny is taken up in the subsequent J story of Genesis 16, which begins with Sarah's request that Abraham bear a child with her slave Hagar.[113] She says explicitly that she is barren—"Yahweh has kept me from bearing" (16:1)—a concept unique to J and introduced in the brief notice of Genesis 11:30.[114] The unified story of 16:4–14 proceeds directly from this initial request; note that the promise of offspring given to Hagar in 16:10 bears a striking resemblance to that given to Abraham in 13:16. The same issue is at the heart of Genesis 18:1–15, the announcement of Isaac's birth. This passage is marked as J not only by virtue of the thematic continuity, but because Genesis 18:1 situates Abraham at the terebinths of Mamre in exclusive accordance with J's statement in 13:18. Yahweh's proclamation that he will cause Sarah to bear a son (18:10–14) can be read as an explicit reversal of Sarah's barrenness, which was equally attributed to Yahweh (16:1). The continuity of the story of the announcement of Isaac's birth with that of the destruction of Sodom and Gomorrah in 18:17–19:38 is effected by 18:16, in which the three "men" who appeared to Abraham in 18:2 depart "and looked down toward Sodom." Yahweh's internal monologue in 18:17–19 hearkens back to his initial speech to Abraham in 12:1–3; note especially the reference to the nations of the earth blessing themselves by Abraham in 18:18—a concept unique in the Pentateuch to J—and the intention in 18:19 to "bring about for Abraham what he had promised him." The story of Lot in Genesis 19 assumes the knowledge that Lot had settled in Sodom, information provided already and only in J in 13:12b. Further, the iniquity of the inhabitants of Sodom and even the destruction of Sodom and Gomorrah were already described and foreshadowed in 13:10, 13. The little town to which Lot flees, Zoar (19:20–22), was also mentioned already, in 13:10, as the extreme edge of the Jordan plain; although at the time the detail seemed unimportant, now its significance becomes clear. Finally, the story of the births of Moab and Ammon in 19:30–38 stands in meaningful contrast to the preceding announcement of Isaac's birth in 18:1–15 and the subsequent birth itself in 21:1: the offspring granted by Yahweh to continue Abraham's threatened lineage will become the people of Israel, while the offspring created through the incestuous scheming of Lot's daughters to continue their father's lineage will become Israel's enemies.

The concentration on progeny continues with the fulfillment of Yahweh's promise of a child to Sarah in Genesis 21:1; we learn too that Abraham's brother Nahor has had children, in 22:20–24. The identities of Abraham's brother and his wife Milcah were already known to us—only in J—from 11:29, a passage that, like the mention of Zoar, seemed unimportant at the time but that is given heightened significance as the story progresses. This genealogy in 22:20–24, ostensibly uninteresting, is in fact crucial to J's narrative, as it establishes the familial relationship between Isaac and Rebekah (22:23). The lengthy continuous episode of Genesis 24 that immediately follows depends on this established relationship, as Abraham makes his servant swear to find Isaac a wife from Abraham's own family (24:2–4). All of the names and relationships in Genesis 24 (see especially 24:10, 15) match J's unique genealogy of 22:20–24. And, most strikingly, in 24:7 Abraham recalls virtually verbatim the promises of 12:1–3, 7.

The story of the birth of Esau and Jacob in Genesis 25:21–26 begins with the notice that Rebekah, like Sarah before her, is barren (25:21). The character traits of the two newborns described in 25:25–26—and unique to J—will be determinative for most of the Jacob and Esau stories to follow, including the immediately following narrative of the sale of Esau's birthright in 25:27–34.

In Genesis 26 we find the fullest narrative about Isaac. It begins with an explicit reference to Genesis 12:10–20: "There was a famine in the land—aside from the previous famine that had occurred in the days of Abraham." Yahweh's first words to Isaac make reference to the same story: "Do not go down to Egypt" (26:2)—as had Abraham (in J alone). Yahweh continues with the promise to Isaac, which is, unsurprisingly, strikingly similar to his promise to Abraham (which is specifically recalled in 26:3); note again the uniquely J idea of the nations blessing themselves by the patriarchal line (26:4). Like his father before him, Isaac too becomes rich in the foreign land (26:12). As with Abraham, so too Isaac's newfound wealth is the catalyst for the subsequent story of land acquisition and separation from neighboring peoples (26:16–17, 19–33).[115] And like Abraham in 12:7, 8 and 13:4, 18, Isaac marks his arrival in secure territory by building an altar and worshipping Yahweh (26:25)—and we may note that the expression used for this worship, "to call on the name of Yahweh," is unique to J (Gen 4:26; 12:8; 13:4). One may debate the extent to which the Abraham and Isaac stories are of independent oral origins; in their literary manifestations in these texts they are deeply interconnected and interdependent.

The story in Genesis 27 of Jacob tricking Isaac into giving him Esau's blessing, which, as already noted, is a unified narrative, depends entirely on J's particular description of Jacob's and Esau's character traits from 25:25–26. Isaac's blessing for Jacob in 27:27–29 ends with a nearly direct quotation from Yahweh's promise to Abraham in 12:3: "cursed be those who curse you, blessed they who bless you." The story ends with Rebekah instructing Jacob to flee to her brother Laban in Haran—the same brother introduced in 24:29. These instructions are fulfilled precisely in 28:10: "Jacob left Beersheba"—where Isaac's family had been living according only to J, in 26:33—"and set out for Haran," which according only to J is where Laban lived. On his journey, Yahweh appears to Jacob and gives him the standard J promise (28:13–15), including, of course, the mention that "all the families of the earth will bless themselves by you and your descendants" (28:14). In 29:1, "Jacob resumed his journey." All of the well-established J locations and characters are mentioned upon his arrival: Haran

(29:4), Laban (29:5), and Nahor (29:5). Laban's reaction upon seeing Jacob, "You are truly my bone and flesh" (29:14), is strikingly similar to Adam's first words upon seeing Eve: "This one at last is bone of my bones and flesh of my flesh" (2:23). The entire J story of Jacob's stay with Laban in Genesis 29–31* is obviously dependent on and continuous with everything that has happened to him from Genesis 27 on; it is perhaps no coincidence that, like Isaac and Abraham, Jacob too becomes wealthy in a foreign land (30:26–42), though, typically for his character according to J, he does so through trickery and deception. Jacob's stay concludes with Yahweh's instructions to him: "Return to the land of your father where you were born [literally, "to the land of your father, to your birthplace"], and I will be with you" (31:3); in this brief sentence, reference is made to both Genesis 12:1 ("the land of your father, your birthplace") and to 28:15 ("I will be with you").

Jacob's departure from Haran begins with his message to Esau in 32:4–6, which recounts precisely what has just occurred in the J story of Jacob and Laban. Jacob's prayer to Yahweh in 32:10–13 begins with a direct recollection of Yahweh's command in 31:3. All of Jacob's careful preparations for meeting Esau, and the meeting itself, described in 32:7–33:16*, depend in turn on the end of Genesis 27: Jacob is afraid of and attempts to appease Esau in consideration of Esau's stated intention to kill Jacob when next they meet (27:41). Furthermore, the possessions that Jacob sends to Esau as gifts (32:14–22; 33:10–11), and that form the basis for Jacob's excuse not to travel with Esau (33:13–14), are the result of Jacob's deception of Laban (30:31–42). The Jacob-Esau and Jacob-Laban stories, sometimes assumed to be tradition-historically separate, are intricately interwoven in the J narrative. Jacob's subsequent journeys through the land in Genesis 34* and 35:21–22a (see case study V) are marked by the violent act of Simeon and Levi and the filial infidelity of Reuben, events that will take on important meaning only in J, and only at the end of Jacob's life.

We have already described in detail, in case study I, the opening of the account of Joseph's life according to J. We may note that the central element of the chapter, the issue of sibling rivalry, has been a consistent feature of J throughout—from Cain and Abel (4:1–16) to Noah's sons (9:21–27) to Ishmael and Isaac (16:4–14), and especially with Jacob and Esau (Gen 27)[116]—and it is no small irony that it is Jacob's own continuation of this rivalry by his favoritism toward Joseph that leads to the tragic ostensible loss of his beloved son in Genesis 37. The imagery in Joseph's first dream of the brothers all being in the field (37:6–7) resonates with the preceding J narratives, in which the brothers are regularly depicted as working in the field (30:14, 16; 34:5, 7). Joseph's dream of the sun, moon, and stars (37:9–10) presupposes that Rachel, Joseph's mother, is still alive, which is the case only in J (see case study V). The manner in which Jacob is deceived in 37:32–33 is an ironic reversal of Jacob's own deception of Isaac in Genesis 27: in both episodes the skin of a goat serves as the means of the deception, and in both the word "recognize" plays an integral part (see 27:23). J's literary account of Joseph cannot be read independently of the preceding stories about Jacob, though they may derive from originally independent oral traditions.

Although the story of Judah and Tamar in Genesis 38 has the character of an interlude in the Joseph story, it is linked with the J narrative: the disclosure of Judah's intercourse with his daughter-in-law in 38:25–26, "Examine these," is a neat parallel to Joseph's brothers' deception of Jacob in 37:32–33: "Examine this," on both the verbal and, more importantly, the thematic level. As already noted, the reference in 39:1 to the Egyptian who bought Joseph from the Ishmaelites who brought him to Egypt connects directly with the J story of 37:28aβb: "They sold Joseph for twenty pieces of silver to the Ishmaelites, who brought Joseph to Egypt." The episode of Joseph and his master's wife in Genesis 39 follows this directly; note again the use of an item of clothing as evidence (39:11–18). The theme of recognition, noted already in 37:32 and 38:25, comes back in Joseph's deception of his brothers in Genesis 42–45 (see especially and explicitly 42:7–8). Jacob's attempts to spare Benjamin from traveling to Egypt in 42:3–4, 36–38 are dependent on his ostensible loss of Joseph in Genesis 37. Joseph's dreams from 37:5–9 are recalled in 42:9. Judah's role in bringing Benjamin to Joseph (43:8–10; 44:18–34) marks the reversal of his leading role in the sale of Joseph in 37:26–27. Joseph refers directly to his brothers' selling of him in his self-revelation in 45:4. The brothers' announcement in 45:26 of having found Joseph alive and Jacob's reaction in 45:28 are a clear reversal of the end of Genesis 37.

The remainder of J's story of Joseph and Jacob follows in nearly perfect continuity and coherence. Jacob goes down to Egypt in 46:5b in the chariots that Joseph had sent for him (45:20–21); he arrives in Goshen—the location of the Israelites in Egypt according only to J—in 46:28, just as Joseph had ordered in 45:10; Jacob and his family come before Pharaoh in 46:31–47:4, just as Pharaoh had instructed Joseph in 45:18; the Israelites are formally settled in Goshen in 47:5a, 6b; Joseph sustains his family according to 47:12, just as he said he would in 45:11. According to J, Jacob's death comes almost immediately upon his arrival in Egypt (47:29–31), in line with Jacob's statements that, having seen Joseph alive, he can finally die in peace (45:28; 46:30). Before he dies, he makes Joseph swear to bury him in Canaan (47:29–31) and delivers his deathbed speech, the poem of Genesis 49:2–27. In this poem the malfeasances of

Simeon, Levi, and Reuben from Genesis 34 and 35:21–22a, told only in J but to this point left unrequited, become the basis for the disinheritance of the three eldest brothers (49:3–7). Upon Jacob's death, Joseph fulfills in 50:1–11 the vow he had made to his father in 47:31 (see especially 50:5–6, where this oath is mentioned explicitly). And finally the attempt of Joseph's brothers to enslave themselves to him as punishment for the wrong they had done him so long ago contains a reference both to their actions in Genesis 37 and to their earlier attempt at self-enslavement in 44:16. Just as Joseph had told them when he revealed himself to them in 45:5–8 that it was God who had brought everything to pass for the good, so he tells them in 50:19–21, again repeating his pledge to sustain them from 45:11. The story of Joseph in J is coherent both internally and externally: within the story itself, all of the historical claims and related themes are interconnected, but the story also has clear continuities with the historical claims and related themes known from other J passages.

The last words of J's account of Joseph's life in Genesis 50:22 state that "Joseph lived one hundred and ten years," and these words lead directly into Exodus 1:6: "And Joseph died, and all his brothers, and all that generation." In Exodus 1:8 the author of J tells us that "a new king arose over Egypt who did not know Joseph"—that is, who did not know Pharaoh's promise to Joseph to provide for his family (Gen 45:17–20; 47:6b). The oppression of the Israelites related in Exodus 1:9–12 is ordered by the new Pharaoh out of fear of the Israelite people becoming too numerous. By this the author of J informs us that part of Yahweh's promise to Abraham, the element of progeny, has been fulfilled; note the use of the word *'aṣûm*, "mighty, populous," in both Exodus 1:9 and in Yahweh's speech in Genesis 18:18. From this point forward, the divine promise to Israel will focus only on the aspect of land, that is, on the unfulfilled portion of the promise to Abraham and his descendants.

The continuous story of Moses killing the Egyptian taskmaster and fleeing to Midian in Exodus 2:11–23aα follows directly from Exodus 1:9–12, both literarily and conceptually.[117] Moses sees the "labors" of the Israelites, *siblōtām*—the very word used in 1:11 (and elsewhere in J).[118] The episode at the well in 2:15–22 that results in Moses's marriage to Zipporah is a literary type-scene that is already known from two previous J passages, and only from J passages: Genesis 24, with Abraham's servant, and Genesis 29:1–14, with Jacob.[119] The author of J has effected a seamless transition between the stories of the patriarchs and that of Moses.

After the king who sought to kill Moses has died (2:23aα), Yahweh appears to Moses in the burning bush (3:2–4a, 5, 6b)—*sᵉneʰ*, a pun on the name Sinai that will become so prominent later in the J story. Yahweh's announcement of his recognition of the Israelites' plight in Egypt and his plan to rescue them in 3:7–8, 16–20 set the stage for everything that is to happen in the J account of the Exodus. Moses is to go to the people, who will listen to him (3:16–18), and is to then go to Pharaoh and request permission to go a three days' distance to worship Yahweh in the wilderness (3:18); Yahweh knows, however, that Pharaoh will not allow the Israelites to leave unless he is coerced (3:19–20). All of these elements are played out to the full in the subsequent narrative. The negotiations between Moses and Yahweh in 4:1–16 begin with Moses's doubt that the Israelites will, in fact, listen to him as Yahweh had said (3:18) and conclude with the appointment of Aaron as Moses's spokesman. In 4:19, Moses is told that it is safe to return to Egypt, in a direct reference to the episode of 2:11–15, and especially to 2:23aα. Moses takes his family with him (4:20a), while Yahweh reminds Moses that he is to perform before Pharaoh the signs with which he has been empowered (4:21)—the very signs that Yahweh used to convince Moses in 4:2–9; Yahweh further predicts the final plague, that of the death of the firstborn son (4:23).

The episode of 4:24–26 is undeniably strange and raises a host of exegetical questions. At the same time, however, it is clearly linked narratively with the preceding J passages: the setting of the episode is "at a night encampment on the way" (4:24), thus assuming the travel to Egypt from 4:20a, and Moses's wife is named Zipporah (4:25), as we know only from J, in 2:21. The meeting of Moses and Aaron in 4:27–28 is the fulfillment of Yahweh's instructions in 4:14; Moses and Aaron assemble the Israelites and perform the signs before them (4:29–30), just as Yahweh had commanded in 3:16–17 and 4:1–9; and the people are convinced (4:31), just as Yahweh had predicted (3:18). The order of events here and the initial commands for which these verses constitute the fulfillment are unique to J. When Moses and Aaron go to Pharaoh and request permission to travel into the wilderness in 5:1, 3, they are again fulfilling Yahweh's instructions to the letter (3:18)—as is Pharaoh when he denies their request (5:2, 4). The entirety of Exodus 5:5–6:1 follows continuously from this initial confrontation.

The J plagues constitute a complete, continuous, and eminently coherent unit,[120] one that follows precisely the prediction of Yahweh in 3:18–20 and that takes 6:1 as its leading statement: "he shall let them go because of a greater might, indeed, because of a greater might he shall drive them from his land." Moses and Aaron ask that Pharaoh let the Israelites go to worship in the wilderness (7:16, 26; 8:16; 9:1, 13; 10:3); Pharaoh refuses of his own free will (7:23; 8:11, 28; 9:7, 34; 10:28). The plagues are all brought about (and ended) by Yahweh himself (8:20; 9:6, 23 [from "and Yahweh sent thunder and hail"]; 10:13 [from

"Yahweh drove an east wind over the land"])—all except the first plague of blood in the Nile, which is brought about by Moses striking the water with his staff and which is, not coincidentally, the one plague that, in J, Yahweh already put in Moses's power (3:9, 21). The J plagues, and only the J plagues, also repeatedly refer to the physical separation between the Israelites and the Egyptians, with the Israelites living by themselves in the land of Goshen (8:18; 9:26), the Israelite territory in Egypt according exclusively to J (Gen 45:10 and elsewhere). The conclusion of the J plagues cycle is just as predicted: Moses tells Pharaoh of the impending death of the firstborn (11:4–8), just as Yahweh had told him to (4:22–23). And upon the infliction of this last plague (12:29–30), Pharaoh indeed drives the Israelites from Egypt (12:31–34, 39), as Yahweh had anticipated (6:1). It was suggested above that the episode of Abraham in Egypt in Genesis 12:10–20 might be taken as a foreshadowing of the Exodus; this suggestion is supported by the final words of Pharaoh to Moses and Aaron in Exodus 12:32: "Take your flocks and your herds, as you said, and begone!"—almost precisely the final words of the king of Egypt to Abraham in Genesis 12:19: "Here is your wife; take her and begone!" As a whole, the plagues in J constitute a beautifully constructed unit of their own accord and are, at the same time, consistently dependent on and referential to earlier J passages, in Exodus and indeed in Genesis as well.

The entrance of the Israelites into the wilderness in J begins with the notice of Yahweh's accompaniment in a pillar of cloud by day and fire by night (Exod 13:21–22); this notice comports with J's earlier statement that Yahweh himself—rather than Moses—would be the one to physically lead the Israelites out of Egypt and into the promised land (3:16–17). This pillar of cloud and fire recurs in J's wilderness account, including in the immediately following episode of the encounter with the Egyptians at the sea (14:19–20, 24). Exodus 14 connects with the preceding J account also in 14:5, in which the king of Egypt realizes that the journey into the wilderness to sacrifice was only a ruse, and in the typically J manner by which it is Yahweh himself who brings about and ends the miracle (14:21 [from "Yahweh drove back the sea"]). (For more detailed analysis, see case study IV.)

The people move from the sea into the wilderness in 15:22a[121] and come to Marah, where Yahweh turns the bitter water sweet (15:23–25a). The use of an everyday object to effect a miracle is reminiscent of the signs Moses does with his staff, his hand, and the water in 4:2–9. This episode marks the first in a series of complaints in J on the part of the Israelites about their hardships in the wilderness. Yahweh takes this opportunity to test the Israelites (15:25b), stating that if they are faithful, then he will be faithful to them in turn (15:26).[122] He then proposes the test referred to in 15:25b: he will provide bread for six days, with a double portion on the sixth day but none on the seventh day, the Sabbath (16:4–5, 26). Perhaps unsurprisingly, the people still try to gather their bread on the seventh day (16:27), to which Yahweh responds angrily (16:28–29), after which the people obey (16:30). The progression from the incident of the bitter waters of Marah to the test of the Sabbath is continued and heightened in the story of Moses getting water from a rock in 17:1 (from "there was no water")–7. The keyword "test" appears here again (17:2), though in an ironic reversal it is the people who are said to be "testing" Yahweh, rather than the reverse. The staff with which Moses strikes the rock is "the rod with which you struck the Nile"—a direct reference to 7:20, "he lifted up the rod and struck the water in the Nile."[123] The J account of the period between Egypt and Sinai as a whole and each individual episode in it are closely linked on the literary level, with both direct cross-references and thematic continuities.

The question that ends the episode in 17:1–7—"Is Yahweh present among us or not?"—provides the impetus for the theophany at Sinai that follows it directly.[124] Unlike in the other sources, in J no law is given at the mountain in the wilderness. It is, at its base, simply a display of Yahweh's presence before the Israelite people. In 19:10–13, Yahweh proclaims the imminent theophany to Moses: "Yahweh will come down, in the sight of all the people, on Mount Sinai" (19:11). The people must be prepared for this event (19:10), and they must be warned not to approach the mountain when they see Yahweh upon it (19:12–13). The assumption is that the people will want to come close to Yahweh and will have to be restrained from encroaching on the divine. This assumption too seems to fit with their doubts and desires as expressed in the question of 17:7. Moses relates Yahweh's message to the people in 19:14–15, and on the third day, as Yahweh had said (19:11), the mountain is full of fire and smoke and Yahweh descends upon it (19:16 [the words "On the third day, as morning dawned"], 18, 20). The dialogue between Yahweh and Moses in 19:21–24 is essentially a repetition of the instructions in 19:12–13, as Moses himself recognizes (19:23). But Moses delivers the message anyway (19:25).

In Exodus 24:1 the author of J relates that Yahweh had previously told Moses to ascend partway up the mountain with Aaron, Nadab, Abihu, and seventy elders, in reference to 19:24; Moses is to come up alone, with the others staying at the lower stage, while the people must again be kept away (24:2). These instructions are fulfilled precisely in 24:9–11. The people as a whole have witnessed the theophany in 19:18, 20; now the most important Israelites have had a particularly close encounter with Yahweh. The point has been made, the question answered: Yahweh is indeed in the midst of the people. This is all that was to happen at Sinai according to Yahweh's plan. He now speaks to Moses individually—presumably after Moses has gone the rest of the way up the mountain, as described in 24:2—to tell him to leave Sinai and enter the promised land (33:1).[125] However, Yahweh himself will not accompany the Israelites any longer but will send a divine messenger instead, for the behavior of the Israelites in the stories of Exodus 15, 16, and 17 has led Yahweh to the conclusion that they are "stiff-necked" and that were he to travel with them he would become enraged and destroy them before they reached Canaan (33:2–3). The negotiations between Moses and Yahweh that follow in 33:12–17 continue from this decision directly. We may observe that Moses's desire for help in leading the Israelites is similar to his argument in 4:1–16; the Moses of J is full of self-doubt.

Once Yahweh has agreed to accompany the Israelites, Moses makes a further request: "Let me behold your presence" (33:18). Yahweh accedes to this also, with some qualifications (33:19–23). His instructions to Moses continue uninterrupted in 34:2–3, again with the restriction on any approach to the mountain by the people or their animals, as in 19:12–13. The private theophany to Moses— continuing the sequence of J theophanies from 19:18, 20 and 24:9–11, each restricted to a more limited group but each more revealing of the deity—occurs in 34:4 ("early in the morning he went up on Mount Sinai") and 34:5 (from "he stood with him there")–9. Yahweh passes before him and proclaims the name Yahweh in 34:6, just as he said he would in 33:19. Moses, faced with the presence of the deity, is moved to exclaim again in 34:9 his plea that Yahweh accompany the Israelites, and Yahweh responds with the proposal of a covenant in 34:10–16: he will drive out the inhabitants of Canaan if the Israelites will not enter into any covenant with the Canaanites.[126] Yahweh instructs Moses to write down the words of this covenant in 34:27.

It should be observed that the entire covenant at Sinai in J and the theophany before Moses were not part of Yahweh's original plan for the Israelites' stop at the mountain. It was to be no more than an appearance of the deity before the people, proving his presence—ironically, just before leaving them. It is Moses's plea that changed the expected course of events. The J Sinai pericope as a whole is inextricably part of the broader narrative context in J. The rationale for it—since it is not based on the need to deliver any laws—derives entirely from the preceding narratives of Israelite complaint in the wilderness; and the major conclusion that emerges from it, that Yahweh will indeed accompany the Israelites, is meaningful only in the context of an extended narrative of travel through the wilderness. Indeed, many of the elements introduced or emphasized in the Sinai pericope play a role in the J passages that follow it.

Once the covenant has been completed in Exodus 34, there is no further business to conduct at Sinai. Thus it is time for the Israelites to depart for Canaan. In Numbers 10:29–32, Moses invites his brother-in-law Hobab—identified as the "son of Reuel the Midianite, Moses's father-in-law," in exclusive accordance with J (Exod 2:18)—to accompany the Israelites. The manner by which they travel through the wilderness is described in Numbers 10:33–36, which mention the exclusively J divine cloud that guides them, as in Exodus 13:21–22 (and in light of Yahweh's agreeing to go with the Israelites in 33:14).[127]

The J stories about the Israelites' journey through the wilderness can be understood, as a whole, as the confirmation of Yahweh's prediction that the people would prove so difficult that he would attempt to destroy them (Exod 33:3). These begin with the brief account of Numbers 11:1–3, in which the people complain and Yahweh sends a fire to punish them. The story of the people's desire for meat in the remainder of Numbers 11 (for the details of the source analysis see case study II) concludes similarly, with the sending of a plague. The J story in Numbers 11 assumes that the people have been eating manna since they entered the wilderness (11:4–9), an assumption that relies on the preceding J story in Exodus 16. The portrayal of Moses is also typical of J, reminiscent of Exodus 4:1–16.

In Numbers 13–14 we find the most extensive J story from the wilderness (excepting the Sinai pericope), that of the spies. The people have arrived at the border of Canaan, and Moses sends some of them to investigate the land (13:17b–20). The spies do so (13:22–24) and return to Moses with their report (13:26–29) that the inhabitants of the land are powerful. Caleb—alone, according exclusively to J—encourages the people despite this description (13:30), but the other spies argue that the land cannot be conquered (13:31, 33). In the face of such negative testimony, the Israelites weep (14:1b), thereby showing their lack of faith in Yahweh's power to fight on their behalf—a power that has already been displayed clearly in Exodus 14. Yahweh's response is angry: he will destroy the people and begin again with Moses (14:11–12); this is nothing less than the fulfillment of Yahweh's prediction in Exodus 33:3 that he would try to destroy the people. Specifically, he threatens to send a "pestilence," *deber*, against the people; this threat coincides beautifully with Yahweh's previous promise that if the people were faithful, he would spare them from the afflictions he had brought on the Egyptians (Exod 15:26), especially considering that the plague of *deber* in Exodus 9:1–7 is exclusive to J. Moses responds to this threat with a plea on behalf of the people (Num 14:13–19). His plea contains two direct connections with other J texts: he mentions in 14:14 the pillar of cloud by day and fire by night in which Yahweh accompanies the Israelites through the wilderness, as in Exodus 13:21–22; and in Numbers 14:17–18 he quotes Yahweh's words from Exodus 34:6–7 back to him: "Let my lord's forbearance be great, as you have declared, saying: 'Yahweh! Slow to anger [better, "Yahweh is slow to anger"] and abounding in kindness.'" Yahweh accedes, in part, but he swears that the entire generation of the Exodus, with the exception of Caleb, will die in the wilderness (Num 14:20–24). In this oath, Yahweh recapitulates virtually the entire J narrative of Exodus: those who will die are those "who have seen my glory," that is, at the theophany at Sinai; "and the signs that I have performed in Egypt," that is, the plagues; "and in the wilderness," that is, the bitter waters turning sweet, the bread raining from the sky, the water from a rock, the quails; "and who have tried me these many times and have disobeyed me," that is, in all of the aforementioned episodes—and note the not inconsequential use of the word "test," which hearkens back directly to the stories of Exodus 15, 16, and 17. The episode of the spies may go back to an independent oral tradition, but the text itself is riddled with cross-references and thematic continuities with the rest of the J narrative.

The episode of the spies concludes with Yahweh's instructions to the Israelites not to attempt to enter Canaan directly, but rather to turn away from the border and go back into the wilderness by way of the road that leads toward the Sea of Reeds (Num 14:25). The news that they will not enter the land causes the Israelites grief (14:39), and they decide to enter Canaan anyway (14:40). Despite Moses's warnings (14:41–43) that they will be defeated because Yahweh will not be with them to fight on their behalf—as he did in Exodus 14—the Israelites attempt to enter the land and, predictably, are soundly defeated (Num 14:44–45). We may note in these verses too the mention of the ark of Yahweh's covenant (14:44), which was mentioned previously by this name, and only in J, in 10:33. In 21:1, the Canaanite king of Arad, taking advantage of Israel's weakened state, takes some of the people captive. The Israelites have learned from their previous experience not to attempt to enter the land and capture their compatriots without Yahweh's assistance, so they make a vow (21:2): if Yahweh will "deliver this people" into their hands, that is, if he will fight for them, then they will proscribe the Canaanite towns—that is, they will not try to settle there, since they have been forbidden from doing so, but rather will utterly destroy them. Yahweh agrees and so it happens (21:3).

When the rescue mission is completed, the Israelites do exactly as Yahweh had instructed them in 14:25 and set out on the road toward the Sea of Reeds (21:4aα). They travel through the wilderness along the itinerary provided in 21:16–20, by the end of which they have arrived at the peak of Mount Pisgah in

Moab, on the eastern border of Canaan. There is nothing left but to enter the land, so Moses gives the people his final speech, the poem of Deuteronomy 33—a clear parallel with the final speech of Jacob in Genesis 49, which is similarly a collection of tribal sayings—after which, in Deuteronomy 34:1–4*, 5*, 6, he dies.

The J document—like all the documents of the Pentateuch—is founded on a variety of traditions, some, if not all, of which were originally independent oral traditions. Yet the written text, the literary work, is so thoroughly interconnected and interdependent; continuous and coherent and well-developed in plot, character, and concept; and full of explicit cross-references and thematic consistencies that it cannot but be considered a unified piece. To say otherwise—to say that in fact what we have here are numerous independent texts that have been linked together only by secondary additions—is to ignore all of the continuities from passage to passage and throughout the J text. The connections observed above cannot be removed from the text without doing irreparable harm to the sense and substance of each passage.

Case Study II

A Complaint in the Wilderness, Numbers 11

¹The people took to complaining bitterly before the Lord. The Lord heard and was incensed: a fire of the Lord broke out against them, ravaging the outskirts of the camp. ²The people cried out to Moses. Moses prayed to the Lord, and the fire died down. ³That place was named Taberah, because a fire of the Lord had broken out against them. ⁴The riffraff in their midst felt a gluttonous craving; and then the Israelites wept and said, "If only we had meat to eat! ⁵We remember the fish that we used to eat free in Egypt, the cucumbers, the melons, the leeks, the onions, and the garlic. ⁶Now our gullets are shriveled. There is nothing at all! Nothing but this manna to look to!" ⁷Now the manna was like coriander seed, and in color it was like bdellium. ⁸The people would go about and gather it, grind it between millstones or pound it in a mortar, boil it in a pot, and make it into cakes. It tasted like rich cream. ⁹When the dew fell on the camp at

¹וַיְהִי הָעָם כְּמִתְאֹנְנִים רַע בְּאָזְנֵי יְהוָה וַיִּשְׁמַע יְהוָה וַיִּחַר אַפּוֹ וַתִּבְעַר־בָּם אֵשׁ יְהוָה וַתֹּאכַל בִּקְצֵה הַמַּחֲנֶה: ²וַיִּצְעַק הָעָם אֶל־מֹשֶׁה וַיִּתְפַּלֵּל מֹשֶׁה אֶל־יְהוָה וַתִּשְׁקַע הָאֵשׁ: ³וַיִּקְרָא שֵׁם־הַמָּקוֹם הַהוּא תַּבְעֵרָה כִּי־בָעֲרָה בָם אֵשׁ יְהוָה: ⁴וְהָאסַפְסֻף אֲשֶׁר בְּקִרְבּוֹ הִתְאַוּוּ תַּאֲוָה וַיָּשֻׁבוּ וַיִּבְכּוּ גַּם בְּנֵי יִשְׂרָאֵל וַיֹּאמְרוּ מִי יַאֲכִלֵנוּ בָּשָׂר: ⁵זָכַרְנוּ אֶת־הַדָּגָה אֲשֶׁר־נֹאכַל בְּמִצְרַיִם חִנָּם אֵת הַקִּשֻּׁאִים וְאֵת הָאֲבַטִּחִים וְאֶת־הֶחָצִיר וְאֶת־הַבְּצָלִים וְאֶת־הַשּׁוּמִים: ⁶וְעַתָּה נַפְשֵׁנוּ יְבֵשָׁה אֵין כֹּל בִּלְתִּי אֶל־הַמָּן עֵינֵינוּ: ⁷וְהַמָּן כִּזְרַע־גַּד הוּא וְעֵינוֹ כְּעֵין הַבְּדֹלַח: ⁸שָׁטוּ הָעָם וְלָקְטוּ וְטָחֲנוּ בָרֵחַיִם אוֹ דָכוּ בַּמְּדֹכָה וּבִשְּׁלוּ בַּפָּרוּר וְעָשׂוּ אֹתוֹ עֻגוֹת וְהָיָה טַעְמוֹ כְּטַעַם לְשַׁד הַשָּׁמֶן: ⁹וּבְרֶדֶת הַטַּל עַל־הַמַּחֲנֶה לָיְלָה יֵרֵד הַמָּן עָלָיו: ¹⁰וַיִּשְׁמַע מֹשֶׁה אֶת־הָעָם בֹּכֶה לְמִשְׁפְּחֹתָיו אִישׁ לְפֶתַח אָהֳלוֹ וַיִּחַר־אַף יְהוָה מְאֹד וּבְעֵינֵי מֹשֶׁה רָע: ¹¹וַיֹּאמֶר מֹשֶׁה אֶל־יְהוָה לָמָה הֲרֵעֹתָ לְעַבְדֶּךָ וְלָמָּה לֹא־מָצָתִי חֵן בְּעֵינֶיךָ לָשׂוּם אֶת־מַשָּׂא כָּל־הָעָם הַזֶּה עָלָי: ¹²הֶאָנֹכִי הָרִיתִי אֵת כָּל־הָעָם הַזֶּה אִם־אָנֹכִי יְלִדְתִּיהוּ כִּי־תֹאמַר אֵלַי שָׂאֵהוּ בְחֵיקֶךָ כַּאֲשֶׁר יִשָּׂא הָאֹמֵן אֶת־הַיֹּנֵק עַל הָאֲדָמָה אֲשֶׁר נִשְׁבַּעְתָּ לַאֲבֹתָיו: ¹³מֵאַיִן לִי בָּשָׂר לָתֵת לְכָל־הָעָם הַזֶּה כִּי־יִבְכּוּ עָלַי לֵאמֹר תְּנָה־לָּנוּ בָשָׂר וְנֹאכֵלָה: ¹⁴לֹא־אוּכַל אָנֹכִי לְבַדִּי לָשֵׂאת אֶת־כָּל־הָעָם הַזֶּה כִּי כָבֵד מִמֶּנִּי: ¹⁵וְאִם־כָּכָה אַתְּ־עֹשֶׂה לִּי הָרְגֵנִי נָא הָרֹג אִם־מָצָאתִי חֵן

night, the manna would fall upon it. ¹⁰Moses heard the people weeping, every clan apart, each person at the entrance of his tent. The Lord was very angry, and Moses was distressed. ¹¹And Moses said to the Lord, "Why have you dealt ill with your servant, and why have I not enjoyed your favor, that you have laid the burden of all this people upon me? ¹²Did I conceive all this people, did I bear them, that you should say to me, 'Carry them in your bosom as a nurse carries an infant,' to the land that you have promised on oath to their fathers? ¹³Where am I to get meat to give to all this people, when they whine before me and say, 'Give us meat to eat!' ¹⁴I cannot carry all this people by myself, for it is too much for me. ¹⁵If you would deal thus with me, kill me rather, I beg you, and let me see no more of my wretchedness!" ¹⁶Then the Lord said to Moses, "Gather for me seventy of Israel's elders of whom you have experience as elders and officers of the people, and bring them to the Tent of Meeting and let them take their place there with you. ¹⁷I will come down and speak with you there, and I will draw upon the spirit that is on you and put it upon them; they shall share the burden of the people with you, and you shall not bear it alone. ¹⁸And say to the people: Purify yourselves for tomorrow and you shall eat meat, for you have kept whining before the Lord and saying, 'If

בְּעֵינֶיךָ וְאַל־אֶרְאֶה בְּרָעָתִי: ¹⁶וַיֹּאמֶר יְהוָה אֶל־מֹשֶׁה אֶסְפָה־לִּי שִׁבְעִים אִישׁ מִזִּקְנֵי יִשְׂרָאֵל אֲשֶׁר יָדַעְתָּ כִּי־הֵם זִקְנֵי הָעָם וְשֹׁטְרָיו וְלָקַחְתָּ אֹתָם אֶל־אֹהֶל מוֹעֵד וְהִתְיַצְּבוּ שָׁם עִמָּךְ: ¹⁷וְיָרַדְתִּי וְדִבַּרְתִּי עִמְּךָ שָׁם וְאָצַלְתִּי מִן־הָרוּחַ אֲשֶׁר עָלֶיךָ וְשַׂמְתִּי עֲלֵיהֶם וְנָשְׂאוּ אִתְּךָ בְּמַשָּׂא הָעָם וְלֹא־תִשָּׂא אַתָּה לְבַדֶּךָ: ¹⁸וְאֶל־הָעָם תֹּאמַר הִתְקַדְּשׁוּ לְמָחָר וַאֲכַלְתֶּם בָּשָׂר כִּי בְּכִיתֶם בְּאָזְנֵי יְהוָה לֵאמֹר מִי יַאֲכִלֵנוּ בָּשָׂר כִּי־טוֹב לָנוּ בְּמִצְרָיִם וְנָתַן יְהוָה לָכֶם בָּשָׂר וַאֲכַלְתֶּם: ¹⁹לֹא יוֹם אֶחָד תֹּאכְלוּן וְלֹא יוֹמָיִם וְלֹא חֲמִשָּׁה יָמִים וְלֹא עֲשָׂרָה יָמִים וְלֹא עֶשְׂרִים יוֹם: ²⁰עַד חֹדֶשׁ יָמִים עַד אֲשֶׁר־יֵצֵא מֵאַפְּכֶם וְהָיָה לָכֶם לְזָרָא יַעַן כִּי־מְאַסְתֶּם אֶת־יְהוָה אֲשֶׁר בְּקִרְבְּכֶם וַתִּבְכּוּ לְפָנָיו לֵאמֹר לָמָּה זֶּה יָצָאנוּ מִמִּצְרָיִם: ²¹וַיֹּאמֶר מֹשֶׁה שֵׁשׁ־מֵאוֹת אֶלֶף רַגְלִי הָעָם אֲשֶׁר אָנֹכִי בְּקִרְבּוֹ וְאַתָּה אָמַרְתָּ בָּשָׂר אֶתֵּן לָהֶם וְאָכְלוּ חֹדֶשׁ יָמִים: ²²הֲצֹאן וּבָקָר יִשָּׁחֵט לָהֶם וּמָצָא לָהֶם אִם אֶת־כָּל־דְּגֵי הַיָּם יֵאָסֵף לָהֶם וּמָצָא לָהֶם: ²³וַיֹּאמֶר יְהוָה אֶל־מֹשֶׁה הֲיַד יְהוָה תִּקְצָר עַתָּה תִרְאֶה הֲיִקְרְךָ דְבָרִי אִם־לֹא: ²⁴וַיֵּצֵא מֹשֶׁה וַיְדַבֵּר אֶל־הָעָם אֵת דִּבְרֵי יְהוָה וַיֶּאֱסֹף שִׁבְעִים אִישׁ מִזִּקְנֵי הָעָם וַיַּעֲמֵד אֹתָם סְבִיבֹת הָאֹהֶל: ²⁵וַיֵּרֶד יְהוָה בֶּעָנָן וַיְדַבֵּר אֵלָיו וַיָּאצֶל מִן־הָרוּחַ אֲשֶׁר עָלָיו וַיִּתֵּן עַל־שִׁבְעִים אִישׁ הַזְּקֵנִים וַיְהִי כְּנוֹחַ עֲלֵיהֶם הָרוּחַ וַיִּתְנַבְּאוּ וְלֹא יָסָפוּ: ²⁶וַיִּשָּׁאֲרוּ שְׁנֵי־אֲנָשִׁים בַּמַּחֲנֶה שֵׁם הָאֶחָד אֶלְדָּד וְשֵׁם הַשֵּׁנִי מֵידָד וַתָּנַח עֲלֵיהֶם הָרוּחַ וְהֵמָּה בַּכְּתֻבִים וְלֹא יָצְאוּ הָאֹהֱלָה וַיִּתְנַבְּאוּ בַּמַּחֲנֶה: ²⁷וַיָּרָץ הַנַּעַר וַיַּגֵּד לְמֹשֶׁה וַיֹּאמַר אֶלְדָּד וּמֵידָד מִתְנַבְּאִים בַּמַּחֲנֶה: ²⁸וַיַּעַן יְהוֹשֻׁעַ בִּן־נוּן מְשָׁרֵת מֹשֶׁה מִבְּחֻרָיו וַיֹּאמַר אֲדֹנִי מֹשֶׁה כְּלָאֵם: ²⁹וַיֹּאמֶר לוֹ מֹשֶׁה הַמְקַנֵּא אַתָּה לִי וּמִי יִתֵּן כָּל־עַם יְהוָה נְבִיאִים כִּי־יִתֵּן יְהוָה אֶת־רוּחוֹ עֲלֵיהֶם: ³⁰וַיֵּאָסֵף מֹשֶׁה אֶל־הַמַּחֲנֶה הוּא וְזִקְנֵי יִשְׂרָאֵל: ³¹וְרוּחַ נָסַע מֵאֵת יְהוָה וַיָּגָז שַׂלְוִים מִן־הַיָּם וַיִּטֹּשׁ עַל־הַמַּחֲנֶה כְּדֶרֶךְ יוֹם כֹּה וּכְדֶרֶךְ יוֹם כֹּה סְבִיבוֹת הַמַּחֲנֶה וּכְאַמָּתַיִם עַל־פְּנֵי הָאָרֶץ: ³²וַיָּקָם הָעָם כָּל־הַיּוֹם הַהוּא וְכָל־הַלַּיְלָה וְכֹל יוֹם הַמָּחֳרָת וַיַּאַסְפוּ אֶת־הַשְּׂלָו הַמַּמְעִיט

only we had meat to eat! Indeed, we were better off in Egypt!' The Lord will give you meat and you shall eat. [19]You shall eat not one day, not two, not even five days or ten or twenty, [20]but a whole month, until it comes out of your nostrils and becomes loathsome to you. For you have rejected the Lord who is among you, by whining before him and saying, 'Oh, why did we ever leave Egypt!'" [21]But Moses said, "The people who are with me number six hundred thousand men; yet you say, 'I will give them enough meat to eat for a whole month.' [22]Could enough flocks and herds be slaughtered to suffice them? Or could all the fish of the sea be gathered for them to suffice them?" [23]And the Lord answered Moses, "Is there a limit to the Lord's power? You shall soon see whether what I have said happens to you or not!" [24]Moses went out and reported the words of the Lord to the people. He gathered seventy of the people's elders and stationed them around the Tent. [25]Then the Lord came down in a cloud and spoke to him; He drew upon the spirit that was on him and put it upon the seventy elders. And when the spirit rested upon them, they spoke in ecstasy, but did not continue. [26]Two men, one named Eldad and the other Medad, had remained in camp; yet the spirit rested upon them—they were among those recorded, but they had not gone out to the Tent—and they

אָסֹף עֲשָׂרָה חֳמָרִים וַיִּשְׁטְחוּ לָהֶם שָׁטוֹחַ סְבִיבוֹת
הַמַּחֲנֶה: [33]הַבָּשָׂר עוֹדֶנּוּ בֵּין שִׁנֵּיהֶם טֶרֶם יִכָּרֵת
וְאַף יְהֹוָה חָרָה בָעָם וַיַּךְ יְהֹוָה בָּעָם מַכָּה רַבָּה
מְאֹד: [34]וַיִּקְרָא אֶת־שֵׁם־הַמָּקוֹם הַהוּא קִבְרוֹת
הַתַּאֲוָה כִּי־שָׁם קָבְרוּ אֶת־הָעָם הַמִּתְאַוִּים:

spoke in ecstasy in the camp. [27]A youth ran out and told Moses, saying, "Eldad and Medad are acting the prophet in the camp!" [28]And Joshua son of Nun, Moses's attendant from his youth, spoke up and said, "My lord Moses, restrain them!" [29]But Moses said to him, "Are you wrought up on my account? Would that all the Lord's people were prophets, that the Lord put his spirit upon them!" [30]Moses then reentered the camp together with the elders of Israel. [31]A wind from the Lord started up, swept quail from the sea and strewed them over the camp, about a day's journey on this side and about a day's journey on that side, all around the camp, and some two cubits deep on the ground. [32]The people set to gathering quail all that day and night and all the next day— even he who gathered least had ten homers—and they spread them out all around the camp. [33]The meat was still between their teeth, nor yet chewed, when the anger of the Lord blazed forth against the people and the Lord struck the people with a very severe plague. [34]That place was named Kibroth-hattaavah, because the people who had the craving were buried there.

Numbers 11 begins with a brief narrative of an indeterminate Israelite complaint against Yahweh. In vv. 1–3, the people's complaint is answered by a fire that destroys the edges of the camp; the people cry out to Moses, and he prays to Yahweh. The fire promptly ends, and the place is named Taberah ("Burning"). This story is little more than an etiology; the details are so slim that there is little other value to the narrative beyond its conclusion. There is no reason to divide these verses; indeed, the story is so concise that any division would render it incoherent.[1]

In v. 4 we are presented with a new complaint: the Israelites wish for meat to supplement their regular diet of manna. Although this is the beginning of a new story, it is connected compositionally with the brief narrative that opens the chapter. The first clause of v. 4 is "The riffraff in their midst felt a gluttonous craving." The word "in their midst" (*bᵊqirbô*, literally, "in its midst") presumes a singular antecedent referring to the people, and this antecedent is found in vv. 1–2: "the people" (*hā'ām*; note the singular verbs: *wayhî* [v. 1] and *wayyiṣ'aq* [v. 2]). Thus v. 4, and the story it begins, is dependent on vv. 1–3 and must be seen as a continuation of the same source.[2]

The complaint that begins in v. 4 continues uninterrupted through the end of v. 6 in a logical progression of the argument. The people as a whole take up the complaint of the "riffraff" among them; they begin with their wish for meat and then look back in v. 5 to the food they enjoyed in Egypt; in v. 6 they contrast their former situation with the present, in which they have nothing but manna to eat. Verses 7–9 are a parenthetical description of the manna: its shape and color, the manner in which it was prepared, its taste, and the way it was delivered. These verses obviously cannot stand alone, as they are explicitly marked as background information and follow directly on the preceding clause at the end of v. 6.[3]

The narrative resumes in v. 10a precisely where it left off. After the people have finished speaking, we are told that Moses hears them weeping. This ties back to the introduction to the direct speech in v. 4: "the Israelites wept." The second half of v. 10 describes Yahweh's anger and Moses's judgment of the people's complaint as "evil" (*rā'*). These expressions resonate with both the story of vv. 4–9 and that of vv. 1–3. Of Yahweh it is said that "he was very angry" (*wayyiḥar-'ap yhwh mᵊ'ōd*); these are the same words used in v. 2 to describe Yahweh's response to the complaint in v. 1 (*wayyiḥar 'appô*).[4] As for Moses, it says that "Moses was distressed," literally, "it [that is, the people weeping for meat] was evil in his eyes" (*ûbᵊ'ênê mōšeʰ rā'*); this phrase echoes not only with the description of the complaint in v. 1, in which the complaint is "evil in the ears of Yahweh" (*ra' bᵊ'oznê yhwh*), but also with the final words of the complaint in v. 6: "There is nothing at all! Nothing but this manna to look to," literally, "our eyes look toward nothing but this manna" (*'ên kōl biltî 'el-hammān 'ênênû*).

Moses's appeal to Yahweh in vv. 11–15 appears to be a direct continuation of the preceding verse. Yet the content of his speech is somewhat confusing. He begins in vv. 11–12 not with any reaction to the people, but rather with a self-oriented inquiry: why have you made me responsible for the entire people? After all, I am not their parent. In v. 13, however, Moses speaks directly to the issue of the people's hunger: where am I supposed to get meat for them? And in vv. 14–15, the meat again goes unmentioned, but Moses returns to his first theme: I am unable to be responsible for all of these people by myself, so either help me or kill me.[5]

Moses appears to raise two distinct issues in this speech. One, in v. 13, relates directly to the people's desire for meat in vv. 4–10. In this verse Moses takes the complaint of the people directly to Yahweh but puts himself forward as the oppressed intermediary; though the people did not ask Moses himself for meat, Moses takes it as a personal attack: where am I to get meat, when they cry before me and say "Give us meat to eat!" We may notice that the theme of the people crying from vv. 4 and 10 is repeated here. And although Moses has reconfigured the people's words to be about him—instead of the people's "If only we had meat to eat," literally, "Who will give us meat to eat?," he has them saying to him "Give us meat to eat!"—the reference in v. 13 directly to v. 4 is undeniable.

On the other hand, vv. 11–12, 14–15 seem to have little connection to the preceding complaint by the people. Nowhere in these verses is meat mentioned, nor even that the people have complained, either specifically as in vv. 4–10 or generally as in v. 1. Rather, Moses's speech is a complaint not about any particularly difficult moment of leading the people, but the act of leading them at all. The four verses are closely linked rhetorically. In both v. 11 and v. 14, the two expressions "bear/burden" (*n-ś-'*) and "all the people" (*kol-hā'ām*) are tied together: "you have laid the burden of all this people upon me" (v. 11) and "I cannot carry [literally, "bear"] all this people by myself" (v. 14).[6] In v. 12, meanwhile, Moses makes clear that his concern is a general one, not one about the issue of meat in particular: it is the entire process of leading the people to the promised land that seems too heavy a burden (again using the verb *n-ś-'*). Similarly, in v. 15, it is equally clear that Moses is speaking on his own behalf, not on that of the people: "let me see no more of my wretchedness." It is not any action of the people that is at stake here, but rather Moses's self-expressed inability to serve as the leader he was chosen to be. The entire speech is framed by the word *ra'*, "evil"—Moses opens by asking "Why have you dealt ill with [literally, "done evil to"] your servant?" (v. 11) and ends by requesting that he no longer be allowed to see "my wretchedness [literally, "my evil"]," that is, the evil that has befallen me (v. 15)—and also by the expression "find favor" (*māṣā' ḥēn bᵊ'ênê*, vv. 11 and 15). This speech is thus a tightly knit rhetorical construction.[7]

If these verses do not in fact belong with the story of the people's desire for meat in this chapter, then to what do they connect? Numbers 11 is the first chapter in any source that takes place in the wilderness; the people have left the mountain in Numbers 10. The occasion for Moses's speech in vv. 11–12, 14–15, then, would not be any specific event, but rather the entire departure from the mountain and entrance into the wilderness. When read in this context, these verses make very good sense: Moses is suddenly faced with the real prospect of leading this enormous populace through the wilderness by himself. The reference to the promise of the land in v. 12 is therefore entirely appropriate. Although a new "story" begins in Numbers 11:11, it is not and never was intended to be read on its own. Thus questions about the narrative's "beginning" are not always useful.[8]

In order to read both of Moses's complaints (v. 13 and vv. 11–12, 14–15) as parts of a smooth narrative, we must recognize that the compiler has made one small adjustment to his received texts in v. 11. The opening words of that verse, "Moses said to Yahweh," are necessary for both stories, yet they appear only once in the canonical text. If we assume that this stereotypical introductory phrase was present in both narratives in their originally independent forms, then we must also assume that the compiler has combined them into a single statement. This is, of course, entirely logical: since the compiler has combined the two speeches into a single speech, he could hardly have two introductions.[9] Further, by doing this, the compiler has not in fact altered either of his original sources, since the words present in both (or either) are still represented in the canonical text.

Yahweh's response to Moses in vv. 16–20 is, like Moses's speech in vv. 11–15, twofold. In vv. 16–17, Yahweh instructs Moses to gather seventy of the elders to the Tent of Meeting so that some of Moses's prophetic spirit may be placed upon them. This is explicitly posed as the solution to Moses's self-doubt: "they shall share the burden of the people with you, and you shall not bear it alone." Yahweh's proposal responds only to vv. 11–12, 14–15; there is, again, no mention of meat, and we may note in particular the recurrence of the keyword *n-ś-'* twice in v. 17.[10] The placing of Moses's prophetic spirit on the elders in no way addresses the people's desire for meat. Verses 18–20, on the other hand, are only about meat (*n-ś-'* does not appear) and directly respond to Moses's question in v. 13: Yahweh instructs Moses to tell the people to purify themselves and prepare to eat meat, but in such quantities that they will regret having ever complained in the first place.[11] Not unexpectedly, we find here yet another two references to the people crying, in vv. 18 and 20, in each case accompanied by a recollection of the people's longing to return to Egypt; these references form bookends to Yahweh's speech and mark it off as a unit. Indeed, they emphasize precisely what is objectionable about the people's complaint: it is not that they wish for meat, but rather that they couch that desire in terms of wanting to return to Egypt.

The same redactional process at work in v. 11 is at work in v. 16. Again, in both sources the same parties are speaking: in this case, Yahweh is speaking to Moses. Again, the compiler had before him two speeches, one from each source, each beginning with the same typical phrase: "Yahweh said to Moses." And again, because he combined the two speeches into one, the compiler simply merged the two identical introductions into a single statement.

The dialogue between Moses and Yahweh in vv. 21–23 directly follows upon the second part of Yahweh's speech in vv. 18–20. Moses questions Yahweh's ability to provide enough meat for the people, and Yahweh tells him to wait and see. We may draw a connection between the words of Moses in these verses and those of v. 13: in both cases, Moses expresses doubt regarding the ability— whether his own or Yahweh's—to feed the entire Israelite population. The difference between this specific doubt and the more general qualms of Moses in vv. 11–12, 14–15 is clear. Although the issue of the size of the Israelite population is raised by Moses in vv. 21–22, it is not in reference to Moses's ability to lead that many people; it is rather a question of Yahweh's ability to feed them.

In v. 24a Moses reports Yahweh's words to the people. Since Yahweh has spoken in both stories, this sentence could in theory belong to either. But there are two strong considerations for linking it with the meat narrative. The first is that Moses's actions here represent a fulfillment of Yahweh's instructions in v. 18: "Say to the people . . ." The second is that only in the story of the meat have the people played any role. In Moses's speech of vv. 11–12, 14–15, and in Yahweh's response in vv. 16–17, the people as a whole are only referred to, never active or even required to act. In the meat story, on the other hand, the people initiate the entire narrative, and it is their complaint to which Moses's words of v. 24a are meant to respond.[12]

This distinction is felt even more keenly when we continue into v. 24b, in which Moses gathers seventy of the elders and brings them to the Tent of Meeting. Just as v. 24a is the fulfillment of Yahweh's command in v. 18 of the meat story, so v. 24b is the direct fulfillment of Yahweh's command to Moses in v. 16. Similarly, v. 25 is the fulfillment of Yahweh's statement in v. 17: Yahweh comes down and places some of Moses's spirit onto the elders. The end of v. 25 tells us that when the spirit was upon the men, they prophesied, although only for a moment.[13] Following the same parallels with vv. 16–17, we may draw an equation between this act of prophesying in v. 25 and Yahweh's promise to Moses in v. 17 that the elders would share some of Moses's burden. The meaning is reasonably clear: if Moses's leadership is derived from his prophetic abilities, then the creation of other prophets from among the Israelite elders would be equivalent to spreading the burden of leadership.[14]

The verses about Eldad and Medad, vv. 26–30, form both a unity and a conclusion to the narrative of the elders.[15] The story of these two elders, who for some reason did not join the others at the Tent but prophesied in the camp anyway, exists mostly as a means of setting up Moses's final line: "Would that all Yahweh's people were prophets." This line is the logical conclusion to the story begun in vv. 11–12, 14–15: there, Moses complained about having to lead all the people; here, he wishes that, in receiving some of the spirit of prophecy, all the people might be able to lead themselves.

The final verses of the chapter (excluding v. 35, which is merely an itinerary notice), vv. 31–34, form the unified conclusion to the story of the meat. As promised, Yahweh provides the people with their meat, in the form of quail, and before the people can finish eating it, Yahweh strikes them with a plague as punishment for their complaining. As with the brief story in vv. 1–3, so too this story ends with an etiology: the place is called Kibroth-Hattaavah, "Graves of Craving."

Numbers 11 thus contains two distinct stories. They begin with two distinct complaints—one by the people, and one by Moses—each with a distinct solution offered by Yahweh in a speech to Moses, and the working out of that solution in reality. One story is about the people's desire for meat and Yahweh's ability to provide it for them. The other is about Moses's doubts regarding his ability to lead the Israelite masses through the wilderness and the prophesying of seventy of Israel's elders. In addition to their disparate plots, each narrative also contains specific keywords: in the story of meat, we find the regular reference to the people crying; in the story of the elders, we see a repetition of the root *n-ś-'*. When the stories are taken individually, we can see that both are complete, coherent, and continuous:[16]

STORY OF THE MEAT	STORY OF THE ELDERS
¹וַיְהִי הָעָם כְּמִתְאֹנְנִים רַע בְּאָזְנֵי יְהוָה וַיִּשְׁמַע	¹¹וַיֹּאמֶר מֹשֶׁה אֶל־יְהוָה לָמָה הֲרֵעֹתָ לְעַבְדֶּךָ
יְהוָה וַיִּחַר אַפּוֹ וַתִּבְעַר־בָּם אֵשׁ יְהוָה וַתֹּאכַל	וְלָמָּה לֹא־מָצָתִי חֵן בְּעֵינֶיךָ לָשׂוּם אֶת־מַשָּׂא כָּל־
בִּקְצֵה הַמַּחֲנֶה: ²וַיִּצְעַק הָעָם אֶל־מֹשֶׁה וַיִּתְפַּלֵּל	הָעָם הַזֶּה עָלָי: ¹²הֶאָנֹכִי הָרִיתִי אֵת כָּל־הָעָם
מֹשֶׁה אֶל־יְהוָה וַתִּשְׁקַע הָאֵשׁ: ³וַיִּקְרָא שֵׁם־הַמָּקוֹם	הַזֶּה אִם־אָנֹכִי יְלִדְתִּיהוּ כִּי־תֹאמַר אֵלַי שָׂאֵהוּ
הַהוּא תַּבְעֵרָה כִּי־בָעֲרָה בָם אֵשׁ יְהוָה:	בְחֵיקֶךָ כַּאֲשֶׁר יִשָּׂא הָאֹמֵן אֶת־הַיֹּנֵק עַל הָאֲדָמָה
⁴וְהָאסַפְסֻף אֲשֶׁר בְּקִרְבּוֹ הִתְאַוּוּ תַּאֲוָה וַיָּשֻׁבוּ	אֲשֶׁר נִשְׁבַּעְתָּ לַאֲבֹתָיו: ¹⁴לֹא־אוּכַל אָנֹכִי לְבַדִּי

וַיִּבְכּוּ גַם בְּנֵי יִשְׂרָאֵל וַיֹּאמְרוּ מִי יַאֲכִלֵנוּ בָּשָׂר:
‎⁵זָכַרְנוּ אֶת־הַדָּגָה אֲשֶׁר־נֹאכַל בְּמִצְרַיִם חִנָּם אֵת
הַקִּשֻּׁאִים וְאֵת הָאֲבַטִּחִים וְאֶת־הֶחָצִיר וְאֶת־
הַבְּצָלִים וְאֶת־הַשּׁוּמִים: ‎⁶וְעַתָּה נַפְשֵׁנוּ יְבֵשָׁה אֵין
כֹּל בִּלְתִּי אֶל־הַמָּן עֵינֵינוּ: ‎⁷וְהַמָּן כִּזְרַע־גַּד הוּא
וְעֵינוֹ כְּעֵין הַבְּדֹלַח: ‎⁸שָׁטוּ הָעָם וְלָקְטוּ וְטָחֲנוּ
בָרֵחַיִם אוֹ דָכוּ בַּמְּדֹכָה וּבִשְּׁלוּ בַּפָּרוּר וְעָשׂוּ אֹתוֹ
עֻגוֹת וְהָיָה טַעְמוֹ כְּטַעַם לְשַׁד הַשָּׁמֶן: ‎⁹וּבְרֶדֶת
הַטַּל עַל־הַמַּחֲנֶה לָיְלָה יֵרֵד הַמָּן עָלָיו: ‎¹⁰וַיִּשְׁמַע
מֹשֶׁה אֶת־הָעָם בֹּכֶה לְמִשְׁפְּחֹתָיו אִישׁ לְפֶתַח
אָהֳלוֹ וַיִּחַר־אַף יְהוָה מְאֹד וּבְעֵינֵי מֹשֶׁה רָע:
‎¹¹וַיֹּאמֶר מֹשֶׁה אֶל־יְהוָה ‎¹³מַאַיִן לִי בָּשָׂר לָתֵת
לְכָל־הָעָם הַזֶּה כִּי־יִבְכּוּ עָלַי לֵאמֹר תְּנָה־לָּנוּ
בָשָׂר וְנֹאכֵלָה: ‎¹⁶וַיֹּאמֶר יְהוָה אֶל־מֹשֶׁה ‎¹⁸אֶל־
הָעָם תֹּאמַר הִתְקַדְּשׁוּ לְמָחָר וַאֲכַלְתֶּם בָּשָׂר כִּי
בְּכִיתֶם בְּאָזְנֵי יְהוָה לֵאמֹר מִי יַאֲכִלֵנוּ בָּשָׂר כִּי־
טוֹב לָנוּ בְּמִצְרָיִם וְנָתַן יְהוָה לָכֶם בָּשָׂר
וַאֲכַלְתֶּם: ‎¹⁹לֹא יוֹם אֶחָד תֹּאכְלוּן וְלֹא יוֹמָיִם
וְלֹא חֲמִשָּׁה יָמִים וְלֹא עֲשָׂרָה יָמִים וְלֹא עֶשְׂרִים
יוֹם: ‎²⁰עַד חֹדֶשׁ יָמִים עַד אֲשֶׁר־יֵצֵא מֵאַפְּכֶם
וְהָיָה לָכֶם לְזָרָא יַעַן כִּי־מְאַסְתֶּם אֶת־יְהוָה אֲשֶׁר
בְּקִרְבְּכֶם וַתִּבְכּוּ לְפָנָיו לֵאמֹר לָמָּה זֶּה יָצָאנוּ
מִמִּצְרָיִם: ‎²¹וַיֹּאמֶר מֹשֶׁה שֵׁשׁ־מֵאוֹת אֶלֶף רַגְלִי
הָעָם אֲשֶׁר אָנֹכִי בְּקִרְבּוֹ וְאַתָּה אָמַרְתָּ בָּשָׂר אֶתֵּן
לָהֶם וְאָכְלוּ חֹדֶשׁ יָמִים: ‎²²הֲצֹאן וּבָקָר יִשָּׁחֵט
לָהֶם וּמָצָא לָהֶם אִם אֶת־כָּל־דְּגֵי הַיָּם יֵאָסֵף
לָהֶם וּמָצָא לָהֶם: ‎²³וַיֹּאמֶר יְהוָה אֶל־מֹשֶׁה הֲיַד
יְהוָה תִּקְצָר עַתָּה תִרְאֶה הֲיִקְרְךָ דְבָרִי אִם־לֹא:
‎²⁴וַיֵּצֵא מֹשֶׁה וַיְדַבֵּר אֶל־הָעָם אֵת דִּבְרֵי יְהוָה
‎³¹וְרוּחַ נָסַע מֵאֵת יְהוָה וַיָּגָז שַׂלְוִים מִן־הַיָּם וַיִּטֹּשׁ
עַל־הַמַּחֲנֶה כְּדֶרֶךְ יוֹם כֹּה וּכְדֶרֶךְ יוֹם כֹּה
סְבִיבוֹת הַמַּחֲנֶה וּכְאַמָּתַיִם עַל־פְּנֵי הָאָרֶץ: ‎³²וַיָּקָם
הָעָם כָּל־הַיּוֹם הַהוּא וְכָל־הַלַּיְלָה וְכֹל יוֹם
הַמָּחֳרָת וַיַּאַסְפוּ אֶת־הַשְּׂלָו הַמַּמְעִיט אָסַף עֲשָׂרָה
חֳמָרִים וַיִּשְׁטְחוּ לָהֶם שָׁטוֹחַ סְבִיבוֹת הַמַּחֲנֶה:
‎³³הַבָּשָׂר עוֹדֶנּוּ בֵּין שִׁנֵּיהֶם טֶרֶם יִכָּרֵת וְאַף יְהוָה
חָרָה בָעָם וַיַּךְ יְהוָה בָּעָם מַכָּה רַבָּה מְאֹד:
‎³⁴וַיִּקְרָא אֶת־שֵׁם־הַמָּקוֹם הַהוּא קִבְרוֹת הַתַּאֲוָה
כִּי־שָׁם קָבְרוּ אֶת־הָעָם הַמִּתְאַוִּים:

לָשֵׂאת אֶת־כָּל־הָעָם הַזֶּה כִּי כָבֵד מִמֶּנִּי: ‎¹⁵וְאִם־
כָּכָה אַתְּ־עֹשֶׂה לִּי הָרְגֵנִי נָא הָרֹג אִם־מָצָאתִי חֵן
בְּעֵינֶיךָ וְאַל־אֶרְאֶה בְּרָעָתִי: ‎¹⁶וַיֹּאמֶר יְהוָה אֶל־
מֹשֶׁה אֶסְפָה־לִּי שִׁבְעִים אִישׁ מִזִּקְנֵי יִשְׂרָאֵל אֲשֶׁר
יָדַעְתָּ כִּי־הֵם זִקְנֵי הָעָם וְשֹׁטְרָיו וְלָקַחְתָּ אֹתָם
אֶל־אֹהֶל מוֹעֵד וְהִתְיַצְּבוּ שָׁם עִמָּךְ: ‎¹⁷וְיָרַדְתִּי
וְדִבַּרְתִּי עִמְּךָ שָׁם וְאָצַלְתִּי מִן־הָרוּחַ אֲשֶׁר עָלֶיךָ
וְשַׂמְתִּי עֲלֵיהֶם וְנָשְׂאוּ אִתְּךָ בְּמַשָּׂא הָעָם וְלֹא־תִשָּׂא
אַתָּה לְבַדֶּךָ: ‎²⁴וַיֶּאֱסֹף שִׁבְעִים אִישׁ מִזִּקְנֵי הָעָם
וַיַּעֲמֵד אֹתָם סְבִיבֹת הָאֹהֶל: ‎²⁵וַיֵּרֶד יְהוָה בֶּעָנָן
וַיְדַבֵּר אֵלָיו וַיָּאצֶל מִן־הָרוּחַ אֲשֶׁר עָלָיו וַיִּתֵּן
עַל־שִׁבְעִים אִישׁ הַזְּקֵנִים וַיְהִי כְּנוֹחַ עֲלֵיהֶם
הָרוּחַ וַיִּתְנַבְּאוּ וְלֹא יָסָפוּ: ‎²⁶וַיִּשָּׁאֲרוּ שְׁנֵי־אֲנָשִׁים
בַּמַּחֲנֶה שֵׁם הָאֶחָד אֶלְדָּד וְשֵׁם הַשֵּׁנִי מֵידָד וַתָּנַח
עֲלֵיהֶם הָרוּחַ וְהֵמָּה בַּכְּתֻבִים וְלֹא יָצְאוּ הָאֹהֱלָה
וַיִּתְנַבְּאוּ בַּמַּחֲנֶה: ‎²⁷וַיָּרָץ הַנַּעַר וַיַּגֵּד לְמֹשֶׁה
וַיֹּאמַר אֶלְדָּד וּמֵידָד מִתְנַבְּאִים בַּמַּחֲנֶה: ‎²⁸וַיַּעַן
יְהוֹשֻׁעַ בִּן־נוּן מְשָׁרֵת מֹשֶׁה מִבְּחֻרָיו וַיֹּאמַר אֲדֹנִי
מֹשֶׁה כְּלָאֵם: ‎²⁹וַיֹּאמֶר לוֹ מֹשֶׁה הַמְקַנֵּא אַתָּה לִי
וּמִי יִתֵּן כָּל־עַם יְהוָה נְבִיאִים כִּי־יִתֵּן יְהוָה אֶת־
רוּחוֹ עֲלֵיהֶם: ‎³⁰וַיֵּאָסֵף מֹשֶׁה אֶל־הַמַּחֲנֶה הוּא
וְזִקְנֵי יִשְׂרָאֵל:

¹The people took to complaining bitterly before the Lord. The Lord heard and was incensed: a fire of the Lord broke out against them, ravaging the outskirts of the camp. ²The people cried out to Moses. Moses prayed to the Lord, and the fire died down. ³That place was named Taberah, because a fire of the Lord had broken out against them. ⁴The riffraff in their midst felt a gluttonous craving; and then the Israelites wept and said, "If only we had meat to eat! ⁵We remember the fish that we used to eat free in Egypt, the cucumbers, the melons, the leeks, the onions, and the garlic. ⁶Now our gullets are shriveled. There is nothing at all! Nothing but this manna to look to!" ⁷Now the manna was like coriander seed, and in color it was like bdellium. ⁸The people would go about and gather it, grind it between millstones or pound it in a mortar, boil it in a pot, and make it into cakes. It tasted like rich cream. ⁹When the dew fell on the camp at night, the manna would fall upon it. ¹⁰Moses heard the people weeping, every clan apart, each person at the entrance of his tent. The Lord was very angry, and Moses was distressed. ¹¹And Moses said to the Lord, ¹³"Where am I to get meat to give to all this people, when they whine before me and say, 'Give us meat to eat!'" ¹⁶Then the Lord said to Moses, ¹⁸"Say to the people: Purify yourselves for tomorrow and you

¹¹Moses said to the Lord, "Why have you dealt ill with your servant, and why have I not enjoyed your favor, that you have laid the burden of all this people upon me? ¹²Did I conceive all this people, did I bear them, that you should say to me, 'Carry them in your bosom as a nurse carries an infant,' to the land that you have promised on oath to their fathers? ¹⁴I cannot carry all this people by myself, for it is too much for me. ¹⁵If you would deal thus with me, kill me rather, I beg you, and let me see no more of my wretchedness!" ¹⁶Then the Lord said to Moses, "Gather for me seventy of Israel's elders of whom you have experience as elders and officers of the people, and bring them to the Tent of Meeting and let them take their place there with you. ¹⁷I will come down and speak with you there, and I will draw upon the spirit that is on you and put it upon them; they shall share the burden of the people with you, and you shall not bear it alone." ²⁴He gathered seventy of the people's elders and stationed them around the Tent. ²⁵Then the Lord came down in a cloud and spoke to him; he drew upon the spirit that was on him and put it upon the seventy elders. And when the spirit rested upon them, they spoke in ecstasy, but did not continue. ²⁶Two men, one named Eldad and the other Medad, had remained in camp; yet the spirit rested upon

shall eat meat, for you have kept whining before the Lord and saying, 'If only we had meat to eat! Indeed, we were better off in Egypt!' The Lord will give you meat and you shall eat. [19]You shall eat not one day, not two, not even five days or ten or twenty, [20]but a whole month, until it comes out of your nostrils and becomes loathsome to you. For you have rejected the Lord who is among you, by whining before him and saying, 'Oh, why did we ever leave Egypt!'" [21]But Moses said, "The people who are with me number six hundred thousand men; yet you say, 'I will give them enough meat to eat for a whole month.' [22]Could enough flocks and herds be slaughtered to suffice them? Or could all the fish of the sea be gathered for them to suffice them?" [23]And the Lord answered Moses, "Is there a limit to the Lord's power? You shall soon see whether what I have said happens to you or not!" [24]Moses went out and reported the words of the Lord to the people. [31]A wind from the Lord started up, swept quail from the sea and strewed them over the camp, about a day's journey on this side and about a day's journey on that side, all around the camp, and some two cubits deep on the ground. [32]The people set to gathering quail all that day and night and all the next day—even he who gathered least had ten homers—and they spread them out all around the camp. [33]The meat

them—they were among those recorded, but they had not gone out to the Tent—and they spoke in ecstasy in the camp. [27]A youth ran out and told Moses, saying, "Eldad and Medad are acting the prophet in the camp!" [28]And Joshua son of Nun, Moses's attendant from his youth, spoke up and said, "My lord Moses, restrain them!" [29]But Moses said to him, "Are you wrought up on my account? Would that all the Lord's people were prophets, that the Lord put his spirit upon them!" [30]Moses then reentered the camp together with the elders of Israel.

was still between their teeth, nor yet
chewed, when the anger of the Lord
blazed forth against the people and
the Lord struck the people with a
very severe plague. [34]That place was
named Kibroth-hattaavah, because
the people who had the craving
were buried there.

When the narratives have been separated in this way, we can ask which
sources they belong to. In order to answer this question, we need to identify the
aspects of each story that are dependent on or continuous with other texts in the
Hebrew Bible. The various assumptions and historical claims of each source
are unique and therefore give us a solid grounding on which to base the source
assignment of any given narrative.

The story of the people's desire for meat—even going back to the brief story
that opens the chapter in vv. 1–3—assumes that the people have already left the
mountain and entered the wilderness. The mountain of Yahweh's revelation
could hardly be renamed by a brief etiological narrative. In only two of the pentateuchal sources have we explicitly read that the Israelites left the mountain: in
P (Num 10:11–28) and in J (Num 11:29–36). We may thus tentatively narrow our
options for this strand to P or J. The content of the meat story provides a more
definitive clue. The Israelites' complaint in Numbers 11 is answered by the appearance of quail. Yet in P, in Exodus 16:11–13, Yahweh has already sent quail to
the people, as part of the provision of manna, in response to the people's desire
for food. The story in Numbers 11, were it from P, not only would be a doublet
of the story in Exodus 16, but it would contain an irreconcilable contradiction:
the people have already been given meat, and been satisfied, yet here they are
begging for meat.

The meat story in Numbers 11 therefore cannot belong to P—but it does have
a connection with Exodus 16. Numbers 11 presumes that the manna has been
a regular feature of the Israelites' existence since the departure from Egypt,
such that they can complain about having had too much of it.[17] Exodus 16
contains both the P and J versions of the giving of the manna, and while the
P version also mentions the quails, the J version does not. The meat story in
Numbers 11 therefore appears to belong to J and depends on the J narrative of
Exodus 16.[18] (Since the manna goes unmentioned in E, it can again be eliminated as a potential source for this story in Num 11.) We may note also the
similar physical descriptions of the manna in the two stories: in Numbers 11:7

we are told that it was like coriander seed, and this precise description, word for word, is found also in Exodus 16:32 (J).[19] The process of collecting the manna described in Numbers 11:8, by which the people go around gathering it, is what was prescribed in Exodus 16:16 (J) and carried out in 16:17. Finally, the process of cooking the manna described in Numbers 11:8, boiling it, was also prescribed in Exodus 16:23 (J).

The isolation of the meat narrative in Numbers 11 is confirmed, at least in large part, by the reference to it in Psalm 78:18–31. In this historical psalm, the elders are not mentioned, but the quails are. All three major elements of the J story are present in Psalm 78: the people's complaint (vv. 19–20), the abundance of quail promised (or threatened) by Yahweh and brought by the wind (vv. 26–29), and the plague that strikes the people before they have run out of meat (vv. 30–31). This psalm thus represents strong evidence for both the correct division of Numbers 11 and for the independence of the J narrative. Indeed, Psalm 78 seems to depend on the same traditional basis as does J throughout its retelling of Israel's history.[20]

Further connections with the larger J narrative are also apparent. The beginning of Yahweh's instructions to Moses in v. 18 have the people purifying themselves for the following day. This is reminiscent of the similar instructions given to Moses before the theophany at Sinai in J in Exodus 19:10. The manner in which Yahweh brings the quail—blowing them in by a wind from the sea—also resonates with J texts. In the J plagues, the locusts arrive via an east wind (Exod 10:13aβ) and are driven away with a strong west wind (10:19). In the J story of the crossing of the sea (see case study IV), Yahweh drives back the sea with a strong east wind (Exod 14:21aβ).

We may also note the character of Moses in this story.[21] After both the people's complaint and Yahweh's initial response, Moses expresses reservations, to put it lightly: he doubts himself and Yahweh, despite Yahweh's clear statements of power. This Moses, something of a whiner, is similar to the Moses we meet in Exodus 4—the Moses who doubts whether the Israelites will believe him (Exod 4:1), who pleads infirmity of speech (4:10), who asks that someone else be chosen (4:13), and who asks why Yahweh sent him to bring harm upon the Israelites (5:22–23). All of these passages, and this depiction of Moses, belong to J. Indeed, in the second of these examples, we have a remarkably close parallel to Numbers 11:21–23. In Numbers 11, Moses wonders whether it is possible that enough food could ever be provided for the people, and Yahweh answers: "Is there a limit to Yahweh's power? You shall soon see whether what I have said happens to you or not." In Exodus 4:10–12, Moses says that he is slow of speech, and Yahweh answers: "Who gives man speech? Who makes him dumb or deaf, seeing or blind? Is it not I, Yahweh? Now go, and I will be with you as you speak and will instruct you what to say." The similarity of theme is unmistakable, and unique to J. We may note also the theme of parenthood; Moses cries that he is not Israel's parent that he should be carrying them through the wilderness; his emphatic use of the pronoun "I" suggests that it is rather Yahweh who is in the parental role. This has been expressed explicitly in J, by Yahweh, to Moses, in Exodus 4:22–23.

We may finally note that in J we find in the narratives of the wilderness wandering a strong emphasis on the repeated railings of the Israelites against Yahweh, especially for lack of suitable provisions. Thus in J we have the manna story in Exodus 16*, the water story in Exodus 17:1bβ–7, and the meat story in Numbers 11.[22] Over the course of these narratives we see Yahweh's response to the Israelites increasing in severity, from no response in Exodus 16–17 to the plague in Numbers 11, and culminating in the final major wilderness narrative in J, that of the spies in Numbers 13–14, in which the entire Exodus generation is doomed to die in the wilderness because the people did not trust that Yahweh could actually lead them successfully into Canaan (Num 14:21–23). These four narratives of intransigence are built around the central J story of Yahweh's theophany at Sinai, in which Yahweh tells Moses that he will not travel with the Israelites because he might destroy them on the way (Exod 33:3), given their difficult nature, evident from the events of Exodus 16–17. Although Moses persuades Yahweh to accompany the Israelites in the wilderness (33:12–17), Yahweh's first word was correct: the continued intransigence of the Israelites after the theophany, in Numbers 11 and 13–14, does indeed lead to the destruction of the people. Thus the J story in Numbers 11 belongs to a larger narrative arc about the people doubting Yahweh's ability to lead them to the promised land—a promise originally made to Moses in J in Exodus 3:8 and thence to the people in 3:16–17—a narrative arc that begins with Exodus 16–17, peaks at Sinai, and reaches its culmination in Numbers 13–14.

Now to the story of the elders. Since the meat story is from J, this one cannot be. If the theory offered above is correct, that this story takes place at the time of the departure from the mountain rather than in the wilderness, then it cannot belong to P either, because in P the Israelites have already entered the wilderness. By process of elimination, this story should belong to E. This conclusion is confirmed by the evidence of D.[23] At the beginning of Moses's historical recollection in Deuteronomy, he recalls Yahweh's command to leave Horeb and take possession of the promised land (Deut 1:6–8). The departure takes place in v. 19. In between, Moses recounts the appointing of judges to help him with the various judicial cases that are brought before him. Although the majority of these verses are dependent on Exodus 18 (which is E, and which also uses the word *n-ś-'* [Exod 18:22][24]), the initial statement of Moses's burden takes its language directly from Numbers 11. In Deuteronomy 1:9, Moses says to the people, "I cannot bear the burden of you by myself"; this is strikingly similar to Numbers 11:14: "I cannot carry ["bear"] all this people by myself."[25] A few verses later, in Deuteronomy 1:12, Moses says, "How can I bear unaided the trouble of you, and the burden, and the bickering?"; this, in turn, resembles Numbers 11:17: "They shall share the burden of the people with you, and you shall not bear it alone." These verses in D, like the elders story in Numbers 11, center on the verb *n-ś-'*. The story of the meat goes entirely unmentioned, which not only confirms the source division presented here, but further clarifies the reason for Moses's grief: it is not any complaint of the people that drives Moses to desperation, but rather the sheer number of them, as Deuteronomy 1:10 makes clear: "Yahweh your God has multiplied you until you are today as numerous as the stars in the sky."

The situating of Moses's speech before the departure from Horeb further supports the theory offered above, that is, that the speech is tied directly to the imminent departure from the mountain and does not take place in the wilderness as does the J narrative. When we recognize that Moses's speech belongs to E, we can be even more specific: the E story of Numbers 11 originally followed on the E narrative of the golden calf, which provides a very fine narrative rationale for Moses's speech. Moses realizes that he is to lead this people, who just violated the first words they heard from Yahweh almost as soon as they heard them, through the wilderness. He expresses his fears immediately after he has restored the covenantal relationship between the people and Yahweh with the second set of tablets in Exodus 34* (see chapter 3). We can see, then, that it is not merely the multitude of the people that worries Moses, but also their disobedient instincts.

The elders themselves are also indicative of E. All the pentateuchal sources mention a select group of Israelites known as the elders.[26] Two of them, J and E, further claim that of these elders there was a special group of seventy who were set apart from the others by virtue of being somehow closer to the deity.[27] The number seventy is no more than a stereotypically meaningful number, as can be seen from its other attestations in the Bible (Gen 46:27; 50:3; Exod 15:27; Judg 1:7; 8:30; 1 Sam 6:19; 2 Kgs 10:1; Isa 23:15; Jer 25:11; Zech 1:12; Dan 9:2; 2 Chr 36:21). It is not unreasonable to suppose that a tradition existed in which seventy of Israel's leaders had a higher status, and it is this tradition that is represented in both J and E. The two narratives in which these elders were selected, however, are by nature contradictory, since they do not locate the selection at the same time or place or as part of the same event. Thus in J, seventy of Israel's elders are chosen to go part of the way up Mount Sinai with Moses, Aaron, Nadab, and Abihu (Exod 24:1, 9). When we come to the elders story in Numbers 11, therefore, with its unique conception of how the seventy elders were chosen, we realize that the story cannot be from J, in which this event has already happened, and under entirely different circumstances.[28]

Further evidence for the attribution of the elders narrative to E is the premise underlying Moses's initial complaint in vv. 11–12, 14–15. Moses realizes that when the Israelites leave the mountain he will have to lead them by himself. In P this is not the case: the Presence of Yahweh resides in the Tabernacle, dwelling among the people at all times (Exod 40:34–38). In J this is also not the case: although Yahweh had threatened not to travel with the Israelites through the wilderness, but rather to send a divine messenger (Exod 33:1–3), Moses pleaded and persuaded Yahweh himself to accompany them on their travels (33:12–17). In E, however, Yahweh does not go with the Israelites; rather, he sends a divine messenger to guide and protect them (Exod 22:20–22; 32:34). This is not a threat as in J: it is a promise, and is meant positively. But the divine messenger does not play a role in supervising the people, nor can it be called upon to assist Moses. Only in E, then, does Yahweh not constantly accompany the people on their journey.

The presence or absence of the deity among the people leads us to a further connection between the elders story in Numbers 11 and E. As noted, in J, Yahweh accompanies the Israelites, in the form of the pillar of cloud (by day) and fire (by night) introduced already in Exodus 13:21–22 and mentioned again in Exodus 14:19–20, 24 and Numbers 14:14. In P, the divine presence dwells in the Tabernacle at all times, as indicated by the cloud that sits in the Tent of Meeting. In E, however, the cloud that signifies the presence of the deity is not constantly present as in J and P; it appears only when Moses goes into the Tent of Meeting to communicate with Yahweh (Exod 33:9–10). It is thus a distinctive feature of E's historical presentation that Yahweh is not present among the people but appears only when called upon by Moses.

This unique concept of the divine appearance at the Tent of Meeting, described in Exodus 33:7–11, is presumed by other aspects of the elders narrative in Numbers 11. In Numbers 11:24b, the seventy elders are gathered around the Tent, and in v. 25 Yahweh comes down in a cloud to speak to Moses and place some of Moses's spirit on the elders. This descent is, as we just observed, a unique feature of E's view of the Tent of Meeting.[29] It is also to be noted that the Tent in the elders story is outside the camp: Eldad and Medad, who are not with the other seventy elders, had "remained in the camp" and "had not gone out to the Tent" (v. 26); after the elders have prophesied, Moses returns with them "to the camp" (v. 30). This conforms to E's placement of the Tent "outside the camp, at some distance from the camp" (Exod 33:7), and not to that of P, which situates the Tent squarely in the middle of the Israelite camp (Num 2); J does not mention the Tent of Meeting at all. Finally in regard to the Tent, we may note the presence of Joshua in Numbers 11:28. In this story, Joshua, though not one of the elders, is with Moses and the elders by the Tent of Meeting; he responds to the message of the youth who brings news of Eldad and Medad out to Moses.[30] Joshua is there not because he is to receive some of Moses's spirit, but because, according to Exodus 33:11, he essentially resides in the Tent at all times, whether Moses is there or not. (It should be further observed that Joshua is not introduced in P until Num 13:8 and that he does not exist at all in J.)

The story of the elders thus can be understood fully only when read in its wider E context. The assumptions about the location of the Tent and the means by which Moses and Yahweh communicate are based solely in the larger E narrative. Beyond these factual matters, however, there is a broader thematic issue at play in our story that belongs squarely to the E source. At stake in Moses's speech, and in Yahweh's solution to it, is Moses's prophetic authority. This theme is unique to E and is played out over a series of narratives in the E document, beginning with Moses's prophetic accreditation at Horeb and continuing through the Elohistic wilderness narrative.[31] At Horeb, the divine revelation occurs for the explicitly stated purpose of investing Moses with prophetic authority: "I will come to you in a thick cloud, in order that the people may hear when I speak with you and so trust you ever after" (Exod 19:9). This is, indeed, what happens: the people, upon hearing Yahweh speak, grant Moses prophetic status: "You speak to us, and we will obey" (Exod 20:16). This prophetic authority granted at Horeb is now to be implemented upon the departure from the mountain, and it is at this precise moment that Moses doubts his own capacity for sole responsibility for the people. In the E narrative of Numbers 11, Moses's prophetic powers are temporarily distributed among the seventy elders, which both relieves Moses of his burden and reconfirms his status as Yahweh's prophet. In the following chapter, Numbers 12, Moses's prophetic authority is again the central issue: Yahweh tells Aaron and Miriam that he communicates with Moses mouth to mouth, without riddles or intermediary visions, and that they should therefore not criticize Moses (Num 12:6–8). And in Numbers 16 (see case study III), Dathan and Abiram challenge the authenticity of Moses's prophetic leadership, and die for it. Finally, E concludes in the Pentateuch with the statement that "never again did there arise in Israel a prophet like Moses—whom Yahweh singled out, face to face" (Deut 34:10–12). Although the

other sources obviously recognize that Moses has prophetic powers, the centrality of this theme — the establishment, challenges to, and restatement of Moses's
prophetic authority — is unique to E.[32]

Usually in the Pentateuch stories are combined when, as in Genesis 37, the
represented sources are telling the same story: such as the flood, the plagues,
the theophany on the mountain, and the spies. In Numbers 11, however, we
have two very distinct narratives in the two sources. In part, this distinctiveness
stands as a rebuttal to the notion that one of the stories was written as a supplement to the other. At the same time, we cannot ignore the fact that someone,
the compiler, did see fit to combine the two stories into a single narrative, and
we must also therefore address the question: what compelled the compiler to
interweave these narratives rather than let them stand on their own?

Some scholars have argued that the similarity between vv. 11–12, 14–15 in E
and v. 13 in J was the driving force behind the combination of the two stories,
but the only words the two passages have in common are "all this people."[33]
Not only is this hardly enough to warrant combining two very different narratives, it is also questionable whether this or any other type of verbal resonance
ever drove the compiler to combine his texts. As a counterexample we might
consider the two stories in which God announces the birth of Isaac to Abraham
and Sarah in Genesis 17–18. Here we have two very similar stories, both containing the pun on Isaac's name (17:17; 18:12–15), and both containing the idea
that Isaac will be born in one year's time (17:21; 18:10, 14) — in short, there are
far more verbal and even narrative resonances between these two stories, yet
they have been left side by side. Verbal resonances as slight as "all this people"
in Numbers 11 can be found across nearly all pentateuchal texts, yet the vast
majority are not interwoven as they are here. We must therefore look elsewhere.

As is always the case, the compiler's work here is done on narrative grounds,
not stylistic grounds. In order to understand the compiler's desire to see in these
two narratives a single story, we must recognize both the temporal identity of
the stories and their divergent narrative settings. Both the J story of the meat
and the E story of the elders are the first major events that take place after the
theophany at the mountain for each source. Further, both have close links to
the preceding Sinai/Horeb pericope. For J, the complaint of the people is the
fulfillment of Yahweh's prediction in Exodus 33:1–3 that the people will be in-
transigent. For E, Moses's concern about leading the people connects to the episode of the golden calf in Exodus 32 and 34. Between the J and E antecedents
in Exodus 32–34 and the stories of Numbers 11 stands the vast priestly section of
Exodus 34:29–Numbers 10:28. For the J story, this break presents little difficulty:
Yahweh's prediction referred to the period of the wilderness wandering and

is relevant only once the people enter the wilderness in Numbers 10. But for E, Moses's speech required the immediately preceding golden calf episode in order to make complete sense. With the interruption of the priestly material — and perhaps more important, with the passage of nearly a year's time in the P narrative — the link between Moses's words in Numbers 11:11–12, 14–15 and the golden calf in Exodus 32 is severed. That scholars have been largely unable to recognize this original link, even when they have identified the sources correctly, testifies to the difficulty created by the insertion of the priestly legislation.

The compiler, having finished writing down the P section from Exodus 34: 29–Numbers 10:28 — which ends with the priestly notice of the Israelites entering the wilderness — would also have had to put down the similar notice in J (Num 10:29–36). Now he had before him the two first post-Sinai/Horeb narratives from J and E — that of the meat in J and the elders in E. Recognizing that the E story has been severed from its original narrative setting, the golden calf, the compiler was no doubt delighted to realize that the temporally equivalent J story also contained an episode in which the people acted badly — an episode that could, in fact, serve as the new rationale for Moses's speech in Numbers 11:11–12, 14–15. In combining the two stories in this way, the compiler also realized a secondary goal: that of making the differing issues in the wilderness — trust in Moses's prophetic authority in E, and trust in Yahweh's ability to bring the people to Canaan in J — into a larger whole.

Despite the distinctive features of the two narratives in Numbers 11, and despite the inner coherence and completeness of each, some scholars have attempted to understand the elders story as somehow dependent on the narrative of the people's desire for meat.[34]

Martin Noth claimed that the story of the elders was not an independent narrative, but rather a secondary insertion into the already extant meat narrative.[35] A key element in this argument for Noth was the judgment that the elders story is incomplete, lacking an initial event to drive Moses's complaint in vv. 14–15 (Noth believed that vv. 11–12 belonged to the meat story).[36] Without a beginning, Noth argued, the story could not be considered independent. Yet, as we have seen, not only does the story make sense within the E context as the first event as the people prepared to depart from Horeb, but this is even the explicit statement of the parallel in Deuteronomy 1:9–18. Erhard Blum similarly argues that the elders story depends on the meat narrative, but the only evidence he produces is the fact that in v. 18 the introduction to Yahweh's speech in v. 16 is assumed;[37] the redactional combination of the two speech formulas, as argued above, is a far simpler explanation, and thus the tenuous thread by which Blum's theory hangs may be swiftly severed. Reinhard Achenbach sees the elders story as part of the latest redactional layer of the Pentateuch, along with the other key texts from E that have been mentioned above.[38] He recognizes that the elders strand tells a very different story and that, especially in vv. 16–17 and 24b–30, it is fundamentally unconnected with the meat narrative. Yet he does not make the crucial argument that the elders story cannot be read independently; without this initial claim, there is no literary basis for reading the narrative as anything other than independently composed.[39]

Although he stands alone in his reconstruction, the argument of Horst See-bass that the elders story is the original narrative and the meat story is a second-ary addition to it is important methodologically.[40] That Seebass, working with the same text and moreover virtually the same source division as those who claim that the elders story is the later supplement, can come to precisely the opposite conclusion highlights the problems with taking either narrative as a secondary addition to the other. The claim that one story is complete while the other is not is revealed as largely subjective and based less on an independent reading of each story on its own than on the a priori belief of the scholar. Both stories are, in fact, complete and coherent on their own terms, and no theory of supplementation is required. We have here, as demonstrated, two independent narratives that have been combined into a single story.

In the case studies of both Genesis 37 and Numbers 11, I have discerned in the canonical Pentateuch two nonpriestly strands, J and E, each of which is complete, coherent, and continuous with other J and E passages elsewhere in the text. Nevertheless, it is common in scholarship to find doubts regarding the existence of E as a separate source. I address these doubts in the next chapter.

Chapter 3

—•••◦⟨∞⟩◦•••—

COHERENCE

The E Source

In the preceding case study of Numbers 11, we saw that the story of the prophesying elders, readily separable from the story of the people's desire for meat with which it has been intertwined, belongs to a larger narrative arc stretching from the theophany at Horeb in Exodus 19 to the episode of Dathan and Abiram in Numbers 16. This overarching narrative is identifiable on the basis of its unique historical claims: the location, purpose, and function of the Tent of Meeting; the role of Joshua; the means of communication between Yahweh and Moses; the existence of Miriam; and the role of the elders. It is further marked by its consistent thematic focus on the prophetic authority of Moses: its establishment at Horeb, the challenges to it in the wilderness, and the proofs of it after each challenge. The episodes that make up this narrative are continuous both chronologically and geographically, and they have a distinctive structural integrity. At no point is it necessary to postulate that any piece of the narrative is missing, either in the individual episodes or in the whole.

This lengthy narrative strand is intertwined, as we have seen, with another nonpriestly strand in Numbers 11—which belongs to its own larger narrative arc, complete with its own unique historical claims and themes—with priestly material in Numbers 16 (see below) and with both priestly and nonpriestly stories in Exodus 19–34 and Deuteronomy 34. Given the ease with which the E source is isolated in each individual case, and given the clear narrative and thematic coherence of the whole and its constituent parts, it is difficult to understand the long-standing conviction in scholarship that the E document is either nothing but a series of secondary insertions or, as is more common today, that it simply doesn't exist at all. The opposition to E stands as a fundamental basis for much antidocumentary scholarship and is frequently accepted even by those who generally hold to the documentary model. It is thus of paramount importance that E be returned to its rightful place in the four-source theory. In this chapter, I discuss and evaluate the problems with the E source—or at least its treatment in classical documentary scholarship—and the resulting arguments against the existence of E, and offer a fresh case for the E document.

CHALLENGES TO E

It is something of an irony in pentateuchal scholarship that the discussion of E's existence takes place entirely on the basis of how it relates to the J document. As already mentioned in chapter 1, the earliest attempts to divide Genesis into its component parts resulted in two strands, the Yahwist (what we now call J) and the Elohist (a combination of what we now call E and P). For the first ventures into source criticism, therefore, the fundamental distinction was not between P and J/E, but rather between J and P/E. The E document, when postulated by Hermann Hupfeld, was not defined against its nonpriestly counterpart J, but rather against its "Elohistic" counterpart P, at least for Genesis 1–Exodus 6. In other words, once J had been isolated, the remaining text was still not a unified whole but resolved, as Hupfeld demonstrated, into two coherent strands. Had scholars followed Hupfeld's procedure and started by identifying J on purely narrative grounds and then, having removed J, continued with the separation of E from P over the rest of the Pentateuch, it is possible that the existence of E would never have been called into question—after all, the priestly source is so recognizable on narrative, thematic, and linguistic grounds that the removal from it of the non-J material should have proceeded with little difficulty. Yet scholarship after Hupfeld quickly turned to isolating P first and then attempting to distinguish E from J, and here numerous methodological problems emerged.

Why did E become associated with, analyzed in relation to, and read in light of J, rather than P? In part, the answer is surely that after Exodus 3, in which the divine name is revealed to Moses, the most easily recognizable distinctive historical claim of E over against J—whether the characters knew and used the proper name Yahweh—could no longer be used, since all three sources now employed the divine name in their narratives. After Exodus 3, the most prominent feature of any of the sources is undoubtedly the distinctive language and priestly focus of the P document, and it was therefore easier to begin by isolating P and then dealing with the nonpriestly text. Perhaps more influential in scholarship, however, was the rise of scholarly attention to the laws rather than the narratives of the Pentateuch. Although there are ostensibly four law codes in the Pentateuch, each of which can be assigned to one of the four sources, the foundational documentary scholars effectively reduced the number to three: the priestly code, the deuteronomic code, and the Covenant Code.[1] The brief laws of Exodus 34, which were generally assigned to J, were considered so similar to the Covenant Code of Exodus 20–23, and so difficult to date relative to that code, that they were either ignored or grouped together with the E legal material.[2] Within this framework, a chronological line of development could be ascertained: first the Covenant Code, then its revision in the deuteronomic laws, and then another revision in the priestly legislation. This scheme formed the basis of the work of the three great pentateuchal scholars of the late nineteenth century, Karl Heinrich Graf, Abraham Kuenen, and Julius Wellhausen, who took the tripartite division of the law and connected it to the narrative, resulting in a similar division into P, D, and "JE" (in reverse chronological order). The statement of Kuenen on this could not be clearer: "We have seen that the division of the whole mass of laws into these three groups must ultimately influence our view of the narratives of the Hexateuch."[3]

Once J and E were associated over against P and D, they began to be treated as a single entity, or at least as very similar entities; Kuenen described them together as the "prophetic" element of the Pentateuch.[4] From this point forward, a substantial portion of scholarship referred to (and continues to refer to) the nonpriestly, nondeuteronomic text as "JE," thereby not only failing to distinguish between the two documents, but actually equating them in a fundamental sense.[5] At the heart of this equation is the claim, frequently explicit, that the J and E documents are so alike in content and style that distinguishing between them is either unnecessary (in terms of their status relative to P and D) or difficult. Kuenen made the first of these arguments—that J and E do not need to be separated—quite clearly: "There can be no objection to our indicating all that is left in the Hexateuch after the withdrawal of R [the common siglum for the Redactor], P, and D, by the combination JE."[6] As to the second point, that the two are difficult to tell apart, Wellhausen stated this categorically: "The final result is that while indeed JE in this section [Genesis 27–36] also must consist of J and E, a thorough-going division is impossible."[7] Wellhausen's admission informed not only his own analysis—in his classic *Prolegomena to the History of Israel* J and E are treated together under the term "Jehovist" until the very end—but also resonated in subsequent generations, even among scholars who undertook the very separation that Wellhausen had proclaimed impossible.[8] The determinative statement on this topic comes from Martin Noth, who, having declared that the nonpriestly material "is considerably more difficult to analyze than is the P narrative,"[9] concludes that "in a case of doubt one is to decide for J rather than E."[10] This ad hoc decision, indefensible on literary grounds, speaks to the relegation of E to a secondary status relative to J, even though the two are equally difficult to separate.

One underlying reason that scholars have found it difficult to separate J from E is that their analyses have generally proceeded along the lines of style or theme, rather than the historical claims intrinsic to each narrative. (As we have seen, and will continue to demonstrate, when the historical claims are taken as the primary evaluative foundation, the two documents are in fact relatively easy to identify.) Whereas P has a very recognizable style, the stylistic features of J and E are, indeed, relatively similar—which makes the reliance on style to distinguish between them even more problematic.[11] Yet this is how scholars have generally sought to disentangle the two sources. Most of all, the use of Elohim rather than Yahweh has retained its force as the primary stylistic distinction between the two. As this was already a problem for the earliest pentateuchal criticism, it is no surprise that it continued to be a problem, with Wellhausen stating, "Only where the different names for God provide a striking criterion as to the author's hand does one succeed in clearly recognizing the double strand."[12] Yet this criterion, useful though it may be at points in Genesis, evaporates after Exodus 3, and without it, the stylistic criteria for separating J from E are slim indeed.[13] This can be seen from the lists of "typical" words and phrases sometimes produced to support various source divisions.[14] In one of the most extensive of these, that of J. Estlin Carpenter and G. Harford-Battersby, twenty-five "characteristic" features of E's language are listed; the first of these is the title Elohim, which they acknowledge is useful only through Exodus 3:15.[15] Of the remainder, their list identifies only three that appear uniquely in E, and even these are problematic.[16] All the rest are words and phrases found frequently in E but also in other sources, including, frequently, J. Of course, once a word is found in more than one source, it can no longer be used as evidence that a given passage is from any specific source. Yet Carpenter and Harford-Battersby, and others dependent on their work, do just that.[17]

While the reliance on style was a feature of E scholarship of the late nineteenth to early twentieth centuries, the mid-twentieth century saw a stronger dependence on the identification of themes in E.[18] We make take, for example, the general statement of Peter Weimar: "Differently from the Jahwist, in which the single stories are joined by a continuous sequence of events, the elohistic work presents itself as a more or less loose sequence of individual stories, which are not connected by a spatial-temporal events frame, but by thematic linkings with each other."[19] A number of works have attempted to describe the overriding theme of E, with a variety of possibilities suggested: the fear of God, the threat of God, the testing of God, faith in God and God's plan for Israel, God's progressive self-revelation, God's providence, the relationship between God and Israel, the relationship between Israel and Canaanite religion, wisdom, and pro-northern political propaganda.[20] Two methodological points should be made in this regard. First, and most obviously, the identification of E passages cannot be carried out on the basis of perceived theme, just as it cannot be carried out on the basis of style. Themes and motifs emerge only after the document has been isolated on narrative grounds. As a corollary to this, it should be emphasized that just because a theme is central to one source does not mean that it must therefore be unattested in another. Two or more sources may share a theme. The recognition in J of a theme central to E does not in any way affect the evaluation of E. Second, it is an oversimplification and a denigration of the ancient Israelite author's literary abilities to identify "the" single theme of E, or of any of the pentateuchal documents. Within the extensive narrative of E it is possible, even highly likely, to find multiple themes at work; these include some or all of those mentioned above, and others as well.[21] We are doing a disservice to E and to our own appreciation of it when we reduce the source to a one-note song.

Of equal importance was the belief of many scholars that the apparent similarity of J and E is such that they must have told precisely the same stories, in almost precisely the same manner.[22] On the face of it, there is little to suggest such a conclusion: J recounts many episodes not found in E, from the entirety of the primeval history in Genesis 2–11 to the wooing of Rebecca in Genesis 24 to the people's complaint in Numbers 11, while E similarly contains narratives not anywhere evident in J, from the sacrifice of Isaac in Genesis 22 to the battle against Amalek in Exodus 17:8–16 to the leprosy of Miriam in Numbers 12. What the two documents have in common is, for the most part, the basic outline of the overarching narrative: the patriarchs, in their established order; the Exodus; and the wilderness wandering. Within this broad framework, the two diverge far more often than they converge. In this respect the difference between J and E is precisely the same as that between either and P. Despite the literary evidence that the two documents were free to narrate Israel's history in unique ways, the difficulty scholars encountered in telling one source from the other led to the conclusion that the two were far more similar than they are. Some scholars went so far as to postulate an earlier *Vorlage*, either oral or written, for J and E, since lost. Noth claimed that "in structure and content the written sources J and E had so much in common that they could not have been composed in complete independence from each other."[23] He therefore postulated "a common basis (Grundlage) for the two sources, from which both—independently of each other—have drawn the nucleus of their content."[24] For Frank Moore Cross, this same idea was expressed as the Israelite oral "epic": "a long and rich poetic epic of the era of the league, underlying JE."[25]

Those who did not come to this conclusion also tended, in their analyses, to go to great lengths to "discover" two parallel nonpriestly stories at almost every turn. This caused significant problems, of course, since a unified narrative with no obvious internal inconsistencies will not easily break down into two coherent strands. Thus, for example, Carpenter and Harford-Battersby attempted to divide the indivisible narrative of Genesis 27:1–45 into J and E, with truly destructive consequences.[26] Their E narrative reads from v. 5a to v. 7b: "Rebecca had been listening as Isaac spoke to his son Esau . . . 'And prepare a dish for me to eat . . . ,'" while the verse in between, in which Rebecca says to Jacob, "I overheard your father speaking to your brother Esau, saying . . . ," they ascribe to J. Or further along, they ascribe parts of vv. 30–31 to E, reading, "No sooner had Jacob left the presence of his father Isaac . . . he too prepared a dish and brought it to his father," in which the subject of the second half is Esau—who was introduced in the clause in between, "his brother Esau came back from his hunt," which they have ascribed to J. Their analysis equally disrupts the J narrative, such that they assign v. 15 and v. 18b to J in succession: "Rebecca then took the best clothes of her older son Esau, which were there in the house, and had her younger son Jacob put them on . . . 'Which of my sons are you?'" In short, such attempts to discern two sources where only one is present, where there are no narrative indications of multiple authorship, but only the critic's a priori belief that J and E must have parallel narratives at nearly every point, are doomed to failure.[27]

One of the primary results of these two methodological problems—the stylistic and thematic grounds for analysis and the attempt to find both J and E in almost every story—was the increasingly fragmentary nature of E in scholarly analyses. When the mere presence of a word or phrase or idea becomes the determinative grounds for source assignment, rather than the narrative in which the word or phrase is found, then a verse, or part of a verse, can be taken as belonging to a source different from that of its narrative context. For example, Carpenter and Harford-Battersby, in their analysis of Genesis 32:25–33,[28] the story of Jacob wrestling with the divine being, ascribe only v. 31 ("Jacob named the place Peniel, meaning, 'I have seen a divine being face to face, yet my life has been preserved'") to E—this despite their attribution of v. 32, in which Jacob passes by Penuel, and the entire narrative etiology for the name Peniel in

vv. 25–30, to J. Their basis for this analysis is the phrase "face to face," which they assign to E (in Exod 33:11; see also Num 12:8 and Deut 34:10). Similarly, in the narrative of Joseph and his master's wife in Genesis 39, only the words in v. 4, "he made him his personal attendant," and in vv. 6–7, "he left all that he had in Joseph's hands" and "Joseph was well built and handsome. After a time . . .," are ascribed to E.[29] Not only is this hardly a story, but the narrative elements introduced in these phrases are central to the rest of the story: the notion that his master left everything in Joseph's hands is repeated by Joseph himself in v. 8, and the notice of Joseph's beauty leads directly to the attraction of his master's wife in the continuation of v. 7. Again, it is the presence of stylistic features they have deemed typical of E that drives their analysis here: the word "to attend" in v. 4, the word "well-built" in v. 6, and the phrase "and it came to pass after these things" in v. 7 are all, according to Carpenter and Harford-Battersby, so closely tied to E that even though these verses cannot, on narrative grounds, be removed from their context, on stylistic grounds they evidently must be.

The requirement that both J and E tell the same stories has negatively affected the critical evaluation of some of the most significant episodes in the pentateuchal narrative. Although it is reasonable to assume that all three sources, J, E, and P, told some version of the story of the Egyptian plagues, this assumption is not a compelling rationale for dividing Exodus 7–10 into three sources. Only the internal literary evidence of the pericope can provide for such an analysis — and it does not: the plagues divide neatly into two coherent, continuous narrative strands, and every attempt to discern three sources in these chapters results in fragmentary narratives (see case study IV). Even if we knew without a doubt that all three sources must have once told this story, if the plagues narrative were judged on internal grounds to be literarily unified we would have no justification for splitting it into three. Similarly, the most potent image in the popular imagination from the law-giving in the wilderness is that of the stone tablets on which the Decalogue is inscribed. Probably for this reason, most scholars have assumed that the tablets must have been part of both the J and E narratives of the wilderness theophany. Yet the attempts to divide the text so that each source contains the tablets again leaves neither in a readable state.[30]

Thus we are confronted with both methodological problems inherent in the classical documentary scholarship regarding E—the reliance on style or theme as a criterion for source division and the a priori belief that nearly every episode must have been told in both J and E—and the consequent failure of the classical approach to result in a coherent E source. It is little wonder, then, that the existence of E became a point of contention in scholarship: it was treated, even by staunch believers in the Documentary Hypothesis, as both the least readily identifiable document on stylistic grounds and the least coherent source on narrative grounds.[31]

Critics of E have justifiably focused on precisely these issues in their arguments.[32] Criticism has focused more on the issue of style than on that of theme, even in the mid- to late-twentieth century. That said, there have been challenges to the thematic identification of E. It should be noted that most adherents of E have not in fact attempted to isolate E on the basis of theme—rather, they have argued for the integrity and coherence of E on the basis of common themes running through the various texts attributed to it by other means. It is perhaps the lack of methodological clarity on this point that has led some critics to read thematic studies of E as equivalent to attempts to identify E texts on the basis of theme. We thus find general statements such as R. Norman Whybray's: "The discovery of a few passages here and there in the Pentateuch with a common theological theme does not in the least constitute proof of the existence of a continuous document"[33]; or specific critiques such as that of John Craghan: "Ultimately the question must be raised: is 'fear of God' an adequate criterion for source division?"[34] When such criticisms are rightfully addressed to those scholars who do attempt to isolate E on thematic grounds, they are certainly valid. As themes, like words, are not restricted to one author, one story, one place, or one time, they are particularly weak grounds for source identification.

The priority of style as a means of identifying E, despite the paucity of terms unique to E (leaving aside for the moment the issue of the divine names), admitted even by a believer in E such as Noth, opened an easy avenue of attack.[35] Some of the stylistic lines along which J and E have been divided were obvious targets. The purported use of "Canaanites" by J and "Amorites" by E to designate the pre-Israelite inhabitants of the promised land[36] is easily shown to be untenable (as the collocation of the two terms in both J [Exod 3:8, 17; 33:2; Num 13:29] and E [Gen 15:21; Exod 23:23] contexts makes abundantly clear).[37] The theory that Jacob is called "Israel" in J and "Jacob" in E after Genesis 32:29[38] is similarly demonstrated to be insupportable.[39]

When these examples of faulty stylistic arguments could be discarded, it became easier for critics similarly to discard authentic examples of E language. The classic distinction between the terms used by J and E for "maidservant," šipḥāʰ and 'āmāʰ, respectively, does seem to hold good in the Pentateuch.[40] Even more so is the designation of the mountain in the wilderness as Horeb or "the mountain of God" clearly unique to E.[41] Although the critics' attempts to argue otherwise may not be convincing, their fundamental argument in this regard is nevertheless valid: when style is taken as the definitive indication of E, and only a handful of terms at best can be brought as proof, stylistic considerations cannot play any role in the determination of a text as E rather than J.[42]

The regular admission of adherents to the E source that their stylistic proofs were shaky at best obviously did not help their case, and these statements were often used against them; equally open to attack were overly strong claims for the stylistic basis of the source division.[43] The criticisms of the stylistic basis for defining E are absolutely correct.

The issue of the alternation of divine designations in J and E is generally treated by both critics and adherents as an element of the question of style, but it is in fact a slightly different, if related, case.[44] Critics focus a considerable amount of attention on the use of Yahweh and Elohim and bring a diverse set of arguments as to why these features cannot function as stylistic indicators of J and E, respectively. Thus it is noted that the Septuagint and the Masoretic Text do not always agree on the divine names and that scholars have relied on whichever version provides the best evidence for their analysis in any given case.[45] The fact that J uses both Yahweh and Elohim in various contexts is also brought as evidence that Elohim is not a mark of E.[46] And the fact that there seem to be places where E uses the name Yahweh is considered a final nail in the coffin.[47]

Each of these arguments may be countered. The first, that scholars use text-critical evidence as the basis for or justification of their analyses is not, on its own, a negative. In cases such as this, the divine name is clearly not the decisive indicator for the assignment of the passage to E (since the "wrong" divine name is used); if it is determined on other grounds that a passage belongs to E, then the presence of versional evidence for the "correct" divine name is relevant. As Emanuel Tov writes: "The quintessence of textual evaluation is the selection from the different transmitted readings of the one reading which is the most appropriate to its context. Within the process of this selection, the concept of the 'context' is taken in a broad sense, as referring to the language, style, and content of both the immediate context and of the whole literary unit in which the reading is found."[48] To criticize adherents of E for following standard text-critical procedure is somewhat disingenuous. In fact, the discernment of textual error even in cases in which there is no versional evidence to support such an assumption is equally valid.[49] When a word, on the basis of a well-founded group of other literary indications, is deemed unlikely to be original, especially in the case of a word (such as the divine designations) that has a well-established record of versional differentiation, it is not unreasonable at least to suggest the possibility of scribal error.

The second and third arguments may be rebutted by stating once again the elementary observation of Hupfeld: the difference in divine designations between J and E (and P, for that matter) is not one of style, but of historical claim.[50] According to J, everyone from the third generation of humanity on knew and used the divine name Yahweh; according to E, the divine name was not known until it was revealed to Moses in Exodus 3. This fundamental aspect of the issue of the divine designations contains within it the response to the critics' arguments: neither J nor E is prohibited in any way from using either divine designation. Both authors knew that Elohim and Yahweh were one and the same. That J uses Elohim in specific circumstances—notably, when interacting with non-Israelites or in foreign settings—is perfectly acceptable, since J, of all the sources, was at liberty to use either Yahweh or Elohim at will. Only slightly more complicated is E's use of the name Yahweh. It must be remembered that the author of E knew that God's proper name is Yahweh—he claims only that his characters did not know it until Exodus 3. Thus if the divine name is used in third-person narration in E before then, it does not present a problem for the claim that the divine designations are indicative of the sources. Of course, the fact that E does not regularly do so both supports and renders problematic this claim. On the one hand, E is more readily identifiable because it does use Elohim in third-person narration far more often than not. On the other hand, this regular use of Elohim has led scholars to the erroneous conclusion that E could not use the name Yahweh under any circumstance. When the distinction between the author of E and the historical claims he makes about his characters is recognized, the arguments of the critics appear to miss the mark.[51]

That said, it is perhaps not the critics' fault that they have attacked the use of Elohim as a stylistic marker—that is, as an inviolable part of E's terminology. As already noted, adherents of E, in pushing stylistic criteria as the basis for identifying E over against J, regularly presented the divine names as the primary example of E's distinctive style.[52] That this feature is present only through Exodus 3 makes it even more problematic, since after Exodus 3 scholars defending E lost their primary stylistic marker. The critics have done little more than react to the manner in which E was defended in scholarship, and in doing so, they have brought to the forefront one of the main problems with the way in which most scholars have isolated E.

Equally important for the critics of E was the traditional attempt to find two versions of most narratives even in ostensibly unified pericopes, and the concomitant fragmentation of the text into disconnected phrases.[53] Again, the critics are undoubtedly correct in their basic assessment. The attempt by some traditional scholars to divide Genesis 27:1–45 into two, as described above, stands as a case in point: Paul Volz pointedly observed that the lexical items that served as the purported grounds for source division in Genesis 27, such as the two terms used for the food to be served to Isaac, *ṣayid* and *maṭ'ammîm,* are hardly probative and that in fact the only reason that scholars attempted to dissect the chapter was because "the source division had already become dogma and one now had to give to each narrator his material from the virtually identical narrative. If one rejects the dogma, this distribution appears completely unnecessary, indeed even unjustified, destroying the artistic and objective intention of a single narrator."[54]

As valid as this criticism is, it must be accepted only with a caveat. The artistic merit or theological intention of a given text cannot override any clear narratological problems. This issue can be approached in two ways. First, there is the case of a text that may have some structural or other artistic integrity, or even a clear theological message, but that contains narrative inconsistencies. Genesis 37 (see case study I) may count in this category: the structural and theological arguments brought to bear on the chapter gloss over the fundamental narrative problems of the text. Although authors can be assumed to have written both artistically and with some broader intention, the primary act of writing in the narrative form is to create a narratologically coherent story. Thus the literary evidence for disjuncture must take priority over the scholar's judgment as to the artistic merit or theological interpretation of the text.

Second, we must be careful not to read a given pericope in total isolation from its broader narrative context. It is not uncommon to find scholars focusing entirely on a single text and arguing for its unity on purely internal grounds.[55] The Pentateuch is not, either in its canonical form or in its constituent parts, a series of unconnected stories, to be read and interpreted individually. When the focus of analysis is a single episode, without any interaction with the texts that precede and follow it, it is easy to miss the presence in that single story of elements that connect to other disparate and mutually contradictory passages. For example, the J story of Genesis 50:1–22 contains no internal contradictions, and read on its own it would appear to be a unity; yet the notice in vv. 12–13 that Jacob's sons buried him in the cave of Machpelah is the fulfillment of Jacob's instructions in P in 49:29–32 and fits into the broader P story and not at all into that of J. Thus although it is frequently the case that the division of an otherwise ostensibly unified text is unjustified, and done on the basis of the methodological errors described above and noted correctly by Volz, we are not at liberty to ignore the larger context of a given episode, or of its constituent narrative elements.

It is perhaps not coincidental that the arguments of E's critics tend to proceed along the same lines as those of scholars who oppose the entire source-critical enterprise.[56] Thus the claim that style is not a viable criterion for source division has been made not only for the question of J and E, but for P and D as well.[57] The fragmentation of the text has also been used as an argument against all textual division.[58] Indeed, some of the anti–source-critical writings have been cited approvingly by scholars who oppose only the existence of E.[59] Yet the critics of E in particular do not oppose the existence of P, even while they adopt the arguments of those who do. This peculiar situation reveals an interesting point: for those opposed to the critical enterprise, the two methodological problems we have identified in the critical analysis of E—the basis of identification on style and the belief that E and J must have told the same stories, and the resulting textual fragmentation—are in fact methodological problems in the critical analysis of the entire Pentateuch. Thus the problems that scholars have had with the evaluation of E are not unique to E but are applicable across the Pentateuch; the problems of E differ, therefore, only in degree, rather than in kind.

We can further see that in none of these cases are scholars—either for or against E—proceeding along the lines argued for in this book: the identification and division of the sources on the basis of consistency of historical claims and narrative flow.[60] When the identification of E is based on elements of style, and when it is assumed that E must be discovered in nearly every narrative episode, it is clear that not only can no case for E be made, but that the case against E is in fact quite strong. David Carr's description of traditional arguments from E bears repeating here: Analysis of E "tends to proceed in two steps: (1) presuppose that E 'must' be in a given section, and (2) use the fund of terminological indicators drawn from other texts to identify Elohistic fragments in the material that can be shaken loose from the Yahwistic context."[61] As Carr rightly states: "Whereas distinction of P materials from non-P materials can draw on numerous explicit cross-references . . . and extensively parallel phraseology, J and E materials are often distinguished by little more than their supposed diverging preferences for certain common words and genres. Yet such an approach is inherently problematic."[62] Any defense of E must, therefore, be carried out on other grounds. This means going back to the first step in its identification and working forward from there, with a renewed focus on the narrative coherence of E.

As Hupfeld demonstrated, when J is isolated and removed from the text of Genesis, what remains is not a unified narrative. The non-J text contains internal contradictions regarding the timing and content of God's covenant with Abraham—whether sacrifices are offered before Sinai/Horeb, where Abraham and the other patriarchs lived and died, why Jacob left Canaan for Aram, when he gave the name Bethel to the place formerly known as Luz, when Jacob's name was changed to Israel, where Jacob arrived first after leaving Aram, and where and how Rachel died. Although Hupfeld showed this only for Genesis, it is even more the case for the rest of the Pentateuch. There are different claims regarding when and where God revealed his true name to Moses, the manner of the divine theophany at the mountain, what Moses was told on the mountain, the content of the laws in whole and in part, the mode of divine communication with Moses, the presence or absence of the deity in the midst of Israel, the nature and location of the Tent of Meeting, when the Israelites were granted meat in the wilderness, and the rationale and timing of the conquest of the Transjordan and the giving of this territory to some of the Israelite tribes.

These distinctions, and the separation of the priestly from the nonpriestly texts in general, are recognized by virtually all commentators. When P is isolated and removed from the Pentateuch, however, what remains is equally unreadable. The nonpriestly text is contradictory with regard to when and where God first appears to Abraham; when and by whom the cult site of Bethel was inaugurated; when and why Hagar is sent into the wilderness; how Jacob grew rich through Laban; what Shechem did or did not do to Dinah, and how Jacob and his sons responded; the manner of Joseph's descent into Egypt; the name of Moses's father-in-law; where and how God first appeared to Moses; when and how the divine name Yahweh is revealed to humanity; the manner in which Moses is to return to Egypt; whether Moses takes his family with him when he returns, and how many sons he had; what and where the place called Horeb is; the manner, purpose, and content of the theophany and covenant at the mountain in the wilderness; when and how the seventy elders were selected from among the people; whether and how God accompanies the Israelites in the wilderness; the manner and content of the people's rebellions in the wilderness; and the itinerary of the wilderness wandering.

Most critics of E accept that the nonpriestly narrative is not unified. They claim, however, that the elements traditionally attributed to E are in fact a series of secondary insertions or supplements to J, from one or more hands.[63] Thus Rolf Rendtorff: "That the doublets or complements at various places in the Pentateuch could be independent of each other is thus not given serious consideration."[64] In order to justify the existence of E as a once-independent document, rather than as a layer or layers of a reworking of J, it must therefore be demonstrated that the non-P, non-J material represents a coherent whole. I am here taking up the challenge of Whybray: "It is necessary to find . . . some connecting links: not merely common theological traits, but something like cross-references or other traces of a narrative thread."[65]

THE E SOURCE

Unlike most previous treatments, both for and against E, the discussion here will begin with the texts already treated above, namely, the interconnected narratives from Horeb through the death of Moses. Virtually every discussion of E from Hupfeld on has started, logically but unfortunately, with Genesis.[66] For Hupfeld, this was a matter of simply following the scholarly discourse: he was reacting to the treatments of Jean Astruc and Johann Eichhorn, which proposed the two-source solution only for Genesis. Once the identification of E had been widened to include the entire Pentateuch, however, most critical responses continued to deal primarily, if not entirely, with Genesis. Thus the seminal work of Paul Volz and Wilhelm Rudolph covers only Genesis 15–50.[67] The arguments from style refer almost exclusively to terms used predominantly in Genesis: the words for female slave, the names for Jacob, and of course the use of Yahweh or Elohim—all these purported distinctions are founded on texts from Genesis. Even scholars writing in defense of E have generally based their identification of E, whether in terms of style, theme, or theology, on the analysis of passages from Genesis.[68] This has led Erhard Blum to observe correctly that "the plausibility of the source model probably from the outset nourished itself here [that is, in Exodus–Numbers] on the extrapolation of the basic paradigm developed in Genesis."[69] Though this is not, in principle, methodologically problematic—after all, there is no reason not to start at the beginning—in fact the most substantial and clearly coherent E material is found in Exodus and Numbers.[70] Carr points out the perils of beginning the analysis with Genesis: "Analyses of E tend to seek certain textual beachheads, such as Genesis 20–22; 28:10–22*; and 37:3–11, 21–30, and then work outward from them to find the missing Elohistic context of these passages. This does not just involve locating passages using the divine name 'Elohim.' Instead, such early Elohistic passages are identified through an ever-expanding range of vocabulary and thematic indicators developed first from the Elohistic beachhead texts, and then from subsequent texts linked with them."[71] The methodological problem that Carr highlights is not the manner of identifying E per se—after all, the classification of distinctive elements from a textual corpus and the subsequent recognition of other texts that also contain those elements are the way that much scholarship proceeds, whether in the identification of P on the basis of seminal texts such as Genesis 1 and 17 or in the attempt to find deuteronomistic passages in Genesis–Numbers (or, indeed, in the very notion of "deuteronomistic" passages outside of Deuteronomy, as in Joshua–Kings). The problem is rather of textual starting point. The "textual beachheads" referred to by Carr, it will be noted, are all in

Genesis and moreover are largely disconnected from each other narratively. One or two isolated chapters are not a firm basis from which to derive an entire source document. If, however, we begin with the extensive E narrative described in the preceding case study of Numbers 11 (and briefly at the beginning of this chapter), we begin our investigation on a more solid footing. Further, as we will concentrate primarily not on "vocabulary and thematic indicators" but rather on the historical claims of the narrative—who, what, when, where, how, and why—we will avoid falling into the same trap as those scholars criticized by Carr; in fact, the typical "textual beachheads" in Genesis will constitute only a very small part of the following argument.

The existence of a coherent E narrative can be shown in two ways: the interdependence of the E texts, and their independence from J (in the following, I will deal only with the nonpriestly text; comparisons with P will be restricted to the notes). As already established, there is a definable and entirely coherent narrative strand beginning with the E Horeb pericope in Exodus 19–24, 32–34 and continuing directly with Numbers 11, 12, and 16. Unlike the usual "beachhead texts" in Genesis, this strand is not a disconnected series of texts with common stylistic features, but rather a complete and continuous narrative, one without discernible gaps at the level of either the individual episodes or the overarching narrative.

The texts that constitute this central E story are as follows:

Horeb	Exodus 19:2b–9a, 16 (except the words "on the third day, as morning dawned")–17, 19
	Exodus 20:1–23:33
	Exodus 24:3–8, 11bβ–15a, 18b
	Exodus 31:18a (only the words "He gave Moses the two tablets"[72]), b–32:14, 15 (except the word *'ēdût*[73])–25, 30–35
	Exodus 33:4, 6–11[74]
	Exodus 34:1, 4 (except the words "early in the morning he went up on Mount Sinai"[75]), 5aα, 28
The prophesying elders	Numbers 11:11–12, 14–17, 24b–30
The leprosy of Miriam	Numbers 12:1–15
The rebellion of Dathan and Abiram	Numbers 16:1b–2aα, 12–15, 25, 27b–34
	(see case study III)

This E narrative is recognizable first and foremost by its unique historical claims:

1. The mountain in the wilderness is identified as Horeb (Exod 33:6) or "the mountain of God" (24:13), as opposed to Sinai in J (19:11, 18, 20, 23; 34:2, 4), in which Horeb is in fact a different place entirely (see below).[76]

2. The purpose of the theophany at Horeb is the establishment of Moses's prophetic authority (Exod 19:9; 20:15) by means of the people's fear of hearing or approaching Yahweh (19:16b–17; 20:15–18), whereas in J the people are so fearless that they need to be restrained from rushing the mountain to see the deity (19:12–13, 21–24; 24:2; 34:3).[77]

3. Yahweh does not travel with the Israelites but sends a divine messenger to lead them, Yahweh descending only on occasion to speak with Moses (Exod 23:20–22; 32:34; Num 11:17, 25; 12:5, 9), whereas Yahweh explicitly agrees to travel with the Israelites in J (Exod 33:2–3, 14–17; Num 10:33–34; 14:13–14).[78]

4. The covenant between Yahweh and Israel is made on the basis of the laws of the Covenant Code (Exod 20:23–23:33) and ratified in a formal ceremony (24:3–8, 11bβ), whereas in J the covenant is made on an entirely different basis (Exod 34:10–16) and is in fact an entirely unintended event—the covenant is made only because Moses persuades Yahweh to travel with the people in the wilderness (Yahweh's original plan was simply to send the people off without a covenant; 33:1–3).[79]

5. Moses ascends the mountain to receive the tablets of the Decalogue, shatters them on account of the golden calf, and goes up again to receive a new set, each time spending forty days and nights (Exod 24:12–15a, 18b; 31:18*; 32; 34:1, 4*, 5aα, 28), whereas in J he ascends Sinai for the purpose of a visual experience of the deity (Exod 24:1–2, 9–10; 33:18–23; 34:2–3, 4*, 5aβb, 6–7) and does not spend any great length of time there.[80]

6. The Tent of Meeting is located outside the camp, Yahweh descends in front of it, and Moses enters the Tent to speak with the deity, and there is no mention of an ark (Exod 33:7–11; Num 11:16–17, 24b–30; 12:4–9); in J, by contrast, it is the Tent of Meeting that does not exist, and the Ark of the Covenant seems to serve to indicate Yahweh's presence (Num 10:33–36; 14:44).[81]

7. Joshua is Moses's servant (Exod 24:13; 32:17; 33:11; Num 11:28–29), whereas in J Joshua is not mentioned at all.[82]

8. The people—including Moses himself—doubt Moses's leadership (Exod 32:1; Num 11:11–12, 14–15; 12:1–2; 16:1–2*, 12–14, 28–30), whereas in J the people doubt not Moses's authority, but rather Yahweh's capacity to lead them through the wilderness (Num 11:1; 14:11–24).[83]

9. The seventy select elders are chosen to be endowed with some of Moses's prophetic spirit after the events at Horeb (Num 11:16–17, 24b–30), whereas in J they are chosen to accompany Moses part of the way up Sinai to visually experience the theophany (Exod 24:1–2, 9–10).[84]

Thus, without any consideration of style, but attending only to the contradictory historical claims in the nonpriestly text, a substantial and coherent E narrative—coherent narratologically, thematically, theologically, and, yes, stylistically—from Exodus 19 through Numbers 16 can be identified, while leaving the J narrative not only intact, but considerably clarified in its details. This lengthy E section provides a far more secure basis for identifying E elsewhere than do the handful of isolated texts in Genesis that usually serve this purpose. As we broaden our textual horizons, we find that numerous other passages share the historical claims listed above and that these texts similarly present contradictions to the narrative of J. (Thematic, theological, and stylistic links, because they are secondary observations that emerge from the narrative analysis, will be treated only in the notes to the following.)

I want to emphasize that it is not my intention in what follows to discuss every text that belongs to E, nor, importantly, is it my aim to demonstrate the continuity of one passage to another, as will be evident from the order in which the following texts are mentioned. What is at stake is the claim that the E texts, from the central section described above and throughout, comprise a distinctive and interlocking set of historical claims, both internally consistent and contradictory to the non-E text. What is required is not an exhaustive listing of every E passage; rather, the identification of a significant number of texts from various parts of the Pentateuch that participate in the unique historical viewpoint of E should serve to challenge the attempt to deny E the status of source document.

We may turn first to the encounter with Edom in Numbers 20:14–22a. This continuous passage, consisting primarily of negotiations between Moses and the king of Edom, contains in vv. 15–16 a description by Moses of the Exodus, in which he says that Yahweh "sent a messenger who freed us from Egypt [literally, and much better, 'who led us out of Egypt']." As we have seen, it is only in E that a divine messenger leads the Israelites (Exod 23:20–22); in J it is Yahweh himself (33:14–17).[85] The E passage of Numbers 20:14–22a is continued directly in 21:4aβ–9, with the opening words "to skirt the land of Edom."[86] The Israelites' encounters with Sihon, king of the Amorites, and Og, king of Bashan, in 21:21–35 belong to the same narrative, as again the Israelites send messengers to ask for passage through a foreign territory; the message sent to Sihon (21:22) is nearly identical to the one sent to Edom (20:17, 19).[87]

Sihon and Og, rather than simply refusing the Israelites passage, engage them in battle and are defeated, such that Israel comes to possess the territory of the Transjordan (21:24–25, 35). The possession of the Transjordan is, in turn, the narrative precursor to the request of the Gadites and Reubenites in the nonpriestly text of Numbers 32 that they might remain there permanently. As there has been no J story in which the Israelites conquer the Transjordan, while E tells precisely of this (as is explicitly recollected in 32:33), the nonpriestly text of Numbers 32 must also belong to E.[88]

In Deuteronomy 31:14–15, Moses is commanded to bring Joshua to the Tent of Meeting for the formal transfer of authority. This is the sole mention of the Tent of Meeting in Deuteronomy, and it conforms precisely to the procedure established elsewhere in E: Moses and Joshua enter the Tent, and the pillar of cloud descends at the entrance to the Tent. (These verses are continued in v. 23, which is the content of Yahweh's speech to Joshua.) This passage marks the predictable culmination of Moses and Joshua's relationship: as Moses's servant throughout, it is only fitting that Joshua should take over upon Moses's death.[89] Since the Tent, the procedure for Yahweh's appearance there, and Joshua are all unknown in J, there can be little question that these verses belong to E. The final verses of Deuteronomy, 34:10–12, also connect directly to the E narrative of Exodus 19–Numbers 16. The description of Moses as a prophet reflects the central concern of E, the establishment of Moses's prophetic authority, and the statement that Yahweh spoke to him "face to face" is identical to that of Exodus 33:11 (and very similar to Num 12:8 — "mouth to mouth" — which is equally dependent on Exod 33:11).

If Deuteronomy 31:14–15, 23 and 34:10–12 represent the end of the story of Moses in E, the beginning is to be found in Exodus 3. In 3:1 Moses is tending the flock of his father-in-law Jethro at "Horeb, the mountain of God." We have already seen that these are the two terms E uses to describe the mountain in Exodus 19–34; here they are formally identified as one and the same. The identification of Moses's father-in-law as Jethro contradicts the preceding J narrative, in which his father-in-law is named Reuel (2:18). The content of God's speech to Moses in 3:9–15 similarly both connects with our established E text and contradicts J. Verses 9–10 are a clear doublet of vv. 7–8: in both passages God announces that he has heard the cry of the Israelites and seen their oppression in Egypt. In vv. 7–8, Yahweh says that he will lead the Israelites out, a concept reflected both in the J plagues, in which Yahweh brings about each plague himself, and in the destruction of the Egyptians at the sea, in which Yahweh fights on behalf of Israel, as well as in the rebellions of the Israelites in the wilderness. In vv. 9–10, God instructs Moses to free the people himself; Moses's leadership is, as we have seen, the focus of much of the E narrative from Horeb on.[90] In Exodus 3:11, Moses doubts his ability to lead the Israelites, much as he does in Numbers 11:11–12, 14–15 (see case study II). The revelation of the divine name in Exodus 3:13–15 is, of course, in stark contradiction to J's claim, borne out throughout J, that the name Yahweh had been known since the first generations of humanity (Gen 4:26).

Exodus 3:12, in which God tells Moses that after Moses has freed the Israelites he is to bring them back to this mountain to worship, is of particular interest. In the J story, the Israelites never worship at Sinai. Although Moses repeatedly tells Pharaoh to let the Israelites go so that they can worship Yahweh (for instance in Exod 3:18; 5:3; 7:26), this is entirely a ruse. They have no intention of actually worshipping, and Pharaoh realizes this when, after three days, the Israelites are still making their way through the wilderness (Exod 14:5). That Moses asks Pharaoh for permission to go three days into the desert to worship, rather than to the mountain, is a further indication that J and E disagree here. In J, the Israelites do not know that they are to go to Sinai; Yahweh announces that it will be the site of the theophany only once the Israelites chance upon it. In E, on the other hand, the Israelites do indeed worship at Horeb. Although most scholars read 3:12 as referring to the covenant ratification ceremony of 24:3–8, it is equally likely that it refers to the sacrifices offered in Exodus 18:12.[91] Whether this is the case or not, Exodus 18, which is for the most part unified,[92] connects with E not only as the fulfillment of 3:12, but also by the presence of Jethro. As we have seen, Jethro is E's name for Moses's father-in-law. The chapter also connects directly by means of its location, at "the mountain of God" (18:5), to the beginning of E in Exodus 19:3: "Israel encamped there in front of the mountain." The word "there" in 19:3 requires the antecedent of 18:5.[93] Again, this is not a matter of style; it is the consistency of historical claim that marks these passages as part of the E document.

Exodus 18 also links with Moses's return to Egypt in 4:18: "Moses went back to his father-in-law Jether [a variant spelling of Jethro] and said to him, 'Let me go back to my kinsmen in Egypt and see how they are faring.' And Jethro said to Moses, 'Go in peace.'" This verse, which stands practically alone in the midst of a J narrative, is identifiable as E not only because it refers to Jethro (and, in its opening words, refers to Moses as having been at Horeb in 3:1), but because it conflicts with the next verse, 4:19, from J in which Yahweh tells Moses to return to Egypt—after Moses has already told Jethro that he is leaving. Moses takes his family and returns to Egypt in 4:20, continuing the J story but contradicting Exodus 18:5: "Jethro, Moses' father-in-law, brought Moses' sons and wife to him in the wilderness." This contradiction, in concert with the clear links between Exodus 18 and the E passages in Exodus 3, supports the assignment of Exodus 18 to E. As part of the E narrative, Exodus 18 also plays a structural role, serving, along with the story of the elders in Numbers 11, as a bookend to the Horeb pericope: just before the events at Horeb, Moses receives assistance in carrying out his judicial functions; just after, he receives assistance in carrying out his prophetic role. Thus the organization of the Israelite leadership in its two main capacities brackets the Horeb pericope.

In Exodus 17:8–15 we find another unified narrative, that of the battle against Amalek. Here we encounter Joshua in his role as Moses's servant. We also encounter the person named Hur, who is associated with Aaron but whose role is otherwise undefined. Although we have not had occasion to mention him thus far, it may be noted that Hur appears only in conjunction with Aaron and only in the E narrative (Exod 24:14).

Of some interest is the preceding episode in this chapter, that of Moses getting water from the rock in vv. 1bβ–7. Although almost always ascribed to E by documentary scholars, largely because of the appearance of the word "Horeb" in v. 6, this passage in fact conflicts with the E narrative, precisely in the use of Horeb.[94] Since for E Horeb is the name of the mountain of God where the theophany and law-giving occurs, it is impossible that it should be the same place where Moses gets water from the rock—because in 17:7, the name of the latter place is changed to Massa and Meribah. Thus, importantly, J also knows of a place called Horeb—but a place different from that in E.[95]

Returning to the nonpriestly story of the plagues, we find another contradiction in the narrative. According to J, Pharaoh's courtiers come to realize that the plagues are destroying their land and property and plead with Pharaoh to let the Israelites go (Exod 10:7), though they subsequently regret their decision (14:5). After the death of the firstborn, Pharaoh finally relents and lets the Israelites go, with all their flocks, and the Egyptians hurry the Israelites out of the country—before their bread even has time to rise (12:31–34). In this story, then, the Egyptians want the Israelites gone as fast as possible, directly after the final plague. Yet in the very next verses, 12:35–36, we are told that Yahweh had made the Egyptians—all of them, not just Pharaoh's courtiers—favorably disposed toward the Israelites, so that they freely gave them their silver and gold. This passage contradicts the J story both in the characterization of the Egyptians' attitude and in plot: there is no point in the J narrative at which this logically could have happened.[96]

Exodus 12:35–36 does not stand alone, however. It is the fulfillment of Yahweh's prediction to Moses in 11:2–3, in virtually identical words. Exodus 11:1–3, in turn, is a clear disruption of the continuous speech of Moses in J from 10:28–29 to 11:4–8. Both 12:35–36 and 11:1–3 belong together with 3:21–22, which is again a nearly verbatim parallel and is the continuation of God's speech to Moses in 3:9–15. The description of the Egyptians in these texts as Israel's "neighbors" (3:22; 11:2) suggests that the Israelites live among the Egyptians, whereas in J they live apart, in Goshen (for example, Gen 45:10; Exod 8:18; 9:26). These three passages are at odds with J, but more importantly they play a role in E. The despoiling of the Egyptians is the means by which the Israelites, who were of course slaves, acquire the precious metals they use to construct the golden calf. Note that in J the Israelites leave with their flocks but nothing else (Exod 12:32–34); in E there is no mention of animals but only and specifically of gold and silver. The connection of the despoiling of the Egyptians and the construction of the golden calf is supported by Yahweh's instructions in 3:22 that the Israelites are to put the silver and gold "on your sons and daughters"—and when the Israelites make the calf, Aaron instructs them to remove the gold that is on "your wives, your sons, and your daughters" (32:2).

In case study I, the sale of Joseph in Genesis 37, we saw an example from Genesis of a nonpriestly passage that breaks down into two complete and coherent narratives: one from J, in which Joseph is sold by his brothers to the Ishmaelites, and one from E, in which Midianite traders kidnap Joseph, taking him out of the pit into which his brothers had thrown him. As already noted, each of these versions is referred to later in the Joseph story: the J version in Genesis 45:4 ("I am your brother Joseph, he whom you sold into Egypt") and the E version in 40:15 ("I was kidnapped from the land of the Hebrews"). This sentence from E does not stand alone, of course, but is part of the larger unified narrative of Joseph interpreting the dreams of Pharaoh's wine steward and baker, which occupies the entirety of Genesis 40. This story continues uninterrupted into Genesis 41, in which the wine steward remembers Joseph and has him brought to interpret Pharaoh's dreams. Joseph's interpretation—seven years of plenty, seven years of famine—and his appointment as second in command over all of Egypt are all part of this continuous narrative. In 41:47–49, Joseph collects the grain from Egypt in anticipation of the famine to come. In vv. 53–54, the seven years of plenty end, and the famine sets in. Between these two passages is the notice of the birth of Joseph's sons, Manasseh and Ephraim. That vv. 50–52 are part of the same E story is indicated by the first clause of v. 50: "Before the years of famine came."[97] The tripartite structure of 41:47–54 is clear. The etiologies Joseph provides for his sons' names also fit perfectly into this E narrative: both names make sense in a story in which Joseph has overcome adversity—his kidnapping and sale into a foreign land—to arrive at a position of wealth and power. That is precisely the story of E in Genesis 37, 40, and 41.

The births of Manasseh and Ephraim in 41:50–52 provide an important basis for recognizing other E texts in the Joseph story. In 48:1, Joseph is informed that his father is ill, and he brings Manasseh and Ephraim to Jacob for blessing. This verse contradicts the preceding verses in 47:29–31: there, Jacob is already on his deathbed, and Joseph is already with him. Moreover, the presence of Manasseh and Ephraim indicates that this verse could not be from J: the birth of Joseph's sons, or anything else about them, is never mentioned in J, neither in the Joseph story nor anywhere else.[98] The blessing of Manasseh and Ephraim, and the reversal of their priority, is a nearly continuous E episode through the end of Genesis 48.[99] Following this same line, the next mention of Ephraim and

Manasseh comes in Joseph's deathbed scene, in Genesis 50:23–26, which probably follows in E directly on the end of Genesis 48. Here we are informed that
Joseph lived to see the grandchildren of Ephraim and Manasseh. (Manasseh's
son Machir, named here in 50:23, is mentioned again in E in Num 32:40.)
Before his death, Joseph addresses his brothers—"So Joseph made the sons of
Israel swear, saying, 'When God has taken notice of you, you shall carry up my
bones from here'"—and then he dies.

Thus in the Joseph story, as in Exodus and Numbers, a coherent E narrative
can be identified, one that is not only internally self-referential, but that contradicts the narrative of J, and again on the primary grounds of historical claims
alone. Crucially, from the end of the Joseph story we can find a direct link into
the Exodus narrative. When the Israelites leave Egypt after the death of the firstborn, we read in Exodus 13:19: "And Moses took with him the bones of Joseph,
who had exacted an oath from the children of Israel, saying, 'God will be sure
to take notice of you: then you shall carry up my bones from here with you.'"
The reference to Genesis 50:26 could not be more direct.

Exodus 13:19, for its part, belongs with 13:17–18, in which we learn that God
did not lead the Israelites on the direct route through Philistine territory to
Canaan, but took them roundabout, through the wilderness; we are also told
that the Israelites went out of Egypt armed for war. As these verses are the narrative antecedent to v. 19—the phrase "Moses took with him" in v. 19 implies a
preceding reference to the departure of the Israelites, found in vv. 17–18—they
too belong to E. Exodus 13:17–18 are explicitly intended to explain why the
Israelites did not go directly from Egypt to Canaan—why they entered Canaan
across the Jordan, from the east, rather than from the south. This tradition of
Israel crossing the Jordan into Canaan is explained also by J, but in very different terms: in J the Israelites wander through the wilderness until the generation
of the Exodus dies, as punishment for the episode of the spies (Num 14:21–23).
According to E, however, it was not a punishment, but by divine design; note
too that there is no required length of wandering according to E, and indeed,
nowhere in E is the idea ever mentioned that the generation of the Exodus died
in the wilderness, or that the wandering took forty years.

The note in Exodus 13:18 that the Israelites left Egypt armed is also of interest.
In the very next section of J, the destruction of the Egyptians at the sea, the Israelites do no fighting—Yahweh fights on their behalf (see case study IV). Later
in J, after the episode of the spies, in Numbers 14:25, 39–46, the same notion
is found: Yahweh tells the Israelites not to go through the territory of the Canaanites and Amalekites, but the Israelites decide to travel that way regardless
of Yahweh's command. Moses, however, warns them, saying that since Yahweh

will not be in their midst—that is, there to fight for them—they will be attacked and beaten. This is, of course, precisely what happens. The Israelites, according to J's story, did not intend to fight, just to cross through the neighboring territory, but when attacked, they had no means to defend themselves, as Yahweh was not with them. In E, on the other hand, as we have already seen, the Israelites do indeed fight: against the Amalekites (Exod 17:8–15) and against Sihon and Og (Num 21:21–35). Thus the description of the Israelites leaving Egypt armed provides an important datum for the E narrative, but not at all for that of J.[100]

As stated above, it is not my intention to work through every bit of nonpriestly text in the Pentateuch, nor do I think it necessary. I have isolated a broad web of interconnected narratives from Genesis 37 through the end of the Pentateuch, narratives that are interdependent in their historical claims and at the same time contradictory to the historical claims of J. This is true both in terms of individual pericopes, such as Genesis 37 and Numbers 11, and in terms of the overarching story. Style, theme, and theology have played only a secondary part in the preceding analysis, although the E narrative is coherent in those as well.

Given the extensive evidence from the texts discussed above, when we find other passages that contradict the claims of the J narrative, it is not unreasonable to wonder whether they might belong to the same coherent E strand. Although the use of Elohim rather than Yahweh has not factored in our identification of E to this point, the knowledge of God's proper name is a fundamental historical claim in the E narrative, and in cases such as the doublet of Hagar's expulsion, in which one version uses the name Yahweh (Gen 16:4–14) and one the title Elohim (Gen 21:9–21), this might be enough to assign the latter passage to E even without other connections. Yet in virtually every such text there are other connections, whether narrative (such as the reference to the Israelites going free from Egypt "with great wealth" in Gen 15:14 [cf., for example, Exod 3:21–22]), thematic (the description of Abraham as a prophet in Gen 20:7, 17 [cf., for example, Deut 34:10]), theological (the fear of God in Gen 20:11; 22:12 [cf. Exod 20:17] or theophanies in dreams or visions in Gen 15:1; 20:3; 28:12; 31:11, 29; 46:2 [cf. Num 12:6]), or stylistic (the repetition of a character's name when called by the deity and the reply "Here I am" in Gen 22:11; 46:2 [cf. Exod 3:4]).

We may thus respond directly to Rendtorff's challenge: the "doublets or complements at various places in the Pentateuch" are not a mere collection of independent secondary additions, unrelated one to the other, but are intricately and integrally connected on substantive narrative grounds. Each depends on those that preceded and is required for those that follow. They form a coherent storyline, with coherent claims about what happened, when, where, why, and how, with, as should only be expected, a coherent set of themes, theology, and style. To propose that these passages are independent of one another requires the belief that each successive textual interpolation was added not as a supplement to the entire nonpriestly narrative, but only to those parts that were also "secondary"—since the E texts agree with and interact with only themselves, and not at all with J. It is far simpler, of course, to recognize that all the E passages described above (and some I have not mentioned) belong to a single composition.

Equally invalid is the argument that E is not an independent document but rather a layer of theologically oriented supplements to and revisions of J.[101] It is not the coherence of E on its own that repudiates this view, but rather its relationship to J. First and foremost, the fact that when the two sources are intertwined, as in Genesis 37, the Horeb pericope, and Numbers 11, E is not a series of interpolations, but a complete and coherent narrative in its own right; E is comprehensible only when isolated from J, and vice versa. In addition, some elements of E cannot be understood as theological updatings of J, such as the identification of the mountain as Horeb rather than Sinai or that of Moses's father-in-law as Jethro rather than Reuel. Rather, these differences must emerge from a variant tradition, as they have no theological value on their own, much less as a reworking of J. Some doublets of J found in E are similarly problematic: it is unclear why an editor would feel the need to repeat, but in slightly different words, God's announcement to Moses of the impending rescue of the Israelites (Exod 3:7–8 and 3:9–10) or provide a second description of Moses departing Midian for Egypt (4:18 and 4:19). The fact that some E passages are located at some textual distance from the J texts that they contradict, such as the selection of the seventy elders (Num 11:16–17, 24b–30 and Exod 24:1–2), is difficult to explain as the result of anything other than an independently written composition, since, in this case, the J description of the selection of the elders precedes that of E and is allowed to stand, thereby rendering the E story redundant. Secondary revisions are intended to reorient the text toward the secondary material, not away from it. On this same principle, in those places where the E and J materials have been interwoven, we frequently find that the general orientation of the passage is toward J, while the E story is somewhat obscured, as in Genesis 37, Exodus 34, or Numbers 11, and in these cases too it is difficult to understand E as a secondary addition. Finally, we may simply note the abundance of stories told by E that are entirely absent from J: Joseph interpreting the dreams in Genesis 40–41; Manasseh and Ephraim in Genesis 48; the war against Amalek in Exodus 17; the visit of Jethro in Exodus 18; the prophesying elders in Numbers 11; Miriam's leprosy in Numbers 12; the rebellion of Dathan and Abiram in Numbers 16; the encounters with

Edom, Sihon, and Og in Numbers 20–21; and the apportioning of the Transjordan in Numbers 32. These are not theological reinterpretations or reworkings of J; they are completely independent narratives, told with no reference to J at all, but only to each other, and intricately so.[102]

One of the primary arguments against E as an originally independent document is its ostensibly fragmentary nature. Even scholars writing in defense of an E document frequently describe it as the fragmentary remains of an originally complete whole.[103] There is some truth to this. E lacks a clear beginning, although when Genesis 15 is recognized as belonging, in whole or in part, to E, this problem is somewhat ameliorated.[104] The story of the Exodus proper, whether it included plagues or something else, is referred to in other E passages (Exod 11:1; 18:8–10) but is missing from E itself; so too the beginning of the Jacob story. As we have seen, however, there are lengthy sections that are as complete as anything we find in J or P: the Joseph story, the Horeb pericope, and the wandering in the wilderness. There may be a number of explanations for the missing pieces of E: they may have been removed in the process of compilation for reasons that are now unclear to us, or, more likely, they may have been missing already in the independent E text when it was taken up into the canonical text by the compiler, hundreds of years after its original composition. The various failures in traditional scholarship show that the solution to this problem does not lie in the attempt to discover bits and pieces of E in the midst of clearly unified J stories. These small fragments of text do not solve the problem of E, except insofar as, by removing elements of J narratives, they render J equally problematic. We must, rather, accept that parts of E are missing and recognize that gaps in a narrative do not necessarily speak to the original completeness of that narrative.[105]

What must be understood in evaluating the completeness of E is that although E is missing some significant pieces, it is not alone in this. Both J and P are also incomplete. J is missing the birth of Isaac and the death of Abraham; is fragmentary from the end of Numbers 14 on, comprising perhaps a handful of verses in Numbers 20–21 before the blessing of Moses in Deuteronomy 33; and is most likely missing a section in the Sinai pericope as well. Kuenen goes so far as to say of J, "It is no more complete than E."[106] P, for its part, lacks the births of Jacob and Esau, Jacob's marriages, and the descent of Joseph to Egypt. The incompleteness we recognize in E, then, is not unique to E: all the sources (with the exception of D) have gaps. E is different only in degree, not in kind. And the various indications of an originally independent and complete composition that we find in J (and P)—cross-references, foreshadowing, narrative recollection, development of characters and themes, chronological and geographical progression, and overall coherence—all of these are equally present in E. E has all the signs of an originally independent document. We may draw an analogy with the Ugaritic story of Kirta (KTU 1.14–16). Despite lacking its opening lines, and despite significant gaps in the text, perhaps comprising one or more entire tablets, the original completeness of the narrative as a whole is not in dispute because it is coherent in all the ways described above.[107] So too is E.

Compelling evidence not only for E as it has been identified above but for its original independence from J is found in Deuteronomy (see further in chapter 4).[108] In Moses's introductory speech in Deuteronomy 1–11, the history of Israel from Horeb to the plains of Moab is recounted, and in virtually every instance D follows the E narrative. The stories told only in E are found also in D: the appointing of judges (Deut 1:9–18); the encounters with Edom, Sihon, and Og (2:2–3:11); and the apportioning of the Transjordan (3:12–20). Far more important are the narratives in D that refer back to passages in which J and E are interwoven: the complaint of Moses from Numbers 11 (Deut 1:9–12), as we have seen case study II, and especially the recollection of the events at Horeb (4:10–14; 5:2–5, 19–28; 9:8–21, 25–10:5). In these cases D contains no trace of the J story, even where J is predominant. Thus, for example, Deuteronomy 4:11 reflects Exodus 19:16–17, the only E verses in 19:10–18, which is otherwise J. Deuteronomy 9:9–10 contains details from Exodus 24:18b and 31:18. Most impressively, Deuteronomy 10:1–5 contains the entirety of E's story from Exodus 34 and nearly verbatim, while the dominant J story in Exodus 34, with the rules against anyone approaching the mountain, the theophany, and the covenant, is completely absent.[109] Unless the author of D had the independent E text before him when writing, it is difficult, if not impossible, to imagine how he was able to follow E so precisely while avoiding J so entirely.

The existence of E as an independent document is evident on both internal and external grounds. Attempts to argue otherwise are based on methodological errors in the identification of E, both by its critics and more so by its defenders. When the historical claims of the narrative, rather than theme or style, are taken as the primary evidence, and when the analysis begins not with a series of disconnected passages but with the substantial, coherent, and continuous narrative from Exodus 19–Numbers 16, the interdependence of the E texts on each other and their independence from J are clear. The existence, scope, and independence of E are further bolstered by the evidence from D. On both the level of the individual episode and that of the overarching narrative, E is distinct from J and coherent in all the ways that an independent document should be.

Chapter 4

COMPLEMENTARITY

The D Source

Uniquely among the pentateuchal sources, the D document is found in the canonical text in almost a single uninterrupted block, contained entirely within the book of Deuteronomy. For this reason, D is generally not subject to the same source-critical analyses as the other three pentateuchal documents; it does not require a fine-toothed comb to extricate D from its canonical setting. Nevertheless, some questions about D remain, particularly regarding its scope: namely, in Deuteronomy is the D source proper to be restricted to the deuteronomic laws alone, or to some or all of the framework around the laws? And in Genesis–Numbers are there passages that are to be ascribed to a deuteronomic author or editor?

THE SCOPE OF D

That the laws of Deuteronomy 12–26 constitute the majority of the D document is not in dispute, and it is clear that the main goal of D is the presentation and promulgation of these laws. The legal block in Deuteronomy is formally distinct from the material that surrounds it, mostly consisting of Moses's historical retrospective and rhetorical exhortations. Formal distinction, however, does not automatically imply compositional distinction. Indeed, the laws of Deuteronomy 12–26 cannot stand on their own literarily. They are presented as Mosaic speech, addressed to the Israelite people in the second person: "Be careful to heed all these commandments that I enjoin upon you" (Deut 12:28). As such, they require at the very least an introductory statement from the narrator, such as "These are the words that Moses addressed to all Israel" (Deut 1:1), or "This is the Torah that Moses set before the Israelites" (Deut 4:45). Obviously, such statements are present in the text; they come, however, not immediately before the laws but as introductions to Moses's historical recollections, to the framework of the laws.

The reason for this is clear enough: in order to persuade the Israelites—both those in the story and those in the audience—to obey the laws, the author is required to present the need for obedience, the obligation of the Israelites to the deity. The literary phenomenon of framing laws with the justification for those laws is well known. We find it in its most extensive form in E and P, the narratives of which lead to the divinely given laws at Horeb/Sinai and justify, primarily through the story of the Exodus, the Israelites' obligation to Yahweh.[1] It is present also in the laws of Hammurabi, which are prefaced with the description of the deity appointing Hammurabi to provide laws for the people. Perhaps the most valuable parallel is to the ancient Near Eastern treaties, on the structure of which D is modeled.[2] These treaties, whether in the Hittite or Mesopotamian form, typically begin with a preamble and historical prologue, the purpose of which is to remind the parties involved of the suzerain's past acts of protection and support and the vassal's prior submission to the suzerain. Just as the historical prologue is a necessary part of the ancient Near Eastern treaty, so too the D equivalent, Moses's historical retrospective in Deuteronomy 1–11, is a necessary part of the D source. And just as the stipulations of the ancient Near Eastern treaty did not exist independently of their framing elements—even though they are distinct in form—so too the laws of D did not exist independently of the material that surrounds them.

Yet there is an obvious literary difficulty in taking Deuteronomy 1–11 as the historical prologue to the laws of Deuteronomy 12–26. As noted above, there are not one but two narrative introductions to Moses's speech to the Israelites:

DEUTERONOMY 1:1–4	DEUTERONOMY 4:45–49[3]
[1]These are the words that Moses addressed to all Israel on the other side of the Jordan.—Through the wilderness, in the Arabah near Suph, between Paran and Tophel, Laban, Hazeroth, and Di-zahab, [2]it is eleven days from Horeb to Kadesh-barnea by the Mount Seir route.—[3]It was	[45]These are the decrees, laws, and rules that Moses addressed to the people of Israel, after they had left Egypt, [46]beyond the Jordan, in the valley at Beth-peor, in the land of King Sihon of the Amorites, who dwelt in Heshbon, whom Moses and the Israelites defeated after they

in the fortieth year, on the first day of the eleventh month, that Moses addressed the Israelites in accordance with the instructions that the Lord had given him for them, ⁴after he had defeated Sihon king of the Amorites, who dwelt in Heshbon, and King Og of Bashan, who dwelt at Ashtaroth [and] Edrei.

had left Egypt. ⁴⁷They had taken possession of his country and that of King Og of Bashan—the two kings of the Amorites—which were on the east side of the Jordan ⁴⁸from Aroer on the banks of the wadi Arnon, as far as Mount Sion, that is, Hermon; ⁴⁹also the whole Arabah on the east side of the Jordan, as far as the Sea of the Arabah, at the foot of the slopes of Pisgah.

Not only are the narrative introductions very similar in wording (and completely alike in function), the Mosaic speeches they each introduce are also strikingly similar. The speech that begins in Deuteronomy 1:6 contains both historical recollection (Deut 1:6–3:29) and rhetorical exhortation regarding obedience to the laws that will follow (Deut 4:1–40).⁴ So too the speech that begins in Deuteronomy 5:2, although here the two elements are more intermingled: historical recollection in Deuteronomy 5:2–28; 9:7–10:11 and rhetorical exhortation in Deuteronomy 5:29–9:6; 10:12–11:31. Both speeches also conclude with a clear transition into the laws proper: "This is the Torah that Moses set before the Israelites" (Deut 4:44); "These are the laws and rules that you must carefully observe in the land that the Lord, God of your fathers, is giving you to possess, as long as you live on earth" (Deut 12:1).

As framing elements for the laws of Deuteronomy 12–26, these two speeches constitute a functional doublet. This observation led many earlier scholars to conclude that what we have here are two strata of D, labeled variously as Dᵍ and Dˢ, or D¹ and D²: an original framework to the laws, usually considered to be the speech introduced in Deuteronomy 4:45, and a later addition, consisting of the speech introduced in Deuteronomy 1:1.⁵ In the mid-twentieth century, Martin Noth argued that in fact Deuteronomy 1:1–4:40 was not from D at all but was the proper introduction to the Deuteronomistic History (Dtr) in Joshua–2 Kings.⁶ This opinion has been followed, with various emendations, by the majority of subsequent scholars.⁷

It seems indisputable that there are in fact two speeches here and that they are compositionally distinct. Indeed, it is even likely that the author of Deuteronomy 1:1–4:40 wrote in full awareness of Deuteronomy 4:45–11:31: the history recalled in the two speeches is complementary, not repetitive. Only the Horeb story is described in any detail in Deuteronomy 4:45–11:31, while the other events of the wilderness period are mentioned only briefly. As an introduction to the law, concentration on the Horeb story makes sense; it was at Horeb, after all, that the Israelites pledged their obedience to Yahweh by making a covenant, and it is the author's claim that what they agreed to were the laws of Deuteronomy 12–26. The author highlights the apostasy of the Israelites in his description of the Horeb narrative, because the duality of obedience and disobedience is at the heart of the deuteronomic ideology. In Deuteronomy 1:1–4:40 the events of the wilderness wandering after Horeb are described at length, while the events of Horeb are mentioned only in passing as an element of the rhetorical section in Deuteronomy 4:1–40 (in 4:10–14). The history recounted in Deuteronomy 1:1–4:40 brings the Israelites from Horeb to the plains of Moab and demonstrates that even after Horeb they were disobedient—it retells the episode of the spies in full—and that they are obligated to Yahweh for his providence throughout the wilderness period, by recalling the victories of the Israelites over their enemies. It looks, therefore, as if the later author consciously supplemented the earlier history, augmenting both aspects of the earlier author's argument.[8]

This very evidence of augmentation may speak to the idea that the later speech is in fact to be attributed to a D author rather than to the Deuteronomistic History. Noth contended that Deuteronomy 1:1–4:40 had "nothing in particular in common with the Deuteronomic law,"[9] yet its complementary function in relation to the original introduction to the law is clear. Other considerations also support the attribution of both speeches to a D author rather than to Dtr. The fact that Deuteronomy 1:1–4:40 is a Mosaic speech, rather than third-person narration of the history, suggests that it was written not to introduce the third-person narrative of the Deuteronomistic History, but rather to introduce the Mosaic speech comprising the laws of Deuteronomy 12–26. Among other rhetorical elements, we may note that the common deuteronomic phrase "at that time" occurs regularly in both speeches.[10] Most tellingly, Deuteronomy 1:1–4:40 refers directly to the laws from an internal perspective, calling them "this Torah" (Deut 1:5; 4:8, 44); the use of the demonstrative "this" indicates that the speech is intended to be read as part of the same document as the laws. As already noted, this is not the case for the Deuteronomistic History, which refers to the entirety of D from an external perspective: "the Torah of Moses" or "the book of Torah," never "this Torah." Thus, although there are two introductions to the law, both are clearly intended to be part of the same written document as the law; hence both can be subsumed under the siglum "D" and distinguished by the sigla "D¹" for Deuteronomy 4:45–11:31 and "D²" for Deuteronomy 1:1–4:40.

Perhaps most notable for our purposes, the relationship to the other pentateuchal documents is identical in both speeches. In all of the history recounted in these speeches from the revelation on the mountain to the plains of Moab, there are no references to any P narratives. The construction of the Tabernacle, the deaths of Nadab and Abihu, the rebellion of Korah, Moses and Aaron getting water from the rock, the death of Aaron on Mount Hor, the zeal of Phinehas, the war against Midian—not one of these is mentioned in either speech. And of those stories that, in Exodus and Numbers, are told in both a P and non-P version—the theophany at the mountain, the spies, the apportioning of the Transjordan—the version in Deuteronomy parallels only the nonpriestly strand, without any P elements.[11] The Deuteronomistic History, on the other hand, contains clear references to priestly material: for example, the claim of the daughters of Zelophehad in Joshua 17:13–14, which refers directly to the P text of Numbers 27:1–11. There is no equivalent in Deuteronomy 1:1–4:40, the purportedly Dtr introduction, despite the many possible stories from P that fit into the time frame of those historical recollections.

Although both Mosaic speeches in Deuteronomy 1–11 are marked by the absence of P elements, they are equally marked by a clear dependence on the nonpriestly narratives, with particular dependence on the stories from E. In the preceding chapters, those texts from Exodus and Numbers that belong to J and E, respectively, were identified on the grounds of narrative continuity and coherence of historical claims. Thus we can see that in D^1, the speech of Deuteronomy 4:45–11:31, which focuses on the Horeb story, it is the E narrative of the theophany on the mountain that forms the basis for the deuteronomic parallel.[12] This is clear almost from the very beginning of the speech. Most obviously, in Deuteronomy 5:2 and throughout, the mountain is identified as Horeb, as is the case only in E. In Deuteronomy 5:5 (and again in 5:20–24), Moses reminds the Israelites that he acted as intercessor between them and Yahweh, for they were afraid to approach the mountain, as is true only in E (Exod 20:15–16). The Decalogue in Deuteronomy 5:6–18 is known only from E (Exod 20:1–14). The tablets on which the Decalogue is written in Deuteronomy 5:19 are exclusive to E (Exod 31:18*). God's command to Moses to come back to the mountain to receive the full set of laws in Deuteronomy 5:28 parallels Moses's reascent to receive the laws in E (Exod 20:18).

When the Horeb narrative picks up again in Deuteronomy 9–10, the same situation obtains. Moses says in 9:9 that he had been on the mountain for forty days and forty nights, without food or water, exactly as in E (Exod 24:18b; 34:28). The tablets are said in 9:10 to be inscribed with the finger of God, just as in E (Exod 31:18*; 32:16). The words God uses to inform Moses of the Israelites' apostasy in 9:12–14 are virtually identical to those he uses in E (Exod 32:7–10)—and, of course, it is only in E that the Israelites make a golden calf. Moses smashes the tablets in 9:17, just as he does in E (Exod 32:19), and then burns the calf, grinds it into powder, and scatters it over the waters in 9:21, just as in E (Exod 32:20). Moses's plea on behalf of the Israelites in 9:26–29 is almost identical to his plea in E (Exod 32:11–13). Finally, his return to the top of the mountain to receive the second set of tablets in 10:1–5 contains virtually every single word of E's narrative in Exodus 34:1–5*, 28.

What is remarkable here is that the Horeb narrative from E is, in the canonical text, interwoven with J's Sinai account; yet the parallel in Deuteronomy makes no mention of any of the J story elements. The prohibition on the Israelites rushing the mountain (Exod 19:10–13, 21–25); the required purity of the people (Exod 19:14–15); the ascent of Moses, Aaron, Nadab, and Abihu (Exod 24:1–2, 9–11bα); the threat that Yahweh will not travel with the Israelites (Exod 33:1–3) and Moses's desperate response (Exod 33:12–17); the personal theophany to Moses on the mountain (Exod 33:18–23; 34:2–5*); the covenant in which Yahweh promises to dispossess the Canaanites as long as the Israelites do not worship the local deities (Exod 34:10–16, 27)—the entirety of the J Sinai narrative goes unmentioned, even in passing, in Deuteronomy.[13]

Yet the author of D[1] does know of J. As noted, the focus even in the retelling of the Horeb story is on the disobedience of the Israelites; when the D[1] author refers to J stories, he does so in order to bolster his case for the intransigence of the Israelite people in the wilderness. Thus in Deuteronomy 6:16, Moses says, "Do not try Yahweh your God, as you did at Massah"—a reference to the J story of Exodus 17:1bβ–7. At the most crucial moment of the Horeb story, when the Israelites have sinned but Moses has not yet interceded on their behalf, the author has Moses remind the Israelites that this was not a singular occurrence: "You provoked Yahweh at Taberah, and at Massah, and at Kibroth-Hattaavah. And when Yahweh sent you on from Kadesh-Barnea, saying, 'Go up and take possession of the land that I am giving you,' you flouted the command of Yahweh your God; you did not put your trust in him and you did not obey him" (Deut 9:22–23). Four stories are referred to here—all exceptionally briefly, and, most importantly, all from J: Taberah (Num 11:1–3), Massah (Exod 17:1bβ–7), Kibroth-Hattaavah (Num 11:4–35*), and the spies (Num 13–14*). The purpose of naming these stories is made clear: "As long as I have known you, you have been defiant toward Yahweh" (Deut 9:24). D[1] tells the E Horeb story and supplements it with references to J stories of Israelite intransigence. It is thus evident, as noted earlier, that this author knew both E and J, but knew them as independent documents.

At the same time as the D¹ author uses E's Horeb story to demonstrate Israel's disobedience, and supplements it with references to J stories that prove the same, he uses the story also to demonstrate Israel's obligation to Yahweh on the basis of the covenant they made there, and supplements this aspect with brief references to other ways in which Yahweh provided for the Israelites during the wilderness period. Thus in Deuteronomy 8:3 Moses tells the Israelites, famously, "He subjected you to the hardship of hunger and then gave you manna to eat, which neither you nor your fathers had known, in order to teach you that man does not live on bread alone, but that man may live on anything that Yahweh decrees." The manna is not part of the E narrative but is told in J (Exod 16:4–5, 26–30; Num 11:4–9). Similarly, the Israelites are exhorted not to "forget Yahweh your God," who preserved them in the wilderness despite the "seraph serpents" and who "brought forth water for you from the flinty rock" (Deut 8:14–16). The reference to the serpents seems to be related to the E story in Numbers 21:4–9, and the water from the rock is from J (Exod 17:1bβ–7). The manna, from J, is mentioned again here also. Finally, Moses reminds the people of Yahweh's "majesty, his mighty hand, his outstretched arm," by recalling "what he did to Egypt's army, its horses and chariots; how Yahweh rolled back upon them the waters of the Sea of Reeds when they were pursuing you," and "what he did to Dathan and Abiram, sons of Eliab son of Reuben, when the earth opened her mouth and swallowed them, along with their households, their tents, and every living thing in their train, from amidst all Israel" (Deut 11:2–6). The destruction of the Egyptians at the sea, as described here, belongs to J (see case study IV); the story of Dathan and Abiram belongs to E (see case study III). Again we have a series of brief references to narratives that demonstrate Yahweh's power and providence in the wilderness, to match the brief references to narratives that demonstrate Israel's intransigence.

When we turn to the speech in D², Deuteronomy 1:1–4:40, we find precisely the same kind of dependence on and use of E and J. As argued above, the author of D² already had before him Deuteronomy 4:45–11:31, in which the Horeb narrative was recounted in full, and so did not have to reassert the Israelites' obligation to Yahweh on the basis of the covenant made at Horeb or their gross disobedience there. What he could do, however, was expand on the elements of obligation and disobedience by telling the story of how the Israelites got from Horeb to the plains of Moab.

As in the earlier speech, there is a reference to Horeb—not Sinai—very early in Deuteronomy 1:1–4:40, in fact immediately after the opening verses that set the scene (Deut 1:6). In Deuteronomy 1:9–12, Moses recalls that he complained to Yahweh that he was unable to bear the enormous number of Israelites by himself, just as he did only in E (Num 11:11–12, 14–15); there are nearly verbatim parallels between the two passages. In Deuteronomy 1:13–18, Moses appoints tribal leaders to act as judges, just as only in E, in Exodus 18; again, elements are nearly word for word. Deuteronomy 1:19–45 recounts the episode of the spies from Numbers 13–14—though of course only the nonpriestly part. Uniquely among the stories recounted by the author of D^2, this narrative is from J, not E. But it is clear why the author would want to tell this of all J stories: it fits perfectly his agenda of demonstrating Israel's disobedience in the wilderness. This episode, the fullest in D^2, stands as the parallel to the Horeb story in the other speech, as it provides evidence that even when they were brought to the very border of the promised land, the Israelites still lacked faith in Yahweh. The version in Deuteronomy 1:19–45 parallels Numbers 13–14 in almost every aspect, frequently using the exact words of J.

The avoidance of the territory of Seir in Deuteronomy 2:2–6 parallels the E story of the same in Numbers 20:14–21, and here the author makes his case for Yahweh's providence in the wilderness: "Indeed, Yahweh your God has blessed you in all your undertakings. He has watched over your wanderings through this great wilderness; Yahweh your God has been with you these past forty years: you have lacked nothing" (Deut 2:7). The Israelites cross the wadi Zered (Deut 2:13) and the wadi Arnon (Deut 2:24), just as they do only in E (Num 21:12–13), upon which they encounter Sihon, king of Heshbon. The Israelites attempt to pass peacefully through Sihon's territory but are forced to fight and defeat him (Deut 2:26–37), precisely as in E (Num 21:21–31). Unlike E, however, the author of D^2 adds to the story the idea that Yahweh has delivered Sihon, and any other opponents, into Israel's power in advance of any encounter (Deut 2:24–25). This notion conforms to the author's goal of demonstrating how Yahweh cared for Israel in the wilderness. Deuteronomy 3:1–7 describes the defeat of Og, as in E (Num 21:33–35), with word-for-word precision. The apportioning of the newly conquered land, recalled in Deuteronomy 3:12–20, is told in E in Numbers 32*.

In short, both Mosaic speeches in Deuteronomy 1–11 show clear dependence primarily on E, but also on the stories of J, which highlight the disobedience of the Israelites despite Yahweh's care for them and their covenantal obligation to him. There is no difference in how the two speeches approach the task of introducing the laws; they simply describe complementary parts of Israel's history leading up to the narrative present on the plains of Moab. As a final piece of the puzzle we may note that the relationship between the introductory speeches and the other pentateuchal documents is the same as that in the laws of Deuteronomy 12–26 themselves. It is well known and generally accepted that the law code of Deuteronomy 12–26 is based on the laws of Exodus 20:23–23:33, the laws at the center of E's Horeb narrative.[14] Beyond that, however, there are explicit references to narratives embedded into the laws. The law of prophets in Deuteronomy 18:15–22 refers back to the Israelites' pleading with Moses to act as intercessor for them at Horeb (18:16), that is, to the E narrative in Exodus 20:15–16. The exclusion of Ammonites and Moabites from the community in Deuteronomy 23:4–5 refers explicitly to the lack of hospitality those nations showed Israel during the wilderness wandering, that is, in E (Num 20:14–21; 22–24). The law of skin disease in Deuteronomy 24:8 is accompanied in 24:9 by a reminder of Miriam's affliction from E (Num 12). Finally, Israel's eternal enmity toward Amalek, prescribed in Deuteronomy 25:17–19, is based on Amalek's attack on Israel after the Exodus, narrated only by E, in Exodus 17:8–16.

Thus not only E's laws, but also its narratives, are at the base of the D law code. This primary dependence on E, and the complete lack of reference to P's narratives, is precisely what we find also in the speeches that introduce the law. Certainly we have two authors at work in the Mosaic speeches, but both, by virtue of their similarities to each other, their similarities to the law, and their dissimilarities with Dtr, belong to D.

The same is true of the material that follows the laws, in Deuteronomy 27: 1–32:47 (with the exception of 31:14–15, 23; see below). It has long been recognized that the blessing and curses in Deuteronomy 27 and 28, the oath in Deuteronomy 29, and the provisions for the deposition of the written document in Deuteronomy 31:24–26 and for the period reading of the document in Deuteronomy 31:9–13 reflect standard elements of the ancient Near Eastern vassal treaty, just as Deuteronomy 1–11 reflect the preamble, historical prologue, and basic stipulations of allegiance, and Deuteronomy 12–26 reflect the terms of the treaty. Thus the chapters that follow the law belong to the fundamental structure of D. These chapters also include many of the same elements we saw in Deuteronomy 1–11: references to E stories (Horeb [Deut 28:69], Sihon and Og [29:6; 31:4], the apportioning of the land [29:7]), self-description as "this Torah" (27:8; 28:58, 61; 29:20, 28; 30:10; 31:9, 12, 24, 26; 32:46), and a wide range of conceptual and linguistic parallels.

Two elements not part of the treaty structure are introduced in these concluding chapters of D: the appointing of Joshua as Moses's successor (Deut 31: 1–8) and the poem of Deuteronomy 32:1–43, with its introduction in 31:16–22. The first of these, the appointing of Joshua, participates fully in the standard D concepts and language: Yahweh's ruling that Moses should not cross the Jordan (31:2, taken verbatim from 3:27), the reference to Sihon and Og (31:4; a key reference throughout D, see 1:4; 4:46–47; 29:6), and the exhortation to follow the laws (31:5). The second, Moses's farewell poem, is probably, like the poems of Genesis 49 and Exodus 15, an originally independent piece. It has, however, been taken up by the D author and framed accordingly. The poem is to be a witness that Yahweh knew beforehand that the Israelites would continue to disobey his laws after Moses's death (Deut 31:16–21). The attention to the Israelites' intransigence is typical of D, as we have seen; these introductory verses also make reference to the curses of Deuteronomy 28 (in 31:17). The poem itself also fits D's purposes nicely; it is in some ways a poetic summation of D's essential message: Yahweh did remarkable things for Israel, and yet Israel has forsaken their god.

The conclusion of D is found in Deuteronomy 32:45–47 (on the remainder of Deuteronomy, see below). Here Moses gives his final words to Israel, the distillation of everything he has said to them on the plains of Moab. "Take to heart all the words with which I have warned you this day" (Deut 32:46)—as D has said throughout (6:6–7; 10:12, 16; 11:13, 18; 13:4; 26:16; 30:1–2, 6, 10, 14). "Enjoin them upon your children, that they may observe faithfully all the terms of this Torah" (Deut 32:46)—a regular instruction in D (4:9–10; 6:1–2, 7, 20–25; 11:19; 31:13). "For this is not a trifling thing for you: it is your very life" (Deut 32:47)—repeating the identification of the laws and life from elsewhere in D (4:1, 4; 30:6, 15, 19–20). "Through it you shall long endure on the land that you are to possess upon crossing the Jordan" (Deut 32:47)—obedience to the law is the prerequisite for lasting possession of the land, as D has said throughout (4:5, 26, 40; 5:16, 30; 6:1–3, 18; 8:1; 11:8–9, 18–21; 30:16).

D contains no notice of Moses's death, nor should we expect it to. It is not the narrative of Moses's life, but the final speech of Moses, and its power comes not from the history it tells—which, in the end, takes place only over a single day—but rather from the rhetoric of Moses's speech. The document does not begin with Moses's birth and end with his death; it begins with the introduction to Moses's speech—"These are the words that Moses addressed to Israel"—and ends with the conclusion of that speech, with the final, powerful exhortation to follow the law.

The siglum "D" stands for not the earliest layer of the document, but for the final form, comprising the central law code, the two introductory speeches, and the concluding material (which is itself probably layered like Deut 1–11). Despite its evident stratification, the D document is a cohesive and coherent whole, with a defined agenda, consistent themes and language, and a recognizable structure. It is, moreover, source-critically consistent: it takes up narratives from E and J, in comprehensible ways, and is entirely ignorant of P. It comprises the entirety of Deuteronomy 1:1–32:47: that is D, the pentateuchal document incorporated into the canonical text by the compiler.

Having described the scope of D, I now turn to the second major source-critical question: is there any D material outside of Deuteronomy? that is, did a deuteronomic author or editor insert any material into Genesis–Numbers, or redact any of the earlier material in a deuteronomic fashion?

D IN GENESIS–NUMBERS

Earlier documentary scholars tended to identify scattered phrases and verses in Genesis–Numbers as "deuteronomic," almost always because they contained language that was considered typical of D. Thus, for instance, Genesis 26:5, "inasmuch as Abraham obeyed me and kept my charge: my commandments, my laws, and my teachings," was assigned by many to a deuteronomic hand because of the collocation of legal terms; so too Exodus 15:26: "He said, 'If you will heed Yahweh your God diligently, giving ear to his commandments and keeping all his laws, then I will not bring upon you any of the diseases that I brought upon the Egyptians, for I Yahweh am your healer.'\"[15] Exodus 19:3b–6, in which Yahweh instructs Moses to tell the Israelites that if they obey him and keep his covenant they will be his treasured possession, a kingdom of priests and a holy nation, was also frequently attributed to a D author, mostly because of the language of obedience and covenant.[16] Because the list of Canaanite nations whom the Israelites are to dispossess is given a full enumeration in Deuteronomy 7:1—"the Hittites, Girgashites, Amorites, Canaanites, Perizzites, Hivites, and Jebusites, seven nations much larger than you"—some scholars claimed that the equally full listing in Genesis 15:19–21, and indeed for some scholars virtually every list of the Canaanite nations, was a deuteronomic addition.[17] In the Covenant Code, the so-called hortatory expansions, such as Exodus 22:20, "for you were strangers in the land of Egypt," were assigned to D because similar expressions are found in the laws of Deuteronomy.[18]

Each of these claims for deuteronomic activity may be readily countered. The legal expressions in Genesis 26:5 and Exodus 15:26 do not belong to D and refer to the deuteronomic laws, as such language does when used in Deuteronomy, but belong rather to J, which typically uses clusters of legal terminology to signify general obedience to the will of Yahweh (since J has no law code to which it might refer).[19] Indeed, there is no logical reason that a deuteronomic editor would insert references to obedience to actual laws, since in both Genesis 26:5 and Exodus 15:26 no laws have yet been given. The language of Exodus 19:3b–6 has affinities with D only in the expressions "obey me faithfully" (19:5; cf. Deut 15:5; 28:1) and "treasured possession among all the peoples" (19:5; cf. Deut 7:6; 14:2; 26:18). None of the other language in these verses has any affinity with that of D.[20] Moreover, to remove Exodus 19:3b–6 from its context would leave a narrative with a gaping hole: "Moses went up to God. . . . Moses came and summoned the elders of the people and put before them all that Yahweh had commanded him" (Exod 19:3a, 7).[21] The full list of the Canaanite nations in Deuteronomy 7:1 is nice for having the classic biblical number seven attached to it, but this is no reason to assume that the list originates with D everywhere it is found, especially as it so rarely contains all seven nations listed in Deuteronomy 7:1. The list in Genesis 15:19–21 is actually more extensive than that of Deuteronomy 7:1, with ten nations. What's more, the Canaanite nations are listed in D only twice: in Deuteronomy 7:1 and again in Deuteronomy 20:17, where in fact only six nations are listed. There is nothing uniquely deuteronomic about the so-called expansions to the Covenant Code; the laws in Exodus 20:23–23:33 are part of the E document, which of course included the Exodus narrative. In fact, in the Covenant Code the language used is always that of being "strangers," *gērîm*, in the land of Egypt, as E says in Genesis 15:13, while in D the equivalent expression uses the term "slaves" (Deut 15:15; 16:12).

Beyond the specifics of each case, there are general principles that speak against the analyses of earlier scholarship. First, as repeatedly noted, style and terminology cannot be the primary criteria for source assignment. No individual words or phrases are, in the abstract, unique to a single author, since all the biblical authors had access to the Hebrew language. As none of these examples is literarily difficult—none poses a contradiction to the source in which it is currently located, none disrupts the narrative flow—there is no pressing reason to assign them to any hand other than that of the source in which they are presently found. In addition, all of these scholars recognized that D based both the narrative and laws on E and J; yet while the content of the earlier material could be taken up into D, the language evidently could not. If D is based on E and J, if the D author knew and read and incorporated into his own text the laws and narratives of E and J, it seems remarkable to assume that he should not have also incorporated E's and J's language. Even if a phrase occurs only once in E and repeatedly in D, once we have established D's dependence on E then there is no reason that D could not have taken up a particular E phrase and made more of it than E did. J. E. Carpenter and G. Harford-Battersby ironically put it best: "The phraseology of D cannot be wholly new; it must have had some basis in prior usage."[22] D's rhetorical strength is undeniable, but it does not require that D invented every phrase or concept in the document. Where there is similar language in both D and its sources, and when there is no narrative reason to exclude a passage from its context, there is no reason not to believe that D is simply adopting the language of its sources.

More recent scholarship, mostly of the European approach, has argued that many if not all of the narratives in Exodus–Numbers that have parallels in D are in fact entirely of deuteronomic origin. We may take two texts as examples: Deuteronomy 1:9–18 and Deuteronomy 10:1–5.[23]

We have already had occasion to note that Deuteronomy 1:9–18 parallels two nondeuteronomic stories: the E narratives of Numbers 11 and Exodus 18. These parallels are evident both in the content of the stories and in the specific language used. In Deuteronomy 1:9–12 Moses recalls his complaint of the burden of leading the large Israelite community by himself, as occurs only in E, in Numbers 11:11–12, 14–17; there are nearly verbatim parallels between Deuteronomy 1:9, 12 and Numbers 11:14, 17. In Deuteronomy 1:13–18, Moses recounts appointing the tribal leaders as judges, as occurs only in E, in Exodus 18; again, there is a pair of nearly word-for-word parallels, between Deuteronomy 1:15, 17 and Exodus 18:25, 26. While the E stories in Exodus 18 and Numbers 11 are quite separate chronologically, textually, and conceptually, their parallels in Deuteronomy 1:9–18 are found in a single narrative, in which Moses's complaint about the burden of the people is resolved by Moses himself deciding to appoint the tribal leaders as judges. We have already assigned the stories in Exodus and Numbers to E and claimed that D's historical retrospective is based on E and J in their independent forms. A number of European scholars, however, who reject the existences of J and E, see the dependence going in the other direction, with the texts in Exodus and Numbers being deuteronomic in one respect or another.[24]

There are two main difficulties with such analyses. The first is structural: we have one deuteronomic text that has been divided into two separate stories and expanded dramatically in both. It is unclear how the single, simple story of complaint and resolution in Deuteronomy 1:9–18 could be taken as related to two distinct events in Israel's past—and moreover, why the resolution (Exod 18) should be placed chronologically before the complaint (Num 11). The second problem is that of the discrepancies between the D story and those of Numbers 11 and Exodus 18. The main bulk of the Numbers 11 story is about the prophesying elders; yet there are no such figures in Deuteronomy, either in Deuteronomy 1:9–18 or anywhere else. In fact, the idea of anyone but Moses prophesying during Moses's lifetime would be contrary to D's basic perspective. In Exodus 18, it is Jethro who brings the idea of appointing judges to Moses, while in Deuteronomy Jethro is never mentioned, and it is Moses himself who takes credit for the idea of the judges. If Exodus 18 is deuteronomic, then we have to reckon with a deuteronomic author who removed credit for something from Moses and gave it to someone else, someone who is never mentioned in D.

I have noted above that Deuteronomy 10:1–5, in which Moses recounts going up to receive the second set of tablets, contains nearly verbatim the entirety of the E narrative of the same event from Exodus 34:1–5*, 28. I took this as an indication that D knew E independently of J, since the E story in Exodus 34 is closely intertwined with, and in fact quite dominated by, a J story that makes no appearance in D. Again, however, for some contemporary scholars the dependence runs in reverse, and the elements of Exodus 34 that resemble Deuteronomy 10:1–5 are to be attributed to a deuteronomic author or editor.[25] The difficulty here is that Exodus 34 is lacking a significant part of the Deuteronomy 10:1–5 narrative: the thrice-repeated reference to the ark (10:1–2, 3, 5). The ark is important to D: it is where the tablets of the Decalogue are stored, and perhaps even more significantly it is where the written copy of the laws in Deuteronomy 12–26 are to be kept (Deut 31:26). When virtually every other aspect of D's text in Deuteronomy 10:1–5 is present in Exodus 34, the absence of the ark stands out even more prominently.

These two examples can stand for the remainder of the parallel texts in D and Exodus–Numbers. Although there are clear similarities and resonances, even verbatim phrases and verses, these do not stand alone; there are substantive and substantial differences between the D and non-D presentations. There are elements in the Exodus and Numbers texts that are considerably more expansive than in D and that contain concepts and historical claims that are not found anywhere in D and may even contradict basic deuteronomic tenets. There are also elements of D that are central to the deuteronomic presentation but that are missing in the Exodus and Numbers parallels. If the Exodus and Numbers texts are attributed to a deuteronomic hand, then we must posit a deuteronomic author or editor who either does not understand D or does not agree with it, thus challenging the very definition of "deuteronomic."

The differences between D and its parallel texts indicate that the parallels are not fundamentally deuteronomic. They also, of course, serve to distinguish D source-critically from the other pentateuchal documents; if there were no differences in historical claim between the historical retrospective in Deuteronomy and the narratives in Exodus–Numbers, we would have no reason to think that it was a different source at all. Thus for both reasons it is worth enumerating at least briefly some of the main ways in which D's historical retrospective differs from the stories narrated in E and J.

We have already observed the discrepancies between Deuteronomy 1:9–18 and the parallels in Numbers 11 and Exodus 18. In Deuteronomy 1:19–45, Moses recalls the episode of the spies, told in J in Numbers 13–14*. The J story is missing its opening lines, probably displaced in light of P's more extensive introduction in Numbers 13:1–17a; D, however, describes the people suggesting that Moses send spies and Moses selecting one person from each tribe (Deut 1:22–23). In J, Moses gives the spies explicit instructions regarding what they are to look for (Num 13:17b–20), an element that is missing in D. The spies' arrival at Hebron, at the wadi Eshcol, described in detail in Numbers 13:22–24 with an etiology of the name Eshcol, is recounted in brief in Deuteronomy 1:24–25a. The spies' report in Numbers 13:27–29 contains both good and bad news: it is a good land, flowing with milk and honey, but its inhabitants are dangerous and many; Caleb urges the people to go up, but the other spies declare any attack to be futile (13:30–31, 33). In D, however, there is no mention of Caleb's encouragement of the Israelites; only that they refused to go up in light of the spies' report (Deut 1:25b–28). D also adds a new complaint on the part of the people, "It is because God hates us that he brought us out of the land of Egypt" (Deut 1:27). Rather than Caleb encouraging the people, D has Moses castigating them for their lack of faith (1:29–33). The dialogue between Yahweh and Moses in Numbers 14:11–25, in which Yahweh threatens to destroy the people and Moses successfully intercedes on their behalf, is reduced in D only to its concluding lines (Deut 1:34–36), which parallel nearly verbatim Numbers 14:22–24. Most interesting here is that in both Numbers 14:24 and Deuteronomy 1:36 Yahweh singles out Caleb as the only one who will enter the promised land—yet in D this is the first mention of Caleb. It is clear from this that D is based on the J story, and not the other way around. Between the text of Numbers 14:24 and 25, D inserts an element foreign to J: Yahweh's determination that Moses too should not enter the land because of the faithlessness of the Israelites (Deut 1:37–38).[26] This is entirely in keeping with D's repeated assertion that Moses was forbidden from entering Canaan because of the people's sins, not because of any of his own (see also Deut 3:26; 4:21). In the concluding section of the narrative, the main difference between the two stories is that in Numbers 14:41–43, Moses tells the people not to attack Canaan of his own accord, while in Deuteronomy 1:42 he is instructed by Yahweh to relay the same message.

In Numbers 20:14–21, Israel attempts to pass through the territory of Edom, but the people are turned away with force. In Deuteronomy 2:2–7, however, Yahweh tells Moses that the Israelites will indeed pass through Edom (which D calls Seir) and that the Edomites will be afraid of the Israelites. D also adds references to Esau, the ancestor of the Edomites; these references are lacking in E's narrative for the crucial reason that E never mentions Esau, and seems not to know of Esau's existence, or the identification of Esau and Edom.[27] Similarly, in the D section that follows, Moses recalls being instructed to avoid the territories of Moab and Ammon, because just as Edom is a possession of the descendants of Esau, so Moab and Ammon are possessions of the descendants of Lot (Deut 2:8–23). Again, there is no mention of these instructions in E—nor is there any mention of Lot, who is also absent from the E document. D also includes in this section two brief surveys of the history of Moab and Ammon that have no parallel in any other pentateuchal text.

For D, the conquest of the territories of Sihon and Og mark the beginning of the occupation of the promised land (Deut 2:24–25). In E, however, the Israelites attempt to pass peacefully through Sihon's territory, conquering it only because Sihon chose to engage them in battle (Num 21:21–32). Moses's message to Sihon in Numbers 21:22 is paralleled very closely in Deuteronomy 2:27–28, but D then adds references to the Israelites having passed through the territories of Seir and Moab (Deut 2:29), which are obviously not present in E as these events occurred only according to D. Sihon's refusal to let the Israelites through is given no explicit rationale in E; in D, however, Yahweh hardens Sihon's heart and repeats the instruction to begin the occupation of the land (Deut 2:30–31).

The defeat of Og is told in Deuteronomy 3:1–3, nearly verbatim with Numbers 21:33–35. But D adds further elements that are not present in E's story: details of the territory conquered (Deut 3:4–5, 8–11) and the massacre of the inhabitants of Sihon's and Og's territories (3:6–7). The apportioning of the newly conquered land immediately follows in D (Deut 3:12–17) and is done at Moses's instigation. In the E parallel of Numbers 32*, however, it is only because the Reubenites and Gadites come to Moses and request the territory as their tribal holding that the land is apportioned to them. This provides something of a parallel to the example of Deuteronomy 1:9–18 and Exodus 18, where in the E story it is Jethro's idea to appoint judges, while in D's version it is Moses's. In Numbers 32*, Moses instructs the Reubenites and Gadites that they have to fight in Canaan proper with the rest of Israel, indeed in the vanguard of the Israelite forces, before they can return to their newly acquired homestead; these instructions precede the actual apportioning of the land. In D, however, the order is reversed; first the land is apportioned (Deut 3:12–17), and only then does Moses give his instructions (3:18–20).

The description of the Horeb episode in D is very similar to that of E; there are some differences, however. D, unlike E, describes Yahweh as appearing in fire (Deut 4:12, 15, 33, 36; 5:4–5, 19–23; 9:10, 15), an element (the only element, in fact) that seems likely to be derived from J's account (Exod 19:18). In D, the covenant between Yahweh and Israel at Horeb is made on the basis of the Decalogue alone—"He declared to you the covenant that he commanded you to observe, the Ten Words" (Deut 4:13), and note also the uniquely D expression "tablets of the covenant" (Deut 9:9, 11)—while in E the covenant is made on the basis of the laws of the Covenant Code (Exod 24:3–8). This is perhaps the most important distinction between the two narratives: D eliminates the Covenant Code from existence, claiming that the Israelites never heard any law code at Horeb, only the Decalogue; the laws that were given to Moses privately at Horeb (Deut 4:14, 5:28) are not the basis of the Horeb covenant, but rather the new covenant made on the plains of Moab—not the laws of the Covenant Code, but the laws of Deuteronomy 12–26 were given at Horeb. Thus there is no D parallel to the covenant ceremony of Exodus 24:3–8, since the laws on which that ceremony was based did not, according to D, exist.

The full narrative of Israel's apostasy with the golden calf in Exodus 32:1–6 is missing in D. Deuteronomy 9:12–14 picks up with Yahweh's pronouncement to Moses of the Israelites' sin, just as in Exodus 32:7–10. At this point another important discrepancy occurs. While in E Moses now pleads on behalf of the people, in Exodus 32:11–13, in D the intercession is delayed until after Moses has descended the mountain and destroyed the calf, in Deuteronomy 9:25–29. The fact that the nearly word-for-word parallel text is found in two different places in the two narratives speaks strongly to the notion that they must derive from different authors, for there is no reason that a deuteronomic author would have placed the material from Deuteronomy 9:25–29 in a different location in the Exodus 32 version.[28]

In Exodus 32:20, Moses makes the Israelites drink the water in which the powdery remains of the calf have been mixed; not so in Deuteronomy 9:21, where there is no mention of the Israelites drinking the water.[29] In Exodus 32:21–25, Moses confronts Aaron about the calf, and Aaron lies to protect himself; there is no threat of punishment for Aaron in the E story. In D, on the contrary, we are told that Moses had to intercede with Yahweh to save Aaron (Deut 9:20)—even though to this point in the D narrative no mention has been made of Aaron's involvement in the making of the calf. Finally, we have already observed that the prominent element of the ark in Deuteronomy 10:1–5 is absent from the E parallel text in Exodus 34:1–5*, 28.

If the parallel stories in D and Exodus–Numbers were from the same deuteronomic hand or school, then there would be no accounting for the wide variety of differences, some quite important, between them. Because D incorporates stories from both J and E, while neither J nor E shows any knowledge of each other, and because D explicitly eliminates the central law code of E, while E does not explicitly reject D, it is clear that D is based on the earlier nonpriestly texts, rather than the other way around. What's more, it is clear that D is written not to supplement the earlier texts, but to replace them.[30] One cannot read D in natural succession with the Exodus–Numbers material; the contradictions, and the outright rejections, are impossible to overcome. D claims that the Covenant Code does not exist; it would be nonsensical for such a claim to be made in a work that includes the Covenant Code and the narrative leading up to it.

THE END OF DEUTERONOMY

I now turn, finally, to the question of how D came to achieve its place in the canonical Pentateuch. For the most part, this is a relatively simple issue, although one that is frequently overlooked. D is not placed at the end for any particular theological aim; it is not intended by the compiler to be the final word, summarizing and reconceptualizing all that came before it. It is placed at the end because, in the D document itself, it constitutes the final words of Moses, his address to the Israelites on the plains of Moab just before the entry into the promised land. D is where it is because, chronologically, it is the only place it could go: Moses's final words can only come at the end of the story.

Yet they are not the very end; all three sources—J, E, and P—contained conclusions to the life of Moses that D did not. D begins and ends with Moses's speech, as we have said; but J, E, and P are narrating the history of Israel, and there is more that happened in that history before the conquest of Canaan.

The last piece of E before Deuteronomy is the apportioning of the Transjordanian territory in Numbers 32*. In E this was followed by the ceremony in which Joshua was appointed Moses's successor (this same order of events can be observed in D's brief proleptic reference to the selection of Joshua just after the apportioning of the Transjordan in Deut 3:21–22). That E narrative is now found in Deuteronomy 31:14–15, 23. The signs of E in these verses are clear: Moses and Joshua are to go to the Tent of Meeting—which is unknown in D—where, in standard E fashion, Yahweh appears in a cloud that rests at the entrance to the tent (31:14–15; see Exod 33:7–11 and other E texts). Deuteronomy 31:16–22 are clearly of a different character, as Yahweh addresses Moses alone and gives instructions relating to the song in Deuteronomy 32; these verses, as already argued, are from D. Yet in 31:23, we read, "He charged Joshua son of Nun: 'Be strong and resolute: for you shall bring the Israelites into the land that I promised them on oath, and I will be with you.'" The subject here is clearly Yahweh, as was the case in 31:15, but not in the immediately preceding canonical verse, 31:22, where the subject is Moses.

D has, unsurprisingly, taken over this short E story in its own way, in Deuteronomy 31:7–9. Much of the language is the same—again, this is to be expected—but D has Moses appoint Joshua as his successor, rather than Yahweh appointing Joshua, and publicly, "in the sight of all Israel," rather than

privately, in the Tent of Meeting. It is clear why the compiler interwove the
E and D accounts into the single narrative of Deuteronomy 31: the two documents related the same historical event, and, as everywhere, singular events told
by multiple authors are combined into a single narrative.

P's last words before Deuteronomy are the summary statement in Numbers 36:13: "These are the commandments and regulations that Yahweh en-
joined upon the Israelites, through Moses, on the steppes of Moab, at the Jordan near Jericho." With the final laws given, and with Moses and the Israelites
located at the border of Canaan in Moab, there is nothing left for P but to
narrate Moses's death. Thus immediately after the last words of D, the conclusion of Moses's speech in Deuteronomy 31:47, the compiler naturally inserted
from P Yahweh's instructions to Moses to ascend Mount Nebo to die there
(32:48–52).[31]

As for J, the last pre-Deuteronomy passage brought the Israelites to the border
of Canaan in Moab (Num 21:16–20). There, Moses gave his deathbed speech,
a tribal poem concluding the Exodus period just as Jacob's deathbed speech in
Genesis 49 concluded the patriarchal period. This J poem is found in Deuteronomy 33. It was placed here by the compiler, after both the entirety of D and
the priestly narrative of Yahweh instructing Moses to ascend Mount Nebo to
die, because it begins by explicitly situating the poem as Moses's last act before
dying: "This is the blessing with which Moses, the man of God, bade the Israelites farewell before he died" (Deut 33:1). This is thus the only logical place for
the poem to be.

All of the events in all of the sources that must have happened before Moses's death are presented in precisely the order that they need to be so as to
preserve the logical narrative chronology. Moses's actual death is told in Deuteronomy 34, by all three nondeuteronomic sources. As all three describe a
singular event—Moses cannot die more than once, after all—the compiler has
interwoven them into a single narrative. Both J and P are present in Deuteronomy 34:1. J reads "Moses went up to the summit of Pisgah, and Yahweh showed
him the whole land," and continues through the end of 34:4. The location at
Pisgah conforms to the end of J's wilderness itinerary in Numbers 21:16–20,
which concludes "at the peak of Pisgah, overlooking the wasteland." The recollection of the patriarchal promise in Deuteronomy 34:4, for its part, is taken
verbatim from Exodus 33:1, a J text. P reads in Deuteronomy 34:1, "Moses went
up from the steppes of Moab to Mount Nebo, opposite Jericho." The location
"the steppes of Moab" is unique to P (cf. Num 22:1; 26:3, 63; 31:12; 35:1; 36:13).
"Mount Nebo, opposite Jericho" is the place of Moses's death according to
Deuteronomy 32:49, a text we have already identified as P.

P, having just identified the location of Moses's death, continues with the first three words of Deuteronomy 34:5: "Moses died there," and with the final clause of the verse, "at the command of Yahweh." This final clause is exclusively priestly, occurring in Exodus 17:1, Leviticus 24:12, and thirteen times in Numbers. It continues and concludes finally with Deuteronomy 34:7–9, with the note of Moses's age of 120 years and physical state at his death, where the age agrees entirely with P's chronology: Moses being eighty years old at the time of the Exodus (Exod 7:7) and the wilderness period lasting forty years (Num 14:34);[32] the thirty-day mourning over Moses, identical to the thirty-day mourning over Aaron in Numbers 20:29; and the new leadership of Joshua, with explicit reference to the P ritual in which Moses laid his hands on Joshua in Numbers 27:23. J must also have contained at least the plain words "Moses died" in Deuteronomy 34:5, or some slight variation, and J concludes with the notice of Moses's burial in 34:6—where the location again matches well with Numbers 21:20, involving a "valley in the land of Moab."

E, for its part, begins in Deuteronomy 34 with the announcement of Moses's death in 34:5—"Moses the servant of Yahweh died there, in the land of Moab"—and continues in 34:10–12, with the assessment of his leadership. The notion of Moses as Yahweh's servant is known from E in Numbers 12:7, while Moses's unique status as prophet and the concept of Yahweh speaking exclusively to Moses "face to face" is, as noted already, typical of E.

Deuteronomy is not a unique case in the Pentateuch by any stretch. All the pieces—including the D document—are ordered logically and chronologically by the compiler. That D exists in an essentially continuous block of text is due to its internal features: it is a single speech, and it takes place in a single day: the last day of the history recounted in the Pentateuch.

Case Study III

The Revolt in the Wilderness, Numbers 16

¹Now Korah, son of Izhar son of Kohath son of Levi, betook himself, along with Dathan and Abiram sons of Eliab, and On son of Peleth— descendants of Reuben—²to rise up against Moses, together with two hundred and fifty Israelites, chieftains of the community, chosen in the assembly, men of repute. ³They combined against Moses and Aaron and said to them, "You have gone too far! For all the community are holy, all of them, and the Lord is in their midst. Why then do you raise yourselves above the Lord's congregation?" ⁴When Moses heard this, he fell on his face. ⁵Then he spoke to Korah and all his company, saying, "Come morning, the Lord will make known who is his and who is holy, and will grant him access to himself; he will grant access to the one he has chosen. ⁶Do this: You, Korah and all your band, take fire pans, ⁷and tomorrow put fire in them and lay incense on them before the Lord. Then the man whom

¹וַיִּקַּח קֹרַח בֶּן־יִצְהָר בֶּן־קְהָת בֶּן־לֵוִי וְדָתָן וַאֲבִירָם בְּנֵי אֱלִיאָב וְאוֹן בֶּן־פֶּלֶת בְּנֵי רְאוּבֵן: ²וַיָּקֻמוּ לִפְנֵי מֹשֶׁה וַאֲנָשִׁים מִבְּנֵי־יִשְׂרָאֵל חֲמִשִּׁים וּמָאתָיִם נְשִׂיאֵי עֵדָה קְרִאֵי מוֹעֵד אַנְשֵׁי־שֵׁם: ³וַיִּקָּהֲלוּ עַל־מֹשֶׁה וְעַל־אַהֲרֹן וַיֹּאמְרוּ אֲלֵהֶם רַב־ לָכֶם כִּי כָל־הָעֵדָה כֻּלָּם קְדֹשִׁים וּבְתוֹכָם יְהוָה וּמַדּוּעַ תִּתְנַשְּׂאוּ עַל־קְהַל יְהוָה: ⁴וַיִּשְׁמַע מֹשֶׁה וַיִּפֹּל עַל־פָּנָיו: ⁵וַיְדַבֵּר אֶל־קֹרַח וְאֶל־כָּל־עֲדָתוֹ לֵאמֹר בֹּקֶר וְיֹדַע יְהוָה אֶת־אֲשֶׁר־לוֹ וְאֶת־הַקָּדוֹשׁ וְהִקְרִיב אֵלָיו וְאֵת אֲשֶׁר יִבְחַר־בּוֹ יַקְרִיב אֵלָיו: ⁶זֹאת עֲשׂוּ קְחוּ־לָכֶם מַחְתּוֹת קֹרַח וְכָל־עֲדָתוֹ: ⁷וּתְנוּ בָהֵן אֵשׁ וְשִׂימוּ עֲלֵיהֶן קְטֹרֶת לִפְנֵי יְהוָה מָחָר וְהָיָה הָאִישׁ אֲשֶׁר־יִבְחַר יְהוָה הוּא הַקָּדוֹשׁ רַב־לָכֶם בְּנֵי לֵוִי: ⁸וַיֹּאמֶר מֹשֶׁה אֶל־קֹרַח שִׁמְעוּ־ נָא בְּנֵי לֵוִי: ⁹הַמְעַט מִכֶּם כִּי־הִבְדִּיל אֱלֹהֵי יִשְׂרָאֵל אֶתְכֶם מֵעֲדַת יִשְׂרָאֵל לְהַקְרִיב אֶתְכֶם אֵלָיו לַעֲבֹד אֶת־עֲבֹדַת מִשְׁכַּן יְהוָה וְלַעֲמֹד לִפְנֵי הָעֵדָה לְשָׁרְתָם: ¹⁰וַיַּקְרֵב אֹתְךָ וְאֶת־כָּל־אַחֶיךָ בְנֵי־לֵוִי אִתָּךְ וּבִקַּשְׁתֶּם גַּם־כְּהֻנָּה: ¹¹לָכֵן אַתָּה וְכָל־עֲדָתְךָ הַנֹּעָדִים עַל־יְהוָה וְאַהֲרֹן מַה־הוּא כִּי תַלִּינוּ עָלָיו: ¹²וַיִּשְׁלַח מֹשֶׁה לִקְרֹא לְדָתָן וְלַאֲבִירָם בְּנֵי אֱלִיאָב וַיֹּאמְרוּ לֹא נַעֲלֶה: ¹³הַמְעַט כִּי הֶעֱלִיתָנוּ מֵאֶרֶץ זָבַת חָלָב וּדְבַשׁ לַהֲמִיתֵנוּ בַּמִּדְבָּר כִּי־תִשְׂתָּרֵר עָלֵינוּ גַּם־הִשְׂתָּרֵר: ¹⁴אַף לֹא אֶל־אֶרֶץ זָבַת חָלָב וּדְבַשׁ הֲבִיאֹתָנוּ וַתִּתֶּן־לָנוּ נַחֲלַת שָׂדֶה וָכָרֶם הַעֵינֵי הָאֲנָשִׁים הָהֵם תְּנַקֵּר לֹא נַעֲלֶה: ¹⁵וַיִּחַר לְמֹשֶׁה מְאֹד וַיֹּאמֶר אֶל־יְהוָה אַל־

the Lord chooses, he shall be the holy one. You have gone too far, sons of Levi!" [8]Moses said further to Korah, "Hear me, sons of Levi. [9]Is it not enough for you that the God of Israel has set you apart from the community of Israel and given you access to Him, to perform the duties of the Lord's Tabernacle and to minister to the community and serve them? [10]Now that he has advanced you and all your fellow Levites with you, do you seek the priesthood too? [11]Truly, it is against the Lord that you and all your company have banded together. For who is Aaron that you should rail against him?" [12]Moses sent for Dathan and Abiram, sons of Eliab; but they said, "We will not come! [13]Is it not enough that you brought us from a land flowing with milk and honey to have us die in the wilderness, that you would also lord it over us? [14] Even if you had brought us to a land flowing with milk and honey, and given us possession of fields and vineyards, should you gouge out those men's eyes? We will not come!" [15]Moses was much aggrieved and he said to the Lord, "Pay no regard to their oblation. I have not taken the ass of any one of them, nor have I wronged any one of them." [16]And Moses said to Korah, "Tomorrow, you and all your company appear before the Lord, you and they and Aaron. [17]Each of you take his fire pan and lay incense on it, and each of you bring his fire pan

תִּפֶּן אֶל־מִנְחָתָם לֹא חֲמוֹר אֶחָד מֵהֶם נָשָׂאתִי
וְלֹא הֲרֵעֹתִי אֶת־אַחַד מֵהֶם: [16]וַיֹּאמֶר מֹשֶׁה אֶל־
קֹרַח אַתָּה וְכָל־עֲדָתְךָ הֱיוּ לִפְנֵי יְהוָה אַתָּה וָהֵם
וְאַהֲרֹן מָחָר: [17]וּקְחוּ אִישׁ מַחְתָּתוֹ וּנְתַתֶּם עֲלֵיהֶם
קְטֹרֶת וְהִקְרַבְתֶּם לִפְנֵי יְהוָה אִישׁ מַחְתָּתוֹ חֲמִשִּׁים
וּמָאתַיִם מַחְתֹּת וְאַתָּה וְאַהֲרֹן אִישׁ מַחְתָּתוֹ:
[18]וַיִּקְחוּ אִישׁ מַחְתָּתוֹ וַיִּתְּנוּ עֲלֵיהֶם אֵשׁ וַיָּשִׂימוּ
עֲלֵיהֶם קְטֹרֶת וַיַּעַמְדוּ פֶּתַח אֹהֶל מוֹעֵד וּמֹשֶׁה
וְאַהֲרֹן: [19]וַיַּקְהֵל עֲלֵיהֶם קֹרַח אֶת־כָּל־הָעֵדָה אֶל־
פֶּתַח אֹהֶל מוֹעֵד וַיֵּרָא כְבוֹד־יְהוָה אֶל־כָּל־
הָעֵדָה: [20]וַיְדַבֵּר יְהוָה אֶל־מֹשֶׁה וְאֶל־אַהֲרֹן
לֵאמֹר: [21]הִבָּדְלוּ מִתּוֹךְ הָעֵדָה הַזֹּאת וַאֲכַלֶּה
אֹתָם כְּרָגַע: [22]וַיִּפְּלוּ עַל־פְּנֵיהֶם וַיֹּאמְרוּ אֵל אֱלֹהֵי
הָרוּחֹת לְכָל־בָּשָׂר הָאִישׁ אֶחָד יֶחֱטָא וְעַל כָּל־
הָעֵדָה תִּקְצֹף: [23]וַיְדַבֵּר יְהוָה אֶל־מֹשֶׁה לֵּאמֹר:
[24]דַּבֵּר אֶל־הָעֵדָה לֵאמֹר הֵעָלוּ מִסָּבִיב לְמִשְׁכַּן
קֹרַח דָּתָן וַאֲבִירָם: [25]וַיָּקָם מֹשֶׁה וַיֵּלֶךְ אֶל־דָּתָן
וַאֲבִירָם וַיֵּלְכוּ אַחֲרָיו זִקְנֵי יִשְׂרָאֵל: [26]וַיְדַבֵּר אֶל־
הָעֵדָה לֵאמֹר סוּרוּ נָא מֵעַל אָהֳלֵי הָאֲנָשִׁים
הָרְשָׁעִים הָאֵלֶּה וְאַל־תִּגְּעוּ בְּכָל־אֲשֶׁר לָהֶם פֶּן
תִּסָּפוּ בְּכָל־חַטֹּאתָם: [27]וַיֵּעָלוּ מֵעַל מִשְׁכַּן־קֹרַח
דָּתָן וַאֲבִירָם מִסָּבִיב וְדָתָן וַאֲבִירָם יָצְאוּ נִצָּבִים
פֶּתַח אָהֳלֵיהֶם וּנְשֵׁיהֶם וּבְנֵיהֶם וְטַפָּם: [28]וַיֹּאמֶר
מֹשֶׁה בְּזֹאת תֵּדְעוּן כִּי־יְהוָה שְׁלָחַנִי לַעֲשׂוֹת אֵת
כָּל־הַמַּעֲשִׂים הָאֵלֶּה כִּי־לֹא מִלִּבִּי: [29]אִם־כְּמוֹת
כָּל־הָאָדָם יְמֻתוּן אֵלֶּה וּפְקֻדַּת כָּל־הָאָדָם יִפָּקֵד
עֲלֵיהֶם לֹא יְהוָה שְׁלָחָנִי: [30]וְאִם־בְּרִיאָה יִבְרָא
יְהוָה וּפָצְתָה הָאֲדָמָה אֶת־פִּיהָ וּבָלְעָה אֹתָם
וְאֶת־כָּל־אֲשֶׁר לָהֶם וְיָרְדוּ חַיִּים שְׁאֹלָה וִידַעְתֶּם
כִּי נִאֲצוּ הָאֲנָשִׁים הָאֵלֶּה אֶת־יְהוָה: [31]וַיְהִי כְּכַלֹּתוֹ
לְדַבֵּר אֵת כָּל־הַדְּבָרִים הָאֵלֶּה וַתִּבָּקַע הָאֲדָמָה
אֲשֶׁר תַּחְתֵּיהֶם: [32]וַתִּפְתַּח הָאָרֶץ אֶת־פִּיהָ וַתִּבְלַע
אֹתָם וְאֶת־בָּתֵּיהֶם וְאֵת כָּל־הָאָדָם אֲשֶׁר לְקֹרַח
וְאֵת כָּל־הָרְכוּשׁ: [33]וַיֵּרְדוּ הֵם וְכָל־אֲשֶׁר לָהֶם
חַיִּים שְׁאֹלָה וַתְּכַס עֲלֵיהֶם הָאָרֶץ וַיֹּאבְדוּ מִתּוֹךְ
הַקָּהָל: [34]וְכָל־יִשְׂרָאֵל אֲשֶׁר סְבִיבֹתֵיהֶם נָסוּ לְקֹלָם
כִּי אָמְרוּ פֶּן־תִּבְלָעֵנוּ הָאָרֶץ: [35]וְאֵשׁ יָצְאָה מֵאֵת
יְהוָה וַתֹּאכַל אֵת הַחֲמִשִּׁים וּמָאתַיִם אִישׁ מַקְרִיבֵי
הַקְּטֹרֶת:

before the Lord, two hundred and fifty fire pans; you and Aaron also [bring] your fire pans." [18]Each of them took his fire pan, put fire in it, laid incense on it, and took his place at the entrance of the Tent of Meeting, as did Moses and Aaron. [19]Korah gathered the whole community against them at the entrance of the Tent of Meeting. Then the Presence of the Lord appeared to the whole community, [20]and the Lord spoke to Moses and Aaron, saying, [21]"Stand back from this community that I may annihilate them in an instant!" [22]But they fell on their faces and said, "O God, source of the breath of all flesh! When one man sins, will you be wrathful with the whole community?" [23]The Lord spoke to Moses, saying, [24]"Speak to the community and say: Withdraw from about the abodes of Korah, Dathan, and Abiram." [25]Moses rose and went to Dathan and Abiram, the elders of Israel following him. [26]He addressed the community, saying, "Move away from the tents of these wicked men and touch nothing that belongs to them, lest you be wiped out for all their sins." [27]So they withdrew from about the abodes of Korah, Dathan, and Abiram. Now Dathan and Abiram had come out and they stood at the entrance of their tents, with their wives, their children, and their little ones. [28]And Moses said, "By this you shall know that it was the Lord who sent me to do all these

things; that they are not of my own
devising: [29]if these men die as all
men do, if their lot be the common
fate of all mankind, it was not the
Lord who sent me. [30]But if the Lord
brings about something unheard-of,
so that the ground opens its mouth
and swallows them up with all that
belongs to them, and they go down
alive into Sheol, you shall know that
these men have spurned the Lord."
[31]Scarcely had he finished speaking
all these words when the ground under them burst asunder, [32]and the
earth opened its mouth and swallowed them up with their households, all Korah's people and all their
possessions. [33]They went down alive
into Sheol, with all that belonged
to them; the earth closed over them
and they vanished from the midst of
the congregation. [34]All Israel around
them fled at their shrieks, for they
said, "The earth might swallow us!"
[35]And a fire went forth from the Lord
and consumed the two hundred and
fifty men offering the incense.

Numbers 16 begins with a list of Israelites who brought claims against Moses in the midst of the wilderness wanderings. We are introduced to Korah, a
member of the Kohathite clan of the tribe of Levi; Dathan and Abiram, two
Reubenites;[1] and 250 unnamed Israelite leaders (vv. 1–2). These men are said
in v. 2 to have risen against Moses;[2] in v. 3, they oppose both Moses and Aaron.[3]
In v. 3, we hear the details of their complaint: Moses and Aaron have elevated
themselves above the rest of the Israelites, even though the entire community
is holy and Yahweh is among them all. The practical meaning of this claim is
elucidated by Moses's response in vv. 5–11. The issue is not simply who is holy
and who is not; it is, rather, who has the standing to minister in the cult, who
has the right to approach the sanctum—and, it should be understood, who has

the right to receive the perquisites of meat and money that come with the priesthood. This will be determined, according to Moses, by a test: those who think themselves worthy of participating in the priestly duties will bring their fire pans and offer incense before Yahweh, and Yahweh himself will determine who may serve him. Moses goes on to accuse his adversaries of trying to rise above their divinely ordained status: it is not enough that the Levites should be allowed to care for the Tabernacle and be the cultic leaders of the community; now they want to act as proper priests as well, offering the sacrifices and performing the rituals. Moses accuses them of revolting not against himself and Aaron, but, insofar as the elevation of Aaron's line to the priesthood was commanded at Sinai, against Yahweh himself.

Although we are introduced to a number of characters in vv. 1–2, from v. 3 on only some are mentioned: Korah and his band—that is, the 250 Israelite leaders (vv. 5, 6, 8). It is also clear that the complaint and Moses's response are about the status of the Levites relative to the priestly descendants of Aaron (vv. 7–10). Since Korah is identified as a Levite, this is sensible; it is less obvious, however, what place Dathan and Abiram, two members of the tribe of Reuben, would have in this argument; and, indeed, they go unmentioned in vv. 3–11.

Verses 3–11 constitute a unified text; its argument is coherent and literarily well crafted. The complaint in v. 3 begins with the accusation "You have gone too far" (*rab lākem*); Moses turns this accusation around and returns it in v. 7, and again, although with a variation, in v. 9 ("is it not enough for you"; *ham'aṭ mikkem*). The complaint is ostensibly directed again Moses and Aaron in v. 3, and the claim is made that Yahweh is equally present for all the Israelites; Moses's final words in response, in v. 11, state the reverse: it is not Moses and Aaron who are being castigated, but rather Yahweh himself (in a clear parallel to the P story of the manna in Exod 16:7–8). The Levites want the right to approach Yahweh cultically (*hiqrîb*), as Moses's proposed test indicates, but Moses cleverly notes in v. 10 that Yahweh had already brought the Levites to him by setting them apart (*hiqrîb*). A similar wordplay is at work when the narrator refers to Korah's band in v. 5 as a "company" (*'ēdāʰ*; better, "congregation"): this word is used almost exclusively elsewhere—and here also, as in v. 9—for the Israelite community as a whole; its use here to designate Korah's group suggests that by attempting to overthrow the divinely imposed hierarchy of priests and Levites, they are in essence constituting a countercommunity and are no longer part of the Israelite congregation.[4]

On narrative grounds alone, these verses can belong only to P. The cultic distinction between the priests and the Levites is presupposed in this text, and this distinction has been introduced only by, indeed is known only to, P.[5]

The method of testing proposed by Moses also presupposes knowledge of how the cult is administered and by whom, and this information too is provided only in P.[6] These verses are also saturated with priestly language: "community" ('*ēdā*ʰ), "holy," "congregation" (*qāhāl*), "approach" (*hiqrîb*) (in the cultic sense), "fire pans," "incense," "serve" ('*ābad*) (cultically), "tabernacle," "minister," "priesthood."[7]

In v. 12, however, we encounter a sudden change. We are told that Moses sends for Dathan and Abiram, the two Reubenites, who refuse to come to him.[8] Reading the text as a whole, this is puzzling: if Dathan and Abiram were authentically part of Korah's group, as vv. 1–2 suggest, then they should have been standing already before Moses; indeed, they should have been addressed already as part of Moses's challenge to the Levites in the preceding verses. That they are apparently elsewhere confirms the suspicion that they play no part in the priestly story of vv. 3–11. Further, just as Dathan and Abiram were absent from vv. 3–11, so too do Korah and the 250 leaders go unmentioned in vv. 12–15. We may, therefore, confidently separate the introduction of Dathan and Abiram in vv. 1b–2aα (through "Moses") from that of Korah in v. 1a. We may also recognize that the continuation of v. 2, describing the 250 tribal leaders, belongs with the mention of Korah in v. 1a; this permits us to understand the first word of the chapter, *wayyiqqaḥ*, not in the abstract sense of "Korah betook himself," as in the New Jewish Publication Society translation, but rather as having the 250 tribal leaders as its object: "Korah, son of Izhar, son of Kohath, son of Levi, took two hundred and fifty Israelites."[9]

The speech of Dathan and Abiram in vv. 13–14 presents an entirely different argument from that of Korah in v. 3.[10] There is no mention of Levites or of the cult at all. Dathan and Abiram accuse Moses not of arrogating to himself any specific duties in which they want to share, but rather of being a dictatorial leader in general, of having taken them from a bountiful land into the desolate wilderness.[11] Since he has brought them nothing but hardship, what right does he have to rule over them single-handedly? Moses's response in v. 15 reflects this new complaint: he tells Yahweh that he has done nothing wrong, that the broad accusation against him of misconduct is groundless.[12] The difference in content and theme of these verses is matched by a similar difference in language. Absent are all the priestly terms and concepts that we encountered in such density in vv. 3–11. Verses 12–15 should be attributed to one of the nonpriestly documents. We may also note that Aaron is not part of the speech of Dathan and Abiram or the response to it; these passages deal with Moses alone. This observation allows us to return again to the beginning of the story, where there are two descriptions of rebellion: "they rose up against Moses" in v. 2, and "they combined against Moses and Aaron" in v. 3. The latter, we have already seen, belongs to the P narrative; we are now in a position to attribute the former to the nonpriestly story.[13]

In vv. 16–17, we find ourselves back in the story of Korah. Moses addresses Korah and instructs him and his people—using the now-expected priestly term "community" (*'ēdāʰ*)—to appear the next day before Yahweh, and Aaron is to be there as well. The details of the test are repeated and given somewhat more detail: Korah, each of the 250 leaders, and Aaron are all to take their fire pans, place incense on them, and bring them before Yahweh. In v. 18 we find the fulfillment of Moses's command in the preceding verses, and in v. 19 we are told that Korah assembled not only his cohort, but the entire Israelite community to witness the proceedings at the Tent of Meeting and that the *kābôd* of Yahweh appeared to the entire community. Strikingly, the precise sequence of words used here for gathering (*q-h-l* [hiphil]) the entire community (*kol-hā'ēdāʰ*) at the Tent of Meeting (*'el-petah 'ōhel mô'ēd*) appear elsewhere only in Leviticus 8:3—at the beginning of the investiture of Aaron and his sons. Thus the priestly author subtly emphasizes the true nature of Korah's rebellion: he is trying to reenact, or perhaps undo, the act by which Aaron was raised above him.[14] Verses 20–22 describe Yahweh's intention to destroy the entire community and Moses and Aaron's plea that Yahweh punish only those who have actually sinned. We may note that Moses's (and Aaron's) reaction to Yahweh's words is to fall on his face; he did the same thing upon hearing Korah's words in v. 4. The author by this mechanism draws a nice parallel between the speeches of Korah and Yahweh: both will lead, whether indirectly or directly, to the destruction of the Israelite community.[15]

This entire section reads as a unity, is the natural continuation of the Korah story from P, and, as we have come to expect, contains language typical of the priestly source. Again, Dathan and Abiram are not mentioned. The situation is more complicated, however, in vv. 23–24. Here Yahweh tells Moses to instruct the community to withdraw from around the dwelling of Korah, Dathan, and Abiram. Although the majority of these verses are still clearly part of the P story—the presence of the entire community connects this passage with what immediately precedes it—the mention of Dathan and Abiram as well as Korah is problematic. The solution, however, is relatively simple: the compiler, in the course of combining the stories of Korah's rebellion and Dathan and Abiram, has inserted the names of the Reubenites here in an effort to create a single narrative out of two. We may note not only the priestly term *miškan*, but also the fact that it is rendered in the singular, for it is only Korah's dwelling that was originally mentioned here.[16]

The redactional status of the words "Dathan and Abiram" in v. 24 is cemented by the following verse, v. 25, in which Moses goes to Dathan and Abiram with the Israelite elders in tow.[17] If the names in v. 24 were authentic, then Moses would not have to go anywhere to confront Dathan and Abiram; they, along with the rest of Korah's band—and the rest of the Israelite community as a whole—should be standing with Moses and Aaron at the entrance to the Tent of Meeting. That Moses has to go to them signals that they were not part of the priestly story. Furthermore, Moses's going to Dathan and Abiram is directly related to the nonpriestly narrative in v. 12 (and v. 14), in which Dathan and Abiram refused to come up to Moses when called. Since they did not come to him, Moses is forced to go to them. Verse 25 therefore picks up directly on the end of v. 15, as the logical continuation of the nonpriestly story.

In v. 26, Moses addresses the community, telling them to move away from the tents of the evildoers so that they will not be punished along with the sinners. The first words of this verse are the direct word-for-word fulfillment of Yahweh's command to Moses in v. 24 and are therefore P. So too is the content of Moses's address: Moses was instructed in v. 24 to tell the community to withdraw from Korah's dwelling, and that is what he does in v. 26. That he does not use the precise words of v. 24 to do so poses little problem: the content of the message is the same and connects not only to Yahweh's speech of v. 24, but also to Moses and Aaron's plea in v. 22, as the keyword "sin" serves to indicate.[18] And indeed, when the people obey in v. 27a, they do so with the expected word-for-word fulfillment of Yahweh's instructions from v. 24: "they withdrew from about the abode of Korah."[19] Note that in v. 27a, again, the compiler has added the names Dathan and Abiram in an effort to bring his two narratives together. It is not coincidence that this redactional move takes place in the exact same context in both verses. It is further noteworthy that just as the insertion in v. 24 is followed by a verse from the nonpriestly story that mentions Dathan and Abiram by name, so too the redactional insertion in v. 27a is followed by the resumption of the nonpriestly story in v. 27b, again with the names Dathan and Abiram prominently mentioned.

In v. 27b, Dathan and Abiram have come out of their tents—note the fact that they are, again, obviously not at the Tent of Meeting with the rest of the Israelites as in P, and that their dwellings are described in the plural, since there are, after all, two of them, as opposed to the singular *miškān* of Korah—along with their families, in a direct continuation from v. 25. The description of them standing (*n-ṣ-b*) by their tents (*petaḥ 'oholêhem*) finds its only true parallel in Exodus 33:8, where all the Israelites stand by the entrances to their tents while Moses communicates with Yahweh in the Tent of Meeting. It is perhaps not coincidental that Dathan and Abiram, who have challenged Moses's authority over them, take up the very position that represents the people's recognition of Moses's direct connection with the deity. In vv. 28–30, Moses puts forth a proposition, another test, though one distinctly different from that of P.[20] Whereas in P the Levites are to bring their fire pans and attempt to engage in the standard priestly cultic procedure, in the nonpriestly story Moses asks Yahweh to do something new and previously unheard-of, that is, to make the earth open up and swallow Dathan and Abiram alive.[21]

It is in Moses's speech here in vv. 28–30 that we understand the precise nature of Dathan and Abiram's challenge. Their objection, in vv. 13–14, was to Moses's leadership; here Moses clarifies that he was acting only as Yahweh instructed him, not on his own or for his own benefit: "By this you shall know that it was Yahweh who sent me to do all these things; that they are not of my own devising." The underlying issue in this story, therefore, is the status of Moses as an authentic prophet.

The nonpriestly story continues from v. 30 directly into vv. 31–33, in which Moses's prediction immediately comes to pass, and in virtually the same language: the ground opens and swallows up Dathan and Abiram and their households, who had been introduced proleptically in v. 27b. We may note the ironic reversal at work here: Dathan and Abiram, who said twice to Moses, "We will not come," literally, "We will not go up," spoke truly: in the end, they "go down" into the earth.[22] In v. 32, we find Korah's name mentioned, as one of the things swallowed by the earth. As Korah has played no part in the nonpriestly narrative to this point, we are again faced with an addition by the compiler.[23] Just as the compiler added the names Dathan and Abiram to the P story in vv. 24 and 27, so too he added the word "Korah" here in v. 32.[24] Again, the purpose of this addition is clear, as is its secondary nature.

Verse 34 relates that "all Israel," who were evidently standing around Dathan's and Abiram's tents, fled in fear that they too would be swallowed up. This verse forms the conclusion to the nonpriestly story, as the mention of the punishment makes clear. We may also note that according to the nonpriestly story, the people—not the community, as in P, but "all Israel"—are standing close enough to the tents of Dathan and Abiram to fear for their lives, such that they flee from the area. This is in contrast to the P story, in which the people have been given specific instructions to move away from the dwelling of Korah and have in fact done so. Verse 34 thus provides another justification for the assignment of vv. 26–27 to P.

Just as v. 34 is the clear conclusion to the nonpriestly story, so v. 35 provides the expected conclusion to the P story: fire goes forth from Yahweh and consumes the 250 men offering incense, that is, Korah's band, who have brought their fire pans to the Tent of Meeting. This verse continues directly from v. 27; the instant that the community at large moves out of harm's way, Yahweh kills Korah and his group.[25] Were we to try to read this chapter as a unity, we would be forced to wonder how it is that Korah was first swallowed by the earth in v. 32 and then burned in v. 35.[26]

As we have seen, the canonical text of Numbers 16 divides neatly into two discrete narrative strands, each of which tells a different story, about a different event, using different language.[27] The two narratives read independently as follows:[28]

P NARRATIVE	NONPRIESTLY NARRATIVE

P NARRATIVE:

¹וַיִּקַּח קֹרַח בֶּן־יִצְהָר בֶּן־קְהָת בֶּן־לֵוִי ²אֲנָשִׁים מִבְּנֵי־יִשְׂרָאֵל חֲמִשִּׁים וּמָאתָיִם נְשִׂיאֵי עֵדָה קְרֻאֵי מוֹעֵד אַנְשֵׁי־שֵׁם: ³וַיִּקָּהֲלוּ עַל־מֹשֶׁה וְעַל־אַהֲרֹן וַיֹּאמְרוּ אֲלֵהֶם רַב־לָכֶם כִּי כָל־הָעֵדָה כֻּלָּם קְדֹשִׁים וּבְתוֹכָם יְהוָה וּמַדּוּעַ תִּתְנַשְּׂאוּ עַל־קְהַל יְהוָה: ⁴וַיִּשְׁמַע מֹשֶׁה וַיִּפֹּל עַל־פָּנָיו: ⁵וַיְדַבֵּר אֶל־ קֹרַח וְאֶל־כָּל־עֲדָתוֹ לֵאמֹר בֹּקֶר וְיֹדַע יְהוָה אֶת־ אֲשֶׁר־לוֹ וְאֶת־הַקָּדוֹשׁ וְהִקְרִיב אֵלָיו וְאֵת אֲשֶׁר יִבְחַר־בּוֹ יַקְרִיב אֵלָיו: ⁶זֹאת עֲשׂוּ קְחוּ־לָכֶם מַחְתּוֹת קֹרַח וְכָל־עֲדָתוֹ: ⁷וּתְנוּ בָהֵן אֵשׁ וְשִׂימוּ עֲלֵיהֶן קְטֹרֶת לִפְנֵי יְהוָה מָחָר וְהָיָה הָאִישׁ אֲשֶׁר־ יִבְחַר יְהוָה הוּא הַקָּדוֹשׁ רַב־לָכֶם בְּנֵי לֵוִי: ⁸וַיֹּאמֶר מֹשֶׁה אֶל־קֹרַח שִׁמְעוּ־נָא בְּנֵי לֵוִי: ⁹הַמְעַט מִכֶּם כִּי־הִבְדִּיל אֱלֹהֵי יִשְׂרָאֵל אֶתְכֶם מֵעֲדַת יִשְׂרָאֵל לְהַקְרִיב אֶתְכֶם אֵלָיו לַעֲבֹד אֶת־ עֲבֹדַת מִשְׁכַּן יְהוָה וְלַעֲמֹד לִפְנֵי הָעֵדָה לְשָׁרְתָם: ¹⁰וַיַּקְרֵב אֹתְךָ וְאֶת־כָּל־אַחֶיךָ בְנֵי־לֵוִי אִתָּךְ וּבִקַּשְׁתֶּם גַּם־כְּהֻנָּה: ¹¹לָכֵן אַתָּה וְכָל־עֲדָתְךָ הַנֹּעָדִים עַל־יְהוָה וְאַהֲרֹן מַה־הוּא כִּי תַלִּונוּ עָלָיו: ¹⁶וַיֹּאמֶר מֹשֶׁה אֶל־קֹרַח אַתָּה וְכָל־עֲדָתְךָ הֱיוּ לִפְנֵי יְהוָה אַתָּה וָהֵם וְאַהֲרֹן מָחָר: ¹⁷וּקְחוּ

NONPRIESTLY NARRATIVE:

¹דָּתָן וַאֲבִירָם בְּנֵי אֱלִיאָב וְאוֹן בֶּן־פֶּלֶת בְּנֵי רְאוּבֵן: ²וַיָּקֻמוּ לִפְנֵי מֹשֶׁה ¹²וַיִּשְׁלַח מֹשֶׁה לִקְרֹא לְדָתָן וְלַאֲבִירָם בְּנֵי אֱלִיאָב וַיֹּאמְרוּ לֹא נַעֲלֶה: ¹³הַמְעַט כִּי הֶעֱלִיתָנוּ מֵאֶרֶץ זָבַת חָלָב וּדְבַשׁ לַהֲמִיתֵנוּ בַּמִּדְבָּר כִּי־תִשְׂתָּרֵר עָלֵינוּ גַּם־הִשְׂתָּרֵר: ¹⁴אַף לֹא אֶל־אֶרֶץ זָבַת חָלָב וּדְבַשׁ הֲבִיאֹתָנוּ וַתִּתֶּן־לָנוּ נַחֲלַת שָׂדֶה וָכָרֶם הַעֵינֵי הָאֲנָשִׁים הָהֵם תְּנַקֵּר לֹא נַעֲלֶה: ¹⁵וַיִּחַר לְמֹשֶׁה מְאֹד וַיֹּאמֶר אֶל־ יְהוָה אַל־תֵּפֶן אֶל־מִנְחָתָם לֹא חֲמוֹר אֶחָד מֵהֶם נָשָׂאתִי וְלֹא הֲרֵעֹתִי אֶת־אַחַד מֵהֶם: ²⁵וַיָּקָם מֹשֶׁה וַיֵּלֶךְ אֶל־דָּתָן וַאֲבִירָם וַיֵּלְכוּ אַחֲרָיו זִקְנֵי יִשְׂרָאֵל: ²⁷וְדָתָן וַאֲבִירָם יָצְאוּ נִצָּבִים פֶּתַח אָהֳלֵיהֶם וּנְשֵׁיהֶם וּבְנֵיהֶם וְטַפָּם: ²⁸וַיֹּאמֶר מֹשֶׁה בְּזֹאת תֵּדְעוּן כִּי־יְהוָה שְׁלָחַנִי לַעֲשׂוֹת אֵת כָּל־הַמַּעֲשִׂים הָאֵלֶּה כִּי־לֹא מִלִּבִּי: ²⁹אִם־כְּמוֹת כָּל־הָאָדָם יְמֻתוּן אֵלֶּה וּפְקֻדַּת כָּל־הָאָדָם יִפָּקֵד עֲלֵיהֶם לֹא יְהוָה שְׁלָחָנִי: ³⁰וְאִם־בְּרִיאָה יִבְרָא יְהוָה וּפָצְתָה הָאֲדָמָה אֶת־פִּיהָ וּבָלְעָה אֹתָם וְאֶת־כָּל־אֲשֶׁר לָהֶם וְיָרְדוּ חַיִּים שְׁאֹלָה וִידַעְתֶּם כִּי נִאֲצוּ הָאֲנָשִׁים הָאֵלֶּה אֶת־יְהוָה: ³¹וַיְהִי כְּכַלֹּתוֹ לְדַבֵּר אֵת כָּל־הַדְּבָרִים הָאֵלֶּה וַתִּבָּקַע הָאֲדָמָה אֲשֶׁר

אִישׁ מַחְתָּתוֹ וּנְתַתֶּם עֲלֵיהֶם קְטֹרֶת וְהִקְרַבְתֶּם
לִפְנֵי יְהוָה אִישׁ מַחְתָּתוֹ חֲמִשִּׁים וּמָאתַיִם מַחְתֹּת
וְאַתָּה וְאַהֲרֹן אִישׁ מַחְתָּתוֹ: 18וַיִּקְחוּ אִישׁ מַחְתָּתוֹ
וַיִּתְּנוּ עֲלֵיהֶם אֵשׁ וַיָּשִׂימוּ עֲלֵיהֶם קְטֹרֶת וַיַּעַמְדוּ
פֶּתַח אֹהֶל מוֹעֵד וּמֹשֶׁה וְאַהֲרֹן: 19וַיַּקְהֵל עֲלֵיהֶם
קֹרַח אֶת־כָּל־הָעֵדָה אֶל־פֶּתַח אֹהֶל מוֹעֵד וַיֵּרָא
כְבוֹד־יְהוָה אֶל־כָּל־הָעֵדָה: 20וַיְדַבֵּר יְהוָה אֶל־
מֹשֶׁה וְאֶל־אַהֲרֹן לֵאמֹר: 21הִבָּדְלוּ מִתּוֹךְ הָעֵדָה
הַזֹּאת וַאֲכַלֶּה אֹתָם כְּרָגַע: 22וַיִּפְּלוּ עַל־פְּנֵיהֶם
וַיֹּאמְרוּ אֵל אֱלֹהֵי הָרוּחֹת לְכָל־בָּשָׂר הָאִישׁ אֶחָד
יֶחֱטָא וְעַל כָּל־הָעֵדָה תִּקְצֹף: 23וַיְדַבֵּר יְהוָה
אֶל־מֹשֶׁה לֵּאמֹר: 24דַּבֵּר אֶל־הָעֵדָה לֵאמֹר הֵעָלוּ
מִסָּבִיב לְמִשְׁכַּן־קֹרַח: 26וַיְדַבֵּר אֶל־הָעֵדָה לֵאמֹר
סוּרוּ נָא מֵעַל אָהֳלֵי הָאֲנָשִׁים הָרְשָׁעִים הָאֵלֶּה
וְאַל־תִּגְּעוּ בְּכָל־אֲשֶׁר לָהֶם פֶּן־תִּסָּפוּ בְּכָל־
חַטֹּאתָם: 27וַיֵּעָלוּ מֵעַל מִשְׁכַּן־קֹרַח מִסָּבִיב 35וְאֵשׁ
יָצְאָה מֵאֵת יְהוָה וַתֹּאכַל אֵת הַחֲמִשִּׁים וּמָאתַיִם
אִישׁ מַקְרִיבֵי הַקְּטֹרֶת:

תַּחְתֵּיהֶם: 32וַתִּפְתַּח הָאָרֶץ אֶת־פִּיהָ וַתִּבְלַע אֹתָם
וְאֶת־בָּתֵּיהֶם וְאֵת כָּל־הָאָדָם 33וַיֵּרְדוּ הֵם וְכָל־
אֲשֶׁר לָהֶם חַיִּים שְׁאֹלָה וַתְּכַס עֲלֵיהֶם הָאָרֶץ
וַיֹּאבְדוּ מִתּוֹךְ הַקָּהָל: 34וְכָל־יִשְׂרָאֵל אֲשֶׁר
סְבִיבֹתֵיהֶם נָסוּ לְקֹלָם כִּי אָמְרוּ פֶּן־תִּבְלָעֵנוּ
הָאָרֶץ:

[1]Now Korah, son of Izhar son of Kohath son of Levi, took [2]two hundred and fifty Israelites, chieftains of the community, chosen in the assembly, men of repute. [3]They combined against Moses and Aaron and said to them, "You have gone too far! For all the community are holy, all of them, and the Lord is in their midst. Why then do you raise yourselves above the Lord's congregation?" [4]When Moses heard this, he fell on his face. [5]Then he spoke to Korah and all his company, saying, "Come morning, the Lord will make known who is his and who is holy, and will grant him access to himself; he will grant access to the one he has chosen. [6]Do this: You, Korah and all your band, take fire pans, [7]and tomor-

[1]Dathan and Abiram sons of Eliab, and On son of Peleth—descendants of Reuben—[2]rose up against Moses. [12]Moses sent for Dathan and Abiram, sons of Eliab; but they said, "We will not come! [13]Is it not enough that you brought us from a land flowing with milk and honey to have us die in the wilderness, that you would also lord it over us? [14]Even if you had brought us to a land flowing with milk and honey, and given us possession of fields and vineyards, should you gouge out those men's eyes? We will not come!" [15]Moses was much aggrieved and he said to the Lord, "Pay no regard to their oblation. I have not taken the ass of any one of them, nor have I wronged any one of them." [25]Moses rose and went to

row put fire in them and lay incense on them before the Lord. Then the man whom the Lord chooses, he shall be the holy one. You have gone too far, sons of Levi!" [8]Moses said further to Korah, "Hear me, sons of Levi. [9]Is it not enough for you that the God of Israel has set you apart from the community of Israel and given you access to him, to perform the duties of the Lord's Tabernacle and to minister to the community and serve them? [10]Now that he has advanced you and all your fellow Levites with you, do you seek the priesthood too? [11]Truly, it is against the Lord that you and all your company have banded together. For who is Aaron that you should rail against him?" [16]And Moses said to Korah, "Tomorrow, you and all your company appear before the Lord, you and they and Aaron. [17]Each of you take his fire pan and lay incense on it, and each of you bring his fire pan before the Lord, two hundred and fifty fire pans; you and Aaron also [bring] your fire pans." [18]Each of them took his fire pan, put fire in it, laid incense on it, and took his place at the entrance of the Tent of Meeting, as did Moses and Aaron. [19]Korah gathered the whole community against them at the entrance of the Tent of Meeting. Then the Presence of the Lord appeared to the whole community, [20]and the Lord spoke to Moses and Aaron, saying, [21]"Stand back from this community that I

Dathan and Abiram, the elders of Israel following him. [27]Now Dathan and Abiram had come out and they stood at the entrance of their tents, with their wives, their children, and their little ones. [28]And Moses said, "By this you shall know that it was the Lord who sent me to do all these things; that they are not of my own devising: [29]if these men die as all men do, if their lot be the common fate of all mankind, it was not the Lord who sent me. [30]But if the Lord brings about something unheard-of, so that the ground opens its mouth and swallows them up with all that belongs to them, and they go down alive into Sheol, you shall know that these men have spurned the Lord." [31]Scarcely had he finished speaking all these words when the ground under them burst asunder, [32]and the earth opened its mouth and swallowed them up with their households, and all their possessions. [33]They went down alive into Sheol, with all that belonged to them; the earth closed over them and they vanished from the midst of the congregation. [34]All Israel around them fled at their shrieks, for they said, "The earth might swallow us!"

may annihilate them in an instant!"
²²But they fell on their faces and said,
"O God, source of the breath of all
flesh! When one man sins, will you
be wrathful with the whole community?" ²³The Lord spoke to Moses,
saying, ²⁴"Speak to the community
and say: Withdraw from about the
abode of Korah." ²⁶He addressed
the community, saying, "Move away
from the tents of these wicked men
and touch nothing that belongs to
them, lest you be wiped out for all
their sins." ²⁷So they withdrew from
about the abode of Korah. ³⁵And a
fire went forth from the Lord and
consumed the two hundred and fifty
men offering the incense.

When read independently, the distinct natures of these two narratives, in content, theme, and language, are readily apparent. The priestly story relates a Levite rebellion against the priestly prerogatives granted solely to the line of Aaron, that is, the priests. Korah, a Levite, gathers a band of Israelite leaders to support his claim for levitical cultic rights. Korah is no ordinary Levite, how-ever: he is from the clan of the Kohathites, the group of Levites responsible for the transportation of the most sacred objects in the Tent of Meeting: the ark, the table, the lampstand, and the altar (Num 4:1–14).²⁹ Although each of the Levite clans is assigned a specific duty with regard to the Tabernacle, each of which is laid out in systematic fashion, only with regard to the Kohathites is a warning given to Moses: he must be particularly careful to prevent them from encroaching on the sacred space, so that they are not cut off from the rest of the Israelites (Num 4:17–20). Though it may be going too far to suggest that this added element in Numbers 4 was meant to refer proleptically to the events of Numbers 16, it is clear that in the priestly view the Kohathites, by virtue of their important responsibilities, were particularly susceptible to precisely the kind of encroachment desired by Korah and his band. It is also important to note that Moses and Aaron are Kohathites as well: their father, Amram, was the brother of Korah's father, Izhar (Exod 6:18–21), so Aaron, chosen to be high priest, and

Korah, a mere Levite, are cousins. This familial relationship provides further background to and justification for the actions of Korah in Numbers 16.

The organization of the levitical groups in Numbers 3–4 gives us further insight into the meaning of the priestly narrative in Numbers 16 in terms of Yahweh's instruction to the people to withdraw from the *miškān* of Korah. According to the priestly narrative, all the people have gathered at the Tent of Meeting to witness the test of the fire pans. Many commentators see a discrepancy between this narrative location and the *miškān* of Korah, since the two *miškān*s are not the same; they therefore emend "*miškān* of Korah" to "*miškān* of Yahweh," or some such variation.[30] Yet according to Numbers 3, the levitical clans have their dwellings immediately around the *miškān* of Yahweh. Thus when the people gather at the Tent of Meeting, they are also gathering by the tents of the Levites, including of course the tents of the Kohathites, which in turn include the tent of Korah.[31] It is therefore perfectly reasonable that Yahweh should require the people to withdraw from the *miškān* of Korah, even though they are said to be gathered around the Tent of Meeting: both are in the same place. Although *miškān* is frequently used in P to refer to the Tabernacle, as the dwelling place of Yahweh, it is used here in its generic sense of habitation—it is not "the" *miškān*, it is the *miškān* of Korah.[32] Some irony may be intended by this designation—as with the similar double use of the standard priestly terms *'ēdāʰ*—but the narrative contains no inconsistency in this regard, either internally or with regard to other parts of P, and requires no emendation.

The test offered by Moses is also integrally connected to other parts of the priestly narrative as a whole. Not only is the bringing of fire before Yahweh a specifically Aaronid right, even within that group the formal process of the incense offering is strictly regulated. The danger of this procedure is well known, both to the Israelites in the story and to the reader of P, since we have already witnessed the fiery deaths of Aaron's sons Nadab and Abihu, who brought incense before Yahweh when they were not commanded to do so (Lev 10:1–3).[33] We are not at all surprised when Korah and his band are engulfed in divine fire. Both the risks of improper cultic procedure and the standard punishment for it, therefore, are well established in the priestly narrative.

This priestly story in Numbers 16 is comprehensible only when read alongside other P texts. It is an integral part of the larger priestly narrative, which includes the laws of sacrifice, the separation of the Levites from the rest of Israel, the separation of Aaron's line from the Levites, and the passages mentioned above. The narrative does not in fact end in Numbers 16, but continues into the next chapter, where the physical remains of the test are removed, the people as a whole continue to challenge Moses and Aaron, and a plague breaks out as punishment—a plague that is stopped by the correct offering of incense by Aaron, in explicit counterdistinction to the incorrect offering of Korah in Numbers 16. The story concludes in Numbers 17 with a sign from Yahweh: the leader of each tribe brings his tribal staff to the Tent, and the next day Aaron's has sprouted almond blossoms, thereby signifying, once and for all, Yahweh's choice of Aaron and his line as the true priests among the people. It is not coincidence that the subsequent chapter, Numbers 18, details the perquisites of Aaron and his sons, the very issue that drove the rebellion in Numbers 16. This chapter of law begins with an explicit statement of Aaronid control over the cult, and with a restatement of the subjugation of the Levites to Aaron's line; reference is even made to the events of Numbers 16–17: "No outsider will approach you as you perform the duties of the shrine and the duties of the altar, so that wrath will not again strike the Israelites" (18:4–5). (Naturally, no reference to Dathan and Abiram is found in Num 17–18.) Further reference to Korah is found in Numbers 27:3, where the daughters of Zelophehad state that their father was not part of Korah's band, using the precise language of 16:11: "he was not one of the faction ['*ēdāʰ*], Korah's faction, that banded together [*hannôʿādîm*] against Yahweh ['*al-yhwh*]."

Central elements of the priestly narrative of Numbers 16 are common to the other major priestly narratives of the wilderness period: the appearance of the presence of Yahweh in the Tent of Meeting as a reaction to some objectionable behavior by the people, accompanied by a communication with Moses (and Aaron), and a subsequent action on the part of Yahweh—all these are found not only in Numbers 16, but also in Exodus 16:10–13 and Numbers 14:10, 26–38; 17:6–15; 20:1–13.[34] The P narrative of Numbers 16 is not only a self-standing coherent story, it is part of the continuous P document.

The nonpriestly story in Numbers 16 is shorter and simpler than that of P, but, with the possible exception of its somewhat convoluted introduction, it is no less complete.[35] There are no references to priestly or levitical activities, regulations, or responsibilities; nor would we expect to find such in a nonpriestly text. We have, rather, a narrative about two Reubenites, Dathan and Abiram, challenging the basis of Moses's leadership of the Israelites: his prophetic credentials. (In the course of doing so, they claim that Moses has raised himself above the rest of the Israelites; this claim stands in sharp contrast, perhaps intentionally, with the clear statements of Moses's humility in the two preceding E narratives: in Num 11:29, Moses wishes that all Israelites could share in his prophetic spirit, while in Num 12:3, Moses is simply described as the most humble man on earth.[36]) As we have already seen in the case of Numbers 11 (see case study II), the theme of Moses's prophetic authority belongs to the E narrative, for it is in E alone that the revelation at the mountain in the wilderness occurs for the explicit purpose of investing Moses with prophetic authority, it is in E that this authority is challenged regularly throughout the wilderness wanderings, and it is in E that this authority is restated as the final word upon the death of Moses in Deuteronomy 34.[37]

Confirmation that this story is separate from that of P, and that it belongs to E, can be found in the brief reference to this narrative in D. As with Numbers 11 and the other passages mentioned in chapter 4, D's description of the events of Numbers 16 reflects only the E story, and does so with language that is nearly verbatim what we find in Numbers 16.[38] Deuteronomy 11:6 recalls "what he [that is, Yahweh] did to Dathan and Abiram, sons of Eliab son of Reuben, when the earth opened her mouth and swallowed them, along with their households, their tents, and every living thing in their train, from amidst all Israel." This text contains direct parallels with Numbers 16:1 and 16:32. Notably, the first of these verses in Numbers 16 contains some P (the introduction of Korah), while the second contains a redactional insertion (the inclusion of Korah among those swallowed by the earth); D, however, makes no mention of either the priestly or the redactional elements in the canonical text. D, therefore, again represents strong evidence not only for the division of the text, but for the independent existence of the E narrative.

As we have seen, in the P narrative of Numbers 16 the test by which Korah and his band are proved in the wrong is simply the standard ritual procedure of the incense offering. In E, however, it is not Dathan and Abiram who are truly being tested; it is Moses. Dathan and Abiram are not instructed to do anything; they simply stand there. Moses's challenge is self-imposed: if he is able to importune Yahweh to make something truly exceptional happen—like the earth opening and swallowing his adversaries—then he, Moses, is proved to be a true prophet. The nature of this test, then, conforms entirely to the larger setting of the story and confirms its place in the E narrative arc from Horeb to the death of Moses. Again, as with P, the E story of Numbers 16 is not only internally coherent, but it is continuous with other E texts that make up a cohesive narrative.[39]

The two stories combined by the compiler in Numbers 16 are not as similar as those of Genesis 37 and Exodus 14, in which a singular event was told in two sources and therefore had to be unified; nor, however, are they as disparate as the two very different narratives of Numbers 11. Numbers 16 contains two rebellions, but they are two very different rebellions. It is for this reason that it is difficult to accept the notion that one story was written as a revision or retelling of the other, but, as in Numbers 11, it does require that we understand why the compiler would have seen them as similar enough to be combined into a single narrative. In this case, the answer is far less complicated than that for Numbers 11. For both P and E, the story told in Numbers 16 is the definitive rebellion against the Israelite leadership; that of the Aaronid priesthood for P, that of Moses in E. After these stories, the question is settled: the authority of Moses and Aaron is never again questioned. Both narratives make this clear not only from the absence of further stories of rebellion in the respective documents, but on grounds internal to the events of Numbers 16 themselves. For P, the conclusion of the story comes with Yahweh's definitive selection of Aaron in Numbers 17:21–26, especially with Yahweh's words in 17:25: "Put Aaron's staff back before the *'ēdût* to be kept as a sign for the rebels, so that their mutterings against me may cease, lest they die." After this, no rebellion against the Aaronid priesthood is possible. E, on the other hand, does not contain so clear a statement, but the finality of the Dathan and Abiram story can be seen in the wondrous act of the earth swallowing them alive. This unheard-of event is the definitive sign of prophetic authority, for Moses just as for Elijah in 1 Kings 18:36–37, where the prophet's bringing about of a seemingly impossible divine act (fire from heaven) is intended to demonstrate his prophetic powers and is utterly convincing: "When they saw this, all the people flung themselves on their faces and cried out, 'Yahweh alone is God, Yahweh alone is God!'" (18:39).

For the compiler, then, there could be little choice but to combine these two stories into one. Just as Joseph could not be sold more than once, just as the Egyptians could not be destroyed more than once, so too the authority of Israel's leadership could not be finally decided more than once. In the course of combining the pentateuchal documents, the compiler had long since confused the distinction between varying types of leadership; Mosaic prophetic authority and Aaronid cultic authority were conjoined already in the canonical Sinai/Horeb pericope, in which both are established. Thus the end of the challenge to the now-singular Israelite authority could also be only singular.

The two narratives that can be isolated in Numbers 16 are, as we have seen, not only internally coherent, but in fact describe two completely different events. Though both are rebellions, or attempted rebellions, they are directed at different parties, on different grounds, with different tests and different results. Their aims are entirely distinct: in one case, to prove, for the first and only time, the cultic legitimacy of the Aaronid priesthood; in the other, to prove, once again, the authentic national prophetic leadership of Moses. Despite these stark differences, some scholars read the priestly narrative as a reworking of the nonpriestly, as a revision and supplement rather than as an independently conceived and executed story.

The most straightforward reading of P as originally supplementary comes from John Van Seters, who, however, does not provide any rationale for his analysis.[40] He has identified the P and nonpriestly stories precisely but does not treat the P narrative in any detail. The brief insertions that we have attributed to the compiler Van Seters attributes to P, in its redactional, rather than authorial, role. We may point out two significant problems with this analysis. First, if P is entirely supplementary, rather than having existed independently, then we ought to see evidence that the P author has used the nonpriestly text as a base on which to build his own story—yet we are able to read P entirely on its own, as a coherent narrative, without any knowledge of the nonpriestly text. Second, if the combination of the two stories is attributable to the author of the latter, that is, to P, then we should not expect to find any major discontinuities in the text—yet the location of the events, whether at the Tabernacle or the tents of Dathan and Abiram, is completely muddled in the canonical text.

The position that P is a supplementary layer is also taken, at least implicitly, by Baruch Levine. In his discussion of vv. 16–24, the part of the P story describing the test of the incense offering, Levine suggests that this passage was written as a conscious extension of or commentary on the E phrase "pay no regard to their *minḥāʰ*" in v. 15.[41] If this were the case, then the earlier reference to this test, in vv. 5–7, must also be part of the same interpretive move by the priestly author. Yet such an assumption seems unwarranted. There is nothing in the priestly story that requires a basis in the E narrative. The bringing of incense has already served as a test of sorts for P, in Leviticus 10:1–3, and it is perfectly in line with the rest of P's worldview that this should be the test here as well. Not only does the priestly text read naturally without any reference to v. 15, it is highly unlikely that a priestly author would draw the connection between the *minḥāʰ* of v. 15 and the incense offering of his own story: *minḥāʰ* in P has the specific meaning of "meal-offering" (Lev 2; 6:7–23).

Jacob Milgrom has also argued for P as a recension, or perhaps for two priestly recensions.[42] He begins his analysis with a putative "penultimate recension," in which both the priestly and the nonpriestly stories are included, then postulates an "ultimate recension" in which the two stories are more closely tied together and some additional priestly material added. His analysis is structural: he argues that the penultimate recension was structured chiastically, a feature that was ruined by the ultimate recension. Yet Milgrom's chiasm is entirely dependent on the removal of those features that ruin the purported structure—and it is those precise features that are attributed to the ultimate recension. Milgrom assigns vv. 5–11 to his ultimate recension, though it is unclear why these verses, particularly vv. 5–7, which introduce the test of the fire pans, are to be separated compositionally from their parallel text in vv. 16–19—except that they don't fit the chiastic pattern. Milgrom also assigns v. 25 to the ultimate recension, although, as we have seen, it is integral to the E narrative and has no connection at all to the P story. Additionally, it is not obvious why the combining of Korah with Dathan and Abiram in vv. 24, 27, and 32 should be part of the ultimate recension and not the penultimate, since these redactional moves are necessary from the moment that the two stories are interwoven and meant to be understood as a single narrative. Most important, Milgrom nowhere demonstrates that the priestly story is dependent on that of E, or is secondary to it in any way; indeed, his penultimate recension is bracketed by the Dathan and Abiram story, rather than the Korah story, which might suggest a nonpriestly compiler. He simply states that P is a recension rather than a source, though, at least for the penultimate recension, there is no basis for such a claim.

Reinhard Kratz takes a similar approach, viewing Numbers 16 as the product of a threefold accumulation of texts.[43] First, he claims, there was the nonpriestly story (vv. 12–15, 25–34) about Dathan and Abiram's rebellion against Moses; then an addition covering the majority of what we have identified as P (vv. 1–7, 16–24, 35), in which Korah, Dathan, Abiram, and On rebel against the priesthood of Moses and Aaron; and finally a layer in which Korah and the Levites rebel against Aaron (with additions over a number of verses). Kratz's first two layers are, for the most part, E and P as we have isolated them above. Like our priestly narrative, Kratz's second layer can be read as a self-standing narrative; it is not dependent on the first layer, and in fact contradicts it in numerous details, as we have seen. Yet for Kratz, this layer is to be read as a supplement, though it is unclear whether he means that it was written independently and then secondarily added or that it was written for the purpose of being attached to the nonpriestly story. A particular difficulty in Kratz's description of his layers is that in the second one, covering vv. 1–7, 16–24, and 35, the main characters are supposed to be Korah and Dathan, Abiram, and On; yet, as we have noted repeatedly, Dathan, Abiram, and On are not mentioned in these verses. We may further note that Kratz's third layer contains additions to a variety of verses, but that all of the affected verses belong to his second stratum, the equivalent to our P. It is therefore unclear why this third layer should be seen as a supplement to the combined first two layers, rather than to the second layer alone—in which case his first layer represents our E, and his second and third represent our P, with a posited internal development.

Erhard Blum's analysis, though following along the same lines, alleviates some of the difficulties of Kratz's presentation.[44] Blum sees two originally independent narratives: the nonpriestly story of Dathan and Abiram and a priestly story about the 250 Israelite leaders who want access to the priesthood (vv. 3–7a, 18, 35). These were combined, according to Blum, by a priestly redactor who also inserted the verses about Korah and his Levite rebellion (vv. 7b–11, 16–17 [as a resumptive repetition preceding v. 18 after the insertion of vv. 7b–15], 19–22) and added the name Korah into the earlier narratives at various points. While there are some appealing elements to this analysis—especially the recognition of originally independent priestly and nonpriestly narratives—it suffers from some of the same problems as that of Kratz. The supposedly redactional layer of Korah's rebellion appears almost exclusively in the context of the purportedly earlier priestly narrative. Thus vv. 7b–11 follow directly on the priestly vv. 3–7a, reconfiguring them (and presumably adding the name Korah in vv. 5 and 6); vv. 19–22 follow on the priestly v. 18; and even vv. 16–17 were inserted for the purpose of linking two priestly sections together (vv. 3–7a and 18). Notably, the additions into the nonpriestly narrative serve only to tie the two stories together; there is no significant change to the content or thrust of the nonpriestly story by these additions. It therefore seems just as easy, if not easier, to argue that Blum's priestly redaction was in fact a secondary stratum within the priestly source; the insertion of Korah into the nonpriestly story would then not be part of a priestly redaction, but would rather be, as argued above, a result of combining the non-priestly narrative with the (already combined) priestly story.[45]

The evidence from Numbers 16 strongly suggests that P was an independent source, rather than a redactional layer. Yet it is clear from the variety of attempts to argue otherwise that the nature of P and its relationship to the nonpriestly materials remains very much in question in pentateuchal scholarship. In the following chapter, I discuss the status of the priestly source as a whole.

Chapter 5

————•◦•✦•◦•————

COMPLETENESS

The P Source

Amid all the various theories regarding the composition of the Pentateuch, the identification of the priestly writings, in terms of historical claims, stylistic tendencies, and scope, has remained almost entirely consistent from early scholarship to the present. Despite this widespread agreement on which texts are to be designated as priestly, however, the nature of P, as broadly defined, has remained an ongoing point of dispute. Two issues in particular are at the heart of the discussion of P: whether P is a redactional layer or a source, and whether P was written as a response to the nonpriestly text.

Until the middle of the second half of the nineteenth century, the question of whether P was redactional or not was moot: P, whether as part of the original "Elohist" source (in combination with E) or on its own, was seen as the earliest layer of the Pentateuch and described as the *Urschrift* or *Grundschrift*. Even when P came to be viewed as the latest of the pentateuchal sources, its status as an independent document was generally accepted. While in the late nineteenth to mid-twentieth centuries the view of P as a redactional layer was held only by a minority of scholars,[1] the latter part of the twentieth century witnessed a marked revival of this claim, particularly in the works of Frank M. Cross, John Van Seters, Rolf Rendtorff, and those who followed them.[2] Direct rebuttals of these scholars have been produced by others, and there is no need to replicate them in detail here.[3] Rather, I will restrict the following discussion to more general observations about the priestly materials.

THE P SOURCE

First, however, it is important to lay out the priestly document as a whole, with a focus on how it functions as a literary work. When read on its own terms, the P document can present something of a challenge to the reader. It does not have the consistent novelistic features of the J and E sources, and a reader expecting to find a fully fleshed-out story will be left unsatisfied. Yet the unique manner in which P describes Israel's history is both artistic and meaningful.[4] Appreciating the priestly document as it is, rather than judging it in light of other sources, allows for a clearer understanding of P's artistry and intention. As J. A. Emerton has written, "Provided we do not begin with a preconceived idea of what to expect, the passages ascribed to P can be read as an intelligible, consecutive document, in which the author stressed what was important to him and said little about other matters."[5]

The primeval history in P comprises the genealogy of humankind from Adam through Abraham, a progression that is slowed to allow for the fuller description of two major episodes: creation and the flood. The creation story of Genesis 1 establishes in majestic form the eternal state of the world, with specific interest in elements that will later become important for the priestly legislation: the division of time and the division of the animal kingdom.[6] It also provides the dominant concept of humanity, in God's blessing of humankind.[7] The flood story is both an undoing and a redoing of creation and contains the first covenant with humankind, in the promise that the work of creation will never be undone again (accompanied by the restatement of the blessing from Gen 1). Here also P presents the first food laws (Gen 9:3–4) and the fundamental law governing human interaction, the prohibition of murder (9:5–6). These episodes are linked by the genealogy from Adam to Noah (ten generations), and the flood story is followed by the priestly Table of Nations in Genesis 10*, which explains how humanity came to spread over the earth. Thus the primeval history for P is the basic presentation of the state of nature and humanity. The elements established in this section are unalterable and serve as the background for the rest of P's history.

The transition from the primeval history to the patriarchal history is accomplished by means of another genealogy, this one from Shem to Abraham (like that of Gen 5, also ten generations). P tells us little about the patriarchs, so what is told is therefore of heightened importance. Abraham's settlement in Canaan is a necessary prerequisite for the story and is told very briefly, with the only extraneous detail being his wealth (Gen 12:4b–5).[8] Once Abraham is settled, P provides only two episodes from his life: the covenant in Genesis 17 (including the intrinsically connected verses 16:1, 3, 15–16 and 21:2–5) and the purchase of the family burial plot in Genesis 23. The importance of Abraham for P boils down to these two key moments. The first, Genesis 17, is the central theological statement of P's patriarchal history, as it establishes for the first time the special status of Abraham's descendants through Sarah as recipients of the divine promise of progeny and land and stands as an important lens through which the rest of the priestly history is to be read.[9] The new use of the divine epithet El Shaddai, as opposed to simply Elohim as with Noah, underscores the advent of a new epoch in Israel's history. The first part of the promise to Abraham begins to be fulfilled immediately, as Isaac is born to Sarah (Gen 21:2–5). Upon this, her part in the history ends, and she dies. The second part of the promise begins to be fulfilled in Genesis 23, with the purchase of the burial plot for Sarah.[10] This parcel of land, small though it may be, is the sole piece of property in Canaan that is to belong to the patriarchs throughout their time in the land; it is an *'aḥuzzāʰ*, a permanent possession.[11] Once these initial steps toward the fulfillment of the divine promise have been taken, Abraham's role comes to an end, and he dies (Gen 25:7–10). Even in P's death notice for Abraham, however, the two main features of his life are recognized: he is buried by his two sons, each of whom will be the father of a nation, in the family burial plot.

Of Ishmael we learn only that what God had promised Abraham had come to pass: he is given a genealogy, which concludes with the notice that his sons were chieftains of tribes—that is, a nation (25:12–17). Of Isaac we hear very little: that he married and had children (25:19–20, 26b), that he was wealthy (26:13–15, 18), and that he died (35:27–29). That Isaac stands for P mostly as the continuation of the promise to Abraham is noted in the first words after Abraham's death: "After the death of Abraham, God blessed his son Isaac" (25:11a). All of the aforementioned notices about Isaac are closely parallel with the same elements in the priestly rendering of Abraham; even in Isaac's death, his two sons—each of whom will go on to be the father of a nation—bury him in the family plot.

Jacob receives a slightly fuller treatment. The first thing we are told about him is that he is sent to Paddan-Aram to marry within the family (26:34–35; 27:46; 28:1–9); thus it is through Jacob that P establishes the principle of endogamy. As with Abraham and Isaac, so with Jacob we are informed that he is wealthy (30:43), and we learn of his wives and children (35:22b–26). Upon Jacob's return to Canaan, God repeats to him the promises made to Abraham in Genesis 17 (35:11–12); Jacob's name is also changed to Israel, thereby marking him as the direct ancestor of the twelve tribes (35:10). Rachel's death is described by P (35:16a, 19) because she is the only one of the patriarchs or matriarchs who was not buried in the family plot. (Just as Ishmael's genealogy served to indicate the fulfillment of God's promise to Abraham that he would be the father of many nations, so too the genealogy of Esau in Gen 36.) As already noted, the Joseph story in P is really the end of the Jacob story. Joseph is merely the mechanism by which the Israelites come to Egypt and settle there. P pays far greater attention to the list of Jacob's descendants (46:8–27), which again stands as evidence of the continuing fulfillment of God's promise. Israel's settlement in Egypt (47:27) is portrayed in terms of the blessing from Genesis 1:28—Israel is fruitful and multiplies greatly. Before his death, Jacob recalls to Joseph what God had promised him and, through a ceremony of adoption, brings Manasseh and Ephraim into the community of the established tribes of Israel (48:3–7, 20). Jacob's final act is to make sure that he is buried in the family plot in Canaan (49:29–33), as indeed comes to pass (50:12–13).

The patriarchal story in P may look different from those of J and E, but it is a masterful narrative in its own right. Every word is carefully chosen; even in its sometimes repetitive style, every repetition is meaningful. Though there are but four major episodes (Gen 1; 6–9*; 17; 23), these extended passages establish the main elements of interest to P: for the primeval history, the state of nature and humanity's place in it; for the patriarchal history, the blessing and promise of progeny and land. As Walter Brueggemann writes, "These narratives . . . are transparently vehicles of a message."[12] Outside of these major episodes, the priestly story is told rapidly, moving quickly through the generations until the Israelites are in Egypt. What P does choose to note along the way, however, is striking: virtually every notice in P is in one way or another an indication of the continuing fulfillment of God's blessing and promise to the patriarchs.[13] Each of the patriarchs marries and has children, who all go on to be tribal leaders or to found nations. Each is buried in the permanent family plot in Canaan. Each is even said to be wealthy, a sign of God's blessing. The genealogies serve this purpose as well. P's patriarchal history is remarkable for both its concision and its precision. It tells only and exactly what it needs to tell in order to establish the historical and theological groundwork for Israel's future.[14] It is not the case, as some have argued (see below), that the priestly narrative in Genesis does not make sense unless one is already familiar with the nonpriestly patriarchal materials. In fact, the priestly narrative in Genesis is entirely sensible on its own terms; it appears to be "missing" elements only when it is read against the canonical text.

The priestly story continues with the Exodus and begins there with the formal notice of the fulfillment of the promise of progeny: from seventy people, Israel grows to fill the land of Egypt (Exod 1:1–5, 7). The enslavement of the

Israelites and God's recognition of their oppression are stated concisely (1:13–14; 2:23aβ–25); the covenant with the patriarchs is recalled and serves as the motivation for God's deliverance of Israel. As Walther Zimmerli observed, "What happens in the time of Moses is also at its core, in terms of the attachment of Yahweh to his people, merely the redemption of the earlier promises to Abraham."[15] God's speech to Moses (6:2–8) revisits the patriarchal promise of the land and adds the revelation of the name Yahweh, marking the third epoch in Israel's history.[16] By their redemption from slavery, the Israelites are to know and accept Yahweh as their god. The genealogy that follows this speech focuses on the priestly lineage, thereby establishing the importance of this tribe for P. Without further ado, the priestly plagues cycle begins. Again, though the plagues make up a significant segment of the priestly narrative, there is no tension in the story: as in the flood, Yahweh announces the course of events beforehand: he will harden Pharaoh's heart, and Pharaoh will not let the people go until Yahweh has thoroughly demonstrated his power (7:3–5). Thus in P the plagues are not really plagues at all, but as P calls them, signs and wonders: they are not intended to persuade Pharaoh to let the people go, but rather only to demonstrate Yahweh's control.[17] The passover in P is both the impetus for the Exodus proper and an indication to the Israelites of Yahweh's power and salvation (12:26–27). The final destruction of the Egyptians at the sea in Exodus 14 is yet another demonstration of Yahweh's might (14:4, 17–18).[18]

The priestly Exodus story, then, introduces a new theme in P: Yahweh's power, which is to be recognized by both the Egyptians and the Israelites. This theme stands as a bridge between what preceded and what follows: Yahweh's salvation of the Israelites is presented as part of the fulfillment of the patriarchal promise of land, while at the same time it establishes Yahweh as Israel's god, to whom they owe obedience and loyalty. The elements of the story that contribute to this theme are given expansive treatment—the speech to Moses, the plagues, the passover, and the crossing of the sea—while those elements that establish the necessary premises on which this story is built are treated far more briefly.

The events at Sinai in P are not about the theophany, which is described very briefly (24:17). Rather, the priestly Sinai pericope is really about the construction of the Tabernacle, the dwelling of Yahweh in it, and the rituals that are required to keep Yahweh in the midst of the people.[19] This is the central theological concern of P, as is evident from the amount of material devoted to it (Exod 25–31, 35 through Num 9) and as is only to be expected from priestly authors for whom these rites, and the theology underlying them, were the very basis of their existence. Everything in P builds to this point: the primeval history, which establishes the natural order that must be ritually maintained; the patriarchal stories, which establish the people of Israel and their claim to the land in which Yahweh will dwell in their midst; and the Exodus story, which establishes Yahweh's power and Israel's obligation to him.[20] As Edgar Brightman correctly stated, "P has a single aim: to teach the ritual law, with its divine historical sanctions."[21]

For generations, scholars have sought to sunder the literary connection between the priestly narrative and the priestly legislation, arguing that the laws are a later addition to the preexisting narrative. Yet the laws, or perhaps better the Sinai pericope as a whole, including the construction of the Tabernacle, are the center and the apex of the priestly narrative. As David Damrosch notes, "Far from interrupting the narrative, the laws complete it, and the story exists for the sake of the laws that it frames."[22] The priestly narrative is unthinkable without the laws; indeed, the difficulty in understanding the priestly narrative without the laws no doubt contributed to the opinion that P was not an independent document. Just as the narrative elements of D frame its laws, establishing Israel's pattern of sin and punishment through the wilderness as the justification for the necessity of obedience to the law, so too in P the narrative frames the law and is imbued with far greater meaning by the presence of the law at its center.[23] The blessings and promises of God to the patriarchs, the destructive power Yahweh wields against the Egyptians, and the sustenance that he provides in the wilderness all speak to the issue of Yahweh's continuing presence in the Tabernacle once the Israelites have settled in Canaan. As Georg Fohrer put it, "the narrative provides the foundation for the eternal law, and the eternal law justifies the presentation of the narrative."[24]

The priestly text from Exodus 25 through Leviticus 16 systematically establishes the cultic system by which Yahweh's presence in the midst of the people is to be maintained. The attention to order and detail is impeccable. Moses is called up to the mountain to receive the blueprint for the Tabernacle (24:18a; 25:1–31:18); the Israelites build the Tabernacle as instructed (35:1–40:33), and Yahweh descends to dwell in it (40:34–38). Only once the Tabernacle is complete, with all the cultic appurtenances, is it sensible to give the laws pertaining to the cultic rituals that will occur there; and of course the laws for the rituals must be known before any can be carried out. So in Leviticus 1–7 we find the definitions of and instructions for the various sacrifices. Before any offering can take place, however, there must be priests: Leviticus 8–9 describes the investiture of the Aaronid priesthood, concluding, finally, with the first formal sacrifice (9:8–24). Immediately thereafter, the priestly text establishes the precision by which these rites are to be carried out through the counterexample of Nadab and Abihu. The laws of Leviticus 11–15 indicate the ways in which the divine presence in the Tabernacle is threatened, through the detailed explanation of the priestly impurity system and the mechanisms by which impurity is to be removed. The rituals for the day of atonement in Leviticus 16, in turn, describe the means by which the contamination of the Tabernacle, caused by the sins of the people, is to be removed.

The priestly legislation is systematic and thorough, and single-minded in its focus on the central question of how Yahweh's presence in the midst of the people is to be maintained. As with the narrative that leads to this legislation, each piece builds on the next. Every element is required for the final picture, and nothing extraneous is added.[25]

The lengthy listing of Israel's tribes in Numbers 1–2—and note especially their impressive numbers, further testimony to the fulfillment of the promise— is followed by the ordering of the tribes around the Tabernacle (Num 3), again emphasizing the centrality of Yahweh in the midst of the people. Before the Israelites can leave Sinai, P provides the instructions for how the Tabernacle is to be disassembled and transported; this requires outlining the roles of the Levites (Num 4). The Levites must further be ritually invested with their cultic rights (Num 8). Finally, the Israelites may depart, and the description of this is provided in Numbers 9–10:28; again, the regular formal listing of the tribes stands as confirmation of everything that P has established to this point.

The narratives that follow the departure from Sinai in P depict the failures of the people, both in their faith in Yahweh and in their adherence to the laws. Just as the story of the Exodus established the grounds for the obedience of the Israelites, the stories of rebellion and misconduct in the wilderness reaffirm the destructive power that Yahweh wields when he is not obeyed. The episode of the spies (Num 13–14*) centers on the people's lack of faith in Yahweh's promise of the land, for which they are punished by forty years of wandering. The provision of manna (Exod 16*) begins with the people's desire to return to Egypt rather than die in the wilderness, as they have just been condemned to do, and simultaneously reinforces the people's obligation to Yahweh: he provides them with food, but does so in a way that takes into account the previously given Sabbath laws.[26] The rebellion of Korah (Num 16–17*) focuses on the singular prerogatives of the Aaronid priests, the challenge to which results in fiery death and a plague. The difficult story of Moses getting water from the rock in Numbers 20:1–13* seems to make the point that Yahweh's word is to be obeyed to the letter, regardless of who is acting: even if it is Moses and Aaron themselves, the repercussions are decisive. Aaron's death follows immediately, and simultaneously and necessarily the investiture of his son Eleazar as the

new high priest (20:23–29). Through these narratives, the priestly author demonstrates the fragility of the blessings and promises to the patriarchs, which are
threatened when the people forget their obligation to Yahweh as established
in the Exodus and disregard their responsibility to safeguard the divine presence. Yet even as the generation of the Exodus is condemned to die in the
wilderness, the promise itself remains firm, simply transferred to the subsequent
generation.[27]

As in Genesis, the priestly text from Exodus through Numbers comprises
individual extended episodes linked by smaller connecting pieces, in the case
of the latter books by travel itinerary notices. The progression of the Israelites
from Egypt to the border of Canaan is paused at various points so that P can
present one of the episodes, each of which contributes to the overall argument
of the priestly document.

Finally, the priestly text turns to the beginning of the possession of the land,
starting with the territory of the Transjordan. The war against Midian in Numbers 31, prepared for in Numbers 25:16–18, explains how the Israelites came to
control the Transjordan; the apportioning of the land in Numbers 32 explains
how the tribes that settled there came to do so. With this matter resolved, and
with the conquest of the land and the final fulfillment of God's promise to the
patriarchs at hand, Moses ascends Mount Nebo and dies, succeeded by Joshua
(Deut 32:48–52; 34:1a$\alpha^1\beta$, 5*, 8–10).

The priestly document, from beginning to end, is a model of precision, clarity, and rhetorical power.[28] The lack of "action" typically associated with narrative is not a weakness of P, but rather a central element of its magisterial style.
Yahweh's control over events is never in doubt.[29] Everything that occurs is fore-
told. P, both in its overall scope and in many of its specifics, can be understood
as a series of divine speeches—commands, promises, and predictions—and the
working out of their fulfillments.[30] The course of Israel's history and the establishment of the priestly cult at its religious center is all according to the divine
plan.[31] The constant reiteration of this overarching theme gives the priestly narrative its force. The individual themes that occur and recur throughout are ex-
emplified through the narrative episodes, and anything that does not contribute
to those themes is omitted. There are no significant gaps in P; what may appear
in light of the canonical text to be missing narrative elements are in fact nothing
of the kind. We may extrapolate Baruch J. Schwartz's description of the priestly
Sinai pericope to cover the entirety of P: "The narrative is thoroughly complete
and coherent. Nothing is out of sequence, nothing is mentioned that has not
been properly introduced, and nothing is introduced that is not developed to its
logical conclusion."[32] What P tells us is precisely what P wants us to concentrate
on, precisely what is necessary for building the theological argument that devel-

ops over the course of the priestly work.[33] What we as canonical readers assume is important is not the same as what P thinks is important, nor should it be. P does not romanticize Israel's history in the slightest. The lives of the patriarchs have importance for P only insofar as they participate in the reception and initial fulfillments of the divine blessings and promises. The enslavement of the Israelites is meaningful only insofar as it serves as a mechanism for God to fulfill his promise and display his power. Antony Campbell insightfully notes: "The text is not the history of Israel that we might write today. . . . The Priestly text is not written for us, however, and there is a coherence to its horizon that we need to note."[34] The priestly document—coherent, independent, and complete—is as worthy of literary respect as any biblical text.

P AS REDACTION

Having laid out the priestly document as a whole, I now turn to some of the broader questions regarding the status of P in pentateuchal scholarship, especially as it relates to the nonpriestly material. Although there are places in which P comprises little more than a notice—of genealogy, of age, of birth, of marriage, of itinerary—when P does relate a fuller episode, these passages are full stories, entirely comprehensible and complete on their own terms. Such episodes include the following:

Creation	Genesis 1:1–2:4a
The flood	Genesis 6–9*
The covenant with Abraham	Genesis 17[35]
The purchase of the cave of Machpelah	Genesis 23
The revelation of Yahweh's name to Moses and the plagues in Egypt	Exodus 6–10*
The crossing of the sea	Exodus 14 (see case study IV)
The giving of manna	Exodus 16*
The entire Sinai event, including the construction of the Tabernacle, the law-giving, and the individual episodes	Exodus 19–Numbers 10*
The spies	Numbers 13–14*
The rebellion of Korah	Numbers 16*
The water from the rock	Numbers 20:1–13*
The death of Aaron	Numbers 20:22–29
The war against Midian	Numbers 31
The apportioning of the Transjordan	Numbers 32*

Each of these stories is self-contained and coherent, consistent both internally and in the larger P context.

This observation can be coupled with the recognition that P tells some stories that have no parallel in the nonpriestly narratives. Only P describes the purchase of a burial plot for the patriarchs and matriarchs (Gen 23), the construction of the Tabernacle (Exod 25–31, 35–40), the rebellion of Korah (Num 16*), the actions of Phinehas (Num 25*), and the war against Midian (Num 31). On a smaller scale, only P tells of the plagues of lice (Exod 8:12–15), boils (9:8–12), and darkness (10:20–23, 27).[36]

Where P and non-P do narrate the same historical events, they are told differently. P's creation story is obviously distinct from that of J (Gen 2:4b–25), not least in terms of the order and purpose of creation. P's flood story differs from that of J in the number of animals brought onto the ark, the chronology of the flood, and the concluding covenant. The covenant with Abraham in P is made on entirely different grounds from that of E (Gen 15). Jacob leaves his father's house for Aram for completely divergent reasons in P (Gen 26:34–35; 27:46–28:9) and in J (27:1–45). The revelation of Yahweh's name to Moses in P occurs at a time and place different from that in E (Exod 3*). P's plagues cycle differs from that of J in the content of the plagues as well as their purpose. The crossing of the sea in P has virtually no resemblance to the destruction of the Egyptians in J besides the fact that both involve water (see case study IV). In P the giving of the manna is the response to the people's complaint, while in J it is a test of the people's faithfulness, as well as an etiology for the Sabbath. The laws of P are entirely different from those of E (Exod 20:23–23:33) and are given in a different place at a different time. Compared with J, the spies in P leave from a different place, go to a different place, and bring back a different report; different characters are involved, and the episodes conclude differently. The episode of Moses getting water from a rock in P takes place at a different place, at a different time, and with very different results from the parallel J story (Exod 17:1bβ–7). The story of the apportioning of the Transjordan in P differs from its counterpart in E with regard to when the tribes will possess the land and who grants it to them.

When these three elements are taken together—that P tells different stories, that P tells the same stories differently, and that in both cases the stories P tells are complete—the case for P as a redactional layer rather than an independent source becomes difficult to maintain. In all three of these respects, P is exactly like J and E. The P stories have all the hallmarks of an independent composition: they have beginnings and endings; they are internally consistent and coherent in plot, theme, and language; and they are distinctive from their nonpriestly counterparts. These P stories, especially those without a parallel in the nonpriestly material, do not participate in any discernible redactional process. They are, rather, clearly reliant on a unique set of traditions, or unique renderings of common traditions. The independence of P comes out clearly in those stories that have a parallel in non-P but are set at a different place and time (and take no notice of the fact that the events they are relating have already happened once before or will happen again later): notably the revelation of Yahweh's name in Exodus 6 and the episode of Moses getting water from the rock in Numbers 20. If P were a mere redactional layer, these episodes would, presumably, occur at the same time as—or, better, before—their nonpriestly counterparts, or even as supplements and revisions to the nonpriestly texts.[37] There is nothing inherent in either story that requires them to be set apart from the nonpriestly versions; they are situated where they are in the P narrative because that is where the P author thought that they occurred. This speaks to the independence of the P narrative from that of non-P.

Equally compelling is the completeness of those P stories that have been interwoven with J and/or E. Such completeness is required only of an independent story; if P were a redaction of non-P, we would expect that it would be unreadable on its own, that it would depend on the content of the nonpriestly story that it supplements. In the episodes mentioned above, this is clearly not the case. P is eminently readable on its own, and it does not require the nonpriestly text to make sense. This is admitted even by Erhard Blum, who considers P a layer rather than a source; for this reason, he describes P as something between a source and a redaction.[38] These independent stories speak to P as a source; for Blum and many others, it is the parts of P that are not so clearly episodic that suggest P as a redaction.

The status of P's independence, however, especially in the case of the smaller notices between the larger narrative episodes, must be judged on the basis of P when read apart from the nonpriestly text; the guiding question must be whether P can be read on its own—whether P requires non-P to make sense. This question is most pertinent in the patriarchal narratives; from Exodus 6 onward, P is far lengthier and fuller than J and E. In Genesis, however, where J and E have substantial narratives, P frequently comprises little more than a brief notice. Thus Abraham's departure for Canaan and his settlement there—told in detail by J in Genesis 12:1–4a, 6–9, complete with the divine promise and the establishment of cultic sites—is told in reportorial form by P in 11:31–32 and 12:4b–5 (and 11:32 is only a genealogical notice). The story of Lot and the destruction of Sodom and Gomorrah, the J story of which covers the majority of Genesis 13, 18, and 19, is represented by only a handful of verses in P: 13:6, 11b–12bα; 19:29.[39] Jacob's travels to and from Aram and the time he spent there, told in such detail by both J and E in chapters 29–33, receive little treatment by P other than the notices of his departure from Canaan (28:1–9), acquisition of wealth (30:43), children (35:22b–26),[40] departure from Paddan-Aram (31:17–18), and arrival back in Canaan (33:18*). P's Joseph story contains none of the plot elements of J or E; it is little more than the notice of Joseph's rise to power (40:45–46a), the list of people who came with Jacob to Egypt (46:6–27), the settlement of Jacob's family in Rameses (47:5–6a, 7–11, 27–28), the blessing of Manasseh and Ephraim (48:3–7, 20), and Jacob's blessing and burial instructions to his sons (49:1a, 28b–33) and their fulfillment of those instructions (50:12–13).[41] From a slightly broader perspective, we may observe that P's Abraham story really comprises only the notice of his journey to Canaan, the covenant with God, the purchase of the burial plot, and his death; the Isaac story contains only the notice of his marriage, his acquisition of wealth (Gen 26:13–15, 18),[42] his blessing and sending off of Jacob (28:1–9), and his death (35:27–29); the Jacob story relates only briefly his time in Paddan-Aram, the blessing he receives upon his return (35:9–13, 15), and his descent to Egypt. These stories are interspersed with genealogies (Gen 25:12–17; 36; 46:8–27).

When P is read in light of the more substantial J and E stories, it is little wonder that it has been considered incomplete. Blum describes P's patriarchal materials as a "caricature of a story rather than a patriarchal history."[43] Van Seters states of the Abraham story in P that it "cannot possibly be construed as an account of Abraham's life, even if P is regarded as 'summarizing' in the extreme."[44] Cross says of P that "its 'narrative' is nothing like the narrative of saga."[45] Yet these critiques are founded on assumptions derived from the nonpriestly patriarchal stories. What constitutes a proper "patriarchal history" for Blum can only be what is found in the nonpriestly text; what counts as a proper "account of Abraham's life" for Van Seters can similarly only be the nonpriestly version of it. Cross's definition of saga is determined by his view of the nonpriestly materials as the literary representations of an early Israelite oral epic. The thoroughness of P's patriarchal history cannot be judged in light of other authors; indeed, it should not be judged at all. Thoroughness is a subjective matter, determined only by comparison with other material. As Klaus Koch cogently put it, the determination that P is incomplete "is based on indirect, abstract considerations about the genre of narrative Hebrew works and about the indispensability of certain subjects within an Israelite recounting of the early history of the people. . . . In the end, that one is put off by the different types of material and an allegedly gap-filled continuity arises from a judgment of taste that inevitably corresponds to modern sentiment and is hardly objective."[46] To put it more broadly, we cannot judge P on the basis of whether it conforms to the modern expectation of the fullness of "narrative," conditioned by our familiarity with the form of the novel—or, for that matter, to any externally imposed concept of what narrative should be. Not only is it possible that what we consider a satisfactory narrative is not what the ancient author or audience would have considered so (as if such a question would have been pressing for the ancient author/audience in any case), but more importantly there is no justification for the requirement that P conform to any given genre in the first place. Not all documents need to be full, novelistic narratives. We cannot judge P against a standard to which the author of P would have felt no obligation to adhere.

What can be judged is the coherence and continuity of the priestly description of the patriarchal era, taken on its own terms. "P may not have been intended to be a narrative document in the same sense as JE," Emerton writes. "It is, however, arguable that it is intelligible when considered in its own right."[47] Without comparison to the nonpriestly text, the patriarchal history in P is, on its surface, entirely comprehensible. It comprises a series of notices of travel, births, deaths, marriages, and genealogies, with some more substantial episodes punctuating the chronological and geographical progression. There is no internal inconsistency in this material, nor are there any significant gaps (see the discussion below); indeed, as Otto Eissfeldt recognized, "the continuity of what is related [in P] is indeed much more strongly brought out than in the other sources."[48] As long as P is not required to tell the same stories as J and E, and more importantly, as long as P is not required to tell the patriarchal history in the same manner as J and E, there is no reason that its patriarchal history should be considered incomplete. Again, Koch: "No a priori postulate regarding genre can be derived that already determines . . . what a proper Hebrew book can and cannot contain."[49]

Beyond the mere comparison with the fuller nonpriestly sources, scholars have claimed that P contains gaps that are understandable only if it was written as a supplement to the nonpriestly accounts. In this regard Cross points to the absence of any story of primordial human rebellion, the sacrifice of Isaac, the endangered ancestress stories, the wooing of Rebekah, the rivalry between Jacob and Esau, the Jacob-Laban cycle, the story of Dinah and Shechem, the Joseph story, the birth of Moses, his flight from and return to Egypt, and the Balaam cycle.[50] These ostensible omissions from P are, in Cross's words, "hard to believe" and "difficult to imagine"; "what remains makes a poor narrative indeed."[51] Most famously, Cross marvels at the lack of a covenant at Sinai in P: "The most stunning omission from the Priestly document is a narrative of the covenant ceremony proper. . . . To suppose that the Priestly tradent simply had no tradition of the covenant rites at Sinai is incredible. To posit a theory that P

had no covenant at all at Sinai is a fortiori beyond credence."[52] Both the subjectivity of Cross's assessments and the patent reliance on the nonpriestly material
as the basis for his judgments render his argument tendentious. We cannot
require P to tell the same stories as J or E, nor can we require that the stories
held in common be told in the same way.

The examples brought by Cross do not in fact represent gaps in P on its own,
but only in comparison with the nonpriestly material. Rendtorff, however, argues that the priestly material in the patriarchal history—consisting of chronological notices and reports of promises and blessings—is lacking any priestly
connections one to the other.[53] In order to argue this, however, he eliminates
the majority of the long-recognized priestly texts that do connect one priestly
passage to another. Tellingly, he does so on the basis not of content, but rather
of style: he makes regular reference to the use of a concordance to demonstrate
that words in verses typically assigned to P are found in other sources;[54] he
describes the issue of Jacob's stay in Paddan-Aram in P, as opposed to Haran
in J, as "linguistic," and the words Paddan-Aram as "an expression."[55] Rendtorff
further removes from P the major episode of Genesis 23, on the basis of style
and theology: "It is, in my opinion, inconceivable that the author of texts like
Genesis 17 and Exod. 6:2–8 should have departed so far from his own style as
to have taken over this purely 'profane' story (there can be no question at all,
in my opinion, of P being the real author), without throwing even the slightest
theological light on it."[56] Despite the fact that the priestly notices of the burials
of the patriarchs all depend on and refer to Genesis 23 (and that no nonpriestly
passage has any connection to it), the style and theology of the chapter (or lack
thereof) evidently render it unfit to be P. Rendtorff thus defines what is "authentically" P on the basis of those texts he is willing to attribute to it; those that do
not fit his paradigm are thereby excluded. It is ironic that he should at the same
time criticize Martin Noth for "[carrying] through his opinion consistently by
excluding all the material that is opposed to it."[57]

Rendtorff further argues that the Moses story in P lacks a beginning, as Moses
is not introduced before God speaks to him in Exodus 6:2 and that therefore
P must presuppose the introduction of Moses in the nonpriestly story.[58] On
general grounds, this is not necessarily a problem. One might assume that, of
all biblical figures, Moses was well enough known by the general Israelite population that he required no formal introduction; of course, for Rendtorff, there
were no such common Israelite traditions (see chapter 2), and so the absence of
an introduction is more problematic for him than it might otherwise be. More
specifically, however, we may note that P does provide a formal introduction for
Moses: it comes in the genealogy of Exodus 6:14–30, which concludes with a

detailed rehearsal of precisely who Moses is, complete with verbatim references back to the dialogue between Yahweh and Moses in 6:2–12.[59] Thus P may not introduce Moses before Exodus 6:2; but P does introduce Moses immediately thereafter, and though the style may not be to Rendtorff's liking, this makes it no less of a formal introduction.

The examples of gaps brought by Cross and Rendtorff are, as we have seen, not valid. They are based on canonical readings of the story, on methodologically flawed source analyses, and on presumptions of how P "should" tell a story. As Jean-Louis Ska observes, "No one asked P to furnish a parallel for each text present in the earlier sources."[60] There are, however, some authentic gaps in P that should not be overlooked. P has no notice of the births of Jacob and Esau (though it does tell us how old Isaac was when they were born, in Gen 25:26b), nor of Jacob's marriages. Though these are relatively minor gaps, given the otherwise complete state of P, they do represent information that, though absent, is crucial to the rest of the P story and contained in the nonpriestly text. Thus they might constitute evidence of P's dependence on non-P.[61] Yet we may also observe what type of material is missing in these places: birth and marriage notices, along with death notices, are a unique category, insofar as they are events that in the compiled Pentateuch cannot, and do not, happen more than once. If more than one source says that Jacob and Esau were born, only one can be preserved in the text, for it is narratively impossible for this to happen twice. Moreover, these are events that cannot really happen in different ways: while both P and J can have a flood story, but told so differently that they could each be preserved in a combined form, the notice of a birth or death is a singular occurrence, told in a single sentence. That these gaps in P are not a problem with P per se, but are rather a function of the compilation of the sources, is evident from the fact that the same gaps occur in the nonpriestly stories. For example, because the compiler used the P version of the birth of Isaac in Genesis 16:2–5, there is no J version of this event, although it is clear that J must have had one (the introduction to it still stands, in 16:1). J similarly lacks an account of Abraham's death, though it is prepared for in 25:1–6; instead, we have P's death notice, in 25:7–10. Thus the only true gaps in P are readily accounted for by the process of compilation and do not signify that P depended on the nonpriestly accounts; indeed, the gaps in J where P contains birth and death notices constitute evidence to the contrary.[62]

Perhaps the most important evidence that P does not require the nonpriestly narrative comes from the referential horizon of the priestly material. To put it briefly, P is consistently self-referential, from beginning to end, but contains virtually no references to the nonpriestly text. The priestly genealogy of Genesis 5 begins with explicit reference to creation in Genesis 1. The priestly flood story portrays the flood as a reversal and renewal of creation, again with reference only to Genesis 1, not to Genesis 2. The priestly covenant between God and Abraham in Genesis 17 presupposes only that Sarah is old (17:17), not that she is barren as in J (11:30; 16:2). All of the deaths and burials of the patriarchs and matriarchs in P presuppose the story of the purchase of Machpelah in Genesis 23. Isaac sends Jacob off to Paddan-Aram in 28:1–9 on the grounds established in P in 26:34–35 and 27:46, with no reference to the lengthy story of Jacob's deception in 27:1–45 or to any rivalry between Jacob and Esau. God's blessing of Jacob in P in 35:9–12 connects directly to Isaac's blessing of Jacob in 28:1–4, and there is no mention of any of the events of Jacob's time in Aram from the J and E sources. Jacob's deathbed speech to Joseph in 48:3–7 refers in detail to the P narrative of Genesis 35, but not at all to any of the events of Jacob's life narrated in the nonpriestly stories (see case study V). The overall chronology of the patriarchs in P is both thoroughgoing and contradictory to the nonpriestly chronology (see chapter 1). The revelation of Yahweh's name in Exodus 6:2–6 refers to the priestly theophanies in Genesis, and not to the nonpriestly ones, which it in fact explicitly contradicts; it is presented as the first revelation of the divine name, as if Exodus 3:9–15 had never happened.[63] The conclusion of the priestly plagues story (Exod 11:9–10) refers verbatim to its beginning (7:3–4), and not to the J version. The crossing of the sea in P resonates entirely with the priestly plagues, not with those of J (see case study IV). The priestly Sinai pericope makes no mention of the Decalogue, the tablets, the Covenant Code, the golden calf, or any other aspect of the nonpriestly accounts. The construction of the Tabernacle and the institution of the Sabbath, on the other hand, have clear connections with the priestly creation in Genesis 1.[64] All of the priestly law-giving and narrative after Exodus 40 presupposes the priestly Tabernacle, with no regard for E's Tent of Meeting (33:7–11). The story of Korah's rebellion, as we have seen, presupposes the priestly ordering of the tribes, the establishment of the Levites as cultic servants, the procedure of the fire pans, and the deaths of Nadab and Abihu. The priestly story of Moses getting water from a rock makes no mention of the idea that this has happened before, in J.

The preceding list could well be extended, and certainly provided with far more details, but the point is clear: the priestly text is full of internal cross-references, is built only on itself, and at virtually no point makes any reference to or shows any dependence on the nonpriestly story. If P is an independent document, this is of course to be expected; if P is a redactional layer, it is almost inconceivable. And then there are the nearly universal contradictions between P and non-P, in almost every aspect of both narrative and law. P does not constitute a reorienting "countercurrent" in the midst of the non-P narrative;[65] it presents an insurmountable dam, preventing anything resembling a coherent meaning in the canonical text. It is unthinkable that the definitive statements of P should have been written in order to coexist alongside their polar opposites.[66]

It is argued that P is a redactional layer because it provides the structural framework for the nonpriestly materials: the new beginning in Genesis 1, the *toledot* formulae ("these are the generations of . . ."), the travel notices in the wilderness.[67] This claim may be addressed on two fronts. First, we must again begin by looking at P on its own terms. The structural elements of the canonical text that belong to P—and there is no question that these do exist—are first and foremost structural elements of the independent P document.[68] The priestly history is highly structured, far more so than its J and E counterparts.[69] The *toledot* formulae contribute to this structure, as does the succession of covenants and promises.[70] The repetition of language from Genesis 1 in the Tabernacle pericope adds a further structural element.[71] When it is recognized that these structural elements are intrinsic to the P document, and not to the nonpriestly sources, then the fact that they serve also as structuring devices for the canonical text changes from an issue of redactional insertion to one of compilation. The compiler simply followed his sources. P has headings and other structural elements, and they have entered the canonical text precisely where they belong, that is, precisely where they were in the original P document. That they serve to structure the canonical whole is only to be expected: the *toledot* formula that begins P's flood story (Gen 6:9), for example, could go nowhere other than at the beginning of the canonical flood story. Even more clearly, P's creation story could hardly go anywhere other than before J's creation story: as jarring as it may be to read Genesis 2 after Genesis 1, the reverse is even less conceivable. Genesis 1 was not placed at the beginning because a priestly redactor wanted to have the first word, but because it belongs first logically and chronologically. The apparent priestly structure of the canonical Pentateuch is no more than the natural result of the combination of one highly structured document, P, with documents lacking such elements. The structure of the Pentateuch is not a sign of priestly redaction, or even some preference for P over the other sources.[72]

The second front on which the claim for P as a structuring redaction may be addressed is the canonical text itself. Although there are indeed places where the canonical text is framed by P, there are many more where this is patently not the case. Thus while the Pentateuch does begin with P in Genesis 1, it does not conclude with P; the last verses of Deuteronomy, 34:10–12, belong to E. The *toledot* of Adam in Genesis 5:1, which introduces Adam's descendants, comes after J's genealogy of Adam in 4:17–26, which covers much of the same ground.

The episodes about Abraham begin not with P, but with the J promise of Genesis 12:1–3. The notice of Isaac's birth is prefaced by J (Gen 21:1), not P. The life of Joseph ends in Genesis 50:23–26 with E; P makes no mention of Joseph's death. The introduction of Moses in the canonical text belongs to E (Exod 2: 1–10), not to P. The plagues are first anticipated not by P, but by J (Exod 3:20; 4:21–23; 6:1). When Moses is called to come up the mountain in the wilderness, this is narrated by J (Exod 24:1) and E (24:12) before it is mentioned by P (24:16). The priestly notice of Israel's departure from the mountain (Num 10:11–28) is followed by the J notice of the same (10:29–36). Even in some places where the priestly text does seem to provide a structuring element, it fits badly with the canonical text. Thus, for example, the heading of 37:2a, "This, then, is the line of Jacob" (better, "This is the story of Jacob"), serves in the canonical text to introduce the story of Joseph. "This is the story of Jacob" is a meaningful heading only for the priestly story that follows, in which Joseph plays a relatively minor role, serving only as the means by which Jacob descends to Egypt; Jacob is far and away the main character in P in Genesis 37–50. As a redactional insertion, this heading makes little sense; as a part of an independent P, it is eminently reasonable.[73] Thus the argument for P as a redactional structuring device for the canonical Pentateuch is overstated. Though in a number of cases priestly texts may stand at the beginning or end of a textual block, they do not do so in any thoroughgoing manner.

We see a similar situation when we examine the individual episodes in the canonical text. Though at times P does seem to predominate, shaping the canonical story and requiring that we read the text through the lens of the priestly presentation, there are also many instances where the historical claims, themes, and theology of P are subjugated to or undermined by those of the nonpriestly text. The covenant in Genesis 17 is, in the priestly document, the first appearance of God to Abraham; yet in the canonical text, God has already promised Abraham the land and progeny (12:1–3; 13:14–17) and made a covenant with him (Gen 15).[74] Similarly, the first appearance of God to Jacob in P, in 35:9–13, is robbed of its force by the fact that God has already appeared to Jacob (28:11–15; 31:3, 10–13; 35:1), just as the change of Jacob's name to Israel in P in 35:10 is rendered redundant by the fact that his name was already changed in 32:29. The priestly notion about why Jacob has to go to Aram—in order to get married—is entirely subsumed by the story of Jacob's deception of Isaac in 27:1–45. The dramatic revelation of the divine name in P in Exodus 6:2–6 is far less impressive when preceded by the revelation of the divine name in 3:14–15. P's presentation of the crossing of the sea does dominate that of J (see case study IV), but it is J's theological statement that is given the final, defining word in the story (Exod 14:31). The priestly version of the theophany at Sinai (Exod 24:16–17) is scarcely noticeable in the context of the nonpriestly versions (19:2b–24:15a). The priestly laws are preceded by the frequently contradictory laws of the Covenant Code (Exod 20:23–23:33) and by the people's affirmation that they will do all that God has commanded (Exod 24:3–8)—as if the giving of the commandments has been completed. (Moreover, it is Deuteronomy that has the last word on the legal front.) The formal priestly installation of the Levites as cultic servants in Numbers 3–4 is indeed mere formality after the Levites have already been selected in Exodus 32:26–29. In P, Joshua is introduced in Numbers 13:16 by the change of his name from Hoshea—a considered restatement by P that the divine name was not known before Moses, yet one that lacks any force after Joshua has been a regular part of the narrative (Exod 17:9–10, 13–14; 24:13; 32:17; 33:11; Num 11:28). As already noted, in P there is supposed to be no sacrifice, no cult of any kind, before it is formally instituted at Sinai; yet Noah (Gen 8:20–21), Abraham (12:7–8; 13:18; 15:9–17; 22:13), Jacob (28:18; 31:54; 35:7, 14; 46:1), Moses (Exod 18:12; 24:4–8), and Aaron (Exod 32:5–6) participate in cultic activities before the formal inauguration of the cult in P (Lev 8:22–24).[75] As William Gilders observes, "The combination of P and non-P ends up subverting and negating P's very ideological point."[76]

If P is a redaction, meant to reorient the existing text according to the priestly worldview, it fails on numerous counts. The canonical text does not speak in the voice of P.

A final argument against the claim that P is a redactional layer is the multilayered nature of P itself. Since the classical period of pentateuchal criticism, scholars have argued that P is not a unified work, but that there are in fact distinct strata of P. These have been variously labeled: P^1, P^2, P^3, etc., or P^g, P^n, P^s. Most convincing is the division of the priestly writings into P and H, the latter siglum representing the Holiness Legislation in Leviticus 17–26 and some related texts elsewhere in the Pentateuch.[77] The stratification of P is a common element of most current scholarship, although, as with most issues, there is little consensus on the precise demarcation of the strata.[78] Regardless of which way the priestly writings are divided into their constituent layers, however, what is common to all of these reconstructions is that the layers are all internal to P. Even when scholars make claims for a second, late layer of P as a redaction— as we saw in case study III—closer inspection reveals that the ostensibly later priestly elements are added only to earlier layers of P.[79] Nowhere does H or any other purportedly secondary priestly redaction supplement, revise, or interact in any discernible way with the nonpriestly text.[80]

The presence of layers in P—even if only two—stands as evidence that P was once an independent document. For if P were written as a supplement or redaction to the nonpriestly text, then a later addition should affect the entire

Pentateuch, priestly and nonpriestly texts alike. If the secondary layers interact exclusively with P, then the only logical way this can be explained is if P once existed on its own, in which state it was revised and supplemented, however many times, before it was combined with the other pentateuchal sources.[81]

P AS REACTION

Even among scholars who understand P as an independent document, it is held as a practically universal claim that P was written as a response to the nonpriestly documents, as a polemical correction of the various theologically problematic (from the priestly standpoint) claims of J and E.[82] This stance is taken by scholars of all schools and approaches; yet the argument rests on logically and methodologically flawed grounds.

In the argument that P writes its history as a response to the nonpriestly material, a crucial a priori claim must be addressed. When it is argued that the priestly text revises the nonpriestly, we ought to ask why the reverse could not be true: why could the nonpriestly text not be a revision of P? For example, it is claimed that in the P version of the flood story when Noah brings onto the ark only a single pair of animals, this is a revision of the J version in which he brings seven pairs so that he has enough to offer a sacrifice afterward. P, which argues that there was no sacrifice before Sinai, therefore is assumed to have eliminated the narrative element of J that stood in opposition to the priestly view.[83] But we ought to ask, if only for the sake of argument, why it is not possible that the J version might be a revision of P—after all, J clearly believes that there was sacrifice throughout Israel's history, and there could hardly be a more appropriate moment than after the flood. J, reading the P version, thereby would have made a conscious theological change to the priestly story, reflecting J's differing outlook.[84] When it is argued that P heightens the role of Aaron over his minimal part in the nonpriestly stories,[85] we ought to ask why the nonpriestly writers could not have intentionally minimized Aaron's role, writing from a counterpriestly perspective. The reason these possibilities go unconsidered—the primary underlying reason that P is regularly thought to be a revision of non-P—is because of the a priori belief that P was familiar with and responding to non-P.

An important initial step in the argument that P is based on, if not a redaction of, the nonpriestly texts is the statement that P follows the narrative outline of the nonpriestly story.[86] From the broadest perspective, this is true: P, like the other pentateuchal sources (and other biblical texts as well), adheres to the traditional sequence of primeval history, patriarchs (in their specific order— Abraham, Isaac, Jacob), Joseph, Exodus, and wilderness (with the theophany at the mountain). Yet within this overarching framework, P does not follow the nonpriestly narratives with any great precision. On the one hand, P, as we have seen, contains stories that are not found in the nonpriestly narratives: the purchase of the cave of Machpelah, the plague of lice, the plague of boils, the plague of darkness, the rebellion of Korah, the war against Midian, and the numerous smaller stories interspersed among the priestly legislation.[87] In these cases, P cannot be said to have followed the nonpriestly text because there is no parallel nonpriestly text to follow. At the same time, P describes events that are paralleled in the nonpriestly narrative but that P has located elsewhere, both geographically and temporally: the promise to Abraham, the revelation of Yahweh's name to Moses, the story of Moses getting water from the rock. In these cases, if P were following the nonpriestly text, we would have to explain why these events do not occur at the same place and time as their nonpriestly counterparts. Once it is admitted, however, that P contains some unique traditions, there is no reason to reject the possibility that it also contains unique versions of common traditions. The geographical and temporal locations of these stories do not need to be explained as a priestly reconceptualization of earlier traditions; they can simply be where and when the priestly author thought these events occurred.

This conclusion can be extrapolated over the entire priestly narrative. Where the priestly and nonpriestly stories diverge (and similarly where the J and E stories diverge), we may attribute the differences to the unique traditional bases on which the authors drew or to the unique renderings of common tradition among different schools and authors. Where the priestly and nonpriestly stories converge, we may attribute the similarities to the common elements of the tradition known to the authors. Only if it is imagined that the nonpriestly authors invented the entirety of the pentateuchal narrative out of whole cloth can it be argued that the similar narratives in P derive from non-P. If, on the other hand, we accept that J and E wrote their narratives on the basis of common Israelite traditions, then there is no reason to believe that P could not have done the same. The claim that P is a reaction to the nonpriestly text cannot be established on the grounds of its general plot outline, at least as long as we take seriously the insights of tradition criticism.

The bulk of the argument for P as reaction lies in its specific differences from non-P. Yet a striking number of these differences have no theological or ideological content; they are simply differences in detail. The genealogy of Genesis 5 presents a variation on that of Genesis 4:17–26, but there is no obvious significance to the variation. In the flood story (and throughout), P has a different chronology from J. Noah sends one raven rather than three doves. P does not name Sodom and Gomorrah specifically, referring only to the "cities of the plain." Rebekah's family is from Paddan-Aram, not Haran or Aram-Naharaim. Benjamin is born in Paddan-Aram rather than in Canaan. Jacob's family settles in Rameses, not in Goshen. One has to go to great lengths to attribute these variations to some purposeful theological statement. These differences are evidence not of any meaningful priestly reaction to non-P, but rather of simple variation in story.

Further, in places where P does seem to have a particular theological interest, it is not always clear why the presentation of the nonpriestly sources would have been problematic. The priestly rationale for Jacob's departure for Aram (Gen 26:34–35; 27:46; 28:1–9) is clearly rooted in the priestly concern for endogamy, but there is nothing in the story of Jacob's deception of Isaac that contradicts this concern; in fact, in the nonpriestly story too Jacob marries within the family (Gen 29:1–14a). This priestly passage is best explained not as a polemical response to the J narrative, but rather as P's independent and unique version of why Jacob went to Aram.

Once it is granted that the P author tells some aspects of his stories without reference to the nonpriestly versions, we must ask whether this phenomenon cannot serve to explain those aspects that have been claimed to be responses to non-P. We may again take as an example the differing claims regarding the number of animals Noah brings onto the ark. Must we read P's number as a deliberate correction of J? Why could this not be equivalent to the different chronology in P, or P's mention of the raven rather than the three doves—that is, why could it not simply be the way that the author tells the story, the way that he has adopted and adapted the traditions known to him? Aaron plays a far larger role in P than in the nonpriestly sources, but this need not be an indication of a deliberate revision of non-P; it may simply be that for the priestly writer, for obvious reasons, Aaron is an important figure and so is given a significant function in the telling of the story. The centrality of the priestly Tent of Meeting and the Tabernacle can be read as P's view of the Tent without it necessarily being understood as a response to the Tent of E. And so on. The major theological differences in P are prima facie indications of nothing more than differences: they are entirely explainable in light of the overall priestly worldview, without any reference to the nonpriestly text at all.

The question in all of these cases is, how else would P tell the story? If the nonpriestly stories did not exist, would the priestly text look any different? What elements are necessarily responses, rather than original presentations of the tradition? In this light the comparison with D's reuse of E can be fruitful. In D, as mentioned in chapter 4, we have a narrative that is clearly based on E but that reworks the earlier text when theological differences arise. The use of E as a basis is clear from the rigor with which D follows E's storyline and by the at times verbatim use of E's language. These close similarities in turn highlight the important theological distinctions in D's revised version. In P, however, as we have seen, the nonpriestly plot is followed only in its barest outlines. In addition, there is virtually no overlap in language such as we find in D with regard to E; at no point does P adopt the nonpriestly text in its purported revision of it.[88] While D is full of indications of its dependence on E, in P these indications are entirely absent.[89]

It is argued that in the stories P does not tell we can see signs of a deliberate silencing of problematic aspects of the nonpriestly narrative. Thus the absence in P of the story of the golden calf, for example, in which Aaron plays a leading (negative) role, is taken as an indication that P purposefully excised the narrative so as to preserve Aaron's reputation.[90] The absence in P of any references to sacrifice before Sinai is understood as the removal of these narrative elements from the nonpriestly story.[91] The absence in P of dreams or divine messengers is read as a polemical expurgation of these features.[92] This argument for deliberate silence is, however, an argument from silence. Because P does not tell a story does not mean that P is deliberately erasing that story. It means only that P does not tell it, or does not know it. Since P claims that there was no sacrifice before Sinai, there will of course be no sacrifice before Sinai in P; this would be true even if the nonpriestly texts did not exist.

The claim that P deliberately omits elements from the nonpriestly narrative is based on a reading of P that is undertaken entirely in light of the nonpriestly material. As with the argument that P is redactional because it does not tell all of the same stories as non-P, this claim too is methodologically problematic because it does not read P on its own first and foremost. P cannot be read through the lens of the nonpriestly text. If P makes an argument—and it makes many—it does so on its own terms, as an argument for the history of Israel as understood according to the priestly worldview. Nothing about P's argument, or that of J or E either, requires a preexisting literary foil. To describe the history of Israel in priestly terms is not necessarily to contradict a nonpriestly version. It is a statement, an interpretation, a rendering of tradition through the priestly lens. As Albert de Pury describes the author of P, "he manifestly was an architect, a conceptor, an innovator, a creator, a sovereign poet who boldly set the stage to put forth his visions of the origins, his conceptions of the beginnings."[93] Were ancient Israel made up only of priests, all of whom thought alike, P would look exactly as it does.

Schwartz's conclusion regarding the lack of dependence by P on the nonpriestly sources in the Sinai pericope may be quoted in full, with some adjustments to extend its argument over the entire priestly document: "Now it might appear that the resemblances are indications of a literary dependence. Yet, when careful comparison is made, the opposite conclusion becomes virtually inescapable. For while a number of similar 'ingredients' are indeed present, their use in P is so thoroughly irreconcilable with their use in the other sources, that it is inconceivable that P was even familiar with the other accounts. . . . Most logically, then, although the Priestly narrator and his non-Priestly colleagues recall and recount the same chapter[s] in Israel's distant past, P draws directly on national memory and on tradition, not on the other sources. The similarity between them is on the level of *Gattung*, not of literary dependence."[94]

The Israelites at the Sea, Exodus 14

¹The Lord said to Moses: ²"Tell the Israelites to turn back and encamp before Pi-hahiroth, between Migdol and the sea, before Baal-zephon; you shall encamp facing it, by the sea. ³Pharaoh will say of the Israelites, 'They are astray in the land; the wilderness has closed in on them.' ⁴Then I will stiffen Pharaoh's heart and he will pursue them, that I may gain glory through Pharaoh and all his host; and the Egyptians shall know that I am the Lord." And they did so. ⁵When the king of Egypt was told that the people had fled, Pharaoh and his courtiers had a change of heart about the people and said, "What is this we have done, releasing Israel from our service?" ⁶He ordered his chariot and took his men with him; ⁷he took six hundred of his picked chariots, and the rest of the chariots of Egypt, with officers in all of them. ⁸The Lord stiffened the heart of Pharaoh king of Egypt, and he gave chase to the Israelites. As the Israelites were departing defiantly,

¹וַיְדַבֵּר יְהֹוָה אֶל־מֹשֶׁה לֵּאמֹר: ²דַּבֵּר אֶל־בְּנֵי יִשְׂרָאֵל וְיָשֻׁבוּ וְיַחֲנוּ לִפְנֵי פִּי הַחִירֹת בֵּין מִגְדֹּל וּבֵין הַיָּם לִפְנֵי בַּעַל צְפֹן נִכְחוֹ תַחֲנוּ עַל־הַיָּם: ³וְאָמַר פַּרְעֹה לִבְנֵי יִשְׂרָאֵל נְבֻכִים הֵם בָּאָרֶץ סָגַר עֲלֵיהֶם הַמִּדְבָּר: ⁴וְחִזַּקְתִּי אֶת־לֵב־פַּרְעֹה וְרָדַף אַחֲרֵיהֶם וְאִכָּבְדָה בְּפַרְעֹה וּבְכָל־חֵילוֹ וְיָדְעוּ מִצְרַיִם כִּי־אֲנִי יְהֹוָה וַיַּעֲשׂוּ־כֵן: ⁵וַיֻּגַּד לְמֶלֶךְ מִצְרַיִם כִּי בָרַח הָעָם וַיֵּהָפֵךְ לְבַב פַּרְעֹה וַעֲבָדָיו אֶל־הָעָם וַיֹּאמְרוּ מַה־זֹּאת עָשִׂינוּ כִּי־שִׁלַּחְנוּ אֶת־יִשְׂרָאֵל מֵעָבְדֵנוּ: ⁶וַיֶּאְסֹר אֶת־רִכְבּוֹ וְאֶת־עַמּוֹ לָקַח עִמּוֹ: ⁷וַיִּקַּח שֵׁשׁ־מֵאוֹת רֶכֶב בָּחוּר וְכֹל רֶכֶב מִצְרָיִם וְשָׁלִשִׁם עַל־כֻּלּוֹ: ⁸וַיְחַזֵּק יְהֹוָה אֶת־לֵב פַּרְעֹה מֶלֶךְ מִצְרַיִם וַיִּרְדֹּף אַחֲרֵי בְּנֵי יִשְׂרָאֵל וּבְנֵי יִשְׂרָאֵל יֹצְאִים בְּיָד רָמָה: ⁹וַיִּרְדְּפוּ מִצְרַיִם אַחֲרֵיהֶם וַיַּשִּׂיגוּ אוֹתָם חֹנִים עַל־הַיָּם כָּל־סוּס רֶכֶב פַּרְעֹה וּפָרָשָׁיו וְחֵילוֹ עַל־פִּי הַחִירֹת לִפְנֵי בַּעַל צְפֹן: ¹⁰וּפַרְעֹה הִקְרִיב וַיִּשְׂאוּ בְנֵי־יִשְׂרָאֵל אֶת־עֵינֵיהֶם וְהִנֵּה מִצְרַיִם נֹסֵעַ אַחֲרֵיהֶם וַיִּירְאוּ מְאֹד וַיִּצְעֲקוּ בְנֵי־יִשְׂרָאֵל אֶל־יְהֹוָה: ¹¹וַיֹּאמְרוּ אֶל־מֹשֶׁה הַמִבְּלִי אֵין־קְבָרִים בְּמִצְרַיִם לְקַחְתָּנוּ לָמוּת בַּמִּדְבָּר מַה־זֹּאת עָשִׂיתָ לָּנוּ לְהוֹצִיאָנוּ מִמִּצְרָיִם: ¹²הֲלֹא־זֶה הַדָּבָר אֲשֶׁר דִּבַּרְנוּ אֵלֶיךָ בְמִצְרַיִם לֵאמֹר חֲדַל מִמֶּנּוּ וְנַעַבְדָה אֶת־מִצְרָיִם כִּי טוֹב לָנוּ עֲבֹד אֶת־מִצְרַיִם מִמֻּתֵנוּ בַּמִּדְבָּר: ¹³וַיֹּאמֶר מֹשֶׁה אֶל־הָעָם אַל־תִּירָאוּ הִתְיַצְּבוּ וּרְאוּ אֶת־יְשׁוּעַת יְהֹוָה אֲשֶׁר־יַעֲשֶׂה לָכֶם הַיּוֹם כִּי אֲשֶׁר רְאִיתֶם אֶת־מִצְרַיִם הַיּוֹם לֹא

boldly, [9]the Egyptians gave chase to them, and all the chariot horses of Pharaoh, his horsemen, and his warriors overtook them encamped by the sea, near Pi-hahiroth, before Baalzephon. [10]As Pharaoh drew near, the Israelites caught sight of the Egyptians advancing upon them. Greatly frightened, the Israelites cried out to the Lord. [11]And they said to Moses, "Was it for want of graves in Egypt that you brought us to die in the wilderness? What have you done to us, taking us out of Egypt? [12]Is this not the very thing we told you in Egypt, saying, 'Let us be, and we will serve the Egyptians, for it is better for us to serve the Egyptians than to die in the wilderness'?" [13]But Moses said to the people, "Have no fear! Stand by, and witness the deliverance which the Lord will work for you today; for the Egyptians whom you see today you will never see again. [14]The Lord will battle for you; you hold your peace!" [15]Then the Lord said to Moses, "Why do you cry out to me? Tell the Israelites to go forward. [16]And you lift up your rod and hold out your arm over the sea and split it, so that the Israelites may march into the sea on dry ground. [17]And I will stiffen the hearts of the Egyptians so that they go in after them; and I will gain glory through Pharaoh and all his warriors, his chariots and his horsemen. [18]Let the Egyptians know that I am Lord, when I gain glory through Pharaoh, his chariots, and

תֹסִיפוּ לִרְאֹתָם עוֹד עַד־עוֹלָם: [14]יְהוָה יִלָּחֵם לָכֶם וְאַתֶּם תַּחֲרִישׁוּן: [15]וַיֹּאמֶר יְהוָה אֶל־מֹשֶׁה מַה־תִּצְעַק אֵלָי דַּבֵּר אֶל־בְּנֵי־יִשְׂרָאֵל וְיִסָּעוּ: [16]וְאַתָּה הָרֵם אֶת־מַטְּךָ וּנְטֵה אֶת־יָדְךָ עַל־הַיָּם וּבְקָעֵהוּ וְיָבֹאוּ בְנֵי־יִשְׂרָאֵל בְּתוֹךְ הַיָּם בַּיַּבָּשָׁה: [17]וַאֲנִי הִנְנִי מְחַזֵּק אֶת־לֵב מִצְרַיִם וְיָבֹאוּ אַחֲרֵיהֶם וְאִכָּבְדָה בְּפַרְעֹה וּבְכָל־חֵילוֹ בְּרִכְבּוֹ וּבְפָרָשָׁיו: [18]וְיָדְעוּ מִצְרַיִם כִּי־אֲנִי יְהוָה בְּהִכָּבְדִי בְּפַרְעֹה בְּרִכְבּוֹ וּבְפָרָשָׁיו: [19]וַיִּסַּע מַלְאַךְ הָאֱלֹהִים הַהֹלֵךְ לִפְנֵי מַחֲנֵה יִשְׂרָאֵל וַיֵּלֶךְ מֵאַחֲרֵיהֶם וַיִּסַּע עַמּוּד הֶעָנָן מִפְּנֵיהֶם וַיַּעֲמֹד מֵאַחֲרֵיהֶם: [20]וַיָּבֹא בֵּין מַחֲנֵה מִצְרַיִם וּבֵין מַחֲנֵה יִשְׂרָאֵל וַיְהִי הֶעָנָן וְהַחֹשֶׁךְ וַיָּאֶר אֶת־הַלָּיְלָה וְלֹא־קָרַב זֶה אֶל־זֶה כָּל־הַלָּיְלָה: [21]וַיֵּט מֹשֶׁה אֶת־יָדוֹ עַל־הַיָּם וַיּוֹלֶךְ יְהוָה אֶת־הַיָּם בְּרוּחַ קָדִים עַזָּה כָּל־הַלַּיְלָה וַיָּשֶׂם אֶת־הַיָּם לֶחָרָבָה וַיִּבָּקְעוּ הַמָּיִם: [22]וַיָּבֹאוּ בְנֵי־יִשְׂרָאֵל בְּתוֹךְ הַיָּם בַּיַּבָּשָׁה וְהַמַּיִם לָהֶם חֹמָה מִימִינָם וּמִשְּׂמֹאלָם: [23]וַיִּרְדְּפוּ מִצְרַיִם וַיָּבֹאוּ אַחֲרֵיהֶם כֹּל סוּס פַּרְעֹה רִכְבּוֹ וּפָרָשָׁיו אֶל־תּוֹךְ הַיָּם: [24]וַיְהִי בְּאַשְׁמֹרֶת הַבֹּקֶר וַיַּשְׁקֵף יְהוָה אֶל־מַחֲנֵה מִצְרַיִם בְּעַמּוּד אֵשׁ וְעָנָן וַיָּהָם אֵת מַחֲנֵה מִצְרָיִם: [25]וַיָּסַר אֵת אֹפַן מַרְכְּבֹתָיו וַיְנַהֲגֵהוּ בִּכְבֵדֻת וַיֹּאמֶר מִצְרַיִם אָנוּסָה מִפְּנֵי יִשְׂרָאֵל כִּי יְהוָה נִלְחָם לָהֶם בְּמִצְרָיִם: [26]וַיֹּאמֶר יְהוָה אֶל־מֹשֶׁה נְטֵה אֶת־יָדְךָ עַל־הַיָּם וְיָשֻׁבוּ הַמַּיִם עַל־מִצְרַיִם עַל־רִכְבּוֹ וְעַל־פָּרָשָׁיו: [27]וַיֵּט מֹשֶׁה אֶת־יָדוֹ עַל־הַיָּם וַיָּשָׁב הַיָּם לִפְנוֹת בֹּקֶר לְאֵיתָנוֹ וּמִצְרַיִם נָסִים לִקְרָאתוֹ וַיְנַעֵר יְהוָה אֶת־מִצְרַיִם בְּתוֹךְ הַיָּם: [28]וַיָּשֻׁבוּ הַמַּיִם וַיְכַסּוּ אֶת־הָרֶכֶב וְאֶת־הַפָּרָשִׁים לְכֹל חֵיל פַּרְעֹה הַבָּאִים אַחֲרֵיהֶם בַּיָּם לֹא־נִשְׁאַר בָּהֶם עַד־אֶחָד: [29]וּבְנֵי יִשְׂרָאֵל הָלְכוּ בַיַּבָּשָׁה בְּתוֹךְ הַיָּם וְהַמַּיִם לָהֶם חֹמָה מִימִינָם וּמִשְּׂמֹאלָם: [30]וַיּוֹשַׁע יְהוָה בַּיּוֹם הַהוּא אֶת־יִשְׂרָאֵל מִיַּד מִצְרָיִם וַיַּרְא יִשְׂרָאֵל אֶת־מִצְרַיִם מֵת עַל־שְׂפַת הַיָּם: [31]וַיַּרְא יִשְׂרָאֵל אֶת־הַיָּד הַגְּדֹלָה אֲשֶׁר עָשָׂה יְהוָה בְּמִצְרַיִם וַיִּירְאוּ הָעָם אֶת־יְהוָה וַיַּאֲמִינוּ בַּיהוָה וּבְמֹשֶׁה עַבְדּוֹ:

his horsemen." [19]The angel of God, who had been going ahead of the Israelite army, now moved and followed behind them; and the pillar of cloud shifted from in front of them and took up a place behind them, [20]and it came between the army of the Egyptians and the army of Israel. Thus there was the cloud with the darkness, and it cast a spell upon the night, so that the one could not come near the other all through the night. [21]Then Moses held out his arm over the sea and the Lord drove back the sea with a strong east wind all that night, and turned the sea into dry ground. The waters were split, [22]and the Israelites went into the sea on dry ground, the waters forming a wall for them on their right and on their left. [23]The Egyptians came in pursuit after them into the sea, all of Pharaoh's horses, chariots, and horsemen. [24]At the morning watch, the Lord looked down upon the Egyptian army from a pillar of fire and cloud, and threw the Egyptian army into panic. [25]He locked the wheels of their chariots so that they moved forward with difficulty. And the Egyptians said, "Let us flee from the Israelites, for the Lord is fighting for them against Egypt." [26]Then the Lord said to Moses, "Hold out your arm over the sea, that the waters may come back upon the Egyptians and upon their chariots and upon their horsemen." [27]Moses held out his arm over the sea, and at daybreak the sea

returned to its normal state, and the
Egyptians fled at its approach. But
the Lord hurled the Egyptians into
the sea. [28]The waters turned back
and covered the chariots and the
horsemen—Pharaoh's entire army
that followed them into the sea; not
one of them remained. [29]But the
Israelites had marched through the
sea on dry ground, the waters forming a wall for them on their right
and on their left. [30]Thus the Lord
delivered Israel that day from the
Egyptians. Israel saw the Egyptians
dead on the shore of the sea. [31]And
when Israel saw the wondrous power
which the Lord had wielded against
the Egyptians, the people feared the
Lord; they had faith in the Lord and
His servant Moses.

The famous episode of the Israelites and Egyptians at the sea,[1] burned into
popular imagination by the visual representations in films such as *The Ten
Commandments* and *The Prince of Egypt*, is described in prose in Exodus 14. As
with so many other parts of the biblical narrative, closer inspection reveals that
the text is not as straightforward as it first seems. Unlike Genesis 37, in which a
small but glaring detail proved to be the key to untangling the two sources, in
Exodus 14 there is no single obvious problem, but rather an extensive network
of contradictions and repetitions that make the historical event being described
almost impossible to re-create.

The order of events at the beginning of the story and the motivations for
them are confusing. In v. 2, the Israelites are commanded to turn back toward
Egypt and encamp by the sea. Pharaoh's predicted reaction to this movement
is described in v. 3: he will assume that the Israelites will die in the wilderness
and that he need not pursue them ("the wilderness has closed in on them"). Yet
Yahweh will force Pharaoh to chase the Israelites anyway ("I will stiffen Pharaoh's heart and he will pursue them"; v. 4).[2] In these verses, then, Pharaoh is
depicted as an unwilling participant in a chase he would not have undertaken

on his own. According to v. 5, however, upon hearing that the Israelites have
fled, Pharaoh realizes of his own accord that he has made a terrible decision in
letting them go and changes his mind ("Pharaoh and his courtiers had a change
of heart") and goes after them (vv. 6–7).³ Even more confusing is the order of
events in vv. 6–8. In vv. 6–7, Pharaoh readies his chariots and his men, because
he has already decided to pursue the Israelites (in v. 5). In v. 8a, however, as
predicted in v. 4, Yahweh stiffens Pharaoh's heart and he pursues the Israelites.
This event is plainly out of sequence with what precedes it; Pharaoh has no
inclination to pursue the Israelites, at least according to vv. 4 and 8a, until Yahweh has stiffened his heart; yet in vv. 6–7, he has already begun preparations for
military action, if not actually taken off in chase.⁴

The reaction of the Israelites to the Egyptian pursuit, and the reactions by
Moses and God to the Israelites, are also difficult to follow. In v. 10, the Israelites cry out "to Yahweh." Yet in v. 11, they speak directly to Moses. It is clear
that they are not using Moses as an intermediary to speak with God, since they
refer to past conversations ("Is this not the very thing we told you in Egypt?"; v.
12), which can only have taken place with Moses. On the other hand, in v. 15,
God criticizes the people for crying out to him, even though in vv. 13–14 Moses
has just responded directly to the people and reassured them. God's speech in
vv. 15–18 reads as a second response to the people, as if Moses had never spoken.⁵

The purpose of the destruction of the Egyptians is unclear in this narrative.
According to vv. 13–14, God will fight on behalf of the Israelites for their deliverance, whereas in vv. 17–18, the Egyptians are to serve as a means by which God
gains greater glory for himself; the Israelites are mentioned only as a mechanism by which this end can be attained. (Like the issue of Pharaoh's free will,
this tension is continued from the plagues narrative earlier in Exodus.) Similarly, the agent of the splitting of the sea is somewhat vague: in vv. 13–14, God
is portrayed as the active character; in v. 16, the seas are to be split by Moses's
gesture with his staff.

The confusion reaches a head in v. 21. Moses splits the sea as he was commanded in v. 16, but God also "drives back" the sea with the east wind. The
sea is said to become "dry ground," by virtue of the wind, before the waters are
said to be split. Who actually controls the movement of the sea is very much
unclear; it is, further, difficult to imagine how an east wind would be able to
split the sea.⁶ Similar difficulties arise in vv. 27–28. Here Moses again uses his
staff to control the waters, but God also acts in throwing the Egyptians into the
sea. Just as the movement of the sea is narrated twice in v. 21, so in vv. 27–28 it
is twice said that the waters "return."

Given the claim that Pharaoh and his army will chase the Israelites into the sea (vv. 16–17), the appearance of the divine messenger and the pillar of cloud in vv. 19–20 is narratively curious. The cloud accomplishes the task of preventing the Egyptians from seeing the Israelites, but this end seems to be at odds with the previously suggested plan: the Egyptians need to see the Israelites passing through the sea in order to have the boldness to go in after them.[7] Further, the overnight delay created by vv. 19–20 between Yahweh's command to Moses in v. 16 and Moses's fulfillment of that command in v. 21 is, to say the least, unexpected.[8] The pillar is once again seemingly awkward in vv. 24–25.[9] In vv. 21–23, the Israelites enter the sea and Pharaoh and his army enter after them; it is perfectly reasonable for the Israelites, upon reaching the other side, to simply turn and close the sea again, as in fact happens in vv. 26–27. The panic of the Egyptians in vv. 24–25 seems to serve no narrative function.[10]

Even granting the notion of the "fog of war," the movement of the Egyptians as they cross the sea is confused. In v. 25, the Egyptians decide to flee from the Israelites, that is, out of the waters and back toward Egypt. If they are indeed passing through the middle of the sea, this means turning around and going back out the same way. Yet the Egyptians are described in v. 27 as fleeing "toward" the sea (a better translation than "at its approach" as in the New Jewish Publication Society translation). Then, in v. 28, the Egyptians are described as still following after the Israelites into the sea, a description that is no longer appropriate to the situation if the Egyptians are in fact fleeing away from the Israelites. At the pinnacle of the story, the destruction of the Egyptians, we are still left with a contradictory story. In v. 27, as the Egyptians flee from the Israelites, God himself throws them into the sea. In v. 28, the waters turn back and cover the Egyptians. The movements of both the Egyptians and the waters are more than unclear—they are incompatible.[11]

These difficulties, like all such narrative problems, have been subjected to a wide range of explanations and interpretations based on the assumption of, or with the intention of proving, textual unity (see the notes to the preceding paragraphs). Critical scholars have long realized, however, that this chapter breaks down neatly into two separate strands, contradictory to one another and each at the same time connected internally on the basis of clear markers of narrative continuity. By following the narrative lines closely, these strands are readily discernible.

The chapter begins with God's speech to Moses in vv. 1–4a and the Israelites' fulfillment of their responsibilities in v. 4b; these verses are an inseparable unit.[12] The reaction of Pharaoh to the departure of the Israelites in v. 5 is incompatible with his reaction (and Yahweh's hardening of his heart) in v. 3. We therefore have in v. 5 a new source. The two sources at the beginning of Exodus 14, vv. 1–4 and v. 5, are readily identifiable as priestly and nonpriestly, respectively, as each is the direct continuation of its immediately preceding narrative line.[13]

In P, Yahweh brings the plagues upon Egypt so that "the Egyptians shall know that I am Yahweh" (Exod 7:5). The plagues are not intended to persuade Pharaoh to release the Israelites from bondage according to P; indeed, Pharaoh is never given the chance, as after each plague God hardens his heart (Exod 7:3, 13, 23; 8:15; 9:12, 35; 10:20, 27; 11:10). In fact, at no point in the priestly story does Pharaoh agree to let the people go; they simply leave (Exod 12:37). The path of their travels is marked in P in 12:37 and 13:20 and leads directly into Exodus 14:1, where Yahweh abruptly changes the natural course of the journey ("turn back").[14]

In the nonpriestly plagues story, on the other hand, the plagues are intended to persuade Pharaoh to let the Israelites go. Over the course of the plagues Pharaoh's resolve gradually weakens: at first he ignores them, but by the end he relents and sends the Israelites away (7:23; 8:11, 28; 9:7, 34; 10:10–11; 12:31–32). In the nonpriestly narrative, Pharaoh is entirely in command of his own will, continuously changing his mind about whether to let the people go (and who among them might go). This process reaches its final stage in 14:5, as Pharaoh, having finally let the Israelites depart, changes his mind for the last and fatal time. Whether this source is J or E depends largely on how one views the non-priestly material in the plagues narrative. I believe the nonpriestly material here and in the plagues narrative to be J and so will designate it as such.[15] (I will provide further support for the identification of the Exod 14 narratives as J and P, particularly in their respective connections to other J and P texts, after the source division.)

Verses 6–7, in which Pharaoh prepares for the chase, follow logically on the decision to pursue the Israelites in v. 5.[16]

In v. 8a we have the word-for-word fulfillment of God's speech in v. 4. The logic of this story—in which Pharaoh pursues the Israelites only after God has hardened his heart—supports the conclusion that vv. 5–7 belong to a different source.[17] The subsequent clause, "the Israelites were departing defiantly" (liter-ally, "with a high hand"), is formally parenthetical in any context (note the dis-junctive word order and the participial form of the verb); its content, however, is sensible only in the priestly narrative. In J's Exodus story, Pharaoh finally al-lows the Israelites to leave, and they leave as quickly as possible (Exod 12:31–34, 39); in the P story, as noted above, they are given no permission to leave Egypt, they simply do so (Exod 12:37–38, 40–51).[18] Their departure in P is an act of defi-ance, a statement of God's power. It is in this context, then, that the designation of the Israelites' departure as "high-handed" makes sense, and this clause thus belongs also to P.[19] Verse 9 is likewise attributable to P, as is made clear by the description of the Israelites' location, which matches that of v. 2 and which is nowhere specified in the J story.[20]

Verse 10 seems at first to be a single statement: the Israelites saw the Egyptians approaching and, frightened, cried out to Yahweh. The Israelites' speech to Moses in vv. 11–12, as already mentioned, seems not to follow directly from the preceding verse, however.[21] The first key to resolving this problem is Moses's response to the people in vv. 13–14. It is clearly directed at the people's speech in vv. 11–12, concluding as it does with the command to be silent. Yet it also begins with the command "have no fear," which seems to be a direct reference to the description of the people in v. 10: "they were very frightened." Indeed, the only element of vv. 10–14 that does not stand in the logical train of events and speeches is the very phrase that we have had occasion to note already, "the Israelites cried out to Yahweh."[22]

Perhaps unsurprisingly, it is this phrase that is directly picked up in God's speech in v. 15: "Why do you cry out to me?" This speech continues in one piece through the end of v. 18 and shows every indication of belonging to the P strand: it contains the priestly notion of the stiffening of Pharaoh's heart (v. 17; cf. v. 4), as well as the distinctly priestly concept of God attaining glory through the destruction of the Egyptians (v. 18; cf. v. 4).[23] These connections allow us to designate vv. 10bβ ("the Israelites cried out to Yahweh") and 15–18 as belonging to P, and vv. 10abα and 11–14 as belonging to J.[24] By this division all of the duplicative and contradictory elements in vv. 10–18 are resolved: the double cry of the people, the double addressee of the cries, and the double response to the cries; the contradictory views of who will act as the agent of the destruction of the Egyptians; and the contradictory rationales given for their destruction. Designating v. 10abα as J also illuminates and eliminates the discrepancy between the announcement of Pharaoh overtaking the Israelites in v. 9 (P) and the statement of his approach in v. 10abα (J). In J, the Israelites complain to Moses before the Egyptians have arrived; in P, they cry out upon the arrival of the Egyptians.[25]

God's command to Moses to lift his staff and arm in order to split the waters in v. 15 is, like virtually every imperative in the Bible, intended to be carried out immediately.[26] It is strange, then, not only to have the action interrupted by the introduction of the pillar of cloud in vv. 19–20, but to have Moses's fulfillment of God's command delayed overnight. These problems are made even more apparent when the beginning of v. 21 seems to contain precisely the fulfillment of God's command that was expected at the end of v. 18: "Moses held out his arm over the sea."[27] When we add to these considerations the need in P for the Egyptians to see the Israelites enter the sea, it is clear that vv. 19–20 belong to the J story.[28] Thus we can see that in P the action happens in one continuous sequence, in a single day: from the Israelites' encampment to the arrival of the Egyptians to the splitting of the sea. In J, on the other hand, there is a clearer sense of passing time: between the arrival of the Egyptians and their destruction a night passes, during which the cloud prevents the Egyptians from seeing or approaching the Israelite camp.[29] This detail provides an important key for disentangling the next few verses.

We have already observed that the first clause of v. 21, "Moses held out his arm over the sea," is the natural, necessary, and immediate fulfillment of God's command in v. 16 and therefore must be P. We might naturally expect that the rest of God's command from vv. 16–17 will similarly be fulfilled; thus we should anticipate that the words following this initial clause in v. 21 be "and he split the sea" or something similar. Indeed, such words are found in v. 21: "and the waters were split"—but they occur at the end of the verse. Between these clauses we are informed that "Yahweh drove back the sea with a strong east wind all that night, and turned the sea into dry ground." There are two clear indications that these words belong not with the first and last clauses of v. 21, from P, but rather to the J story. Most obvious is the reference to "all that night"; as we have seen, it is only in J that a night passes. Less obvious, but still important, is the description of how God affects the waters. First, it is noteworthy that here it is God who acts; this conforms precisely to Moses's description of God's deliverance of the Israelites in vv. 13–14 (J). Second, God "drove back" the waters with a strong east wind according to the J story, while Moses "split" them according to P. Unless we read the J story in light of the P story, we are not at all compelled to understand these verbs to mean the same thing. What seems to be pictured here in J is not the splitting of the sea, but something akin to a very strong tide: the wind pushing the sea—probably imagined as part of the Mediterranean—back from the shore, revealing the seabed underneath.[30] This view is confirmed in the continuation of the J story below.

Verses 22–23 continue with the fulfillment of God's command in vv. 16–17, again nearly word for word.[31] Here, according to P, the Israelites go into the midst of the sea, with the Egyptians chasing after them.[32] Verse 24, however, begins with the temporal clause "at the morning watch," thus marking it as belonging to the J story, as the presence in the verse of the pillar of fire and cloud confirms. The Egyptian army panics, and God prevents them from fleeing by locking their chariot wheels (v. 25).[33] Not only is this narrative element unnecessary in the P story, it stands as the fulfillment of Moses's prediction of these events earlier in the J story: "Yahweh will battle for you" (v. 14).[34] Even the Egyptians recognize this, at the end of v. 25: "Let us flee from the Israelites, for Yahweh is fighting for them against Egypt."[35]

God's command to Moses in v. 26 to hold out his arm so that the waters will come back upon the Egyptians is priestly in every respect that we have come to recognize in this chapter. As in v. 21, the beginning of v. 27 is the fulfillment of the priestly command: "Moses held out his arm over the sea" — and once again, the expected continuation, "and the waters came back upon the Egyptians," is delayed.[36] The rest of v. 27 conforms perfectly to the J story: there is the temporal marker, "at daybreak"; there is the description of the Egyptians fleeing, as they decided to do in v. 25; and there is God's direct action, throwing the Egyptians into the sea, again fulfilling the prediction "Yahweh will battle for you."[37]

The P fulfillment of God's command in v. 26 continues from the first clause of v. 27 in v. 28, just as expected, again nearly word for word.[38] The description of the Israelites passing through the sea in v. 29 is a direct parallel of the same description in v. 22, also from P. The concluding verses, 14:30–31, as they contain the narrative summary of Yahweh's deliverance of Israel, belong with the J story that has emphasized that concept from the beginning (vv. 13–14).[39] Further, there is a lovely reversal in these verses: whereas at the beginning of the story the Israelites saw the Egyptians approaching and were afraid (v. 10), at the end of the J narrative they see the Egyptians dead on the shore and the deity's power, and they fear Yahweh (v. 31); whereas at the beginning they doubted Yahweh's ability to save them in the wilderness (vv. 11–12), at the end they believe in Yahweh and Moses his servant (v. 31).[40]

The two strands of Exodus 14, P and J, thus break down into the following:[41]

P NARRATIVE

¹וַיְדַבֵּר יְהֹוָה אֶל־מֹשֶׁה לֵּאמֹר: ²דַּבֵּר אֶל־בְּנֵי יִשְׂרָאֵל וְיָשֻׁבוּ וְיַחֲנוּ לִפְנֵי פִּי הַחִירֹת בֵּין מִגְדֹּל וּבֵין הַיָּם לִפְנֵי בַּעַל צְפֹן נִכְחוֹ תַחֲנוּ עַל־הַיָּם: ³וְאָמַר פַּרְעֹה לִבְנֵי יִשְׂרָאֵל נְבֻכִים הֵם בָּאָרֶץ סָגַר עֲלֵיהֶם הַמִּדְבָּר: ⁴וְחִזַּקְתִּי אֶת־לֵב־פַּרְעֹה וְרָדַף אַחֲרֵיהֶם וְאִכָּבְדָה בְּפַרְעֹה וּבְכָל־חֵילוֹ וְיָדְעוּ מִצְרַיִם כִּי־אֲנִי יְהֹוָה וַיַּעֲשׂוּ־כֵן: ⁸וַיְחַזֵּק יְהֹוָה אֶת־לֵב פַּרְעֹה מֶלֶךְ מִצְרַיִם וַיִּרְדֹּף אַחֲרֵי בְּנֵי יִשְׂרָאֵל וּבְנֵי יִשְׂרָאֵל יֹצְאִים בְּיָד רָמָה: ⁹וַיִּרְדְּפוּ מִצְרַיִם אַחֲרֵיהֶם וַיַּשִּׂיגוּ אוֹתָם חֹנִים

J NARRATIVE

⁵וַיֻּגַּד לְמֶלֶךְ מִצְרַיִם כִּי בָרַח הָעָם וַיֵּהָפֵךְ לְבַב פַּרְעֹה וַעֲבָדָיו אֶל־הָעָם וַיֹּאמְרוּ מַה־זֹּאת עָשִׂינוּ כִּי־שִׁלַּחְנוּ אֶת־יִשְׂרָאֵל מֵעָבְדֵנוּ: ⁶וַיֶּאְסֹר אֶת־רִכְבּוֹ וְאֶת־עַמּוֹ לָקַח עִמּוֹ: ⁷וַיִּקַּח שֵׁשׁ־מֵאוֹת רֶכֶב בָּחוּר וְכֹל רֶכֶב מִצְרַיִם וְשָׁלִשִׁם עַל־כֻּלּוֹ: ¹⁰וּפַרְעֹה הִקְרִיב וַיִּשְׂאוּ בְנֵי־יִשְׂרָאֵל אֶת־עֵינֵיהֶם וְהִנֵּה מִצְרַיִם נֹסֵעַ אַחֲרֵיהֶם וַיִּירְאוּ מְאֹד ¹¹וַיֹּאמְרוּ אֶל־מֹשֶׁה הֲמִבְּלִי אֵין־קְבָרִים בְּמִצְרַיִם לְקַחְתָּנוּ לָמוּת בַּמִּדְבָּר מַה־זֹּאת עָשִׂיתָ לָּנוּ לְהוֹצִיאָנוּ מִמִּצְרָיִם: ¹²הֲלֹא־זֶה הַדָּבָר אֲשֶׁר דִּבַּרְנוּ אֵלֶיךָ בְמִצְרַיִם

לֵאמֹר חֲדַל מִמֶּנּוּ וְנַעַבְדָה אֶת־מִצְרָיִם כִּי טוֹב
לָנוּ עֲבֹד אֶת־מִצְרַיִם מִמֻּתֵנוּ בַּמִּדְבָּר: ¹³וַיֹּאמֶר
מֹשֶׁה אֶל־הָעָם אַל־תִּירָאוּ הִתְיַצְּבוּ וּרְאוּ אֶת־
יְשׁוּעַת יְהוָה אֲשֶׁר־יַעֲשֶׂה לָכֶם הַיּוֹם כִּי אֲשֶׁר
רְאִיתֶם אֶת־מִצְרַיִם הַיּוֹם לֹא תֹסִפוּ לִרְאֹתָם עוֹד
עַד־עוֹלָם: ¹⁴יְהוָה יִלָּחֵם לָכֶם וְאַתֶּם תַּחֲרִישׁוּן:
¹⁹וַיִּסַּע מַלְאַךְ הָאֱלֹהִים הַהֹלֵךְ לִפְנֵי מַחֲנֵה
יִשְׂרָאֵל וַיֵּלֶךְ מֵאַחֲרֵיהֶם וַיִּסַּע עַמּוּד הֶעָנָן
מִפְּנֵיהֶם וַיַּעֲמֹד מֵאַחֲרֵיהֶם: ²⁰וַיָּבֹא בֵּין מַחֲנֵה
מִצְרַיִם וּבֵין מַחֲנֵה יִשְׂרָאֵל וַיְהִי הֶעָנָן וְהַחֹשֶׁךְ
וַיָּאֶר אֶת־הַלָּיְלָה וְלֹא־קָרַב זֶה אֶל־זֶה כָּל־
הַלָּיְלָה: ²¹וַיֵּט מֹשֶׁה אֶת־הַיָּם בְּרוּחַ קָדִים עַזָּה
כָּל־הַלַּיְלָה וַיָּשֶׂם אֶת־הַיָּם לֶחָרָבָה ²⁴וַיְהִי
בְּאַשְׁמֹרֶת הַבֹּקֶר וַיַּשְׁקֵף יְהוָה אֶל־מַחֲנֵה מִצְרַיִם
בְּעַמּוּד אֵשׁ וְעָנָן וַיָּהָם אֵת מַחֲנֵה מִצְרָיִם: ²⁵וַיָּסַר
אֵת אֹפַן מַרְכְּבֹתָיו וַיְנַהֲגֵהוּ בִּכְבֵדֻת וַיֹּאמֶר
מִצְרַיִם אָנוּסָה מִפְּנֵי יִשְׂרָאֵל כִּי יְהוָה נִלְחָם לָהֶם
בְּמִצְרָיִם: ²⁷וַיָּשָׁב הַיָּם לִפְנוֹת בֹּקֶר לְאֵיתָנוֹ
וּמִצְרַיִם נָסִים לִקְרָאתוֹ וַיְנַעֵר יְהוָה אֶת־מִצְרַיִם
בְּתוֹךְ הַיָּם: ³⁰וַיּוֹשַׁע יְהוָה בַּיּוֹם הַהוּא אֶת־יִשְׂרָאֵל
מִיַּד מִצְרַיִם וַיַּרְא יִשְׂרָאֵל אֶת־מִצְרַיִם מֵת עַל־
שְׂפַת הַיָּם: ³¹וַיַּרְא יִשְׂרָאֵל אֶת־הַיָּד הַגְּדֹלָה אֲשֶׁר
עָשָׂה יְהוָה בְּמִצְרַיִם וַיִּירְאוּ הָעָם אֶת־יְהוָה
וַיַּאֲמִינוּ בַּיהוָה וּבְמֹשֶׁה עַבְדּוֹ:

עַל־הַיָּם כָּל־סוּס רֶכֶב פַּרְעֹה וּפָרָשָׁיו וְחֵילוֹ עַל־
פִּי הַחִירֹת לִפְנֵי בַּעַל צְפֹן: ¹⁰וַיִּצְעֲקוּ בְנֵי־יִשְׂרָאֵל
אֶל־יְהוָה: ¹⁵וַיֹּאמֶר יְהוָה אֶל־מֹשֶׁה מַה־תִּצְעַק
אֵלָי דַּבֵּר אֶל־בְּנֵי־יִשְׂרָאֵל וְיִסָּעוּ: ¹⁶וְאַתָּה הָרֵם
אֶת־מַטְּךָ וּנְטֵה אֶת־יָדְךָ עַל־הַיָּם וּבְקָעֵהוּ וְיָבֹאוּ
בְנֵי־יִשְׂרָאֵל בְּתוֹךְ הַיָּם בַּיַּבָּשָׁה: ¹⁷וַאֲנִי הִנְנִי
מְחַזֵּק אֶת־לֵב מִצְרַיִם וְיָבֹאוּ אַחֲרֵיהֶם וְאִכָּבְדָה
בְּפַרְעֹה וּבְכָל־חֵילוֹ בְּרִכְבּוֹ וּבְפָרָשָׁיו: ¹⁸וְיָדְעוּ
מִצְרַיִם כִּי־אֲנִי יְהוָה בְּהִכָּבְדִי בְּפַרְעֹה בְּרִכְבּוֹ
וּבְפָרָשָׁיו: ²¹וַיֵּט מֹשֶׁה אֶת־יָדוֹ עַל־הַיָּם וַיְבַּקְעוּ
הַמָּיִם: ²²וַיָּבֹאוּ בְנֵי־יִשְׂרָאֵל בְּתוֹךְ הַיָּם בַּיַּבָּשָׁה
וְהַמַּיִם לָהֶם חוֹמָה מִימִינָם וּמִשְּׂמֹאלָם: ²³וַיִּרְדְּפוּ
מִצְרַיִם וַיָּבֹאוּ אַחֲרֵיהֶם כֹּל סוּס פַּרְעֹה רִכְבּוֹ
וּפָרָשָׁיו אֶל־תּוֹךְ הַיָּם: ²⁶וַיֹּאמֶר יְהוָה אֶל־מֹשֶׁה
נְטֵה אֶת־יָדְךָ עַל־הַיָּם וְיָשֻׁבוּ הַמַּיִם עַל־מִצְרַיִם
עַל־רִכְבּוֹ וְעַל־פָּרָשָׁיו: ²⁷וַיֵּט מֹשֶׁה אֶת־יָדוֹ עַל־
הַיָּם ²⁸וַיָּשֻׁבוּ הַמַּיִם וַיְכַסּוּ אֶת־הָרֶכֶב וְאֶת־
הַפָּרָשִׁים לְכֹל חֵיל פַּרְעֹה הַבָּאִים אַחֲרֵיהֶם בַּיָּם
לֹא־נִשְׁאַר בָּהֶם עַד־אֶחָד: ²⁹וּבְנֵי יִשְׂרָאֵל הָלְכוּ
בַיַּבָּשָׁה בְּתוֹךְ הַיָּם וְהַמַּיִם לָהֶם חֹמָה מִימִינָם
וּמִשְּׂמֹאלָם:

¹The Lord said to Moses: ²"Tell the Israelites to turn back and encamp before Pi-hahiroth, between Migdol and the sea, before Baal-zephon; you shall encamp facing it, by the sea. ³Pharaoh will say of the Israelites, 'They are astray in the land; the wilderness has closed in on them.' ⁴Then I will stiffen Pharaoh's heart and he will pursue them, that I may gain glory through Pharaoh and all his host; and the Egyptians shall know that I am the Lord." And they

⁵When the king of Egypt was told that the people had fled, Pharaoh and his courtiers had a change of heart about the people and said, "What is this we have done, releasing Israel from our service?" ⁶He ordered his chariot and took his men with him; ⁷he took six hundred of his picked chariots, and the rest of the chariots of Egypt, with officers in all of them. ¹⁰As Pharaoh drew near, the Israelites caught sight of the Egyptians advancing upon them.

did so. [8]The Lord stiffened the heart of Pharaoh king of Egypt, and he gave chase to the Israelites. As the Israelites were departing defiantly, boldly, [9]the Egyptians gave chase to them, and all the chariot horses of Pharaoh, his horsemen, and his warriors overtook them encamped by the sea, near Pi-hahiroth, before Baal-zephon. [10]The Israelites cried out to the Lord. [15]Then the Lord said to Moses, "Why do you cry out to me? Tell the Israelites to go forward. [16]And you lift up your rod and hold out your arm over the sea and split it, so that the Israelites may march into the sea on dry ground. [17]And I will stiffen the hearts of the Egyptians so that they go in after them; and I will gain glory through Pharaoh and all his warriors, his chariots and his horsemen. [18]Let the Egyptians know that I am Lord, when I gain glory through Pharaoh, his chariots, and his horsemen." [21]Then Moses held out his arm over the sea. The waters were split, [22]and the Israelites went into the sea on dry ground, the waters forming a wall for them on their right and on their left. [23]The Egyptians came in pursuit after them into the sea, all of Pharaoh's horses, chariots, and horsemen. [26]Then the Lord said to Moses, "Hold out your arm over the sea, that the waters may come back upon the Egyptians and upon their chariots and upon their horsemen." [27]Moses held out his arm over the sea. [28]The waters

They were greatly frightened, [11]and they said to Moses, "Was it for want of graves in Egypt that you brought us to die in the wilderness? What have you done to us, taking us out of Egypt? [12]Is this not the very thing we told you in Egypt, saying, 'Let us be, and we will serve the Egyptians, for it is better for us to serve the Egyptians than to die in the wilderness'?" [13]But Moses said to the people, "Have no fear! Stand by, and witness the deliverance which the Lord will work for you today; for the Egyptians whom you see today you will never see again. [14]The Lord will battle for you; you hold your peace!" [19]The angel of God, who had been going ahead of the Israelite army, now moved and followed behind them; and the pillar of cloud shifted from in front of them and took up a place behind them, [20]and it came between the army of the Egyptians and the army of Israel. Thus there was the cloud with the darkness, and it cast a spell upon the night, so that the one could not come near the other all through the night. [21]The Lord drove back the sea with a strong east wind all that night, and turned the sea into dry ground. [24]At the morning watch, the Lord looked down upon the Egyptian army from a pillar of fire and cloud, and threw the Egyptian army into panic. [25]He locked the wheels of their chariots so that they moved forward with difficulty. And the Egyptians said, "Let us flee from turned back and covered the chariots and the horsemen—Pharaoh's entire army that followed them into the sea; not one of them remained. [29]But the Israelites had marched through the sea on dry ground, the waters forming a wall for them on their right and on their left.

the Israelites, for the Lord is fighting for them against Egypt." [27]At daybreak the sea returned to its normal state, and the Egyptians fled at its approach. But the Lord hurled the Egyptians into the sea. [30]Thus the Lord delivered Israel that day from the Egyptians. Israel saw the Egyptians dead on the shore of the sea. [31]And when Israel saw the wondrous power which the Lord had wielded against the Egyptians, the people feared the Lord; they had faith in the Lord and His servant Moses.

With the sources thus separated, we can see more clearly the distinct representations of this event according to each author.

The P story is built on a structure of three divine speeches and their fulfillments. Everything that happens proceeds according to the divine plan, with the stated purpose of glorifying Yahweh's name. The route toward the sea is entirely unnecessary for the Israelites' escape, as Yahweh's command in v. 2 makes clear; they are in fact retracing their steps for the sole purpose of luring the Egyptians toward the water, where Yahweh will destroy them.[42] Though Pharaoh has no real reason to pursue the Israelites, Yahweh hardens his heart, forcing him against his will to do so. Yahweh instructs Moses to lift his arm over the waters and split the sea so that the Israelites can pass through the middle of the waters; the Egyptians will follow. Immediately upon receiving these instructions Moses carries them out, lifting his arm and splitting the sea, and the Israelites pass between the walls of water with the Egyptians in pursuit. As soon as the Egyptians are in the midst of the sea, Yahweh commands Moses to lift his arm again and return the waters; again Moses immediately fulfills this command, and the waters cover the Egyptians and destroy them. The destruction of the Egyptians, like the wonders that preceded them in the priestly plagues narrative, occurs solely for the glorification of Yahweh.[43]

The J story is substantially different. The structure is not provided by divine speeches, as there are none; rather, there are two crucially placed speeches by the Egyptians, one at the beginning of the story and one at the end (vv. 5, 25). The narrative takes place over two days rather than one. Pharaoh, discovering to his horror that the Israelites have not taken three days' leave but have in fact fled their servitude, decides of his own free will to pursue them, repenting of his misinformed decision to let them go. The Israelites have, according to this story, been fleeing Egypt along the coast of the Mediterranean, as is geographically sensible, and the Egyptians have been following them along that path. (Note that in neither P nor J is it assumed that the Israelites have to cross a body of water to reach Canaan from Egypt; both authors are perfectly aware of the regional geography.) When the Egyptians arrive, it is nightfall, and the Israelites halt and strike camp; the pillar of cloud moves between the camps to prevent the Egyptians from overrunning the Israelites. During this night, the pillar of cloud also prevents the Egyptians from seeing that Yahweh is blowing back the waters from the shore by a strong east wind, thereby essentially moving the coastline. When dawn comes, Yahweh begins the battle against the Egyptians, impelling them to flee and at the same time making it difficult for them to move with the necessary speed. The Israelites, as Moses told them (v. 13), do not need to move at all; there is no crossing of the sea in this story.[44] When the Egyptians do try to turn back to Egypt, thinking they are retracing their steps along the water's edge, they are in fact traveling along a false shore, and when the sea returns to its former state, the Egyptians are washed away. In their divinely created confusion, they even run unknowingly toward the water. Unlike in the P story, however, they are close enough to land that they have a chance of escaping; it is necessary therefore that God throw them back into the sea.[45]

When the text is divided into two separate stories according to these narrative indications, a number of elements of style and terminology resolve into one of the two stories as well.[46] These are, however, only secondary support for the source division; they are, as we have seen, entirely unnecessary for the argument. Far more important are the connections between the two stories in Exodus 14 and the rest of the J and P narratives, particularly the plagues. As already noted, the P narrative begins in 14:1–2 with the direct continuation of the itinerary notice from P in 13:20. Further, as we have seen, the hardening of Pharaoh's heart in v. 4, by which Yahweh reverses or undermines Pharaoh's will, is one of the major defining features of the priestly plagues narrative. The end of v. 4, "and the Egyptians shall know that I am Yahweh," hearkens back to the beginning of the plagues narrative, in Exodus 7:5: "And the Egyptians shall know that I am Yahweh." Also, as noted, the parenthetical comment of v. 8b, "the Israelites were departing defiantly," belongs only to the priestly narrative of the Exodus and is in fact contradictory to the J story.[47]

In the second and third paragraphs of P, we find Yahweh's instruction to Moses to lift his staff and arm over the sea and split it or cause it to return. The use of Aaron's or Moses's hands or staff as the instrument of God's actions is an essential element of each of the priestly signs in the plagues narrative (cf. Exod 7:9, 19; 8:1, 12; 9:8, 22; 10:12, 20). Not only the manner of Moses's action, but indeed the entire form of the P story in Exodus 14 resembles that of the priestly plagues. In the P plagues story, each individual event is introduced by instructions from Yahweh to Moses, followed immediately by their fulfillment, with no notice of any intervening action; so too the crossing of the sea in Exodus 14.

The J story in Exodus 14 also belongs firmly to the larger J narrative. As observed earlier, the motif of Pharaoh changing his mind, indeed of Pharaoh having a will of his own at all, evident in 14:5, recurs throughout the J plagues. Note also in v. 5 the presence of Pharaoh's courtiers (*ʿᵃbādāyw*), who have an active role in the plagues story only in the nonpriestly strand (cf. Exod 7:20, 28, 29; 8:5, 7, 17, 20, 25, 29; 9:14, 20, 21, 30, 34; 10:1, 6, 7; 11:8; 12:30). Of particular interest in this regard is Exodus 10:7, in which the courtiers attempt to persuade Pharaoh to let the Israelites go (see also 12:31); this part of the story is almost certainly in mind when Pharaoh and his courtiers have a change of heart in 14:5.[48] In their sole appearance in P, in 7:10, the servants are silent witnesses to the first sign; they do not reappear thereafter.

The pillar of cloud and fire in vv. 19–20, 24 was introduced in J at the end of the previous chapter (Exod 13:21–22). This J concept of the pillar that accompanies the Israelites recurs in Numbers 14:14 and stands in opposition to the priestly notion of the divine cloud (Exod 40:34–38), which hovers over or resides in the Tabernacle, indicates the Presence of Yahweh, and functions as the means by which the Israelites know whether to travel or to encamp; it differs also from the presentation of E, in which the cloud is not a constant presence as in J and P but appears only at the Tent of Meeting and only when Yahweh descends to speak with Moses (Exod 33:7–11; see case study II). According to J, the pillar appears as cloud during the day and as fire during the night; P does not describe the cloud as a pillar, and the fire at night appears within the cloud, not in place of it. The very concept of Yahweh personally leading the Israelites through the wilderness, introduced in 13:21–22 and assumed here, is part of a continuing J motif: Yahweh threatens to cease accompanying the Israelites in Exodus 33:1–3; Moses pleads for Yahweh to relent in 33:12–16; and Yahweh agrees to continue leading them in 33:17.

In the analysis above, an important piece of evidence for separating the sources was the distinction between J's view that the events took place over the course of two days and the intervening night, and P's view that the events all took place in a single day. The different views of passing time in J and P are not restricted to this chapter but are yet another continuation of details from the two versions of the plagues narrative. In the P version, there is no indication of any passing time between one plague and the next; as Pharaoh's heart is hardened after each one, the next plague follows immediately. In J, on the other hand, each plague is followed by a period during which Pharaoh is given the chance to allow the people to leave, and there are regular indicators that time passes between each plague (see 7:15, 25; 8:16, 19, 25; 9:13, 18; 10:4, 13b; 11:4).[49]

Whereas in the priestly plagues, and the P story of Exodus 14, it is the action of Moses (and Aaron, in the plagues) that brings about the plagues, in the J plagues narrative it is Yahweh himself who is responsible for initiating them (see Exod 8:20; 9:6, 23aβ; 10:13aβ; even the plague of blood, which is marked by Moses striking the Nile, is attributed to Yahweh, 7:25). Further, the means by which Yahweh moves the sea in J, that is, with the wind (14:21aβ), resonates with other texts from J. It is with a wind that Yahweh brings the locusts (Exod 10:13aβ) and with a wind that he drives them away (10:19); later, it is with a wind that Yahweh brings the quails to feed the people in the wilderness (Num 11:31; see case study II).

Through these textual relationships we can see that the J and P narratives in Exodus 14 cannot and should not be read on their own, but rather fit into a larger narrative arc and can be fully understood only when read in light of the passages that precede them.

When we have separated this chapter into two strands, we can see clearly that each story is entirely complete, continuous, and coherent. With this in mind, we can turn to the question of whether it is preferable, or indeed even possible, to see the priestly material in this chapter as a redactional layer, imposed upon the J material, rather than as an independent source.[50]

The assessment of P as a redactional layer has long been based on the belief that it is not complete, continuous, or coherent in its own right and that it therefore must require the nonpriestly materials in order to be sensible. Yet as already argued in this book, such a view depends on a reading of the priestly source through the lens of the canonical whole. In fact, when viewed independently, and judged on its own terms, the priestly source is indeed complete, continuous, and coherent—considerably more so, in fact, than either J or E. Upon reading the priestly text of Exodus 14, the same conclusion seems evident. How, then, have those scholars who believe P to be a redactional layer made that argument in this particular chapter?[51]

Some scholars try to have it both ways, claiming on the one hand that P redacted and supplemented the nonpriestly material and on the other hand that P is, in this chapter at least, a continuous and self-standing narrative.[52] Erhard

Blum, acknowledging the fullness of the priestly story, does see a gap between the Israelites' cry to Yahweh in v. 10 and Yahweh's response in v. 15 in which he accuses Moses of crying out; Blum concludes from this that the priestly story, though almost entirely free of gaps, is here dependent on a preexisting narrative.[53] Yet there are two problems with this argument. First, this gap is hardly significant enough to demonstrate that P was written as a supplement to a preexisting text.[54] Second, and more important, the prepriestly text on which Blum assumes the P narrative was based also does not include any notice of Moses crying out to Yahweh. Moses's speech in vv. 13–14 is entirely directed to the people and cannot in any way be construed as "crying out to Yahweh."[55]

John Van Seters claims that P was written exclusively to supplement J, but his conclusion is based on a considerably different source division.[56] He argues that the priestly story lacks a locale, since it depends on "the J itinerary (13:20) at its beginning."[57] The itinerary notice in 13:20, however, has a word-for-word parallel in Numbers 33:6 (P).[58] He assigns v. 9aα (through *'al-hayyām*) to J, ostensibly because it would stand as J's narration of Pharaoh's pursuit;[59] as a result, Van Seters asks, "How did Israel get to the other side of the sea, since they are located as 'encamped beside the sea' (v. 9)?"[60] This is a problem, of course, only when v. 9aα is assigned to J, despite the fact that the concluding words of this clause, "encamped by the sea," are a direct quotation of the priestly notice of the Israelites' location in v. 2 (even according to Van Seters's own source division). He conflates the Israelites' cry to Yahweh in v. 10 and their complaint to Moses in vv. 11–12, attributing both to J; this has the effect of making Yahweh's response to the cry in v. 15 appear to be lacking an antecedent in the priestly narrative[61] but also results, as we have seen, in a confusing sequence of events and responses. Finally, Van Seters dislikes the sequence of vv. 27b and 30 in J, claiming that "the description of the Egyptians' overthrow is not complete without the explicit statement of v. 28,"[62] a judgment that is more revealing of Van Seters's literary style than of that of the biblical author. He thus assigns the entirety of v. 28 to J, severing its connection with v. 26 and damaging the priestly scheme of command and fulfillment. This attribution results in the necessity for the Israelites to cross the sea in J as well as in P and requires Van Seters to bring vv. 22a and 23 also into the J narrative.[63] At this point, what was once the straightforward narrative of J is considerably more complicated, incorporating numerous variant elements and themes, while the complete narrative of P is obliterated. With this source division as his basis, it is no wonder that Van Seters considers P to be redactional. Yet the problems with his analysis are numerous and manifest, and as a result the conclusions he draws from it are problematic as well.[64]

More interesting are those scholars who agree with the basic source division presented here yet still hold to the view that P is a redactional layer. Jan Wagenaar describes P in Exodus 14 as "a redactional adaptation of the Yahwistic Sea Narrative."[65] His basis for this conclusion, however, is somewhat opaque: "The Priestly version of the Sea Narrative mainly consists of the three-fold speech of Yahweh to Moses and the subsequent execution of the divine commands. . . . The Priestly texts, therefore, can hardly be seen as an independent and self-contained story."[66] It is decidedly unclear as to why this should be so. If the priestly source contained only the direct discourse of the divine speeches, without their narrative execution, it would certainly be problematic; as it stands, however, the P story is eminently readable, coherent, and complete. The argument that a text consisting of only speeches and their fulfillments is not a self-contained narrative seems to be grounded in an a priori formal view of what a "narrative" should look like—and an odd one at that—rather than on the content of the text itself. The fact that Wagenaar is able to reconstruct and explain the priestly story,[67] without noting any obvious or even less than obvious gaps, and without noting any actual dependence on the J narrative, in itself speaks against his conclusion.

The strongest voice in contemporary scholarship for P as a redactional layer is that of Marc Vervenne. Like Wagenaar, his conclusion in this regard depends heavily on his aesthetic evaluation of the priestly story: "the attentive reader will notice that it is not thrilling literature."[68] He too notes the structure of speech and execution, to which he adds the observation that "the vocabulary is very stereotypic."[69] Further, "this strand is without the effects of surprise nor does it move towards a real *dénouement.*"[70] These assessments are entirely subjective and moreover have no bearing on the status of the story as independent or redactional; even thrill-less literature can be authentically authorial. Similar is Vervenne's observation that "only the first two speeches of Yhwh reach a climax in the motive of 'knowing'";[71] this observation also speaks only to the inner workings of the priestly text and not to its status relative to the nonpriestly narrative.[72] Vervenne goes on to argue that "the end of the 'story' is ineffective. The miracle seems to be unsuccessful. It is not told that the Egyptians finally ידעו יהוה [know Yahweh]."[73] First, it should be noted that P does not expect the Egyptians to "know Yahweh," but rather to know "that I am Yahweh" (Exod 7:5). It is not P's intention that the Egyptians should be converted to the Yahwistic faith, but that they should come to know firsthand who controls earthly events. More to the point, perhaps, I would argue that the priestly author assumes that the Egyptians, in the very act of dying by divine agency, come to know "that I am Yahweh" in the most direct of ways. Yet Vervenne seems to be demanding some sort of formal resolution to the narrative, even though one is tempted to think that if such a direct conclusion were provided in the priestly text, it would be judged as yet another example of the speech-and-execution formula, and hence as not particularly good literature.

Vervenne brings a few more detailed arguments in support of his claim. He asserts that the motif of the hardening of Pharaoh's heart in v. 4 is surprising, since this motif reached its logical conclusion in the final plague in Exodus 12:29–32.[74] Even leaving aside the fact that Exodus 12:29–32 is nonpriestly, and makes no mention of the hardening of Pharaoh's heart, Vervenne has made an artificial break between the plague and sea stories, one that is expressly contradicted by the language and themes of the priestly source. According to P, it is not Yahweh's intention to stop with the deaths of the Egyptian firstborn and the exodus of the Israelites; the Egyptians must die as well. When Vervenne states that "the motive of the hardening of the heart reappears unannounced in 14,4, for we nowhere read that Pharaoh and the Egyptians resisted again,"[75] he is neglecting or misreading the preceding verse, in which, as I have argued, Pharaoh proclaims himself disinclined to chase the Israelites. Pharaoh's heart must be hardened, since he is resisting—ironically, not the urge to let the people go, but the urge to chase them in the wilderness.[76]

Vervenne finds it "difficult to explain why Aaron, who was alongside his brother Moses in the preceding 'plague' sections, is no longer present in the Sea narrative."[77] Unless we are to believe that the priestly redactor had an anti-Aaron perspective—a hard conclusion to draw given the well-known focus on Aaron in the priestly work as a whole—it is unclear why this should be an indication that the priestly story is redactional. Further, it is to be noted that Aaron's role in the priestly plagues narrative diminishes gradually and consistently over the course of the story;[78] his absence here is no more than the logical continuation of that trend.

Finally, Vervenne correctly notes two places where the priestly material and the nonpriestly material stand in some conflict, and where, in his view, the priestly text "frames" the nonpriestly text, namely, vv. 21 and 27–28.[79] He observes correctly that the priestly notice of the splitting of the sea at the end of v. 21 is somewhat awkward after it has already been said earlier in the verse that the sea was turned into dry ground. Similarly, he sees the returning of the waters according to P in v. 28 as redundant after the waters have already been said to return in v. 27. He goes on to claim that the placement of the priestly text in these passages reveals "a profound and deliberate redactional activity in the Sea narrative."[80] This is similar to Blum's claim and can be answered similarly. These redundancies are in fact the result of redactional activity, but not on the part of the priestly writer. Rather, the placement of the priestly passages is entirely due to the necessary logic of the combined text. As awkward as the order of v. 21 may be, the alternative, in which the notice of the waters being split would precede the wind and the revealing of the dry ground, is far worse; the same is true for any reorganization of vv. 27–28.

It seems very difficult to accept the notion that the priestly text as identified above is not an independent source. It is only when one enters the discussion having already decided that P is a redactional layer that such a possibility even arises. Apparently aware of how groundless this view is, Vervenne finds it necessary to bolster it by asserting that "this P material can barely be read as a complete whole."[81] Yet this view is so thoroughly at odds with the plain evidence of the text, and the majority of scholarly opinion, that it can hardly be taken as a definitive argument.

Because the J and P narratives of Exodus 14 describe a singular event—one that happened at a specific historical moment, and could happen only once—the fact that they were combined into a single story is hardly surprising. It is important, however, to recognize how they were combined. The opening sections of each story (vv. 1–4 and v. 5) could hardly be placed in any other order: only vv. 1–4 contain the important geographical information and the prediction of Pharaoh's actions, which obviously has to precede Pharaoh's actual actions. Similarly, vv. 6–7, in which Pharaoh readies his army, have to precede v. 8, in which the actual pursuit is narrated. The pursuit and overtaking of the Israelites in v. 9 is similarly a prerequisite for the Israelites seeing the Egyptians approaching in v. 10abα. The two statements of Israel's fear in v. 10 could theoretically be put in either order and still make sense (although putting the stative sentence "they were very afraid" after the active "the Israelites cried out to Yahweh" might be read as somewhat redundant); there is no reason that the compiler should have switched from one source to the other here. As we have seen, the general rule is that one source is followed as long as possible, until the next section of the other source has to be inserted.

The people's speech in vv. 11–12 has to precede both Moses's and Yahweh's reactions to it, while Moses's speech, insofar as it is actually addressed to the people, logically follows. Either way, Moses's speech in vv. 13–14 and Yahweh's speech in vv. 15–18 contradict each other, with Moses telling the people to stand still and Yahweh telling them to move; it is far more acceptable, however, for Yahweh to contradict Moses than vice versa. Verses 19–20, about the pillar of cloud, explicitly take place before the episode at the sea and so have to be placed before that event begins in v. 21. In v. 21, Moses stretching his arm over the sea cannot follow Yahweh driving back the water, for it would be rendered entirely useless. The end of this verse is another case where, since either order of "he turned the sea into dry ground" and "the waters were split" results in a striking redundancy, the compiler seems to have followed the usual procedure of simply following the same source until it is necessary to change.

The Israelites and Egyptians must enter the sea in vv. 22–23 before Yahweh causes the Egyptians to panic in vv. 24–25: since in their panic they try to flee, they have to have already entered the water in the canonical text. In vv. 26–27 Moses holding his arm over the sea had to be placed before the return of the waters and the attempt of the Egyptians to flee; on the other hand, the attempt of the Egyptians to flee had to come before their final destruction in v. 28. The final sections, v. 29 and vv. 30–31, could hardly be placed in a different order: v. 29 is still concluding the narrative, albeit in retrospective fashion, while vv. 30–31 read as the summation and moral of the entire story.

The compiler, in combining these two narratives into a single story, was able to preserve the entirety of his sources, without adding, subtracting, or changing a word. He simply put the pieces in their logical and chronological order. At each step, his choices were fairly clear; indeed, they were hardly choices at all. It is hard to imagine how the various elements could have been put in any different order without creating an even more problematic narrative. We have seen this same procedure at work in the previous case studies as well; in the following chapter I discuss the work of the compiler in detail.

Chapter 6

―――――――•·◄∞►·•―――――――

COMPILATION

The Combining of the Sources

The preceding chapters have argued for, and the case studies have demonstrated, the literary grounds for the hypothesis that the canonical Pentateuch is the product of the combination of four originally independent documents. At this point it is appropriate to address the question of how these documents were brought together into the Pentateuch we now have. The question is, decidedly, "how," rather than when, where, why, or by whom. For it is only the literary evidence that the Documentary Hypothesis takes up, and the literary evidence can answer only the question of how the sources were combined. This is not to say that the other questions we may ask are invalid—they are certainly worth asking—but, as with the isolation and identification of the source documents themselves, we must begin at the literary level, for the Pentateuch is, first and foremost, a literary work, and it is the literary problems inherent in the canonical text that require addressing. What we can and cannot say in regard to the other questions will be dealt with only after we have established how the sources were combined.

THE EXPANDED ROLE OF THE REDACTOR

Any study of the redaction of the Pentateuch must begin with an observation that is self-evident, but the ramifications of this observation are often overlooked or ignored: the idea of the redactor(s) of the Pentateuch is necessitated only by the existence of four continuous, coherent, originally independent documents that have been combined into a single story in the canonical text. That is, if there are four sources in the Pentateuch that have been interwoven, then we must postulate a redaction that effected their combination into the text we now have. The redactor is a necessary logical outgrowth of the identification of the pentateuchal documents.

This initial observation has important consequences for how we identify redactional work in the Pentateuch and conceive of the redactor(s). First, it means that the analysis must begin with the identification and isolation of the sources before any investigation of how they were put together can proceed. There obviously can be no accurate evaluation of how the sources were combined before we have a full picture of what texts each of the sources comprises. Second, and as a corollary to the first, we must assume that a given text belongs to one of the sources unless the impossibility of such an assignment can be conclusively demonstrated. In other words, every effort must be made to understand a given passage as part of one of the four documents, with the attribution to a redactor being a last resort. Every time we assign a bit of text to a redactor, we run the risk of having taken part of the literary work of a genuine author, whose words and work are well established, and given it to a considerably more nebulous figure who owes his existence solely to the theory. Third, the activity attributed to the redactor cannot outstrip the simple function required of him by the theory: the combination of the four source documents into a single text. The redactor owes his existence only to the fact that the documents have been combined and is defined by this role; we cannot assign to him anything beyond his single necessary function (although, as we will see, this function can be manifested in a variety of forms). For this reason I have referred throughout to the redactor as "compiler," for this term emphasizes the authentic role required of this figure. Fourth, any text attributed to a redactor must serve the purpose of redaction; that is, it must participate in the process of combining the sources. If a redactor is given credit for authoring texts that do not contribute to the combination of the sources, then he becomes something other than a redactor, and that something is not required by the theory.

As already noted, these logical consequences of the recognition that the redactor emerges from the identification of the sources, rather than being on a par with them, have not affected the majority of pentateuchal scholarship, even (especially) among classical source critics. Rather, we can observe within scholarship a trend toward the expansion of the redactor's role, from the simple combination of sources to a full-blown author and theologian in his own right.[1]

For some of the earliest pentateuchal critics, the redactor did little more than put his sources (however many there may have been) down in some rough order. In the seventeenth century, Baruch Spinoza claimed that the redactor (for him, Ezra) took the historical documents available to him and presented them without attempting to reconcile their contradictions, without overlaying them with his own historical, theological, or ideological viewpoint; rather, Spinoza claimed that Ezra "simply set them down, leaving their examination and arrangement to posterity."[2] So too Johann Vater, despite (or because of) his identification of very many fragments making up the Pentateuch, considered the redactor to have merely put the fragments into chronological order, contradictions notwithstanding.[3] Jean Astruc even claimed that Moses had arranged the sources of Genesis in columns, just as he himself had, in chronological order.[4] For these scholars, there was no text that could be attributed to the hand of the redactor.

Johann Eichhorn, in the early nineteenth century, recognized that the redactor was almost entirely faithful to his sources, preserving them as completely as possible: "Did ever a historian handle his sources more religiously and reverently than did the arranger of these?"[5] Yet he also noted that there were places where the redactor had adjusted his received texts ever so slightly, for the sole purpose of improving the connection between them in the final form. Eichhorn offered as an example the change of "he bore Noah" to "he bore a son" in Genesis 5:28 (P), a change necessitated by the etymology of Noah's name in 5:29 (J).[6]

In the mid-nineteenth century Hermann Hupfeld assigned a new role to the redactor: author of interpretive glosses. Though Hupfeld recognized that the redactor made insertions into his text for the purpose of resolving some contradictions, such as the word "again" in Genesis 35:9 (see case study V), he also attributed to the redactor phrases or verses that he could not fit into any of his three source documents. Thus he brought as an example Genesis 20:18, the final line of the story of Isaac and Rebecca in the court of Abimelech. Since he could not find a place for it in either J or E—for terminological reasons: the verse is set in an E context but uses the divine name Yahweh—Hupfeld decided that it must be a gloss from the redactor.[7] Thus a new era for the redactor began, one in which he could be held responsible for passages that did not contribute to the process of redaction proper; now the redactor served as a means of solving problems in a scholar's analysis, terminological or otherwise. The redactor became an analytical tool, to be wielded when the going got too tough. The high point (or low point) of this sort of use of the redactor may be Julius Wellhausen's analysis (or lack thereof) of Exodus 32–34, which, after admitting to great difficulty in separating the sources, he assigned in toto to the redactor.[8]

While the redactor's role in scholarship changed, from the logical outgrowth of the existence of the sources to the solution to difficult passages, his literary role was dramatically altered as well: no longer a compiler, who made small adjustments for the purpose of a better final text, the redactor now became an author in his own right. Thus the passages that could be ascribed to him were expanded from those that served the process of compilation to virtually any text at all; there was no longer any limit on what type of text could be, in theory, the work of a redactor. In this way almost any passage that could be removed without grossly disturbing its context could be attributed to a redactor. These passages, frequently described as "secondary additions," comprise a wide range of genres, styles, and content: from seemingly repetitive statements, as in Exodus 3:14, to prolepsis, as in Exodus 4:21–23; from historical referents in the Covenant Code to the patriarchal promises.[9] Though some of these "secondary additions" contain little in the way of new ideas, some, particularly the patriarchal promises, carry significant theological weight. These passages were not assigned to the redactor because they were theological, necessarily, but rather on stylistic or terminological grounds or because they could be removed from their contexts without breaking the flow of the narrative. Yet because they do contain theological concepts, the redactor became—almost by accident—not just an author, but an active, regularly intervening, theologically minded author. The distance between this active theologian and the compiler necessitated by the theory is difficult to overstate.

It is also clear that the dramatic expansion of the redactor's role in classical source-critical scholarship found its logical conclusion in the European approach, in which the equation of redactors with theologically intentional authors is made explicit. To a certain extent, the European approach deserves credit for recognizing the degree to which the redactor had taken on a new role and embracing it, placing the authorial and theological aspects of the redactor's role in the forefront of his work, rather than leaving them as unstated attributes. We can also see in the European approach the way in which the redactor performs a great variety of literary tasks: compiler of disparate materials, inserter of words and phrases to connect these materials, interpreter and glossator of older texts, author of entirely new sections, and above all ideological, political, and theological reviser. As we have seen in chapter 2, in this approach the genuine literary activity of the Pentateuch belongs to the redactors, not to the "authors," who are relegated to an ephemeral prehistory of the text. Again, the lack of control over what text can be attributed to a redactor is at the heart of the matter, both for the European approach and for its classical predecessors.

HOW MANY COMPILERS?

If I am advocating in this book for a return to the classical four-source hypothesis, I am also advocating for a return to the earliest concepts of how the

redactor, that is, the compiler, worked. In recognizing the ways in which the redactor's role expanded, we are able to recognize the ways in which it must now
be reduced. As I have argued, the compiler belongs to the documentary theory
as a necessary outgrowth of the identification of the four sources, as the required
figure who combined them. All that we can and should ask of the compiler is
the combination of the sources into a single story—no more, no less. What we
attribute to the compiler can be only those elements that contribute to the process of compilation. This has been the practice in the case studies to this point,
and I further define these elements below.

First, however, we must address a fundamental point: how many compilers
of the Pentateuch were there? From Wellhausen to Richard Elliott Friedman,
virtually all adherents of the Documentary Hypothesis have posited three distinct redactions: J and E into "JE," by a redactor "R^{JE}"; "JE" and D into "JED"
by a redactor "R^{JED}"; and JED and P into the canonical Pentateuch by the final
redactor, "R." Given how widespread this claim is, it is necessary to inquire why
scholars have thought that there must be more than one compiler.

The first reason, and the most theoretical (rather than literary), is the theory
of the evolutionary growth of the Pentateuch posited by Wellhausen and others
of his era. When Israelite religion is reduced to a monolith, the entire culture
developing in lockstep with a single concept of religion at any given moment,
then the textual representation of that religion also must exist only in a single
form at any given time. Although each document was written to supplant the
one that preceded it, the authoritative status of the earlier document evidently
meant that it could not simply disappear. And since the coexistence of two
competing religious worldviews could hardly be thinkable from the evolutionary perspective, the later document was combined with the earlier, thereby preserving not only the latest manifestation of Israelite religion but also the history
of its development. This evolutionary framework is highly conditioned by the
period in which it arose, and it assumes a theory of religious development that
is largely unattested in societies ancient or modern. We can no longer assume
that disparate religious views could not have existed side by side at a single moment in ancient Israel.

On more substantial literary grounds, scholars have argued for the separate
redactions of J and E and of JE and D because these combined works seem to
be the basis for the later documents written to replace them. Thus it is claimed
that D knew of and wrote on the basis of the combined JE text, and that P
knew of and wrote in response to the combined JED text. Such claims would
be very powerful indeed, if they could be demonstrated to be true. Yet, as we
have already seen, neither claim is confirmed by the literary data. We have

seen that although the author of D did indeed know J and E, he knew them separately. This is demonstrated by his use of the E stories of Numbers 11 and especially of the Horeb pericope without any reference to the J texts with which they have been intermingled (see chapter 3).[10] We have also treated at length, in chapter 5, the independence of P from the nonpriestly material. To some extent, as argued in chapter 5, the literary claims for the dependence of the later sources on the earlier are inextricably linked with the theoretical claims for the evolutionary growth of the text. If we do not assume the latter, we are able to see more clearly that the literary evidence in fact stands in opposition to the former.

Wellhausen also argued that there was a discernible difference between the combination of J and E and that of JE and P. The difference he found, however, was both subjective and logically problematic: he claimed that because it was more difficult, at times even impossible, for him to separate J from E, while it was very easy to isolate P, J and E must have been combined at an earlier stage.[11] The subjectivity is evident in the first part of the argument: it is because Wellhausen was unable to separate J and E that some explanation is required. If, however, one does not have great difficulty separating J and E, then the basis for his redactional argument is eliminated. The logical problem comes in the second part: it is unclear why difficulty in separating two sources should be an indication that they were either combined in a separate redactional event or that their redaction must be ascribed to an earlier stage. Wellhausen's difficulty in separating J from E has many explanations—they are not as stylistically distinct as P, they are more similar in genre than P, they overlap narratively more than P—but none of them requires a separate redaction of J and E. And certainly the relative timing of this purported redaction has no bearing on anything: if J and E were combined early or late, the combination would presumably look the same. Despite the many scholars who followed Wellhausen in his conclusion, his logic in reaching that conclusion is not without its faults.

Friedman has recently combined some versions of these three arguments into a more coherent argument for separate redactors than has previously been attempted.[12] He argues for a distinction between R^{JE} and R on the basis of the different way in which they have each treated the material that came down to them. It should first be noted that Friedman begins from the assumption that there are different redactors, and works from there, thus to a certain extent arguing in a circle. Moreover, the clear line he attempts to draw between the methods of R^{JE} and those of R do not hold up. Friedman claims that R^{JE} had a fairly free hand in reworking his source texts and was willing to delete some material from each, whereas R was concerned with retaining his sources in full.[13] Yet this does not account for the many contradictions and other narrative problems that remain in the purported "JE" text that should have been fixed by this unconstrained editor. On the other side, the places where P and "JE" have been combined, but part of one or the other has been eliminated (as in the birth of Isaac, the death of Abraham, or the marriages of Jacob), belie Friedman's description of the maximally retentive R.

In reengaging the question without any preconceived notions, either theoretical or literary, as to how many compilers there were, we must begin with another relatively simple methodological point: we should assume, unless proved otherwise, only as many compilers as are necessary to put the four sources together—in other words, one. With this assumption as the starting point, the question changes somewhat. We now need to ask what literary evidence we might find that would point to more than one compiler.

It is not coincidental that the process of identifying multiple compilers is parallel to that of finding more than one author in the Pentateuch. Indeed, the two types of analysis require the same sorts of questions, mutatis mutandis. We identify the four authors of the Pentateuch by virtue of their disparate historical claims, which, as I have argued, constitute the primary mark of authorship. Where we see distinct historical claims, so we see distinct authors. When we turn to the compiler, we follow the same path: the primary mark of a compiler is the method by which he combines his sources, in both major and minor ways. If we find disparate methods of compilation between the various sources—that is, if the method of combining J and E is clearly distinct from the method of combining J and P, P and E, etc.,—then, and only then, can we justifiably argue for separate compilers.

As has perhaps become evident from the preceding case studies and chapters, such disparate methods are nowhere to be found. In terms of the broader ways that the sources have been combined, we see entire narratives from one source placed beside entire narratives from another: the P and J creation stories in Genesis 1 and 2–3, the J and E stories in Genesis 19 and 20, the E and P stories in Genesis 22 and 23. Narratives from each source are interwoven with another, in every possible variety, as the case studies have shown: J and E in Genesis 37 and Numbers 11, P and E in Numbers 16, P and J in Exodus 14.

In more detailed terms, we may consider those places where the compiler has inserted a word or phrase into one source to correct a glaring discrepancy with another. This has been done in J with regard to an E story (the insertion of "Potiphar, a courtier [better: eunuch] of Pharaoh and his chief steward" in Gen 39:1); in E with regard to a J story (the insertion of "from the bush" in Exod 3:4); in P with regard to an E story (the insertion of "the two tablets" in Exod 34:29); in E with regard to a P story (the insertion of "Korah" in

Num 16:32); in P with regard to a J story (the insertion of "Goshen" in Gen 47:27); in J with regard to a P story (the insertion of "I will harden his heart" in Exod 4:21). We may also consider places where two sources used the same phrase, and the compiler set it down only once. This can be seen in combinations of E and P (Exod 31:18), J and E (Num 11:11), and J and P (Num 13:26).

There is, in short, no literary reason to assume more than one compiler for the canonical Pentateuch. The methods of combining the documents, from the broadest to the most minute, are identical across J, E, and P, regardless of which two sources are being combined.[14] August Dillmann, one of the very few scholars to argue for a single compiler, made this point clearly: "It is just the thorough similarity in the method of combining J with E and E with P . . . that speaks strongly in favor of the idea that the same hand effected both combinations."[15] If the Pentateuch were as consistent in its historical claims as its compilation is with regard to method, we would never have needed to hypothesize the existence of four sources. The existence of the four sources, in turn, in no way necessitates the existence of three compilers. With no evidence to the contrary, we should abide by the most economical explanation: one compiler, who did his work thoroughly and uniformly across the four documents of the Pentateuch.

THE COMPILER'S METHOD

I now turn to the question of precisely what it was that the compiler did—not solely in the mechanical sense, but in the broader picture. I begin, however, by recognizing not what the compiler did, but what he did not do.

The compiler did not resolve the vast majority of contradictions between the sources. If he had, of course, we would never have known that there were sources to begin with. Even so, the extent of contradiction that the compiler allowed to stand in his combined text is extraordinary. The laws, for instance, with all of their disparities, were left untouched. The competing notions of what and where the Tent of Meeting was; the competing numbers of animals Noah was to take onto the ark; the different names of Moses's father-in-law; the different names for the mountain in the wilderness—all of these and many more were evidently not deemed problematic enough to warrant correction. Given the compiler's clear aversion to fixing the contradictions in the final text, we must be very cautious in attributing to him texts that seem to present "solutions" to the conflicting sources.

We may note, however, that the compiler does intervene in certain circumstances. As we have already observed, the categories of birth, death, and marriage reports are unique: none is told more than once, though it is almost certain that J, E, and P all told them. The distinctive feature of these categories is not only that they could not have happened twice, but also their relatively fixed formulation: that someone was born, or died, or was married is told in virtually the same words regardless of source. In the case of the flood, which also could not have happened twice, the story is told in very different ways, indeed in very different words, by J and P. The death of Abraham, however, could hardly be told other than in the words "Abraham died," or some variation thereof. Thus the compiler intercedes, albeit very lightly, by setting down only one of the competing reports. In this way, however, he did not truly alter his source texts, because the information, indeed probably the very words, were identical in both (or all three).

The compiler also makes a change when he combines two stories that take place in irreconcilable locations. Importantly, changes are not made when the sources use two names for the same functional place: Sinai and Horeb are both names for the mountain in the wilderness where the theophany and law-giving occurred, and whether they are in fact the same place in the minds of their respective authors, it is certainly easy enough to consider them two names for a single location. This is the case also with Rebecca's homeland, called Haran (J) or Paddan-Aram (P), or the Transjordanian territory, ascribed to the Edomites and Amorites (E) or Midianites (P). But when two locations are described, rather than simply named, then a real problem exists. According to E, Joseph is sold into the house of Potiphar, Pharaoh's eunuch and chief steward; according to J, he is sold into the house of an unnamed Egyptian and ends up in prison. When these stories converge, Joseph would appear to be in two places at once. Thus the compiler equates Potiphar's house with the prison in Genesis 40:3, 5. Similarly, according to J, God called to Moses from the burning bush; according to E, he almost certainly called to Moses from heaven. When the compiler combined these two speeches into one, he could not have God in both places at once and so inserted "from the bush" into the E story. We may note that the same principle applies to people as well as places: though one person can have two different names, as with Moses's father-in-law, two clearly differentiated people cannot serve the same narrative function. Thus Potiphar and the un-named Egyptian, each of whom is, according to E and J respectively, the one who purchased Joseph, are identified as one and the same person by the compiler's insertion in Genesis 39:1. So too with the combination of Korah with Dathan and Abiram in Numbers 16:24, 27, 32 (see case study III).

Though this certainly does not exhaust the list of places where the compiler alters his sources or inserts material into the text, it does give some sense of how restrictive the compiler was in his interventions and therefore how careful we must be in ascribing text to him. It is clear that the compiler's primary goal was not to resolve contradictions, and that only a select few cases qualified as problematic enough to require some redactional work.

Along the same lines, the compiler did not rearrange his source materials, but rather kept the contents of the documents in their original order. Again, this is demonstrated by the presence of chronological disparities in the final text that result from the preservation of the sources in their original order. Isaac's deathbed blessing of Jacob in Genesis 27 (J) should have been followed by the notice of his death, but his death does not come in P until after Jacob's return from Paddan-Aram, thus leaving Isaac at death's door for twenty years. The compiler could have moved the notice of Isaac's death from the end of Genesis 35 to the end of Genesis 27, but he didn't; the resulting disordering of P's original text would evidently have been worse than the narrative oddity (but not impossibility) in the canonical Pentateuch. The other major indication of the compiler's fidelity to the order of his sources is that when the sources are read in isolation, they read in perfect logical and chronological order. If the compiler had displaced text regularly, then the individual sources would be left in a state of disarray. This is not the case.

There are, however, exceptions to this general rule as well, though they occur in easily defined situations. Again, the fundamental issue is what can or cannot have happened twice. In many cases, the events that take place in more than one source that cannot happen more than once do, generally, take place at the same time in each source: the flood, for instance, or the theophany in the wilderness, or the sending of the spies. But in some rare cases, singular events occur at different times in the sources. An easy example of this is the destruction of Sodom and Gomorrah (J), or the cities of the plain (P). According to J, this destruction took place after Abraham had lived in Canaan for some time, after the expulsion of Hagar, after he had been promised a child by Yahweh, after the negotiations to save the cities. According to P, however, the cities of the plain were destroyed almost immediately upon Abraham and Lot's arrival and split from each other in Canaan. Since the same place can be destroyed only once, the compiler had no choice but to move P's report of the destruction to coincide with the J account (Gen 19:29). Such cases are very few and far between, however, and insofar as they occur only under these special circumstances, they even serve to highlight just how faithful the compiler is to the order of his sources otherwise.

The compiler is not an author: he does not create new material, but rather uses the words and phrases of his sources when he makes insertions. When he inserts Potiphar into Genesis 39:1, he uses the exact words of E in 37:36. When he inserts the reference to the prison into Genesis 40:3, 5, he uses the same words as in his source, J, in 39:20. When he inserts the reference to Joseph's wife in Genesis 41:50, he uses the exact words as P in 46:20. When he inserts the proleptic description of the hardening of Pharaoh's heart in Exodus 4:21, he does so in the very words of P from Exodus 7:3. When he inserts the reference to the tablets into Exodus 34:29, he does so with the same phrasing of E in Exodus 34:4. The direct borrowing of language evident in the compiler's insertions speaks to both his fidelity to his sources and his desire to create a text that does not look as if an editorial hand has worked on it.[16] The wide conceptual gap between this silent compiler and the active theological redactors of the European approach is worth noting.

It should also be noted that the compiler's insertions are very brief and tend to use the language of only a single source, rather than a combination of elements from more than one. Thus some lengthier passages that seem to draw on language from multiple sources are, most likely, not to be attributed to the compiler. Foremost among these are the laws of Exodus 34:17–26, which combine elements of E, P, and D legislation.[17] Not only does this passage not conform to the usual formal protocol for the compiler's insertions, it is a theologically interpretive text, and, crucially, does not contribute to the combination of the sources. As such, it is probably to be ascribed to later hands.

If the compiler does not resolve the majority of contradictions, does not rearrange his source texts, and is not an author, then what is he? He is, first and foremost, a preservationist. As we have already seen, the compiler is willing to allow significant contradictions, discontinuities, and chronological problems to exist in the combined text, intervening only on very rare occasions. His toleration of these contradictions speaks to his desire to retain as much of his source material as possible. As far as we can tell, he has done a fine job of it: with few exceptions, the sources all read continuously and coherently for the majority of their extent. Where they read perfectly, it is important to note, is in the laws, where the compiler has not touched a word. (The first attempts to bring the disparate and contradictory laws into line with one another happen only in the late biblical period, in Chronicles, Ruth, and the late text of Exod 34:17–26.[18]) As it happens, the three major law codes of the Pentateuch—the Covenant Code, the priestly laws, and the laws of Deuteronomy—were all, according to their own sources, given at different times and places and so presented no true literary difficulties for the compiler; they could all be left precisely where and how they were. It may also be the case, however, that the preservation of the sources was primarily the preservation of the laws contained in them. Whether or not we accept as historical in any literal sense the stories of Ezra and Nehemiah, we can at least be certain that for the authors of those stories living in the late biblical period, the relevant parts of the "scroll of the Torah of Moses" (Neh 8:1) were the laws (see especially Neh 10). The narratives that, in the original sources, framed the laws and gave them their historical credentials as having been given by Yahweh to Moses do the same in the final form. As we have seen, the narratives are integrally linked with the laws—and vice versa—and they even contain some scattered laws themselves (as in Gen 9:6; 17; 32:33, for example). Thus the compiler, naturally, retained the narratives along with the central law codes; but the truly comprehensive fidelity to the text of the laws remains, perhaps, a mark of their status in the final text.

The compiler's evident attempt to preserve as much of his sources as possible, even retaining blatant contradictions, speaks also to the question of apparent gaps in the sources after they have been separated. This question is most pertinent with regard to E, which, for example, is clearly missing its beginning (though how much is missing is unknown). Given that the compiler has attempted everywhere to preserve in the canonical text every word of his sources, it is unlikely that the lack of a beginning in E is the result of an excision of text by the compiler. We should rather consider strongly the possibility that the compiler really did preserve nearly every word of his sources—but that, in some cases, the texts he worked from were incomplete. This is not unthinkable; the temporal gap between the original authorship of the documents and the compiler's work may be as much as four hundred years. Given the medium, papyrus, and the Levantine climate, it would be nearly miraculous if a document could have survived for any extended period without some damage.[19] And given further the fact that it is the beginning of the text that is missing, and that we are imagining a scroll—individual sheets of papyrus stitched together—it is not unreasonable to assume that the first sheet or sheets of the scroll, those on the outside, would have been the ones to undergo the most severe damage. Gaps in the sources should not therefore automatically be attributed to the compiler; in fact, the compiler's tendency everywhere to preserve virtually everything suggests that this should be the last option considered.

It is clear, however, that the compiler did not simply preserve his sources: if this had been the sole aim, he could have simply set them down one after the other. The sources have been combined into a single story, and in this the compiler reveals himself as a master of narrative logic. As we have seen in the preceding case studies, the manner in which the compiler has interwoven his sources is deceptively simple: he set them down in the only logical, chronological order possible. What has to come first, comes first, from beginning to end. The decision of which texts to leave as blocks and which to interweave into a single narrative is part of this process: if two sources told stories that the compiler deemed to be recounting the same historical moment, they had to be interwoven—such as the flood, the sale of Joseph, the plagues, and the theophany in the wilderness. If something could logically happen twice, even if it seems literarily infelicitous to the modern reader, the compiler left it twice: Moses getting water from the rock, for example, or the expulsion of Hagar. Again, contradictions are not the issue: the creation of a single chronologically coherent story is apparently what drove the compiler's method.

Recognition of the fundamentally literary nature of the compiler's work illuminates those places where he has intervened in his texts. In a single story, one character cannot be in two places—in his master's house and in prison—at the same time. In a single story, two different characters—Potiphar and an unnamed Egyptian—cannot fill the same functional role. In a single story, events that could not happen twice—the destruction of the cities of the plain—do not happen twice. In a single story, the same words—"Moses said to Yahweh"—are not written twice in a row. The historical claims and theological arguments of the individual sources are left to stand in blatant contradiction to each other. But the combined whole had to read in chronological order, and does, even when that chronology seems at times impossible (as in the lengthy death of Isaac).

From large blocks to individual verses and even smaller units, the compiler was remarkably consistent in his method throughout. At every stage, at practically every word, he was faced with a decision: is there something in another source that needs to come before the next words of this one? If not, then he could continue with the same source until the question arose again. If so, then he switched sources, and was immediately faced with the same question again. The intricacy of this process cannot be overstated, but at the same time neither can its simple logic. How else would one make a single story out of four, sometimes quite different, sometimes quite similar texts, while still preserving their original words and order as much as possible? For each of the interwoven chapters that we have analyzed in the case studies above—and for every other part of the Pentateuch—there is really no other order in which the sources could have been placed that would have resulted in a more coherent whole. The compilation of the Pentateuch was a fundamentally literary activity: the combination of four literary works into a single literary whole, a combination guided by literary sensibilities.

THE COMPILER'S INTENTION

We may therefore posit yet another thing that the compiler is not. He is not a historian—he is not concerned with giving the one accurate account of Israel's early history. And above all he is not an interpreter; he does not create new theological concepts. This aspect of the compiler's work is the most difficult to recognize and accept. It must be remembered, however, that the minimal requirement of the compiler, the sole activity that must be attributed to him, is the combination of the sources into a single whole. Any theological intentionality that one might ascribe to the compiler must therefore be demonstrated literarily, not assumed.

If we keep in mind the strict chronological order that the compiler follows throughout, the means by which theological intentionality could be demonstrated is clear: we would have to be able to locate places where the compiler has deviated from the chronological order in order to bring the sources together in a theologically meaningful way. Such places, I posit, do not exist anywhere in the Pentateuch. It is not enough to observe, as in canonical or redaction criticism, that the collocation of two sources in a given passage results in a new theological message; for if the sources are, in such a passage, also put in chronological order, then it must be assumed that, as elsewhere, it was the chronology that guided the compiler, not the resulting meaning. For example, the placement of J's covenant in Exodus 34 after the sin of the golden calf has been read as an important theological message from the compiler: after the destruction of the golden calf and the tablets of the E covenant, the compiler has placed the J covenant, based on grace and mercy (Exod 34:6–7), thereby giving the canonical text a new meaning—the renewal of the covenant in the loftier spiritual terms of sin and forgiveness.[20] This may be the best reading of the canonical text, but it does not mean that the compiler created this concept of the "renewed covenant" with any theological intentionality. In fact, the J covenant is set down in the only place possible according to the chronology of the original sources and the combined whole. It is the job of the canonical interpreter to find meaning in the final form of the text; it does not follow, however, that it was the intention of the compiler to create that meaning.

We may draw an analogy: Imagine a bookcase full of books on a wide variety of topics. All of the books are ordered alphabetically by author, from beginning to end. In the midst of one shelf are three books in a row, all biographies of George Washington. These books, too, are in alphabetical order; that is, they belong to the overarching organizational scheme of the entire bookcase. Now, there are two options for understanding this arrangement. Either these biographies have been intentionally put side by side because they deal with the same subject, and they just happen to be in alphabetical order; or the entire bookcase was arranged alphabetically and it is a coincidence that the biographies happen to be together. The evidence points to the latter. So too with the Pentateuch: over its entire length, the sources have been set down in chronological order.

If occasionally—and only occasionally—this chronological ordering coincides with a second level of meaning, we cannot therefore assume that the meaning drove the arrangement of the sources. Rather, it emerges from the compiler's literary logic. This does not mean that the compiler did not recognize that, in his ordering of the sources, he had created at points a novel theological message; it means only that this message was not his intention, or, at the very least, that it cannot be proved that this was his intention.

It would be a mistake, however, to think of the compiler as merely a mechanical orderer of texts, or to think of the compilation of the Pentateuch as a theologically meaningless exercise. Quite the contrary. The theological intentionality is not to be found in the text of the compiled Pentateuch, but rather in the very act of compilation itself. By preserving four discrete and distinct documents, each of which relates its own version of the early history of Israel and argues for a particular view of Israelite religion, the compiler has made an important theological statement. No one source, no one viewpoint, captures the entirety of the ancient Israelite religious experience. No single document describes the full panoply of ancient Israelite culture. No one aspect of Israel's culture, in fact, represents the whole. The competing voices preserved in the Pentateuch are, in fact, complementary, even as they disagree. Only when they are read together is the picture complete. Furthermore, no one religious voice is given more credence than another; all four sources are preserved completely, and all four are ordered chronologically, thereby providing a level playing field. As we have come to recognize that there is no single "biblical theology," we are also coming to recognize that there was no single "Israelite religion." Both of these elements are manifested in the compiler's work. The compilation of the Pentateuch sends a clear and resounding message about the diversity of ancient Israelite religious thought and the importance of giving equal voice to all of its disparate representations. To attempt to read the canonical Pentateuch as having a single theological message, be it that of the compiler or one of his sources, is to gravely misunderstand the meaning of the final form of the text, of the compiler's work.

Now that we have addressed the literary questions of what the compiler did and how he did it, we may return briefly to the other questions raised at the beginning of the chapter: what can we know about who the compiler was, when and where he did his work, and why? The short answer is: virtually nothing. Or, at the very least, the literary evidence of the Pentateuch and the literary method of analyzing the Pentateuch, the Documentary Hypothesis, provide few means of answering these questions.

The one question that we may address, although only in part, is that of why the compiler put his sources together this way. We have already noted that the laws are the one place that the compiler has made no adjustments of any kind and suggested that this might speak to a special status for the laws within the text. We may go further, however, and posit that the preservation of the laws stands at the center of the compiler's work. This supposition is supported by the manner in which the canonical Pentateuch ends. A distinction must be drawn between the end of the Pentateuch and the end of its sources. Given the trajectories of the J, E, and P documents, it is highly likely that each included at least the history of the settlement of the promised land, for it is to this end that the patriarchal promises point. The compiler, however, has ended his work before the ends of his source documents. He ends it, pointedly, with the final laws and the death of the law-giver, Moses. Once the laws were set down in their entirety and, with the death of Moses, the possibility of any further laws was eliminated, the compiler's work was complete. The compiler produced a law book. What drove him to do so is another question the Documentary Hypothesis cannot answer.

What the literary analysis of the Pentateuch provides is the answer to how the compiler put the sources together. That answer is invariable; while the who, when, where, and why may change as more extraliterary evidence comes to light, or as scholarly trends develop, the literary evidence of the Pentateuch will remain firm. In other words, whether it is someday proved that the compilation of the Pentateuch took place in the pre-exilic period or the postexilic period or by the Dead Sea community, how the compilation of the Pentateuch took place would be no different. The identity and location, geographical or temporal, of the compiler are fundamentally nonliterary questions. We may very much want to know the answers, but whatever the answers may be, they will not change any aspect of the literary analysis. From the perspective of the Documentary Hypothesis, any answers to those questions are legitimate as long as the conclusions regarding how the compiler worked are maintained.

Case Study V

Jacob Returns to Bethel, Genesis 35

[1]God said to Jacob, "Arise, go up to Bethel and remain there; and build an altar there to the God who appeared to you when you were fleeing from your brother Esau." [2]So Jacob said to his household and to all who were with him, "Rid yourselves of the alien gods in your midst, purify yourselves, and change your clothes. [3]Come, let us go up to Bethel, and I will build an altar there to the God who answered me when I was in distress and who has been with me wherever I have gone." [4]They gave to Jacob all the alien gods that they had, and the rings that were in their ears, and Jacob buried them under the terebinth that was near Shechem. [5]As they set out, a terror from God fell on the cities round about, so that they did not pursue the sons of Jacob. [6]Thus Jacob came to Luz—that is, Bethel—in the land of Canaan, he and all the people who were with him. [7]There he built an altar and named the site El-bethel, for it was there that God had re-

וַיֹּאמֶר אֱלֹהִים אֶל־יַעֲקֹב קוּם עֲלֵה בֵית־אֵל ¹
וְשֶׁב־שָׁם וַעֲשֵׂה־שָׁם מִזְבֵּחַ לָאֵל הַנִּרְאֶה אֵלֶיךָ
בְּבָרְחֲךָ מִפְּנֵי עֵשָׂו אָחִיךָ: ²וַיֹּאמֶר יַעֲקֹב אֶל־בֵּיתוֹ
וְאֶל כָּל־אֲשֶׁר עִמּוֹ הָסִרוּ אֶת־אֱלֹהֵי הַנֵּכָר אֲשֶׁר
בְּתֹכְכֶם וְהִטַּהֲרוּ וְהַחֲלִיפוּ שִׂמְלֹתֵיכֶם: ³וְנָקוּמָה
וְנַעֲלֶה בֵּית־אֵל וְאֶעֱשֶׂה־שָּׁם מִזְבֵּחַ לָאֵל הָעֹנֶה
אֹתִי בְּיוֹם צָרָתִי וַיְהִי עִמָּדִי בַּדֶּרֶךְ אֲשֶׁר הָלָכְתִּי:
⁴וַיִּתְּנוּ אֶל־יַעֲקֹב אֵת כָּל־אֱלֹהֵי הַנֵּכָר אֲשֶׁר
בְּיָדָם וְאֶת־הַנְּזָמִים אֲשֶׁר בְּאָזְנֵיהֶם וַיִּטְמֹן אֹתָם
יַעֲקֹב תַּחַת הָאֵלָה אֲשֶׁר עִם־שְׁכֶם: ⁵וַיִּסָּעוּ וַיְהִי
חִתַּת אֱלֹהִים עַל־הֶעָרִים אֲשֶׁר סְבִיבֹתֵיהֶם וְלֹא
רָדְפוּ אַחֲרֵי בְּנֵי יַעֲקֹב: ⁶וַיָּבֹא יַעֲקֹב לוּזָה אֲשֶׁר
בְּאֶרֶץ כְּנַעַן הִוא בֵּית־אֵל הוּא וְכָל־הָעָם אֲשֶׁר־
עִמּוֹ: ⁷וַיִּבֶן שָׁם מִזְבֵּחַ וַיִּקְרָא לַמָּקוֹם אֵל בֵּית־אֵל
כִּי שָׁם נִגְלוּ אֵלָיו הָאֱלֹהִים בְּבָרְחוֹ מִפְּנֵי אָחִיו:
⁸וַתָּמָת דְּבֹרָה מֵינֶקֶת רִבְקָה וַתִּקָּבֵר מִתַּחַת
לְבֵית־אֵל תַּחַת הָאַלּוֹן וַיִּקְרָא שְׁמוֹ אַלּוֹן בָּכוּת:
⁹וַיֵּרָא אֱלֹהִים אֶל־יַעֲקֹב עוֹד בְּבֹאוֹ מִפַּדַּן אֲרָם
וַיְבָרֶךְ אֹתוֹ: ¹⁰וַיֹּאמֶר־לוֹ אֱלֹהִים שִׁמְךָ יַעֲקֹב לֹא־
יִקָּרֵא שִׁמְךָ עוֹד יַעֲקֹב כִּי אִם־יִשְׂרָאֵל יִהְיֶה שְׁמֶךָ
וַיִּקְרָא אֶת־שְׁמוֹ יִשְׂרָאֵל: ¹¹וַיֹּאמֶר לוֹ אֱלֹהִים אֲנִי
אֵל שַׁדַּי פְּרֵה וּרְבֵה גּוֹי וּקְהַל גּוֹיִם יִהְיֶה מִמֶּךָּ
וּמְלָכִים מֵחֲלָצֶיךָ יֵצֵאוּ: ¹²וְאֶת־הָאָרֶץ אֲשֶׁר נָתַתִּי
לְאַבְרָהָם וּלְיִצְחָק לְךָ אֶתְּנֶנָּה וּלְזַרְעֲךָ אַחֲרֶיךָ
אֶתֵּן אֶת־הָאָרֶץ: ¹³וַיַּעַל מֵעָלָיו אֱלֹהִים בַּמָּקוֹם
אֲשֶׁר־דִּבֶּר אִתּוֹ: ¹⁴וַיַּצֵּב יַעֲקֹב מַצֵּבָה בַּמָּקוֹם
אֲשֶׁר־דִּבֶּר אִתּוֹ מַצֶּבֶת אָבֶן וַיַּסֵּךְ עָלֶיהָ נֶסֶךְ

vealed himself to him when he was fleeing from his brother. ⁸Deborah, Rebekah's nurse, died, and was buried under the oak below Bethel; so it was named Allon-bacuth. ⁹God appeared again to Jacob on his arrival from Paddan-aram, and he blessed him. ¹⁰God said to him, "You whose name is Jacob, you shall be called Jacob no more, but Israel shall be your name." Thus he named him Israel. ¹¹And God said to him, "I am El Shaddai. Be fertile and increase; a nation, yea an assembly of nations, shall descend from you. Kings shall issue from your loins. ¹²The land that I assigned to Abraham and Isaac I assign to you; and to your offspring to come will I assign the land." ¹³God parted from him at the spot where He had spoken to him; ¹⁴and Jacob set up a pillar at the site where he had spoken to him, a pillar of stone, and he offered a libation on it and poured oil upon it. ¹⁵Jacob gave the site, where God had spoken to him, the name of Bethel. ¹⁶They set out from Bethel; but when they were still some distance short of Ephrath, Rachel was in childbirth, and she had hard labor. ¹⁷When her labor was at its hardest, the midwife said to her, "Have no fear, for it is another boy for you." ¹⁸But as she breathed her last—for she was dying—she named him Ben-oni; but his father called him Benjamin. ¹⁹Thus Rachel died. She was buried on the road to Ephrath—now Bethlehem.

וַיִּצֹק עָלֶיהָ שָׁמֶן: ¹⁵וַיִּקְרָא יַעֲקֹב אֶת־שֵׁם הַמָּקוֹם אֲשֶׁר דִּבֶּר אִתּוֹ שָׁם אֱלֹהִים בֵּית־אֵל: ¹⁶וַיִּסְעוּ מִבֵּית אֵל וַיְהִי־עוֹד כִּבְרַת־הָאָרֶץ לָבוֹא אֶפְרָתָה וַתֵּלֶד רָחֵל וַתְּקַשׁ בְּלִדְתָּהּ: ¹⁷וַיְהִי בְהַקְשֹׁתָהּ בְּלִדְתָּהּ וַתֹּאמֶר לָהּ הַמְיַלֶּדֶת אַל־תִּירְאִי כִּי־גַם־זֶה לָךְ בֵּן: ¹⁸וַיְהִי בְּצֵאת נַפְשָׁהּ כִּי מֵתָה וַתִּקְרָא שְׁמוֹ בֶּן־אוֹנִי וְאָבִיו קָרָא־לוֹ בִנְיָמִין: ¹⁹וַתָּמָת רָחֵל וַתִּקָּבֵר בְּדֶרֶךְ אֶפְרָתָה הִוא בֵּית לָחֶם: ²⁰וַיַּצֵּב יַעֲקֹב מַצֵּבָה עַל־קְבֻרָתָהּ הִוא מַצֶּבֶת קְבֻרַת־רָחֵל עַד־הַיּוֹם: ²¹וַיִּסַּע יִשְׂרָאֵל וַיֵּט אָהֳלֹה מֵהָלְאָה לְמִגְדַּל־עֵדֶר: ²²וַיְהִי בִּשְׁכֹּן יִשְׂרָאֵל בָּאָרֶץ הַהִוא וַיֵּלֶךְ רְאוּבֵן וַיִּשְׁכַּב אֶת־בִּלְהָה פִּילֶגֶשׁ אָבִיו וַיִּשְׁמַע יִשְׂרָאֵל בְּנֵי יַעֲקֹב שְׁנֵים עָשָׂר: ²³בְּנֵי לֵאָה בְּכוֹר יַעֲקֹב רְאוּבֵן וְשִׁמְעוֹן וְלֵוִי וִיהוּדָה וְיִשָּׂשכָר וּזְבוּלֻן: ²⁴בְּנֵי רָחֵל יוֹסֵף וּבִנְיָמִן: ²⁵וּבְנֵי בִלְהָה שִׁפְחַת רָחֵל דָּן וְנַפְתָּלִי: ²⁶וּבְנֵי זִלְפָּה שִׁפְחַת לֵאָה גָּד וְאָשֵׁר אֵלֶּה בְּנֵי יַעֲקֹב אֲשֶׁר יֻלַּד־לוֹ בְּפַדַּן אֲרָם: ²⁷וַיָּבֹא יַעֲקֹב אֶל־יִצְחָק אָבִיו מַמְרֵא קִרְיַת הָאַרְבַּע הִוא חֶבְרוֹן אֲשֶׁר־גָּר־שָׁם אַבְרָהָם וְיִצְחָק: ²⁸וַיִּהְיוּ יְמֵי יִצְחָק מְאַת שָׁנָה וּשְׁמֹנִים שָׁנָה: ²⁹וַיִּגְוַע יִצְחָק וַיָּמָת וַיֵּאָסֶף אֶל־עַמָּיו זָקֵן וּשְׂבַע יָמִים וַיִּקְבְּרוּ אֹתוֹ עֵשָׂו וְיַעֲקֹב בָּנָיו:

²⁰Over her grave Jacob set up a pillar; it is the pillar at Rachel's grave to this day. ²¹Israel journeyed on, and pitched his tent beyond Migdal-eder. ²²While Israel stayed in that land, Reuben went and lay with Bilhah, his father's concubine; and Israel found out. Now the sons of Jacob were twelve in number. ²³The sons of Leah: Reuben—Jacob's first-born—Simeon, Levi, Judah, Issachar, and Zebulun. ²⁴The sons of Rachel: Joseph and Benjamin. ²⁵The sons of Bilhah, Rachel's maid: Dan and Naphtali. ²⁶And the sons of Zilpah, Leah's maid: Gad and Asher. These are the sons of Jacob who were born to him in Paddan-aram. ²⁷And Jacob came to his father Isaac at Mamre, at Kiriath-arba—now Hebron—where Abraham and Isaac had sojourned. ²⁸Isaac was a hundred and eighty years old ²⁹when he breathed his last and died. He was gathered to his kin in ripe old age; and he was buried by his sons Esau and Jacob.

In the entirety of Genesis, no chapter contains such a profusion of disparate narrative elements as does chapter 35. Over its course we are told about God's instructions to Jacob to return to Bethel and the fulfillment of those instructions (vv. 1–7); the death of Deborah, Rebekah's nurse (v. 8); the blessing of Jacob and the changing of his name (vv. 9–14); the naming of Bethel (v. 15); the death and burial of Rachel and the birth of Benjamin (vv. 16–20); Reuben sleeping with Bilhah (vv. 21–22a); the listing of Jacob's sons (vv. 22b–26); and the death of Isaac (vv. 27–29). This variety of topics means that there is perhaps less opportunity to identify narrative problems within the chapter itself, since no story is told for more than a few verses. On the other hand, almost every one of its lines connects directly and clearly to other texts in Genesis, which are themselves readily identifiable as belonging to their respective source documents. Most of the analysis of Genesis 35, therefore—with one exception discussed below—must be carried out in light of the surrounding narratives in Genesis.

The first narrative block of Genesis 35 is Jacob's return to Bethel, vv. 1–7. The section begins with God telling Jacob to go to Bethel and build an altar to the deity who appeared to him there when he was fleeing from Esau. In this command is a direct reference to a previous theophany at Bethel, one that took place before Jacob fled to Laban's household. That theophany was narrated in Genesis 28:10–22. Although Genesis 28:10–22 is a composite text, and a particularly complicated one at that, the basic elements of an E story are fairly readily isolated: Jacob had a dream theophany; recognized upon waking that he was in a holy place, a "house of God," a *bêt ʾᵉlōhîm*; in the morning set up a pillar and anointed it; and named the place, which had previously been called Luz, Bethel—"house of God." He finally vowed to turn his impromptu cultic site into a proper sanctuary and to tithe. The signs of E are evident. The theophany in a dream or vision is standard procedure only in E (cf. Gen 15:1; 20:3; 31:10–11, 24; 41:25; 46:2), and the central pun of the chapter is a play on the title Elohim.[1] These events are recalled further in Jacob's dream, recounted in 31:10–13; in the last of these verses God is said to have spoken to Jacob as follows: "I am the God of Bethel, where you anointed a pillar and where you made a vow to me."

With this E narrative in mind, God's command to Jacob in 35:1 is entirely comprehensible. Now that Jacob has returned from his sojourn abroad, he is obligated to fulfill the vow he made at the beginning of his journey: he must set up a true sanctuary at Bethel by building an altar there.[2] Jacob instructs his family to rid themselves of their pagan idols—since they are Arameans, they have not been following the customs of Abraham[3]—and recounts nearly verbatim God's instructions (vv. 2–3). The family does so in v. 4.[4] The end of this verse, in which Jacob buries his family's idols under a tree near Shechem, marks this narrative as the direct continuation of the preceding story in Genesis 34, that of Dinah and Shechem.

Genesis 34 is also a composite text, and while the precise delineation of the sources in it is not necessary here, its two narratives can be quickly summarized. According to the J narrative in Genesis 34, Shechem abducts Dinah; Jacob waits until his sons return from the field to give them the news; Simeon and Levi, alone among the brothers, kill Hamor and Shechem and retrieve Dinah; Jacob objects to their act, but the brothers defend themselves strongly. According to E, Shechem falls in love with Dinah and does not take her by force (or at all); he attempts in good faith to marry her; the brothers—all of them—trick the Shechemites into being circumcised; and while they are in pain, Jacob's sons slaughter and plunder the town. Genesis 35:4, by placing the action outside of

Shechem, could theoretically connect to either of the strands in Genesis 34. Verse 5, however, tells us that as Jacob's family set out for Bethel, the surrounding cities were struck by a terror from God so that they did not pursue Jacob's sons—not Simeon and Levi, or Jacob (as we would expect from 34:30), but his sons as a whole, that is, the protagonists of the E narrative in Genesis 34.⁵ This connection is not unexpected, of course, since 35:1–4, in which Jacob goes to Bethel, is E, as we have already established, and v. 5 assumes the departure from Shechem to Bethel; indeed, in J, as we will have occasion to state further, the family has not yet left Shechem at this point in the story.⁶

Verses 6–7 are the fulfillment of God's command in v. 1: Jacob comes to Bethel—here identified as having formerly been called Luz, as we knew from Genesis 28:19—and builds an altar, which he calls El-Bethel.⁷ Even the rationale for building the altar, stated twice already in vv. 1 and 3, is repeated here nearly word for word in v. 7. We can thus securely identify Genesis 35:1–7 as being a coherent, continuous narrative from the E source.⁸ It connects to the other E narratives in Genesis 28:10–22 and Genesis 34 via substantive narrative claims: that Jacob experienced a theophany at Bethel, that he had an obligation to found a proper cultic site there, that he had just been in Shechem, that his sons had acted in such a way that the family needed protection upon leaving Shechem, and, of course, that he had changed the name of the city to Bethel from Luz.

The death and burial of Deborah, Rebekah's nurse, in v. 8 seems to have little connection with anything else that happens in this chapter. It seems to be a reflex of an otherwise unmentioned tradition. Regardless, this tree, and the death and burial associated with it, is explicitly located at Bethel, which is important: only in E, in the verses we have just read, is Jacob's family in Bethel. We can therefore assign 35:8 to E as well.

In v. 9, the markers of E apparent to this point in the chapter are replaced by definitive signs of P. God's appearance to Jacob here is described as happening "on his arrival from Paddan-Aram." It is only in P that Rebekah's family lives in Paddan-Aram. In Genesis 27:1–45, from J, Jacob is forced to flee to his mother's family to escape the wrath of Esau after having stolen his brother's blessing, and in this J passage Laban lives in Haran (27:43; see also 28:10, 29:4). In P, on the other hand, Jacob goes to Laban—in Paddan-Aram—not because he is fleeing, but rather because Isaac and Rebekah do not want Jacob to marry outside the family, as Esau has shamefully done (26:34–35). Thus Rebekah tells Isaac to send Jacob off to get married (27:46); Isaac does so, explicitly telling Jacob to go to Paddan-Aram (28:1–5; see also 28:6–9). The P narrative of Jacob's stay in

Paddan-Aram is exceptionally brief; all that we can assign to it with certainty are 30:43 and 31:17–18, in which Jacob grows wealthy and takes his wives and children and the other possessions he has acquired in Paddan-Aram and sets out to return to Isaac in Canaan.[9] His arrival back in Canaan is narrated by P in 33:18a, again with the explicit mention of Paddan-Aram (see further below). Thus in 35:9, the mention of Paddan-Aram identifies the verse immediately as being from P.

Further, the last clause of 35:9, "he blessed him," is also indicative of P. Although the concept of blessing is obviously not restricted to only one of the sources—it is, in fact, the central theme of the patriarchal promises in J[10]—the verb *wayyibbarēk* with God as the subject is a distinctively P element (cf. Gen 1:22, 28; 2:3; 5:2; 9:1; 25:11; 48:3).[11] The subsequent speech of God in 35:10–12 consists of two distinct parts: the changing of Jacob's name to Israel (v. 10) and the promise of progeny and land (vv. 11–12). Each part is recognizable as priestly.[12] The change of Jacob's name to Israel in v. 10 is very similar to the change of Abraham's name in Genesis 17:5;[13] moreover, in E Jacob's name had already been changed to Israel in the encounter with the divine being in 32:29.[14] The promise in vv. 11–12 begins with God's self-identification as El Shaddai; this is the name that, according to P in Exodus 6:2–6, God used with the patriarchs before revealing his true name to Moses (cf. Gen 17:1; 28:3; 48:3). The command to "be fruitful and multiply" is among the most famous of P elements, known from Genesis 1:22, 28; 9:1, 7; 17:20; 28:3; 48:4. The wording of the promise, with the idea that a "community" (*qāhāl*) of nations and kings will descend from the patriarch, is also exclusively part of the P promises (cf. Gen 17:6, 16; 28:3; 48:4). Genesis 35:9–12, then, can be securely assigned to P.

This source assignment finds external support from another passage in Genesis, 48:3–4. Here Jacob, on his deathbed, says to Joseph: "El Shaddai appeared to me at Luz in the land of Canaan, and he blessed me, and said to me, 'I will make you fertile and numerous, making of you a community of peoples, and I will assign this land to your offspring to come for an everlasting possession.'" This is a direct recollection of precisely Genesis 35:9–12, complete with the use of the name El Shaddai, the wording of "be fruitful and multiply," the notion of a "community" descending from Jacob, and the promise of the land. Similarly, God's speech to Jacob in 35:10–12 is anticipated by Isaac's final words to Jacob before he leaves for Paddan-Aram in 28:3–4: "May El Shaddai bless you, make you fertile and numerous, so that you become an assembly of peoples. May he grant the blessing of Abraham to you and your offspring, that you may possess the land where you are sojourning, which God assigned to Abraham." This

P section of Genesis 35, then, is both anticipated and recollected, narratively, thematically, and verbally, elsewhere in the P patriarchal narrative.

In v. 13, God leaves Jacob "at the spot where he had spoken to him." In the chapter to this point, it is only in P that God has spoken with Jacob, and this verse therefore can belong only to P (see below). Further, the language used to describe God's departure, *wayya'al mē'ālāyw*, literally, "he went up from upon him," is found elsewhere only in P, and strikingly so in Genesis 17:22, when God finishes speaking with Abraham (see also Num 16:27a). In v. 14, Jacob sets up a pillar and anoints it. That this cannot be P is clear enough, since in P there is no cult before its inauguration at Sinai.[15] It is equally clear that it is part and parcel of the E narrative, the establishment of the cultic site at Bethel. This official pillar stands as the replacement for (or supplement to) the ad hoc pillar Jacob erected in Genesis 28:18.[16] Moreover, pillars play a recurring role in Jacob's travels in E: from the first in Genesis 28:18 to the one he erects as a witness to his agreement with Laban in 31:45 to this one in 35:14.[17] In v. 15, Jacob names the place where God had spoken to him Bethel. Since, as we have seen, it is only in P that God has spoken to Jacob in this chapter, this verse makes sense only in P. More obviously, in E Jacob has already named the place Bethel, in 28:19.[18]

The departure from Bethel, the birth of Benjamin, and the death and burial of Rachel in vv. 16–20 could, in theory, belong to either P or E. That this section is not from J is clear from the identification of the point of departure as Bethel—as we have already had occasion to note, in J the family is still, as far as we know, in Shechem. The pillar Jacob erects over Rachel's grave in v. 20 points to E, which, as we have seen, contains a series of pillars marking Jacob's journeys. On the other hand, the death of Rachel is recalled by Jacob in the same deathbed speech to Joseph that we have already referred to, in Genesis 48:7: "When I was returning from Paddan, Rachel died, to my sorrow, while I was sojourning in the land of Canaan, when still some distance short of Efrat, and I buried her there on the road to Efrat—now Bethlehem."[19] What Jacob mentions in this recollection—and equally, if not more so, what he leaves out—makes clear which parts of 35:16–20 belong to P, and which to E. The departure from Bethel and the location on the road to Efrat in v. 16a are from P; the hard labor and birth of Benjamin in v. 16b–18, unmentioned in 48:7, are from E; the death and burial of Rachel on the road in v. 19 belong to P;[20] the pillar over her grave in v. 20, as already said, belongs to E.[21]

This division leaves two perfectly coherent stories of Rachel's death, but two quite different ones. According to P, Rachel died on the road from Bethel to Efrat and was buried there. That is the extent of it, but it is important for P to tell, since only P takes great care to describe the burials of all the other patriarchs and especially the matriarchs whose burials are not described anywhere in the nonpriestly material (all the patriarchs and matriarchs are, according to P, laid to rest in the family plot in the cave of Machpelah; see Gen 23; 25:9–10; 49:29–31; 50:12–13). According to E, on the other hand, Rachel dies while giving birth to Benjamin—still, as far as we can tell, in Bethel—where, according to the tradition known to E, a pillar still exists to mark the spot, the pillar that Jacob placed over her grave.[22]

Verses 21–22a contain two narrative items: Jacob's journey to Migdal-Eder and Reuben sleeping with Bilhah. These verses are linked by the thrice-repeated use of the name Israel for Jacob, unique in this chapter. To which source they belong is a separate issue. That they are not from P is clear from the notice that Jacob "pitched his tent"; in P, the word "tent" is not used until the construction of the Tabernacle (first in Exod 26:7), where it obviously has a very distinct meaning. This leaves J and E as the remaining possibilities. If these verses were from E, they would describe Jacob leaving Bethel; if from J, they would describe Jacob leaving Shechem, where he has been since the end of Genesis 34. Two elements point to J. First, the use of the word "dwell," *š-k-n*, is used only in J to refer to human dwelling (cf. Gen 9:27; 16:12; 25:18; 26:2; 49:13); it is used in P exclusively for the dwelling of the divine presence on Sinai or in the Tabernacle (cf. Exod 24:16; 25:8; 29:45–46; 40:35; Num 5:3; 9:17, 18, 22; 10:12; 35:34; and of course the priestly term for the Tabernacle, *hammiškān*).[23] Second, and far more telling, is the reference to this moment in Genesis 49:3–4, Jacob's "blessing" of Reuben. The poem of Genesis 49 is an older independent piece, but it has been incorporated into the J narrative;[24] J is fond of using traditional elements as parts of his stories, from the song of Lemech in Genesis 4:23–24 to the song of the sea in Exodus 15, from the song of the well in Numbers 21:17–18a to the blessing of Moses in Deuteronomy 33. The removal of Reuben, Simeon, and Levi as potential recipients of Jacob's blessing in this poem paves the way for the ascendance of Judah, which is a central theme for J.[25] In this light, it is not coincidental that the section of J that immediately precedes 35:21–22a is Jacob's condemnation of Simeon and Levi in 34:30; the J narrative and the poem of Genesis 49 are integrally connected, with the narratives setting the stage for Jacob's disinheritance of his eldest three sons on his deathbed.[26] And the sudden use of Israel in 35:21–22a, though not probative—J and E both use Jacob's two names interchangeably[27]—does at least suggest that there is a distinction between these verses and the rest of the chapter, in which the name Israel is not used. These verses, alone in Genesis 35, belong to J.

The list of Jacob's sons in vv. 22b–26 provides little new information; the names of Jacob's sons, their mothers, and their birth order are already known to us from the J and E narratives of Genesis 30–31. It is in the last line of this section, v. 26b, that we encounter an important and new item: "These are the sons of Jacob who were born to him in Paddan-Aram." As we have already seen, Paddan-Aram is exclusive to P, and this list therefore belongs to P as well. But this sentence also contains a startling contradiction to what we have just read in vv. 16–20: whereas, according to the E narrative of Rachel's death, Benjamin was born in Bethel, here P states directly that Benjamin, like all of Jacob's sons, was born in Paddan-Aram.[28] This statement confirms the source division in vv. 16–20, where, as we have seen, the birth of Benjamin is told only in E; Benjamin's birth is not mentioned in connection with Rachel's death in P, neither in vv. 16–20 nor in Jacob's recollection in 48:7. Now it is clear why: according to P, Benjamin was born in Paddan-Aram, well before Rachel's death.[29]

The final section of Genesis 35 is the death of Isaac in vv. 27–29. It begins by telling us that Jacob came to his father Isaac. This appears to be the final stage of Jacob's journey from Paddan-Aram in P, since it said in 31:17–18 that Jacob took his family and possessions "to go to his father Isaac in the land of Canaan."[30] Isaac's location in "Mamre, at Kiriath-Arba—now Hebron—where Abraham and Isaac had sojourned" is also clearly from P. Mamre—that is, Hebron—is where Abraham bought the cave of Machpelah, as P repeatedly mentions (Gen 23:17, 19; 25:9; 49:30; 50:13), and where, according to P, all the patriarchs lived. Although not all age notices are from P, they are common in P, and v. 28 connects directly to v. 29, which contains two lexical items unique to P. The word "breathed his last [expired]," *g-w-ʿ*, is used only in P, and regularly: of humanity in the flood (Gen 6:17; 7:21), of Abraham (25:8), of Ishmael (25:17), of Jacob (49:33), and of Aaron (Num 20:29).[31] And the phrase "gathered to his kin" is similarly a P phrase for burial: for Abraham (Gen 25:8), Ishmael (25:17), Jacob (49:33), and Aaron and Moses (Deut 32:50). The burial of Isaac by Jacob and Esau implicitly assumes that Esau is still living in Hebron; this stands in contradiction to the J narrative, in which Esau has already moved to Seir/Edom (32:4);[32] note also that Isaac and Ishmael similarly bury Abraham together in 25:8. This final section of Genesis 35 belongs to P.[33]

Though, with one exception, Genesis 35 is not a particularly self-contradictory chapter, we have seen that almost every line contains a clear and direct connection to other narratives in Genesis, and the source division may be carried out successfully along those lines. Not unexpectedly, when we have separated the E and P narratives, they are both internally consistent and continuous, as can be seen from the following division:[34]

P NARRATIVE

⁹וַיֵּרָא אֱלֹהִים אֶל־יַעֲקֹב בְּבֹאוֹ מִפַּדַּן אֲרָם וַיְבָרֶךְ אֹתוֹ: ¹⁰וַיֹּאמֶר־לוֹ אֱלֹהִים שִׁמְךָ יַעֲקֹב לֹא־יִקָּרֵא שִׁמְךָ עוֹד יַעֲקֹב כִּי אִם־יִשְׂרָאֵל יִהְיֶה שְׁמֶךָ וַיִּקְרָא אֶת־שְׁמוֹ יִשְׂרָאֵל: ¹¹וַיֹּאמֶר לוֹ אֱלֹהִים אֲנִי אֵל שַׁדַּי פְּרֵה וּרְבֵה גּוֹי וּקְהַל גּוֹיִם יִהְיֶה מִמֶּךָּ וּמְלָכִים מֵחֲלָצֶיךָ יֵצֵאוּ: ¹²וְאֶת־הָאָרֶץ אֲשֶׁר נָתַתִּי לְאַבְרָהָם וּלְיִצְחָק לְךָ אֶתְּנֶנָּה וּלְזַרְעֲךָ אַחֲרֶיךָ אֶתֵּן אֶת־הָאָרֶץ: ¹³וַיַּעַל מֵעָלָיו אֱלֹהִים בַּמָּקוֹם אֲשֶׁר־דִּבֶּר אִתּוֹ: ¹⁵וַיִּקְרָא יַעֲקֹב אֶת־שֵׁם הַמָּקוֹם אֲשֶׁר דִּבֶּר אִתּוֹ שָׁם אֱלֹהִים בֵּית־אֵל: ¹⁶וַיִּסְעוּ מִבֵּית אֵל וַיְהִי־עוֹד כִּבְרַת־הָאָרֶץ לָבוֹא אֶפְרָתָה ¹⁹וַתָּמָת רָחֵל וַתִּקָּבֵר בְּדֶרֶךְ אֶפְרָתָה הִוא בֵּית לָחֶם: ²²וַיִּהְיוּ בְנֵי־יַעֲקֹב שְׁנֵים עָשָׂר: ²³בְּנֵי לֵאָה בְּכוֹר יַעֲקֹב רְאוּבֵן וְשִׁמְעוֹן וְלֵוִי וִיהוּדָה וְיִשָּׂשכָר וּזְבוּלֻן: ²⁴בְּנֵי רָחֵל יוֹסֵף וּבִנְיָמִן: ²⁵וּבְנֵי בִלְהָה שִׁפְחַת רָחֵל דָּן וְנַפְתָּלִי: ²⁶וּבְנֵי זִלְפָּה שִׁפְחַת לֵאָה גָּד וְאָשֵׁר אֵלֶּה בְּנֵי יַעֲקֹב אֲשֶׁר יֻלַּד־לוֹ בְּפַדַּן אֲרָם: ²⁷וַיָּבֹא יַעֲקֹב אֶל־יִצְחָק אָבִיו מַמְרֵא קִרְיַת הָאַרְבַּע הִוא חֶבְרוֹן אֲשֶׁר־גָּר־שָׁם אַבְרָהָם וְיִצְחָק: ²⁸וַיִּהְיוּ יְמֵי יִצְחָק מְאַת שָׁנָה וּשְׁמֹנִים שָׁנָה: ²⁹וַיִּגְוַע יִצְחָק וַיָּמָת וַיֵּאָסֶף אֶל־עַמָּיו זָקֵן וּשְׂבַע יָמִים וַיִּקְבְּרוּ אֹתוֹ עֵשָׂו וְיַעֲקֹב בָּנָיו:

E NARRATIVE

¹וַיֹּאמֶר אֱלֹהִים אֶל־יַעֲקֹב קוּם עֲלֵה בֵית־אֵל וְשֶׁב־שָׁם וַעֲשֵׂה־שָׁם מִזְבֵּחַ לָאֵל הַנִּרְאֶה אֵלֶיךָ בְּבָרְחֲךָ מִפְּנֵי עֵשָׂו אָחִיךָ: ²וַיֹּאמֶר יַעֲקֹב אֶל־בֵּיתוֹ וְאֶל כָּל־אֲשֶׁר עִמּוֹ הָסִרוּ אֶת־אֱלֹהֵי הַנֵּכָר אֲשֶׁר בְּתֹכְכֶם וְהִטַּהֲרוּ וְהַחֲלִיפוּ שִׂמְלֹתֵיכֶם: ³וְנָקוּמָה וְנַעֲלֶה בֵּית־אֵל וְאֶעֱשֶׂה־שָּׁם מִזְבֵּחַ לָאֵל הָעֹנֶה אֹתִי בְּיוֹם צָרָתִי וַיְהִי עִמָּדִי בַּדֶּרֶךְ אֲשֶׁר הָלָכְתִּי: ⁴וַיִּתְּנוּ אֶל־יַעֲקֹב אֵת כָּל־אֱלֹהֵי הַנֵּכָר אֲשֶׁר בְּיָדָם וְאֶת־הַנְּזָמִים אֲשֶׁר בְּאָזְנֵיהֶם וַיִּטְמֹן אֹתָם יַעֲקֹב תַּחַת הָאֵלָה אֲשֶׁר עִם־שְׁכֶם: ⁵וַיִּסָּעוּ וַיְהִי חִתַּת אֱלֹהִים עַל־הֶעָרִים אֲשֶׁר סְבִיבֹתֵיהֶם וְלֹא רָדְפוּ אַחֲרֵי בְּנֵי יַעֲקֹב: ⁶וַיָּבֹא יַעֲקֹב לוּזָה אֲשֶׁר בְּאֶרֶץ כְּנַעַן הִוא בֵּית־אֵל הוּא וְכָל־הָעָם אֲשֶׁר־עִמּוֹ: ⁷וַיִּבֶן שָׁם מִזְבֵּחַ וַיִּקְרָא לַמָּקוֹם אֵל בֵּית־אֵל כִּי שָׁם נִגְלוּ אֵלָיו הָאֱלֹהִים בְּבָרְחוֹ מִפְּנֵי אָחִיו: ⁸וַתָּמָת דְּבֹרָה מֵינֶקֶת רִבְקָה וַתִּקָּבֵר מִתַּחַת לְבֵית־אֵל תַּחַת הָאַלּוֹן וַיִּקְרָא שְׁמוֹ אַלּוֹן בָּכוּת: ¹⁴וַיַּצֵּב יַעֲקֹב מַצֵּבָה מַצֶּבֶת אָבֶן וַיַּסֵּךְ עָלֶיהָ נֶסֶךְ וַיִּצֹק עָלֶיהָ שָׁמֶן: ¹⁶וַתֵּלֶד רָחֵל וַתְּקַשׁ בְּלִדְתָּהּ: ¹⁷וַיְהִי בְהַקְשֹׁתָהּ בְּלִדְתָּהּ וַתֹּאמֶר לָהּ הַמְיַלֶּדֶת אַל־תִּירְאִי כִּי־גַם־זֶה לָךְ בֵּן: ¹⁸וַיְהִי בְּצֵאת נַפְשָׁהּ כִּי מֵתָה וַתִּקְרָא שְׁמוֹ בֶּן־אוֹנִי וְאָבִיו קָרָא־לוֹ בִנְיָמִין: ¹⁹וַתָּמָת רָחֵל ²⁰וַיַּצֵּב יַעֲקֹב מַצֵּבָה עַל־קְבֻרָתָהּ הִוא מַצֶּבֶת קְבֻרַת־רָחֵל עַד־הַיּוֹם:

⁹God appeared to Jacob on his arrival from Paddan-aram, and he blessed him. ¹⁰God said to him, "You whose name is Jacob, you shall be called Jacob no more, but Israel shall be your name." Thus he named him Israel. ¹¹And God said to him, "I am El Shaddai. Be fertile and increase; a nation, yea an assembly of nations, shall descend from you. Kings shall issue from your loins. ¹²The land that I assigned to Abraham and Isaac I as-

¹God said to Jacob, "Arise, go up to Bethel and remain there; and build an altar there to the God who appeared to you when you were fleeing from your brother Esau." ²So Jacob said to his household and to all who were with him, "Rid yourselves of the alien gods in your midst, purify yourselves, and change your clothes. ³Come, let us go up to Bethel, and I will build an altar there to the God who answered me when I was in

sign to you; and to your offspring to come will I assign the land." [13]God parted from him at the spot where he had spoken to him; [15]Jacob gave the site, where God had spoken to him, the name of Bethel. [16]They set out from Bethel; but when they were still some distance short of Ephrath, [19]Rachel died. She was buried on the road to Ephrath—now Bethlehem. [22]Now the sons of Jacob were twelve in number. [23]The sons of Leah: Reuben—Jacob's first-born—Simeon, Levi, Judah, Issachar, and Zebulun. [24]The sons of Rachel: Joseph and Benjamin. [25]The sons of Bilhah, Rachel's maid: Dan and Naphtali. [26]And the sons of Zilpah, Leah's maid: Gad and Asher. These are the sons of Jacob who were born to him in Paddan-aram. [27]And Jacob came to his father Isaac at Mamre, at Kiriath-arba—now Hebron—where Abraham and Isaac had sojourned. [28]Isaac was a hundred and eighty years old [29]when he breathed his last and died. He was gathered to his kin in ripe old age; and he was buried by his sons Esau and Jacob.

distress and who has been with me wherever I have gone." [4]They gave to Jacob all the alien gods that they had, and the rings that were in their ears, and Jacob buried them under the terebinth that was near Shechem. [5]As they set out, a terror from God fell on the cities round about, so that they did not pursue the sons of Jacob. [6]Thus Jacob came to Luz—that is, Bethel—in the land of Canaan, he and all the people who were with him. [7]There he built an altar and named the site El-bethel, for it was there that God had revealed Himself to him when he was fleeing from his brother. [8]Deborah, Rebekah's nurse, died, and was buried under the oak below Bethel; so it was named Allon-bacuth. [14]Jacob set up a pillar, a pillar of stone, and he offered a libation on it and poured oil upon it. [16]Rachel was in childbirth, and she had hard labor. [17]When her labor was at its hardest, the midwife said to her, "Have no fear, for it is another boy for you." [18]But as she breathed her last—for she was dying—she named him Ben-oni; but his father called him Benjamin. [19]Thus Rachel died. [20]Over her grave Jacob set up a pillar; it is the pillar at Rachel's grave to this day.

Not only are these two narratives internally consistent, they also belong firmly to the larger contexts of their respective sources, as we have seen. The P story fits into the continuum from Jacob's departure for Paddan-Aram in Genesis 27:46–28:9, including Isaac's anticipatory blessing of Jacob, through Jacob's stay in Paddan-Aram, and his departure from there to return to his father in the land of Canaan.[35] It connects further with Jacob's deathbed recollection to Joseph in 48:3–7 of the events of this chapter. The blessing, the changing of Jacob's name, the promise of progeny and land, the burial of the matriarch, and Isaac's death are all part of the regular priestly telling of the patriarchal story, in theme and language. These continuities are the markers of an independent, coherent priestly narrative.[36]

The E story has even broader connections with its original source context. Jacob's return to Bethel is linked directly to his first visit there in Genesis 28:10–22, including his obligation to inaugurate a proper cultic site. The departure from Shechem connects this story to the preceding E narrative in Genesis 34. Jacob's journeys in E form a complete arc, from Bethel back to Bethel, the beginning and end each marked by the establishment of a cultic site there, with a series of pillars erected along the way.

Even the brief J text in vv. 21–22a is well integrated in the larger J narrative. The objectionable action of Reuben follows directly on Jacob's condemnation of Simeon and Levi in 34:30, and these two moments form the narrative precursors to the sequential disinheritance of the three sons in Genesis 49:3–7.

The source division of Genesis 35 is relatively straightforward when the chapter is read in light of the other narratives in Genesis. What is of particular interest in this chapter is the way that the compiler has gone about his work. Genesis 35 contains a variety of excellent examples of different aspects of the redactional process. First, it should be noted that the combination of the P and E stories in this chapter is readily understandable: in both sources, Jacob went to Bethel after his sojourn abroad in Aram, and it was only natural that the compiler should have considered these to have been the same visit; in both sources, Rachel died, and this assuredly could have happened only once. In more specific terms, the compiler had no choice but to put the E section of vv. 1–8 before the P passage in vv. 9–12: in the first, Jacob is told to go to Bethel, makes preparations to do so, and arrives at the site; in the second, he is already there.[37] The instructions and movement toward Bethel in E have to precede the events that take place there in P. In vv. 16–20, the P geographical notice has to come first; the childbirth in E must precede the actual death and burial from P; and the pillar over the grave must come last. There is simply no other order in which the pieces could possibly be arranged.

Yet beside these broad observations, which we have seen are applicable to every pentateuchal narrative, the compiler also made a series of important smaller moves that demand special attention. Verse 9, as noted, is the beginning of the P narrative of Jacob's brief visit to Bethel. In the P narrative, God appears to Jacob only once, in this chapter, just as God appeared to Abraham only once, in Genesis 17.[38] Yet the canonical text reads "God appeared again to Jacob." Since there has been no previous theophany to Jacob in P, the word "again" makes no sense as part of the P narrative. In the canonical context, however, it is not only understandable, it is almost necessary: this is not the first time that God has appeared to Jacob in the compiled text. The first theophany was in Genesis 28:10–22, and there have been still others from the nonpriestly sources, in 31:10–13, 32:2–3, 27–30. Thus the compiler, in order to bring his sources into line, added the single word "again," *'ôd*, into the original P text of 35:9.[39]

It may be noted that although the P story in Genesis 35 is decidedly set in Bethel, as v. 15 makes clear, there is no notice in this chapter that Jacob has actually come to Bethel, or to the place previously called Luz. In order to explain this, we must go back a bit to Genesis 33:18a. In the canonical text, this verse reads "Jacob arrived safe in the city of Shechem which is in the land of Canaan—having come thus [better, "on his arrival"] from Paddan-Aram." It is clear from the reference to Paddan-Aram that there is some P in this verse, but there are also indications that it is not entirely from P. The concept of Jacob traveling safely is foreign to the P narrative: in P, Jacob goes to Paddan-Aram to get married and returns; it is only in the nonpriestly stories that Jacob is fleeing from Esau and worried for his safety.[40] Additionally, the reference to Shechem in this verse makes little sense in P; the story of Dinah and Shechem in Genesis 34 contains no P, only J and E.[41] The next P verse after this one is 35:9, which, as we have seen, already takes place in Bethel. Taking these observations together, we can surmise that the compiler has combined two separate accounts here: one from P, describing Jacob's return from Paddan-Aram, and one from E, describing Jacob's arrival in Shechem, which leads via 33:18b–20 into the narrative of Genesis 34. The E verse would have read: "Jacob arrived safe in the city of Shechem"; the P verse would have read "Jacob arrived in X in the land of Canaan on his arrival from Paddan-Aram." Where Jacob arrived according to P we cannot know from this verse alone, since the compiler has covered P's location with that of Shechem from E, logically enough since the next narrative takes place in Shechem. Yet Genesis 48:3 provides us with the answer: there, Jacob says, "El Shaddai appeared to me at Luz in the land of Canaan." We can thus fill in the blank in 33:18a and reconstruct the original P verse there as "Jacob arrived in Luz in the land of Canaan on his arrival from Paddan-Aram."[42] If we read this in succession with the subsequent P verse in 35:9, we can see that they fit together perfectly: "Jacob arrived in Luz in the land of Canaan on his arrival from Paddan-Aram, and God appeared to Jacob on his arrival from Paddan-Aram." In this way the narrative of P in Genesis 35 is provided with its location—and further, it is precisely what we expected, that is, the previous name of Bethel, which Jacob changes in 35:15.[43] This leaves us with a final question: why did the compiler not simply leave the E verse in 33:18a where it stands, as the introduction to Genesis 34, and put the P verse with the rest of the P narrative in Genesis 35? The answer comes from the phrase "in the land of Canaan": the P verse in 33:18a describes Jacob's first arrival in the land of Canaan after his sojourn abroad.[44] Since the compiler, and everyone else, knows that Shechem is in Canaan, Jacob's entry into the land could not come after Genesis 34 but had to come before it. Yet he also could not simply leave the P verse as it was because it explicitly had Jacob arriving not in Shechem, but in Luz, that is, Bethel. Thus the compiler took his two verses from E and P and made them into one: Jacob's first arrival in the land of Canaan (in P) became equated with his safe arrival in Shechem (in E). Despite the cleverness of this solution, it is unclear how the compiler could have done anything different here without either having Jacob's entry into the land according to P come after his time in Shechem (if he put the P verse in Gen 35) or having Jacob arrive in Luz according to P and then suddenly be in Shechem (if he left the word Luz in 33:18a).[45]

As we have seen, in vv. 13 and 15 from P reference is made to "the place where (God) had spoken to him," a reference that, as noted, makes sense only in the priestly narrative, since it is only in P that God speaks with Jacob in Bethel in Genesis 35. Yet the phrase is found also in v. 14, which is otherwise clearly from E, since it describes the erecting and anointing of a pillar. In E, the phrase is out of place narratively; even in E's own language, Jacob is to establish the cultic site at Bethel not because God has spoken to him, but because God has "appeared" to him (35:1).[46] Indeed, even in the first theophany in E, in Genesis 28:10–22, God does not actually speak to Jacob; Jacob sees only the vision of the divine messengers ascending and descending the ladder. Thus any reference to God having spoken to Jacob in Bethel cannot belong to the original E document. It seems likely, then, that the compiler has inserted the phrase from P into E here, for essentially the same reason that he inserted "again" into the P verse in 35:9: he is creating a single story out of two, one in which God appeared to Jacob more than once, and one in which God spoke to Jacob.[47] At the same time, it is certainly possible, if not provable, that the occurrence of the phrase "where he had spoken to him" in v. 14 is not redactional at all, but rather scribal; that is, a copyist would have accidentally inserted the phrase into v. 14 under the influence of its appearance in the two surrounding verses.[48]

In the compiled vv. 16–20, both sources tell their version of Rachel's death. The words "Rachel died" in v. 19, however, appear only once. This being the central event for both stories, it is very likely that both contained this phrase.

The compiler, of course, could not possibly have the words occur twice in a row. Indeed, there would be no need to do so: even in removing one version of this phrase, he would not have actually altered the original text of either, since both probably had these exact words in this exact place.

The compiler's final step in the creation of the canonical text of Genesis 35 is perhaps his most significant. The list of Jacob's sons in vv. 22b–26, though clearly from P, does not seem to fit into the natural flow of the P narrative at this point. Why should the list of Jacob's sons born in Paddan-Aram have been given by P after Jacob had left Paddan-Aram? It is probably the case that it wasn't: rather, this section originally would have stood somewhere before Genesis 31:17–18.[49] In those verses, Jacob puts his wives and sons on camels to return to his father in Canaan. Thus according to 31:17–18, Jacob's sons have already been born; it is difficult to imagine that P could refer to Jacob's children without at least having enumerated them first—and that enumeration is provided by 35:22b–26. This leaves the question of why the compiler saw fit to take the drastic step of relocating a text from its original source context, a move that occurs only very rarely in the Pentateuch. The answer, however, is clear: according to E in 35:16–20, Benjamin isn't born until Bethel, after Jacob has left Paddan-Aram. The compiler could not have Benjamin born in P before he was born in E, and thus the text in which Benjamin's birth was reported in P had to be placed after that of E (which, indeed, it follows almost directly).[50] Especially notable about this move is what it tells us about the compiler's priorities: Benjamin could not be born twice, or before his time; but the compiler's respect for his sources was such that he did not change the text of vv. 22b–26, despite its contradiction with vv. 16–20. This again points to the compiler's work as being a narrative process, the placing of his sources in the best possible logical and chronological order, with the specific contradictions inherent in his combined text being left to speak for themselves. It further speaks against the idea that P is a redactional layer: such a blatant contradiction, and in such an odd place, would make little sense as a secondary addition.[51] It is only sensible as an originally independent notion of when and where Jacob's sons were born.

As a whole, Genesis 35 therefore contains examples of a number of specific redactional techniques the compiler used in bringing his sources together into a single narrative. We have seen in 35:9 the addition of a single word, "again"; in 33:18a the replacement of one geographical location with another, "Luz" with "Shechem"; in 35:14 the insertion of a phrase from one source into the other, "at the place where he had spoken to him"; in v. 19 the single use of a phrase that appeared originally in both sources, "Rachel died"; and in vv. 22b–26 the relocation of a block of text, the list of Jacob's sons. Each of these redactional moves, judged individually, is not only sensible, but in fact practically required by the nature of the sources themselves. And although Genesis 35 presents a rare combination of all of these techniques in a single chapter, each of them is attested elsewhere throughout the Pentateuch. The compiler's work in Genesis 35 is not unique; it is identical to the methods he employs everywhere: creating from his disparate source documents a single logically and chronologically sequential text.

Conclusion

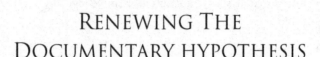

RENEWING THE DOCUMENTARY HYPOTHESIS

In the preceding pages I have presented, both in theory and in practice, the argument for the Documentary Hypothesis. The hypothesis, in its most basic form, postulates four originally independent documents that have been combined into the single text of the canonical Pentateuch. Yet it will be noted that the methods I have used in this book to argue for the hypothesis, and the conclusions that derive from them, differ in some considerable ways from the classical source theory of Julius Wellhausen and his successors. Identifying the differences from the classical theory will perhaps clarify the unique claims espoused in this book and the analytical benefits that proceed from them.

1. The basis on which the sources are identified. Classical scholarship more frequently than not took stylistic and terminological criteria as the starting point for the division of the text, with special reliance on the divine names as an element of style. This resulted in the creation of lengthy lists of words "belonging" to each source, which then formed the basis for subsequent source assignments. Themes and theology were also often used as guides for source division: a given source "could not" have said something, and therefore the passage in question could not be assigned to it. I have argued here for placing the historical claims of the narrative at the forefront of the analysis, with style, theme, and theology playing only secondary, supporting roles. The mark of an author is his creation of and adherence to a distinctive and definable set of historical claims: who did what, when, where, and how. Where these claims are contradictory, we must consider that a different author is at work; where they are the same, there is no need to pursue any source division.

2. What the narratives tell. Among the driving forces behind much classical source analysis was the implicit or explicit understanding that all of the sources basically told the same story, not only in the broader sense of the overarching narrative from the patriarchs through the wilderness, but even in many of the individual episodes making up that history. This resulted in unnecessary fragmentations of the text and faulty source divisions. We should, on the contrary, recognize that the sources in fact tell very different stories within the same larger framework, with different episodes, in different orders, and with very different viewpoints. This recognition allows for literarily unified passages to remain so, and also allows for simpler source divisions.

3. The literary nature of the task. For generations now, the Documentary Hypothesis has been considered synonymous with Wellhausen's reconstruction of the evolutionary growth of ancient Israelite religion. Almost more than the source division, the placement of the sources in a straight line of development from earliest to latest, from naturalistic to legalistic, has been taken as the fundamental claim of the hypothesis. This is demonstrated by the attempts in scholarship to debunk the Documentary Hypothesis by arguing against Wellhausen's view of Israelite religion, as if the former depended on the latter. On the contrary, however, it was Wellhausen's source division in *Composition of the Hexateuch* that allowed for his historical reconstruction in *Prolegomena to the History of Israel*. In the first book, he addressed only the literary evidence; in the second, he addressed only the historical questions. The approach described in this book returns to the first stage and leaves the second unconsidered. The literary question is primary and is in fact the only question that can be answered by the documentary theory. Even if one disagrees with or disproves the arguments of Wellhausen's *Prolegomena*, the literary analysis of the Pentateuch stands on its own merits.

4. The dating of the sources. In the classical model, the sources were understood as representing discrete historical periods and were therefore dated accordingly. The order J-E-D-P was almost universally accepted and was made the basis for much of the analysis. In the Documentary Hypothesis as espoused here, the absolute dating of the sources is not a topic of investigation. There is little in the sources themselves that allows for any absolute dating. What is possible is relative dating, though only in one particular case. The relationship of D to E and J makes clear that D was written after the other two nonpriestly documents. Yet whether J or E came first and how P fits into this picture are questions that the literary data simply do not provide evidence for. Nor does the theory rest on any specific dating of the documents: if all four were written within twenty years of each other, the literary evidence would not change; if

J were written in the tenth century and P in the Middle Ages, the literary evidence would not change. The dating of the sources does not affect the Documentary Hypothesis.

5. What stage of the documents is addressed. The classical source theory was often concerned with identifying the various strata that made up the individual sources, positing J^1, J^2, etc. These strata frequently came to be considered independent sources in their own right and even were given separate sigla. Further, the presence of strata in the sources was used to solve supposed internal discrepancies within the sources. The Documentary Hypothesis as presented in this book is concerned only with the penultimate form of the text: what the compiler had at hand when he put the four documents together. This approach allows for a far greater clarity in addressing the question of how the Pentateuch came to be this way, for it goes back only a single step. It is crucial to note, however, that the Documentary Hypothesis does not dispute the internal growth of the sources; it is simply unconcerned with it. Like so much else, how each source came to look as it does is a secondary question. The Documentary Hypothesis does not deny that each source has a history, nor does it deny that the Pentateuch itself has a history after the compilation of the documents. It is a restricted answer to a restricted question.

6. The singularity of the compiler. The classical approach posited at least three redactors for the Pentateuch, each responsible for one stage in the evolutionary growth of the text. These redactors acquired over the generations roles entirely unsuited to the combination of the four documents: glosses, insertions, theological revisions. In stark contrast, I have argued that the evidence requires but a single compiler, who was responsible for the combination of all four sources. The compiler's work was entirely literary: it was no more than the combination of the four documents into a single story, with the rare small adjustments and insertions that contributed to that process. This approach highlights the fundamental distinction between an author and an editor and keeps each in its proper place.

7. Economy. The classical theory began as a fairly simple proposition. Over time, however, it expanded dramatically, so that even within a generation of Wellhausen the analysis of the Pentateuch required innumerable sigla, regular divisions of the text into half-verses and even single words, and highly complex theories about redaction. The unwieldiness of this theory inevitably led in part to opposition, as it could no longer be said that the Documentary Hypothesis was a particularly economical or elegant solution to the problems of the pentateuchal text. I have tried in this book to restore the economy of the earlier scholarship. The Documentary Hypothesis presented here requires precisely four sources and one compiler.

The major point I have emphasized throughout this book is that the Documentary Hypothesis, in general and in its particulars, is a literary solution to a literary problem, and no more than that. It does not begin with the search for sources in the text: the sources are the conclusion of the theory, not its beginning. It begins with the canonical text and the literary problems that require explanation. Why the Pentateuch is incoherent, that is the driving question of all critical enquiries into the composition of the text, and the Documentary Hypothesis is the simplest and best answer to that question.

NOTES

INTRODUCTION

1. In the translation of the Hebrew texts in the case studies, I use the New Jewish Publication Society (NJPS) translation of the Hebrew Bible as an aid to the reader. In the discussion of the texts, I occasionally deviate from the NJPS translation to provide what I consider a better rendering of the Hebrew; such instances are marked.

2. For a more detailed and comprehensive survey of the narrative problems in the canonical text of Gen 37, see Schwartz, "Joseph's Descent." See also Seebass, *Genesis III*, 24–25.

3. The novelty of Judah's proposal is the idea of profiting from Joseph's death; Reuben had already argued that if the brothers were going to kill Joseph, they should not do it with their own hands, but rather by leaving him to die, probably by drowning, in a pit (vv. 21–22). Although most translations read "Let us not take his life" in v. 21, such a reading is illogical in the context of the narrative. Reuben intends to save Joseph secretly when he returns to the pit (v. 29); he does not try to persuade his brothers not to kill him at all, only to kill him bloodlessly (v. 22). (It seems most likely that the brothers are supposed to think Joseph has drowned in the pit, while Reuben alone knows, as does the reader, that the pit is in fact empty [v. 24].) While the phrase *hikkāʰ nepeš* most commonly means simply "kill" in the Bible (cf. Lev 24:17–18; Num 35:11, 15, 30; Deut 19:6; Josh 20:3, 9; Jer 40:14–15), this is almost certainly an abbreviation from the fuller expression found in Deut 19:11, *wᵉhikkāhû nepeš wāmēt*, "[if] he strikes him and he dies." This example seems to demonstrate that the original meaning of the phrase *hikkāʰ nepeš* was simply to physically assault, probably with intent to kill, which is more sensible in the context of Gen 37:21. Even if the phrase does imply the taking of life, we must understand Reuben here to be saying that the brothers should not take Joseph's life by striking him; rather, they should kill him by throwing him into the pit.

4. The Hebrew in v. 28 is a series of *wayyiqtol* verbs, only the first of which has a stated subject (the Midianites); this syntax suggests that the Midianites are indeed the subject throughout the verse. To claim that it is in fact the brothers who pull Joseph from

the pit or sell him to the Ishmaelites is to read somewhat against the grammar of the text, though this is how the passage has been understood in the majority of instances (see below). Such a reading also raises the question of what function the Midianites serve in the narrative.

5. The Masoretic Text employs in 37:36 the unique gentilic *hammᵉdānîm*, technically "the Medanites." Most commentators have understood this as a shortened form of "Midianites"; the correction to *hammidyānîm* appears already in the Septuagint and the Samaritan Pentateuch. (The name Medan is attested elsewhere in the Bible only as a personal name, as one of the sons of Abraham and his second wife Keturah, in Gen 25:1 and 1 Chr 1:32.) See the opposite viewpoint of some commentators below. The argument of Knauf, "Medan," that the different spelling in 37:36 is intended "to mark this verse as a gloss" is difficult to accept; not only is it unclear how a misspelling marks a gloss, but it is equally clear that this purported marking was missed by all readers for at least two millennia.

6. On the assumptions of early biblical interpreters regarding the text, see Kugel, *Traditions*, 1–30 (esp. 14–19).

7. See particularly the *Testaments of the Twelve Patriarchs* (perhaps originally from the second century BCE), in which this episode is regularly referred to, and always with the Ishmaelites alone. Cf. *T. Sim.* 2:9; *T. Zeb.* 3:9, in which the plot to sell Joseph is not formed upon seeing the Ishmaelites as in Gen 37, but rather three days in advance (4:3); *T. Gad* 2:3; *T. Benj.* 2:1, 3. Some of the testaments mention the sale, but not the Ishmaelites by name: cf. *T. Dan* 1:5; *T. Naph.* 7:4.

8. *Ant.* II.32–39.

9. *T. Jos.* 15, 27.

10. *On Joseph*, 15.

11. *Bib. Ant.* 8:9. This ostensibly novel reading of the story may, however, be the result of Pseudo-Philo's brevity here, rather than of a conscious effort to smooth over the biblical text.

12. *Ber. Rab.* 84:22.

13. Rashi on Gen 37:28.

14. Rashi therefore read "Midianites" for "Medanites" in v. 36.

15. See Leibowitz, *Genesis*, 401. She also notes the interpretation of Ḥizquni, which involves four sales, two of which are clandestine (the brothers to the Midianites and the Ishmaelites to the Medanites) because Joseph was considered potentially stolen property, and which reads "from the hand of the Ishmaelites" as meaning that the Ishmaelites gave the guarantee that Joseph's purchase and subsequent sales were in order (ibid., 402).

16. On the development of interpretive strategies in the medieval Jewish commentators, see Greenstein, "Medieval Bible Commentaries."

17. Rashbam on 37:28. All translations of Rashbam are taken from Lockshin, *Genesis*.

18. Rashbam was so certain that the verbs in Hebrew indicate that the Midianites pulled Joseph from the pit that he went to great lengths to defend it in his commentary on v. 28: "Even if one were to insist on saying that they sold Joseph to the Ishmaelites

means that Joseph's brothers sold him, one would still have to say that Joseph's brothers first commanded the Midianites to pull Joseph out of the pit, and then sold Joseph to the Ishmaelites."

19. This also accounts for Reuben's mystification upon returning to the pit in 37:29–30; neither he nor any of the brothers were present when Joseph was removed and sold to Egypt.

20. Rashbam on 37:36.

21. Ibn Ezra on 37:28. Translation from Strickland and Silver, *Genesis*.

22. The same solution was proposed by Radak on 37:28.

23. The lack of the definite article on *midyānîm* in 37:28 — in fact, the entire description of this group as "men, Midianite merchants" — suggests grammatically that this is the first appearance of this entity in the narrative. Cf. Wellhausen, *Composition*, 52; Dillmann, *Genesis*, 2:340; Simpson, *Pentateuchal Criticism*, 78–79; Cassuto, *Questione*, 358.

24. Naḥmanides, *Commentary*, 459, on 37:25. He is followed by Sforno on 37:28.

25. Ibid., 460.

26. See further Leibowitz, *Genesis*, 402–4.

27. Augustine, *Quaestionum*, 48 (question 124).

28. And not before wishing that he could avoid the question altogether: "These matters have been dealt with by Augustine and others irrelevantly. I would certainly prefer that questions should be raised about more serious and useful matters" (Luther, *Genesis*, 387).

29. Ibid.

30. Ibid.

31. Ibid.

32. Calvin, *Genesis*, 270–71.

33. Ibid.

34. Brooke and McLean, *The Old Testament in Greek*, 1:108; cf. Anbar, "Changement," 223–24. Dahse, in his *Textkritische Materialen*, 1:131, used these data to argue that the text of the Masoretic Text is unstable enough to render it unsuitable for inquiry into its composition.

35. Cave, *Inspiration*, 201.

36. Ibid. Note that Cave silently assumed that the brothers are the subject of the verbs in this verse, (unconsciously) with Rashi and against Rashbam.

37. Finn, *Unity*, 54. See also Green, "Pentateuchal Question. III," 8–9, who acknowledged that Ishmaelites and Midianites were different tribes but stated that "tribal names are not always used with definite exactness" (8). His solution was that "they were recognized in the distance as an Ishmaelite caravan, but it was not till they actually came up to them that the Ishmaelites were discovered to be specifically Midianites" (9). He also explicitly rejected the possibility that the Midianites pulled Joseph from the pit: "in the connection in which it stands, such a sense is simply impossible" (9). See also Keil and Delitzsch, *Commentary*, 217; Kitchen, *Ancient Orient*, 119–20, and Mendenhall, "Midian," 815: "The term Midianite alternates with the term

Ishmaelite, probably to be explained by the fact that at the time the narrative reached its present form, the Midianites had ceased to exist as a distinct ethnic group but were identified with an ethnic group later called Ishmaelites."

38. Jacob, *Genesis*, 706–7, and in greater detail his *Quellenscheidung*, 16–22. Jacob's interpretation was followed almost to the letter by Wilhelm Rudolph (in Volz and Rudolph, *Elohist*, 154). So also Römer, "Joseph approche," 77.

39. Jacob, *Genesis*, 709. Jacob also explicitly denied that the "Medanites" are a group distinct from the Midianites, citing the variation of *dōtān* and *dōtāynā*[h] in the same verse in this very chapter (v. 17).

40. Other difficulties with this solution—where were the brothers when the Midianites stole Joseph from the pit? why was only Reuben surprised that the pit was empty, when all the brothers would have thought Joseph was there? why does the story even bother to mention the plan of the brothers to sell Joseph?, among others—were raised in objection by Cassuto, *Questione*, 357.

41. Green, "*What Profit?*," 49.

42. Ibid., 60. She derives this second option from Adele Berlin's analysis of repetition of information in biblical narrative. Berlin treated the similarity between 37:36 and 39:1 as a means of signaling the return of the narration to an earlier point (in this case with the interlude of Gen 38), but from a different viewpoint (Berlin, *Poetics*, 76). Berlin, however, deals only with the repetition of Joseph being sold in Egypt to Potiphar; she explicitly leaves aside what she terms "the Midianite-Ishmaelite problem" (ibid.). In a similar study of the function of 39:1 as a resumptive repetition of 37:36 bracketing Gen 38, Talmon argued that "in the present context, as also in other settings [e.g., Judg 8:24], the designations 'Ishmaelites' and 'Midianites' are devoid of any ethnic connotation, but rather are coterminous and both equivalent to 'caravan traders' ("Synchroneity," 19).

43. Similar investigations of this narrative have been undertaken by Good (*Irony*, 107) and Ackerman ("Joseph," 99), who take the position that the Midianites beat the brothers to the sale of Joseph, and White ("Joseph Story," 64–65; see also White, "Reuben," 73–97) and Wenham (*Genesis 16–50*, 354–55), who equate the Midianites and Ishmaelites, accepting as grammatically possible but rejecting as narratively implausible the Midianite usurpation of Judah's plan to sell Joseph to the Ishmaelites. None of these authors reckons with the difficulties such conclusions entail. Neither Good nor Ackerman, for instance, mentions the notice in 39:1 that Potiphar bought Joseph from the Ishmaelites, and White falls back on the argument from Judg 8:24, familiar to us from ibn Ezra. See Ska, *Introduction*, 67–68.

44. Fokkelman, *Reading*, 80.

45. Greenstein, "Equivocal Reading," 114–25.

46. Ibid., 119.

47. Ibid., 123.

48. Longacre, *Joseph*, 29–30. "Perhaps 'Ishmaelites' was sometimes used as a more generic term (= Bedouin nomad), while 'Midianite' is more specific and ethnic" (29). He provides no evidence for this possibility. See also his article on this passage, "Who Sold Joseph." Longacre's argument is closely followed by Marconi, "Contributi," al-

though Marconi, like Greenstein, claims to be providing merely a mechanism for reading the canonical text, rather than an argument for its unitary composition.

49. Ibid., 30.

50. Ibid.

51. Campbell and O'Brien, *Rethinking*, 65. It is hard to see how their first option, of Joseph simply being left to die in the pit, has any narrative plausibility.

52. Ibid., 64.

53. Humphreys, *Joseph*, 36.

54. Ibid.

55. Revell, "Midian," 75.

56. Ibid. Revell bases his argument on what he perceives as similar pairings in the Jacob-Joseph stories, though in none of the other examples he brings is there a question of narrative incoherence as a result of the alternation. For a similar comparison of Gen 37 with other interchanges of proper names in both biblical and extrabiblical literature, see Anbar, "Changement," and Abramski, "Ishmaelites," 128–29.

57. Revell, "Midian," 87.

CHAPTER 1. THE DOCUMENTARY HYPOTHESIS

1. On the Christian side, similar questions had been raised in the early centuries CE and well into the Reformation; see the detailed overviews provided in Pfeiffer, *Introduction*, 135–36, and Hayes, *Introduction*, 106–15.

2. Hobbes, *Leviathan*, 173.

3. Simon, *Histoire Critique*, 32 (translation mine): "Je sçai qu'on peut apporter des réponses à la plus-part de ces passages & à quelques autres qu'il seroit inutile de produire: mais pour peu de reflexion qu'on veüille faire sur ces réponses, on les trouvera plus subtiles que veritables; & je ne croi pas qu'il soit necessaire, ni même judicieux, d'avoir recours à ces sortes de fuites, puis que les plus sçavans Peres ont avoüé librement, que le Pentateuque, au moins de la maniere qu'il est maintenant, pouvoit n'être pas attribué tout entier à Moïse." On Simon's life and work, see Steinmann, *Richard Simon*. The majority of Simon's book is devoted to text-critical investigation and comment on the nature of biblical translation, and it is certain that his innovation and effect in this area was far greater than his influence on the question of pentateuchal composition. On this aspect of Simon's work, see especially McKane, *Selected Christian Hebraists*, 111–50.

4. At least from the rabbinic standpoint, this view may be understood as a necessary element of the midrashic method: in order for new laws and interpretations to be validated, they have to emerge from a text that is ultimately of divine origin. The divine authorship of the Torah, then, became more than a historical claim; it became a necessary creed in rabbinic thought. This is evident in the strong statement of *b. Sanh.* 99a: "Even if one maintains that the whole Torah is from heaven except a certain verse which the Holy One, blessed be He, did not speak, but rather Moses himself," he is denied participation in the world to come.

5. See also Exod 12:49; Lev 6:7, 18; 7:1, 7, 11, 37; 11:46; 12:7; 13:59; 14:2, 32, 54, 57; Num 5:29, 30; 6:13, 21; 15:16, 29; 19:2, 14; 31:21.

6. See also Deut 1:5; 4:44; 17:18, 19; 27:3, 8, 26; 28:58, 61; 29:28; 31:9, 11, 12, 24; 32:46, and the similar expression "this book of Torah," Deut 29:20; 30:10; 31:26; cf. Najman, *Seconding Sinai*, 29–31.

7. See also Josh 8:32; 23:6; 1 Kgs 2:3; 2 Kgs 14:6; 23:25, and similarly Josh 1:7, 22:5; 2 Kgs 21:8. It is also described as the "Torah of Yahweh" (2 Kgs 10:31). Cf. Haran, *Biblical Collection*, 2:291–92.

8. Cf. Ezra 6:18; 7:6; 10:3; Neh 8:2, 3, 7, 9, 13, 14; 9:14; 10:35, 37; 12:44; 13:1, 3. In Chronicles the same situation seems to apply; cf. 2 Chr 23:18; 25:4; 30:16. On the equation of Chronicles-Ezra-Nehemiah's "Torah" with the Pentateuch as a whole (rather than any individual elements thereof), cf. Myers, *Ezra-Nehemiah*, lix–lxii.

9. For an overview of Reformation scholarship on the literary problems of the Pentateuch, see Carpenter and Harford-Battersby, *Hexateuch*, 1:22–28.

10. If we take the first words of Deut 10:8, "at that time," to refer to the immediately preceding verse, which narrates the journey of the Israelites from Gudgod to Jotbath, then this is where the Levites were invested. However, even if we read "at that time" as referring to the main narrative of Deut 10, that is, the second giving of the tablets—the description of which begins in 10:1–5 and resumes in 10:10, forming a bracket around the notices of Aaron's death and the investiture of the Levites in vv. 6–9—we are still faced with a contradiction, although perhaps a lesser one: according to Deuteronomy, in this reading, the Levites were invested while Moses was on the mountain receiving the second set of tablets, while Num 3–4 places the same event not on top of the mountain, but in the Tent of Meeting at the foot of the mountain. Moses descends from the mountain for the last time in Exod 34:29. No matter how we choose to understand the phrase "at that time," the story in Deuteronomy and the story in Numbers do not agree.

11. Or, following the explicit chronological notices carefully, perhaps even eighty years passed between Isaac's deathbed scene and his actual death. According to Gen 25:26, Isaac was sixty years old when Jacob and Esau were born. In 26:34, we learn that Esau was forty when he married his Hittite wives, making Isaac one hundred. Since, according to 27:46, it is Esau's marriage that precipitates Jacob's departure, we know that the events of Gen 27 (the deathbed scene) took place at that time. When Isaac dies, he is said to be 180 (35:28–29). Thus between Gen 27 and 35, between the deathbed and the actual death, eighty years must have passed.

12. Some early critical scholars, who identified the various contradictions in the biblical narrative, recognized that the Pentateuch must be made up of distinct written elements but did not attempt to produce a full theory as to how those elements were put together. Thus Isaac La Peyrère described the pieces of the Pentateuch as "diversely written, being taken out of several authors" and supposed that these pieces had been put together by Moses but were subsequently misarranged in the course of transmission, resulting in "a heap of Copie confusedly taken" (*Theological systeme*, 210, 208). On La Peyrère's life and work as a whole, see Popkin, *Isaac La Peyrère*. Similarly, Baruch Spinoza argued that the contradictions prove that the Pentateuch was com-

piled from disparate and contradictory historical documents and followed La Peyrère
in claiming that these disparate texts had been placed out of their correct order in
the final text: "all the materials were very promiscuously collected and heaped together" (*Treatise*, 135). It is known that Spinoza had La Peyrère's book in his library;
see Frampton, *Spinoza*, 208. For a survey of La Peyrère's influence on Spinoza, see
Strauss, *Spinoza's Critique*, 64–85. Also see Frampton and Strauss for an overview of
Spinoza's view of the Bible and religion as a whole, as well as the historical and intellectual setting of his work.

In the late eighteenth century, Alexander Geddes proposed that the Pentateuch
was a collection of diverse historical writings collected during the Solomonic era,
gathered together by an anonymous figure who had "collected from such documents
as he could find, either among his own people, or among the neighboring nations"
(*Holy Bible*, xviii–xix). Geddes did not provide any details for this process; these were
to wait only a short while until the work of Johann S. Vater in the early nineteenth
century, in his *Commentar*. On the historical and cultural setting of Geddes and his
work, see Fuller, *Alexander Geddes*.

Vater put forward a series of rationales by which the various segments of the Pentateuch could be isolated: headings, such as the *toledot* formula, "these are the generations of . . . ," found in Genesis; clearly independent pieces, such as the itinerary
of Num 33; concluding formulae, such as Lev 7:37–38; repetitions, as in Gen 1 and 2;
contradictions in fact, for example, the varying accounts of when the town of Luz was
renamed Bethel (Gen 28:19 and 35:15); differences in tone, again using Gen 1 and 2
as the prime example; differences in expression, such as the use of the name Horeb
in Deuteronomy for the mountain in the wilderness, as opposed to Sinai in the preceding books; and the different divine appellations (*Commentar*, 396–413). Vater was
careful to state that the ability to separate one passage from another did not necessarily
mean that they were to be separated; at the same time, the fact that so many pieces
could be separated suggested to Vater that there were indeed separations to be made
(ibid., 417). Vater gave significant weight to the question of form, rather than content.
Thus the various *toledot* formulae, despite their common wording, are potentially
attributable to different authors, since they introduce distinct passages (ibid., 397).
Similarly, Vater saw Num 7, in which the various tribes bring their gifts for the inauguration of the Tabernacle, as an independent piece, despite the fact that it assumes
the construction of the Tabernacle at the end of Exodus (Num 7:1) as well as the
assignment in Num 3–4 of specific roles to the levitical groups (7:6–9) (ibid.). At the
same time, Vater viewed the plagues narrative in Exod 7–11, despite its many internal
contradictions, as a single segment (ibid., 448).

Using the aforementioned criteria, Vater isolated a large number of fragments
across all five books of the Pentateuch. When it came to the question of the relationships among these pieces, Vater was reticent to draw any conclusions; he erred on the
side of independence rather than connection: "If the individual pieces have in this
commentary been called 'fragments,' this is only to say that they are individual pieces
without mutual connection; since who could possibly be able to show precisely whether
and in what relation to a larger whole such ancient articles once stood?" (ibid., 395 n.;

translation mine). [Wenn die einzelnen Stücke in diesem Commentare: Fragmente, überschrieben worden sind, so soll damit nur gesagt werden, daß sie einzelne Stücke ohne gegenseitigen Zusammenhang sind; denn wer möchte von so uralten Aufsätzen genau angeben können, ob und in welchem Verhältnisse sie einst zu grösseren Ganzen gestanden haben?] With Vater, then, the ideas of Geddes were developed into a full-blown theory, that is, many originally independent fragments, collected and arranged in vague chronological order to form the Pentateuch as we now have it.

For good overviews of the early history of pentateuchal scholarship, see Houtman, *Pentateuch*; Kraus, *Geschichte*; Westphal, *Sources*.

13. Fewer than twenty years after Vater's commentary was published, an extensive and persuasive refutation of the Fragmentary Hypothesis was produced by Ewald in his *Komposition*, 122–190. Although in this early work Ewald defended the unity of the text, in his later writings he became one of the forefathers of the Supplementary Hypothesis (see chapter 2).

14. This approach is connected primarily with the scholars Jean Astruc, in *Conjectures*, and Johann Gottfried Eichhorn, in *Einleitung*. Astruc recognized the various narrative difficulties identified by his seventeenth-century predecessors; however, he argued that the variation in divine appellations—in one place the title "Elohim," or "God," and in another place the divine name proper, "Yahweh"—should be seen as yet another textual problem to be explained. (The alternation of divine names in Gen 1 and 2 and the recognition on that basis that these chapters must be the work of two distinct authors had already been noted in the early eighteenth century by Henning Bernhard Witter, in *Jura Israelitarum in Palaestinam*; this work, however, was unknown in scholarship until it was rediscovered and described by Lods [*Jean Astruc*, 54–55].) Astruc proceeded simply to divide Genesis into two columns: one including those texts that employed the title Elohim, and one with those that used the name Yahweh. The strength of Astruc's analysis derived not only from his division of the text, but in large part from his insight in recognizing that passages which regularly use one name over against the other can be connected into a larger narrative: "Upon these reflections, it was natural to try to take apart Genesis, to separate all the different bits that are confounded there, to reunite those that are of the same kind and that appear to have belonged to the same Memoires, and in this way to restore these original Memoires which I believe Moses had. The enterprise was not so difficult as one might believe" (*Conjectures*, 143) (translation mine). [Sur ces réflexions, il était naturel de tenter de décomposer la Genèse, de séparer tous les différents morceaux qui y sont confondus, de réunir ceux qui sont d'une même espèce et qui paraissent avoir appartenu aux mêmes Mémoires, et par ce moyen de rétablir ces Mémoires originaux que je crois que Moïse a eus. L'enterprise n'était pas aussi difficile, qu'on aurait pu le croire.] In this way, Astruc was the first to describe "documents" rather than individual fragments. On Astruc and his place in scholarship, see Lods, *Jean Astruc*, and Smend, *From Astruc to Zimmerli*, 1–14.

Eichhorn not only accepted Astruc's arguments regarding the division of Genesis into two documents, he claimed Astruc as his guide: "Finally Astruc, a famous doctor, has done what no critic of the profession wanted to venture, and disassembles the entirety of Genesis into individual fragments. I too have done the same investigation; however, I have let nothing influence my viewpoints without taking Astruc as my guide" (*Einleitung*, 22–23) (translation mine). [Endlich hat Astrük, ein berühmter Arzt, das gethan, woran sich kein Kritikus von Profession wagen wollte, und die ganze Genesis in einzelne Fragmente zerlegt. Auch ich habe dieselbe Untersuchung angestellt; aber, um mein Gesichtspunkte durch nichts verrücken zu lassen, ohne Astrük zu meinem Führer oder Geleitsmann zu wählen.] Eichhorn, however, went beyond Astruc in the precision of his analysis, as well as in his correlation of the two documents with the narrative inconsistencies in the text. It was with regard to Eichhorn's work that the term "Documentary Hypothesis" began to be used. Eichhorn's *Einleitung* is widely seen as providing the model for all subsequent introductions to the Hebrew Bible.

Despite recognizing that the motivating factor behind the division of Genesis into multiple sources was the issue of narrative inconsistency, Astruc's and Eichhorn's divisions of the text began with and stayed entirely true to the alternation of divine appellations. The problems solved in this manner were, indeed, those of narrative inconsistency, but the resolution of the textual issues became, in their analysis, a proof of the correctness of the division according to divine appellation. So Eichhorn: "The alternating names of God, Jehovah and Elohim, remain the leaders; the character of both documents, their own phraseology, their favorite idioms, and the other peculiarities enumerated above make the road more sure and the progress more certain" (ibid., 105) (translation mine). [Die wechselnden Namen Gottes, Jehova und Elohim, bleiben Hauptführer; der Charakter der beiden Urkunden, ihre eigene Phraseologie, ihre Lieblingswendungen, und die andern oben aufgezählten Eigenheiten werden die Bahn sicherer und die Fortschritte gewisser machen.] At times, the primary focus on the divine appellations created difficulties rather than solving them: Eichhorn, for instance, isolated the second creation story in Gen 2:4–3:24 as not belonging to either the Yahweh document or the Elohim document because it uses the unique designation "Yahweh Elohim" throughout (ibid., 39–41).

15. Eichhorn, *Einleitung*, 91. Astruc went to great lengths to argue that Exod 6:2–6 (the second revelation of Yahweh's name to Moses) is not evidence that the patriarchs did not know the divine name (*Conjectures*, 387–95). Given that his Elohist source was described entirely on the basis of that name never being used, it is perhaps surprising that he did not connect Exod 6:2–6 with the Elohist. Eichhorn argued similarly that Exod 6:2–6 is about the change of God's persona from the distant omnipotent deity to the more personal God of the Israelites (*Einleitung*, 145–46). For both scholars it is likely that the sources discovered in Genesis were thought to end in Exod 2 not only because the divine appellations cease to function as a distinguishing feature after the revelation of the divine name in Exod 3, but also because they attributed the texts that dealt with the adult life of Moses (Exod 3–Deut 34) to Moses himself. In this we see the continuation of the arguments of La Peyrère, who observed that although Moses certainly could have written what happened in his own lifetime, he would not have been privy to the detailed information about the events of Genesis, all of which happened hundreds if not thousands of years before his time (*Theological system*, 213–14).

16. Astruc, *Conjectures*, 257–58, 286, 293–94.
17. See Hupfeld, *Quellen*, 87–88, who directly criticized Astruc for his "apologetic" interpretation of Exod 6:2–6.
18. Credit for the first move in this direction belongs to Karl D. Ilgen, in *Urkunden*. His analysis was widely seen as flawed, however, and gained little traction in the field. The scholar to whom we are indebted for the fullest and most persuasive separation of the "Elohist" source into two documents is Hupfeld, in his seminal *Quellen*. Hupfeld not only separated Genesis into its three component documents, he also provided a detailed analysis of each, highlighting the differences among them in narrative, theme, and language.
19. For example, Johann G. Eichhorn and Wilhelm M. L. de Wette.
20. Hupfeld, *Quellen*.
21. Wellhausen, in *Composition*, designated the priestly narratives with the siglum Q (from the Latin *quatuor*, for the four covenants he discerned therein), and the priestly laws by the siglum PC (for "Priestercodex"). The move to P as the standard siglum for all the priestly material was made by Kuenen, *Hexateuch*, 64–65 n. 34.
22. Indeed, J, which calls the mountain Sinai, knows of a place called Horeb—but it is not the mountain of the theophany. It is, rather, the name of the rock in the wilderness from which Moses brings forth water, and its name is changed after that event to "Massah and Meribah" (Exod 17:1bβ–7).
23. The most substantial of these lists was produced by Carpenter and Harford-Battersby, *Hexateuch*, 1:185–221.
24. Hendel, "'Begetting.'"
25. The attempt to draw conclusions regarding the development of Israelite religion on the basis of the Pentateuch had already been undertaken before the Documentary Hypothesis was put forth, particularly in the works of Wilhelm M. L. de Wette, Carl P. W. Gramberg, and Johann F. L. George. On these scholars, see particularly Rogerson, *Old Testament Criticism*, 28–49, 57–68. Ewald, employing a documentary/supplementary model, moved even further in this direction in *Geschichte*. On Ewald, see Rogerson, *Old Testament Criticism*, 91–103. It was Ewald's student, Wellhausen, in *Prolegomena*, who argued most forcefully for the Documentary Hypothesis as the key to understanding the course of Israelite religious thought.
26. McEvenue, "Return," 386.
27. See Friedman, "Torah (Pentateuch)."
28. This type of analysis was present already in the seminal work of Kuenen, *Hexateuch*, and was implemented in depth by Carpenter and Harford-Battersby, *Hexateuch*, vol. 2. In the twentieth century the discernment of multiple strata within the sources reached its fullest expression in the work of Smend, *Erzählung*, and Simpson, *Early Traditions*. It was this secondary division of the sources that gave rise in the mid-twentieth century to a series of attempts to isolate a third nonpriestly, nondeuteronomic source alongside J and E. Thus we find arguments for a lay source (L) by Eissfeldt, *Old Testament*; a Kenite source (K) by Morgenstern, "Oldest Document"; a Seir source (S) by Pfeiffer, "Non-Israelite Source"; and a nomadic source (N) by Fohrer, *Überlieferung*.

29. Although Klostermann (*Pentateuch*) is frequently given credit for identifying the Holiness Code of Lev 17–26, this is in fact inaccurate. His contribution was merely the nomenclature, as he was the first to designate this corpus as the "Holiness Laws" (*Heiligkeitsgesetzes*). The recognition that these chapters in Leviticus are a distinctive block within the priestly laws was already well known by the time of Kuenen (see *Hexateuch*, 88 n. 24, for a brief history of scholarship). Virtually all scholars believed H to be the earliest layer of the priestly legislation until the crucial contribution of Knohl, *Sanctuary of Silence*, who demonstrated that H is in fact a later addition to and redaction of P. Knohl's thesis has been accepted by the majority of current critics, most importantly by Jacob Milgrom.

CASE STUDY I. THE SALE OF JOSEPH, GENESIS 37:18–36

1. See Speiser, *Genesis*, 293: "The work of a competent writer surely presupposes an inner consistency of theme and details. Yet [these verses], as they now read, are marked by inconsistency, duplication, and discrepancies."
2. Thus even a scholar fundamentally opposed to source criticism must admit the difficulty here: "The alternative roles played by the Ishmaelite and Midianite traders in the affair seemed to provide the clearest case of a double account" (Whybray, *Making*, 89). See also Eerdmans, *Alttestamentliche Studien I*, 66.
3. For further details of the following source division, see Schwartz, "Joseph's Descent." For a useful summary and analysis of critical views on the composition of this chapter and the Joseph narrative as a whole, see Paap, *Josephsgeschichte*.
4. See Simpson, *Early Traditions*, 128. The repetition of the direct object yet again in v. 28b, on the other hand, is not unexpected, as the subject has changed to the Ishmaelites and the direct object is provided again for clarity.
5. Note the use of "our brother," *'āḥînû*, at the beginning and the end, the parallel places of "cover his blood" and "let our hand not be against him," the centrality of "let's sell him to the Ishmaelites," and the use of the monetary terms "profit" and "sell" at the beginning of each sentence.
6. If this case (and that of vv. 21–22 and 24; see below) is seen to fit into the common biblical pattern of command and fulfillment—in this case with the command coming in the form of the cohortative rather than the imperative—it may provide yet another reason to view v. 28aα as an intrusion into the expected sequence of events. See Baden, "Narrative Pattern."
7. Many scholars separate v. 18a (which is seen as linked to vv. 19–20) from 18b, though this severs the logical connection between the brothers seeing Joseph "from afar," *mērāḥōq*, and the drawing up of their plan before he "drew near," *yiqrab*. See Kautzsch and Socin, *Genesis*, 87; Addis, *Documents*, 1:73; Bacon, *Genesis*, 186; Holzinger, *Genesis*, 224; Carpenter and Harford-Battersby, *Hexateuch*, 2:59; Procksch, *Elohimquelle*, 41; Gunkel, *Genesis*, 388; Brightman, *Sources*, 66; Skinner, *Genesis*, 446; Ruppert, *Josephserzählung*, 29; Schmidt, *Josephsgeschichte*, 147; Graupner, *Elohist*, 320.
8. Kebekus, *Joseferzählung*, 8–9; Schwartz, "Joseph's Descent," 12–13.
9. Note the same framing device, in this case the reference to "the dreamer" and "his

dreams" at the beginning and end of the speech. We might view Judah's replacement of "the dreamer" with "our brother" as an intentional softening of the brothers' original language, reminding them that he is more than a pest with ambition, but their own flesh and blood first and foremost.

10. It is unnecessary to claim, as some have, that v. 28b, "they brought Joseph to Egypt," refers to the Midianites and belongs with v. 28aα, rather than as the continuation of the Ishmaelite strand in v. 28aβ (see Hupfeld, *Quellen,* 68–69; Wellhausen, *Composition,* 53 n. 1; Kautzsch and Socin, *Genesis,* 88; Bacon, *Genesis,* 187; Dillmann, *Genesis,* 2:339–40; Holzinger, *Genesis,* 224; Carpenter and Harford-Battersby, 2:60; Gunkel, *Genesis,* 389; Driver, *Genesis,* 325; Skinner, *Genesis,* 448; Ruppert, *Josephserzählung,* 30; Kebekus, *Joseferzählung,* 10; Graupner, *Elohist,* 320–21). The notice that the Midianites brought Joseph to Egypt is provided in v. 36 for the first time; this preserves for the reader the same suspense and uncertainty exhibited by Reuben in vv. 29–30: where has Joseph gone? The frequent claim among the older critics that one strand uses *b-w-'* (v. 28b) and the other *y-r-d* (vv. 25, 39:1) to describe the movement to Egypt is based on far too little evidence and is typical of the early-twentieth-century tendency to divide texts on the basis of minute terminological variations. The attempt of Kebekus (*Joseferzählung,* 27–29) to connect v. 36 with the Judah/Ishmaelite strand is incomprehensible.

11. Some scholars separate v. 21 from v. 22, assigning the first to story A and the second to story B, on the basis of the double speech marker and the ostensibly difficult *wayyiqtol wayyaṣṣilēhû;* this, however, forces them to read "Judah" for "Reuben" in v. 21 (see Wellhausen, *Composition,* 53–54; Kautzsch and Socin, *Genesis,* 87; Addis, *Documents,* 1:73 n. 3; Bacon, *Genesis,* 186–87; Dillmann, *Genesis,* 2:338; Holzinger, *Genesis,* 224; Carpenter and Harford-Battersby, *Hexateuch,* 2:59; Gunkel, *Genesis,* 388, 392; Driver, *Genesis,* 324; Smend, *Erzählung,* 100; Procksch, *Elohimquelle,* 42; Brightman, *Sources,* 66; Skinner, *Genesis,* 447; Simpson, *Early Traditions,* 127; Noth, *Pentateuchal Traditions,* 30, 35; Ruppert, *Josephserzählung,* 30; von Rad, *Genesis,* 353; Schmidt, *Josephsgeschichte,* 146–47). Carr (*Fractures,* 284, 287) allows for either v. 21b or 22 to be an addition, though without providing any rationale for either option.

Neither problem is a true difficulty: for the first, double speech markers are not uncommon in biblical narrative, even within the same source (see, for example, the triple speech marker in Gen 17:3, 9, and 15 in a unified P text; see Septimus, "Iterated Quotation Formulae," 371–75); for the second, as has long been recognized, this *wayyiqtol* can and should be read as a conative, "he attempted to save him"; see Speiser, *Genesis,* 291. The difficulty of the emendation of "Judah" for "Reuben" in v. 21, and the assignment of that verse to story A, is perhaps the best argument against this analysis: Judah does not save Joseph at this point in the story, but rather only after the Ishmaelite caravan is seen in v. 25, and then only from the motivation of profit. See Graupner, *Elohist,* 320. Recognizing these difficulties, Schmitt (*Josephsgeschichte,* 23–24 n. 76) proposed that v. 21 was a later addition, intended to put Reuben in a better light, since in v. 22 Reuben still ostensibly wants Joseph dead, whereas in v. 21 he tries to prevent the death altogether (Schmitt is followed by Kebekus, *Joseferzählung,* 10–12). This argument is based, however, on a misunderstanding of the phrase *hikkā^h nepeš*; see the introduction. Whatever the justification, separating these verses also ruins the artistic composition of the unit, with the verb *n-ṣ-l* (hiphil), "to save," in the narrator's voice both preceding and following Reuben's speech (see Seebass, *Genesis III*, 22).

12. See Gunkel, *Genesis*, 392; Simpson, *Early Traditions*, 127.

13. Thus the analysis of Addis (*Documents*, 1:74), in which the words "they pulled Joseph up out of the pit" in v. 28 belongs to story A, is impossible, as Joseph is not, in story A, in any pit from which the brothers might draw him—even in Addis's own source division. His analysis also leaves *wayyimš^{e}kû*, "they pulled," without an object.

14. Dillmann's assignment of vv. 19–20 to the same strand as vv. 21–22 (*Genesis*, 2:337) ignores the intimate connections of vv. 19–20 and 26–27. So also Graupner, *Elohist*, 320. The theory of Redford (*Joseph*, 139–43) that vv. 26–27 are secondarily built on v. 22 and that vv. 19–21 are a yet later addition to the text is even more egregious.

15. Schwartz, "Joseph's Descent," 5–6. Schwartz also highlights the difference in the verbal root used to signify the killing of Joseph in the two stories: in story B (v. 18), *m-w-t* (hiphil); in story A (vv. 20, 26), *h-r-g* (ibid., 13). Note also that this verbal distinction emerges from the analysis of the text on narrative grounds; it is supportive, rather than determinative, of the analysis.

16. See the positive argument for the unity of this section in Graupner, *Elohist*, 321. These verses are seen as an addition even within story A by Kratz (*Composition*, 277), not because they conflict with anything in the narrative strand but, presumably, because they are linked verbally with Gen 38, which Kratz sees as a secondary insertion into the narrative. Among the older commentators, the common sin of excessive source division afflicted them in the analysis of these verses, such that this tightly constructed section was divided into two strands, neither completely coherent; see Kautzsch and Socin, *Genesis*, 88; Addis, *Documents*, 1:74; Bacon, *Genesis*, 187–88; Carpenter and Harford-Battersby, *Hexateuch*, 2:60, who may have the most incoherent strands at this point; Smend, *Erzählung*, 101; Procksch, *Elohimquelle*, 42; Brightman, *Sources*, 66; Simpson, *Early Traditions*, 129; Dillmann, *Genesis*, 2:340–41, whose separation of vv. 34a and 35b from 34b–35a leaves *'ōtô* in v. 35b completely without an antecedent. Dillmann is followed precisely by Gunkel, *Genesis*, 389; Skinner, *Genesis*, 448–49; Ruppert, *Josephserzählung*, 30; Schmidt, *Josephsgeschichte*, 148.

17. Schwartz, "Joseph's Descent," 17.

18. See Westermann, *Genesis 37–50*, 40. Schwartz, "Joseph's Descent," 3–4, 12–13, has cogently argued that the doublet of the brothers' motivation for killing Joseph in the first part of the chapter is not, as almost always claimed, between the dreams and the tunic, but rather between their father's special love for Joseph (represented by both the dreams and the coat) and his habitual spying on them and reporting back to Jacob.

19. Note that in vv. 19 and 23 the same verb is used in the Hebrew, *bā'*, while in v. 18 the brothers plan to kill Joseph before he "draws near," *yiqrab*.

20. Although some scholars seem to suppose precisely this; see Addis, *Documents*, 1:73; Gunkel, *Genesis*, 388–89; Brightman, *Sources*, 66.

21. As already understood by Hupfeld, *Quellen*, 69.

22. The same source division can be found in Friedman, *Sources Revealed*, 93–94, and Schwartz, "Joseph's Descent," 14–15.

23. Friedman, *Sources Revealed*, 94.

24. Ibid.

25. Von Rad, *Genesis*, 353–54; Schwartz, "Joseph's Descent," 18.

26. Note especially J's focus on Judah's development in character from the callous sale of Joseph in chapter 37, through the embarrassing events of chapter 38, to the self-sacrifice for the sake of Benjamin in chapter 44 (see Scharbert, *Genesis 12–50*, 242). It is also of no small relevance that E does not seem to refer to or even recognize the existence of Ishmael at any point in its narrative. On the narrative connections from the J and E stories in Gen 37 through Gen 39–41, see Jenks, *Elohist*, 28–29. Friedman (*Sources Revealed*, 94) claims that the birth notice of Medan and Midian in Gen 25:2 is from E, but his evidence for this claim is the use of the tribal names here in Gen 37, thus creating a distinctly circular argument. Gen 25:1–6 is most likely from J, as it narrates the second marriage of Abraham after the reference to the death of Sarah at the end of Gen 24 (J).

27. Schwartz, "Joseph's Descent," 17.

28. For the following, see in greater detail Schwartz, "Joseph's Descent," 19–27.

29. Schwartz, "Joseph's Descent," 23.

30. The presence of both the Ishmaelites and Midianites in the narrative could have been understood by the compiler in either of the standard ways we have encountered in the introduction if we imagine him being concerned with this at all. Either he thought that the Midianites were the ones who sold Joseph to the Ishmaelites, confusing as this is (and contradictory with 37:36), or, more likely, he simply saw the two groups as the same, not only because they may have been conflated in Israelite thought by the time the compiler worked (as Gunkel would have it [*Genesis*, 393]; this is a far better use of the evidence of Judg 8:24 than is made by those who argue for an authorial equation of the two groups), but because they fulfilled precisely the same function in both stories: the Arab caravan that brought Joseph to Egypt.

31. See Cassuto, *Documentary Hypothesis*.

32. Cassuto, *Questione*, 358.

33. Coats, *Genesis*, 271. See similarly Kessler, "Querverweise," 150, followed by Blum, *Vätergeschichte*, 244–45; Carr, *Fractures*, 287–88; Schmid, "Josephsgeschichte," 105–6. A critique of Coats, and of many of the supplementary approaches discussed below, can be found in White, "Reuben and Judah," 73–83.

34. Donner, "Josephsgeschichte," 114–15.

35. He was preceded in this by Volz and Rudolph, *Elohist*, 154, and Kessler, "Querverweise," 155, and followed by Willi-Plein, "Josefsgeschichte"; Schmitt, *Josephsgeschichte*, 23 n. 75; Coats, *Genesis*, 271; Blum, *Vätergeschichte*, 245; Carr, *Genesis*, 288. Willi-Plein, however, followed Jacob in seeing v. 28, and the rest of the nonpriestly text of the chapter, as a unity.

36. Thus some scholars do not even bother to address the question; see, for example, Kratz, *Composition*, 275–76. This argument, along with others, against the supplementary approach is found also in Seebass, *Genesis III*, 26–27.

37. Westermann, *Genesis 37–50*, 41–42. So also Redford, *Joseph*, 138–46; Tengström, *Hexateucherzählung*, 163; Yoreh, "Elohistic Source, 91–98, who also attributes vv. 31–35 to the J supplement.

38. Westermann, *Genesis 37–50*, 35. This is reminiscent of some of the literary solutions described in the introduction, especially those of Campbell and O'Brien and Humphreys. Mowinckel (*Erwägungen*, 62) recognized the irreconcilability of the Midianite and Ishmaelite traditions but, seeing it largely as a tradition-critical rather than a literary-critical problem, believed it possible that J (the single author of the Joseph narrative, in his view) might have known and included both versions.

39. The same verses are treated by Scharbert, *Genesis 12–50*, 240–42, who uses the term "J-Variant" to refer to vv. 25–27 and 28aβb. His J, however, is obviously not the continuous document usually indicated by the siglum: what precedes and follows these verses in the narrative? There is nothing with which to connect them, no context in which to place them; in short, they do not seem to be part of a narrative whole at all. To his credit, Scharbert does recognize that there is significant E material in this chapter; however, he vastly overstates the case. Seebass (*Genesis III*, 25–27) subscribes to the documentary approach to this chapter, albeit somewhat half-heartedly, but he also ascribes the entirety of vv. 3–24 to E, leaving J, which he begins in v. 25, without any background, nor even a subject for the verbs.

40. Loewenstamm, "Reuben and Judah," 35–41.

41. Coote, *Defense*, 29–30 and passim; Dietrich, *Josephserzählung*, 19–22 and passim.

42. Coote, *Defense*, 29 n. 1.

43. Thus the suggestion of Simpson, *Early Traditions*, 600–3, that E is not a supplement to but a complete rewriting of J (which has subsequently been combined with the text it was intended to replace), conforms better to the state of E's narrative. This treatment too is problematic, however, as the many substantial and insubstantial "changes" that E is to have made to the J story each need to be explained and provided with some meaning. Simpson's struggles in this regard are evident in his analysis.

44. Schmitt, *Josephsgeschichte*, 23–32. Schmitt sees the Reuben layer as a supplementation in part because he claims that it is fragmentary, while the Judah layer is complete (26); even given that his separation of the two strands is partially incorrect, his Reuben layer is, to my eye at least, perfectly comprehensible as an independent narrative.

45. The same reading of the E narrative, without any hint of the supplementary approach, is found in Ruppert, *Josephserzählung*, 231. Twenty years after the publication of his book, however, Ruppert bowed to the pressures of the general European adherence to the supplementary approach and claimed that the material he had previously identified as J was, in fact, a secondary revision, in the J style, of the underlying (and complete) E narrative strand in Gen 37 ("Aporie").

46. Credit for the most fragmentary analysis of the passage belongs to Levin (*Jahwist*, 265–73). He claims that in the earliest layer of the narrative the brothers planned to kill Joseph (vv. 18a, 19–20), stripped him of his coat (v. 23abα), threw him into the pit (v. 24a), bloodied his tunic (v. 31), and sent it to their father (v. 32aα^1), who recognized it (v. 33) and wept (v. 35b). This layer has its difficulties, especially in that the plan according to vv. 19–20 was to kill Joseph and throw his body into the pit, whereas in

the execution they don't kill him first but throw him in alive, with no reason given for doing so. More problematic by far is Levin's claim that 39:1a ("Joseph was taken down to Egypt") belongs to this original layer; there is no explanation for how this happened, as neither the Ishmaelites nor Midianites make an appearance in these verses. This original layer, according to Levin, was supplemented by the appearance of the Ishmaelites (v. 25) and the sale of Joseph to them (v. 28aβb); yet whence the decision to sell Joseph to the Ishmaelites if Judah's plan in vv. 26–27 was not part of this layer? And what role does the meal at the beginning of v. 25 play in this narrative? The only part of the story that Levin attributes to his "J" is vv. 26–27, which are yet another supplement, despite their intimate connection to vv. 19–20, 25, and 28aβb. Like Coote and Schmitt, Levin sees the entire Reuben story, vv. 18b, 22, 24b, 28aα, and 29–30 (and 34–35a, which have, however, no obvious connection to the rest of the verses in this layer), as a later addition, "post-final-redactional," intended (as argued by Coats) to demonstrate that the Israelite brothers were not responsible for the sale of Joseph, but that it was the Midianites, non-Israelites, who sold Joseph to the Ishmaelites. Verse 21 is considered an addition to this much-expanded story (see above), and v. 36 as well, linked with 39:1 (see above). Levin's analysis is unsustainable, and moreover unnecessary, at every stage.

47. Those who see E as the original layer and J as a revision include Ruppert, "Aporie," Dietrich, *Josephserzählung,* 19–22 and passim; Kebekus, *Joseferzählung,* 6–30; Ska, *Introduction,* 207.

48. See Speiser, *Genesis,* 294: "Each source is entirely self-consistent thus far, and goes on to build on its own set of data, which hold up meaningfully as the story unfolds. Indeed, each version gains in significance and impact when viewed as a unit unto itself."

49. Ibid., 291.

CHAPTER 2. CONTINUITY

1. Rendtorff, *Problem,* 108–32; Gertz, Schmid, and Witte, eds., *Abschied;* Dozeman and Schmid, eds., *Farewell.*
2. On the history of form-critical study, see Bentzen, *Introduction,* 1:102–8; Wilcoxen, "Narrative"; Knierim, "Criticism"; Ljungberg, "Genre"; Butler, "Narrative Form Criticism"; Buss, "Form Criticism"; Sweeney, "Form Criticism," 60–69; Buss, *Biblical Form Criticism.*
3. On the genres of the psalms, see Gunkel, *Psalms,* 1–21 and passim; Weiser, *Psalms,* 52–91; Limburg, "Psalms," 531–34.
4. On the analysis of Ps 30, see Weiser, *Psalms,* 265–73.
5. See Buss, *Biblical Form Criticism,* 234–35.
6. See Coats, *Genesis,* 4: "The terms for the genres have been drawn by and large from fields of literature outside the OT [Old Testament], indeed, from outside the period of time that produced the principal narratives. They apply, therefore, to OT literature only with a limited degree of accuracy."

7. Compare, for example, Bentzen, *Introduction*, 203–51; Eissfeldt, *Old Testament*, 11–56; Coats, *Genesis*, 5–10.
8. Gunkel, *Genesis*, vii–lxix and passim.
9. See Coats, *Genesis*, 4; Knierim, "Criticism," 136–46; Tucker, *Form Criticism*, 12–13; Ljungberg, "Genre."
10. See Coats, *Genesis*, 223–24.
11. See Barton, *Reading*, 31–34.
12. See Muilenburg, "Form Criticism"; Barton, *Reading*, 45–60.
13. See Koch, *Growth*, 111–32; Sweeney, "Form Criticism." See especially Alter, *Art*, 47–62: "A coherent reading of any art work, whatever the medium, requires some detailed awareness of the grid of conventions upon which, and against which, the individual work operates. . . . Through our awareness of convention we can recognize significant or simply pleasing patterns of repetition, symmetry, contrast; we can discriminate between the verisimilar and the fabulous, pick up directional clues in a narrative work, see what is innovative and what is deliberately traditional at each nexus of the artistic creation" (47).
14. See Houtman, "Jacob," 40.
15. See Noth, *Pentateuchal Traditions*, 92–94.
16. Ibid., 103.
17. Ibid., 107–8.
18. Ibid., 5.
19. See Gunkel, *Genesis*, lxix–lxx; von Rad, "Form-Critical Problem," 1–3; Noth, *Pentateuchal Traditions*, 1–4.
20. See Coats, *Genesis*, 303–5.
21. Ibid., 206–9; Westermann, *Genesis 12–36*, 453.
22. See Noth, *Pentateuchal Traditions*, 84, though he seems to read the adoption of Manasseh and Ephraim as part of E even while attributing vv. 5–6 to P (ibid., 18); Westermann, *Genesis 37–50*, 185.
23. See Noth, *Pentateuchal Traditions*, 84; Westermann, *Genesis 37–50*, 188.
24. See Noth, *Pentateuchal Traditions*, 84–85.
25. See Gunkel, *Genesis*, 382; von Rad, "Joseph Narrative."
26. See, for example, Whybray, "Joseph Story"; Coats, *Genesis*, 263–66; Donner, "Literarische Gestalt."
27. See Whybray, "Joseph Story," 525: "It is, to say the least, very difficult to believe that a novel of superlative merit could be the result of a conflation of two other novels. . . . If the Joseph story as we have it now is a literary masterpiece . . . it must be a complete literary unity both in conception and execution; if it is a conflation of two sources, then von Rad's estimate of its high qualities as a novel must be largely illusory."
28. Whybray, "Joseph Story," 528, says simply that "it would be foolish to deny that there are problems here," though this acknowledgment does not seem to have any effect on his conclusion that the text is a unity.
29. Coats, *From Canaan*, 57.
30. See ibid., 61; Westermann, *Genesis 37–50*, 49–50.

31. Coats, *From Canaan*, 53.
32. See ibid., 52–53; Westermann, *Genesis 37–50*, 173–74.
33. Nicholson, "Interpretation," "Antiquity," "Origin."
34. Nicholson, "Antiquity," 78.
35. Ibid.
36. We would be more accurate to refer here to Exod 24:1–2, 9–11bα; the words "they ate and drank" at the end of v. 11 belong in fact as the conclusion to the covenant story in vv. 3–8.
37. Ska, "Vision," 179.
38. This transitional moment has been noted by Boorer, *Promise*, 102, in regard to Rendtorff's literary application of Westermann's preliterary analysis of the promise formulae.
39. See Rendtorff, *Problem*, 24–31.
40. Blum, *Vätergeschichte* and *Studien*.
41. Levin, *Jahwist*.
42. Kratz, *Composition*.
43. For example, Ska, *Introduction*; Schmid, *Erzväter*.
44. Carr, *Fractures*; Gertz, *Exoduserzählung*; Nihan, *Priestly Torah*; Achenbach, *Vollendung*; Römer, *Israels Väter*. All of these scholars have produced numerous other works devoted to the application of the European approach.
45. Rendtorff, *Problem*, 62.
46. Ibid., 23.
47. Ibid.
48. We may compare Rendtorff's stance with that of Noth, *Pentateuchal Traditions*, 5: "On the whole, however, our access to the beginnings of the Pentateuchal tradition does, in fact, necessarily begin with the literary end-product. . . . Consequently it would be fallacious to play off traditio-historical research against literary-critical research, and to regard the latter as unimportant in comparison with the former."
49. See Wynn-Williams, *State*, 242: "Whereas the Documentary Hypothesis is predisposed to expect connections between different parts of the Pentateuch, Rendtorff's approach can be said to be predisposed toward its fragmentation." See also McEvenue, "Return," 388: "I would characterize the Wellhausen approach as attentive to the material continuities of the text, whereas the approach of Blum looks more to questions of horizon, meaning, and form."
50. Blum, *Vätergeschichte*, 88–98. The difficult source-critical analysis of Gen 28:10–22 is well recognized in the history of scholarship but does not impinge on the discussion here.
51. There are, however, other parts of Gen 28:10–22 that are connected with external texts. For instance, 28:10, containing the location of Jacob at Beersheba and his destination of Haran, is obviously linked to 26:23–33, in which Isaac dwells at Beersheba, and 27:43, in which Rebekah instructs Jacob to flee to her family in Haran. The promise God makes to Jacob in 28:13–15 is thematically, stylistically, and verbally similar, in parts identical, to the promises in Gen 12:1–3; 13:14–17; 18:18; 24:7; 26:3–5, 24; and 32:13. Not surprisingly, these verses are also eliminated from the text as "secondary"

by Blum. We may note, however, two other items. The setting sun in 28:11, as Jacob is leaving Canaan, is paralleled by the rising sun upon his return in 32:32 (Baruch J. Schwartz, personal communication). And the odd locution *niṣṣāb ʿālāyw* in 28:13, meaning to "stand beside," is found elsewhere in the Torah only in Gen 18:2 and 45:1 (both J passages).

52. Blum, *Vätergeschichte*, 307–11; so too Levin, *Jahwist*, 141–42; Kratz, *Composition*, 271, 297 n. 37.

53. Blum, *Vätergeschichte*, 286. We may, however, note that 13:10, which refers to the plain of Jordan as well watered "like the garden of Yahweh, like the land of Egypt," seems to have as its reference points the Eden story of Gen 2–3 and the episode of 12:10–20, in which the plenty of Egypt is contrasted with the famine of Canaan. Furthermore, the sojourn in Egypt provides the explanation for how Abraham acquired vast flocks and herds (12:16); this plot element is crucial to the story of Abraham's separation from Lot in 13:2, 6–9.

54. Levin, *Jahwist*, 202–4.

55. Ibid., 205; see also Kratz, *Composition*, 269, 297 n. 33 (on Gen 26:1).

56. Blum, *Studien*, 119, suggests that the "messenger" referred to in Num 20:16 is in fact supposed to be Moses; given that Moses is the speaker, this theory is hard to accept. Blum further supposes that Num 20:14–21 is later than its almost exact parallel in 21:21–25; here the obvious literary relationship between the two is taken as evidence that one is secondary to the other, rather than that both are from the same hand.

57. Achenbach, *Vollendung*, 342–43; see also Blum, *Studien*, 118–20; Kratz, *Composition*, 283; Ska, *Introduction*, 192–93.

58. See the two collections of essays on this topic, *Abschied vom Jahwisten* (Gertz, Schmid, and Witte, eds.) and *A Farewell to the Yahwist?* (Dozeman and Schmid, eds.). The topic is given a full treatment in Schmid, *Erzväter*. A rebuttal to this notion is provided by Nicholson, *Pentateuch*, 125–30.

59. See Noth, *Pentateuchal Traditions*, 47, 55–56.

60. Rendtorff, *Problem*, 65–70.

61. Ibid. Rendtorff also takes passages that seem to be related to the themes of Genesis and interprets them otherwise, thereby avoiding the necessity of marking them as secondary. In the case of Exod 1, for example, in which there are repeated references to the great increase of the Israelite people (according to the Documentary Hypothesis, this repetition is due to the presence of J, E, and P in this chapter), Rendtorff claims that as there is no explicit reference to the patriarchal promises of offspring in Genesis, the author is obviously not aware of such traditions (*Problem*, 66; a similar argument from silence is made regarding Exod 3). If Rendtorff expected to see the narrator explicitly state that the Israelites increased in accordance with the divine promise to the patriarchs, he was bound to be disappointed; the theme of the promise is present only in direct speech, never in narration. Further, it is only the doubting modern who requires such explicit markers of reference; it seems clear enough according to the plain meaning of the text that the description of Israel's increase at the beginning of Exodus is in fact nothing other than the notice of the fulfillment of that aspect of the patriarchal promises from Genesis.

62. See Blum, *Studien*, 363–65; Schmid, *Erzväter*, 230–33; Römer, "Recherches actuelles," 209; Gertz, "Transition," 80–81; Ska, *Introduction*, 201–2. See the counterarguments of Ausloos, "Deuteronomist"; Carr, "What Is Required," 169–72; Van Seters, "Report," 151: "Why should an editor take it upon himself to construct all of these interconnections in the text as if he were the author of the text? The interconnections are exactly what one would expect an author . . . to do if he were composing a comprehensive history. The prediction that we have in 50:24–26 has its parallel in the predictions to Jacob in Gen 46:3–4 and to Abraham in 15:13–16. This is a well-known historiographic technique in classical literature and one that is also employed here." For Van Seters, all these texts belong to his late J; it is not a coincidence that they are all classically (and correctly) assigned to E.

63. See Crüsemann, "Eigenständigkeit."

64. Deut 1:8, 35; 4:37–38; 6:10, 18, 23; 7:8, 12; 8:1, 18; 9:5, 27–28; 10:11, 15; 11:9, 21; 19:8; 26:3; 28:11; 29:12; 30:20; 31:7; 31:20.

65. This position was first taken by Van Seters, "Confessional Reformulation," and argued most fully by Römer, *Israels Väter*.

66. Deut 1:8; 6:10; 9:5, 27; 29:12; 30:20. See Römer, *Israels Väter*, 153–67, 196–201, 218–22, 231–35, 256–65.

67. Graupner, *Elohist*, 6 (translation mine): "Die Einsicht in die üeberlieferungsgeschichtliche Selbständigkeit der Pentateuchthemen ist keineswegs neu, sondern durch G. von Rad und M. Noth vorgegeben. In dieser Perspektive sind Texte, die themenüebergreifende Zusammenhänge herstellen, zweifeloss sekundär. Gilt diese Urteil aber auch in literarkritischer Perspektive? Auch im nichtpriesterschriftlichen Tetrateuch lassen sich die Themenblöcke nur noch separieren, wenn man eindeutige, im Worltaut greibare Zusammenhänge ausscheidet oder übergeht. Inzwiefern ist ein solches Verfahren aber noch methodisch zulässig und sinnvoll?"

68. See Wynn-Williams, *State*, 220–25.

69. Yet even the isolated Jacob at Bethel story, for example, is not a coherent, self-contained narrative; see ibid., 114–24. See also the critique of Blum's division of this pericope in McEvenue, "Return."

70. McEvenue, "Return," 377 n. 6.

71. Wynn-Williams, *State*, 207.

72. Here we might see the crucial distinction between these local narratives and, for example, the short book of Obadiah: for the prophetic corpus, it is certainly conceivable that the *ipsissima verba* of the prophet were considered so important that they had to be preserved in writing to ensure their correct transmission.

73. See Wynn-Williams, *State*, 118–19.

74. Noth already recognized this when he argued that the association of Jacob with Bethel came about only as an application or transfer of the larger, preexisting Jacob tradition to the local site of Bethel (*Pentateuchal Traditions*, 80–81).

75. One might compare in length such texts as Arad Ostraca 24, 40; Lachish Ostraca 3, 4, 6; Yavneh Yam Ostracon 1; Horvat 'Uza Ostracon 2 (all probably between fifty-five and seventy-five words, about the length of Blum's Jacob at Bethel story). These ostraca measure, in general, no more than six inches on their longest side.

76. The most famous wall inscription, that of the Siloam Tunnel, is not comparable to the purported Jacob at Bethel story, as it commemorates a single historical moment contemporary with the writing of the inscription itself, that is, the completion of the tunnel. There are, to my knowledge, no examples of narrative inscriptions found engraved into the wall of an Israelite sanctuary.

77. See Haran, "Book-Scrolls in Israel" and "More Concerning Book-Scrolls."

78. On typical scroll length in ancient Israel, see Haran, "Book-Size." Even if we assume that the priestly source is itself a collection of smaller scrolls kept in the Temple archives (see Haran, "On Archives" and "Book-Scrolls at the Beginning"; Haran is followed in this by Knohl, *Sanctuary*, 6 and passim), none of the component elements of the priestly source is nearly as short as the proposed Jacob at Bethel story. More important is the observation that the dimensions of ancient scrolls were considerably smaller than is usually imagined, small enough probably to fit in one's hand even in the case of entire biblical books (see Haran, "Scrolls of the Torah"). The corollary to this observation is that a piece of papyrus of only a few lines would be extraordinarily small and therefore all too susceptible to destruction or misplacement.

79. See the major collections of ancient Hebrew inscriptions: Renz and Röllig, *Handbuch*; Davies, *Ancient Hebrew Inscriptions*; Dobbs-Allsopp et al., *Hebrew Inscriptions*; Aḥituv, *HaKetav veHaMiktav*.

80. On the Supplementary Hypothesis, see Briggs, *Higher Criticism*, 60–68; Houtman, *Pentateuch*, 91–95.

81. Ewald, *Geschichte*, 1:94–193.

82. Compare, for example, the general treatments of Blum, *Vätergeschichte* and *Studien*, who identifies a first patriarchal history (Vg^1), a second patriarchal history (Vg^2), a thoroughgoing deuteronomistic layer (K^D), a priestly layer (K^P), and a postpriestly hexateuchal redaction; Gertz, *Exoduserzählung*, who sees in Exod 1–15 a prepriestly layer (with supplements), a priestly layer (with supplements), and an *Endredaktion* (with supplements); and Achenbach, *Vollendung*, who identifies in Numbers alone a predeuteronomistic layer, a Hexateuch redaction, a Pentateuch redaction, and four distinct theological reworkings (*Theokratische Bearbeitungen*).

83. Levin, *Jahwist*, 207–15.

84. Kratz, *Composition*, 279–93.

85. Ibid., 293.

86. Ibid.

87. Ibid., 326 (chart).

88. Ibid., 267–74.

89. Vermeylen, "Le vol."

90. Blum, *Vätergeschichte*, 80–88.

91. Wellhausen, *Composition*, 7–8, also recognized the role of orality in the creation of the Pentateuch: "In themselves, heterogeneous components do not exclude the unity and naturalness of a written connection; it is possible that already the first recording of the oral tradition associated all kinds of matter that had no internal connection" (translation mine). [An sich schliessen heterogene Bestandteile die Einheit und Ursprünglichkeit eines schriftlichen Zusammenhanges nicht aus; es ist möglich,

dass schon die erste Aufzeichnung der mündlichen Tradition allerlei in Verbindung brachte, was in keiner innerlichen Verwandtschaft stand.]

92. On orality and tradition criticism, see Wynn-Williams, *State*, 211–13; note especially his observation that "in terms of the supposed oral antecedents, the unity of a source can be expected to be constituted not primarily by a homogeneity of style or by the perfect harmony of all the various tradition elements that have been incorporated into the whole, but rather by its narrative coherence and continuity" (212).

93. See Wynn-Williams, *State*, 201–2.

94. See the analysis of Gertz, *Exoduserzählung*, 308–9 and passim, in which he argues that the original nonpriestly Exodus story contained no mention of Aaron. The story of Aaron being appointed Moses's spokesman in Exod 4:13–16, 27–31, is attributed to a redactional layer (according to Gertz, the *"Endredaktion"*); the mentions of Aaron in 5:1, 3, 4 are attributed to insertions from the same layer, along with the narrative sections of 5:6–6:1, 8:21–27, 9:27–29, 10:12–20, and 12:31–32, all of which make mention of Aaron. Further references to Aaron in the plagues cycle are deemed insertions even into the *Endredaktion*: Exod 8:4, 8; 10:3, 8. Here we see yet another example of defining the character of a narrative by the systematic elimination of a feature that is deemed uncharacteristic.

95. See Whybray, *Making*, 208–10: "In this respect, then, Rendtorff is not a tradition-historian at all in the sense in which the term is usually understood. The process which he assumed in his discussion of the promises in Genesis could only have taken place with regard to a written text" (208).

96. Blum, *Vätergeschichte*, 282–89. See the criticism of Nicholson, *Pentateuch*, 120–21, in which he demonstrates that even the etiological elements in the supposedly independent smaller units are complementary—the Abraham-Lot cycle contains the etiologies of Israel's relationship to Ammon and Moab, the Jacob cycle those regarding Aram and Edom—which leads him to the conclusion that "the connections and complementarity between the 'smaller units' belong to their substance and cannot plausibly be accounted for in terms of a secondary editorial linking together of independent narratives composed in isolation from one another. Put differently, in so far as we can discern or conjecture originally independent stories (*Sagen*) or 'cycles' of such stories in Genesis 12–37, they have evidently been thoroughly worked over to create a continuous and cumulative story of Israel's ancestors" (120).

97. Blum, *Vätergeschichte*, 290–91, 352–59, 400–5.

98. Noth, *Pentateuchal Traditions*, 56–58. Noth even surmised that local traditions excluded from preservation in the biblical material may have contained the theme of "promise to the patriarchs" with regard to their own tribal forefathers (ibid., 102 n. 300). In this he relied heavily on the work of Alt, "Gott der Väter." The centrality of the patriarchal promises in the narratives of Genesis was first challenged by Hoftijzer, *Verheissungen*.

99. For Rendtorff and those who followed him, all of these categories essentially fall under the title "theological," such that every redactional layer, every secondary addition, has a "theological" purpose. This may broaden the notion of "theology" beyond its natural borders.

100. Gunkel, "Israelite Literary History," 34.
101. Davies, "Composition," 81.
102. See Otto, "Nachpriesterschriftliche Pentateuchredaktion," 91–92; Achenbach, *Vollendung*, 290–98; Levin, *Jahwist*, 368.
103. Far more than traditional source critics, scholars of the European approach rely on an astonishingly exacting level of stylistic similarity in acknowledging the continuity of passages. This is most evident in Rendtorff's analysis of the patriarchal promises (*Problem*, 55–84), in which the order of three words — *lᵊkā 'ettᵊnennāʰ ûlᵊzarʿekā* against *lᵊkā ûlᵊzarʿekā 'ettēn* — is seen as evidence of distinct layers (57–59; see the critique of this analysis by Nicholson, *Pentateuch*, 114–15). As Wynn-Williams puts it (*State*, 214), "the sorts of sources they [i.e., Rendtorff and Blum] are looking for — and do not find — are literary unities that could be distinguished as though their authors had used different dialects." A similar point is made by McEvenue, "Return," 388 n. 26: "Blum seems to expect narrative, not only to be free from internal contradictions, but also to be ruled by the rigid focus of a theologian rather than the freedom of a storyteller."
104. Rendtorff, *Problem*, 173.
105. Ibid., 108.
106. Here and throughout, an asterisk after a biblical reference signifies that only part of the text referred to is intended. In this case, the J narrative is interwoven in Gen 6–9 with that of P; it is simpler to describe J's portion as "Gen 6–9*" than to provide the full details of the source-critical analysis.
107. A prominent theme in J's primeval history is that of names and naming. Adam names the animals Yahweh creates for him (2:19–20); he names the woman (2:23); he calls her Eve (3:20); the names of Adam's children are provided with meaningful etymologies (Cain, 4:1; Seth, 4:25; even Abel, although only implicitly, as the name means "nothingness," fittingly enough for a character whose existence is defined by his death); the beginning of worship of Yahweh is described as "calling on Yahweh by name" (4:26); Noah's name is imbued with meaning, connecting directly to the theme of the earth (5:29); and of course humankind builds the Tower of Babel explicitly in order to "make a name" for themselves (11:4).
108. See Spina, "'Ground.'" Throughout J's version of the primeval history we see an intense focus on the earth and its fruitfulness, marked by a dense repetition of the words "earth," *'ereṣ*, and "ground," *'ᵃdāmāʰ*. Unlike the account of P in Gen 1, in which the proto-world is a watery chaos from which the land emerges, in J the original state of the earth is dry and barren and requires water (2:4b–6). From the earth man and animals are formed (2:7, 19) and trees grow (2:9). The serpent is cursed to crawl on the ground (3:14), and the earth itself is cursed on account of Adam's eating of the tree of the knowledge of good and evil (3:17–19). Humans are banished from the garden to work the ground (3:23). Cain's offering, of the fruits of the earth, is rejected precisely because it came from the cursed ground (4:3–5). Abel's blood cries to Yahweh from the ground, and Cain in turn is cursed "more than the ground," so that he cannot even derive produce from it as his father Adam did (4:10–12). Noah's birth is supposed to provide relief from Yahweh's curse on the earth (5:29). Even when Yahweh realizes that humankind is inherently wicked, the earth remains at the center of attention:

note the repetition of the word in Gen 6:5–7, and indeed throughout the J flood narrative, culminating in Yahweh's promise of Gen 8:21–22. Noah is a "tiller of the soil" (9:20). The Tower of Babel story in Gen 11:1–9 describes the inhabitation of the entire earth and not coincidentally begins and ends with the word "earth" (11:1, 9).

109. J's primeval period is one of origins and etiologies: man and animals are formed from the ground (2:7, 19); woman is made from man's rib (2:21–22); the serpent goes about on its belly because of Yahweh's curse (3:14); women experience pain in childbirth because of Eve's actions (3:16); humans are forced to work the earth to produce food because of Adam's actions (3:17–19); the first city is built, by Cain (4:17); the Bedouin lifestyle is inaugurated by Jabal (4:20); music is invented by Jubal (4:21) and metallurgy by Tubal-Cain (4:22); formal worship of Yahweh is begun by Enosh (4:26); humans' lifespan is limited by Yahweh (6:3); viniculture is begun by Noah (9:20); the first empire is created by Nimrod (10:8–12); human languages are differentiated and humankind is spread across the earth (11:8–9).

110. It is possible that the distinctly strange episode of Gen 6:1–4 should also be seen as influencing Yahweh's decision to bring the flood, although the rationale given in 6:5, that humankind must be destroyed because of its wickedness, does not seem to have much relationship to the events of the immediately preceding verses, in which it is the divine beings who are the main actors. The placement of the episode, however, does seem to suggest that it was understood as being related to the inception of the flood.

111. See Schwartz, "Flood Narratives."

112. Ibid., 152.

113. Although Gen 14 is typically believed to be a late insertion into the Pentateuch, it should be noted that it does in fact contain some elements that situate it specifically into the context of the J narrative. In 14:12 Lot is said to have settled in Sodom, as only J has related (13:12b). In 14:13, Abraham is said to be settled at the terebinths of Mamre, as is the case in J (13:18). It is thus possible that Gen 14 (with the exception of 14:18–20, which are clearly distinct from the rest of the story) may be part of the J document.

114. In the E source, no reason is given for Sarah's lack of offspring; when God promises Abraham that he will have a son of his own, that is, Isaac (Gen 15:4), there is no mention of relieving Sarah of barrenness. P is more explicit: Isaac's birth is miraculous because of Abraham's and Sarah's advanced ages, not barrenness (Gen 17:16–19). Again, there is no mention of Sarah having been unable to bear children before this.

115. Gen 26:15, 18 have long been recognized as out of place in this chapter; they are most likely to be assigned to P. See Baden, *Redaction*, 213–18.

116. We may even perhaps include the rivalry of Leah and Rachel (see, for example, 30:14–16). The entire theme of sibling rivalry is absent in P (see case study V) and is significantly less prominent in E than in J.

117. The opening words of Exod 2:11, literally, "In those days, Moses grew up," meaning, probably, "achieved adulthood," cannot refer to the immediately preceding text of Exod 1:15–2:10, which end with Moses being only a small child (and which are from E). They refer, rather, to the reign of the Pharaoh who enslaved the Israelites in 1:8–12. The words "Moses grew up" constitute J's introduction of the character of Moses. Although brief, there is nothing improbable about such an introduction, especially for

a character as well known in Israelite tradition as Moses. It is equivalent to a modern American historian describing the state of American society in the early nineteenth century before writing "That was the period in which Abraham Lincoln came of age." The ramifications of recognizing the continuity between 1:8–12 and 2:11–23aα in J are substantial: according to J, Moses was not raised in the Egyptian court, but was rather a common Israelite; moreover, according to J, the period of Israelite enslavement in Egypt did not last for hundreds of years, but merely for a single generation, that between Joseph and Moses. It may be noted in this regard that whereas E puts the period of Israel's stay in Egypt at 400 years (Gen 15:13) and P at 430 years (Exod 12:40), J has no equivalent. For fuller treatment of Exod 1–2 see Baden, "From Joseph to Moses."

118. This is not to argue that the word *siblōtām* is exclusive to J; the use of the word in Exod 1:11 and 2:11 is not a rationale for assigning both to J. The word does not belong to only one author, but that does not rule out the possibility that its use in these two J passages is meaningful within the single source.

119. Note that these scenes are not merely repeated in identical terms, but that there is rather a progression from one to the next, an intensification: whereas Abraham's servant arrives at the well and is assisted by Rebekah, when Jacob arrives at the well he assists Rachel and Laban's shepherds in removing the rock from the top of the well; and when Moses arrives at the well, he actually fends off hostile shepherds to assist Reuel's daughters. All of these stories play in to a certain extent to the general J concern with hospitality (e.g., Gen 18–19).

120. The plagues in J are blood (Exod 7:14–18, 20 [from "he lifted up the rod"]–21, 23–24); frogs (7:25–29; 8:4–11); insects (8:16–28); pestilence (9:1–7); hail (9:13–21; 23 [from "Yahweh sent thunder and hail"], 24 ["the hail was heavy" and "such as had not fallen on the land of Egypt since it had become a nation"], 26–30, 33–34); locusts (10:1–11, 13 [from "Yahweh drove an east wind"], 14 [from "they settled within all the territory of Egypt"], 15 [through "the land was darkened"], 16–19, 24–26, 28–29); and death of the firstborn (11:4–8; 12:21a, 27b, 29–34).

121. The song of Exod 15:1–18, though an independently composed hymn, was inserted into the narrative by the author of J and should thus be considered part of the J document.

122. Note that Yahweh uses the legal terms "commandments," *miṣwôt*, and "laws," *ḥuqqîm*, even though no laws have been given (in any of the sources to this point). This use of legal terminology to denote general obedience is typical of J; see Gen 18:19 and 26:5, and in the next J section, 16:28.

123. On the use of the name "Horeb" in Exod 17:6, see chapter 3.

124. The question in 17:7 is usually taken not as an actual question asked by the Israelite people, but rather as something of an interpretive comment on the preceding episode by the narrator; it is understood as belonging to the etymological explanation of the name "Massah and Meribah." Yet this is not the only possible reading; it could also be the continuation of the first clause of 17:7: "They named the place Massah and Meribah . . . saying, 'Is Yahweh present among us or not?'" In this reading, the question would in fact have actually been asked, presumably at the time that the place was named, that is, at the end of the episode. This reading is, admittedly, somewhat

forced, though we may note the example of 1 Sam 4:21–22, in which Phinehas's wife, upon giving birth, names her son Ichabod, and the narrator provides the name with an etymological explanation: "the glory has departed from Israel"; having done so, the woman then goes on to actually repeat the explanation as a normal statement: "She said, 'the glory has departed from Israel.'" We might thus postulate that a similar repetition on the part of the Israelites of the narrator's etymology for Massah and Meribah in Exod 17:7 is assumed by J; or, more speculatively, that it was actually in the original J text but was dropped by a (rather understandable) scribal error of haplography. Even if neither of these possibilities is accepted, the question of 17:7 still stands as the conceptual basis for the succeeding Sinai theophany in J.

125. The strange episode in Exod 32:26–29 is commonly assigned to the J source, if only because it clearly does not fit into either the E or P narratives at this point. At the same time, however, it fits equally poorly in the J story. Although one might assume that there is a gap in J here, it is impossible to reconstruct what might have plausibly stood before these verses. It is also possible that this section of text has been moved to this point from elsewhere in the J document by the compiler, in order to bring J's description of the investiture of the Levites to the same general time as in P, though it is, again, difficult to surmise where in J this text would have been previously.

126. Although there is some evidence that the text of Exod 34:10–16 has been retouched by a later hand, it is still probable, to my mind at least, that there is a core of authentic J material here; see Schwartz, "Reexamining the Fate," 154. The same cannot be said, however, of the laws in 34:17–26 (see Bar-On, "Festival Calendars"), which are a postcompilational insertion.

127. In this passage we also find the first mention in J of the "ark of the covenant of Yahweh" (Num 10:33). Although this item has not been introduced previously in J, once it had been stated in J that Moses wrote down the words of the covenant (Exod 34:27), it may simply have been presumed that there had to be a vessel in which that covenant document would have been carried. This is particularly plausible given the nature of the covenant, with its central feature of Yahweh driving out Israel's enemies, and the practical use of the ark, as a palladium to be carried before the people as they travel toward the promised land. The ark of Num 10:33 is certainly not to be equated with the ark of P, which is the central cultic item, not a palladium as in J.

CASE STUDY II. A COMPLAINT IN THE WILDERNESS, NUMBERS 11

1. The rare attempt to see layers in this story is made, though without any convincing success, by Holzinger, *Numeri*, 43; Levin, *Jahwist*, 374; and Achenbach, *Vollendung*, 209–19.
2. Note also the word order of the opening of v. 4: as a disjunctive clause, beginning with the subject, it is syntactically dependent on the preceding narrative.
3. These verses are sometimes seen as a secondary addition, although there is no reason that they cannot be original. Noth (*Numbers*, 86) claims that their secondary status is clear because the present context has nothing to do with manna; yet as the manna

is mentioned in the second-to-last word of v. 6, this argument seems ill-founded. See also Dillmann, *Numeri*, 54; Baentsch, *Exodus-Leviticus-Numeri*, 504; Holzinger, *Numeri*, 42; Gressmann, *Mose*, 124–25 n. 2; Rudolph, "*Elohist,*" 66–67; Coats, *Rebellion*, 97; Fritz, *Israel*, 16; de Vaulx, *Nombres*, 149; Scharbert, *Numeri*, 47; Levin, *Jahwist*, 375.

4. Although some have argued that Yahweh's anger is out of place narratologically and is therefore to be seen as secondary (e.g., Gray, *Numbers*, 106; Smend, *Erzählung*, 190; Gressmann, *Mose*, 124–25 n. 2; Eissfeldt, *Hexateuch-Synopse*, 39; Rudolph, "*Elohist,*" 67–68; Noth, *Numbers*, 86), I see no reason why this should be the case.

5. A similar sentiment is expressed by Moses in Exod 32:32, although perhaps more obliquely.

6. Although "all the people" admittedly occurs in v. 13, it does so without any connection to the concept of burden and therefore belongs to the common use of the phrase. In no other way does v. 13 connect with the surrounding verses.

7. See Fritz, *Israel*, 16. Attempts to assign vv. 11–12 to one strand and vv. 14–15 to another (or vv. 11–13, 15 to one and v. 14 to another), or to a secondary addition, are therefore problematic and contrary to the evidence. See Wellhausen, *Composition*, 99; Kuenen, *Hexateuch*, 158; Addis, *Documents*, 1:161–62; Carpenter and Harford-Battersby, *Hexateuch*, 2:202; Baentsch, *Exodus-Leviticus-Numeri*, 504; Smend, *Erzählung*, 189–91; Eissfeldt, *Hexateuch-Synopse*, 39; Rudolph, "*Elohist,*" 65; Noth, *Numbers*, 86–87; see also the arguments for the unity of vv. 11–15 by Wenham, *Numbers*, 108; Sommer, "Reflecting," 604; Seebass, *Numeri*, 2:38.

8. See Sommer, "Reflecting," 607 n. 13, who claims that if the elders strand begins in v. 16, it forms a sensible whole, whereas if it begins in v. 11, it does not.

9. See Fritz, *Israel*, 16–17; Sommer, "Reflecting," 607 n. 13. This redactional move is attested elsewhere; cf. Gen 35:19 ("Rachel died"; discussed in case study V); Exod 31:18 ("He gave Moses"), 32:15 ("Moses went down"), 34:4 ("he went up"); and Num 13:26 ("they came to Moses"), 32:2 ("they said to Moses"), 32:6 ("Moses replied"), 32:16 ("they said"), 32:20 ("Moses said to them").

10. See Rashi on Num 11:17.

11. On the process of sanctification before an encounter with the deity, see Milgrom, *Numbers*, 384–86.

12. It has been suggested that vv. 18–24a are a secondary expansion of the meat story, since the threat by Yahweh in these verses does not match precisely with the punishment in v. 33 (see Wellhausen, *Composition*, 100; Kuenen, *Hexateuch*, 254; Dillmann, *Numeri*, 55; Baentsch, *Exodus-Leviticus-Numeri*, 504; Seebass, *Numeri*, 2:35). Although there may be a discrepancy between the two parts of the story (though perhaps not; see Rudolph, "*Elohist,*" 68–70; Van Seters, *Life of Moses*, 233), it is not necessary to view them as separate recensions; indeed, one wonders why a later author or redactor, with the freedom to alter the narrative, would create a problem rather than resolve one. See Coats, *Rebellion*, 109–10.

13. The briefness of the prophetic spirit among the elders creates some confusion: how does a momentary bout of prophesying relieve Moses's burden throughout the wilderness wandering? It seems most likely to me that the intention here is to demonstrate

the possibility of support for Moses, so that if he should ever feel particularly burdened, he can know that such a moment of prophetic inspiration might be repeated. Naḥmanides (on Num 11:17) similarly suggests that this story was meant to serve as a description of what happened every time Moses received divine instructions: the elders would also know what was said to Moses and would pass the divine communication to their various tribes.

14. Thus we cannot accept the claim of Gray, *Numbers*, 98, 111, that vv. 11–12, 14–15, and 17b (those that describe Moses's complaint and his burden) are not literarily connected with the story of the elders. The meaning here was correctly understood by Noth, *Numbers*, 87.

15. Arguments for these verses being a secondary addition have been made (see de Vaulx, *Nombres*, 149; Levin, *Jahwist*, 374; Achenbach, *Vollendung*, 262–66; Seebass, *Numeri*, 2:34–35, 52–53), yet the episode, despite some uncertainties as to the specifics, partakes fully of the spirit of the elders narrative as a whole; see Blum, *Studien*, 84.

16. The source division presented here (with the exception of the first three verses, which are frequently assigned to E) is agreed on, in the main, by most commentators. See Kuenen, *Hexateuch*, 158; Carpenter and Harford-Battersby, *Hexateuch*, 2:201–3; Gray, *Numbers*, 97–119; Holzinger, *Numeri*, 41–43; Smend, *Erzählung*, 189–91; Brightman, *Sources*, 99–100, 170–71; Meyer, *Israeliten*, 66; Fritz, *Israel*, 16–18; Blum, *Studien*, 83; Sommer, "Reflecting," 604. The rare argument for reading the chapter as a unity is made by Levine, *Numbers 1–20*, 327–28 (although he recognizes the presence of two distinct subject matters); Noth, *Pentateuchal Traditions*, 128 n. 360; Van Seters, *Life of Moses*, 228–29; Friedman, *Sources Revealed*, 258–60.

17. It is thus not, as Friedman (*Sources Revealed*, 259) suggests, a "triplet" of the J and P stories about the manna from Exod 16. Num 11 does not describe the giving of manna—it presumes it and refers back to it.

18. Many early scholars, although they attributed the meat narrative to J, assigned vv. 1–3 to E, despite the grammatical dependence of v. 4 on vv. 1–3. Usually the rationale for the attribution of vv. 1–3 to E was the depiction of Moses acting as intercessor with Yahweh, and particularly the use of the verb *hitpallēl*, which is otherwise found only in E before Deuteronomy (Gen 20:7, 17; Num 21:7). Yet the scant number of examples of the verb is hardly grounds for source assignment (see Rudolph, "Elohist," 64), and the depiction of Moses acting as a prophet, though typical of E, is not restricted to E: as noted in chapter 1, J also portrays Moses pleading with Yahweh and being heard, most notably in the J plague narratives (Exod 8:8, 26; 9:33; 10:18).

19. In Exod 16:31 the manna is also described as being white, whereas in Num 11:7 it is described as being like bdellium. The two descriptions may in fact be different ways of noting the brilliance of the manna: it gleams white like a precious stone (Levine, *Numbers 1–20*, 322), or it may simply be that bdellium, which is a type of resin, is white-ish in color (Milgrom, *Numbers*, 84).

20. See Sommer, "Reflecting," 605.

21. See the extensive discussion of this topic by Sommer, "Reflecting," 611–14.

22. These stories contain what has come to be called the "murmuring tradition," frequently seen as both tradition-historically and compositionally secondary to an origi-

nally positively oriented narrative—in this case, the quails story would be seen as a story originally about Yahweh's providence in the wilderness, only secondarily to be transmuted into a tale of "murmuring" and punishment. See Noth, *Pentateuchal Traditions*, 123–30; Coats, *Rebellion*, 99–115. However, de Vries, "Origin," criticizes this view.

23. See Baden, *Redaction*, 106–14.
24. The difficulty some scholars have in reconciling Exod 18, in which Moses appoints tribal leaders to serve as judges, and Num 11, in which some of the elders are chosen to prophesy, is groundless. The two narratives are about two very different issues: in Exod 18, it is specifically Moses's role as arbiter of Israelite disputes that is the source of the problem; in Num 11, as argued here, it is the burden of leading the people through the wilderness (see Scharbert, *Numeri*, 50; Eissfeldt, *Hexateuch-Synopse*, 41). The two stories are complementary, not contradictory, and stand as bookends to the story of the theophany at Horeb; each takes place at the mountain, and in combination they represent the establishment of both judicial and prophetic leadership among the Israelite elders. See Kuenen, *Hexateuch*, 251; Dillmann, *Numeri*, 55; Addis, *Documents*, 1:160–61; Carpenter and Harford-Battersby, *Hexateuch*, 2:202; Holzinger, *Numeri*, 42; Rudolph, *"Elohist,"* 65–66; Fritz, *Israel*, 17; Levin, *Jahwist*, 374; Seebass, *Numeri*, 2:42–45.
25. Although it was noted that the phrase "all the people" plays a central role in Num 11:11–12, 14–15, it should be added that it is a regular refrain throughout the E narrative from Horeb on (though, as a common phrase, it is certainly not unique to E); see Exod 18:14, 21, 23; 19:8, 16; 20:18; 23:27; 24:3; 32:3; 33:8, 10.
26. In J: Exod 3:16, 18; 4:29; 12:21; 17:5, 6; in E: Exod 18:12; 19:7; 24:14; Num 16:25; in P: Lev 4:15; 9:1; in D: Deut 5:23; 27:1; 29:9; 31:9.
27. In Ezekiel, on the other hand, seventy of the elders are set apart as particularly sinful (Ezek 8:11).
28. The rabbis, recognizing that the seventy elders could not be selected twice, solved the problem by claiming that the first seventy, those chosen in Exod 24:1, had died. According to one midrash, the elders died for positive reasons: trying to prevent the Israelites from building the golden calf, they were killed by the angry mob. According to another midrash, they died for negative reasons, because in Exod 24:9–11 they looked upon the deity and were punished for it in the fire at Taberah (Num 11:1–3). See *Midrash Tanḥuma'* Beha'aloteka 14, 16.
29. On the Tent of Meeting in E, see Haran, *Temples*, 260–75.
30. Joshua's response to the prophesying of Eldad and Medad is reminiscent of his response to the making of the golden calf in Exod 32:17 (E).
31. This prophetic theme, as well as the image of the Tent of Meeting and the various textual connections described above and in the following, have been keenly observed by Blum, *Studien*, 76–82, 194–97, although he does not call these related passages E; so too Gunneweg, "Gesetz"; Achenbach, *Vollendung*, 246–47, both of whom ascribe these texts to the last redactional stratum of the Pentateuch. A key element of their argument, however, is that these texts cannot stand on their own as independent narratives; as we have seen, however, they can indeed.

32. E also famously describes Abraham in prophetic terms; see Gen 20:7, 17. See also Jenks, *Elohist*.

33. The use of the phrase "all this people" can even less stand as evidence for a single author, as argued by Van Seters, *Life of Moses*, 228.

34. These attempts have been more fully discussed and aptly criticized by Sommer, "Reflecting," 607–8.

35. Noth, *Numbers*, 83–91.

36. Ibid., 83.

37. Blum, *Studien*, 83 n. 169.

38. Achenbach, *Vollendung*, 237–51.

39. Similarly Römer, "Nombres 11–12," in assigning the chapter to a very late redactional stage, claims that the two stories cannot be convincingly reconstructed.

40. Seebass, "Num. xi, xii."

CHAPTER 3. COHERENCE

1. See especially Kuenen, *Hexateuch*, 49–55.

2. See Kaufmann (*Religion of Israel*, 166), who refers to "the JE code of Exodus." In fact, the identification of three law codes is correct: it has been persuasively demonstrated by Bar-On, "Festival Calendars," that the laws in Exod 34 are a late insertion into the text, after the compilation of the sources, and constitute a reworking of legal material from the Covenant Code, D, and P.

3. Kuenen, *Hexateuch*, 55.

4. Ibid., 138 and passim; see also Bacon, *Genesis*, 59; Driver, *Introduction*, 117.

5. On the history of the idea of the "JE" document, see Baden, *Redaction*, 11–43.

6. Kuenen, *Hexateuch*, 64. See also Driver, *Exodus*, xii: "J and E, as they are very similar in character and tone, may, for many practical purposes, be grouped together as a single stratum."

7. Wellhausen, *Composition*, 35 (translation mine): "Das Endergebnis ist, dass JE zwar auch in diesem Abschnitt aus J und E bestehen muss, dass aber eine durchgeführte Scheidung unmöglich ist."

8. See, for example, von Rad, *Genesis*, 27; Levine, *Numbers 1–20*, 49.

9. Noth, *Pentateuchal Traditions*, 20.

10. Ibid., 27. Here he follows the principle of Wellhausen, *Composition*, 22: "J is laid as the foundation and from E is supplied that which was not found in J, or not in the same manner" (translation mine). [Dabei ist J zu Grunde gelegt und aus E das mitgeteilt, was sich in J entweder überhaupt nicht oder nicht so fand.] So too Ruppert, "Elohist," 108.

11. See Noth, *Pentateuchal Traditions*, 21: "Not even an examination of the language and style is of any decisive assistance in the analysis of the old Pentateuchal tradition [i.e., J and E]. For, owing to the scantiness of material at our disposal, and the lack of truly characteristic terms and idioms in the predominantly simple and vernacular manner of speech, a division of the total material according to linguistic and stylistic

considerations alone is not feasible." Note that for Noth, even while he admits the difficulty, considerations of language and style are assumed to be the primary means of distinguishing between J and E. See also Jenks, *Elohist*, 39: "The reliable stylistic constants of E are few."

12. Wellhausen, *Composition*, 35 (translation mine): "Nur wo die verschiedenen Gottes-namen ein auffallendes Kriterium an die Hand geben, gelingt es die doppelte Strö-mung klarer zu erkennen."

13. Although some scholars continued to use the divine names as a criterion for source division after Exod 3, at least in some passages; see Carpenter and Harford-Battersby on Exod 13:17–19 (*Hexateuch*, 2:99); Kuenen, *Hexateuch*, 141; Addis, *Documents*, 1:liv; Schmidt, *Old Testament Introduction*, 90.

14. See Holzinger, *Einleitung*, 93–110, 181–91, 283–91, 338–49; Carpenter and Harford-Battersby, *Hexateuch*, 1:185–221; Driver, *Genesis*, vii–xi, xiii; McNeile, *Exodus*, iii–v, vii–ix; Simpson, *Early Traditions*, 403–9; Skinner, *Genesis*, l–li; Friedman, *Sources Revealed*, 8–10.

15. Carpenter and Harford-Battersby, *Hexateuch*, 1:190–92.

16. Thus the phrase "messenger of Elohim," which is attributed exclusively to E, is found in Exod 14:19, which belongs to J (see case study IV); the word "here I am," *hinnēnî*, is not, as Carpenter and Harford-Battersby claim, exclusive to E, but occurs in clear J contexts in Gen 27:1, 18 and Num 14:40 (what is exclusive to E is the use of this word after God calls to a character using the character's name twice, as in Gen 22:11; 46:2; Exod 3:4); the verb "to interpret" and its related nouns are indeed found only in E, but also only in the continuous narrative of Gen 40–41, and thus this word is more dependent on context than on authorship.

17. See the acute criticism of Coats, *From Canaan*, 56: "An argument from vocabulary cannot serve as the *decisive* appeal for making source distinctions, especially when the word under question appears in a limited number of texts."

18. See Schmitt, "Gen 22,1–19*," 88: "To prevent an incorrect development of a myth—above all spreading from Heidelberg [i.e., from Rendtorff and Blum]—one must once again stress in reviewing the last century of pentateuchal scholarship that in the classical Pentateuch theory—with a few exceptions—there has been no mechanistic application of the so-called 'God's name criterion,' but that the isolation of an 'elo-histic' Pentateuch layer was always founded primarily on the statement of a similar theological intention" (translation mine). [Um einer—vor allem in Heidelberg sich ausbreitenden—falschen Legendenbildung vorzubeugen, wird man gerade im Rück-blick auf die Pentateuchforschung des letzten Jahrhunderts noch einmal betonen müssen, daß es in der klassischen Pentateuchtheorie—von wenigen Ausnahmen abgesehen—keine mechanistische Anwendung des sog. 'Gottesnamenskriteriums' gab, sondern daß die Ausscheidung einer 'elohistischen' Pentateuchschicht immer primär in der Feststellung einer gleichen theologischen Intention begründet war.]

19. Weimar, *Redaktionsgeschichte*, 109 (translation mine): "Anders als der Jahwist, bei dem die einzelnen Geschichten zu einem kontinuierlichen Handlungsablauf zu-sammengefügt sind, bietet sich das elohistische Werk als einen mehr oder mindere

lockere Aneinanderreihung von Einzelgeschichte dar, die nicht durch einen raum-
zeitlichen Geschehensrahmen, sondern durch thematische Verknüpfungen mitein-
ander verbunden sind."

20. Wolff, "Elohistic Fragments"; Vermeylen, "Premières étapes littéraires," 151–60 (fear of God); Schmitt, "Menschliche Schuld" (threat of God); Ruppert, "Motiv" (testing of God); Kilian, *Vorpriesterlichen Abrahamsüberlieferungen*, 64–65 and passim (faith in God and God's plan); Graupner, "Erzählkunst" (self-revelation); McEvenue, "Elohist" (providence); Ruppert, "Elohist"; Schüpphaus, "Volk Gottes"; Schmitt, "Erzählung" (God and Israel); Jaroš, *Stellung* (Israel and Canaanite religion); Schmidt, "Weisheit" (wisdom); Coote, *Defense*; White, "Elohistic Depiction" (propaganda).

21. See the variety of themes described by Zenger, *Sinaitheophanie*, 161–63; Seebass, "Elohist,"; and even more extensively by Zimmer, *Elohist*, 163–227.

22. This is evident in the common refrain that J and E are parallel accounts, have the same general outlines, are very similar, etc.; see Wellhausen, *Composition*, 16; Kuenen, *Hexateuch*, 144; Addis, *Documents*, 1:liii; Carpenter and Harford-Battersby, *Hexateuch*, 1:110; Gray, *Numbers*, xxx–xxxi; Gunkel, *Genesis*, lxxiv; Driver, *Genesis*, xvi; McNeile, *Exodus*, vi; Brightman, *Sources*, 121; Skinner, *Genesis*, xlv; Speiser, *Genesis*, xxx; Propp, *Exodus 1–18*, 49.

23. Noth, *Pentateuchal Traditions*, 38.

24. Ibid., 39; Noth is followed by Fohrer, *Introduction*, 127–32. See also Kuenen, *Hexateuch*, 139; Bacon, *Genesis*, 62.

25. Cross, *Canaanite Myth*, 124 n. 38. In this he followed his teacher, William F. Albright (*Stone Age*, 189): "J and E must reflect two recensions of an original epic narrative, the nucleus of which had presumably been recited by Hebrew rhapsodists before the Exodus."

26. Carpenter and Harford-Battersby, *Hexateuch*, 2:39–42. See too their divisions of Gen 26:21–34; 41:28–40; and the nonpriestly text of Num 13–14 (*Hexateuch*, 2:37–38, 64–65, 205–10).

27. The comments of Addis, *Documents*, 1:47–48, on Gen 27 are telling: "It is a combination of a Jahvist and Elohist account. . . . It is impossible to make any complete severance between the Jahvist and Elohist. Each has adopted and told substantially the same story." So too Bacon, *Genesis*, 156: "J and E are here so nearly identical and so closely interwoven as to make an exact separation impossible. The most critics feel sure of is that both J and E related the same story of the usurpation of Jacob."

28. Carpenter and Harford-Battersby, *Hexateuch*, 2:51.

29. Ibid., 2:61–62; so too Addis, *Documents*, 1:77; Bacon, *Genesis*, 191.

30. See Bacon, *Triple Tradition*, 154–55; Carpenter and Harford-Battersby, *Hexateuch*, 2:134; Brightman, *Sources*, 97; Driver, *Exodus*, 364–66; Friedman, *Sources Revealed*, 177.

31. As observed by Schmidt, *Old Testament Introduction*, 55: "The fact that as source analysis becomes more detailed it no longer wins general acceptance is due not only to the situation of the text itself but also to the working of a general law that also applies to literary criticism: The more extravagant and complicated a theory is, the more improbable it becomes."

32. On the development of scholarly opposition to E, see Jenks, *Elohist*, 9–12; Knight, "Pentateuch," 282–83; Zimmer, *Elohist*, 21–32.

33. Whybray, *Making*, 115.

34. Craghan, "Elohist," 27; see also Lichtenstein, "Dream-Theophany," 46–47 (and the response to Lichtenstein by Gnuse, "Dreams").

35. See Engnell, *Rigid Scrutiny*, 54–56; Rendtorff, *Problem*, 117–19; Carr, *Fractures*, 147.

36. See Holzinger, *Einleitung*, 182; Addis, *Documents*, 1:lvi; Carpenter and Harford-Battersby, *Hexateuch*, 1:190; Driver, *Genesis*, xiii; Brightman, *Sources*, 113; Skinner, *Genesis*, li; Eissfeldt, *Old Testament*, 183.

37. See Volz and Rudolph, *Elohist*, 18.

38. See Kuenen, *Hexateuch*, 145; Addis, *Documents*, 1:lv; Holzinger, *Einleitung*, 182; Gunkel, *Genesis*, lxxv; Driver, *Genesis*, xiii; Brightman, *Sources*, 114; Skinner, *Genesis*, li.

39. See Volz and Rudolph, *Elohist*, 18, 149–50.

40. Contra Volz and Rudolph, *Elohist*, 17–18; Mowinckel, *Erwägungen*, 4. See Rendtorff, *Problem*, 118: "When the claim that the sources J and E differ from each other in their use of language is reduced after all to the statement that there are two (or three!) different designations for the slave woman, it can only be due to the principle of inertia that this argument is still used at all."

41. Contra Volz and Rudolph, *Elohist*, 19.

42. The statement of Van Seters, *Abraham*, 156, is particularly applicable: "This criterion [i.e., terminology] may be helpful in the task of source *identification* but rarely in source division; that is, not for the purpose of separating the sources from one another but of grouping the various units belonging to a particular source, only after the separation." See also the sensible arguments of Zimmer, *Elohist*, 40–45.

43. See Volz and Rudolph, *Elohist*, 8–10; Rendtorff, *Problem*, 117–18.

44. See Van Seters, *Abraham*, 156: "I am very skeptical about making a division between two verses or parts of verses within the same unit only on the basis of vocabulary, such as the alternation of the divine names Yahweh and Elohim." Similarly Blum (*Vätergeschichte*, 471–75), in his extensive argument against the use of the divine designations as a marker of source division, uses the terms "style marker" (*Stilmerkmal*) and "style variation" (*Stilvariante*) (474).

45. See Volz and Rudolph, *Elohist*, 14; Engnell, *Rigid Scrutiny*, 55.

46. See Volz and Rudolph, *Elohist*, 15–16, 148–49.

47. Ibid., 15.

48. Tov, *Textual Criticism*, 309.

49. See Hendel, *Text of Genesis 1–11*, 6–9, and the scholars cited there.

50. See Graupner, *Elohist*, 5.

51. See McEvenue, "Return," 386 n. 23, in his criticism of Blum's attack on the use of the divine names as a basis for source division: "Blum develops the thesis that the divine name cannot be used as an a priori argument for source division, in isolation from other indications. In this, he is fighting straw men: no serious source critic ever did that."

52. See Addis, *Documents*, 1:lv; Holzinger, *Einleitung*, 181–82; Carpenter and Harford-Battersby, *Hexateuch*, 1:190; Driver, *Genesis*, xiii; Gunkel, *Genesis*, lxxiv–lxxv; McNeile,

Exodus, viii; Skinner, *Genesis*, l–li; Wolff, "Elohistic Fragments," 68; Jenks, *Elohist*, 66; Friedman, "Torah (Pentateuch)," 610; Seebass, "Elohist."

53. See Volz and Rudolph, *Elohist*, 6–7, 23–24; Van Seters, *Abraham*, 126–27; Carr, *Fractures*, 146–47.

54. Volz and Rudolph, *Elohist*, 16–17 (translation mine): ". . . die Quellenscheidung schon Dogma gewesen ware und man nun jedem Erzähler der im übrigen fast gleichlautenden Erzählung hätte seinen Stoff geben müssen. Sieht man vom Dogma ab, so erscheint diese Verteilung als vollständig unnötig, ja als unberechtigt, die künstlerische und sachlich Absicht des einen Erzählers zerstörend." See also Mowinckel, *Erwägungen*, 59: "It must also be admitted that in many isolated cases the differentiation has been carried out between J and E because one was convinced from other cases of the existence of two sources and was now required to be able to carry out the differentiation everywhere" (translation mine). [Es muss auch zugegeben werde, dass in vielen Einzelfällen die Unterscheidung zwischen einem J und einem E nur deshalb vorgenommen worden ist, weil man aus anderen Fällen von der Existenz zweier Quellen üeberzeugt und nun bestrebt war, die Unterscheidung überall durchführen zu können.]

55. See Van Seters, *Abraham*, 157: "So each unit of tradition must be scrutinized from the viewpoint of internal consistency and continuity and with the use of form-critical and structural analysis to arrive at an evaluation of its unity or division into primary and secondary sources." See also Zenger, *Sinaitheophanie*, 49–51; Coats, *From Canaan*, 59.

56. The confessional outlook of many anticritical writers is, to a certain extent, echoed even in the works of critical scholars writing in opposition to E. Volz argued that the Pentateuch existed for the purpose of religious instruction—"one wanted to use the splendid narrative book in lessons and in worship" (*Elohist*, 23 [translation mine]; [wollte man das prachtvolle Erzählungsbuch im Unterricht und im Gottesdienst gebrauchen])—and Rudolph argued against the division of J and E (but not P) on the grounds that most of the doublets (in the Joseph story, at least) are in religiously unimportant details and therefore can be ignored (*Elohist*, 147).

57. See Green, *Higher Criticism*, 113–18; Finn, *Unity*, 378–83; Kyle, *Problem*, 145–90; Cassuto, *Documentary Hypothesis*, 42–54; Segal, *Pentateuch*, 14–19.

58. See Finn, *Unity*, 358–63.

59. See the reference to Green by Volz and Rudolph, *Elohist*, 177, and the references to Cassuto by Mowinckel, *Erwägungen*, 4, and Engnell, *Rigid Scrutiny*, 56 n. 9.

60. Indeed, Mowinckel, *Erwägungen*, 5, even criticized Volz and Rudolph for approaching the question from too literary a perspective. In an overview of scholarship on E in the middle of the twentieth century, Craghan ("Elohist") discusses numerous methodological approaches to E, but the issue of continuity of historical claims is nowhere mentioned.

61. Carr, *Fractures*, 146.

62. Ibid., 147.

63. So Volz and Rudolph, *Elohist*; Mowinckel, *Erwägungen*.

64. Rendtorff, *Problem*, 172.

65. Whybray, *Making*, 115.
66. Graupner, *Elohist*, deserves credit for beginning with the call of Moses in Exod 3.
67. Though Rudolph continued the treatment into the rest of the Pentateuch (*"Elohist"*), his book assumes the conclusions of the first, rather than attempting to demonstrate them anew.
68. See, for example, Jenks, *Elohist*, 19–39.
69. Blum, *Studien*, 4 (translation mine). [. . . die Plausibilität des Quellenmodells nährte sich hier wohl von Anfang an aus der Extrapolation des an der Genesis entwickelten Grundparadigmas.]
70. See Friedman, "Torah (Pentateuch)," 619; Propp, *Exodus 1–18*, 50.
71. Carr, *Fractures*, 146.
72. In Exod 31:18 the canonical text represents the conflation of two similar notices, one by P and one by E. The E verse here read, "He gave Moses two tablets, stone tablets inscribed with the finger of God," while the P verse read, "When he finished speaking with him on Mount Sinai, he gave Moses the *'ēdût.*" The words "he gave to Moses" were part of both P and E independently and were not repeated in the compiled text.
73. Exod 32:15 presents a similar situation to 31:18. In both P and E, Moses has to descend from the mountain, and the compiler logically combined the two notices of his descent into a single sentence. Thus E originally read, "Moses turned and went down from the mountain bearing the two tablets," and P originally read, "Moses went down from the mountain bearing the *'ēdût.*"
74. The description of the Tent of Meeting in Exod 33:7–11 does not present a particular moment, but rather, as the verbal forms in the Hebrew indicate, the regular mechanism by which Yahweh would communicate with Moses in the future.
75. In Exod 34:4, where J reads "he went up on Mount Sinai," E would have originally read "he went up the mountain"; see below.
76. In P, the mountain is also called Sinai; cf. Exod 24:16; 31:18; 34:29, 32; Lev 7:38; 25:1; 26:46; 27:34; Num 3:1; 28:6.
77. In P, the Israelites are afraid only momentarily, and only of Moses's appearance after speaking with Yahweh (Exod 34:30). See Schwartz, "Priestly Account," 127–28.
78. In P, Yahweh takes up permanent residence among the Israelites after the construction of his dwelling, the Tabernacle (Exod 29:45–46; 40:34) and remains there throughout the wilderness period. When P regularly refers to cultic items or actions taking place in the Tent or Tabernacle "before Yahweh," this is to be taken literally (see Exod 16:33; 27:21; 34:34; Lev 1:3; Num 16:7, 16, 17, and elsewhere.).
79. In P, there is no covenant with the people at Sinai, as famously observed (though while drawing the wrong conclusions) by Cross, *Canaanite Myth*, 318–20. See also Schwartz, "Priestly Account," 130–32.
80. In P, Moses ascends the mountain (Exod 24:18a) in order to receive the blueprint for the Tabernacle and the *'ēdût* (on the meaning of which see Schwartz, "Priestly Account," 126 n. 52). He does not ascend the mountain again; the construction of the Tabernacle (Exod 35–40) and the giving of all of the laws to Moses (Lev 1–Num 9) occur at the foot of the mountain, in the newly constructed Tabernacle; Lev 25:1,

26:46, and 27:34 should be read "at Mount Sinai" rather than "on Mount Sinai" (see Schwartz, "Priestly Account," 123).

81. The Tent of Meeting in P is located in the middle of the camp (Num 1:53–2:34), and Yahweh dwells within it (see above). On the distinctions between the priestly and nonpriestly Tents, see Haran, *Temples*, 260–75.

82. In P, Joshua is not introduced until Num 13:8, 16; that this is his first appearance in P is clear from the change of his name from Hosea to Joshua. Joshua is mentioned in P only in connection with the episode of the spies, in which he and Caleb proved themselves loyal to Yahweh (Num 14:6–9, 30, 38; 26:65; 32:12), until the moment that he is chosen by Yahweh to succeed Moses as leader of the Israelites (Num 27:18–23; 32:28; 34:17).

83. P relates a variety of Israelite offenses in the wilderness: complaint about lack of provisions (Exod 16:3), lack of faith in Yahweh's ability to overcome the Canaanites (Num 14:2–4), the cultic rebellion of Korah (Num 16:3; see case study III), and the sin of Zimri with the Midianite woman (Num 25:6–18).

84. The elders of Israel are mentioned only twice in P: Lev 4:15 and 9:1. There is no special selection of seventy elders in P, as is sensible, since in P the priests serve as the leaders of the people.

85. The phrase "all the hardships that have befallen us" in 20:14 is attested elsewhere in the Pentateuch only in Exod 18:8 (and otherwise only in Neh 9:32). The collocation of the terms "fields and vineyards" in 20:17 is part of E's vocabulary (cf. Exod 22:4; Num 16:14).

86. The episode of the Nehushtan in 21:4b–9 has distinctive structural parallels to the leprosy of Miriam in Num 12: a complaint against Moses, a plague, a plea on behalf of the affected party for Moses to intercede, the intercession, and a mechanism by which the plague is relieved. See Culley, *Studies*, 102–6.

87. Note the cohortative of '-*b-r* in 21:22, found in the Pentateuch only in E (20:17 [in the plural], 19) and D (Deut 2:27, 28; 3:25), and "the King's Highway," only in 21:22 and 20:17; "field and vineyard," see the note above. The phrase "went out against" (with hostile intent) is a regular trope of E in Num 20–21; see 20:20; 21:23, 33.

88. On the source division of Num 32, see Baden, *Redaction*, 141–48. The priestly account of the apportioning of the Transjordan in Num 32 connects not with the conquests in Num 21, but with the war against Midian in Num 31.

89. In P, as already mentioned, Yahweh selects Joshua as Moses's successor on the basis of his loyalty during the episode of the spies in Num 13–14 and is invested in Num 27:18–23. In E, no single act defines Joshua as the next leader of the Israelites; it is simply taken for granted that as Moses's servant he will succeed him.

90. Additionally, the word for "oppress" in 3:9, *l-ḥ-ṣ*, is found elsewhere in the Pentateuch only in the Covenant Code, Exod 22:20; 23:9—both times with reference to the oppression in Egypt.

91. See Schwartz, "Visit," 46–47; Propp, *Exodus 1–18*, 631.

92. On possible redactional insertions in Exod 18, see Schwartz, "Visit," 35 n. 17.

93. See ibid., 45.

94. See Baden, *Redaction*, 176–77.

95. In fact, it is likely, if not provable, that the two uses of the name Horeb derive from the two distinct meanings of the root *ḥ-r-b*: that in J from the meaning "dry," and that of E from the meaning "waste, desolation" (Baruch Schwartz, personal communication). Further, the "rod with which you struck the Nile" in v. 5 refers back to a J story (Exod 7:17–18, 20aβb¹) and is to be distinguished from the "rod of God" in E in 17:9, which is the staff Yahweh gave to Moses in E in Exod 4:17 (in the continuation of Yahweh's speech from 3:22) and which Moses took with him when he left for Egypt in 4:20b. Note also that the episode in 17:1bβ–7, with its theme of "trying Yahweh" (v. 2), fits squarely into the larger wilderness narrative of J.

96. This was pointed out to me by Jeffrey Stackert (personal communication).

97. Gen 41:50b is patently an insertion of the compiler on the basis of P. In E, Potiphar is the Egyptian to whom Joseph is sold by the Midianites, whereas in P he is the priest of On and Joseph's father-in-law; the compiler has taken 41:50b directly from the priestly genealogy in 46:20, which itself reflects Joseph's marriage to Asenath in P in 41:45.

98. In fact, after Exod 1:6, none of the twelve sons of Jacob, or any of their descendants, is ever mentioned again by name in J. The Israelites are only called the Israelites, as a united people, no longer identified by tribe (the exception is the investiture of the Levites in Exod 32:26–29, which is, I think, exceptional). In E, on the other hand, Dathan and Abiram are identified as Reubenites in Num 16, and the Reubenites and Gadites are the protagonists of the E story in Num 32, where the descendants of Manasseh are mentioned as well. P, of course, contains extensive genealogies delineating the descendants of the sons of Jacob. If one were so inclined, one might suggest that J is making a political point by referring to the Israelites only as a unified body, if J was, in fact, written in support of the United Monarchy (whether during the time of Solomon or any time thereafter).

99. Gen 48:3–7 belong to P; see case study V. Probably 48:20 is also from P, as this verse represents a second blessing of Ephraim and Manasseh after the E blessing of vv. 15–16.

100. The rare word for "armed" used here, *ḥᵃmušîm*, is probably also to be read in Num 32:17 (E) in place of the otherwise bizarre *ḥûšîm* (see Ehrlich, *Miqra ki-peshuto*, 1:303–4).

101. This theory is held by both critics of E (Volz and Rudolph, Mowinckel) and some ostensible adherents (McEvenue, "Elohist"; Coote, *Defense*; Zimmer, *Elohist* [and see his discussion of other scholars who hold this view, 35–38]).

102. See Fohrer, *Introduction*, 155; Graupner, *Elohist*, 8–10.

103. See Kuenen, *Hexateuch*, 140; Wolff, "Elohistic Fragments"; Seebass, "Elohist"; Schmidt, *Old Testament Introduction*, 86; Graupner, *Elohist*. Gnuse, "Redefining," 215, describes E as a collection of "loose pools of Elohist tradition."

104. Although Gen 15 has long been a focal point of source-critical dispute, the connections between elements of this chapter and other E passages are numerous. In terms of historical claims, the statement that the Israelites will leave Egypt with great wealth (15:14) refers to the despoiling of the Egyptians in E (Exod 3:21–22; 11:2–3; 12:35–36). In terms of theme and language, we may note the prophetic address to Abraham in 15:1 (see the depiction of Abraham as a prophet in Gen 20:7, 17); the appearance of God in

a vision; the linking of the promise with a reference to the enslavement in and Exodus from Egypt (15:13–16; see Gen 46:3–4); the self-identification of Yahweh in 15:7, which is strikingly parallel to that of the Decalogue in Exod 20:2; the description of Yahweh as appearing in smoke and fire in 15:17, as in Exod 20:18—the only two pentateuchal texts in which the rare word *lappîd* appears; and the presence of a formal ceremony to mark the making of a covenant, elsewhere only in E (Exod 24:3–8). There is certainly some difficulty with the use of the divine name in 15:2, 7, 8; yet the numerous other E indicators strongly outweigh the evidence of the divine names, which, as we have noted above, cannot be used as the primary evidence for source division.

105. See Graupner, *Elohist*, 11: "The gapped connection of the elohistic texts is therefore not a serious argument against the existence of an E source, but merely a statement about its condition" (translation mine) [Der lückenhafte Zusammenhang der elohistischen Texte ist darum kein ernsthaftes Argument gegen die Existenz einer Quelle E, sondern lediglich eine Aussage über ihren Erhaltungszustand]"; Speiser, *Genesis*, xxxiv: "Fragmentary preservation of a work cannot be used as an argument about its original scope."

106. Kuenen, *Hexateuch*, 140.

107. See Gibson, *Canaanite Myths*, 19–20; Gray, *KRT Text*, 1–2; Pardee, "Kirta Epic," 333; Wyatt, *Religious Texts*, 177–78; Margalit, "Legend," 203–4.

108. On the relationship of D to E, see Baden, *Redaction*, 99–195, and the scholarship cited there.

109. The recognition of the dependence of Deut 10:1–5 on E's text in Exod 34 allows for a more certain separation of J and E in Exod 34, especially regarding phrases that could logically fit into either. Thus in particular the words "he went up on Mount Sinai" in 34:4, which are attributed to J because they refer to Sinai, must cover the original E clause, "he went up the mountain"—which is represented in Deut 10:3 ("I went up the mountain"). The following clause in Exod 34:4, "as Yahweh had commanded him," could also fit into either J or E, but because it finds its parallel in Deut 10:5, it is more likely part of E. See Baden, *Redaction*, 166–72.

CHAPTER FOUR. COMPLEMENTARITY

1. In E, see Exod 19:4–5; in P, Exod 6:6–8.

2. On the relationship of D to ancient Near Eastern treaty patterns, see Weinfeld, *Deuteronomy and the Deuteronomic School*, 59–157.

3. There is some debate as to whether the second speech begins in Deut 4:45 or one verse earlier, in 4:44. Two main arguments speak in favor of 4:45. First, the term "Torah" in 4:44 to describe the laws of Deut 12–26 is used elsewhere in Deut 1–11 only in the first speech (1:5, 4:8), and the occurrences in 1:5 and 4:44 serve to bracket the first historical speech of Moses. Second, 4:45 begins with the word *'ēlleʰ*, "these"; if it were written as an appositional phrase to 4:44, we would expect the coordinating conjunction *waw* before the word (especially as the *waw* is found before the first word of 4:44: *wᵉzōʼt*, "and this"). See Haran, *Biblical Collection*, 52–54.

4. It is almost universally acknowledged that the passage in Deut 4:41–43, in which Moses assigns the cities of refuge, is a later insertion or is otherwise out of place, as it has no relation to either the first or second speech as it currently stands.

5. See, for example, Kuenen, *Hexateuch*, 117–23; Addis, *Documents*, 1:19–25; Carpenter and Harford-Battersby, *Hexateuch*, 2:247–48; Eissfeldt, *Old Testament*, 226; Fohrer, *Introduction*, 171. Driver, *Deuteronomy*, lxvii–lxxii, was almost alone in arguing for a unity of authorship in Deut 1–11. Some have attempted to delineate two strata throughout D on the basis of the alternation between the use of the second-person singular and plural; see, for example, de Tillesse, "Sections." Yet most recent scholars have correctly concluded that such a feature is probably due to stylistic choice on the part of a single author (a style that may have been mimicked by subsequent strata); see Weinfeld, *Deuteronomy 1–11*, 15–16; Römer, *Deuteronomistic History*, 73–74.

6. Noth, *Deuteronomistic History*, 29–33. Noth considered Deut 4:1–40 to be a special case: "it is questionable whether Deut. 4.1–40 is to be attributed to Dtr. [the Deuteronomistic History] or seen as a later addition" (ibid., 57); yet he seems to conclude that at least a significant bulk of the chapter is indeed from Dtr.

7. See, for example, Weinfeld, *Deuteronomy 1–11*, 13–14; Rofé, *Deuteronomy*, 9; Nelson, *Deuteronomy*, 8; Schmidt, *Old Testament Introduction*, 126; Ska, *Introduction*, 5; Pfeiffer, *Introduction*, 185.

8. We can perhaps see a sign of this supplementary motive in the transition between Deut 4:44 and 4:45. If 4:45 was the original introduction to the second speech, beginning "these are the decrees, laws, and rules that Moses addressed to the people of Israel," then the author of the first speech may have composed 4:44, the conclusion of his speech, as a deliberate echo of the beginning of the one to follow: "This the Torah that Moses set before the Israelites." Haran (*Biblical Collection*, 54–58) suggests that in fact Deut 1:1–4:44 was composed as an alternative introduction to the laws, independently of 4:45–11:31; so too, in fact, Wellhausen (*Composition*, 193). Yet this theory does not take into account the complementary histories related in the two speeches.

9. Noth, *Deuteronomistic History*, 29.

10. See Deut 1:9, 16, 18; 2:34; 3:4, 8, 12, 18, 21, 23; 4:14; 5:5; 9:20; 10:1, 8.

11. The one clear exception occurs in Deut 1:39, which is taken almost verbatim from P's spies narrative in Num 14:31. The very exceptionality of this P element in D highlights the absence of such elements elsewhere; this verse is probably an insertion from the compiler. Scholars have tended also to see priestly resonances in Deut 4:16–18, which seems to be similar to the priestly creation account in Gen 1, and in 4:32, which also has possible priestly overtones in the phrase "ever since God created man on earth," using the same word for "create," *b-r-'*, as P. It is possible that Deut 4 has undergone some expansion after the compilation of the Pentateuch, though the majority of the text remains firmly deuteronomic in character.

12. For a more expansive treatment of the parallels between D and its nonpriestly sources, see Baden, *Redaction*, 99–195.

13. The only exception is the element of fire from J's account in Exod 19:18 (see below).

14. See Levinson, *Deuteronomy*.

15. For Gen 26:5, see, for example, Kuenen, *Hexateuch*, 259; Addis, *Documents*, 1:45; Dillmann, *Genesis*, 2:203; Bacon, *Genesis*, 153; Carpenter and Harford-Battersby, *Hexateuch*, 2:38; Brightman, *Sources*, 53; for Exod 15:26, see Kuenen, *Hexateuch*, 259; Addis, *Documents*, 1:132; Bacon, *Triple Tradition*, 88; McNeile, *Exodus*, 94; Brightman, *Sources*, 154.

16. See, for example, Bacon, *Triple Tradition*, 101; Carpenter and Harford-Battersby, *Hexateuch*, 2:110; McNeile, *Exodus*, 110–11.

17. On Gen 15:19–21, see, for example, Carpenter and Harford-Battersby, *Hexateuch*, 2:23; on every such list, see Bacon, *Triple Tradition*, 22 and elsewhere; McNeile, *Exodus*, 17 and elsewhere (both initially commenting on Exod 3:8).

18. See, for example, Kuenen, *Hexateuch*, 261–62; Bacon, *Triple Tradition*, 113–26; McNeile, *Exodus*, 135–46; Brightman, *Sources*, 159 n. 23.

19. See, in addition to Gen 26:5 and Exod 15:26, Gen 18:19 and Exod 16:28.

20. The next closest resemblance is in the phrase "keep my covenant," *ûš^emartem 'et-b^erîtî* (19:5). The word *ûš^emartem* is a common one in Deuteronomy, but never with the direct object of "covenant" (once with the object "words of this covenant," Deut 29:8); almost always the word is followed by a form of the verb '-*ś-h* (Deut 4:6; 5:1, 32; 7:12; 11:32). Expressions like "what I did to the Egyptians" and "I bore you on eagles' wings" (Exod 19:4), "all the earth is mine" (19:5), and "kingdom of priests" and "holy nation" (19:6) have no parallels in D.

21. Those scholars who attribute Exod 19:7–8 to the same deuteronomic hand (such as Kuenen, *Hexateuch*, 246–47) solve this difficulty but are faced with a deuteronomic addition that uses distinctly E language, in the people's response: "All that Yahweh has spoken we will do!" (see Exod 24:3, 7).

22. Carpenter and Harford-Battersby, *Hexateuch*, 2:83.

23. For a more detailed argument in this regard, see Baden, "Deuteronomic Evidence."

24. See Rose, *Deuteronomist*, 224–63, and Johnstone, *Chronicles and Exodus*, 253–55, for whom all of Num 11 and part of Exod 18 is from D; Crüsemann, *Torah*, 89; Blum, *Studien*, 156–58, for whom Num 11 and Exod 18 are taken up in the larger "D-Komposition." The argument that Num 11 is later than and dependent on D is made by Römer, "Nombres 11–12," 489; Aurelius, *Fürbitter*, 176–81; Schmid, *Sogenannte Jahwist*, 70–75; Perlitt, *Deuteronomium*, 59. Rendtorff, *Problem*, 98–100, attributes Num 11:11–15 to a deuteronomic layer.

25. See Vermeylen, "L'affaire," who argues that Exod 32–34 is the product of multiple deuteronomic redactions and that the first of these actually preceded and formed the basis for the redaction of Deut 9–10; Johnstone, *Chronicles and Exodus*, 154–55; Perlitt, *Bundestheologie*, 203–16; Aurelius, *Fürbitter*, 51–52; Blum, *Studien*, 54–75, for whom Exod 32–34 is taken up into the "D-Komposition"; Blenkinsopp, "Deuteronomic Contribution," 108–9. For a summary of some theories of a deuteronomi(sti)c redaction in the Sinai pericope as a whole, see Schmid, "Israel am Sinai," 22–35; Van Seters, "Is There Evidence."

26. As already noted, Deut 1:39 is most likely from the hand of the compiler.

27. None of the main stories about Esau derive from E. The narrative of Jacob and Esau's birth in Gen 25:21–26a is from J; the sale of Esau's birthright in 25:27–34 is from J; the

theft of Esau's blessing in Gen 27:1–45 is from J; Esau's marriage in 28:6–9 is from P; Jacob's preparations to encounter Esau in 32:4–22 are from J; the encounter itself in 33:1–17 is from J; the notice that Jacob and Esau together buried Isaac in 35:29 is from P; the genealogy of Esau in Gen 36 is from P. The only two references to Esau in E are in Gen 35:1—"Built an altar there to the God who appeared to you when you were fleeing from your brother Esau"—and 35:7—"it was there that God had revealed himself to him when he was fleeing from his brother." As the story of Jacob fleeing from Esau is told only in J it seems likely that these two very similar clauses are the work of the compiler. This is especially probable in light of the E text in 31:13, in which God also reminds Jacob of the theophany in Gen 28, but without any mention of Esau at all: "I am the God of Bethel, where you anointed a pillar and where you made a vow to me."

28. This is especially so since, as many commentators have noted, the intercession in Exod 32:11–13 comes at an awkward place—Moses intercedes before even having discovered what the Israelites have done—while that in Deut 9:25–29 is far more natural. We would have to assume that a D author created a slightly confusing narrative from one that was not at all so, an assumption that makes little sense. It should be noted, however, that the E story is not in fact so strange; Moses pleads on behalf of the people before he has witnessed the calf, it is true, but he intercedes immediately after Yahweh's threat to destroy the Israelites. It seems perfectly natural for Moses to try to assuage Yahweh's anger right away, rather than risk any delay.
29. See Begg, "Destruction," 475: "All the distinctive features of Deut 9,21 can more readily and satisfactorily be accounted for in terms of a rewriting of Exod 32,20 than on the reverse supposition." This statement can be broadened to cover the entirety of D's relationship to E.
30. See Stackert, *Rewriting*, 211–25.
31. The identification of this text as P is hardly in dispute: it has a nearly exact parallel in Num 27:12–14; only P refers to a place known as Abarim (Num 21:11; 27:13); the references to the death of Aaron on Mount Hor and the episode at Meribath-Kadesh are too exclusively P texts (Num 20:23–29 and 20:1–13*, respectively).
32. Note also the unique priestly syntactical construction in Deut 34:7, using the age followed by *b-* and the infinitive construct, *ben-mēʾaʰ wᵊʿeśrîm šānāʰ bᵊmōtô*; cf. the analogous constructions in Gen 12:4; 17:24, 25; 21:5; 25:20, 26; 41:46; Exod 7:7.

CASE STUDY III. THE REVOLT IN THE WILDERNESS, NUMBERS 16

1. The text of Num 16:1 identifies Dathan and Abiram as the sons of Eliab and also seems to introduce a third character, On the son of Peleth, who is not mentioned again in the narrative. This has long been recognized as a textual corruption; the genealogy in Num 26:8–9 identifies Dathan and Abiram as the sons of Eliab, who was in turn the son of Pallu, who was one of Reuben's sons. See Gray, *Numbers*, 194–95. We should probably therefore emend the text in Num 16:1 to read "Dathan and Abiram, the sons of Eliab, the son of Pallu, the son of Reuben" (so Addis, *Documents*, 1:168; Gray, *Numbers*, 195; Rudolph, "*Elohist*," 83; Noth, *Numbers*, 118; Eissfeldt, *Hexateuch-Synopse*,

277; Schmidt, *Priesterschrift*, 117–18). Since Deut 11:6 identifies Dathan and Abiram only as the sons of Eliab, son of Reuben, while the inclusion of Pallu is known only from a few priestly texts (Num 26:8–9; Gen 46:9; Exod 6:14), we may consider the possibility that the full genealogy is the creation of the compiler (see Simpson, *Early Traditions*, 238) or a gloss (Rudolph, "Elohist," 83–84; Achenbach, *Vollendung*, 41). Certainly in Num 26:8–11 the entire reference to Dathan and Abiram and their story seems a secondary addition on formal grounds alone (so too the reference to the narrative of Gen 38 in Num 26:19).

2. The Hebrew expression used here, *qûm lipnê*, is rare but seems to be used for hostile confrontations; cf. Lev 26:37; Josh 7:12–13.

3. Similarly, the expression here, *q-h-l* (niphal) *'al*, also describes an antagonistic scenario; cf. Exod 32:1; Num 17:7; 20:2.

4. See Noth, *Numbers*, 124.

5. Num 3:5–10. It is therefore difficult, if not impossible, to accept the claim of Wellhausen (*Composition*, 105) that some of these verses belonged to the "JE" redactor.

6. Exod 30:7–9; Lev 10:1–3; 16:12–13.

7. Many scholars have argued for multiple strata in this priestly story, although the precise identification of the strata differs widely. This analysis began with the work of Kuenen, "Bijdragen," and was widely adopted thereafter; see Addis, *Documents*, 2:408–10; Bacon, *Triple Tradition*, 192–93; Carpenter and Harford-Battersby, *Hexateuch*, 2:212–15; Baentsch, *Exodus-Leviticus-Numeri*, 541–42; Gray, *Numbers*, 192; Holzinger, *Numeri*, 66; Gressmann, *Mose*, 251–52 n. 3; Eissfeldt, *Hexateuch-Synopse*, 277; Rudolph, "Elohist," 81–82; Driver, *Introduction*, 64–65; Simpson, *Early Traditions*, 240–42; Coats, *Rebellion*, 156–63; Noth, *Numbers*, 121–22; Fritz, *Israel*, 25–26; Milgrom, *Numbers*, 417–20; Scharbert, *Numeri*, 65; Schmidt, *Priesterschrift*, 135–46; Seebass, *Numeri*, 2:175–78. I see no need to assume more than one priestly author in this text (see also Levine, *Numbers 1–20*, 405–6); nevertheless, since these scholars claim that the growth of the P narrative took place before its combination with the nonpriestly story, such analyses do not detract from the main point here (for theories in which the author responsible for the second priestly layer is responsible also for the redaction of the entire chapter, see below). The Documentary Hypothesis, as already stated, is concerned with the penultimate stage of the Pentateuch, and as such any internal developments within a document are a secondary concern.

8. The use of the verb *'-l-h* to signify going to a superior is attested also in Gen 46:31. There is no need to read anything further into the word, whether cultic or geographical; see Rudolph, "Elohist," 84.

9. See Eissfeldt, *Hexateuch-Synopse*, 277. This requires the simplest of textual emendations: the removal of the *waw*, "and," before "two hundred and fifty Israelites" (see Gressmann, *Mose*, 251–52 n. 3; Friedman, *Sources Revealed*, 268). The New Jewish Publication Society translation is apparently based on *Midrash Tanḥuma' Qoraḥ* 3; see also Rashi and ibn Ezra on Num 16:1. The midrash draws the connection between Korah's "taking" himself, that is, separating himself from the community, and Moses's "taking" of the Levites from among the Israelites in Num 8:6 to serve as assistants to the Aaronid priests. This connection may be maintained even when we understand

that Korah "takes" the 250 tribal leaders: this is the means by which Korah attempts to undo the separation of the Levites as cultic secondaries and assert their role as priests. Ibn Ezra mentions an unnamed grammarian who understood the 250 Israelite leaders as the object of "took," but ibn Ezra does not agree. Naḥmanides (on Num 16:1) understands this correctly. Keil and Delitzsch (*Commentary*, 722) also read the verb and object correctly, although they take Dathan, Abiram, and On as belonging to the subject. Once the stated object of *wayyiqqaḥ* is recognized, the various attempts to emend the text (see Milgrom, *Numbers*, 312–13 n. 2) become unnecessary.

10. On the rhetorical artistry of this speech, see Blum, *Studien*, 131 n. 122; Achenbach, *Vollendung*, 44. Their analyses speak loudly against the attempts of some scholars to divide this speech among J and E (see Carpenter and Harford-Battersby, *Hexateuch*, 2:213–14).

11. The reference to "gouging out eyes" refers to a known punishment for runaway slaves, prisoners, and vassals (Levine, *Numbers 1–20*, 414) and is therefore used pointedly here to illustrate Moses's exalted position over the rest of the Israelites. The use here of the common expression "land of milk and honey" to refer not to Canaan but rather to Egypt (v. 13) is unique and wonderfully ironic.

12. The opening phrase, "Pay no regard to their oblation" (better, "Pay no attention to their offering"), is a *crux interpretum*. No specific offering has been mentioned in the nonpriestly story (and this certainly cannot refer to any part of the priestly narrative). Even if we take *minḥāʰ* in its broader sense of gift (as in Gen 32:19, for example), we are still at a loss to identify the antecedent. Levine, *Numbers 1–20*, 426–27, and more expansively in "Offerings," suggests that this phrase is part of an ancient Near Eastern tradition of curses and threats for treaty violators: may their offerings not be accepted. This may be the best understanding of the expression in our chapter; see also Rudolph, "*Elohist*," 83. The second part of Moses's statement, that he has not taken the donkey of any of them, is known also from 1 Sam 12:3. Levine, *Numbers 1–20*, 425–26, also brings a wonderful parallel to Moses's self-defense from the Amarna letters, in which a vassal writing to his suzerain claims that he has not misappropriated a single person, ox, or mule. If this sort of statement is to be seen as part of a broader ancient Near Eastern rhetorical tradition, then Moses, by using the same language, is reversing the claims of his adversaries: he is taking upon himself the role of vassal, rather than that of suzerain as Dathan and Abiram are arguing. These interpretations of the ostensibly confusing phrases in v. 15 permit us to assign it to the nonpriestly story, contra Schmidt, *Priesterschrift*, 120–21. The assignment to P of v. 15 by Friedman, *Sources Revealed*, 269, or v. 15a by Gressmann, *Mose*, 251–52 n. 3, is idiosyncratic.

13. Despite the various difficulties in vv. 1–2, it seems unnecessary to claim that they have been rewritten by a priestly editor, as suggested by Levine, *Numbers 1–20*, 424; indeed, the very fact that they are so difficult belies the argument that they have been rewritten by a single hand.

14. Mirguet, "Numbers 16."

15. Note the use of the same expression in Num 17:10, again after Yahweh threatens to destroy the people. The phrase seems to mark impending danger in P; cf. Lev 9:24, where it immediately precedes the deaths of Nadab and Abihu; Num 14:5, in the

episode of the spies; and Num 20:6, where it precedes the episode of Moses getting water from the rock. We need not, therefore, presume that some threat or action against Moses has been omitted here, as claimed by Liver ("Korah," 190). The one positive use of the phrase in P is in Gen 17:3, 17, where it relates to the covenant of circumcision and the promise of a son for Abraham and Sarah.

16. Note that the Septuagint omits the names Dathan and Abiram here (and also in v. 27; see below). This is almost certainly not because the Septuagint is preserving an earlier text, but rather because the two major discrepancies represented by this phrase—that Korah, Dathan, and Abiram all shared a single dwelling and that the tents of Dathan and Abiram are obviously elsewhere—were judged insurmountable. Thus the Septuagint seems to have made an editorial decision here very much in line with the source-critical analysis.

17. These are to be identified with the seventy elders selected to receive part of Moses's prophetic spirit in Num 11:16–17, 24b–30; see case study II.

18. It is a regular feature of biblical narrative that statements by one character that are then repeated by another are not repeated verbatim; see, for example, Gen 2:16–17 and 3:3; Gen 28:13–15 and 32:13; Gen 42:10–20 and 42:29–34 (and 43:5); Num 11:4 and 13, discussed in case study II; Judg 13:5 and 7. In these examples, the original statement is altered in ways that change its emphasis so as to serve the purposes of the second speaker; we may suggest that the same is happening in Num 16.

    This verse would be very problematic in the nonpriestly narrative, as it essentially gives away the ending for the audience: Moses already would be telling the people that Dathan and Abiram are going to die (though this is precisely what Schmidt claims the nonpriestly author intends [*Priesterschrift*, 134]). We may also wonder what the "sin" of Dathan and Abiram would have been in the nonpriestly narrative; questioning Moses's authority may be wrongheaded, but would it have qualified as a sin? Schmidt (*Priesterschrift*, 133–34) argues that, for the author of this story, the fact that rebellion against Moses constituted a sin was so obvious that it didn't need to be spelled out; this seems to be an admission of a lack of evidence more than a positive argument. Furthermore, it makes little sense for Moses to have brought the elders to the tents of Dathan and Abiram in v. 25 only to tell them immediately to leave in v. 26.

19. On the command-fulfillment pattern in vv. 24–27, and for a critique of the various attempts to assign part of vv. 26–27 to the nonpriestly story, see Baden, "Narrative Pattern," 52–54.

20. Schmidt, *Priesterschrift*, 123–26, claims that these verses (including v. 31) are redactional, intended to bring the priestly and nonpriestly stories together. Yet this speech on the one hand contains the central point of the nonpriestly story—Moses's claim that his actions are in fact divinely ordained—and, more to the point, contains not a trace of the priestly narrative. Schmidt argues that the earth swallowing Dathan and Abiram is by these verses changed from an unintroduced divine punishment into an ordeal, thereby creating a parallel with the priestly ordeal in vv. 16–18. As we have stated, however, the earth swallowing Dathan and Abiram is not an ordeal at all; the victims are not the ones being tested, which is the main identifying feature of the ordeal. Schmidt also focuses on the use of "ground" in vv. 28–31 as opposed to "earth"

in vv. 32–34; this hardly seems reason enough to distinguish two authorial hands, especially as the first set of verses are in direct speech and the second in narrative.

21. On the rhetorical construction of this speech, see Blum, *Studien*, 131 n. 124.

22. See Rashi, on Num 16:12; Alter, *Art*, 136.

23. The theory of Coats, *Rebellion*, 160, that vv. 32–34 belong to P since only Korah is mentioned, is untenable on multiple grounds. The first is grammatical: v. 32 begins by stating that the earth swallowed "them with their households," and continues on, "and all Korah's people." The "them" in the first clause cannot refer to either Korah (who is, after all, singular), nor to his people, who are the third stated object in the sentence. The second problem is narratological and twofold: Coats claims that only Korah dies in v. 32, while the rest of his band dies by fire in v. 35; yet on the one hand, Korah's people are explicitly named in v. 32 as being swallowed by the earth, and thus would die twice, and on the other hand, v. 32 definitively does not state that Korah himself died—only his people. The third problem is methodological: Coats assumes that the priestly and nonpriestly narratives are so similar that the rebels in each suffer the same fate, that is, being swallowed by the earth; not only is this highly unlikely, especially since Coats acknowledges that the two narratives are independent of each other, but it overlooks the centrality of the prophetic test of Moses in the nonpriestly story and the cultic setting in the priestly narrative.

24. This was already observed by ibn Ezra (on Num 16:35), who acknowledged that, contrary to the plain statement of the text, Korah was not with Dathan and Abiram when they died but was offering incense at the Tabernacle. The phrase originally would have read "all their people," that is, Dathan's and Abiram's (see Milgrom, *Numbers*, 416; Knohl, *Sanctuary*, 78–79). That "all Korah's people" cannot have been the redactional insertion here (as posited by many) is evident from the contradiction such an insertion would create with v. 35, in which Korah's band perishes in the fire. Although the compiler does leave contradictions in the text, there is no reason to believe that he would have created them unnecessarily. Though some commentators suggest that the entire phrase, through "and all their possessions," is also redactional (see Carpenter and Harford-Battersby, *Hexateuch*, 2:215; Gray, *Numbers*, 207; Scharbert, *Numeri*, 69; Friedman, *Sources Revealed*, 270), this seems unnecessary; although the term $r^e k\hat{u}\check{s}$ is frequently used in P (cf. Gen 12:5; 13:6; 31:18; 36:7; 46:6; Num 35:3), it is not unique to that source (cf. Gen 14:11, 12, 16, 21; 15:14). Addis, *Documents*, 2:410, conjectures that this phrase originally belonged at the end of v. 35.

25. Although Korah is not explicitly mentioned in v. 35, it is clear that he is to be understood as having been burned with the rest of his company: in the subsequent chapter, which in fact continues the priestly narrative from Num 16, we read in Num 17:5 that Korah and his band had a single fate. The syntax of the Hebrew here (a disjunctive clause with the subject fronted) is not due to the compiler, as Friedman suggests (*Sources Revealed*, 270), but rather indicates the simultaneity of the people withdrawing and the fire going forth.

26. The rabbis of the Talmud attempted to solve this problem both ways: R. Joḥanan said that Korah was neither swallowed up nor burnt, while an anonymous Tanna said that Korah was both swallowed up and burnt (*b. Sanh.* 110a). The very existence of this

discussion illuminates the problem in the canonical text. Ibn Ezra (on Num 16:35) understood that only Dathan and Abiram were swallowed up by the earth, while Korah and his company were burned.

27. Some early commentators attempted to find two stories in the nonpriestly strand, one assigned to J and one to E. See Wellhausen, *Composition*, 103–4; Bacon, *Triple Tradition*, 193–95; Carpenter and Harford-Battersby, *Hexateuch*, 2:212–15; Baentsch, *Exodus-Leviticus-Numeri*, 543; Holzinger, *Numeri*, 67; Gray, *Numbers*, 190–91, 206–7; Procksch, *Elohimquelle*, 103; Brightman, *Sources*, 173; Gressmann, *Mose*, 251–52 n. 3. One of the main bases for this analysis seems to have been the mention of "On the son of Peleth" in v. 1; as we have seen, this is almost certainly a textual corruption. The other common rationale for finding J and E is the *minḥāʰ* in v. 15 (see above). The various attempts to isolate three stories in this chapter are part of the general trend in documentary scholarship already noted: the belief that every story must have been told by every source, even when the literary evidence to support such a claim is thin at best, and more frequently, as here, nonexistent. More recently, Levin (*Jahwist*, 377) has argued that the nonpriestly story has two stages of development: one in which Dathan and Abiram's complaint is simply the continuation of the nonpriestly story in Num 13–14, and a second in which their narrative-specific resistance is widened into a broader rebellion against Moses's leadership. There is no textual evidence for this.

28. This source division, at least in the separation of nonpriestly and priestly material, is, with minor variations noted above, agreed on by Kuenen, *Hexateuch*, 95, 154; Dillmann, *Numeri*, 88; Addis, *Documents*, 1:168–69, 2:408–10; Bacon, *Triple Tradition*, 190–95; Carpenter and Harford-Battersby, *Hexateuch*, 2:212–15; Gray, *Numbers*, 186–208; Holzinger, *Numeri*, 66; Smend, *Erzählung*, 200–5; Brightman, *Sources*, 173–74, 340–42; Simpson, *Early Traditions*, 237–42; Driver, *Introduction*, 63; Meyer, *Israeliten*, 99; Noth, *Numbers*, 120–29; Fritz, *Israel*, 24–26; Blum, *Studien*, 130 n. 119; Scharbert, *Numeri*, 65; Levine, *Numbers 1–20*, 405; Van Seters, *Life of Moses*, 239–44; Seebass, *Numeri*, 2:183–84.

29. Knohl's view (*Sanctuary*, 71–85) that all references to Levites in the P corpus are to be attributed to H—and that therefore elements of Num 16 and the entirety of Num 1:48–5:10 are H, not P—has been convincingly rejected by Milgrom (*Leviticus 17–22*, 1334–37).

30. See Addis, *Documents*, 2:410; Bacon, *Triple Tradition*, 192; Carpenter and Harford-Battersby, *Hexateuch*, 2:214; Gray, *Numbers*, 204; Gressmann, *Mose*, 251–52 n. 3; Rudolph, "*Elohist*," 81; Simpson, *Early Traditions*, 241; Driver, *Introduction*, 65; Milgrom, *Numbers*, 136. Blum, *Studien*, 266–67 n. 143, correctly sees this phrase as deriving from the process of redaction.

31. Ibn Ezra (on Num 16:24) attempts to conjoin the two narratives by placing the *miškān* of Korah and the tents of Dathan and Abiram near each other. His only means of doing so, however, is to claim (without any justification) that Korah had a separate tent for his household and wealth, one that was far from the regular camp of the Levites, that is, beside the Tent of Meeting, but in fact very near to the tents of Dathan and Abiram.

32. See Levine, *Numbers 1–20*, 415–16.

33. See Rashi, on Num 16:6. As in the story of Nadab and Abihu, the ritual procedure itself is not the issue: offering incense in fire pans is a legitimate cultic act. It is, rather, the question of who offers and under what circumstances that provides the rationale for the fiery destruction of both Aaron's sons and Korah and his band. See Haran, *Temples*, 232–33.

34. Blum, *Studien*, 267.

35. Contra Noth, *Pentateuchal Traditions*, 15, 125, who claims that the Dathan-Abiram story is preserved only in fragments.

36. See Magonet, "Korah Rebellion," 15.

37. The connection between Num 16:27b and Exod 33:8 already noted lends further support to the identification of the nonpriestly strand in Num 16 as E.

38. See Baden, *Redaction*, 183.

39. Some terminology typical of E is found in Num 16: "fields and vineyards," v. 14 (cf. Exod 22:4; Num 20:17; 21:22).

40. Van Seters, *Life of Moses*, 239–44.

41. Levine, *Numbers 1–20*, 427.

42. Milgrom, "Korah's Rebellion."

43. Kratz, *Composition*, 107.

44. Blum, *Studien*, 265–66. In this analysis he follows very closely on those of Kuenen, "Bijdragen"; Smend, *Erzählung*, 201–4; and Ahuis, *Autorität* (though Blum swiftly and correctly dismisses Ahuis's assignment of the final Korah redactional layer to a deuteronomistic hand). A similar analysis, at least of the priestly material, is undertaken by Albertz, *History*, 2:633 n. 143; Levin, *Jahwist*, 377; Knohl, *Sanctuary*, 73–79; Achenbach, *Vollendung*, 66–82; Levin, however, like Kratz, sees both priestly layers as redactional additions to the nonpriestly story, with the first one still taking Dathan and Abiram (along with On and the 250 leaders) as the instigators. Blum's analysis is essentially reversed by Schorn, "Rubeniten," who posits that the Dathan-Abiram story was written and inserted by the final editor as a supplement to the already combined priestly text; it may be observed that even the possibility that such a theory could be argued suggests that neither version of the supplementary model is firmly grounded in the text. Even more complicated solutions have been proposed, but they are only more improbable; see de Vaulx, *Nombres*, 189–93; and especially Lehming, "Versuch."

45. This is, in fact, nearly precisely the argument of Schmidt (*Priesterschrift*, 135–46, esp. 146), who even agrees almost entirely with the division of the two priestly layers proposed by Blum; see also Baentsch, *Exodus-Leviticus-Numeri*, 539–44; Holzinger, *Numeri*, 66; Fritz, *Israel*, 25–26.

CHAPTER 5. COMPLETENESS

1. See the bibliography in Nicholson, *Pentateuch*, 197 n. 1.

2. Cross, *Canaanite Myth*, 293–325; Van Seters, *Abraham*, 279–95; Rendtorff, *Problem*, 136–70. See the bibliographies in Nicholson, *Pentateuch*, 198 n. 2; Lemmelijn, "'Priestly' Layer," 485–86 n. 13; de Pury, "P^g," 105 n. 20; and the extended discussions

in Emerton, "Priestly Writer," 382–84; Vervenne, "'P' Tradition," 67–76 ; Campbell, "Priestly Text," 35–45; Lemmelijn, "'Priestly' Layer," 486–92.

3. See Lohfink, "Priestly Narrative," 146–47 n. 31; Schmidt, *Priesterschrift,* 1–206; Nicholson, *Pentateuch,* 196–221; Schwartz, "Priestly Account," 106–110; and see the bibliographies in Nicholson, *Pentateuch,* 198 n. 3; de Pury, "Pᵍ," 105 n. 20.

4. See Schmidt, *Old Testament Introduction,* 93.

5. Emerton, "Priestly Writer," 392–93.

6. See Firmage, "Genesis 1."

7. On the way in which P can be read through the lens of this initial blessing, see Brueggemann, "Kerygma."

8. P refers laconically to the destruction of the cities of the plain, in little more than a notation, but as this story was well known in ancient Israel (cf. Isa 13:19; Jer 49:18; 50:40; Amos 4:11; Lam 4:6), it was important to include at least a brief reference to it; this reference further establishes Abraham's place in the proper part of the land.

9. The centrality of Gen 17 for the rest of P, particularly for the key passages of Exod 6:2–8 and 29:45–46, has been demonstrated in detail by Schmid, *Erzväter,* 257–64.

10. See von Rad, "Promised Land," 90.

11. In a culture in which common agricultural property and hereditary landholdings were distinct, the burial plot was one of the foremost markers of private, permanent possession. See von Rad, "Promised Land," 85; Stager, "Archaeology," 23; van der Toorn, *Family Religion,* 199.

12. Brueggemann, "Kerygma," 102.

13. See Elliger, "Sinn," 124: "The presentation pauses nowhere except to highlight the great promise" (translation mine). [Nirgendwo hält sich die Darstellung auf, es sei denn, um die große Verheißung ins Licht zu rücken.]

14. See Driver, *Introduction,* 12: "These passages present an outline of the antecedents and patriarchal history of Israel, in which only important occurrences . . . are described with minuteness, but which is sufficient as an introduction to the systematic view of the theocratic institutions which is to follow in Ex.-Nu., and which it is the main object of the author of this source to exhibit." So too Carpenter and Harford-Battersby, *Hexateuch,* 1:123: "The 'fathers' have thus become ideal types, of whom nothing must be related that does not become the dignity of progenitors of a race which God will hereafter summon to be holy like himself."

15. Zimmerli, "Sinaibund," 276 (translation mine): "Was in der Mosezeit geschieht, ist auch in seinem innersten, in der Weise der Verbundenheit Jahwes mit seinem Volk, lediglich Einlösung des schon Abraham Verheißenen."

16. That Exod 1:1–5, 7, 13–14; 2:23aβ–25; 6:2–8 are literarily continuous is recognized by Blum, *Studien,* 240–42.

17. Thus the opinion of Kratz (*Composition,* 242), that "the plagues are not among the leading theological texts" in P, is to be rejected; as Kratz himself observes, "the first aim is . . . to demonstrate the power of Yhwh before and in Egypt." This is certainly theological.

18. See Elliger, "Sinn," 138: "Opposition can, indeed, should, according to God's intention—Pᵍ dares to put forth this paradoxical consequence of his belief in God—

serve only to demonstrate God's absolute superiority, to show that he is Yahweh" (translation mine). [Widerstand kann, ja soll nach Gottes Absicht—diese paradoxe Konsequenz wagt P^g aus seinem Gottesglauben zu ziehen—nur dazu dienen, Gottes absolute Überlegenheit zu demonstrieren, zu zeigen, daß er Jahwe ist.]

19. See de Pury, "P^g," 111: "Within Elohim's nations of the earth, Israel has one mission only: to establish and keep the dwelling that will allow Yhwh (i.e. Elohim in his ultimate identity) to reside among humanity in the midst of the Israelites." The argument that Yahweh does not literally dwell in the Tabernacle in the priestly conception (see Ackroyd, *Exile*, 100; Fohrer, *Introduction*, 184–5; Cross, *Canaanite Myth*, 299) is groundless and is contradicted by P's own explicit statements: Exod 29:45 and 40:34–38, and the very many references to cultic practices carried out "before Yahweh" (see chapter 3).

20. See Mowinckel, *Erwägungen*, 25: "What P wanted, with his combined history and ritual-law work, was to write the prehistory and early history of the covenant people from creation through the final installation in the land of the patriarchs, with its center in the foundation of the covenant and the law-giving at Sinai. . . . He wants to tell how the valid divine instructions were instituted, and only this" (translation mine). [Was P mit seinem kombinierten Geschichts-und Ritualgesetzwerke gewollt hat, ist, die Vor-und Frühgeschichte des Bundesvolkes von der Schöpfung bis zur endlichen Installierung in dem Lande der Väter, mit ihrem Zentrum in der Bundesstiftung und Gesetzgebung am Sinai, zu schreiben. . . . Wie die geltenden göttlichen Ordnungen instituiert worden sind, will er erzählen, und nur das.]

21. Brightman, *Sources*, 205. See also Dillmann, *Genesis*, 1:7–8; Carpenter and Harford-Battersby, *Hexateuch*, 1:122.

22. Damrosch, *Narrative Covenant*, 262. See also Mowinckel, *Erwägungen*, 21.

23. On the interaction of ritual and history in P, see Gorman, "Priestly Rituals," 64: "For the Priestly traditions, the world is founded in and through ritual. At the same time, these ritual acts of founding are related to the Priestly understanding of history. Cosmos, history, and ritual converge in Priestly theology."

24. Fohrer, *Introduction*, 183. See also Addis, *Documents*, 1:lxvi; Gunkel, *Genesis*, lxxxii; Pfeiffer, *Introduction*, 190: "The purely historical sections, the strictly legal parts, and the stories which purport to have the validity of legal precedents . . . have the same purpose and point of view."

25. Even if it is conjectured that some parts of the priestly legislation were once independent, such as Lev 1–7 (see, for example, Kuenen, *Hexateuch*, 81–82), this does not speak against the systematic unity of the whole: these independent pieces, if such they are, were set into the priestly work by a priestly author at precisely the appropriate place. See Nihan, *Priestly Torah*.

26. This episode is out of place in the canonical text, where it appears before the Israelites have left Sinai; numerous indicators in the passage, however, make very clear that it has been moved by the compiler from later in the original priestly narrative, somewhere after Num 13–14 but before Num 20. Whether it originally stood before or after the rebellion of Korah in Num 16–17 is difficult to judge. See Baden, "Original Place."

27. See Elliger, "Sinn," 138: "God masterfully ignores all human inadequacy and sin and does not discard his plan to give the land of Canaan to Israel. If it is not this generation that enters, then the next" (translation mine). [Im übrigen setzt Gott sich souverän über ale menschliche Unzulänglichkeit und Sünde hinweg und stößt seinen Plan nicht um, Israel das Land Kanaan zu geben. Ist's nicht diese Generation, die hinein- kommt, dann die nächste.]

28. The unique style of P has been treated most fully and respectfully by Paran, *Forms*.

29. See McEvenue, *Narrative Style*, 182: "Action is replaced by idea, dialogue by dis- course, suspense by symmetry, aspects of personal interiority and psychological inter- change are simply eliminated, dramatic values give way to rhetorical ones." Hendel, "Tangled Plots," 48–49, has aptly termed P's narrative "meta-historical": "P's intertex- tuality . . . serves to structure the plot above or outside the ordinary relations of time, relating a serialized divinen consonance of creation."

30. See McEvenue, *Narrative Style*, 185; Carr, *Fractures*, 128. The pattern of command and fulfillment extends even to the precise words P uses for the individual actions within the stories; see Elliger, "Sinn," 129–30.

31. See Addis, *Documents*, 1:lxvi–viii.

32. Schwartz, "Priestly Account," 117. The only texts in P that appear to be "out of se- quence" are those that have been moved by the compiler (Gen 19:29; 35:22b–26 [see chapter 6 and case study V]; Exod 16).

33. See Lohfink, "Priestly Narrative," 142–43.

34. Campbell, "Priestly Text," 35.

35. The priestly episode of the covenant with Abraham in fact includes material beyond Gen 17 proper; Gen 16:1, 3, 15 provide the necessary introduction to the covenant, as these verses establish Sarah's inability to bear children and the birth of Ishmael to Hagar, and Gen 21:2–5 are in turn the fulfillment of God's promise to Abraham regarding the birth of Isaac. When read without the intervening nonpriestly material, it is clear that these sections are all continuous and all participate in the story of God's covenant with Abraham. The claim of Carr, *Fractures*, 117, that a priestly redactor placed the covenant with Abraham after the birth of Ishmael for theological reasons apparently disregards the fact that within P itself, even as identified by Carr (ibid., 111), the birth of Ishmael already precedes the covenant of Gen 17.

36. On the importance of these uniquely P plagues for the question of P's independence, see Blum, *Studien*, 250.

37. See Schmidt, *Old Testament Introduction*, 95.

38. Blum, *Studien*, 229–85 (so too Childs, *Introduction*, 123; Rofé, *Introduction*, 40–41; Ska, *Introduction*, 147). Note the title of Blum's section: "The priestly layer: Neither 'source' nor 'redaction'" [Weder "Quelle" noch "Redaktion"]. Throughout his analy- sis, Blum's exposition of the ways in which the priestly layer is internally coherent and self-dependent is far more convincing than his arguments for P's interaction with the nonpriestly materials. In the latter cases, Blum brings a variety of subjective and largely ad hoc interpretations of the purpose of P in light of non-P. For the revelation of the name Yahweh in Exod 3 and 6, Blum suggests that the priestly version, although

it is clearly written as if this were the first such revelation, provides an interpretive key for the reader, a guide to understanding, according to P, what actually happened in Exod 3 (ibid., 234–35). The episode of Moses getting water from the rock in Num 20, Blum argues, may be a priestly "midrash" on Deut 33:8 (ibid., 276–77; it is, however, unclear why the priestly author would expand a saying about how the Levites came to achieve their special status into a tale of how Aaron, the priestly progenitor, came to deserve his premature death in the wilderness). In this story Blum also sees an intentional framing of the Sinai pericope, with the nonpriestly story of Moses getting water from the rock set before and the priestly version set after (ibid., 278). Yet this "framing" happens only with this story, and not with others, and hardly provides an explanation for why the priestly version occurs so far in time and space from the nonpriestly.

39. It has long been recognized that 19:29 originally stood in P directly after 13:12bα. It has been displaced by the compiler because the destruction of Sodom and Gomorrah in J does not occur until chapter 19. So already Bacon, *Genesis*, 135.

40. On the displacement of these verses, see case study V.

41. It is likely that the notice of Joseph's descent in P is to be found in 39:1a, "Joseph was taken down into Egypt." Although this clause as currently found certainly belongs to J, this is probably a place where both J and P had virtually identical sentences, and the compiler rendered them only once in the canonical text (Schwartz, "Joseph's Descent," 19).

42. On the assignment of Gen 26:13–15, 18 to P, see Baden, *Redaction*, 217–18.

43. Blum, *Vätergeschichte*, 427.

44. Van Seters, *Abraham*, 285.

45. Cross, *Canaanite Myth*, 294. See also ibid., 305: "If one examines the Priestly material in Genesis, he is soon struck by the paucity of narrative . . . it is at best epitomized history." As Emerton ("Priestly Writer," 392) observes, "P is indeed different from 'the narrative of saga,' but it need not be assumed that the author intended to write saga."

46. Koch, "P," 454 (translation mine): "beruht . . . auf indirekten, abstrakten Überlegungen zur Gattund erzählender hebräischer Werke und zur Unentbehrlichkeit bestimmter Themen bei einem israelitischen Rekurs auf die frühe Volksgeschichte. . . . Die Befremdung über unterschiedliche Stoffdichte und einen vorgeblich lückenhaften Zusammenhang schliesslich entspringt einem Geschmacksurteil, daß notwendig modernen Gefühl entspricht und sich schwer objektivieren läesst."

47. Emerton, "Priestly Writer," 392.

48. Eissfeldt, *Old Testament*, 205.

49. Koch, "P," 455 (translation mine): "Kein vorgängiges Gattungspostulat abgeleitet werden, das . . . schon festsetzt, was ein entsprechendes hebräisches Buch enthalten kann und was nicht."

50. Cross, *Canaanite Myth*, 306–7, 317–18.

51. Ibid., 306, 318, 307.

52. Ibid., 318–20.

53. Rendtorff, *Problem*, 138–53.

54. Ibid., 141–42, 144–45, 149–50, 151–52.

55. Ibid., 142–44.

56. Ibid., 156. See also Kratz, *Composition*, 239. This opinion has been rebutted by Emerton, "Priestly Writer," 388–90.

57. Rendtorff, *Problem*, 137. See also his attacks on the circular reasoning of other scholars (ibid., 138–39).

58. Ibid., 157. See also Pfeiffer, *Introduction*, 207; Blum, *Studien*, 231; Ska, *Introduction*, 147. For a brief rebuttal, see Kratz, *Composition*, 241.

59. Blum, *Studien*, 231, unsurprisingly removes Exod 6:14–30 from the priestly text, attributing this section to a yet later secondary insertion.

60. Ska, *Introduction*, 146. See also Carr, *Fractures*, 119–20: "One must once again be careful not to presuppose that certain things would be in P because they occur in non-P texts."

61. As argued by Ska, *Introduction*, 147.

62. The similar gaps in both P and non-P also speak against Noth's theory (*Pentateuchal Traditions*, 13–14) that the P-oriented redactor regularly suppressed elements of the nonpriestly text in favor of those from P. See Dillmann, *Genesis*, 1:20.

63. That P presents the revelation of the divine name in Exod 6 as if it were the first such revelation is admitted even by Blum, *Studien*, 234. See also Kratz, *Composition*, 241: "The revelation of the name of Yhwh makes sense only in the framework of an independent Priestly Writing."

64. See Blenkinsopp, "Structure"; Kearney, "Creation."

65. See Blum, *Studien*, 238.

66. See Kuenen, *Hexateuch*, 302: "However far we suppose R's activity to have extended we can never make it probable or even conceivable that he enriched the narrative of JE in Gen i.–Ex.vi. with statements and details unconnected with or even contradicting it, simply out of his own head and without the documents supplying the smallest occasion for it." The argument that the priestly theology does not in fact contradict that of non-P, but that a priestly editor would have readily taken up the nonpriestly materials into his final work (so Amit, *History and Ideology*, 77–80), is based on a canonical reading in which the priestly and nonpriestly elements are already set beside each other and ignores the blatant discrepancies in historical claims between the two corpora.

67. See Cross, *Canaanite Myth*, 301–5, 308–17. On the *toledot* in particular, see Tengström, *Die Toledotformel*.

68. See Eissfeldt, *Old Testament*, 205–6; Driver, *Introduction*, 12; Lohfink, "Priestly Narrative," 151 n. 38.

69. On the structure of P, see especially Blenkinsopp, "Structure."

70. The ostensible inconsistency in the precise use of the *toledot* formulae—sometimes superscriptions, sometimes subscriptions, sometimes referring to genealogies, sometimes to narratives—has led some scholars to claim that some *toledot* formulae are original to P and some belong to a redactional layer. The requirement that the priestly author use the *toledot* formula in the same way every time is an unnecessary scholarly imposition on the literary freedom of the ancient author; why the phrase could not be used for a range of purposes is unclear. At the same time, even if some of the *toledot*

are original and some secondary, they provide no evidence for a priestly redaction; see Koch, "P," 452–53; Emerton, "Priestly Writer," 394–96.

71. See Blenkinsopp, "Structure," 280–82.

72. The theory of Noth (*Pentateuchal Traditions*, 12) that P provided the framework into which the nonpriestly sources were placed is therefore not entirely inaccurate: the priestly text does supply something of a framework for the canonical whole, but only insofar as P contains the framing devices that the compiler necessarily took up in the final text. See Schmidt, *Old Testament Introduction*, 96: "Precisely because P was often so schematic, it made sense to fill it out by fitting the older texts into it"; we might adjust this statement by changing the phrase "it made sense" to "there was no choice other than."

73. We may also note the possibility that the *toledot* of Jacob is intended to cover not only the life of Jacob himself, but of all of his descendants, that is, the entire people of Israel into Exodus and beyond. See Lohfink, "Priestly Narrative," 151 n. 38; Schmid, *Erzväter*, 265. If this is the case, then the ostensible lack of agreement between the heading of Gen 37:2 and the canonical Joseph story is eliminated; it does not, however, imply therefore that the heading is redactional, as it still fits well within P by itself.

74. The claim that the covenant of Gen 17 is to be considered redactional because it provides the interpretive key for the entire Abraham story (so Ska, "Quelques remarques," 114–15) is subjective and methodologically difficult: just because a text can serve as the lens through which one reads other passages does not mean that it was written to be so. One may find numerous examples of such key passages in the nonpriestly material without much effort: for example, the "fall of man" in Gen 3, the promise to Abraham in Gen 12:1–3, and the Decalogue in Exod 20. Ska's reading is essentially canonical.

75. See Gilders, "Sacrifice."

76. Ibid., 69.

77. See Knohl, *Sanctuary*; Milgrom, *Leviticus 17–22*, 1319–64, and the scholarship cited therein.

78. See the recent volume dedicated to this topic: Shectman and Baden, eds., *Strata*.

79. This is clearly seen in the claim that a redactor from the Holiness school is responsible for the redaction of the canonical Pentateuch (so Knohl, *Sanctuary*, 101–3; Milgrom, "H_R"): although there may be H passages outside of Lev 17–26 (though undoubtedly far fewer than Knohl asserts; see Blum, "Issues and Problems," 33–34), they are supplements and revisions only to P texts.

80. We may note the important arguments of Stackert, *Rewriting*, regarding the use of both the Covenant Code and Deuteronomy by the authors of H. If Stackert's conclusions are accepted, then H would indeed revise the nonpriestly text. However, Stackert argues, convincingly, that H was intended not to supplement the nonpriestly laws, but to replace them—the literary corpus that H supplements, in fact, even in its interaction with the nonpriestly legislation, is P.

81. See the comprehensive monograph of Nihan, *Priestly Torah*, which argues for a successive growth of priestly strata in Leviticus, only the last stage of which can properly

be called P, and only the last stage of which was the document taken up into the Pentateuch as a whole.

82. See the general state of the field expressed by de Pury and Römer, "Le Pentateuque en question," 71: "Everyone recognizes that P knows and reinterprets the prepriestly texts" (translation mine). [Tout le monde reconnaît que P connaît et réinterprète les textes présacerdotaux.] This statement is true over a wide range of scholarly approaches and eras; see, for example, Kuenen, *Hexateuch*, 299; Wellhausen, *Prolegomena*, 336; Brightman, *Sources*, 211; Mowinckel, *Erwägungen*, 26–34; Fohrer, *Introduction*, 181; McEvenue, *Narrative Style*, passim; Friedman, "Torah (Pentateuch)," 616; Schmidt, *Priesterschrift*, 1–206; Carr, *Fractures*, 114, 127–29; Gertz, *Exoduserzählung*, 390–91; Kratz, *Composition*, 244–45; Halpern, "Historiography," 105–8. The rare but crucial rebuttal of this claim has been made by Schwartz, "Priestly Account," 121–30, and *Holiness Legislation*, 12 and passim.

83. See McEvenue, *Narrative Style*, 24–36; Friedman, "Torah (Pentateuch)," 616; Schmidt, *Old Testament Introduction*, 94–95. See the rebuttal of this view in Baden, *Redaction*, 200–1.

84. The argument that the nonpriestly flood story is in fact later than that of P has in fact been made; see Blenkinsopp, *Pentateuch*, 78–87; Ska, "Flood"; de Pury, "P^g," 114: "There are a number of features in [the nonpriestly flood story]—e.g. the extension of the number of couples required for pure animals (Gen 7,2–3)—that clearly wish to correct what he [the nonpriestly author] perceived as an error in the P^g narrative." Similarly, it has been argued that Gen 2–3 is a later supplement to Gen 1; see Otto, "Paradieserzählung"; de Pury, "P^g," 114–15. There is a small trend of scholars returning almost entirely to the classical Supplementary Hypothesis, arguing that P is the original literary work throughout Genesis, while all of the nonpriestly material is added secondarily (so de Pury, "P^g"; Blenkinsopp, *Pentateuch*, 93, and "P and J"). Along the same lines, Wenham ("Priority") argues that P was one of the sources J used in creating Genesis. That such arguments can be made on the basis of the very same texts serves to indicate the lack of literary evidence for the relative dating of the sources.

85. See Friedman, "Torah (Pentateuch)," 616.

86. Wellhausen, *Prolegomena*, 336; Noth *Pentateuchal Traditions*, 12; Lohfink, "Priestly Narrative," 147–48 n. 32; Kohata, *Jahwist*, 75; Friedman, "Torah (Pentateuch)," 616; Gertz, *Exoduserzählung*, 390–91.

87. We may also include in the list of traditions unique to P the detailed lists of people and places, in genealogies and itineraries, throughout the Pentateuch. As Mowinckel (*Erwägungen*, 38–42) has noted, these elements must derive from some source other than the extant nonpriestly narratives.

88. Individual words or brief phrases held in common between P and non-P hardly qualify as evidence of dependence. Thus the use of the word *mabbûl*, "flood," in both P and J (see McEvenue, *Narrative Style*, 26; Carr, *Fractures*, 60; see also the discussion of this in Baden, *Redaction*, 200–1) or "Tent of Meeting" in both P and E (see Cross, *Canaanite Myth*, 300).

89. See Baden, *Redaction*, 197–207.

90. See Friedman, "Torah (Pentateuch)," 616.
91. See Gunkel, *Genesis*, lxxxii–lxxxiii; Friedman, "Torah (Pentateuch)," 616; Schmidt, *Old Testament Introduction*, 95.
92. See Friedman, "Torah (Pentateuch)," 616.
93. de Pury, "Pᵍ," 102.
94. Schwartz, "Priestly Account," 122.

CASE STUDY IV. THE ISRAELITES AT THE SEA, EXODUS 14

1. At no point in this chapter is the sea referred to explicitly as the "Sea of Reeds" (Hebrew *yam sûp*).
2. Pharaoh's statement in v. 3 is commonly seen as a reflection of his intentions to pursue the Israelites, that is, because they are now vulnerable, being lost in the wilderness (see Rashi, on Exod 14:3, and most commentators since). Such a reading does not take into account, however, the need for Yahweh to further harden Pharaoh's heart in v. 4. The divine instruction to the Israelites in v. 2 to encamp before the sea is similarly intended not so much as a temptation for Pharaoh (as argued by Rashi and ibn Ezra, on Exod 14:2) but rather as a necessary mechanism by which Yahweh ensures the destruction of the Egyptians, by forcing the action to take place at the sea.
3. The interpretation of Adele Berlin (*Poetics*, 66), in which v. 5 represents the interior monologue of Pharaoh and his servants, corresponding to the narrated description in vv. 4 and 8, does not account for the chronological problem of Pharaoh changing his own heart before Yahweh hardens it; see below.
4. In Jubilees, Pharaoh is pushed to go after the Israelites not by God, but by Mastema (Jub 48:9–12, 17). Josephus, in his recounting of these events (*Ant.* II.320), does not mention the motif of God hardening Pharaoh's heart, thereby removing this problem. The classical rabbinic commentary on Exodus, the *Mekhilta de-Rabbi Ishmael* (Beshallah 2), suggests that despite his preparations (vv. 6–7) Pharaoh was not entirely convinced that he wanted to pursue the Israelites until God hardened his heart (Rashi, on 14:8, follows this reading).
5. In Philo (*Moses*, 1.173), these dialogues happen simultaneously: Moses communicates orally with the people and mentally with the deity (so also Augustine, *Quaestionum*, 94 [question 52]). The tension between the two cries of the people was also felt by Abarbanel (on Exod 14:10). See Ska, *Introduction*, 69, who also points out that in Moses's address to the people, he tells them to stand still (v. 13), while Yahweh's first instruction to Moses is to have the people move (v. 15).
6. See Bacon, *Triple Tradition*, 72; Ska, *Introduction*, 70. Nahmanides (on Exod 14:21) explains that the wind was a ruse to make the Egyptians think that the splitting of the sea was a natural occurrence rather than a miracle (and thus incite them to enter the waters); he states plainly that a wind could not split the sea into two parts. In Josephus's recounting Moses strikes the sea with his staff to make it split (*Ant.* II.338–39), but when the waters return Moses's actions go unmentioned, and the sea returns of its own accord (II.343–44). Pseudo-Philo has God command both Moses and the sea

(*Bib. Ant.*, 10:5–6). Abarbanel (on Exod 14:21) correctly wonders at the dual agents of the splitting of the sea, Moses's arm and the east wind. According to Calvin (*Commentaries on the Four*, 1:249–50), the conflation of images in v. 21 is due to Moses (as author) not wishing to take credit for God's action: even though he had been commanded to use his staff, he nevertheless states that it was God who, by virtue of the wind, split the sea. Sarna (*Exodus*, 73) concludes that Moses's gesture is the signal for the wind to commence. A similar view seems to be argued by Houtman (*Exodus*, 2:228). A modern opponent of source criticism, M. H. Segal, wonders "how could the Israelites and their Egyptian pursuers walk into the divided sea if a space had not been dried up by some such agent as the east wind?" (*Pentateuch*, 38). He further directs our attention to the double mention of Moses's hand and the east wind in the plague of locusts, Exod 10:13 as a proof for his claim of textual unity and Mosaic authorship; the critical view, of course, is that 10:13 is also divided between J and P, along precisely these lines. Similarly, Cassuto (*Exodus*, 167–68), despite denying that he is rationalizing the biblical text, argues for the rare confluence of natural phenomena: "an exceptionally low tide" and "the east wind blowing violently all night," which would "have dried up the little water left in the narrow channel of the lake." The biblical miracle, he claims, is that these phenomena occurred at precisely the necessary moment. See also in this vein Keil and Delitzsch, *Commentary*, 350–51. Fischer ("Exodus 1–15," 170–71) argues that the miracle of the parting of the sea is no different from the miracles that precede it in the narrative—the burning bush, Moses's staff, his leprous hand, and the plagues—and, on this basis, denies the source-critical division of v. 21 (and the rest of the chapter as well). In making this claim, however, he ignores, intentionally or not, the crucial doublet of Moses's hand and God's wind in the verse.

7. Pseudo-Philo is forced to deny this explicitly, stating that God prevented the Egyptians from recognizing that they were walking through the sea (*Bib. Ant.*, 10:6).

8. See Bacon, *Triple Tradition*, 71–72: "Did Moses stretch out his hand with the rod over the sea on the evening before, and nothing happen for several hours?" Josephus explains the delay as being due to the exhaustion of the Egyptians (*Ant.* II.334), an explanation nowhere in evidence in the biblical text. Ibn Ezra (on Exod 14:19) reads the verbs in vv. 19–20 in the pluperfect in order to make sense of the narrative, despite the fact that they are *wayyiqtol* forms.

9. Cassuto claims, somewhat remarkably, that the pillar of fire and cloud in this verse is not the same pillar of fire and cloud from vv. 19–20, but is rather a description of a hurricane (*Exodus*, 169).

10. Philo rearranges the narrative in order to make sense of these various details (*Moses*, I.176–79), but his reconstruction is not a considerable improvement. According to Philo, first the wind blew back the waters, then the cloud made it difficult to see at night, then Moses struck the sea and divided the waters, then the cloud moved behind the Israelite camp to prevent the Egyptians from approaching, then the tide rolled back, then the sea came back together. Artapanus combines the two motifs into a two-pronged destruction: the waters rushed in on the Egyptians, and fire came forth from the cloud to consume them (3:37; trans. John J. Collins; in Charlesworth, ed., *Pseudepigrapha*, 2:889–903). See similarly Rashi, on Exod 14:24–25.

11. Jubilees tries to have it both ways (48:13–17): the Israelites walk through the midst of the sea, but the Egyptians are never said to actually follow them through that path; God simply throws them into the sea. *Mek.* Beshallaḥ 7 interprets the Hebrew of v. 27 (*liqra'tô*) almost metaphorically, suggesting that whatever direction the Egyptians fled, the water would rush upon them (see also *b. Soṭah* 11a; Rashi, Rashbam, and ibn Ezra, on Exod 14:27).

12. Note the structure of God's speech, marked by the precise use of verbal forms. From the initial encampment of the Israelites facing the sea (v. 2), everything follows successively, as marked by the use of the *weqatal* form: Pharaoh will respond to the movement of the Israelites; God will act in response to Pharaoh; and Pharaoh will act again, this time in (unwilling) response to God (vv. 3–4aα[1] [*wᵊrādap 'aḥᵃrêhem*]). These actions occur for the express purpose that God will gain glory through Pharaoh and the Egyptians (v. 4aα[2] [*wᵊ'ikkābdā*ʰ]-β); the purpose is marked in this case by the abandonment of the *weqatal* form in favor of the resumption of the volitive (here the cohortative), continuing from the imperative and jussives of v. 2.

13. The attempt by some early scholars to remove v. 3 from P, on the grounds that it is overly "psychological," ignores the necessity of this verse as the antecedent to the hardening of Pharaoh's heart (as argued above); for this claim see Bacon, *Triple Tradition*, 76; Baentsch, *Exodus-Leviticus-Numeri*, 121; Smend, *Erzählung*, 139; Gressmann, *Mose*, 108–9 n. 1; Simpson, *Early Traditions*, 182; Childs, *Exodus*, 220; and more recently, and on different grounds, Levin, "Source Criticism," 45.

   The argument of Weimar, *Meerwundererzählung*, 39 n. 42, that v. 2b does not belong to the original priestly layer depends on the switch from the third person in v. 2a to the second person in v. 2b (he is followed by Schmidt, *Priesterschrift*, 19–22; Krüger, "Erwägungen," 531; Gertz, *Exoduserzählung*, 199–200). There are two problems with this analysis. First, it is unclear why such a switch is naturally or necessarily attributable to a redactor rather than an author; why would the redactor choose to add these words, and with this difference? Second, this type of change is a well-known feature of the priestly author's style; see Paran, *Forms*, 71–73. Schmidt pursues this overly fine analysis throughout his discussion of the priestly source in Exod 14; further examples occur in his dissection of vv. 9, 16, and 26. Similar analyses were common in earlier scholarship, with the typical tendency of that era to find reasons for separation, rather than connection, whenever possible, especially on minute stylistic and terminological grounds; see Simpson, *Early Traditions*, 182–86, and Fuss (*Pentateuchredaktion*, 297–306), who attributes v. 2b to R[P], though in his view the redactor worked on the basis of the originally Elohistic (!) text of v. 2a (at 298–99).

   A forceful argument against the subdivision of vv. 1–4 is made by Noth, "Schauplatz," 182–83.

14. The assignment of vv. 1–4 to P is strongly supported by formal and stylistic features. The opening words of God's speech, *dabbēr 'el-bᵊnê yiśrā'ēl*, "Tell the Israelites," are a common feature of P — in fact, every other occurrence of this phrase in the Bible is from the priestly writings (see Exod 25:2; 31:13; Lev 1:2; 4:2; 7:23, 29; 12:2; 18:2; 23:2, 10, 24, 34; 25:2; 27:2; Num 5:6, 12; 6:2; 9:10; 15:2, 18, 38; 17:17; 19:2; 33:51; 35:10; Josh 20:2). Note also that the use of the imperative of "speak" or "say" or "command" followed

by the jussive, with the meaning "instruct [someone] to do *x*," is also typical of the priestly writer; see Exod 6:11; 25:2; 27:20; Lev 22:2; Num 5:2; 17:2; 19:2. See Paran, *Forms*, 93. The clause indicating the fulfillment of the command to the Israelites, *wayya'ăśû-kēn*, is also predominantly priestly (this is especially true in the preceding plagues narrative: see Exod 7:10, 20, 22; 8:3, 13, 14).

15. With Kohata, *Jahwist*, 93–126; contra Propp, *Exodus 1–18*, 286–92; Friedman, *Sources Revealed*, 130–42. Those scholars who saw three sources in the plagues narrative generally see three here as well, though, as in the preceding chapters of Exodus, the passages they attribute to E (usually parts or all of vv. 3, 7, 9, 10, 15, 16, 19, and 20) are fragmentary at best and should be reassigned to either J or P. See Addis, *Documents*, 1:127–29; Bacon, *Triple Tradition*, 66–78; Dillmann, *Exodus*, 144–68; Carpenter and Harford-Battersby, *Hexateuch*, 2:100–3; Baentsch, *Exodus*, 119–27; McNeile, *Exodus*, xix–xxi; Brightman, *Sources*, 152; Driver, *Exodus*, 114–22; Simpson, *Early Traditions*, 182–86; Noth, *Pentateuchal Traditions*, 25, and *Exodus*, 106; Fuss, *Pentateuchredaktion*, 297–326; Childs, *Exodus*, 220; Scharbert, "'Schilfmeerwunder,'" 398–99. The fundamental argument for only two sources in the plagues narrative is that of Greenberg, *Understanding Exodus*, 183–92 (esp. 185–86). Kohata (*Exodus 3–14*, 280 n. 19), despite finding no E in the plagues narrative, does attribute Exod 14:5a and 19a to E (so also Graupner, *Elohist*, 87–88). Similarly, although Friedman finds only one nonpriestly source in the plagues narrative (E, in his view), he also separates Exod 14 into three stories—though in his summary of the different accounts (*Sources Revealed*, 142), he mentions only the J and P versions. See the comment of Jenks (*Elohist*, 42): "In Exod 14 we cannot be at all certain that E narrative material forms part of the complex of traditions." The desire among scholars to find E in this chapter is to be attributed to the assumption that all the sources told essentially the same story, and that as a result there had to be an E account of the encounter at the sea. This assumption took precedence over both the lack of any substantive reason to divide the story into three sources and the lack of continuity or coherence in the proposed E narrative. Von Rabenau ("Die beiden Erzählungen," 7–12), recognizing this lack of coherence, describes many of these same passages as "glosses."

16. Virtually all scholars view v. 6 as the natural continuation of v. 5. Many claim, however, that the enumeration of Pharaoh's forces in v. 7 is redundant after the general statement of v. 6 and therefore derives from another hand; see Carpenter and Harford-Battersby, *Hexateuch*, 2:100; Baentsch, *Exodus*, 122; Gressmann, *Mose*, 108–9 n. 1; McNeile, *Exodus*, xix; Meyer, *Israeliten*, 20; Noth, *Exodus*, 106; Fuss, *Pentateuchredaktion*, 302–3; Weimar, *Meerwundererzählung*, 34–38; Propp, *Exodus 1–18*, 477–78; Gertz, *Exoduserzählung*, 215; Graupner, *Elohist*, 82. This is an example of the tendency toward unnecessary atomization, particularly in classical source-critical scholarship.

17. In addition, vv. 4b and 8, read in succession, serve as the fulfillment of God's command and speech in vv. 2–4a, thus strongly suggesting that the material in the intervening vv. 5–7 belongs to a different strand. See Baden, "Narrative Pattern."

18. See Driver, *Exodus*, 116; Van Seters, *Life of Moses*, 130.

19. See the direct reference to this in the priestly itinerary of the wilderness wandering, Num 33:3.

20. See Blum, *Studien*, 256. The beginning of v. 9, "The Egyptians pursued them," basically a repetition of v. 8aβ, is probably best understood as a resumptive repetition following the brief parenthesis of v. 8b (see Cassuto, *Exodus*, 162; Propp, *Exodus 1–18*, 478). It is worth remembering that resumptive repetition is not, as is too often assumed uncritically, an automatic sign of interpolation; it is first and foremost an authorial technique used to set off digressions or parentheses, and it is borrowed from the realm of the authorial by later editors who thereby mark off the insertion of secondary material. For the assignment of part of v. 9 to the nonpriestly story, presumably on the basis of the ostensibly awkward resumption, see Addis, *Documents*, 1:128; Dillmann, *Exodus*, 162; Carpenter and Harford-Battersby, *Hexateuch*, 2:100; Simpson, *Early Traditions*, 182–83; Noth, *Exodus*, 105; Fuss, *Pentateuchredaktion*, 304; Childs, *Exodus*, 220; Friedman, *Sources Revealed*, 143. Driver (*Exodus*, 116) reads these words as a gloss, while Gertz (*Exoduserzählung*, 200–1, 215–16) correctly recognizes them as a resumptive repetition but believes them to stem from the hand of a late redactor, framing the late addition of v. 8b. Weimar (*Meerwundererzählung*, 39) sees v. 9b as a redactional insertion, as it depends on v. 2b (which he also considers redactional; see above).

21. As noted by Vervenne ("Protest Motif," 260), this is the only place in which the Israelites cry out to Yahweh and then turn to criticism of Moses.

22. In his highly detailed analysis of the literary structure of Exod 14, Auffret ("Ex 14," 58) observes a chiastic structure in vv. 10–14—a structure that takes into account every word of the verses except "the Israelites cried out to Yahweh." This is, however, the only place in his study that the source division seems to have had any effect on the literary analysis. In general, the ability of a literary critic to discern macro- or microliterary structures, such as chiasms, is not a positive argument for the unity of a text, and indeed Auffret makes no claims in that regard (so also Bachra, "Structural Regularities"). Cf. Baden, "Tower of Babel."

23. Note the similarity of the list of Egyptians in v. 18 to that in v. 9 (P), as opposed to that in vv. 6–7 (J). The verbal structure is also strikingly similar to that of God's initial speech in P in vv. 2–4, including the use of the construction "speak" + jussive (see above).

24. Vervenne ("Protest Motif") oddly concludes that the people's protest to Moses in vv. 11–12 should be connected with Yahweh's response to the cry in v. 15, while the people's cry to Yahweh in v. 10 should be connected with Moses's reassurances in vv. 13–14. This seems a complete reversal of the natural relationship of the elements, in terms of both content and verbal connection. More confusingly, Vervenne claims that vv. 11–12 are a proto-deuteronomic redactional insertion, as they do "not have a formal relation with what precedes" (ibid., 269; see the similar analysis of Weimar, *Meerwundererzählung*, 51–55). Yet they are the direct and natural response of the people to the threat of Pharaoh's approaching forces and are necessary for Moses's response in vv. 13–14, which itself provides the major theological theme for the entire J narrative.

25. Weimar (*Meerwundererzählung*, 31–32), Kohata (*Exodus 3–14*, 279), Gertz (*Exoduserzählung*, 201), and Friedman (*Sources Revealed*, 143), in assigning v. 10a to P, muddy this distinction.

26. The recurring attempt in scholarship to see the presence of the staff in this verse as a secondary insertion (on the grounds that it does not come up again in the narrative) is without merit (see Schmidt, *Priesterschrift*, 19–20; Krüger, "Erwägungen," 532; Gertz, *Exoduserzählung*, 198; Levin, "Miracle," 53–54). Indeed, no one who makes this claim has been able to provide any reasonable grounds on which this concept would be added into the story; ironically, it is the fact that the staff does not occur again in the narrative which makes it difficult to find a legitimate reason for its secondary inclusion.

27. Baden, "Narrative Pattern," 47–48.

28. The appearance of both the "messenger of God" and the pillar of cloud in the same verse has bothered numerous commentators and led to unnecessary splitting of this verse into multiple nonpriestly strands; see Dillmann, *Exodus*, 164–65; Carpenter and Harford-Battersby, *Hexateuch*, 2:101–2; Baentsch, *Exodus*, 124–25; Gressmann, *Mose*, 108–9 n. 1; McNeile, *Exodus*, xx; Driver, *Exodus*, 118–19; Simpson, *Early Traditions*, 184; Meyer, *Israeliten*, 21–22; Noth, *Exodus*, 114–15; Childs, *Exodus*, 220; Scharbert, "'Schilfmeerwunder,'" 398–99; Weimar, *Meerwundererzählung*, 46–51; Blum, *Studien*, 258; Propp, *Exodus 1–18*, 480; Gertz, *Exoduserzählung*, 218–20; Friedman, *Sources Revealed*, 143; Graupner, *Elohist*, 82. See, however, the cogent explanation of Abraham Kuenen (*Hexateuch*, 151): "But is not this account of the column of cloud and fire really the indispensable explanation of the statement about the 'angel of Elohîm' in *v.* 19a? What is the meaning of his changing his place from before to behind the camp of Israel, if not that the column placed itself between the two camps . . . ? If *v.* 19a had meant anything else some kind of explanation would at least have been indicated. 'The angel,' then, must be identified with 'the column.'" So also Van Seters, *Life of Moses*, 130.

29. See Ska, *Introduction*, 69; Levin, "Miracle," 50.

30. See the two possibilities (ebb tide and divine splitting of the sea) provided by Artapanus (3:35–36). Ibn Ezra's commentary on this passage (on Exod 14:27) includes a diatribe against an earlier commentator, Hiwi al-Balkhi, who evidently claimed that Israel had passed through during the low tide, while the Egyptians were destroyed by the incoming high tide.

31. See in addition the repetition in *v.* 23 of the description of the Egyptians—"Pharaoh, his chariots, and his horsemen"—from vv. 17 and 18. Note, however, that Weimar (*Meerwundererzählung*, 40–41 n. 47) and Gertz (*Exoduserzählung*, 198–99) remove precisely these words from all three verses, on the grounds that the text reads more smoothly without them and in order to create a closer parallel with v. 4. This analysis forces the P writer into a formal consistency evidently desired by scholars but not necessarily by the author himself.

32. The Egyptians may, according to this story, have realized that there was something unusual about the Israelites going in the midst of the sea, but because Yahweh was essentially forcing their actions by hardening Pharaoh's heart, they followed nonetheless. See Josephus, *Ant.*, II.340–42; Nahmanides, on Exod 14:21; Calvin, *Commentaries on the Four*, 1:247.

33. In fleeing, the Egyptians reveal again their control over their own will and actions as portrayed in the J story; in P the Egyptians have no chance to get away because they cannot even decide to flee.

34. See Cassuto, *Exodus*, 170; von Rabenau, "Schilfmeerwunder," 16; Ska, *Passage*, 79; Propp, *Exodus 1–18*, 481.

35. The argument of Carpenter and Harford-Battersby (*Hexateuch*, 2:102) that the end of v. 24 is somehow awkward in its context and therefore should be attributed to E is due in part to their desire to find more E in the chapter, in order to outline an at least plausible E story, and in part to their tendency to find doublets in any twofold description of a single event, even when the two descriptions are complementary rather than contradictory. Similar, perhaps, is the assignment of v. 25a to E by Addis, *Documents*, 1:129; Bacon, *Triple Tradition*, 78; Dillmann, *Exodus*, 167; Baentsch, *Exodus*, 126; Brightman, *Sources*, 152; Scharbert, "'Schilfmeerwunder,'" 399; Friedman, *Sources Revealed*, 144. Gertz (*Exoduserzählung*, 221) considers v. 25a a late redactional insertion.

36. See Blum, *Studien*, 256.

37. Kratz (*Composition*, 246–47, 324), who otherwise identifies P correctly, assigns the entirety of v. 27 to P, despite the numerous connections to the J narrative.

38. Some scholars attribute v. 28b to the nonpriestly story (see Addis, *Documents*, 1:129; Bacon, *Triple Tradition*, 78; Propp, *Exodus 1–18*, 481). It fits well into either at this point, however, and so it is simplest to assume that it belongs to the source in which it is embedded in the canonical text. Weimar (*Meerwundererzählung*, 59 n. 102) claims that the clause cannot be from P because without it vv. 28–29 form a closer parallel with vv. 22–23. It may also be noted that the closest equivalent examples of the phrase "not one of them remained" are found in the J plagues narrative (Exod 8:27; 10:10). These arguments are hardly probative; nevertheless, the assignment of v. 28b to the nonpriestly story remains possible, if not necessary.

39. The mention of the Egyptians dead "on the shore" also conforms best to the J story; since the Israelites have had no direct contact with the Egyptians, the sight of the destroyed enemy serves as the confirming indication that Yahweh has in fact delivered them as promised (see Noth, *Exodus*, 118; Kohata, *Exodus 3–14*, 283–84).

40. See Dillmann, *Exodus*, 167; Cassuto, *Exodus*, 172; Ska, *Passage*, 117–19; Mann, *Book of the Torah*, 92; Ska, *Introduction*, 74. We might, in this light, read the words "You hold your peace!" in v. 14 in the future tense: when Yahweh delivers you from the Egyptians, you will no longer complain in this manner (so Abarbanel on Exod 14:14). The thematic connection between 14:13–14 and 30–31 is seen also by Blum (*Studien*, 30–31), although he sees these verses as deriving from an editor, either deuteronomistic (ibid.; for similar analysis of at least v. 31, see also Baentsch, *Exodus*, 127–28; McNeile, *Exodus*, xx; Fuss, *Pentateuchredaktion*, 323–26; Schmid, *Der sogenannte Jahwist*, 54–60; Ska, "Exode xiv," 466; Kohata, *Exodus 3–14*, 294–95) or postpriestly (Blum, "Die literarische Verbindung," 134, and "Literary Connection," 95 n. 20; so also Krüger, "Erwägungen," 528–29; Gertz, *Exoduserzählung*, 222–28, and "Abraham," 80; Nihan, "La Mort de Moïse," 166; Levin, "Miracle," 44). The notion that

these verses must be a later redactional layer stems from the a priori belief, prevalent in current European scholarship, that all indications of an overarching theology (in this case the concept of "belief in Yahweh") must be secondary to the original story; see Rendtorff, *Problem*, 186.

41. This division, at least in terms of the separation of priestly from nonpriestly material, differs little, if at all, from that of the following scholars (some differences of opinion are noted in the preceding footnotes): Nöldeke, "Die s.g. Grundschrift," 45–46; Kuenen, *Hexateuch*, 70; Addis, *Documents*, 1:127–29; Bacon, *Triple Tradition*, 75–78; Dillmann, *Exodus*, 145; Carpenter and Harford-Battersby, *Hexateuch*, 2:100–3; Baentsch, *Exodus*, 119–27; Gressmann, *Mose*, 108–10 n. 1; McNeile, *Exodus*, xix–xxi; Driver, *Exodus*, 114–22; Brightman, *Sources*, 238–39; Elliger, "Sinn," 121; Noth, *Pentateuchal Traditions*, 18, and *Exodus*, 103–4; von Rabenau, "Schilfmeerwunder," 12–16; Childs, *Exodus*, 220; Scharbert, "'Schilfmeerwunder,'" 407–8; Weimar, *Meerwundererzählung*, 32; Kohata, *Exodus 3–14*, 278–79; Ska, *Passage*, 13; Blum, *Studien*, 256–57; Vervenne, "'P' Tradition," 79 (and in slightly different form, without explanation, at 85); Schmidt, *Priesterschrift*, 21; Lohfink, "Priestly Narrative," 145 n. 29; Wagenaar, "Crossing," 464; Krüger, "Erwägungen," 520 n. 9; Propp, *Exodus 1–18*, 461–63; Gertz, *Exoduserzählung*, 195–206; Graupner, *Elohist*, 79–81; Campbell and O'Brien, *Rethinking*, 76; Friedman, *Sources Revealed*, 142–44; Ska, *Introduction*, 68–75; Levin, "Miracle," 39–61. For the rare argument that there is no P at all in this chapter, see Smend, *Erzählung*, 139–43 (esp. 143), who divides it among his J¹, J², and E; Eissfeldt, *Old Testament*, 189, who sees J, E, and his L source; Fohrer, *Überlieferung*, 97–110, who sees J, E, and his N source. Note that these are three of the main scholars who advocated for three nonpriestly, nondeuteronomic documents; it is tempting to believe that they removed P from Exod 14 in large part to provide more material for their newly discovered sources. The same is not true, however, of the recent revival of this theory by Yoreh ("Elohistic Source," 171–74), whose view that J is a redactional layer of E is, however, similarly idiosyncratic. Wellhausen, while accepting that there were traces of P in vv. 1, 2, 4, 8b, 9, 10, and 16, doubted the existence of P elsewhere in the chapter and assigned the rest of what most scholars consider priestly to E (*Composition*, 75–77). His arguments were roundly rejected in subsequent scholarship; see, for example, Kuenen, *Hexateuch*, 71–72.

42. As recognized by ibn Ezra, on Exod 14:2.

43. See Lohfink, "Original Sins," 103.

44. As noted by Simpson, *Early Traditions*, 184–85; Noth, *Exodus*, 118; Meyer, *Israeliten*, 22–23; Childs, *Exodus*, 221; Scharbert, "'Schilfmeerwunder,'" 397–98; Schmidt, *Exodus, Sinai und Mose*, 63; Kohata, *Exodus 3–17*, 281; Blenkinsopp, *Pentateuch*, 158; Wagenaar, "Crossing," 464; Campbell and O'Brien, *Rethinking*, 77–78; Friedman, *Sources Revealed*, 142. In support of this reading, Scharbert ("'Schilfmeerwunder,'" 399–407) lists several other texts (Deut 11:4; Josh 24:6–7; Exod 15:21; Exod 15:1–18; Ps 114:3, 5; Nah 1:4; Ps 66:6; Ps 18:16) in which the episode at the sea is referred to seemingly without describing the crossing of the Israelites. Blum (*Studien*, 257 n. 96) also notes the possibility, though he is reticent to accept it completely. He approaches the

issue from a tradition-critical standpoint, suggesting that in the earlier tradition this story was simply about the destruction of the Egyptians, with the passage through the sea being a later development. Though he is correct to see a tradition in which the emphasis is on the destruction of the Egyptians, this is not a sign of any tradition-historical development per se, but rather of divergent manifestations of the single tradition of the destruction of the Egyptians by water. He does not take into account the fact that in the P story the Israelites are not really saved, as they were never in any real danger to begin with; the passage through the sea is a mechanism of destruction, not salvation. Propp (*Exodus 1–18*, 552–53) argues that the nonpriestly text must have mentioned the crossing of the sea, either in a missing passage or in the poem that follows in Exod 15, because otherwise he cannot understand "whence did the Priestly Writer receive the tradition that Israel crossed the Sea, if not from JE?" Such a question not only assumes a model in which P is dependent on a preexisting nonpriestly text, but problematizes every other instance in which the priestly story describes a new narrative element, as in fact it does in almost every case. Following this logic, we would have to assume that P also derives the notion of the patriarchal burial site of the cave of Machpelah from the nonpriestly text, although it is nowhere mentioned.

45. It is possible also to understand the verb *n-ʿ-r* in v. 27 as meaning that Yahweh caused the Egyptians to be tossed about in the sea, rather than that Yahweh actually threw them into the sea; this reading would suggest that there was no escape available to the Egyptians but that they were overwhelmed by the returning waters, as by a tidal wave. Houtman (*Exodus*, 2:274) imagines a scenario in which "the Egyptians fled pell-mell; colliding with the onrushing waves, they are knocked over and pulled along." This view may also conform somewhat better to the standard meaning of the verb "to shake" (Baruch Schwartz, personal communication).

46. In brief: P uses the term *yābāšā*ʰ for "dry land" (vv. 16, 22, 29; cf. Gen 1:8, 10; 8:14), while J uses the word *ḥārābā*ʰ (v. 21); the collocation of Pharaoh's chariots and his horsemen is found repeatedly and only in P (vv. 9, 17, 18, 23, 26, 28); the phrase "in the midst of the sea," using the word *tôk*, occurs only in P (vv. 16, 22, 23, 29). All of the terminology of salvation occurs in P, while all the military terminology (excepting the regular listing of Pharaoh's army corps) is in J.

47. We may also point to the phrase "the Israelites cried out to Yahweh" in 14:10. The root *z/ṣ-ʿ-q*, "to cry out," occurs in P only in this chapter (in vv. 10 and 15) and in Exod 2:23: "The Israelites were groaning under the bondage and cried out." It seems likely that by using these terms only in these places, the priestly author is drawing an explicit connection between the beginning of the Israelite enslavement in Egypt and the end of it (or the Israelites' fear that the arrival of the Egyptian army signifies a renewed enslavement). It should be noted that the distinction between *z-ʿ-q* and *ṣ-ʿ-q* is not important for source-critical analysis: both forms occur also, in close conjunction, in J (in Gen 18:20 and 18:21, respectively).

48. So already Rashi, on 14:5.

49. This and the many other connections to the plagues narrative, in both J and P, make Blum's contention (*Studien*, 261 n. 121) that there is no obvious link between the story

in Exod 14 and any other narrative, including the plagues, somewhat perplexing. For a detailed counterargument to Blum, see Schmidt, *Priesterschrift*, 25–34.

50. We may set aside as idiosyncratic those scholars who view P as the basic stratum of Exod 14 and the nonpriestly material as secondarily inserted; see Schmitt, "Geschichtsverständnis," 150–55.

51. There are, of course, scholars who hold the priestly stratum to be redactional, but without dealing in detail with Exod 14. See Cross, *Canaanite Myth*, 310.

52. So Kratz, *Composition*, 244–45.

53. Blum, *Studien*, 260.

54. Explanations for Yahweh's statement in v. 15 have included the early view that Moses was praying silently while the Israelites were crying aloud, the assumption that Moses cried with the Israelites, and the idea that Yahweh accuses Moses as the leader and representative of the people. Any of these, or numerous other suggestions, are more credible explanations for the text of v. 15 than the idea that it is a sign of redaction.

55. Blum also argues that the "Dramaturgie" of the canonical text is dominated by the priestly story, and he points to vv. 21–29 as a section where the priestly narrative seems to be given disproportionate emphasis (*Studien*, 261). Yet his admission that for most of the chapter the order of the compilation proceeds along necessary chronological grounds (ibid.) is true here as well; as is the case everywhere in the Pentateuch, the compiler's decisions are forced by the logical and chronological demands of his sources, and it is difficult, if not impossible, to reorder the pieces in such a way as to produce a story anywhere near as sensible as the one we have before us.

56. Van Seters, *Life of Moses*, 128–34.

57. Ibid., 131.

58. While Van Seters argues that Num 33 is a very late combination of both J and P itinerary notices (ibid., 154–61), the majority of scholars have long recognized the intimate connections between Num 33 and P, to the exclusion of any nonpriestly material; even Van Seters, in his analysis of Num 33, sees far more connections with P than with J. He further undermines his own argument by acknowledging that Num 33:7–8a matches with the priestly narrative in Exod 14:2 (ibid., 154–55). It is true, however, that the status of Num 33 remains something of an open question in pentateuchal scholarship.

59. Ibid., 130–31.

60. Ibid., 131–32.

61. Ibid., 131.

62. Ibid., 132.

63. Ibid.

64. A similar assessment can be made of the analysis of Fuss, *Pentateuchredaktion*, 297–326. He attributes much of what we have identified as P to the nonpriestly authors, particularly E, and leaves P with only a few key phrases (the enumeration of Pharaoh, his chariots, and his horsemen, for instance). Much else of what we have labeled P he assigns to R^P, though he does not provide any clear basis for either the distinction between P and R^P or the motivation for R^P's work.

65. Wagenaar, "Crossing," 465.
66. Ibid.
67. Ibid.
68. Vervenne, "'P' Tradition," 79.
69. Ibid.
70. Ibid.
71. Ibid.
72. Vervenne to some extent relies on the work of Weimar (*Meerwundererzählung*) for these arguments. Vervenne claims that Weimar also holds P to be a redactional layer rather than an independent narrative (ibid., 82–85), yet I think Vervenne has misread Weimar to some extent here. Weimar undertakes a detailed analysis of the priestly text of Exod 14 with the aim of demonstrating that it contains numerous formal irregularities (*Meerwundererzählung*, 175–84). He concentrates much of his attention on the differences between the three divine speeches and the notices of their executions and argues that these variations cannot be the work of a single hand. (This argument, however, relies on a far-too-formal view of the nature of the priestly writings; see the important dictum of McEvenue, *Narrative Style*, 50: "[P's] essence is variety within system.") Weimar's conclusion is that the final priestly narrative is indeed the product of a redactional process, but one contained entirely within the priestly text itself; in other words, there was an earlier priestly narrative, one that was, he presumes, schematic and repetitious, that has been reworked by a later, but also priestly, redactor, resulting in basically the P story as identified above. At no point does Weimar suggest that the priestly text, or any part of it, is dependent on or in any other way related to the nonpriestly narrative; rather, the two stories first come into contact with the work of the final redactor. It is no wonder, then, that Vervenne's arguments too, based as they are on Weimar, speak only to the internal issues of the P narrative and do not prove the redactional nature of P vis-à-vis J.
73. Vervenne, "'P' Tradition," 79.
74. Ibid., 85.
75. Ibid.
76. Along the same lines, Vervenne finds the use of the word "return" in v. 2 to be "only understandable taking into consideration the (redactional) exposition to the Sea narrative in 13,17–22 and the chain of itinerary notes" (ibid., 85–86). Even if one were inclined to see 13:17–22 as redactional (and there is no good reason to do so), the word "return" in 14:2 is dependent only on the idea that the Israelites have left Egypt, not on any particular itinerary for their travels through the wilderness. If one wants to remove the narrative of Exod 14 from the departure from Egypt altogether, the entire story is rendered senseless.
77. Ibid., 86.
78. Aaron is the main actor in the first wonder, the rod that turns into a serpent (Exod 7:8–13); in the turning of water into blood (7:19–20a); in the frogs (8:1–3); and in the lice (8:12–15). Moses begins to take over in the story of the boils, in which both he and Aaron are commanded to take handfuls of soot, but only Moses is to throw his toward the sky (9:8–12); and Aaron is absent altogether in the episodes of hail (9:22–23a),

locusts (10:12–13a), and darkness (10:21–23). See Greenberg, *Understanding Exodus*, 186–87.

79. Vervenne, "'P' Tradition," 87.

80. Ibid.

81. Ibid., 85.

CHAPTER 6. COMPILATION

1. An extensive and valuable history of the concept of the "editor" in biblical scholarship can be found in Van Seters, *Edited Bible*, though his conclusions differ from mine.

2. Spinoza, *Treatise*, 133.

3. Vater, *Commentar*, 3:505–12.

4. Astruc, *Conjectures*, 486–91.

5. Eichhorn, *Einleitung*, 3:101 (translation mine): "Ging je ein Geschichtsforscher religiöser und heiliger mit seinen Quellen um, als der Ordner von diesen?"

6. Ibid., 3:100.

7. Hupfeld, *Quellen*, 202–3. On this verse, the scholars who followed Hupfeld in assigning it to a redactor, and the rebuttal to them, see Baden, *Redaction*, 228–30.

8. Wellhausen, *Composition*, 94–95. For other examples of this type of analysis, see Baden, *Redaction*, 224 nn. 47, 49.

9. See Baden, *Redaction*, 236–47, and the scholarship cited therein.

10. See also ibid., 99–195.

11. Wellhausen, *Composition*, 35.

12. Friedman, "Three Major Redactors."

13. Ibid., 38–39.

14. Though I have dealt here only with J, E, and P, it should be noted that D too, though something of a special case, also conforms to the methods described above. It is largely set down as a block, of course, but in Deut 31 it is interwoven with E (E comprises Deut 31:14–15, 23), Deut 33 as a whole probably belongs to J, and there is an insertion on the basis of P in Deut 1:39.

15. Dillmann, *Genesis*, 1:146. I have silently changed Dillmann's sigla for J, E, and P (C, B, and A, respectively).

16. This aspect of the compiler's work is recognized, to a degree, by the many scholars who have argued that Gen 14 does not belong to one of the sources or to the compiler: it simply does not seem to contain any language that can be associated with one of the four documents and therefore cannot belong to the compiler of the documents, either, for he speaks in the language of his sources.

17. See Bar-On, "Festival Calendars."

18. In Chronicles, see famously 2 Chr 35:13, which combines legislation from Deut 16:7 and Exod 12:8–9; on Ruth, see Chavel, "Law and Narrative," 241–47; on Exod 34:17–26, see above.

19. On the fragility of papyrus as a medium, see Haran, "Book-Scrolls," 164–65.

20. See Childs, *Exodus*, 608; Propp, *Exodus 19–40*, 152.

CASE STUDY V. JACOB RETURNS TO BETHEL, GENESIS 35

1. These basic outlines of the E narrative, if not the specifics of it, are recognized by Kuenen, *Hexateuch*, 144–45; Addis, *Documents*, 1:51–52; Skinner, *Genesis*, 375–80.

2. The argument (Blum, *Vätergeschichte*, 38; Boecker, *1. Mose*, 122) that Jacob's altar in 35:7 is not built in fulfillment of his vow in 28:22 because an altar is not a temple ("Ein Altarbau ist wohl etwas anderes als die Errichtung eines Tempels" [Blum, ibid.]) is overly literal, especially as Jacob does not vow to build a temple in 28:22, but to turn his ad hoc pillar into a "house of God," to be taken in the broadest sense as a site of proper cultic worship (cf. Judg 17:5). Moreover, it is argued (Blum, ibid., 37–38; Boecker, ibid.) that the absence of any direct reference to Jacob's vow in 35:1–7 indicates that his actions are not intended as a fulfillment of it. Yet the narrative and thematic continuity and verbal similarity between 28:10–22, 31:10–13 (where the vow is explicitly mentioned) and 35:1–7 render also this argument difficult to maintain: if God's instructions to Jacob in 31:10–13 and 35:1–7 match the content of Jacob's vow in 28:10–22, and if Jacob's actions in 35:1–7 in turn match both his own vow and God's commands, is the word "vow" in 35:1–7 really necessary to establish the narrative connection among the texts? See the rebuttal of this view by Graupner, *Elohist*, 293–94, and the argument for the centrality of the vow in the E Jacob story by Richter, "Das Gelübde," 42–52.

   Similarly, the argument that 35:1–7 is a secondary construction that originally was unconnected with the events of Gen 28:10–22, or was written as an explicit countertext (see Otto, "Jakob in Bethel," 178–82; Köhlmoos, *Bet-El*, 250), depends on the removal not only of the connective elements of 35:1–7, but also those of 28:10–22, especially the vow at the end. Such analyses seem to be aimed less at reading the narratives, and more at disproving the clear continuity of the Jacob story over many chapters. One could certainly perform such analyses at will if one desired: it is easy enough to remove the connective literary markers between two texts and then say that the remaining passages were once independent and that the links between them are secondary—but it would not, and does not, constitute an argument for anything more than the creativity of the scholar.

3. See Driver, *Genesis*, 308; Speiser, *Genesis*, 270. If one wishes to see in the giving over of the earrings here an oblique reference to the episode of the golden calf, in which the people give their earrings to Aaron, but for a very different purpose (see Graupner, *Elohist*, 299; Köhlmoos, *Bet-El*, 258), this is possible: Exod 32 is also from E.

4. Various attempts have been made to see in vv. 2–4, or 2–5, a secondary insertion, usually on the grounds that the idea of putting away the foreign gods has its closest parallels in deuteronomistic texts (see Boecker, *1. Mose*, 160 n. 73; Levin, *Jahwist*, 261–62; Schmidt, "El," 146–47; Koenen, *Bethel*, 160). (For the same reason, Blum, *Vätergeschichte*, 43–44, assigns all of vv. 1–7 to a deuteronomistic layer; so too Köhlmoos, *Bet-El*, 255–63.) Yet deuteronomistic parallels are not a reason to call a text deuteronomistic; especially given the close connections between E and D, it is certainly plausible that E might have contained this notion as well. In this particular instance,

the easy manner in which the burial of the foreign gods fits into the narrative context does not call for any assumption of a secondary insertion.

5. Note that the divine terror here is paralleled conceptually, if not verbally, by the terror that God promises to send before the Israelites when they depart from Horeb in Exod 23:27 (E).

6. In J, the founding of the cultic site in Bethel is not attributed to Jacob at all but to Abraham, who builds an altar there upon his arrival in Canaan (Gen 12:8; 13:3–4). There is no notice of the change of the name from Luz to Bethel in J; it is called Bethel from the beginning. Further, no one ever returns to Bethel in J: the theophany that Jacob experiences in the J text of Gen 28:10–22 is not located at any specific place, but rather occurs at some undefined location on the way from Beersheba to Haran (28:10). The idea that J's theophany here takes place in Bethel is a mistaken reading of the E narrative into that of J; one frequently also finds in the older analyses the assignment of 28:19, in which Jacob names Bethel, to J, despite the obvious pun on *bêt ᵉlōhîm* in v. 17, which was universally assigned to E (see Hupfeld, *Quellen*, 40; Wellhausen, *Composition*, 31; Bacon, *Genesis*, 161–62; Carpenter and Harford-Battersby, *Hexateuch*, 2:43; Holzinger, *Genesis*, 191–92; Procksch, *Elohimquelle*, 22; Gunkel, *Genesis*, 312; Smend, *Erzählung*, 70; Driver, *Genesis*, 266; Brightman, *Sources*, 56–57; Skinner, *Genesis*, 378; Simpson, *Early Traditions*, 97).

   Many scholars have taken v. 5 as a redactional insertion precisely because it refers to the events of Gen 34; they believe either that Gen 34 is itself a later insertion into the text or that there was no E in the chapter (see Dillmann, *Genesis*, 2:303; Carpenter and Harford-Battersby, *Hexateuch*, 2:55; Otto, "Jakob," 178–79 n. 65; Levin, *Jahwist*, 263–64; Graupner, *Elohist*, 295). When an E text is recognized in Gen 34, however, these assumptions are entirely unnecessary. Further, the claim that because there is no reference to the events of Shechem in 35:1–4 those verses must have been written without the preceding chapter in mind (see Kuenen, *Hexateuch*, 326; Skinner, *Genesis*, 425–26) is somewhat prejudicial: the events of a preceding narrative do not have to be explicitly rehashed in order to prove that it actually stood there; if the reader has just finished the story of Dinah and Shechem, then explicit reference to that narrative in the following five verses is certainly not required. And, of course, the events of Gen 34 are referred to in vv. 4–5.

7. That this is the name of the altar, not the site, has been recognized by Dillmann, *Genesis*, 2:304; Keil and Delitzsch, *Commentary*, 203; Blum, *Vätergeschichte*, 64–65; Sarna, *Genesis*, 240; Koenen, *Bethel*, 161. The name that Jacob gives to this altar, El-Bethel, is strikingly similar in form to the name he gives to the altar he built at Shechem in 33:20: El-Elohei-Yisrael.

8. The coherent structure of 35:1–7 (though not its attribution to E) is demonstrated by Blum, *Vätergeschichte*, 36–37.

9. The assignment of 30:43 to P is based on three elements. First, though similar in theme to the J and E narratives in which Jacob grows wealthy through Laban, the idea that Jacob acquired "maidservants and menservants, camels and asses" seems not to fit with the nonpriestly stories, in which Jacob only increases his holdings of Laban's flocks. Second, the phrase "exceedingly," *mᵊᵓōd mᵊᵓōd*, occurs elsewhere in the

Pentateuch only in P (Gen 7:19; 17:2, 6, 20; Exod 1:7; Num 14:7). Finally, the camels mentioned in this verse are, presumably, the same camels on which Jacob places his wives and children in 31:17–18.

10. See Gen 12:2–3; 18:18; 26:3–4, 24; 28:14.

11. See Rose, "L'itinérance," 117–18.

12. That both v. 10 and vv. 11–12 are introduced with the formula "God said to him" is no reason to suggest that there is an insertion or any other type of redactional activity here (see de Pury, *Promesse*, 533–34). As some have recognized (Gross, "Jakob," 331; Blum, *Vätergeschichte*, 266; Rapp, *Jakob*, 28–29), the repetition of "God said to him" is required by the narrator's words "he named him Israel" in v. 10bβ. Even leaving this aside, the repetition of a speech introduction, which frequently marks a shift in topic, is paralleled in Gen 17, where there are in fact three successive speech introductions, each marking shifts in topic, within a single divine address to Abraham (17:3, 9, 15).

13. See McEvenue, *Narrative Style*, 165.

14. The assumption of some scholars that the absence of an etymological explanation of the new name, as in Gen 17:5 with Abraham, indicates that this verse somehow depends on the previous story of Jacob's name change in 32:29 (see Carpenter and Harford-Battersby, *Hexateuch*, 2:55; Gross, "Jakob," 330; Blum, *Vätergeschichte*, 266; Boecker, *1. Mose*, 127; Wenham, *Genesis 16–50*, 325) is groundless (cf. Rose, "L'itinérance," 119). In 17:15 God changes Sarah's name without any explanation. Seebass (*Genesis II*, 446) is virtually alone in ascribing v. 10 to E; a detailed response to this proposal is provided by de Pury, *Promesse*, 538–44.

15. Those scholars who attribute v. 14 to P by claiming that a libation offering does not contradict P's clear rejection of sacrifice before Sinai (see Carr, *Fractures*, 89 n. 24; Gomes, *Sanctuary*, 89) misunderstand the thrust of P's claim: it is not only that those cultic rites to be performed in the Temple are not practiced before the construction of the Tabernacle, but in fact that the Israelites did not have any mechanism by which to perform any kind of cultic act—and nowhere in P is any cultic act permitted anywhere other than the Tabernacle (= Temple). Furthermore, libation offerings are part of the priestly sacrificial system (in which they are always an accompaniment to another kind of offering) and thus do in fact belong to the priestly Temple service (see Exod 37:16; Lev 23:13, 18, 37; Num 4:7; 6:15, 17; 15:5, 7, 10, 24; 28:7–10, 14–15, 24, 31; 29:6, 11, 16, 18–19, 21–22, 24–25, 27–28, 30–31, 33–34, 37–39). Were we to accept the assignment of v. 14 to P, it would constitute the single cultic act before Sinai in P (see Dillmann, *Genesis*, 306–7; yet Dillmann's assignment of the verse to J is highly unlikely given the complete lack of narrative context in J for such an event [he is followed by Driver, *Genesis*, 310; Haran, *Temples*, 52–53]).

16. Ibn Ezra (on Gen 35:14) reads this not as a second pillar, but rather as a pluperfect, referring back to the pillar of 28:18: "Jacob had erected a pillar"; he is followed by Naḥmanides, on Gen 35:14. Attempting to solve the same problem of the two pillars, one from 28:18 and one here in 35:14, Cornill, "Beiträge," 15–19, attaches the pillar to the grave of Deborah from v. 8; he is followed by Addis, *Documents*, 2:225–26; Holzinger, *Genesis*, 216–17; Gunkel, *Genesis*, 366–67; Skinner, *Genesis*, 425. Although these verses are continuous in E, the anointing of the pillar in v. 14 gives it a decidedly

cultic aspect; note that the libations and the anointing are not mentioned in regard to the pillar set up over Rachel's grave in v. 20, and it is difficult to imagine that Jacob was more elaborate in his mourning for Rebekah's nurse than he was for his beloved wife. See further criticisms of Cornill's argument in de Pury, *Promesse*, 554–55. Köhlmoos (*Bet-El*, 265–67) argues that vv. 14–15 are the latest addition to the chapter, and so she must also (and does) assign 28:22, for which vv. 14–15 are the narrative fulfillment, to the same late layer. There are no literary grounds for this.

17. See Addis, *Documents*, 2:225–26.
18. The repeated naming of Bethel was already felt as a problem by Rashbam, on 35:7, who claimed that Jacob named three separate places Bethel (in 28:19, 35:7 [El-Bethel], and 35:15). Naḥmanides (on Gen 35:15) suggests that "he gave the site the name of Bethel" in 35:15 does not mean that he named it again, but that he continuously called it by the name he had given it already in 28:19.
19. Note that the identification of Efrat as being related to Bethlehem, frequently seen as a later gloss (see Addis, *Documents*, 1:70; Bacon, *Genesis*, 181; Carpenter and Harford-Battersby, *Hexateuch*, 2:57; Holzinger, *Genesis*, 218; Gunkel, *Genesis*, 369; Simpson, *Early Traditions*, 122; Blum, *Vätergeschichte*, 207; Westermann, *Genesis 12–36*, 555; Levin, *Jahwist*, 262; Carr, *Fractures*, 261; Gomes, *Sanctuary*, 92), is in fact present in both 35:19 and 48:7, thereby marking it not as a secondary insertion, but rather as part of the original P document. If it is a gloss, therefore, it is one that was written into P when it was still independent of the other sources.
20. Although the similarity between v. 19 (P) and v. 8 (E) is undeniable (see Blum, *Vätergeschichte*, 204–5; Carr, *Fractures*, 260–61), it is built on a common series of words: "X died and was buried at Y location." This phrasing is familiar not only from these two verses, but also from Num 20:1b; Judg 8:32; 10:2, 5; 12:7, 10, 12, 15.
21. See Nöldeke, "Die s.g. Grundschrift," 28–29 (though he also problematically ascribes v. 20 to P). Very many scholars, recognizing the connection between 35:16–20 and 48:7, stand firmly on the identification of 35:16–20 as a unified nonpriestly narrative and are thereby driven to claim that 48:7 is a redactional insertion (see Hupfeld, *Quellen*, 36; Budde, "Genesis 48,7"; Kuenen, *Hexateuch*, 327; Addis, *Documents*, 2:232–33; Bacon, *Genesis*, 215; Carpenter and Harford-Battersby, *Hexateuch*, 2:75; Smend, *Erzählung*, 108; Blum, *Vätergeschichte*, 251–52; Scharbert, *Genesis*, 287; Friedman, *Sources Revealed*, 113). This is a far less satisfying solution, as the central theme of the priestly account isolated in 35:16–20, and its recollection in 48:7, fits squarely in the context of the larger priestly concern for describing the burials of not only all of the patriarchs, but all of the matriarchs as well; see further below. Unrecognized in such arguments is the twofold nature of the recollection in 48:7: it does clearly connect with parts of 35:16–20, but it also ignores what may be the central element of the passage—the birth of Benjamin. See particularly the remarkable statement of Carr (*Fractures*, 91), who describes "the note in Gen. 48:7 about Benjamin's birth in Canaan"—which is precisely the element of 35:16–20 that 48:7 does not mention. Most problematic of all are those scholars who simply assign 35:16–20 to E and 48:7 to P, without noting the relationship between the two passages; see Dillmann, *Genesis*, 2:437–38; Driver, *Genesis*, 376; Skinner, *Genesis*, 504; Speiser, *Genesis*, 358–59.

22. It is worth noting that there is no tradition of Rachel's death in J. Moreover, the narratives of Rachel's death in E and P here in Gen 35 are directly contradicted in J in Gen 37:9–10, Joseph's second dream: the sun, moon, and eleven stars are explicitly interpreted by Jacob as signifying himself, Rachel, and Joseph's brothers. The assumption of both the dream and its interpretation is that here, in Gen 37, Rachel is still alive; see Carpenter and Harford-Battersby, *Hexateuch*, 2:56; Smend, *Erzählung*, 89; von Rad, *Genesis*, 352.

23. See Speiser, *Genesis*, 273.

24. See Wellhausen, *Composition*, 60; Addis, *Documents*, 1:100–1; Bacon, *Genesis*, 220; Dillmann, *Genesis*, 2:450; Carpenter and Harford-Battersby, *Hexateuch*, 2:76; Gunkel, *Genesis*, 453; Driver, *Genesis*, 381; Skinner, *Genesis*, 512; Speiser, *Genesis*, 371; Friedman, *Sources Revealed*, 114.

25. Carr (*Fractures*, 252–53) suggests, not entirely implausibly, that the original old poem of Gen 49 was in fact altered in its first four sayings so as to elevate Judah at the expense of his three older brothers.

26. Against many commentators, it is not necessary to assume that there is some continuation of the story of Reuben and Bilhah that is missing from the text (see Holzinger, *Genesis*, 219; Gunkel, *Genesis*, 370; Skinner, *Genesis*, 427; von Rad, *Genesis*, 340). The story, brief as it is, is perfectly clear: Reuben slept with Bilhah, and Jacob heard about it. The supposition that the story originally contained a curse on Reuben for this act is impossible: the disinheritance of Reuben in 49:3–4 is the (poetic) conclusion to this narrative. Similarly, it is mistaken to read Jacob's condemnation of Simeon and Levi in 34:30 as equivalent to a curse; again, the disinheritance that proceeds from their actions is delayed until 49:5–7. Dillmann, *Genesis*, 2:309–10, recognizes that, lacking nothing, 35:22a is intended as a narrative precursor to 49:3–4 (cf. Blum, *Vätergeschichte*, 209–10, though he also considers these texts, along with Gen 34 and 38, to be secondary pro-Judahite insertions into the text [ibid., 228–29]; he is followed by Carr, *Fractures*, 251–53).

27. See Westermann, *Genesis 12–36*, 554.

28. This discrepancy was noted in the seventeenth century by Simon, *Histoire*, 37. Ibn Ezra (on Gen 35:26), recognizing the contradiction, assumes that "these are the sons of Jacob who were born to him in Paddan-Aram" describes the majority of the sons, rather than all of them; the ad hoc nature of this solution is evident. He is followed by Bekhor Shor, on Gen 35:26; Dillmann, *Genesis*, 2:310; Driver, *Genesis*, 312; Wenham, *Genesis 16–50*, 328.

29. Thus the contradiction that Carr (*Fractures*, 91) sees between 48:7 and 35:22b–26 is, in fact, nowhere in evidence.

30. Noted already by Hupfeld, *Quellen*, 31–32.

31. See also the use of this word in the wailing of the people in the wilderness in P, Num 17:27–28; 20:3.

32. See Hupfeld, *Quellen*, 41; Nöldeke, "Die s.g. Grundschrift," 26–27; Holzinger, *Genesis*, 185; Skinner, *Genesis*, 428; Boecker, *1. Mose*, 131–32; Scharbert, *Genesis*, 233; Lohfink, "Original Sins," 100–1; Graupner, *Elohist*, 303.

33. The report of Isaac's death in P here fits with the larger priestly chronology and assumes that the time between Jacob's departure for Paddan-Aram and his return was

eighty years: Isaac was 60 years old when Jacob and Esau were born (Gen 25:20); Esau married his Hittite wives when he was 40, and Isaac was thus 100 (26:34); assuming that Jacob left at this time, the age of Isaac at his death, 180 (35:28), indicates that Jacob was gone for eighty years. The discrepancy between this chronology and that of the J story could hardly be greater: the lengthy scene of Jacob stealing Esau's blessing in Gen 27:1–45 assumes that Isaac is on his deathbed (27:1: "When Isaac was old and his eyes were too dim to see"). It is thus fairly impossible to imagine that Isaac lay on his deathbed for eighty years until Jacob's return. Far more likely is the possibility that Isaac's death actually took place within the original J story of Gen 27, specifically between vv. 40 and 41: in v. 41 Esau says "Let but the mourning period of my father come, and I will kill my brother Jacob." Since this obviously means that Esau plans to wait until the period for mourning Isaac has passed (not just begun) before going after Jacob, it is reasonable to assume that Isaac's death should have been narrated here. See Bacon, *Genesis*, 160. The compiler, however, would have had little choice but to remove the report of Isaac's death because Isaac does not die and is not buried until the end of Gen 35 in P.

34. Because the J text of Gen 35 comprises only vv. 21–22a, I do not lay it out in full here.

35. The assumption of many scholars that the brevity of the P narrative of Jacob's stay in Paddan-Aram is evidence that P was written as a supplement to the longer J and E narratives (see Westermann, *Genesis 12–36*, 556) is based on the faulty premise that not only the broad outlines of a story but even its particular literary manifestation must be common to all the sources that tell it. The P story of Jacob in Paddan-Aram is brief only because there was little story to tell according to P: Jacob went there to get married, he did so, had children, and returned. The drama of the nonpriestly narrative is not assumed; it is simply not part of the priestly story. Gunkel's drastic rearrangement of the P story (*Genesis*, 372–74) is entirely unnecessary.

36. See Graupner, *Elohist*, 300. Contra Cross, *Canaanite Myth*, 305–6.

37. Blum (*Vätergeschichte*, 269–70) argues that the placement of the P passages after Jacob's return to Bethel (in his view 35:9–15) and before Jacob's departure for Bethel (27:46–28:9) is indicative of a priestly redaction which, by placing its texts as a frame around the nonpriestly story, requires that the reader or audience interpret the events through the priestly lens. Since, however, these P passages are, according to the theory presented above, in the only places they could possibly be, Blum's argument does not prove a priestly redaction; rather, it assumes it.

38. See von Rad, *Genesis*, 339. If P narrated a divine appearance to Isaac, it is ostensibly missing; the notice in Gen 25:11a that God blessed Isaac, however, may be an allusion to such an event, on the basis of the parallel passages of God blessing the patriarchs in P. See Nöldeke, "Die s.g. Grundschrift," 26.

39. See Hupfeld, *Quellen*, 56, 203; Nöldeke, "Die s.g. Grundschrift," 28; Kuenen, *Hexateuch*, 326–27; Addis, *Documents*, 2:225; Bacon, *Genesis*, 181; Dillmann, *Genesis*, 2:305; Holzinger, *Genesis*, 184; Smend, *Erzählung*, 88; Eissfeldt, *Hexateuch-Synopse*, 72*; von Rad, *Genesis*, 339; Westermann, *Genesis 12–36*, 553; Rose, "L'itinérance," 120; Levin, *Jahwist*, 263; Seebass, *Genesis II*, 445; Graupner, *Elohist*, 300–1; Köhlmoos, *Bet-El*, 251 n. 90; Baden, *Redaction*, 267–68.

40. Though many scholars have felt the need to emend or remove the word "safe" in 33:18a, or to read it as a place name, "Shalem"—to which no further reference is made—(see Carpenter and Harford-Battersby, *Hexateuch*, 2:52; Westermann, *Genesis 12–36*, 528; Blum, *Vätergeschichte*, 206; Wenham, *Genesis 16–50*, 300) there is no need to do so, as the word, though perhaps a rare usage, makes good contextual sense. See Skinner, *Genesis*, 415–16; Carr, *Fractures*, 259–60; Graupner, *Elohist*, 288.

41. Contra Addis, *Documents*, 2:222–25; Dillmann, *Genesis*, 2:293–301; Carpenter and Harford-Battersby, *Hexateuch*, 2:52–54; Driver, *Genesis*, 303–8; Skinner, *Genesis*, 418; Simpson, *Early Traditions*, 116–21.

42. Scholars, acknowledging the presence of both P and E elements in 33:18a, have frequently attempted to divide the text into two without recognizing that some of the text must have been present in both sources, as suggested above; such divisions inevitably result in one of the sources in this verse being a mere fragment. Frequently only the words "which is in the land of Canaan—on his arrival from Paddan-Aram" are ascribed to P—but a prepositional phrase does not a sentence make, and this fragment is left unconnected with any other P text. See Skinner, *Genesis*, 416; Eissfeldt, *Hexateuch-Synopse*, 69*; von Rad, *Genesis*, 328. The proposal that the phrase is a redactional insertion is groundless, as no rationale for such an insertion can be provided. See Westermann, *Genesis 12–36*, 528; Blum, *Vätergeschichte*, 62 n. 3; Seebass, *Genesis II*, 416; Levin, *Jahwist*, 263; Carr, *Fractures*, 107 n. 58; Graupner, *Elohist*, 289.

43. In this light there is no need to assign all or part of 35:6 to P; see Bacon, *Genesis*, 181; Holzinger, *Genesis*, 184; Carpenter and Harford-Battersby, *Hexateuch*, 2:55; Procksch, *Elohimquelle*, 39; Gunkel, *Genesis*, 373; Smend, *Erzählung*, 87; Brightman, *Sources*, 226; Eissfeldt, *Hexateuch-Synopse*, 72*; Simpson, *Early Traditions*, 121; Speiser, *Genesis*, 270; Noth, *Pentateuchal Traditions*, 13; Weimar, "Aufbau und Struktur," 185; Otto, "Jakob," 178–79 n. 65; Gross, "Jakob," 325; Schmidt, "El," 147 n. 44; de Pury, *Promesse*, 532–33; Westermann, *Genesis 12–36*, 551–52; Boecker, *1. Mose*, 122; Scharbert, *Genesis*, 230; Seebass, *Genesis II*, 444–45; Lohfink, "Priestly Narrative," 145 n. 29; Graupner, *Elohist*, 295; Koenen, *Bethel*, 197; Köhlmoos, *Bet-El*, 251; Gomes, *Sanctuary*, 86. To remove the arrival in Bethel in v. 6 from E and assign it to P creates two substantial problems: first, there is no longer any notice of Jacob's fulfillment of the instruction in 35:1 to go to Bethel, no notice of his arrival at the place; second, there are then two notices in P of Jacob's arrival from Paddan-Aram, in 35:6 and 33:18a. "Luz" in 35:6 is not an indication of P as some have argued, since it is known first from E in 28:19; in this verse it is used again to mark clearly Jacob's return to the precise place where he had experienced the theophany in 28:10–22. The name is also associated with Bethel in Judg 1:22–26. For further arguments against assigning v. 6 to P, see Rapp, *Jakob*, 27–28; Carr, *Fractures*, 107 n. 58.

44. This prepositional phrase, which occurs in 33:18a and 48:3 in P, is probably an insertion of the compiler in 35:6 (E), where its insertion would have been triggered by the reference to Luz (see Levin, *Jahwist*, 263, though he ascribes the occurrence in 33:18a to a secondary insertion also). It may also be a scribal addition, again on the basis of the two P examples. The words "(which is) in the land of Canaan," though certainly common enough to be expected in any of the sources, are in fact found almost

exclusively in P (see Gen 13:12; 16:3; 23:2, 19; 36:5, 6; 37:1; 46:6, 12; 48:3, 7; 49:30; Num 26:19; 32:30; 33:40; 34:29; 35:14); the exceptions come entirely from the Joseph narrative (see Gen 42:5, 13, 32; 46:31; 47:4; 50:5), where the setting in the foreign land of Egypt makes the references to "the land of Canaan" readily understandable. On the priestly use of this phrase, see de Pury, *Promesse*, 532–33 n. 225.

45. See Baden, *Redaction*, 265–67.

46. Already Rashi (on Gen 35:14) had expressed his inability to understand the meaning of this phrase.

47. See Skinner, *Genesis*, 424–25, who calls the phrase in v. 14 a "gloss"; Eissfeldt, *Hexateuch-Synopse*, 72*; Simpson, *Early Traditions*, 122.

48. See Cornill, "Beiträge," 19; Smend, *Erzählung*, 88–89; Seebass, *Genesis II*, 445; Koenen, *Bethel*, 197–98 n. 7. It is in fact likely that the repetition of the phrase in both v. 13 and v. 15 is not original to the P document. It fits best in v. 15, to designate the place that Jacob named Bethel; it fits considerably less well in v. 13, where the idea that God left Jacob "at the spot where he had spoken to him" seems redundant—where else would God have left him? We may therefore have a rare but significant example of scribal dittography within the independent P document, the phrase having been erroneously copied into v. 13 from v. 15 (which would have been sequential in the original P text, of course). See Kuenen, *Hexateuch*, 327; Carpenter and Harford-Battersby, *Hexateuch*, 2:55; Skinner, *Genesis*, 425; Simpson, *Early Traditions*, 121. If this possibility is accepted, it has important ramifications for clarifying the independent existence of the P document: vertical dittography can take place only if the text once existed without v. 14 in the middle. Further, scribal errors are a function of the process of transmission, which indicates not only that the priestly document was originally independent, but that it was copied and recopied before it was combined with the other sources. That the phrase makes little sense in v. 13 was noted by Ehrlich, *Miqra*, 97 (who, however, claimed that it was a vertical dittography from v. 14; so too Bacon, *Genesis*, 181; Holzinger, *Genesis*, 185; Procksch, *Elohimquelle*, 40; Gunkel, *Genesis*, 373; Speiser, *Genesis*, 271; de Pury, *Promesse*, 558 n. 337; Seebass, *Genesis II*, 445). Westermann (*Genesis 12–36*, 553) correctly rejects the idea that the appearance of the phrase in v. 15 is a dittography from v. 14.

Blum (*Vätergeschichte*, 268) and Gross ("Jakob," 335–37 n. 4) are virtually alone in arguing that all three occurrences are original (and that all three belong to P). They claim that this redundancy is an intentional repudiation of the idea in 28:10–22 that God actually dwells at the site; here, in their view, P is polemically emphasizing the temporary nature of God's appearance there. Although P certainly would not ascribe to the view that God dwells anywhere but the Tabernacle (which has obviously not been built yet), the temporary nature of God's appearance at Bethel need not be taken as a response to an alternative view (as it is not a response in Gen 17, either). In addition, Blum's attempt to read "God parted from him" in v. 13 as contributing to this priestly polemic fails on the grounds of the parallel in Gen 17:22, where there is no earlier tradition for the priestly author (or editor, in Blum's view) to counter.

49. See Holzinger, *Genesis*, 185; Smend, *Erzählung*, 87–88; Skinner, *Genesis*, 422–23; Westermann, *Genesis 12–36*, 556. This P section, wherever we situate it, provides us

with an exegetical insight into the meaning of "be fruitful and multiply": this blessing does not refer to the immediate descendants of the generation to which it is addressed (as supposed by von Rad, *Genesis*, 339; Kratz, *Composition*, 240), but rather implies the long-term growth of the individual into a fully fledged people (cf. Jacob, *Genesis*, 238). This is particularly clear from the parallel in Gen 17:6: the blessing "be fruitful and multiply" is given, as in 35:9–12, as an accompaniment to the promise of land (vv. 3–8), a discourse distinct from that in which Abraham is promised a son with Sarah (vv. 15–21). The placement of "be fruitful and multiply" after eleven of Jacob's twelve children were born was raised as a question already in *Ber. Rab.* 82.4.

50. As recognized by Westermann, *Genesis 12–36*, 556.

51. See Blum, *Vätergeschichte*, 446. Carr, *Fractures*, 89, correctly sees that "the P narrative in Gen. 35:9–15 appears to have been designed to replace, rather than supplement, its non-P counterpart."

BIBLIOGRAPHY

Abramski, Samuel. "Ishmaelites and Midianites [Hebrew]." *Eretz-Israel* 17 (1984): 128–34.

Achenbach, Reinhard. *Die Vollendung der Tora: Studien zur Redaktionsgeschichte des Numeribuches im Kontext von Hexateuch und Pentateuch.* Beihefte zur Zeitschrift für altorientalische und biblische Rechtsgeschichte 3. Wiesbaden: Otto Harrassowitz, 2003.

Ackerman, James S. "Joseph, Judah, and Jacob." Pages 85–113 in *Literary Interpretations of Biblical Narratives.* Vol. 2. Edited by Kenneth R. R. Gros Louis with James S. Ackerman. Nashville: Abingdon, 1982.

Ackroyd, Peter R. *Exile and Restoration.* Old Testament Library. Philadelphia: Westminster, 1968.

Addis, W. E. *The Documents of the Hexateuch.* 2 vols. London: David Nutt, 1892.

Aḥituv, Shmuel. *HaKetav veHaMiktav: Handbook of Ancient Inscriptions from the Land of Israel and the Kingdoms beyond the Jordan from the Period of the First Commonwealth* [Hebrew]. The Biblical Encyclopaedia Library 21. Jerusalem: Mosad Bialik, 2005.

Ahuis, Ferdinand. *Autorität im Umbruch: Ein formgeschichtlicher Beitrag zur Klärung der literarischen Schichtung und der zeitgeschichtlichen Bezüge von Num 16 und 17.* Calwer Theologische Monographien 13. Stuttgart: Calwer, 1983.

Albertz, Rainer. *A History of Israelite Religion in the Old Testament Period.* Translated by John Bowden. 2 vols. Old Testament Library. Louisville, Ky.: Westminster John Knox, 1994.

Albright, William F. *From the Stone Age to Christianity: Monotheism and the Historical Process.* 2nd ed. Baltimore: Johns Hopkins Press, 1957.

Alt, Albrecht. "Der Gott der Väter." *Beiträge zur Wissenschaft vom Alten und Neuen Testament.* 3rd Folge, Heft 12. Stuttgart: W. Kohlhammer, 1929.

Alter, Robert. *The Art of Biblical Narrative.* New York: Basic Books, 1981.

Amit, Yairah. *History and Ideology: An Introduction to Historiography in the Hebrew Bible.* Translated by Yael Lotan. The Biblical Seminar 60. Sheffield: Sheffield Academic, 1999.

Anbar, Moshe. "Changement des noms des tribus nomades dans la relation d'un même événement." *Biblica* 49 (1968): 221–32.

Astruc, Jean. *Conjectures sur les memoires originaux: Dont il paroit que Moyse s'est servi pour composer le Livre de la Genese*. Brussels: Fricx, 1753. Repr., Paris: Éditions Noêsis, 1999.

Auffret, Pierre. "Essai sur la structure littéraire d'Ex 14." *Estudios bíblicos* 41 (1983): 53–82.

Augustine. *Quaestionum in Heptateuchum*. Corpus Christianorum, Series Latina 33: Aurelii Augustini Opera. Vol. 5. Turnholt: Typographi Brepols Editores Pontificii, 1958.

Aurelius, Erik. *Der Fürbitter Israels: Eine Studie zum Mosebild im Alten Testament*. Coniectanea biblica: Old Testament Series 27. Stockholm: Almqvist & Wicksell International, 1988.

Ausloos, Hans. "The Deuteronomist and the Account of Joseph's Death (Gen 50,22–26)." Pages 381–96 in *Studies in the Book of Genesis*. Edited by André Wenin. Bibliotheca Ephemeridum Theologicarum Lovaniensium 155. Leuven: University Press, 2001.

Bachra, Bernard N. "Structural Regularities in the Story of the Passage through the Sea (Exod 13,17–22 and Exod 14)." *Scandinavian Journal of the Old Testament* 16 (2002): 246–63.

Bacon, Benjamin W. *The Triple Tradition of the Exodus*. Hartford: Student Publishing, 1894.

——. *The Genesis of Genesis*. Rev. ed. Hartford: Student Publishing, 1893.

Baden, Joel S. "From Joseph to Moses: The Narratives of Exodus 1–2." *Vetus Testamentum* (forthcoming).

——. "The Deuteronomic Evidence for the Documentary Theory." Pages 327–44 in *The Pentateuch: International Perspectives on Current Research*. Edited by Tom Dozeman, Konrad Schmid, and Baruch J. Schwartz. Tübingen: Mohr Siebeck, 2011.

——. "The Original Place of the Priestly Manna Story in Exodus 16." *Zeitschrift für die Alttestamentliche Wissenschaft*122 (2010): 491–504.

——. *J, E, and the Redaction of the Pentateuch*. Forschungen zum Alten Testament 68. Tübingen: Mohr Siebeck, 2009.

——. "The Tower of Babel: A Case Study in the Competing Methods of Historical and Modern Literary Criticism." *Journal of Biblical Literature* 128 (2009): 209–24.

——. "A Narrative Pattern and Its Role in Source Criticism." *Hebrew Studies* 49 (2008): 41–54.

Baentsch, Bruno. *Exodus-Leviticus-Numeri übersetzt und erklärt*. Handkommentar zum Alten Testament I/2. Göttingen: Vandenhoeck & Ruprecht, 1903.

Bar-On, Shimon. "The Festival Calendars in Exodus xxiii 14–19 and xxxiv 18–26." *Vetus Testamentum* 48 (1998): 161–95.

Barton, John. *Reading the Old Testament: Method in Biblical Study*. 2nd ed. Louisville, Ky.: Westminster John Knox, 1996.

Begg, Christopher T. "The Destruction of the Golden Calf Revisited (Exod 32,20/Deut 9,21)." Pages 469–80 in *Deuteronomy and Deuteronomic Literature: Festschrift C. H. W. Brekelmans*. Edited by Marc Vervenne and Johan Lust. Bibliotheca Ephemeridum Theologicarum Lovaniensium 133. Leuven: Leuven University Press, 1997.

Bentzen, Aage. *Introduction to the Old Testament.* 2 vols. Copenhagen: G. E. C. Gad, 1959.

Berlin, Adele. *Poetics and Interpretation of Biblical Narrative.* Bible and Literature Series 9. Sheffield: Almond, 1983.

Blenkinsopp, Joseph. "Deuteronomic Contribution to the Narrative in Genesis-Numbers: A Test Case." Pages 84–115 in *Those Elusive Deuteronomists.* Edited by Linda S. Schearing and Steven L. McKenzie. Journal for the Study of the Old Testament Supplements 286. Sheffield: Sheffield Academic, 1999.

——— . "P and J in Genesis 1:1–11:26: An Alternative Hypothesis." Pages 1–15 in *Fortunate the Eyes That See.* Edited by Astrid Beck, Andrew H. Bartelt, Paul R. Raabe, and Chris A. Franke. Grand Rapids, Mich.: Eerdmans, 1995.

——— . *The Pentateuch: An Introduction to the First Five Books of the Bible.* Anchor Bible Reference Library. New York: Doubleday, 1992.

——— . "The Structure of P." *Catholic Biblical Quarterly* 38 (1976): 275–92.

Blum, Erhard. "Issues and Problems in the Contemporary Debate regarding the Priestly Writings." Pages 31–44 in *The Strata of the Priestly Writings: Contemporary Debate and Future Directions.* Edited by Sarah Shectman and Joel S. Baden. AThANT 95. Zurich: TVZ, 2009.

——— . "The Literary Connection between the Books of Genesis and Exodus and the End of the Book of Joshua." Pages 89–106 in *A Farewell to the Yahwist? The Composition of the Pentateuch in Recent European Interpretation.* Edited by Thomas B. Dozeman and Konrad Schmid. Society for Biblical Literature Symposium Series 34. Atlanta: SBL, 2006.

——— . "Die literarische Verbindung von Erzvätern und Exodus: Ein Gespräch mit neueren Endredaktionshypothesen." Pages 119–56 in *Abschied vom Jahwisten: Die Komposition des Hexateuch in der jüngsten Diskussion.* Edited by Jan C. Gertz, Konrad Schmid, and Markus Witte. Beiheifte zur Zeitschrift für die Alttestamentliche Wissenschaft 315. Berlin: Walter de Gruyter, 2002.

——— . *Studien zur Komposition des Pentateuch.* Beihefte zur Zeitschrift für die Alttestamentliche Wissenschaft 189. Berlin: Walter de Gruyter, 1990.

——— . *Die Komposition der Vätergeschichte.* Wissenschaftliche Monographien zum Alten und Neuen Testament 57. Neukirchen-Vluyn: Neukirchener Verlag, 1984.

Boecker, Hans J. *1. Mose 25,12–37,1: Isaak und Jakob.* Zurich: TVZ, 1992.

Boorer, Suzanne. *The Promise of the Land as Oath: A Key to the Formation of the Pentateuch.* Beihefte zur Zeitschrift für die Alttestamentliche Wissenschaft 205. Berlin: Walter de Gruyter, 1992.

Briggs, Charles A. *The Higher Criticism of the Hexateuch.* New York: Charles Scribner's Sons, 1893.

Brightman, Edgar S. *The Sources of the Hexateuch.* New York: Abingdon, 1918.

Brooke, Alan E., and Norman McLean. *The Old Testament in Greek.* Cambridge: University Press, 1906.

Brueggemann, Walter. "The Kerygma of the Priestly Writers." Pages 101–14 in *The Vitality of Old Testament Traditions.* 2nd ed. Atlanta: John Knox, 1982.

Budde, Karl. "Genesis 48,7 und die benachbarten Abschnitte." *Zeitschrift für die Alttestamentliche Wissenschaft* 3 (1883): 56–86.

Buss, Martin. *Biblical Form Criticism in Its Context.* Journal for the Study of the Old Testament Supplement Series 274. Sheffield: Sheffield Academic, 1999.

———. "Form Criticism, Hebrew Bible." Pages 406–13 in *Dictionary of Biblical Interpretation.* 2 vols. Edited by John H. Hayes. Nashville: Abingdon, 1999.

Butler, Trent C. "Narrative Form Criticism: Alive or Dead?" Pages 39–59 in *A Biblical Itinerary: In Search of Method, Form and Content.* Edited by Eugene E. Carpenter. Journal for the Study of the Old Testament Supplement Series 240. Sheffield: Sheffield Academic, 1997.

Calvin, John. *Commentaries on the Four Last Books of Moses Arranged in the Form of a Harmony.* 2 vols. Translated by Charles William Bingham. Grand Rapids, Mich.: Baker, 1979.

———. *Commentaries on the First Book of Moses, Called Genesis.* Vol. 2 Translated by John King. Grand Rapids, Mich.: Eerdmans, 1948.

Campbell, Antony F. "The Priestly Text: Redaction or Source?" Pages 32–47 in *Biblische Theologie und Gesellschaftlicher Wandel.* Edited by Georg Braulik, Walter Gross, and Sean McEvenue. Freiburg: Herder, 1993.

Campbell, Antony F., and Mark A. O'Brien. *Rethinking the Pentateuch: Prolegomena to the Theology of Ancient Israel.* Louisville, Ky.: Westminster John Knox, 2005.

Carpenter, J. Estlin, and G. Harford-Battersby. *The Hexateuch According to the Revised Version.* 2 vols. New York: Longmans, Green, 1900.

Carr, David. "What Is Required to Identify Pre-Priestly Narrative Connections between Genesis and Exodus? Some General Reflections and Specific Cases." Pages 159–80 in *A Farewell to the Yahwist? The Composition of the Pentateuch in Recent European Interpretation.* Edited by Thomas B. Dozeman and Konrad Schmid. SBL Symposium Series 34. Atlanta: Society of Biblical Literature, 2006.

———. *Reading the Fractures of Genesis: Historical and Literary Approaches.* Louisville, Ky.: Westminster John Knox, 1996.

Cassuto, Umberto. *A Commentary on the Book of Exodus.* Translated by Israel Abrahams. Jerusalem: Magnes, 1997.

———. *The Documentary Hypothesis.* Translated by Israel Abrahams. Jerusalem: Magnes, 1959.

———. *La Questione della Genesi.* Pubblicazioni della R. Università degli studi di Firenze. Facoltà di lettere e filosofia. III ser., vol. I. Florence: Felice le Monnier, 1934.

Cave, Alfred. *The Inspiration of the Old Testament Inductively Considered.* The Seventh Congregational Union Lecture. London: Congregational Union of England and Wales, 1888.

Charlesworth, James H., ed. *The Old Testament Pseudepigrapha.* 2 vols. Anchor Bible Reference Library. New York: Doubleday, 1985.

Chavel, Simeon. "Law and Narrative in Four Oracular Novellae in the Pentateuch: Lev. 24:10–23; Num 9:1–14; 15:32–36; 27:1–11." Ph.D. diss., Hebrew University, 2006.

Childs, Brevard S. *Introduction to the Old Testament as Scripture.* Philadelphia: Fortress, 1979.

———. *The Book of Exodus.* Old Testament Library. Louisville, Ky.: Westminster, 1974.

Coats, George W. *Genesis with an Introduction to Narrative Literature.* Forms of the Old Testament Literature 1. Grand Rapids, Mich.: Eerdmans, 1983.

———. *From Canaan to Egypt: Structural and Theological Context for the Joseph Story.* Catholic Biblical Quarterly Monograph Series 4. Washington, D.C.: Catholic Biblical Association of America, 1976.

———. *Rebellion in the Wilderness.* Nashville: Abingdon, 1968.

Coote, Robert B. *In Defense of Revolution: The Elohist History.* Minneapolis: Fortress, 1991.

Cornill, C. H. "Beiträge zur Pentateuchkritik." *Zeitschrift für die Alttestamentliche Wissenschaft* 11 (1891): 1–34.

Craghan, John F. "The Elohist in Recent Literature." *Biblical Theology Bulletin* 7 (1977): 23–35.

Cross, Frank M. *Canaanite Myth and Hebrew Epic: Essays in the History of the Religion of Israel.* Cambridge, Mass.: Harvard University Press, 1973.

Crüsemann, Frank. *The Torah: Theology and Social History of Old Testament Law.* Translated by Allan W. Mahnke. Edinburgh: T & T Clark, 1996.

———. "Die Eigenständigkeit der Urgeschichte: Ein Beitrag zur Diskussion um den 'Jahwisten.'" Pages 11–29 in *Die Botschaft und die Boten.* Edited by Jorg Jeremias and Lothar Perlitt. Neukirchen-Vluyn: Neukirchener Verlag, 1981.

Culley, Robert C. *Studies in the Structure of Hebrew Narrative.* Philadelphia: Fortress, 1976.

Dahse, Johannes. *Textkritische Materialen zur Hexateuchfrage.* Vol. 1. Giessen: Alfred Töpelmann, 1912.

Damrosch, David. *The Narrative Covenant: Transformations of Genre in the Growth of Biblical Literature.* Ithaca, N.Y.: Cornell University Press, 1987.

Davies, Graham I. *Ancient Hebrew Inscriptions: Corpus and Concordance.* 2 vols. Cambridge: Cambridge University Press, 1991–2004.

———. "The Composition of the Book of Exodus: Reflections on the Theses of Erhard Blum." Pages 71–86 in *Texts, Temples, and Traditions: A Tribute to Menahem Haran.* Edited by Michael V. Fox, Victor Avigdor Hurowitz, Avi Hurvitz, Michael L. Klein, Baruch J. Schwartz, and Nili Shupak. Winona Lake, Ind.: Eisenbrauns, 1996.

de Pury, Albert. "P^g as the Absolute Beginning." Pages 99–128 in *Les dernières rédactions du Pentateuque, de l'Hexateuque et de l'Ennéateuque.* Edited by Thomas Römer and Konrad Schmid. Bibliotheca Ephemeridum Theologicarum Lovaniensium 203. Leuven: University Press, 2007.

———. *Promesse divine et légende cultuelle dans le cycle de Jacob: Genèse 28 et les traditions patriarcales.* Paris: J. Gabalda, 1975.

de Pury, Albert, and Thomas Römer. "Le Pentateuque en question: Position du problème et brève histoire de la recherche." Pages 9–80 in *Le Pentateuque en question.* 3rd ed. Edited by Albert de Pury and Thomas Römer. Le monde de la Bible 19. Geneva: Labor et Fides, 2002.

de Tillesse, G. M. "Sections 'tu' et sections 'vous' dans le Deuteronome." *Vetus Testamentum* 12 (1962): 29–87.

de Vaulx, J. *Les Nombres*. Sources bibliques. Paris: J. Gabalda, 1972.

de Vries, Simon J. "The Origin of the Murmuring Tradition." *Journal of Biblical Literature* 87 (1968): 51–58.

Dietrich, Walter. *Die Josephserzählung als Novelle und Geschichtschreibung: Zugleich ein Beitrag zur Pentateuchfrage*. Biblisch-theologisch Studien 14. Neukirchen-Vluyn: Neukirchener Verlag, 1989.

Dillmann, August. *Die Bücher Exodus und Leviticus*. 3rd ed. Kurzgefasstes exegetisches Handbuch zum Alten Testament 12. Leipzig: S. Hirzel, 1897.

——. *Genesis Critically and Exegetically Expounded*. 2 vols. Translated by William B. Stevenson. Edinburgh: T & T Clark, 1897.

——. *Die Bücher Numeri, Deuteronomium und Josua*. 2nd ed. Kurzgefasstes exegetisches Handbuch zum Alten Testament. Leipzig: S. Hirzel, 1886.

Dobbs-Allsopp, F. W., J. J. M. Roberts, C. L. Seow, and R. E. Whitaker. *Hebrew Inscriptions: Texts from the Biblical Period of the Monarchy with Concordance*. New Haven, Conn.: Yale University Press, 2005.

Donner, Herbert. "Die literarische Gestalt der alttestamentlichen Josephsgeschichte." Pages 76–120 in *Aufsätze zum Alten Testament aus vier Jahrzehnten*. Beihefte zur Zeitschrift für die Alttestamentliche Wissenschaft 224. Berlin: Walter de Gruyter, 1994.

Dozeman, Thomas B., and Konrad Schmid, eds. *A Farewell to the Yahwist? The Composition of the Pentateuch in Recent European Interpretation*. Society of Biblical Literature Symposium Series 34. Atlanta: Society of Biblical Literature, 2006.

Driver, S. R. *Introduction to the Literature of the Old Testament*. New York: Meridian, 1957.

——. *The Book of Exodus*. Cambridge Bible Commentary. Cambridge: University Press, 1918.

——. *The Book of Genesis*. 12th ed. London: Methuen, 1912.

——. *A Critical and Exegetical Commentary on the Book of Deuteronomy*. 3rd ed. International Critical Commentary. Edinburgh: T & T Clark, 1901.

Eerdmans, B. D. *Alttestamentliche Studien I: Die Komposition der Genesis*. Giessen: Alfred Töpelmann, 1908.

Ehrlich, Arnold B. *Miqra ki-peshuto*. 3 vols. New York: Ktav, 1969.

Eichhorn, Johann G. *Einleitung in das Alte Testament*. Vol. 3. 4th ed. Göttingen: Carl Eduard Rosenbusch, 1823.

Eissfeldt, Otto. *The Old Testament: An Introduction*. Translated by Peter R. Ackroyd. New York: Harper & Row, 1965.

——. *Hexateuch-Synopse*. Leipzig: J. C. Hinrich, 1922.

Elliger, Karl. "Sinn und Ursprung der priesterlichen Geschichtserzählung." *Zeitschrift für Theologie und Kirche* 49 (1952): 121–43.

Emerton, J. A. "The Priestly Writer in Genesis." *Journal of Theological Studies* 39 (1988): 381–400.

Engnell, Ivan. *A Rigid Scrutiny: Critical Essays on the Old Testament*. Translated by John T. Willis. Nashville: Vanderbilt University Press, 1969.

Ewald, Heinrich. *Geschichte des Volkes Israel*. 8 vols. Göttingen: Dieterichschen Buchhandlung, 1864–1868.

——. *Die Komposition der Genesis kritisch untersucht.* Braunschweig: Ludwig Lucius, 1823.

Finn, A. H. *The Unity of the Pentateuch: An Examination of the Higher Critical Theory as to the Composite Nature of the Pentateuch.* 3rd ed. London and Edinburgh: Marshall Brothers, 1928.

Firmage, Edwin. "Genesis 1 and the Priestly Agenda." *Journal for the Study of the Old Testament* 82 (1999): 97–114.

Fischer, G. "Exodus 1–15—Eine Erzählung." Pages 149–78 in *Studies in the Book of Exodus.* Edited by Marc Vervenne. Bibliotheca Ephemeridum Theologicarum Lovaniensium 126. Leuven: University Press, 1996.

Fohrer, Georg. *Introduction to the Old Testament.* Nashville: Abingdon, 1968.

——. *Überlieferung und Geschichte des Exodus: Eine Analyse von Ex 1–15.* Beihefte zur Zeitschrift für die Alttestamentliche Wissenschaft 91. Berlin: Alfred Töpelmann, 1964.

Fokkelman, J. P. *Reading Biblical Narrative: An Introductory Guide.* Translated by Ineke Smit. Louisville, Ky.: Westminster John Knox, 1999.

Frampton, Travis L. *Spinoza and the Rise of Historical Criticism of the Bible.* New York: T & T Clark, 2006.

Friedman, Richard E. "Three Major Redactors of the Torah." Pages 31–44 in *Birkat Shalom: Studies in the Bible, Ancient Near Eastern Literature, and Post-Biblical Judaism.* Edited by Chaim Cohen, Victor Avigdor Hurowitz, Avi Hurvitz, Yochanan Muffs, Baruch J. Schwartz, and Jeffrey Tigay. Winona Lake, Ind.: Eisenbrauns, 2008.

——. *The Bible with Sources Revealed: A New View into the Five Books of Moses.* San Francisco: HarperSanFrancisco, 2003.

——. "Torah (Pentateuch)." Pages 605–22 in vol. 6 of *The Anchor Bible Dictionary.* 6 vols. Edited by D. Noel Freedman. New York: Doubleday, 1992.

Fritz, Volkmar. *Israel in der Wüste: Traditionsgeschichtliche Untersuchungen der Wüstenüberlieferung des Jahwisten.* Marburg: N. G. Elwart, 1970.

Fuller, Reginald C. *Alexander Geddes, 1737–1802: A Pioneer of Biblical Criticism.* Historic Texts and Interpreters in Biblical Scholarship 3. Sheffield: Almond, 1984.

Fuss, Werner. *Die deuteronomistiche Pentateuchredaktion in Exodus 3–17.* Beihefte zur Zeitschrift für die Alttestamentliche Wissenschaft 126. Berlin: Walter de Gruyter, 1972.

Geddes, Alexander. *The Holy Bible; or the Books accounted sacred by Jews and Christians; otherwise called the Books of the Old and New Covenants; faithfully translated from corrected texts of the originals, with various readings explanatory notes and critical remarks.* Vol. 1. R. Faulder and J. Johnson, 1792.

Gertz, Jan C. "The Transition between the Books of Genesis and Exodus." Pages 73–88 in *A Farewell to the Yahwist? The Composition of the Pentateuch in Recent European Interpretation.* Edited by Thomas B. Dozeman and Konrad Schmid. SBL Symposium Series 34. Atlanta: Society of Biblical Literature, 2006.

——. "Abraham, Mose und der Exodus: Beobachtungen zur Redaktionsgeschichte von Gen 15." Pages 63–81 in *Abschied vom Jahwisten: Die Komposition des Hexateuch in der jüngsten Diskussion.* Edited by Jan C. Gertz, Konrad Schmid, and Markus Witte. Beihefte zur Zeitschrift für die Alttestamentliche Wissenschaft 315. Berlin: Walter de Gruyter, 2002.

————. *Tradition und Redaktion in der Exoduserzählung: Untersuchungen zur Endredaktion des Pentateuch.* Forschungen zur Religion und Literatur des Alten und Neuen Testaments 186. Göttingen: Vandenhoeck & Ruprecht, 2000.

Gertz, Jan C., Konrad Schmid, and Markus Witte, eds. *Abschied vom Jahwisten: Die Komposition des Hexateuch in der jüngsten Diskussion.* Beihefte zur Zeitschrift für die Alttestamentliche Wissenschaft 315. Berlin: Walter de Gruyter, 2002.

Gibson, J. C. L. *Canaanite Myths and Legends.* 2nd ed. Edinburgh: T & T Clark, 1977.

Gilders, William K. "Sacrifice before Sinai and the Priestly Narratives." Pages 57–70 in *The Strata of the Priestly Writings: Contemporary Debate and Future Directions.* Edited by Sarah Shectman and Joel S. Baden. Abhandlungen zur Theologie des Alten und Neuen Testaments 95. Zurich: TVZ, 2009.

Gnuse, Robert K. "Redefining the Elohist." *Journal of Biblical Literature* 119 (2000): 201–20.

————. "Dreams in the Night—Scholarly Mirage or Theophanic Formula?: The Dream Report as a Motif of the So-Called Elohist Tradition." *Biblische Zeitschrift* 39 (1995): 28–53.

Gomes, Jules F. *The Sanctuary of Bethel and the Configuration of Israelite Identity.* Beihefte zur Zeitschrift für die Alttestamentliche Wissenschaft 368. Berlin: Walter de Gruyter, 2006.

Good, Edwin M. *Irony in the Old Testament.* 2nd ed. Bible and Literature Series 3. Sheffield: Almond, 1981.

Gorman, Frank H. "Priestly Rituals of Founding: Time, Space, and Status." Pages 47–64 in *History and Interpretation.* Edited by M. Patrick Graham, William P. Brown, and Jeffrey K. Kuan. Journal for the Study of the Old Testament Supplement Series 173. Sheffield: JSOT, 1993.

Graupner, Axel. "Die Erzählkunst des Elohisten: Zur Makrostruktur und Intention der elohistischen Darstellung der Gründungsgeschichte Israels." Pages 67–90 in *Das Alte Testament und die Kunst.* Edited by John Barton, J. Cheryl Exum, and Manfred Oeming. Münster: Lit, 2005.

————. *Der Elohist: Gegenwart und Wirksamkeit des transzendenten Gottes in der Geschichte.* Wissenschaftliche Monographien zum Alten und Neuen Testament 97. Neukirchen-Vluyn: Neukirchener Verlag, 2002.

Gray, George B. *A Critical and Exegetical Commentary on Numbers.* International Critical Commentary. Edinburgh: T & T Clark, 1903.

Gray, John. *The KRT Text in the Literature of Ras Shamra: A Social Myth of Ancient Canaan.* 2nd ed. Leiden: Brill, 1964.

Green, Barbara. *"What Profit for Us?": Remembering the Story of Joseph.* Lanham, Md.: University Press of America, 1996.

Green, William Henry. *The Higher Criticism of the Pentateuch.* New York: Charles Scribner's Sons, 1902.

————. "The Pentateuchal Question. III. Gen. 37:2–Ex. 12:51." *Hebraica* 7 (1890): 1–38.

Greenberg, Moshe. *Understanding Exodus.* New York: Behrman House, 1969.

Greenstein, Edward L. "Medieval Bible Commentaries." Pages 213–59 in *Back to the Sources: Reading the Classic Jewish Texts.* Edited by Barry W. Holtz. New York: Simon & Schuster, 1984.

———. "An Equivocal Reading of the Sale of Joseph." Pages 114–25 in *Literary Interpretations of Biblical Narratives*. Vol. 2. Edited by Kenneth R. R. Gros Louis with James S. Ackerman. Nashville: Abingdon, 1982.

Gressmann, Hugo. *Mose und seine Zeit: Ein Kommentar zu den Mose-Sagen*. Forschungen zur Religion und Literatur des Alten und Neuen Testaments 1. Göttingen: Vandenhoeck & Ruprecht, 1913.

Gross, Walter. "Jakob, der Mann des Segens: Zu Traditionsgeschichte und Theologie der priesterschriftlichen Jakobsüberlieferungen." *Biblica* 49 (1968): 321–344.

Gunkel, Hermann. "Israelite Literary History." Pages 31–41 in *Water for a Thirsty Land: Israelite Literature and Religion*. Edited by K. C. Hanson. Minneapolis: Fortress, 2001.

———. *An Introduction to the Psalms*. Translated by James D. Nogalski. Mercer Library of Biblical Studies. Macon, Ga.: Mercer University Press, 1998.

———. *Genesis*. Translated by Mark E. Biddle. Mercer Library of Biblical Studies. Macon, Ga.: Mercer University Press, 1997.

Gunneweg, A. H. J. "Das Gesetz und die Propheten: Eine Auslegung von Ex 33,7–11; Num 11,4–12,8; Dtn 31,14f.; 34,10." *Zeitschrift für die Alttestamentliche Wissenschaft* 102 (1990): 169–80.

Halpern, B. "Biblical versus Greek Historiography: A Comparison." Pages 101–27 in *Das Alte Testament ein Geschichtsbuch?* Edited by Erhard Blum, William Johnstone, and Christoph Markschies. Altes Testament und Moderne 10. Münster: Lit, 2005.

Haran, Menahem. "Scrolls of the Torah and Scrolls of the Bible in the First Centuries C.E. [Hebrew]." Pages 316–29 in *The Bible and Its World: Selected Literary and Historical Studies*. Jerusalem: Magnes, 2009.

———. *The Biblical Collection* [Hebrew]. 3 vols. Jerusalem: Magnes, 1996–2008.

———. "On Archives, Libraries, and the Order of the Biblical Books." *Journal of the Ancient Near Eastern Society* 22 (1993): 51–61.

———. *Temples and Temple-Service in Ancient Israel*. Winona Lake, Ind.: Eisenbrauns, 1985.

———. "Book-Size and the Device of Catch-Lines in the Biblical Canon." *Journal of Jewish Studies* 36 (1985): 1–11.

———. "More Concerning Book-Scrolls in Pre-Exilic Times." *Journal of Jewish Studies* 35 (1984): 84–85.

———. "Book-Scrolls at the Beginning of the Second Temple Period: The Transition from Papyrus to Skins." *Hebrew Union College Annual* 54 (1983): 111–22.

———. "Book-Scrolls in Israel in Pre-Exilic Times." *Journal of Jewish Studies* 33 (1982): 161–73.

Hayes, John H. *An Introduction to Old Testament Study*. Nashville: Abingdon, 1979.

Hendel, Ronald S. "'Begetting' and 'Being Born' in the Pentateuch: Notes on Historical Linguistics and Source Criticism." *Vetus Testamentum* 50 (2000): 38–46.

———. *The Text of Genesis 1–11: Textual Studies and Critical Edition*. New York: Oxford University Press, 1998.

———. "Tangled Plots in Genesis." Pages 35–51 in *Fortunate the Eyes That See*. Edited by Astrid Beck, Andrew H. Bartelt, Paul R. Raabe, and Chris A. Franke. Grand Rapids, Mich.: Eerdmans, 1995.

Hobbes, Thomas. *Leviathan, or The Matter, Form, and Power of a Commonwealth, Ecclesiastical and Civil.* 2nd ed. London: George Routledge and Sons, 1886.

Hoftijzer, Jacob. *Die Verheissungen an die Väter.* Göttingen: Vandenhoeck & Ruprecht, 1976.

Holzinger, H. *Numeri.* Kurzer Hand-Commentar zum Alten Testament 4. Tübingen: J. C. B. Mohr (Paul Siebeck), 1903.

———. *Genesis.* Kurzer Hand-Commentar zum Alten Testament 1. Freiburg i.B.: J. C. B. Mohr (Paul Siebeck), 1898.

———. *Einleitung in des Hexateuch.* Freiburg i.B.: Mohr (Siebeck), 1893.

Houtman, Cornelius. *Exodus.* 3 vols. Translated by Johan Rebel and Sierd Woudstra. Historical Commentary on the Old Testament. Kampen: Kok, 1993–2000.

———. *Der Pentateuch: Die Geschichte seiner Erforschung neben einer Auswertung.* Kampen: Kok Pharos, 1994.

———. "Jacob at Mahanaim: Some Remarks on Genesis xxxii 2–3." *Vetus Testamentum* 28 (1978): 37–44.

Humphreys, W. Lee. *Joseph and His Family: A Literary Study.* Columbia: University of South Carolina Press, 1988.

Hupfeld, Hermann. *Die Quellen der Genesis und die Art ihrer Zusammensetzung.* Berlin: Wiegandt und Grieben, 1853.

Ilgen, Karl D. *Die Urkunden des ersten Buchs von Moses in ihrer Urgestalt: zum bessern Verständniss und richtigern Gebrauch derselben: in ihrer gegenwärtigen Form aus dem Hebräischen mit kritischen Anmerkungen und Nachweisungen auch einer Abhandlung über die Trennung der Urkunden.* Halle: Hemmerde und Schwetschke, 1798.

Jacob, Benno. *Das erste Buch der Tora: Genesis.* Berlin: Schocken, 1934. Repr., New York: Ktav, 1974.

———. *Quellenscheidung und Exegese im Pentateuch.* Leipzig: M. W. Kaufmann, 1913.

Jaroš, Karl. *Die Stellung des Elohisten zur kanaanäischen Religion.* Orbis biblicus et orientalis 4. Freiburg: Universitätsverlag, 1974.

Jenks, Alan W. *The Elohist and North Israelite Traditions.* Society of Biblical Literature Monograph Series 22. Missoula, Mont.: Scholars Press, 1977.

Johnstone, William. *Chronicles and Exodus: An Analogy and Its Application.* Journal for the Study of the Old Testament Supplements 275. Sheffield: Sheffield Academic, 1998.

Kaufmann, Yehezkel. *The Religion of Israel: Its Beginnings to the Babylonian Exile.* Translated and abridged by Moshe Greenberg. Chicago: University of Chicago Press, 1960.

Kautzsch, E., and A. Socin. *Die Genesis mit äusserer Unterscheidung der Quellenschriften.* Freiburg i.B.: J. C. B. Mohr (Paul Siebeck), 1888.

Kearney, Peter J. "Creation and Liturgy: The P Redaction of Ex 25–40." *Zeitschrift für die Alttestamentliche Wissenschaft* 89 (1977): 375–87.

Kebekus, Norbert. *Die Joseferzählung: Literarkritische und redaktionsgeschichtliche Untersuchungen zu Genesis 37–50.* Internationale Hochschulschriften. Münster: Waxmann, 1990.

Keil, C. F., and F. Delitzsch. *Commentary on the Old Testament, Volume 1: The Pentateuch.* Edinburgh: T & T Clark, 1866–1891. Repr., Peabody, Mass.: Hendrickson, 1996.

Kessler, Rainer. "Die Querverweise im Pentateuch: Überlieferungsgeschichtliche Untersuchung der expliziten Querverbindungen innerhalb des vorpriesterlichen Pentateuchs." Ph.D. diss., Ruprecht-Karl-Universität, 1972.

Kilian, Rudolf. *Die vorpriesterlichen Abrahamsüberlieferungen: Literarkritisch und traditionsgeschichtlich untersucht.* Bonner biblische Beiträge 24. Bonn: Peter Hanstein, 1966.

Kitchen, Kenneth A. *Ancient Orient and Old Testament.* Downers Grove, Ill.: InterVarsity, 1966.

Klostermann, August. *Der Pentateuch: Beiträge zu seinem Verständnis und seiner Entstehungsgeschichte.* Leipzig: Deichert, 1907.

Knauf, Ernst A. "Medan." Page 656 in vol. 4 of *The Anchor Bible Dictionary.* 6 vols. Edited by D. Noel Freedman. New York: Doubleday, 1992.

Knierim, Rolf. "Criticism of Literary Features, Form, Tradition, and Redaction." Pages 123–65 in *The Hebrew Bible and Its Modern Interpreters.* Edited by Douglas A. Knight and Gene M. Tucker. Society of Biblical Literature, The Bible and Its Modern Interpreters 1. Chico, Calif.: 1985.

Knight, Douglas A. "The Pentateuch." Pages 263–96 in *The Hebrew Bible and Its Modern Interpreters.* Edited by Douglas A. Knight and Gene M. Tucker. Society of Biblical Literature, The Bible and Its Modern Interpreters 1. Chico, Calif.: 1985.

Knohl, Israel. *The Sanctuary of Silence: The Priestly Torah and the Holiness School.* Minneapolis: Fortress, 1995.

Koch, Klaus. "P—Kein Redaktor! Erinnerung an zwei Eckdaten der Quellenscheidung." *Vetus Testamentum* 37 (1987): 446–67.

——. *The Growth of the Biblical Tradition: The Form-Critical Method.* Translated by S. M. Cupitt. New York: Charles Scribner's Sons, 1969.

Koenen, Klaus. *Bethel: Geschichte, Kult und Theologie.* Orbis biblicus et orientalis 192. Göttingen: Vandenhoeck & Ruprecht, 2003.

Kohata, Fujiko. *Jahwist und Priesterschrift in Exodus 3–14.* Beiheifte zur Zeitschrift für die Alttestamentliche Wissenschaft 166. Berlin: Walter de Gruyter, 1986.

Köhlmoos, Melanie. *Bet-El—Erinnerung an eine Stadt: Perspektiven der alttestamentlichen Bet-El-Überlieferung.* Forschungen zum Alten Testament 49. Tübingen: Mohr Siebeck, 2006.

Kratz, Reinhard G. *The Composition of the Narrative Books of the Old Testament.* Translated by John Bowden. London: T & T Clark, 2005.

Kraus, Hans-Joachim. *Geschichte der historisch-kritischen Erforschung des Alten Testaments.* 3rd ed. Neukirchen: Neukirchener Verlag, 1982.

Krüger, Thomas. "Erwägungen zur Redaktion der Meerwundererzählung (Exodus 13,17–14,31)." *Zeitschrift für die Alttestamentliche Wissenschaft* 108 (1996): 519–33.

Kuenen, Abraham. *An Historico-Critical Inquiry into the Origin and Composition of the Hexateuch.* Translated by Philip H. Wicksteed. London: Macmillan, 1886.

——. "Bijdragen tot de critiek van Pentateuch en Jozua. IV. De opstand van Korach, Dathan en Abiram." *Theologische Tjidschrift* 12 (1878): 139–62.

Kugel, James L. *Traditions of the Bible: A Guide to the Bible as It Was at the Start of the Common Era.* Cambridge, Mass.: Harvard University Press, 1998.

Kyle, Melvin G. *The Problem of the Pentateuch: A New Solution by Archaeological Methods*. Oberlin, Ohio: Bibliotheca Sacra, 1920.

La Peyrère, Isaac. *Theological system upon the presupposition, that men were before Adam*. London: [n.p.], 1665. Translation of *Systema theologicum, ex preadamitarum hypothesi*. Amsterdam: [n.p.], 1655.

Lehming, Sigo. "Versuch zu Num 16." *Zeitschrift für die Alttestamentliche Wissenschaft* 74 (1962): 291–321.

Leibowitz, Nehama. *Studies in the Book of Genesis*. Translated and adapted by Aryeh Newman. Jerusalem: World Zionist Organization, 1972.

Lemmelijn, Bénédicte. "The So-Called 'Priestly' Layer in Exod 7,14–11,10: 'Source' and/or/nor 'Redaction'?" *Revue Biblique* 109 (2002): 481–511.

Levin, Christoph. "Source Criticism: The Miracle at the Sea." Pages 39–61 in *Method Matters: Essays on the Interpretation of the Hebrew Bible in Honor of David L. Petersen*. Edited by Joel M. LeMon and Kent H. Richards. Society for Biblical Literature Resources for Biblical Study 56. Atlanta: Society for Biblical Literature, 2009.

———. *Der Jahwist*. Forschungen zur Religion und Literatur des Alten und Neuen Testaments 157. Göttingen: Vandenhoeck & Ruprecht, 1993.

Levine, Baruch A. "Offerings Rejected by God: Numbers 16:15 in Comparative Perspective." Pages 107–16 in *"Go to the Land I Will Show You."* Edited by Joseph E. Coleson and Victor H. Matthews. Winona Lake, Ind.: Eisenbrauns, 1996.

———. *Numbers 1–20*. Anchor Bible 4. New York: Doubleday, 1993.

Levinson, Bernard M. *Deuteronomy and the Hermeneutics of Legal Innovation*. Oxford: Oxford University Press, 1998.

Lichtenstein, Murray. "Dream-Theophany and the E Document." *Journal of the Ancient Near Eastern Society* 1 (1969): 45–54.

Limburg, James. "Psalms, Book of." Pages 522–36 in *The Anchor Bible Dictionary*. 6 vols. Edited by D. Noel Freedman. New York: Doubleday, 1992.

Liver, Jacob. "Korah, Dathan and Abiram." Pages 189–217 in *Studies in the Bible*. Edited by Chaim Rabin. Scripta Hierosolymitana 8. Jerusalem: Magnes, 1961.

Ljungberg, Bo-Krister. "Genre and Form Criticism in Old Testament Exegesis." Pages 415–33 in *Biblical Hebrew and Discourse Linguistics*. Edited by Robert D. Bergen. Dallas, Tex.: Summer Institute of Linguistics, 1994.

Lockshin, Martin I. *Rabbi Samuel ben Meir's Commentary on* Genesis: *An Annotated Translation*. Jewish Studies 5. Lewiston/Lampeter/Queenston: Edwin Mellen, 1989.

Lods, Adolphe. *Jean Astruc et la critique biblique au XVIIIᵉ siècle*. Strasbourg: Librairie Istra, 1924.

Loewenstamm, Samuel E. "Reuben and Judah in the Cycle of Joseph Stories." Pages 35–41 in *From Babylon to Canaan: Studies in the Bible and Its Oriental Background*. Jerusalem: Magnes, 1992.

Lohfink, Norbert. "Original Sins in the Priestly Historical Narrative." Pages 96–115 in *Theology of the Pentateuch: Themes of the Priestly Narrative and Deuteronomy*. Minneapolis: Fortress, 1994.

———. "The Priestly Narrative and History." Pages 136–72 in *Theology of the Pentateuch: Themes of the Priestly Narrative and Deuteronomy*. Minneapolis: Fortress, 1994

Longacre, Robert E. *Joseph: A Story of Divine Providence: A Text Theoretical and Textlinguistic Analysis of Genesis 37 and 39–48.* 2nd ed. Winona Lake, Ind.: Eisenbrauns, 2003.

———. "Who Sold Joseph into Egypt?" Pages 75–91 in *Interpretation and History.* Edited by R. Laird Harris, Swee-Hwa Quek, and J. Robert Vannoy. Singapore: Christian Life Publishers, 1986.

Luther, Martin. *Commentary on Genesis.* Volume 6 of *Luther's Works.* Edited by Jaroslav Pelikan. St. Louis, Mo.: Concordia, 1955–1986.

Magonet, Jonathan. "The Korah Rebellion." *Journal for the Study of the Old Testament* 24 (1982): 3–25.

Mann, Thomas W. *The Book of the Torah: The Narrative Integrity of the Pentateuch.* Atlanta: John Knox, 1988.

Marconi, Nazzareno. "Contributi per una lettura unitaria di Gen 37." *Rivista Biblica* 39 (1991): 277–303.

Margalit, Baruch. "The Legend of Keret." Pages 203–33 in *Handbook of Ugaritic Studies.* Edited by Wilfred G. E. Watson and Nicolas Wyatt. Handbuch der Orientalistik I/39. Leiden: Brill, 1999.

McEvenue, Sean E. "A Return to Sources in Genesis 28,10–22?" *Zeitschrift für die Alttestamentliche Wissenschaft* 106 (1994): 375–89.

———. "The Elohist at Work." *Zeitschrift für die Alttestamentliche Wissenschaft* 96 (1984): 315–32.

———. *The Narrative Style of the Priestly Writer.* Analecta biblica 50. Rome: Biblical Institute Press, 1971.

McKane, William. *Selected Christian Hebraists.* Cambridge: Cambridge University Press, 1989.

McNeile, A. H. *The Book of Exodus.* 2nd ed. Westminster Commentaries. London: Methuen, 1917.

Mendenhall, George E. "Midian." Pages 815–16 in vol. 4 of *The Anchor Bible Dictionary.* Edited by D. Noel Freedman. New York: Doubleday, 1992.

Meyer, Eduard. *Die Israeliten und ihre Nachbarstämme: Alttestamentliche Untersuchungen.* Darmstadt: Wissenschaftliche Buchgesellschaft, 1967.

Milgrom, Jacob. "H_R in Leviticus and Elsewhere in the Torah." Pages 24–40 in *The Book of Leviticus: Composition and Reception.* Edited by Rolf Rendtorff and Robert A. Kugler. Supplements to Vetus Testamentum 93. Leiden: Brill, 2003.

———. *Leviticus 17–22.* Anchor Bible 3A. New York: Doubleday, 2000.

———. *The JPS Torah Commentary: Numbers.* Philadelphia: Jewish Publication Society, 1990.

———. "Korah's Rebellion: A Study in Redaction." Pages 135–46 in *De la Tôrah au Messie: Études d'exégèse et d'herméneutique bibliques offertes à Henri Cazelles pour ses 25 années d'enseignment à l'Institut Catholique de Paris (Octobre 1979).* Edited by Maurice Carrez, Maurice Carrez, Joseph Doré, and Pierre Grelot. Paris: Desclée, 1981.

Mirguet, Françoise. "Numbers 16: The Significance of Place—An Analysis of Spatial Markers." *Journal for the Study of the Old Testament* 32 (2008): 311–30.

Morgenstern, Julius. "The Oldest Document of the Hexateuch." *Hebrew Union College Annual* 4 (1927): 1–138.

Mowinckel, Sigmund. *Erwägungen zur Pentateuch Quellenfrage*. Oslo: Universitetsfor-
    laget, 1964.
Muilenburg, James. "Form Criticism and Beyond." *Journal of Biblical Literature* 88
    (1969): 1–18.
Myers, Jacob M. *Ezra-Nehemiah*. Anchor Bible 14. New York: Doubleday, 1965.
Nahmanides (Moses ben Nachman). *Commentary on the Torah*. Vol. 1. Translated by
    Charles B. Chavel. New York: Shilo, 1971.
Najman, Hindy. *Seconding Sinai: The Development of Mosaic Discourse in Second Temple
    Judaism*. Supplements to the Journal for the Study of Judaism 77. Leiden: Brill, 2003.
Nelson, Richard D. *Deuteronomy*. Old Testament Library. Louisville, Ky.: Westminster
    John Knox, 2002.
Nicholson, Ernest W. *The Pentateuch in the Twentieth Century: The Legacy of Julius Well-
    hausen*. Oxford: Clarendon, 1998.
———. "The Origin of the Tradition in Exodus xxiv 9–11." *Vetus Testamentum* 26 (1976):
    148–60.
———. "The Antiquity of the Tradition in Exodus xxiv 9–11." *Vetus Testamentum* 25 (1975):
    69–79.
———. "The Interpretation of Exodus xxiv 9–11." *Vetus Testamentum* 24 (1974): 77–97.
Nihan, Christophe. *From Priestly Torah to Pentateuch: A Study in the Composition of the
    Book of Leviticus*. Forschungen zum Alten Testament II/25. Tübingen: Mohr Siebeck,
    2007.
———. "La Mort de Moïse (Nb 20,1–13; 20,22–29; 27,12–23) et l'édition finale du livre des
    Nombres." Pages 145–82 in *Les dernières rédactions du Pentateuque, de l'Hexateuque
    et de l'Ennéateuque*. Edited by T. Römer and K. Schmid. Bibliotheca Ephemeridum
    Theologicarum Lovaniensium 203. Leuven: University Press, 2007.
Nöldeke, Theodor. "Die s.g. Grundschrift des Pentateuchs." Pages 1–144 in *Untersuchun-
    gen zur Kritik des Alten Testaments*. Kiel: Schwers'sche Buchhandlung, 1869.
Noth, Martin. *The Deuteronomistic History*. 2nd ed. Journal for the Study of the Old Testa-
    ment Supplements 15. Sheffield: Sheffield Academic, 1991.
———. *A History of Pentateuchal Traditions*. Translated by Bernhard W. Anderson. Engle-
    wood Cliffs, N.J.: Prentice-Hall, 1972. Repr., Chico, Calif: Scholars Press, 1981.
———. *Numbers*. Translated by James D. Martin. Old Testament Library. Philadelphia:
    Westminster, 1968.
———. *Exodus: A Commentary*. Translated by J. S. Bowden. Old Testament Library. Phila-
    delphia: Westminster, 1962.
———. "Der Schauplatz des Meereswunders." Pages 181–90 in *Festschrift Otto Eissfeldt*.
    Edited by Johann Fück. Halle an der Saale: Max Niemeyer, 1947.
Otto, Eckart. "Die nachpriesterschriftliche Pentateuchredaktion im Buch Exodus."
    Pages 61–112 in *Studies in the Book of Exodus*. Edited by Marc Vervenne. Bibliotheca
    Ephemeridum Theologicarum Lovaniensium 136. Leuven: Peeters, 1996.
———. "Die Paradieserzählung Genesis 2–3: Eine nachpriesterschriftliche Lehrerzählung
    in ihrem religionshistorischen Kontext." Pages 167–92 in *"Jedes Ding hat seine Zeit . . .":
    Studien zur israelitischen und altorientalischen Weisheit*. Edited by Anja A. Diesel,

Reinhard G. Lehmann, and Eckart Otto. Beiheifte zur Zeitschrift für die Alttestament-liche Wissenschaft 241. Berlin: Walter de Gruyter, 1996.

———. "Jakob in Bethel: Ein Beitrag zur Geschichte der Jakobüberlieferung." *Zeitschrift für die Alttestamentliche Wissenschaft* 88 (1976): 165–90.

Paap, Carolin. *Die Josephsgeschichte Genesis 37–50: Bestimmungen ihrer literarischen Gattung in der zweiten Hälfte des 20. Jahrhunderts.* Frankfurt am Main: Peter Lang, 1995.

Paran, Meir. *Forms of the Priestly Style in the Pentateuch: Patterns, Linguistic Usages, Syntactic Structures* [Hebrew]. Jerusalem: Magnes, 1989.

Pardee, Dennis. "The Kirta Epic." Pages 333–43 in *The Context of Scripture.* Vol. 1. Edited by William W. Hallo. 3 vols. Leiden: Brill, 1997–2002.

Perlitt, Lothar. *Deuteronomium.* Biblischer Kommentar Alten Testament 5. Neukirchen-Vluyn: Neukirchener Verlag, 1990.

———. *Bundestheologie im Alten Testament.* Wissenschaftliche Monographien zum Alten und Neuen Testament 36. Neukirchen-Vluyn: Neukirchener Verlag, 1969.

Pfeiffer, Robert H. *Introduction to the Old Testament.* London: Adam and Charles Black, 1952.

———. "A Non-Israelite Source of the Book of Genesis." *Zeitschrift für die Alttestament-liche Wissenschaft* 48 (1930): 63–73.

Popkin, Richard H. *Isaac La Peyrère (1596–1676): His Life, Work, and Influence.* Brill's Studies in Intellectual History 1. Leiden: Brill, 1987.

Procksch, Otto. *Das nordhebräische Sagenbuch die Elohimquelle übersetzt und untersucht.* Leipzig: J. C. Hinrichs'sche Buchhandlung, 1906.

Propp, William H. C. *Exodus 19–40.* Anchor Bible 2A. New York: Doubleday, 2006.

———. *Exodus 1–18.* Anchor Bible 2. New York: Doubleday 1999.

Rapp, Hans A. *Jakob in Bet-El: Gen 35,1–15 und die jüdische Literatur des 3. und 2. Jahrhunderts.* Freiburg: Herder, 2001.

Redford, Donald B. *A Study of the Biblical Story of Joseph (Genesis 37–50).* Supplements to Vetus Testamentum 20. Leiden: Brill, 1970.

Rendtorff, Rolf. *The Problem of the Process of Transmission in the Pentateuch.* Translated by John J. Scullion. Journal for the Study of the Old Testament Supplement Series 89. Sheffield: Sheffield Academic, 1977.

Renz, Johannes, and Wolfgang Röllig. *Handbuch der althebräischen Epigraphik.* 3 vols. Darmstadt: Wissenschaftliche Buchgesellschaft, 1995.

Revell, E. J. "Midian and Ishmael in Genesis 37." Pages 70–91 in *The World of the Aramaeans I: Biblical Studies in Honour of Paul-Eugène Dion.* Edited by P. M. Michèle Daviau, John W. Wevers, and Michael Weigl. Journal for the Study of the Old Testament Supplements 324. Sheffield: Sheffield Academic Press, 2001.

Richter, Wolfgang. "Das Gelübde als theologische Rahmung der Jakobsüberlieferungen." *Biblische Zeitschrift* 11 (1967): 21–52.

Rofé, Alexander. *Deuteronomy: Issues and Interpretation.* Old Testament Studies. London: T & T Clark, 2002.

———. *Introduction to the Composition of the Pentateuch.* Biblical Seminar 58. Sheffield: Sheffield Academic, 1999.

Rogerson, John. *Old Testament Criticism in the Nineteenth Century: England and Germany*. Philadelphia: Fortress, 1984.

Römer, Thomas. *The So-Called Deuteronomistic History: A Sociological, Historical and Literary Introduction*. London: T & T Clark, 2005.

——. "Recherches actuelles sur le cycle d'Abraham." Pages 179–212 in *Studies in the Book of Genesis*. Edited by André Wenin. Bibliotheca Ephemeridum Theologicarum Lovaniensium 155. Leuven: University Press, 2001.

——. "Nombres 11–12 et la question d'une rédaction deutéronomique dans le Pentateuque." Pages 481–500 in *Deuteronomy and Deuteronomic Literature*. Edited by Marc Vervenne and Johan Lust. Bibliotheca Ephemeridum Theologicarum Lovaniensium 133. Leuven: University Press, 1997.

——. "Joseph approche: Source du cycle, corpus, unité." Pages 73–85 in *Le livre de traverse de l'exégèse biblique à l'anthropologie*. Edited by Olivier Abel and Françoise Smyth. Paris: Les éditions du Cerf, 1992.

——. *Israels Väter: Untersuchungen zur Väterthematik im Deuteronomium und in der deuteronomistischen Tradition*. Orbis biblicus et orientalis 99. Freiburg: Universitätsverlag, 1990.

Rose, Martin. "L'itinérance du Iacobus Pentateuchus: Réflexions sur Genèse 35,1–15." Pages 113–26 in *Lectio Difficilior Probabilior? L'exégèse comme expérience de décloisonnement*. Edited by Thomas Römer. Dielheimer Blätter zum Alten Testament und seiner Rezeption in der Alten Kirche 12. Heidelberg: Esprint, 1991.

——. *Deuteronomist und Jahwist: Untersuchungen zu den Berührungspunkten beider Literaturwerke*. Abhandlung zur Theologie des Alten und Neuen Testaments 67. Zurich: Theologischer Verlag, 1981.

Rudolph, Wilhelm. *Der "Elohist" von Exodus bis Josua*. Beiheifte zur Zeitschrift für die Alttestamentliche Wissenschaft 68. Berlin: Alfred Töpelmann, 1938.

Ruppert, Lothar. "Die Aporie der gegenwärtigen Pentateuchdiskussion und die Josefserzählung der Genesis." *Biblische Zeitschrift* 29 (1985): 31–48.

——. "Das Motiv der Versuchung durch Gott in vordeuteronomischer Tradition." *Vetus Testamentum* 22 (1972): 55–63.

——. "Der Elohist—Sprecher für Gottes Volk." Pages 108–17 in *Wort und Botschaft: Eine theologische und kritische Einführung in die Probleme des Alten Testaments*. Edited by Josef Schreiner. Würzburg: Echter Verlag, 1967.

——. *Die Josephserzählung der Genesis: Ein Beitrag zur Theologie der Pentateuchquellen*. Studien zum Alten und Neuen Testament 11. Munich: Kösel, 1965.

Sarna, Nahum. *The JPS Torah Commentary: Exodus*. Philadelphia: Jewish Publication Society, 1991.

——. *The JPS Torah Commentary: Genesis*. Philadelphia: Jewish Publication Society, 1989.

Scharbert, Josef. *Numeri*. Neue Echter Bibel 27. Würzburg: Echter, 1992.

——. *Genesis 12–50*. Würzburg: Echter Verlag, 1986.

——. "Das 'Schilfmeerwunder' in den Texten des Alten Testaments." Pages 395–417 in *Mélanges bibliques et orientaux en l'honneur de M. Henri Cazelles*. Edited by A. Caquot and M. Delcor. Alter Orient und Altes Testament 212. Neukirchen: Neukirchener Verlag, 1981.

Schmid, Hans Heinrich. *Der sogenannte Jahwist: Beobachtungen und Fragen zur Pentateuchforschung.* Zurich: Theologischer Verlag, 1976.

Schmid, Konrad. "Die Josephsgeschichte im Pentateuch." Pages 83–118 in *Abschied vom Jahwisten: Die Komposition des Hexateuch in der jüngsten Diskussion.* Edited by Jan C. Gertz, Konrad Schmid, and Markus Witte. Beiheifte zur Zeitschrift für die Alttestamentliche Wissenschaft 315. Berlin: Walter de Gruyter, 2002.

———. "Israel am Sinai: Etappen der Forschungsgeschichte zu Ex 32–34 in seinen Kontexten." Pages 9–40 in *Gottes Volk am Sinai: Untersuchungen zu Ex 32–34 und Dtn 9–10.* Edited by Matthias Köckert and Erhard Blum. Veröffentlichungen der Wissenschaftlichen Gesellschaft für Theologie 18. Gütersloh: C. Kaiser, 2001.

———. *Erzväter und Exodus: Untersuchungen zur doppelten Begründung der Ursprünge Israels innerhalb der Geschichtsbücher des Alten Testaments.* Wissenschaftliche Monographien zum Alten und Neuen Testament 81. Neukirchen-Vluyn: Neukirchener Verlag, 1999.

Schmidt, Ludwig. "El und die Landverheissung in Bet-El." Pages 137–49 in *Gesammelte Aufsätze zum Pentateuch.* Beiheifte zur Zeitschrift für die Alttestamentliche Wissenschaft 263. Berlin: Walter de Gruyter, 1998.

———. "Weisheit und Geschichte beim Elohisten." Pages 209–25 in *"Jedes Ding hat seine Zeit . . ."* Edited by Anja A. Diesel, Reinhard G. Lehmann, and Eckart Otto. Beiheifte zur Zeitschrift für die Alttestamentliche Wissenschaft 241. Berlin: Walter de Gruyter, 1996.

———. *Studien zur Priesterschrift.* Beiheifte zur Zeitschrift für die Alttestamentliche Wissenschaft 214. Berlin: Walter de Gruyter, 1993.

———. *Literarische Studien zur Josephsgeschichte.* Beiheifte zur Zeitschrift für die Alttestamentliche Wissenschaft 167. Berlin: Walter de Gruyter, 1986.

Schmidt, Werner H. *Old Testament Introduction.* Berlin: Walter de Gruyter, 1995.

———. *Exodus, Sinai und Mose.* Erträge der Forschung 191. Darmstadt: Wissenschaftliche Buchgesellschaft, 1983.

Schmitt, Hans-Christoph. "Menschliche Schuld, göttliche Führung und ethische Wandlung. Zur Theologie von Genesis 20,1–21,21 und zum Problem des Beginns des 'Elohistischen Geschichtswerks.'" Pages 259–70 in *Gott und Mensch in Dialog.* Vol. 1. Edited by Markus Witte. 2 vols. Beiheifte zur Zeitschrift für die Alttestamentliche Wissenschaft 345. Berlin: Walter de Gruyter, 2004.

———. "Die Erzählung von der Versuchung Abrahams Gen 22,1–19 und das Problem einer Theologie der elohistischen Pentateuchtexte." *Biblische Notizen* 34 (1986): 82–109.

———. *Die nichtpriesterlicher Josephsgeschichte.* Beiheifte zur Zeitschrift für die Alttestamentliche Wissenschaft 154. Berlin: Walter de Gruyter, 1980.

———. "'Priesterliches' und 'prophetisches' Geschichtsverständnis in der Meerwundererzählung Ex 13,17–14,31: Beobachtungen zur Endredaktion des Pentateuch." Pages 139–55 in *Textgemäß: Aufsätze und Beiträge zur Hermeneutik des Alten Testaments.* Edited by A. H. J. Gunneweg and Otto Kaiser. Göttingen: Vandenhoeck & Ruprecht, 1979.

Schorn, Ulrike. "Rubeniten als exemplarische Aufrührer in Num. 16f*/Deut. 11." Pages 251–68 in *Rethinking the Foundations: Historiography in the Ancient World and in the Bible*. Edited by Steven L. McKenzie and Thomas Römer. Berlin: Walter de Gruyter, 2000.

Schüpphaus, Joachim. "Volk Gottes und Gesetz beim Elohisten." *Theologische Zeitschrift* 31 (1975): 193–210.

Schwartz, Baruch J. "Joseph's Descent into Egypt: The Composition of Genesis 37 [Hebrew]." Pages 1–30 in *The Joseph Story in the Bible and throughout the Ages*. Edited by Lea Mazor. Beth Mikra 55. Jerusalem: Bialik, 2010.

——. "The Visit of Jethro: A Case of Chronological Displacement? The Source-Critical Solution." Pages 29–48 in *Mishneh Todah: Studies in Deuteronomy and Its Cultural Environment*. Edited by Nili S. Fox, David A. Glatt-Gilad, and Michael J. Williams. Winona Lake, Ind.: Eisenbrauns, 2009.

——. "The Flood Narratives in the Torah and the Question of Where History Begins." Pages 139–54 in *Shai le-Sara Japhet: Studies in the Bible, Its Exegesis and Its Language*. Edited by Moshe Bar-Asher, Dalit Rom-Shiloni, Emanuel Tov, and Nilil Wazana. Jerusalem: Bialik, 2007.

——. "Reexamining the Fate of the 'Canaanites' in the Torah Traditions." Pages 151–70 in *Sefer Moshe*. Edited by Chaim Cohen, Avi Hurvitz, and Shalom M. Paul. Winona Lake, Ind.: Eisenbrauns, 2004.

——. *The Holiness Legislation: Studies in the Priestly Code* [Hebrew]. Jerusalem: Magnes, 1999.

——. "The Priestly Account of the Theophany and Lawgiving at Sinai." Pages 103–34 in *Texts, Temples, and Traditions: A Tribute to Menahem Haran*. Edited by Michael V. Fox, Victor Avigdor Hurowitz, Avi Hurvitz, Michael L. Klein, Baruch J. Schwartz, and Nili Shupak. Winona Lake, Ind.: Eisenbrauns, 1996.

Seebass, Horst. *Numeri*. 2 vols. Biblischer Kommentar Altes Testament IV. Neukirchen-Vluyn: Neukirchener Verlag, 2003.

——. *Genesis III: Josephgeschichte (37,1–50,26)*. Neukirchen-Vluyn: Neukirchener Verlag, 2000.

——. *Genesis II: Vätergeschichte II (23,1–36,43)*. Neukirchen-Vluyn: Neukirchener Verlag, 1996.

——. "Elohist." *Theologische Realenzyklopädie* 9 (1982): 520–24.

——. "Num. xi, xii und die Hypothese des Jahwisten." *Vetus Testamentum* 28 (1978): 214–23.

Segal, M. H. *The Pentateuch: Its Composition and Its Authorship and Other Biblical Studies*. Jerusalem: Magnes, 1967.

Septimus, Bernard. "Iterated Quotation Formulae in Talmudic Narrative and Exegesis." Pages 371–98 in *The Idea of Biblical Interpretation: Essays in Honor of James L. Kugel*. Edited by Hindy Najman and Judith H. Newman. Supplements to the Journal for the Study of Judaism 83. Leiden: Brill, 2004.

Shectman, Sarah, and Joel S. Baden, eds. *The Strata of the Priestly Writings: Contemporary Debate and Future Directions*. Abhandlungen zur Theologie des Alten und Neuen Testaments 95. Zurich: TVZ, 2009.

Simon, Richard. *Histoire Critique du Vieux Testament*. Rotterdam: [n.p.], 1685. Repr., Frankfurt: Minerva, 1967.

Simpson, Cuthbert A. *The Early Traditions of Israel: A Critical Analysis of the Pre-Deuteronomic Narrative of the Hexateuch*. Oxford: Basil Blackwell, 1948.

Simpson, D. C. *Pentateuchal Criticism*. London: Hodder and Stoughton, 1914.

Ska, Jean-Louis. "The Story of the Flood: A Priestly Writer and Some Later Editorial Fragments." Pages 1–22 in *The Exegesis of the Pentateuch: Exegetical Studies and Basic Questions*. Forschungen zum Alten Testament 66. Tübingen: Mohr Siebeck, 2009.

——. "Vision and Meal in Exodus 24:11." Pages 165–83 in *The Exegesis of the Pentateuch: Exegetical Studies and Basic Questions*. Forschungen zum Alten Testament 66. Tübingen: Mohr Siebeck, 2009.

——. *Introduction to Reading the Pentateuch*. Translated by Pascale Dominique. Winona Lake, Ind.: Eisenbrauns, 2006.

——. "Quelques remarques sur Pg et la dernière rédaction du Pentateuque." Pages 95–125 in *Le Pentateuque en question*. 3rd ed. Edited by Albert de Pury and Thomas Römer. Le monde de la Bible 19. Geneva: Labor et Fides, 2002.

——. *Le passage de la mer: Étude de la construction, du style et de la symbolique d'Ex 14,1–31*. Analecta biblica 109. Rome: Biblical Institute Press, 1986.

——. "Exode xiv contient-il un récit de 'guerre sainte' de style deutéronomistique?" *Vetus Testamentum* 33 (1983): 454–67.

Skinner, John. *A Critical and Exegetical Commentary on Genesis*. 2nd ed. International Critical Commentary. Edinburgh: T & T Clark, 1930.

Smend, Rudolf. *From Astruc to Zimmerli: Old Testament Scholarship in Three Centuries*. Translated by Margaret Kohl. Tübingen: Mohr Siebeck, 2007.

Smend Rudolf. *Der Erzählung des Hexateuch auf ihre Quellen untersucht*. Berlin: George Reimer, 1912.

Sommer, Benjamin D. "Reflecting on Moses: The Redaction of Numbers 11." *Journal of Biblical Literature* 118 (1999): 601–24.

Speiser, E. A. *Genesis*. Anchor Bible 1. New York: Doubleday, 1964.

Spina, Frank A. "The 'Ground' for Cain's Rejection (Gen 4): *'ᵃdāmāh* in the Context of Gen 1–11." *Zeitschrift für die Alttestamentliche Wissenschaft* 104 (1992): 319–332.

Spinoza, Baruch. *A Theologico-Political Treatise*. Translated by R. H. M. Elwes. New York: Dover, 1951.

Stackert, Jeffrey. *Rewriting the Torah: Literary Revision in Deuteronomy and the Holiness Legislation*. Forschungen zum Alten Testament 52. Tübingen: Mohr Siebeck, 2007.

Stager, Lawrence E. "The Archaeology of the Family in Ancient Israel." *Bulletin of the American Schools of Oriental Research* 260 (1985): 1–35.

Steinmann, Jean. *Richard Simon et les origines de l'exégèse biblique*. Bruges: Desclée de Brouwer, 1960.

Strauss, Leo. *Spinoza's Critique of Religion*. Translated by E. M. Sinclair. New York: Shocken, 1965.

Strickland, H. Norman, and Arthur M. Silver. *Ibn Ezra's Commentary on the Pentateuch: Genesis (Bereshit)*. New York: Menorah, 1988.

Sweeney, Marvin. "Form Criticism." Pages 58–89 in *To Each Its Own Meaning: An Intro-duction to Biblical Criticisms and Their Application*. Edited by Steven L. McKenzie and Stephen R. Hayes. Louisville, Ky.: Westminster John Knox, 1999.

Talmon, Shemaryahu. "The Presentation of Synchroneity and Simultaneity in Biblical Narratives." Pages 9–26 in *Studies in Hebrew Narrative Art throughout the Ages*. Edited by Joseph Heinemann and Shmuel Werses. Scripta Hierosolymitana 27. Jerusalem: Magnes, 1978.

Tengström, Sven. *Die Toledotformel und die literarische Struktur der priesterlichen Er-weiterungsschicht im Pentateuch*. Coniectanea Biblica Old Testament Series 17. Lund: CWK Gleerup, 1981.

———. *Die Hexateucherzählung: Eine literaturgeschichtliche Studie*. Coniectanea Biblica Old Testament Series 7. Lund: Gleerup, 1976.

Tov, Emanuel. *Textual Criticism of the Hebrew Bible*. 2nd ed. Minneapolis: Fortress, 2001.

Tucker, Gene M. *Form Criticism of the Old Testament*. Guides to Biblical Scholarship. Philadelphia: Fortress, 1991.

van der Toorn, Karel. *Family Religion in Babylonia, Syria and Israel: Continuity and Change in the Forms of Religious Life*. Studies in the History and Culture of the Ancient Near East 7. Leiden: Brill, 1996.

Van Seters, John. *The Edited Bible*. Winona Lake, Ind.: Eisenbrauns, 2006.

———. "The Report of the Yahwist's Demise Has Been Greatly Exaggerated!" Pages 143–57 in *A Farewell to the Yahwist? The Composition of the Pentateuch in Recent European Interpretation*. Edited by Thomas B. Dozeman and Konrad Schmid. SBL Symposium Series 34. Atlanta: Society of Biblical Literature, 2006.

———. "Is There Evidence of a Dtr Redaction in the Sinai Pericope (Exod 19–24, 32–34)?" Pages 160–70 in *Those Elusive Deuteronomists*. Edited by Linda S. Schearing and Steven L. McKenzie. Journal for the Study of the Old Testament 286. Sheffield: Sheffield Academic, 1999.

———. *The Life of Moses: The Yahwist as Historian in Exodus-Numbers*. Louisville, Ky.: Westminster John Knox, 1994.

———. *Abraham in History and Tradition*. New Haven, Conn.: Yale University Press, 1975.

———. "Confessional Reformulation in the Exilic Period" *Vetus Testamentum* 22 (1972): 448–59.

Vater, Johann S. *Commentar über den Pentateuch*. Vol. 2. Halle: Maisenhaus, 1802–1805.

Vermeylen, Jacques. "Les premières étapes littéraires de la formation du Pentateuque." Pages 149–97 in *Le Pentateuque en question*. Edited by Albert de Pury and Thomas Römer. 3rd ed. Le Monde de la Bible 19. Geneva: Labor et Fides, 2002.

———. "Le vol de la bénédiction paternelle: Une lecture de Gen 27." Pages 23–40 in *Pen-tateuchal and Deuteronomistic Studies*. Edited by C. Brekelmans and Johan Lust. Bib-liotheca Ephemeridum Theologicarum Lovaniensium 94. Leuven: University Press, 1990.

———. "L'affaire du veau d'or (Ex 32–34): Une clé pour la 'question deutéronomiste'?" *Zeitschrift für die Alttestamentliche Wissenschaft* 97 (1985): 1–23.

Vervenne, Marc. "The 'P' Tradition in the Pentateuch: Document and/or Redaction? The 'Sea Narrative' (Ex 13,17–14,31) as a Test Case." Pages 67–90 in *Pentateuchal and Deu-*

teronomistic Studies. Edited by C. Brekelmans and Johan Lust. Bibliotheca Ephemeridum Theologicarum Lovaniensium 94. Leuven: University Press, 1990.

———. "The Protest Motif in the Sea Narrative (Ex 14,11–12): Form and Structure of a Pentateuchal Pattern." *Ephemerides theologicae lovanienses* 63 (1987): 257–71.

Volz, Paul, and Wilhelm Rudolph. *Elohist als Erzähler: Ein Irrweg der Pentateuchkritik?* Beiheifte zur Zeitschrift für die Alttestamentliche Wissenschaft 63. Giessen: Alfred Töpelmann, 1933.

Von Rabenau, Konrad. "Die beiden Erzählungen vom Schilfmeerwunder in Exod. 13,17–14,31." *Theologische versuche* 1 (1966): 7–29.

Von Rad, Gerhard. *Genesis.* Translated by John H. Marks. Old Testament Library. Philadelphia: Westminster, 1972.

———. "The Form-Critical Problem of the Hexateuch." Pages 1–78 in *The Problem of the Hexateuch and Other Essays.* Translated by E. W. Trueman Dicken. New York: McGraw-Hill, 1966.

———. "The Joseph Narrative and Ancient Wisdom." Pages 292–300 in *The Problem of the Hexateuch and Other Essays.* Translated by E. W. Trueman Dicken. New York: McGraw-Hill, 1966.

———. "The Promised Land and Yahweh's Land in the Hexateuch." Pages 79–93 in *The Problem of the Hexateuch and Other Essays.* Translated by E. W. Trueman Dicken. New York: McGraw-Hill, 1966.

Wagenaar, Jan. "Crossing the Sea of Reeds (Exod 13–14) and the Jordan (Josh 3–40): A Priestly Framework for the Wilderness Wandering." Pages 461–70 in *Studies in the Book of Exodus.* Edited by Marc Vervenne. Bibliotheca Ephemeridum Theologicarum Lovaniensium 126. Leuven: University Press, 1996.

Weimar, Peter. *Die Meerwundererzählung: Eine redaktionkritische Analyse von Ex 13,17–14,31.* Ägypten und Altes Testament 9. Wiesbaden: Otto Harrassowitz, 1985.

———. *Untersuchungen zur Redaktionsgeschichte des Pentateuch.* Beihefte zur Zeitschrift für die Alttestamentliche Wissenschaft 146. Berlin: Walter de Gruyter, 1977.

———. "Aufbau und Struktur der priesterschriftlichen Jakobsgeschichte." *Zeitschrift für die Alttestamentliche Wissenschaft* 86 (1974): 174–203.

Weinfeld, Moshe. *Deuteronomy and the Deuteronomic School.* Winona Lake, Ind.: Eisenbrauns, 1992.

———. *Deuteronomy 1–11.* Anchor Bible 5. New York: Doubleday, 1991.

Weiser, Artur. *The Psalms.* Translated by Herbert Hartwell. Old Testament Library. Philadelphia: Westminster, 1962.

Wellhausen, Julius. *Prolegomena to the History of Israel.* Atlanta: Scholars Press, 1994. Reprint of *Prolegomena to the History of Israel.* Translated by J. Sutherland Black and Allan Enzies, with preface by W. Robertson Smith. Edinburgh: Adam & Charles Black, 1885.

———. *Die Composition des Hexateuchs und der historischen Bücher des Alten Testaments.* Berlin: G. Reimer, 1885. Repr., Berlin: Walter de Gruyter, 1963.

Wenham, Gordon J. "The Priority of P." *Vetus Testamentum* 49 (1999): 240–58.

———. *Genesis 16–50.* Word Biblical Commentary. Dallas, Tex.: Word Book, 1994.

———. *Numbers: An Introduction and Commentary.* Leicester: Inter-Varsity, 1981.

Westermann, Claus. *Genesis 37–50.* Translated by John J. Scullion. Continental Commentaries. Minneapolis: Fortress, 2002.

——. *Genesis 12–36.* Translated by John J. Scullion. Continental Commentaries. Minneapolis: Fortress, 1995.

Westphal, Alexandre. *Les sources du Pentateuque: Étude du critique et d'histoire.* Vol. 1. Paris: Librarie Fischbacher, 1888.

White, Hugh C. "The Joseph Story: A Narrative Which 'Consumes' Its Context." *Semeia* 31 (1985): 49–69.

——. "Reuben and Judah: Duplicates or Complements?" Pages 73–97 in *Understanding the Word.* Edited by James T. Butler, Edgar W. Conrad, and Ben C. Ollenburger. Journal for the Study of the Old Testament Supplement Series 37. Sheffield: JSOT Press, 1985.

White, Marsha. "The Elohistic Depiction of Aaron: A Study in the Levite-Zadokite Controversy." Pages 149–59 in *Studies in the Pentateuch.* Edited by J. A. Emerton. Supplements to Vetus Testamentum 41. Leiden: Brill, 1990.

Whybray, R. Norman. *The Making of the Pentateuch: A Methodological Study.* Journal for the Study of the Old Testament Supplement Series 53. Sheffield: JSOT Press, 1987.

——. "The Joseph Story and Pentateuchal Criticism." *Vetus Testamentum* 18 (1968): 522–28.

Wilcoxen, Jay A. "Narrative." Pages 57–98 in *Old Testament Form Criticism.* Edited by John H. Hayes. San Antonio, Tex.: Trinity University Press, 1974.

Willi-Plein, I. "Historiographische Aspekte der Josefsgeschichte." *Henoch* 1 (1979): 305–31.

Wolff, Hans W. "The Elohistic Fragments in the Pentateuch." Pages 67–82 in *The Vitality of Old Testament Traditions.* 2nd ed. Atlanta: John Knox, 1982.

Wyatt, N. *Religious Texts from Ugarit: The Words of Illimilku and His Colleagues.* The Biblical Seminar 53. Sheffield: Sheffield Academic, 1998.

Wynn-Williams, Damian J. *The State of the Pentateuch: A Comparison of the Approaches of M. Noth and E. Blum.* Beihefte zur Zeitschrift für die Alttestamentliche Wissenschaft 249. Berlin: Walter de Gruyter, 1997.

Yoreh, Tzemah. "The Elohistic Source: Unity and Structure [Hebrew]." Ph.D. diss., Hebrew University, 2003.

Zenger, Erich. *Die Sinaitheophanie: Untersuchungen zum jahwistischen und elohistischen Geschichtswerk.* Forschung zur Bibel 3. Würzburg, Echter Verlag, 1971.

Zimmer, Frank. *Der Elohist als weisheitlich-prophetische Redaktionsschicht: Eine literarische und theologiegeschichtliche Untersuchung der sogenannten elohistischen Texte im Pentateuch.* Frankfurt am Main: Peter Lang, 1999.

Zimmerli, Walther. "Sinaibund und Abrahambund: Ein Beitrag zum Verständnis der Priesterschrift." *Theologische Zeitschrift* 16 (1960): 268–280.

INDEX OF MODERN AUTHORS

Dietrich, Walter, 265n41, 266n47
Dillmann, August, 221, 253n23, 262n10,
262n11, 263n14, 263n16, 277n3, 277n12,
279n24, 290n15, 296n28, 299n21, 302n62,
308n15, 309n20, 310n28, 311n35, 311n40,
312n41, 316n15, 318n6, 318n7, 319n15,
320n21, 321n24, 321n26, 321n28, 322n39,
323n41
Dobbs-Allsopp, F. W., 271n79
Donner, Herbert, 41, 264n34, 267n26
Dozeman, Thomas B., 266n1, 269n58
Driver, S. R., 262n10, 262n11, 280n4, 280n6,
281n14, 282n22, 282n30, 283n36, 283n38,
283n52, 289n5, 292n7, 296n28, 296n30,
298n14, 302n68, 308n15, 308n18, 309n20,
310n28, 312n41, 317n3, 318n6, 319n15,
320n21, 321n24, 321n28, 323n41

Eerdmans, B. D., 261n2
Ehrlich, Arnold B., 287n100, 324n48
Eichhorn, Johann, 116, 216, 258n14, 259n14,
259n15, 260n19, 316n5, 316n6
Eissfeldt, Otto, 181, 260n28, 267n7, 277n4,
277n7, 279n24, 283n36, 289n5, 291n1,
292n7, 292n9, 301n48, 302n68, 312n41,
322n39, 323n42, 323n43, 324n47
Elliger, Karl, 298n13, 298n18, 300n27,
300n30, 312n41
Emerton, J. A., 170, 181, 298n2, 301n45,
301n47, 302n56, 303n70
Engnell, Ivan, 283n35, 283n45, 284n59,
298n5
Ewald, Heinrich, 61, 258n13, 260n25,
271n81

Finn, A. H., 9, 253n27, 284n57, 284n58
Firmage, Edwin, 298n6
Fischer, G., 306n6
Fohrer, Georg, 174, 258n13, 260n28,
282n24, 287n102, 289n5, 299n19, 299n24,
304n82, 312n41
Fokkelman, J. P., 10, 253n44
Frampton, Travis L., 257n12

Friedman, Richard Elliott, 218, 219,
260n27, 264n22, 264n23, 264n24, 264n26,
278n16, 278n17, 281n14, 282n30, 284n52,
285n70, 292n9, 293n12, 295n24, 295n25,
304n82, 304n83, 304n85, 304n86,
305n90, 305n91, 305n92, 308n15,
309n20, 309n25, 310n28, 311n35, 312n41,
312n44, 316n12, 316n13, 320n21, 321n24
Fritz, Volkmar, 277n3, 277n7, 277n9,
278n16, 279n24, 292n7, 296n28, 297n45
Fuller, Reginald C., 257n12
Fuss, Werner, 307n13, 308n15, 308n16,
309n20, 311n40, 314n64

Geddes, Alexander, 257n12
George, Johann F. L., 260n25
Gertz, Jan, 54, 266n1, 268n44, 269n58,
270n62, 271n82, 272n94, 304n82, 304n86,
307n13, 308n16, 309n20, 309n25, 310n26,
310n28, 310n31, 311n35, 311n40, 312n41
Gibson, J. C. L., 288n107
Gilders, William K., 303n75, 303n76
Gnuse, Robert K., 283n34, 287n103
Gomes, Jules F., 319n15, 320n19,
323n43
Good, Edwin M., 254n43
Gorman, Frank H., 299n23
Graf, Karl Heinrich, 104
Gramberg, Carl P. W., 260n25
Graupner, Axel, 58, 261n7, 263n14, 263n16,
270n67, 282n20, 283n50, 285n66,
287n102, 287n103, 288n105, 308n15,
308n16, 310n28, 312n41, 317n2, 317n3,
318n6, 321n32, 322n36, 322n39, 323n40,
323n42, 323n43
Gray, George B., 277n4, 278n14, 278n16,
282n22, 291n1, 292n7, 295n24, 296n27,
296n28, 296n30
Gray, John, 288n107
Green, Barbara, 9, 10, 254n41, 254n42
Green, William Henry, 253n37, 284n57,
284n59
Greenberg, Moshe, 308n15, 316n78

INDEX OF BIBLICAL CITATIONS

Psalms (*continued*)

114:3	312*n*44
114:5	312*n*44
116	46
118	46
138	46

LAMENTATIONS

4:6	298*n*8

DANIEL

9:2	97

EZRA

6:18	256*n*8
7:6	256*n*8
10:3	256*n*8

NEHEMIAH

8:1	225
8:2	256*n*8
8:3	256*n*8

8:7	256*n*8
8:9	256*n*8
8:13	256*n*8
8:14	256*n*8
9:14	256*n*8
9:32	286*n*85
10	225
10:35	256*n*8
10:37	256*n*8
12:44	256*n*8
13:1	256*n*8
13:2	256*n*8

1 CHRONICLES

1:32	252*n*5

2 CHRONICLES

23:18	256*n*8
25:4	256*n*8
30:16	256*n*8
35:12–13	15
35:13	316*n*18
36:21	97